The Hudson Valley & Catskill Mountains

Includes Saratoga Springs & Albany

The Hudson Valley & Catskill Mountains

Includes Saratoga Springs & Albany

Joanne Michaels

The Countryman Press ✳ Woodstock, Vermont

FIFTH EDITION

We welcome your comments and suggestions. Please contact Explorer's Guide Editor, The Countryman Press, P.O. Box 748, Woodstock, VT 05091, or e-mail countrymanpress@wwnorton.com.

Fifth Edition

ISBN: 0-88150-595-1
ISSN: 1553-6867

Maps by Moore Creative Design, © 2004 The Countryman Press
Cover and text design by Bodenweber Design
Composition by PerfecType, Nashville, TN
Cover and title page photographs © Hardie Truesdale, photographer of *Hudson River Journey: Images from Lake Tear of the Clouds to New York Harbor*, available from The Countryman Press. To order, call 800-245-4151.

Published by The Countryman Press, P.O. Box 748, Woodstock, Vermont 05091

Distributed by W. W. Norton & Company,
500 Fifth Avenue, New York, NY 10110

Printed in the United States of America

10 9 8 7 6 5 4 3

To the people in my life who have supported, loved, and believed in me through the years, particularly Renee, Lawrence, Nancy, Erik, and Robert. I have been very fortunate in my family and friends.

ACKNOWLEDGMENTS

It is never possible to thank everyone who helps a book of this kind come to life; for every person I mention, several more were behind the scenes, answering questions, mailing brochures, offering suggestions, and opening their homes to me.

The following people, who regularly travel throughout the Hudson Valley and Catskills, gave me excellent recommendations: Nancy Arena, Robert Bombardieri, Ronnie DeCanio, John Heard, Nancy Michaels, Bruce Moor, Gail and Alan Paley, Sally Savage, Richard Segalman, Lynne Turk, and Linda Way-Hartmann. I sincerely appreciate their input. Joseph Puglisi traveled to far-flung areas of the region to photograph some of the sights described here. Jillian Laks, Michael Nardi, Christina Tharp, and Mary Zanko, college interns who assisted in the research, spent time on the phone and the computer, tracking down some of the necessary information for this edition. I would also like to thank Kermit Hummel, Jennifer Thompson, Dale Gelfand, and David Corey for their guidance through the publishing process.

Many people gave their opinions and the names of their favorite spots, based on years of growing up and living in their respective towns. They probably didn't realize at the time how helpful they were. These "locals" got me off the beaten track, and I discovered charming neighborhood restaurants, tranquil back roads, and a swimming spot or hiking area I probably never would have found on my own. So this book, aside from being the best guide to this phenomenal region, is also a gift to all the people of the Hudson Valley and Catskills.

A NOTE TO THE READER

No entries for any of the establishments appearing in the *Explorer's Guide* series have been solicited or paid for. I have selected lodging and dining places for mention in this book based on their merits alone: there is no charge to inn-keepers or restaurant owners for inclusion. The decision to include a place here has to do with quality alone: the book is the *best* of the Hudson Valley and Catskill Mountains.

PRICES

Please do not hold me or the owners of various establishments mentioned responsible for any prices listed as of press time in 2004. Some changes are inevitable. State and local taxes should be added to all prices, as well.

The price rating system is simple and provides general guidelines to travelers. By their nature, restaurants included in the Eating Out group are generally inexpensive. For entrées in the Dining Out and Eating Out sections, in general:

$ means most entrées are $15 and under

$$ means $15–$25

$$$ means above $25

For inns and bed & breakfasts (per room before tax):

$ means most rooms run $125 and under

$$ means $125–$175

$$$ means above $175

SMOKING

All B&Bs, inns, and restaurants are now smoke-free. If this is an issue for you, do inquire when you call. Assume that all establishments do not permit smoking anywhere.

READER RESPONSE

Over the 15 years that this book has been in print, I have received many letters from readers throughout the country. If you would like to share any of your experiences, please contact me at P.O. Box 425, Woodstock, NY 12498, or e-mail jmichaels2@hvc.rr.com.

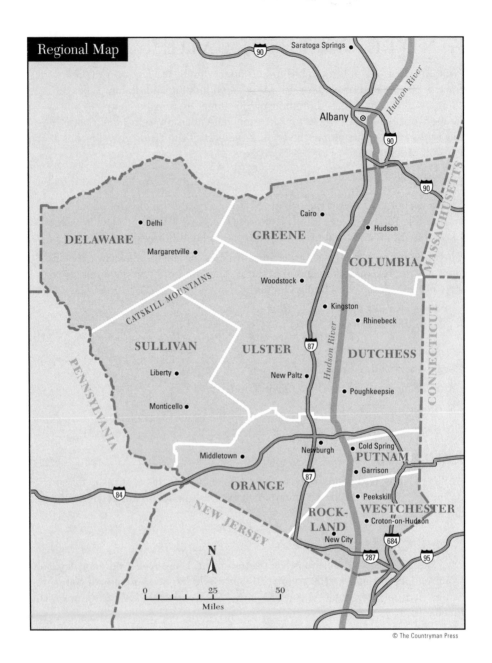

© The Countryman Press

CONTENTS

LIST OF MAPS

INTRODUCTION

Although I am certainly not the first traveler to recognize the scenic wonders of the Hudson Valley and Catskills, I am proud to say that I have remained at the forefront of reminding people that some of the most beautiful sights in the world are, literally, at their back doors. A close friend once commented that by writing about these regional treasures, I am causing them to be overrun with tourists; he suggested I keep these special places to myself, or they will risk being ruined. I cannot deny that there are times when I have the impulse not to include a deserted swimming place I frequent in the summer or an "undiscovered" eatery on a back road I stopped at one day, but I know that sharing this information is what makes my book the best one available.

After 15 years, various editions of this guide have enriched the travels of tens of thousands of people visiting the region. Once in a while readers take the time to write a letter, sharing their experience of a particular inn or historic site. I have never heard anything but praise for the beauty of the Hudson Valley and Catskills—even if, on occasion, a particular restaurant didn't live up to their expectations.

When people think of this area, many imagine mysterious mountains where Rip Van Winkle slept away the years or lush valleys where bobcats roamed or even huge hotels where the entertainment and food never stopped. True, these are part of the region's story, but after traveling tens of thousands of miles on back roads and main roads, in snow, fog, sun, and rain, I have come to the conclusion that practically nowhere else in this country can one enjoy the startling beauty, the rich history, and the culture that can be found here.

And because there is so much to see and do, I chose to include only what I consider "the best"—be it food, inns, parks or history. At historic sites or places of interest, I looked for unusual exhibits or special events. When evaluating restaurants, inns, hotels and B&Bs, I looked for value, distinctiveness, quality, cleanliness, and courtesy. Farm stands, whether large or small, had to show pride in their produce. I traveled the area in all seasons, talked to hundreds of people, and visited every historic and cultural site. In a few cases, if I couldn't experience a place myself, I talked to experts whose judgment I relied on to ensure that you are getting the recommendations of "the best" people, as well.

I know that there are many different types of travelers, so this book offers a

RIVER RAFTING IN ORANGE COUNTY

Orange County Tourism, Inc.

large number of places for visiting and dining. I have tried to select a wide variety of places in order to please people of all ages, all backgrounds, all budgets. Some places are free, others are rather expensive, but all are the best of their type.

I have to emphasize, however, that dollar ratings sometimes change between the time a book is written and the time it appears in the bookstore. Remember that lunches may cost considerably less than dinners, that single-lodging rates may be higher or lower depending on the establishment, and that in some places special rates are available for groups, senior citizens, and midweek. If a site or restaurant does not appear in this book, this omission does not reflect a negative review. Perhaps I didn't know about it, or it may only recently have opened, or I might just have missed it. Tell me about it so that future editions of this guidebook will be as complete and as accurate as possible.

All the sites included in this book are within a day's drive of New York City and New Jersey, and many are a few hours by car from Boston and Philadelphia. The book is arranged by county, beginning with those on the west side of the Hudson

River, heading north to Albany and Saratoga, and continuing south of Albany on the east side of the Hudson. You can be where the action is, or be utterly alone. You can consume crunchy apples and creamy goat cheese, hike, kayak, or just take a walk. The climate is temperate, and the views are extraordinary.

Many places of interest are seasonal as are the outdoor activities, but many sites are open year-round throughout the region. Summer events in particular are often held rain or shine, but I strongly suggest that you plan ahead and check schedules before taking a long trip. At the beginning of each chapter, I have listed phone numbers and websites for tourism departments in every county.

The Hudson Valley and Catskills offer such a range of sights and activities, virtually all visitors will enjoy their stay here. Take your time exploring my favorite region—my childhood home, and where I have lived for the past 25 years. And remember to send your suggestions and discoveries to me at **P.O. Box 425, Woodstock, NY 12498** or email jmichaels2@hvc.rr.com. Keep this book in your car to assist you while traveling through this special place on the planet!

—Joanne Michaels, Woodstock, NY

Rockland County

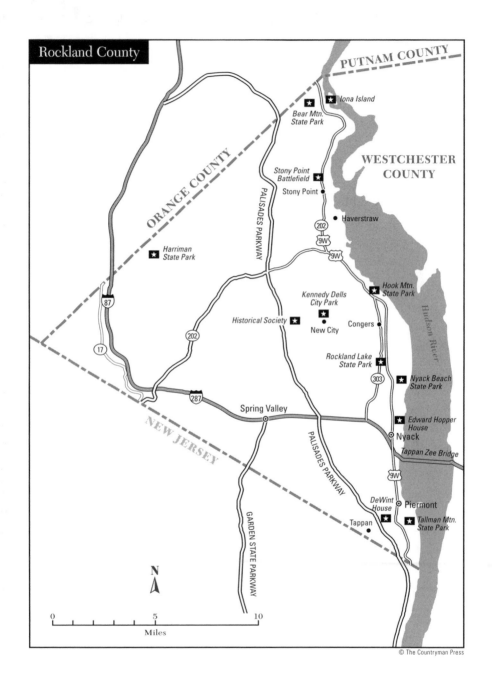

Rockland County

PUTNAM COUNTY

Iona Island

Bear Mtn.
State Park

WESTCHESTER
COUNTY

ORANGE COUNTY

Stony Point
Battlefield
Stony Point

PALISADES PARKWAY

Haverstraw

202
9W

9W

Harriman
State Park

Hook Mtn.
State Park

Kennedy Dells
City Park

Hudson River

Historical Society
New City

Congers

202

Rockland Lake
State Park

Nyack Beach
State Park

303

287

Spring Valley

Edward Hopper
House
Nyack

NEW JERSEY

Tappan Zee Bridge

PALISADES PARKWAY

9W

DeWint
House

Piermont

Tappan

Tallman Mtn.
State Park

GARDEN STATE PARKWAY

N

0   5   10

Miles

© The Countryman Press

ROCKLAND COUNTY

Only 176 square miles in size, Rockland County packs a lot into its area. It seems that everywhere you look in Rockland there is a park, from the tiny vest-pocket squares of green in towns and villages to the great spaces of Bear Mountain. Only 30 miles north of New York City, Rockland has preserved many of its forests, wetlands, mountains, and historical sites and still offers residents and visitors 32,000 acres of parkland. Wealthy patrons, civic leaders, and citizen activists joined forces to prevent Bear Mountain and High Tor from becoming a prison site and a quarry, respectively. Today, the fruits of those early environmental battles are seen and enjoyed by all. Hundreds of miles of hiking and biking trails wind through estuarine marshes, along the Hudson River, and up and over dramatic peaks. Lakes and streams teem with wildlife, and plant lovers will delight in the explosion of color and scent that marks the spring wildflower season. Stony Point Battlefield, the mountaintop meadow where American troops defeated the British Redcoats, is very much as it was more than 200 years ago. In small towns and villages throughout the county, houses have been preserved with such care and such a sense of history that visitors feel as if they have stepped back in time. While touring Rockland, you will hear again and again the names of those who made history and are still remembered in ceremonies and festivals throughout the county: George Washington, Benedict Arnold, John Andre, and even Captain Kidd!

GUIDANCE **Rockland County Tourism** (845-353-5533; 1-800-295-5723), 18 New Hempstead Road, New City, 10956; www.rockland.org.

Chamber of Commerce of the Nyacks (845-353-2221), 6 Park Street, Nyack, 10960; www.thenyacks.net.

Arts Council of Rockland County (845-426-3660), 7 Perlman Drive, Spring Valley, 10977; www.artscouncilofrockland.org.

Historical Society of Rockland County (845-634-9629), 20 Zukor Road, New City, 10956; www.rocklandhistory.org.

GETTING THERE *By car:* From the upper deck of the George Washington Bridge, follow signs to the Palisades Parkway. Take exit 9E, the New York State

Thruway, which leads into I-287 South to 87 South. Get off at exit 11, Nyack, the last exit before the Tappan Zee Bridge. Make a left off the exit onto Route 59, which becomes Main Street.

By bus: **Rockland Coaches** (845-356-0877) operates buses that travel daily from the Port Authority in Manhattan at 20 minutes past the hour, to Route 9W in Nyack. **Transportation of Rockland** (845-364-3333) operates a bus line that services 10 routes within Rockland County and offers service to the Westchester towns of Tarrytown and White Plains. Some of these buses stop at the Metro North train station, where travelers can make connections to Manhattan.

MEDICAL EMERGENCY **Nyack Hospital** (845-348-2000), North Midland Avenue, Nyack.

Good Samaritan Hospital (845-368-5000), 255 Lafayette Avenue, Suffern.

Complete Medical Lab (845-947-2266), 49 South Route 9W, West Haverstraw.

Health Med (845-623-4000), 104 Route 59, Nanuet.

Poison Control Center (1-800-336-6997); **Rabies Information** (845-364-2585/2000).

✳ Villages

Nyack. Located off the NYS Thruway at exit 11, the last exit before the Tappan Zee Bridge. First settled by the Nyack Indians, who moved there from Brooklyn, Nyack soon became home to the Dutch, who began to farm the region. When steamboats arrived, making river travel easier, Nyack became a center for shipping and boatbuilding. The town is now known as an antiques and arts center, home to dozens of shops that offer the finest furniture, jewelry, crafts, and artwork (see *Selective Shopping*).

To see Nyack's charming architectural heritage, begin at South Broadway near the **Nyack Public Library,** one of the libraries built with funds from the Carnegie Foundation at the turn of the 20th century. Next to the library is a Queen Anne-style house with a tower and fine shingle work. Heading north, at 46 South Broadway, **Couch Court** is an unusual late-19th-century building that sports a towerlike cupola. The Presbyterian church was built in 1838 in the Greek Revival style, in which columns and symmetry were used in an effort to capture what was considered the ancient purity of Greece. Down the street a little farther, look for the **Tappan Zee Theatre,** built when movies were silent and vaudeville shows were the rage. Across the street, the Reformed church has a clock tower that dates back to 1850. On Burd Street a plaque on the bank tells a little of the history of Nyack. On North Broadway you'll see the **Congregation of the Sons of Israel**, a synagogue founded in 1870. A side trip down and around Van Houten Road (it turns into Castle Heights) runs past riverfront homes and offers a magnificent view of the Hudson. Continue your drive up North Broadway, passing splendid mansions and lovely 18th-century homes, to **Hook Mountain State Park.**

The village of Nyack sponsors special events throughout the year, including a farmers market every Thursday, May through November, 8:30 AM–2:30 PM, in the municipal lot at Main and Cedar Streets, rain or shine; there are arts and antiques street fairs during the spring and fall, a Halloween parade, and other happenings. A series of spring walking tours includes a guided walk through Oak Hill Cemetery, which contains the burial sites of Helen Hayes, Edward Hopper, Ben Hecht, Carson McCullers, and many other fascinating people who made Nyack their home. For information regarding dates and times, call 845-268-3838.

Piermont. Many travelers neglect to take a detour to this charming village, located about 4 miles south of Nyack. It is one of my favorite places in Rockland County. Just follow Piermont Avenue from Nyack, which takes you along the Hudson River right into town; 9W South is an alternate route. The village became somewhat renowned in recent years after Woody Allen filmed *The Purple Rose of Cairo* here. **The Flying Wheel Art Gallery** on the pier is just one of many intriguing places to see fine art and photography. The best way to experience Piermont is to park the car and wander along Piermont Avenue and the waterfront; the village is chock full of interesting shops and galleries.

Haverstraw. North of Nyack, the brickworks that lined the Hudson in the 19th century made this town known as the brick-making capital of the world. At the time, barges carried the bricks to New York City. Then cement became a more popular building material, and the town deteriorated, like many places with economies based around changing industries. Today, however, Haverstraw is in the midst of an exciting renaissance. Upscale businesses and restaurants are moving into newly renovated storefronts. A downtown walking tour offers a sample of some fine Central American cuisine. At 91 Broadway a restored brick firehouse is now the **Arts Alliance of Haverstraw** (845-786-0253), open Monday–Saturday 1–4. At 28 First Street is **Gallery on the Hudson** (845-942-1535), which features photography, including an exhibit that documents the revitalization of Haverstraw. Don't miss the **Garnerville Arts and Industrial Center** (845-947-1155), 55 Railroad Avenue, a renovated factory complex filled with an array of art galleries, crafts shops, and cabinetmakers. **The Haverstraw Brick Museum** at 12 Main Street gives a detailed overview of the town's past, when it was home to over 40 brickyards. **Emeline Park,** at the foot of Main Street, is the perfect place to rest after strolling; you will be treated to wonderful river views. There is now ferry service to Ossining, across the Hudson in Westchester, for commuters to get to Metro North—or for travelers to enjoy a river outing.

FIRST SETTLED BY THE NYACK INDIANS, NYACK IS NOW KNOWN AS AN ANTIQUES AND ARTS CENTER.

Bob Vergera

Tappan. The local government here was the first in New York State to establish by ordinance an historic district, with the result that a walk down Main Street in Tappan will reveal many 18th- and 19th-century structures. The **Tappan Library,** a frame house dating from the mid-18th century, boasts a restored colonial garden.

John Andre was imprisoned in the **Yoast Mabie Tavern,** built in 1755, although Washington's instructions were that Andre be treated civilly. Just beyond the tavern look for the **Killoran House,** a town house built in 1835 with the bricks taken from a dismantled church. In the middle of Main Street, where it meets Old Tappan Road, the village green was the site of the public stocks and the liberty pole, depending on the mood of the townspeople at the time. The nearby **Reformed Church of Tappan** stands on the site where Andre was tried and convicted of spying. Although Andre requested that he be shot as a soldier, the tribunal ordered him hanged as a spy, since to do otherwise would have been to cast doubt upon his guilt. In the nearby burying grounds you will find many old tombstones. Farther up the road is the **Demming-Latelle House,** best known as the home of the man who manufactured the first canned baby food.

✳ To See

Edward Hopper House and Hopper House Art Center (845-358-0774), 82 North Broadway, Nyack. Open Thursday through Sunday 1–5. Donation suggested. The American realist painter Edward Hopper was born in Nyack in 1882 and as a youth spent much of his time in the village. Several of his paintings feature local landmarks, and he taught painting classes at the house, which was built by his grandfather. When he died in 1967, Hopper was buried in the Oak Hill Cemetery. His boyhood home was rescued from demolition not long after his death, and today it is a community arts and cultural center. Exhibits include works by Hopper and other American painters, and concerts are given in the gardens of the Hopper House each summer. The site also sponsors a local garden tour. There are art classes and workshops for both adults and children, so call for an updated schedule.

HISTORIC HOME DeWint House National Shrine (845-359-1359), 20 Livingston Avenue, near Oak Tree Road in Tappan. Open daily year-round, 10–4. Free. Constructed in 1700 of Holland brick and sandstone, the DeWint House boasts the pitched roof and tile fireplace common in well-to-do Dutch homes of the period. Although the house is important architecturally, it is best known as George Washington's headquarters and as a shrine to Washington's participation in the fraternal organization known as the Masons. It was also here that Washington—after refusing to commute the sentence—stayed the day that British spy Major John Andre was hanged. It is recorded that Washington asked that the shutters to his room be closed—the same shutters that cover the window today. When the house was purchased by the Masons, the owner said family tradition held that several of the items in the house were there at the time of Washington's visits. Today the house offers a look into Washington's day-to-day life during the war, along with the story of his participation in the Masons. A small carriage house museum also contains period artifacts and exhibits, and trees around the site have been marked with identification tags. A self-guided walking tour of Tappan is also available at the carriage house.

HISTORIC SITES Camp Shanks World War II Museum (845-638-5419), South Greenbush Street, Orangeburg. Open April through October, Saturday and Sunday 10–3. Free. This site was the processing center for more than a million soldiers who shipped overseas from the Piermont Pier to Normandy. Now a small museum, it tells the story of military life at the camp through exhibits and a visit to a barracks.

Historical Society of Rockland County (845-634-9629), 20 Zukor Road, off New Main Street in New City. Open Tuesday through Sunday; hours of the gallery and house vary with the season, so call for information. Admission fee. This society offers both history and art to visitors, along with year-round special events. Changing exhibits in the gallery feature works by local and other artists. The house is well-known for its demonstrations of open-hearth cooking. Special events may include folklife or jazz festivals and a house tour. The shop offers a large selection of local publications and maps.

Holocaust Museum & Study Center (845-356-2700), 17 South Madison Avenue, Spring Valley. Open Sunday through Thursday noon–4; closed on Sundays mid-June through Labor Day weekend; also closed on national and Jewish holidays. Free. Visitors to this small museum will be humbled and moved by powerful images of the Holocaust and the strength shown by its survivors. A permanent exhibit examines the history and effects of the Holocaust, while videos and artwork bring home the personal horrors of this period. A research library is available for public use.

Stony Point Battlefield (845-786-2521), located on Park Road, off Route 9W, Stony Point. Open mid-April through October 31, Wednesday through Saturday 10–5, Sunday 1–5. Closed Monday and Tuesday except Memorial Day, Independence Day, and Labor Day. Free, but a fee is charged for special events. When George Washington felt he had to demonstrate that American troops were determined to stand up to the superior British forces in the Hudson Highlands, he sent in General "Mad Anthony" Wayne to prove the point. In July 1779 Wayne led the elite troops of the Corps of Light Infantry in an attack on the British at Stony Point. During a midnight raid, the Americans routed the British from their beds and challenged their reputation as an invincible fighting force. A self-guided walking tour of the battlefield takes visitors through a wildly beautiful park, where remnants of British fortifications still survive. Trails are marked with plaques explaining the battle, and you will pass the 1826 Stony Point Lighthouse, used for more than a century to aid ships on the Hudson; it was restored in 1995. The newly renovated museum offers a slide show that depicts events leading up to the battle and is accompanied by exhibits and original memorabilia illustrating the tactics and strategies that brought victory to the Americans.

THE 1826 STONY POINT LIGHTHOUSE AT STONY POINT BATTLEFIELD

Ken Karlewicz

Dogwoods bloom along the paths, and special events, like military encampments and holiday celebrations, are held in the spring.

✳ To Do

BICYCLING Both **Bear Mountain State Park** and **Harriman State Park** offer a number of challenging bike routes. However, both of these areas can get extremely congested on weekends. You might want to try **Rockland Lake** and **Tallman State Park,** which both have paved bicycle paths. Another option is **Nyack Beach State Park,** located off Route 9W with access from Broadway in Upper Nyack. This park runs along the river, and the paths are flat with fine views of the Hudson. **Hook Mountain State Park** also has biking paths with scenic views of the Hudson. To get there go east on North Broadway in Nyack; the park is located at the end of the road.

FARM STANDS AND PICK-YOUR-OWN FARMS Even though Rockland County is small, you can still discover some terrific outlets for local fruits and vegetables.

Auntie El's Farm Market (845-753-2122), Route 17, Sloatsburg. Open daily year-round, this market offers an enormous array of fruits and vegetables from Rockland County farms.

Dr. Davies Farm (845-268-7020), Route 9W, Congers (open year-round); Route 304, Congers (open May through November). You can pick your own apples in the fall and then select from a wide variety of berries, pumpkins, plums, and other goodies at the farm stand.

Fellowship Community (845-356-8494), 241 Hungry Hollow Road, Chestnut Ridge. Organic fruits and vegetables sold Fridays only, noon–5.

Nyack Farmers Market, the municipal parking lot at Main and Cedar Streets, Nyack. Every Thursday, May through November, 8:30–2:30, rain or shine. This is a great place to stock up for the weekend. The market attracts farmers from throughout the region and offers an enormous variety of produce as well as specialty foods.

The Orchards at Concklin (845-354-0369), South Mountain Road, Pomona. Open March–December. This farm has been in business since 1712. Today you can harvest your own fruits on weekends (10–5), and pick a pumpkin at Halloween.

Schimpf Farms (845-623-2556), Germond Road, West Nyack, has a roadside market from mid-July through October.

Van Houten Farms (845-735-4689), 12 Sickletown Road, Pearl River, is open April through November, with fruits, vegetables, and holiday greenery.

Van Ripers Farm (845-352-0770), 121 College Road, Suffern, is open until Thanksgiving. You can pick raspberries in season, or select from a wide variety of fruits, vegetables, and bedding plants.

FISHING The state parks allow fishing, but you will have to check with them for their individual regulations and restrictions. Fishing is also allowed in the

Ramapo River, which has a long trout season. Route 17 has parking areas, and the waters north of Ramapo are considered good fishing spots. On Route 202 near Suffern watch for the **Mahwah River** and the parking areas along its bank. **Minisceongo Creek** has good fishing from the Rosman Bridge upstream to the Palisades Mountain Parkway Bridge.

GOLF **Blue Hill Golf Course** (845-735-2094), Blue Hill Road, Pearl River. Open 7 AM to dusk on weekdays; 6:30 AM to dusk on weekends. Operated by the town of Orangetown, this pleasant course boasts 27 holes. A good choice for beginners.

The Practice Tee (845-358-5557), 624 Route 303, Blauvelt. Open daily, 8 AM–11 PM. There are 41 turf tees and 25 grass tees at this driving range, with a miniature golf course.

Rockland Lake Champion Golf Course (845-268-7275), Route 9W, Congers. Open 7 AM to dusk on weekdays and 6 AM to dusk on weekends and holidays. There are actually two golf courses at this state park, including an 18 hole par 3 course and an 18 hole full-sized course. It is advised call 10 days in advance to reserve weekend tee times.

Philip J. Rotella Golf Course (845-354-1616), Thiells Mt. Ivy Road, Thiels. Open 7 AM–7 PM weekdays, 6 AM–7 PM on weekends. Named for a former Haverstraw town supervisor, this challenging 18-hole championship golf course recently underwent a $3 million renovation. Duffers will enjoy a view of the Hudson River from one of the tees. Owned and operated by the town of Haverstraw.

Spook Rock Golf Course (845-357-6466), 199 Spook Rock Road, Suffern. Open 7 AM–dusk weekdays; 6 AM–dusk weekends. This 18-hole championship course was built in 1969; it is owned and operated by the town of Ramapo.

Tappan Golf (845-359-0642), 116 Route 303, Tappan. Open 6 AM–11 PM, this 18-hole miniature golf course is a great place to go with the kids.

HIKING AND WALKING Almost every park has hiking trails that wind through the woods or over mountains. Some unusual trails, set up to commemorate the American Revolution, also provide ways to get to know local history. The 1777 Trail, the 1777E Trail, and the 1777W Trail—known collectively as the **Bicentennial Trails**—are all under 3 miles in length. Located in Bear Mountain and Harriman State Parks, the trails are accessed from Route 9W, 1 mile north of Tomkins Cove. Look for the diamond-shaped white blazes with red numbers. This is also the starting area for the **Timp-Torne Trail,** a 10-mile hike that offers spectacular views down the Hudson River all the way to New York City. The trail ends at the Bear Mountain Lodge.

The shorter **Anthony Wayne Trail**—a 3-mile loop marked with white blazes—can be found along Seven Lakes Drive in Bear Mountain State Park, near the traffic circle. Another popular trail is the **Pine Meadow Trail,** which begins at the Reeve Meadow visitors center on Seven Lakes Drive. If you want to climb Bear Mountain, take the **Major Welch Trail** from the Bear Mountain Inn (see *Lodging*).

Buttermilk Falls Park, in Nyack, has trails from the parking lot to the falls themselves, lovely in early spring.

Kennedy Dells Park, Main Street, 1 mile north of New City (watch for signs), was once part of film producer Adolph Zukor's estate. Along with hiking trails, there is also a trail for people with disabilities.

Dutch Garden, at the County Office Building, New Hempstead Road, New City, is a 3-acre historic site with gardens and paths.

Shorter walks may be taken in **Betsy Ross Park,** Tappan; **Tackamack North** and **Tackamack South Parks,** Clausland Mountain Road, Blauvelt; and along the **Erie Trail,** which runs from Sparkill to Grandview along abandoned railroad tracks. **Mount Ivy,** off Route 202, Pomona, is a rails-to-trails park, with hiking along the old tracks and a wetlands and nature study center.

✳ Green Space

Bear Mountain State Park (845-786-2701). Take the Bear Mountain exit off the Palisades Parkway or Route 6 and 9W. Open daily year-round; parking fee. Part of the vast Palisades Interstate Parks System, Bear Mountain shares almost 54,000 acres with its neighbor, **Harriman State Park.** Noted on maps since the mid-18th century, Bear Mountain has been known as Bear Hill, Bread Tray, and Bare Mountain (presumably because of a bald peak). Once the site of Revolutionary War Forts Clinton and Montgomery, the area the park now covers was slated to become the home of Sing Sing Prison until public outcry and political pressure persuaded the state to change its plans early in the 20th century. Since then a parkway system has made the park accessible to the hundreds of thousands who visit each year, and several lakes add to the park's outdoor appeal. Visitors to the park will find a four-season outdoor wonderland featuring a wide program of activities and special events, including swimming, fishing, miniature golf, hiking, boating, sledding, and cross-country skiing. At the **Trailside Museum, Nature Trail, and Zoo,** located next to the Bear Mountain Inn (watch for signs; also see *Lodging*), exhibits and programs describe the Native American, military, and natural history of the area. (There are even mastodon remains!) Open daily 9–5 year-round. Admission is free. Across the field from the Bear Mountain Inn, a beautiful new **carousel** has been built, housed in a stone-and-timber Adirondack-style building. Children may climb aboard carved animals native to the Hudson Valley—raccoons, bear, deer, eagles, fox, river otters, and bobcats—for an old-fashioned ride on this full-size merry-go-round.

The self-guided trail is the oldest continuously run trail in the country. The short trail also features a unique zoo with wildlife in natural settings, including a beaver lodge (which has been cut away for easy viewing), a reptile house, and trees, shrubs, and plants with identification tags. On into the park, visitors may want to bike or drive along the scenic interpark roads or rent a paddle- or row-boat at one of the lakes. (Canoes are subject to an inspection.) Three lakes—Welch, Sebago, and Tiorati—have swimming, picnicking, and other recreational areas, and special events are scheduled throughout the year at the Bear Mountain Inn and in the park. In the past there have been winter holiday fairs, orienteering meets, crafts and ethnic festivals, professional ski-jumping competitions, even stargazing nights.

In recent years Harriman State Park, with rock formations dating back one billion years, has become a center for geology buffs. For many years geological researchers neglected the New York region, but that has changed recently, thanks in large part to the efforts of Dr. Alexander Gates, who discovered garnets in the park dating back over two million years. Gates and his research team are doing geological mapping at Harriman, which is pretty much as it was 12,000 years ago when the last glacier retreated. Gates is working on making Harriman a geological park; his efforts will be of particular interest to travelers with children, so inquire as to his progress and any exhibits.

Hook Mountain State Park and **Nyack Beach Park** (845-268-3020). To reach Hook Mountain State Park, take North Broadway, in Nyack, east to the end; follow signs. To reach Nyack Beach Park, take Route 9W from Broadway. Both parks are open daily dawn to dusk; free. Hook Mountain was once referred to by the Dutch as Verdrietige (tedious) Hook because the winds could change rapidly and leave a boat adrift in the river. The area was also a favorite campground of Native Americans because of its wealth of oysters. For modern visitors the park provides a place to picnic, hike, bike, and enjoy scenic views of the Hudson. A hawk watch is held every spring and fall, and the park is said to be haunted by the ghost of the Guardian of the Mountain, a Native American medicine man who appears during the full moon each September and chants at the ancient harvest festival. Nyack Beach is open for swimming, hiking, and fishing; the views of the river are outstanding, and cross-country ski trails are available in winter.

Piermont Marsh and **Tallman State Park** (845-359-0544), Route 9W in Sparkill, near Piermont, north of Palisades Interstate Parkway, exit 4. Piermont Marsh can be reached through Tallman State Park by following the bike path or from the Erie Pier in the village of Piermont. Admission fee. This nature preserve covers more than 1,000 acres of tidal marsh, mountain, and river and is considered one of the most important fish-breeding areas along the Hudson. Wildflowers, such as the spectacular rose mallow, abound in portions of the marsh, and this is a prime bird-watching locale in all seasons. The area along the marsh is a marvelous place to view the river, and a hike up the mountain offers a spectacular panorama for photographers. Tallman State Park is a wonderful place to spend a summer day—along with its natural wonders, the park has complete recreational facilities, including bike paths, a swimming pool, tennis courts, and hiking trails. Even some human-made ponds have become home for many varieties of reptiles and amphibians; ironically, the ponds were to have been part of a tank storage area for a large oil company earlier in the century. Today, especially in spring, the ponds hum with the sounds of frogs, and the woods come alive with birdcalls.

Rockland Lake State Park (845-268-3020), Route 9W, Rockland Lake exit, Congers. Open daily year-round, although the Nature Center is closed October through May. Use fee. Another jewel in the crown of the Palisades Interstate

Parks System, this popular recreation area is located at the base of Hook Mountain. The lake was once the site of an ice farm, which provided a harvest of pure, clear ice for nearly a century before the advent of modern refrigeration. The park is a wonderful place to explore—in addition to hiking you can enjoy swimming, jogging, fishing, biking, boating, and golf. Rowboats are available to rent by the hour. During the winter, go ice skating on the lake or cross-country skiing and sledding on some of the challenging hills. At the Nature Center you will discover live animals and exhibits, special-events programs throughout the summer, and guided tours along the wetlands walkway (it's about 3.25 miles around the lake). Just outside the center, marked nature trails run along a boardwalk and contain Braille interpretation stops for the blind and visually impaired. Wildflowers and birds are particularly vibrant during the spring, but there are wonders to discover here any time of year.

✳ Lodging

Bear Mountain Inn (845-786-2731), off Route 9W, 9A, 9D and 6, Bear Mountain 10911. ($$) Located in the heart of Bear Mountain State Park, the 77-year old inn's rustic charm makes it a fine place to relax. The stone-and-wood building complements this panoramic spot, and all the facilities of the park can be enjoyed, as well. There are 60 guest rooms at the inn, all with private bath. This is a large establishment in a public park, so it is best to visit in the off-season when the crowds have disappeared. Open year-round.

Best Western Nyack on Hudson (845-358-8100), 26 Route 59, Nyack 10960. ($$) There are 80 rooms and a family restaurant, open from 6 AM–1 AM, at this establishment. A good choice for those traveling with children, it is located only 1 mile from the Palisade Center Mall and within walking distance to Nyack's attractions.

Cove House (845-429-9695), P.O. Box 81, Tomkins Cove 10986. ($$) This ranch house on 3 acres offers one of the best views around of the Hudson River. There are three rooms; one has a private bath, and two share a bathroom. Open year-round.

Holiday Inn of Orangeburg (845-359-7000), 329 Route 303, Orangeburg 10962. ($$) Close to Piermont and Nyack, and the 167 guest rooms have all the amenities. A nice feature is the outdoor pool; also here is a fitness room with sauna. Open year-round.

Super 8 Motel of Nyack (845-353-3880), 47 West Main Street, Nyack 10960. ($$) There are 43 spacious rooms, with king-sized-beds in many of the singles. Nice features are the restaurant next door—and that you are near the center of Nyack.

✳ Where to Eat

DINING OUT Café Portofino (845-359-7300), 587 Piermont Avenue, Piermont. ($$) Open daily for dinner 5–10. Regional Italian cooking served in a warm, friendly atmosphere by the chef-owner. The daily specials include veal, chicken, fish, and seafood dishes. Save room for dessert; all are homemade.

The Clarksville Inn (845-358-8899), 1 Strawtown Road, West Nyack. ($$) Open daily except Monday for lunch noon–2; dinner 5–9; Sunday brunch 11–4. This restaurant is situated on a historic property circa 1850. Both Martin Van Buren and Washington

Irving spent time here. The New American cuisine is prepared fresh daily, and menus change seasonally. One of the specialties of the house is spiced, grilled Ahi tuna served with couscous. All desserts are made on the premises. My favorite: s'mores, which are topped with a layer of pecan crusted Godiva chocolate. The coconut crème brûlée is also superb.

Cornetta's Restaurant and Marina (845-359-0410), 641 River Road, Piermont. ($) Open daily noon–10 PM. Closed Monday and Tuesday December through March. Italian family restaurant specializing in steaks and seafood. The lobster and crab legs are recommended by the chef.

Freelance Café and Wine Bar (845-365-3250), 506 Piermont Avenue, Piermont. ($$) Open daily for lunch noon–3; dinner from 5:30; Sunday brunch noon–3. Right next to Xavier's, this informal eatery offers specialties like coconut shrimp in a sharp mustard sauce, grilled chicken salad, and tiramisu.

Giulio's (845-359-3657), 154 Washington Street, Tappan. ($$) Open for lunch Monday through Friday 11:30–2:30; dinner Monday through Friday 5–10, Saturday until 11, Sunday 2–9. Fine Northern Italian cuisine is served in this 100-year-old Victorian house. There is a romantic candlelit setting at dinner and a strolling entertainer weekday evenings. Sample the Valdostana vitello (veal stuffed with prosciutto and cheese in a champagne sauce) or the scampi Giulio (jumbo shrimp sautéed with fresh mushrooms). Children are welcome. Reservations suggested for dinner.

Ichi Riki (845-358-7977), 110 Main Street, Nyack. ($$) Open for lunch Tuesday through Friday, noon–2:30;

dinner Tuesday through Sunday, 5–10. Whether you prefer tempura, sushi and sashimi, or teriyaki, this is the place to go in Rockland County for fine Japanese cuisine. Tatami room and sushi bar.

Il Portico (845-365-2100), 89 Main Street, Tappan. ($$) Open daily for lunch noon–3; dinner 5–10. There are different fish specials every day at this cozy spot featuring Northern Italian cuisine. The most popular dishes are the veal D'Vinci (with prosciutto and mozzarella) and the linguini a la Genovese (with pesto). The tiramisu and ricotta cheesecake are made fresh on the premises. Children are welcome.

King and I (845-353-4208) 93 Main Street, Nyack. ($$) Open daily from 11:30. Enjoy the spicy, sophisticated flavors of Thai cuisine at this delightful restaurant. Chicken and vegetarian specialties are offered, and the colorful decor makes for a festive, upbeat atomosphere. Try fried curry paste, shrimp simmered in coconut milk, or twice-cooked sliced chicken. The dishes range in spiciness from mild to dangerous. A unique dining experience in Rockland.

La Maisonette (845-735-9000), 500 Veterans Memorial Drive, Pearl River. ($$) Breakfast (6:30–11:30), lunch (11:30–3), and dinner (5–10) daily. Within the Pearl River Hilton, this elegant restaurant has a strong local following. The dining room overlooks a golf course, and the relaxing view further enhances the gracious cuisine. Continental and American entrées, served with homemade bread, include mushrooms filled with crabmeat and spinach and broiled tuna on eggplant. Don't skip their luscious desserts (try the rich chocolate peanut butter pie). Reservations suggested for dinner.

The Landing (845-398-1943), on the waterfront, Piermont. ($$) Open for lunch and dinner Tuesday through Saturday noon–10; Sunday brunch 11–3; dinner until 8. This is primarily a steakhouse, and I suggest the aged porterhouse steak, a favorite of the chef. There are also tasty seafood and lobster dishes to be enjoyed, with a view of the park and Hudson River from the dining room.

Lanterna Tuscan Bistro (845-353-8361), 3 South Broadway, Nyack. ($$) Open daily for lunch 11–3:30; dinner 4:30–10. Chef-owner Roassano Giannini specializes in terrifically imaginative dishes from his native town of Lucca in Tuscany, so don't expect the usual Italian restaurant menu selections. The cheese basket is literally a basket made of cheese filled with fresh mixed green salad and topped with prosciutto. Calamari is served with endive, radicchio, tomato, and a touch of pesto. The seafood over homemade pasta is first-rate; do try the ostrich, rabbit, wild boar, rabbit, or venison in-season. The atmosphere is casual; children are welcome.

Lu Shane's (845-358-5556), 8 North Broadway, Nyack. ($$$) Open Tuesday through Friday for lunch noon–3; dinner 5:30–10:30, Saturday until 11:30, Sunday 4:30–9:30. This modern-American bistro with French and Asian influences is known in the neighborhood for their sesame-seared tuna and porterhouse steak for two. The full raw bar offers a variety of clams and oysters, and the martini menu is extensive, including a watermelon martini in the summer months. It's a dimly lit place with a long copper-clad bar. The appetizers are excellent, and the desserts should not be missed—try the berry napoleon. There's live jazz on Sundays; a place to go when traveling *without* the kids.

Marcello's Ristorante (845-357-9108), 21 Lafayette Avenue, Suffern. ($$) Open for lunch Monday through Friday noon–2; dinner daily 5–9:30. The chef-owner, Marcello, travels to Italy twice each year and brings back new ideas for the continually changing menu. Every dish at this elegant spot is cooked to order, and all pastas are homemade. The seafood ravioli and veal chop with sage are just a couple of the superb house specialties.

Montebello (845-365-6900), 500 Route 340, Sparkill. ($$) Open for lunch Tuesday through Friday noon–2:30; dinner served Tuesday through Sunday 5–10. The Italian cuisine here features pasta, veal, and chicken specialties as well as homemade desserts. On the property is the oldest white ash tree in the country, believed to be at least 400 years old.

Old '76 House (845-359-5476), 110 Main Street, Tappan. ($$) Open daily, except Monday, for lunch at 11:30; dinner at 5. Located in a restored 1753 sandstone-and-brick house, this restaurant boasts beamed ceilings, fireplaces surrounded by Dutch tiles, and a real colonial atmosphere. (Legend says British Major John Andre was imprisoned here during the Revolution.) The food is American and Continental, and entrées include veal Antoinette, steaks, and seafood selections.

Pasta Amore (845-365-1911), 200 Ash Street, Piermont. ($$) Open daily for lunch and dinner noon–10. Over 20 delectable pasta dishes are on the menu here. One of my favorites is the bowtie pasta with shrimp and vodka sauce. The menu is huge, and there is an array of meat, chicken, and fish dishes, as well. The chicken Amore is a popular entrée with local patrons.

The River Club (845-358-0220), the foot of Burd Street on the Hudson, Nyack. ($$) Open Tuesday through Saturday for lunch noon–3; dinner 5–10; Sunday brunch 11–3; dinner 5–9. Waterfront restaurant with outdoor dining, featuring seafood, ribs, chicken, and steak. A great place to go for drinks any time. Children are welcome.

Romolo's (845-268-3770), 77 Route 303, Congers. ($$) Open for lunch Tuesday through Friday 11:30–2:30; dinner Tuesday through Sunday from 5. Find a full range of Italian and Continental specialties here. The veal verbena is an interesting dish: veal with prosciutto, asparagus, and mozzarella cheese in a wine sauce. There are nightly salmon specials. A good place for fine casual dining.

The Turning Point (845-359-1089), 468 Piermont Avenue, Piermont. ($$) Open for lunch Wednesday through Saturday 11:30–3; dinner Wednesday through Sunday from 6; Sunday brunch 11:30–3. Lunch menu served after dinner hours. Relax and enjoy a fine meal while listening to live music. The restaurant has been a hangout for creative people for years, and it is a popular local spot. For dinner, try fettuccine with goat cheese and sliced duck or poached salmon; 15 herbal teas and over 20 kinds of beer are listed on the menu. For brunch on Sunday there are buttermilk pancakes or French toast. Check the continually changing evening performance schedule—some well-known folksingers have appeared—by visiting the web site: www.turningpoint cafe.com.

Wildflower Restaurant at Bear Mountain (845-786-2731), Route 9W, Bear Mountain. ($$) Open Monday through Saturday for lunch at 11; dinner at 5; open Sunday for brunch 11–3, dinner 5–9. Regional American cuisine and views of lovely Hessian Lake and the Hudson Valley. A great time to come here is for brunch, when waffles with ice cream are served. Your best bet is lunch, especially when traveling with children.

Xavier's at Piermont (845-359-7007), 506 Piermont Avenue, Piermont. ($$$) Open Wednesday through Sunday for dinner at 6; Sunday brunch noon–2:30. An intimate, elegant spot, this is a perfect place for people who enjoy fine dining. The imaginative menu featuring Continental cuisine has included roast pigeon with truffle sauce and fettuccine with fennel sausage and white grapes. For dessert, there is maple walnut soufflé, a house specialty. Not recommended for children.

EATING OUT **Café Dolce** (845-357-2066), 24 Lafayette Avenue, Suffern. ($$) Open Monday through Thursday 11–10; Friday and Saturday noon–midnight; Sunday 4–9. This European-style café serves cocktails, coffees of all kinds, tea, and light fare in a relaxed yet elegant ambience.

Easy Gourmet (845-680-2688), 646 Main Street, Sparkill. ($) Open daily 11–9:30. This is a great spot to grab a quick lunch or early dinner. There are many pastas, pizzas, wraps, salads, and quesadillas from which to choose. From noon–2 on weekends, children are allowed to make their own pizzas (and there is no charge for them!). A fun place to go with the kids.

El Bandito (845-425-6622), 27 East Center Avenue, Route 45, Spring Valley. ($) Open daily 11 AM–midnight. Strolling guitar players add to the fun atmosphere at this colorful Mexican eatery, where the portions are generous, and the margaritas are first-rate.

Hudson House (845-353-1355), 134 Main Street, Nyack. ($$) Open for lunch Tuesday through Friday 11:30–2:30, Saturday until 3. Sunday brunch is served 11:30–3. Dinner is served Tuesday through Thursday 5:30–10, Friday and Saturday until 11, and Sunday 5–9. Located across the street from the Helen Hayes Performing Arts Center, this building was originally a firehouse in the 19th century and later became the Nyack Village Hall. The chef, a Culinary Institute graduate, features contemporary American cuisine served with an imaginative flair.

Khan's Mongolian Garden (845-359-8004), 588 Route 303, Blauvelt. ($) Open daily for lunch and dinner noon–10. Just off the NYS Thruway exit 12, this is one of the better Mongolian barbecue restaurants I have tried. Choose your own ingredients and sauces, and watch while the chef creates a delectable meal before your eyes. The buffet includes appetizers, soup, barbecue, and dessert. The all-inclusive price is exceedingly reasonable. Don't miss this if you are traveling with children.

Krum's Chocolatiers (845-735-5100), 4 Dexter Plaza, Pearl River. ($) Open Tuesday-Saturday 10–4. In business since 1901, selling moderately priced chocolates throughout the world (find them at Bloomingdale's), this establishment offers candies, pastries, and jelly squares in addition to chocolates and truffles of all kinds, made daily on the premises. A good place to take out dessert.

La Bamba (845-365-1859), 627 Main Street, Sparkill. ($) Open daily 10:30–9:30. This restaurant offers home-cooked Mexican specialties prepared by the owners of the adjoining grocery. The enchiladas, tacos, and fajitas are delicious, and the price is right. Children of all ages will enjoy this informal eatery.

Latin Star Restaurant (845-429-1113), 39 Broadway, Haverstraw. ($) Open daily 6 AM–10 PM. The menu is quite extensive in this dinerlike establishment, serving Spanish specialties for breakfast, lunch, and dinner.

Mandarin Gourmet (845-352-9090), 212 Route 59, Monsey. ($) Open daily noon–10. The Szechuan, Mandarin, and Hunan specialties are all particularly good.

The Mountain House (845-359-9191), 333 Route 340, Sparkill. ($) Open daily for lunch and dinner noon–10. While the fare is basic Italian-American—burgers, salads, and pastas—the specialty of the house is the thin-crust pizza. A perfect place to go with young children.

Soup Stone Café (845-942-4010), 2 Main Street, Haverstraw ($) Open Monday–Thursday 6:30–2:30, Friday until 8, Saturday 7–3. The American cuisine is prepared by a Culinary Institute–trained chef who offers up excellent grilled Buffalo chicken wraps with blue cheese dressing, homemade soups, chili, salads, and freshly baked muffins and desserts. The freshly prepared stone soup is actually chicken soup with lots of vegetables, and it's slightly different every day. The owner says it contains an eclectic mix of ingredients, "just like the new Haverstraw."

Tacos Marianita (845-942-1295), 10 West Street, Haverstraw. ($) Open daily 11:30–10. If you want authentic tacos, fajitas, enchiladas, or burritos that taste exactly like those to be found in Mexico, this is the place to go. If you crave those traditional Mexican favorites, don't miss this spot.

Temptations (845-353-3355), 80½ Main Street, Nyack. ($) Open Monday through Saturday for lunch and dinner at 11, Sunday at noon. The shop is open late on summer evenings. Those with a sweet tooth won't want to miss this café. There are scores of dessert selections in addition to a wide variety of ice creams, frozen yogurts, cappuccinos, and exotic coffees. The light menu features soups, quiches, salads, and sandwiches.

✳ Selective Shopping

In Nyack

Nyack has many shops that are worth a visit, and an entire day can be spent strolling the shopping district and enjoying the antiques and artwork on view. Most shops are open daily except Monday, but call ahead if you are planning to visit. The following establishments are just some of the highlights of the area, but there are many more offering great shopping.

Hand of the Craftsman (845-358-6622), 152 North Main Street, carries work from more than 200 artists and craftspeople, including an unusual selection of kaleidoscopes and jewelry.

The Original Christopher's Antiques (845-358-9574), 71 South Broadway, is a fine gift shop with all kinds of unique items, including antiques and dried flowers.

Hickory, Dickory Dock (845-358-7474), 43 South Broadway, has clocks that tick, clocks that tock—hundreds of selections, so pity the poor mouse!

Liberty Crafts (845-358-3864), 13 South Broadway. Silver and gems, unique clothing, and a bead-and-findings section to help you create wearable art to suit your style.

Mary Grace's Antique & Country Pine (845-358-3273), 222 Main Street. Pine and fine antiques from Europe.

My Doll House (845-358-4185), 7 South Broadway, has everything for the miniature doll furniture and doll lover.

The Natural Eclectic (845-353-3464), 98 Main Street. Art, gifts, and accessories inspired by nature, including fountains, fossils, gargoyles, aromatherapy candles, oils, and soaps.

Nyack Tobacco Company (845-358-9300), 140 Main Street. For the cigar aficionado, this is the place. One of the most extensive selections outside Manhattan.

Oh, You Beautiful Doll (845-354-6835), 30 North Broadway, specializes in dolls and accessories.

Squash Blossom (845-353-0550), 49 Burd Street, offers Native American jewelry and crafts.

The Palisades Center (845-348-1000), 1000 Palisades Center Drive, West Nyack. This 3-million-square-foot, four-level shopping mall offers over 250 shops under one roof. In addition, there are 25 eateries and restaurants, a NHL-sized ice skating rink, a 68-foot Ferris wheel, a 21-screen movie complex, and an IMAX theater. Located off exit 12 of the NYS Thruway, at the junction of Routes 303 and 59, the mall is open Monday–Saturday 10–9:30, Sunday 11–7.

In Piermont

Piermont is smaller than Nyack, yet both are ideal for shopping excursions. The following are some of my favorite shops in this picturesque village, which is best experienced by wandering down Piermont Avenue and around the waterfront.

America House (845-359-0106), 466 Piermont Avenue, has a good selection of crafts by artisans from throughout the country.

The Mole Hole & Kitchen Too! (845-365-2154), 486 Piermont Avenue, offers wonderful unique gifts.

Piermont Wines & Liquors (845-359-0700), is one of those shops where you will find an amazing selection of wines from around the world. The owner is particularly helpful in providing assistance.

Sow's Ear (845-398-9865), 500 Piermont Avenue, features old-fashioned American items for both children and adults.

✳ Special Events

To get on the mailing list for special events in Rockland County, published quarterly, just call 845-638-5800, or go to the web site www.travelhudson-valley.org. Make sure to do this a couple of weeks in advance if you are planning a stay in the county. Visitors will enjoy dozens of fairs, festivals, walking tours, and special celebrations throughout the year, and it is impossible to list them all. Some of my favorite events include the **Nyack Winter Carnival** in February, the **Annual Art Expo** at Haverstraw's Garnerville Arts & Industrial Center in June, the **International Dance Festival** in Nyack in July, and the **Hawk Watch** at Hook Mountain in September.

Orange County

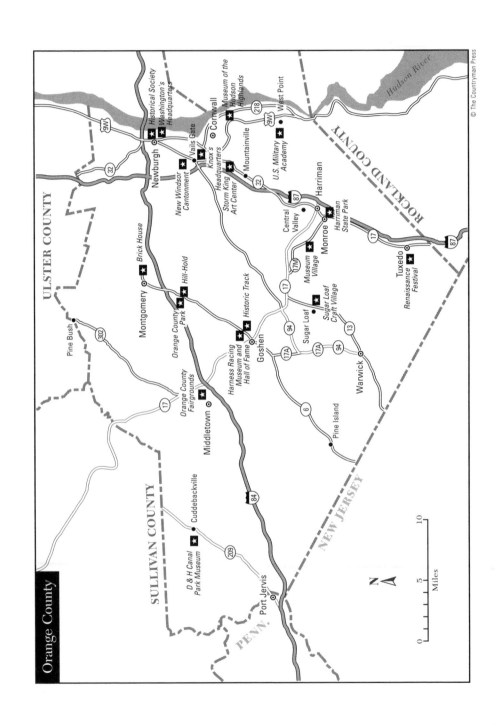

Orange County

© The Countryman Press

ORANGE COUNTY

Visitors are reminded in every village and every park in Orange County that this is a place that cherishes its history. Museums, restorations, and historic exhibits are everywhere, from the Native American displays in the Goshen Courthouse to the collection of military equipment at West Point. You can imagine the life of a Revolutionary War soldier as he waited out the bitter winters in a wooden hut, or watch as a costumed group of interpreters reenacts a battle that helped turn the tide of the American Revolution.

Orange County is also a place where the agricultural heritage of New York is still strong, a place where vegetable farming is a way of life for families and has been for generations. Stop at a farm and take home some just-picked peaches, or join in the fun at the Onion Festival. The Black Dirt area is a unique farming district where some of the best of New York's produce is grown, and a drive through the region in early summer gives new meaning to the word *bountiful*.

GUIDANCE **Orange County Tourism** (845-291-2136), 30 Matthews Street, Suite 111, Goshen 10924; www.orangetourism.org.

Palisades Parkway Tourist Information Center (845-786-5003), between exits 16 and 17 on the Palisades Interstate Parkway. This center offers trail and road maps, hiking and travel information, including NYS fishing licenses. Open daily April through October, 8–6; November through March, 8–5.

GETTING THERE *By car:* Orange County is accessible from exits 16 (Harriman) and 17 (Newburgh) off I-87, the New York State (NYS) Thruway, coming from the north or south, as well as from I-84 coming from points east and west. Route 17, which joins the Thruway at Suffern, is another route that goes into the county.

By bus: **Adirondack Trailways** (800-858-8555) runs buses regularly through Newburgh. **New Jersey Transit** (973-762-5100) runs buses to Greenwood Lake and Warwick. **Short Line** (800-631-8405) runs day trips and extended weekend trips stopping at several Orange County towns.

By train: **Metro North** (800-638-7646) stops in Beacon going to and from Grand Central Station in Manhattan. An inexpensive bus shuttle service across the Hudson from Newburgh connects with the trains.

By air: **Stewart International Airport** (845-564-7200), off NYS Thruway exit 17, on Route 207, in New Windsor, services major cities throughout the eastern U.S.

MEDICAL EMERGENCY **Arden Hill Hospital** (845-294-2170), 4 Harriman Drive, Goshen.

Orange Regional Medical Center (800-467-8666 or 845-342-7504), 60 Prospect Avenue, Middletown.

St. Anthony Community Hospital (845-986-2276), 15 Maple Avenue, Warwick.

St. Luke's Cornwall Hospital (845-561-4400), 70 Dubois Street, Newburgh; (845-534-7711), 19 Laurel Avenue, Cornwall.

✳ To See

Harness Racing Museum and Hall of Fame (845-294-6330/7542), 240 Main Street, Goshen. Open year-round 10–6; closed Christmas, Thanksgiving, and New Year's Day. Admission fee. Messenger and Hambletonian, pacers, trotters, and standardbreds—all call to mind the speed and grace to be found on a trotting track, and the history and color of the sport can be discovered at this unique museum established in 1951. Trotters and pacers (trotters move their right front and left rear legs at the same time; pacers move both legs on one side at the same time) have long been a part of American history. Such notable figures as George Washington, Abraham Lincoln, and Ulysses S. Grant spent time breeding and racing these swift horses. At the Harness Racing Museum and Hall of Fame, the history of the sport can be traced through dioramas, prints, exhibits, and statues displayed throughout the former Good Time Stables building. Galleries contain permanent displays of Currier and Ives prints, famous racing silks, and the amazing Hall of the Immortals, where dozens of small, lifelike statues recall the greatest participants (human and four-legged) in the sport. Restored stalls have full-sized replicas of horses and their equipment, while you can see the sulkies and sleighs the horses once pulled (it wasn't unheard of to drive a horse many miles, then race it, then drive it home to the farm). There is even a room that reproduces the interior of the clubhouse from the nearby Historic Track. The room is so well maintained that you expect to hear the rustle of programs and the voices of members discussing the best bet of the day. There are films and shows in the auditorium, changing gallery exhibits, and the world's only 3-D harness racing simulator that makes you feel you are the driver in a race (you can even feel the wind blowing through your hair!).

Historic Track (845-294-5333), located directly behind the Harness Racing Museum and Hall of Fame. The only sports facility in the country that is a National Historic Landmark, the Historic Track has been hosting meets since the 1830s. Although the Grand Circuit races visit here only once a year, the track is used as a training facility, so you may be able to see pacers, trotters, and a local blacksmith at work, no matter when you visit. The track is such a local institution that some of the private boxes have been passed down in families for generations.

Museum of the Hudson Highlands (845-534-7781), The Boulevard, Cornwall-on-Hudson. From Route 9W, take Route 218 east, turn onto Payson Road, and follow signs. Open year-round Thursday–Saturday 10–4, Sunday noon–4. Hours sometimes vary with the season, so call before you go. Donation suggested. Established in 1959 as a children's educational center, the Museum of the Hudson Highlands has expanded its natural history and environmental programs to include such special concerns as returning the bald eagle and peregrine falcon to the Hudson Valley and creating a detailed environmental "reference collection" of animals and plants from the region. Nature trails on the museum grounds wander through forests, glens, and an unusual tall-grass prairie. The museum itself is a wonderful place for parents and kids to get to know the local environment and the creatures that inhabit it. The natural wing, with its high, vaulted ceilings and tall windows, houses an indoor mini zoo, home to local snakes, mice, moles, turtles, owls, and crows, along with taxidermic mounts. The Ogden Gallery shows the work of local artists. Throughout the year the museum hosts special events, which include exploration days, workshops, and nature walks. The museum also owns **Kenridge Farm** (Route 9W, Cornwall; watch for the sign; 845-534-5506), where visitors can enjoy evening speakers, workshops, and classes, including those for young naturalists. There are also wonderful art exhibits and a good number of hiking trails that are ideal for families.

Museum Village of Orange County (845-782-8247), exit 129 off Route 17, Museum Village Road, Monroe (follow signs). Open May through December; hours vary with the season, so call ahead. Special events are held throughout the year; call for a schedule. Admission fee. The daily life of preindustrial America has been preserved and re-created at this fascinating museum comprised of buildings and equipment moved to the site from other parts of the Hudson Valley. Set up like a small crossroads village, the museum is considered to have one

THE DAILY LIFE OF PREINDUSTRIAL AMERICA HAS BEEN PRESERVED AT MUSEUM VILLAGE OF ORANGE COUNTY.

Orange County Tourism

of the largest sites devoted to the folk arts of everyday America. More than 35 buildings house crafts, equipment, and agricultural displays. At the blacksmith's shop, artisans hammer and pound hot metal into a door latch or horseshoe. The *thump-thump* of a foot-powered loom comes from the weaver's loft, where you may have a chance to try out the treadles yourself. In the newspaper office the master printer and the printer's devil (apprentice) are composing the weekly newspaper, and in the potter's workshop butter churns and mugs take shape on the wheel. Costumed guides answer questions; photos, prints, and tools trace the history of Orange County. The museum is a favorite place for children, and special events (Weekends on the Green), offered throughout the season, have included a Celtic Festival, America's birthday, and more. For a fun time set even farther back in history, visit the mastodon, the most complete skeleton of this 11,000-year-old animal in New York State. Every Labor Day weekend there is a Civil War encampment, the largest in the Northeast, and it includes battles, camping demonstrations, and drills.

Storm King Art Center (845-534-3115), Mountainville. Take the NYS Thruway to exit 16; the center is off Route 32 north, on Old Pleasant Hill Road—watch for signs. Open April 1–November 15; indoor galleries open mid-May. The sculpture park is open Saturday in June, July, and August until 8 PM, with an admission fee charged from 5 to 8. Call regarding special events. There are classical concerts, plays, and garden talks as well as family activities throughout the season. This 400-acre park and museum has one of the world's largest displays of outdoor sculpture. The permanent collection contains more than 120 works by 90 contemporary artists, including Isamu Noguchi, Louise Nevelson, Alexander Calder, David Smith, and Mark di Suvero. The surrounding landscape is lovely, with a backdrop of Schunnemunk Mountain. This is truly one of the most impressive stops in the region and shouldn't be missed. (Trams and elevators now make the grounds handicapped accessible.)

HISTORIC HOMES **Brick House** (845-457-4921), Route 17K, Montgomery. Open mid-May through October Saturday and Sunday 10–4. Admission fee. A treasure trove of early-American furniture and decorative arts owned by the same family since 1768. Now run by the county, the house—a red Georgian mansion constructed with bricks imported from England—is considered one of the finest private homes built between New York City and Albany in the 18th century. It was a meeting site for colonial officers during the Revolution, and many of the original furnishings are still intact. Pieces include a very rare 17th-century chest from Connecticut, fine crystal, Lafayette china (produced to honor the French hero), chairs that may have belonged to the Washingtons, and an Eli Terry shelf clock. Brick House is also the site of a large autumn antiques show.

David Crawford House Museum (845-561-2585), 189 Montgomery Street, Newburgh. Open April through October Sunday 1–4 or by appointment. Admission fee. Maintained and run by the Historical Society of Newburgh Bay and the Highlands, Crawford House, a neoclassical-style structure, was built in 1830. There are changing exhibits in the gallery. Visitors will enjoy the spectacular river views and the collection of pint-sized Hudson River sloop and ship models.

Gomez Mill House (845-236-3126), 11 Millhouse Road, Marlboro. Open April through October, Wednesday through Sunday, 10-5. Admission fee. The oldest surviving Jewish residence in the United States, and the oldest manor house in Orange County, this was the home of Lewis Moses Gomez, who arrived in America in 1703 and became a prosperous businessman. He built a stone trading post north of Newburgh, the site of the house, in 1714. In addition to the home, visitors will see the ice house, root cellar, and restored mill and dam. Continuously inhabited for 290 years, the Gomez house has been a fur trading post and a home to merchants, farmers, and craftsmen.

Hill-Hold (845-291-2404), Route 416, Campbell Hall. Open mid-May through October, Wednesday through Sunday 10–4. Admission fee. Once a section of a 30,000-acre estate, the land Hill-Hold stands on was presented to William Bull, an English stonemason, as a wedding present in the early 18th century. His son, Thomas Bull, built the home. Fortunately for lovers of 18th-century architecture later family members donated the house and most of its furnishings to the county. The large Georgian mansion is graced by elegant wood and stonework, with barrel-backed cupboards, paneling, and deep-silled windows. Rooms are furnished with many original Chippendale, Queen Anne, and Empire pieces. Two kitchens are still extant in the house: one in the basement and a newer one, added in 1800, in a separate stone wing. Like most manor houses of the era, Hill-Hold was also the center of a thriving farm. Surrounding the farmhouse are the original outbuildings, including the granary, barn, summer kitchen, wagon house, smokehouse, and, of course, the privy. On the working farm sheep, cows, chickens, and geese are tended. Children will enjoy the farm animals, and flower lovers should spend some time in the summer gardens. Also on the site is the Goosetown School, a one-room schoolhouse still used for educational programs on daily life in the 19th century.

HISTORIC SITES Clove Furnace (845-351-4696), Arden Road, south of Harriman (accessible from Route 17). Admission fee. Open year-round Monday through Friday 8–4:30, weekends by appointment. Although not a very active site, this is an unusual one: a small museum devoted to the history of iron making in rural New York. The restored hot-blast furnace dates from 1854 and was used to produce artillery pieces during the Civil War. Exhibits outline the story of iron making and mining, and there are displays related to Orange County history (some include rare Parrott artillery pieces). An enlightening stop for those interested in the commercial development of what was once a major industry in America.

Constitution Island and the Warner House (845-446-8676). Take Route 9W to West Point, enter the U.S. Military Academy gate, and take the first right past the Hotel Thayer. The dock and a large parking lot are at the end of the street. (Since September 11, 2001, there are restrictions on touring the USMA site independently, so call ahead to check current regulations.) Tours are offered mid-June through late September, Wednesday and Thursday at 1 and 2 only. Call for reservations—only 40 people per tour. Admission fee. To visit this Hudson River island, take the boat from West Point to Constitution Island. There you will find a 17-room Victorian mansion, home to the Warner family from 1836 to 1915. The daughters, Anna and Susan, grew up on the island and were best known for their writing; Anna penned many hymns, including "Jesus Loves Me," and Susan's *Wide Wide World* was a best-seller. After their father lost his fortune, the sisters stayed on in their home, living frugally and teaching Sunday school courses to West Point cadets, who never forgot the two spinsters. Their home is now a museum filled with their original possessions. Also on the island are the remains of **Fort Constitution,** a Revolutionary War-era fort, and the **Anna B. Warner Memorial Garden,** which is particularly lovely in late June. The surrounding Hudson is glorious anytime. If you visit the West Point cemetery, look for the sisters' graves; they were buried near their beloved home.

Knox's Headquarters (845-561-5498), Forge Hill Road, Route 94, Vails Gate. Open Memorial Day through Labor Day, Wednesday through Saturday 10–5, Sunday 1–5; grounds open daily. Admission fee. For several periods during the Revolution, the Ellison family's stone house served as headquarters for the colonial officers in the area. Generals Henry Knox, Horatio Gates, and Nathanael Greene were only a few of the men who met in the house and planned campaigns in the gracious rooms. Today it is furnished with military camp beds and folding desks such as those that displaced the Ellisons' fine 18th-century furniture. There is also a small plant sanctuary on the grounds, dedicated to the memory of America's first woman botanist.

New Windsor Cantonment (845-561-1765), Temple Hill Road, off Route 32 and 300, Vails Gate. Open April through October, Wednesday through Saturday 10–5, Sunday 1–5. Admission fee. Washington's troops waited out the last months of the Revolutionary War here in anticipation of an announced cessation of hostilities. More than 10,000 soldiers, officers, cooks, and blacksmiths, along with their wives and other camp followers, constructed the snug log cabins, outbuildings, and a meeting hall, and here Washington quelled a mutiny of his troops, who resented Congress's slowness with wages and pensions. After the war, the buildings were auctioned off for the lumber, and the land remained unused until the state acquired 70 acres and began restoration of the site.

A visit to the cantonment today provides a look into the everyday life of Revolutionary soldiers. At the orientation center a slide show is given on the history of the area during the war, and displays depict the difficulties faced by both the troops and their leaders. One fascinating display is of an original Badge of Military Merit, now known as the Purple Heart, which Washington presented to several soldiers. A walkway leads from the orientation center to the rebuilt parade grounds and buildings. Costumed guides go about their business blacksmithing, drilling, cooking, and even entertaining (a fife player may be on hand). There are also demonstrations of 18th-century medical procedures. Although many of the buildings have been reconstructed from sketches that remain from the era, one is original. It had been carted away to become an addition to a local house, and there it remained for a century and a half, until its importance was realized, and it was returned to the site. Just across the road, on the west side of Route 300, are a small museum and re-created campground that illustrate the lives of the enlisted men during the war.

THE UNITED STATES MILITARY ACADEMY AT WEST POINT

United States Military Academy (visitors center 845-938-2638), located off Route 9W, just north of Bear Mountain State Park; follow the signs. The visitors center is open 9–4:45 daily except Thanksgiving, Christmas and New Year's Day. The post is open year-round except major holidays; the museum opens daily at 10:30 except Christmas and New Year's Day. Admission is free, but there is a charge for a bus tour of the post. (Since September 11, 2001, visitors are no longer permitted to travel as freely within the academy, so an organized tour may now be the best way to go. Call 845-938-2638/7049 for current information.) Situated on the bluffs overlooking the Hudson River, this is where the nation's army officers have been trained since 1802; where Benedict Arnold attempted to bring the British to power; where such distinguished cadets as Robert E. Lee, Ulysses S. Grant, and Douglas MacArthur once marched; and where undistinguished cadets like James Whistler and Edgar Allan Poe discovered their other talents. Tradition is important at West Point, and tradition is what you will find here, from the Long Gray Line of cadets to the quiet cemetery and imposing stone barracks.

It is very difficult to see all of West Point in one visit—there are statues, museums, chapels, and points of interest everywhere you turn. But even if you can't stay overnight, use your time well, and make your first stop the visitors center on Main Street near the Thayer Gate entrance. Maps, schedules of events, and a display and movie about the cadets' lives at the Point are available at the center, where you can also pick up the USMA bus tour, which leaves every 20 minutes and lasts nearly an hour in the summer season. (The frequency of the tours changes seasonally.)

A must-see is the **West Point Museum** (845-938-2203), which is in Olmstead Hall. This is the oldest military museum in the country, and its holdings are among the largest in the world. Dioramas, permanent and changing exhibits, and thousands of artifacts are found throughout vast galleries, each with its own theme: the history of war, American warfare, weapons, the history of West Point. Visitors may see anything from a Stone Age hunting ax to the equipment used in Vietnam. Because the museum has so many collections, displays are changed frequently. Outside on the post itself, Trophy Point recalls the dead of the Civil War; there is also a 150-ton chain that was used to close off the Hudson River to British ships during the American Revolution. Although the attempt was unsuccessful, the chain represents the ingenuity that made America the victor. To the rear of the memorial is the Plain, the drilling area once used by Baron von Steuben to train and parade troops. It is still used on Saturday for full-dress parades by the cadets.

The **Cadet Chapel** contains stained-glass windows, the largest church organ in the world, and an overpowering sense of the men and women who have worshiped there. Another restored section of the Point is Fort Putnam, which was used as a fortification in the Revolutionary War and offers exhibits on the lives of Revolutionary soldiers and a show about the battles fought in the area. It also offers a panoramic view of the surrounding mountains. (Currently, the only way for travelers to see the chapel is with an organized tour, due to increased security within the Academy.)

West Point is famous for its football games, played at Michie Stadium; tickets almost always have to be purchased in advance. In addition to football, there are basketball, hockey, and lacrosse games. Call the box office for a complete schedule (845-446-4996).

Concerts are given throughout the summer at various sites on the post; most are free and include the West Point Military Band. The concerts alone are well worth the trip. **Eisenhower Hall Theatre,** on the grounds of West Point, has shows that range from musical revivals and classic country to dramatic theater and just plain classics; call 845-938-4159 for schedules and ticket information.

Just south of the Academy is a Revolutionary War site, **Fort Montgomery Historic Site** (845-786-2701, ext. 226) that offers magnificent views of the Hudson River, interpretive signs describing the "turning-point" battle that occurred here centuries ago, and a pedestrian suspension bridge permitting access to nearby Fort Clinton at the Bear Mountain Zoo. This is a wonderful destination for history buffs; the site is maintained by the Palisades Interstate Park Commission.

Washington's Headquarters (845-562-1195), 84 Liberty Street, Newburgh. Take Route 17 from the NYS Thruway to downtown Newburgh; watch for signs. Open mid-April through October (the rest of the year by appointment), Wednesday through Saturday 10–5; Sunday 1–5. Call for the schedule of special celebrations. If Jonathan Hasbrouck's stone mansion set on a bluff overlooking the Hudson River could speak, it would say that Martha and George slept here. In fact, the end of the American Revolution was announced on the grounds. Construction began in 1750 but was not finished until 1782, when Washington's troops added a gunpowder laboratory, a barracks, a privy, and a larger kitchen. Washington remained here for nearly a year and a half, waiting for the British to leave New York under the terms of surrender. The house and grounds were acquired by the government in 1848, and on opening day, July 4, 1850, Washington's Headquarters became America's first National Historic Site.

In the adjacent museum, opened in 1910, is an exhibit called "First in the Nation," which highlights the site's history of over 150 years. The galleries here recall the events of 1782–83, including the establishment of the Badge of Military Merit, forerunner of the Purple Heart. A section of the chain and boom that was stretched across the Hudson at West Point, a life-size portrait of George Washington—and even a lock of his hair—are just a few of the many fascinating items on display. (For vision impaired and blind visitors, a Braille tour is available.)

The story of the Revolution truly comes alive inside Hasbrouck House, where Washington is seen as a man who endured problems, boredom, and loss of the privacy that was so dear to him. (The house was owned by Tryntje Hasbrouck, a widow, who received notice of her eviction with a "sullen silence"—or so history records.) Visitors are guided through the eight rooms in which Washington and his staff lived and worked. The dining room where George and Martha ate their meals still contains the original jambless Dutch fireplace, open on three sides. The plain bedrooms and offices are sparsely furnished, and a field bed with its tentlike covering speaks clearly of the winter cold, while bedrooms show that not everyone was fortunate enough to have a room. The grounds are well kept and offer wide views up and down the Hudson. Special events are held throughout the year and include kite-flying days, Martha Washington's birthday celebration, and, of course, George Washington's birthday festivities.

SCENIC DRIVES The term *scenic drive* in Orange County is almost redundant; there are so many well-maintained roads where the pace is unhurried and the views are lovely that just about any drive around the county is certain to please. Even the Thruway softens up a bit as it moves through the Harriman area—drivers will see deer at twilight and apple blossoms in the spring. Route 9W is an attractive road, but the section known as Old Storm King Highway, between West Point and Cornwall, is spectacular.

For a lovely country drive past lakes and trees, start at Harriman and take

WASHINGTON'S HEADQUARTERS IN NEWBURGH BECAME AMERICA'S FIRST NATIONAL HISTORIC SITE.

Orange County Tourism

HAWK'S NEST DRIVE

Route 6 east across Bear Mountain State Park to the Bear Mountain Bridge; from there 9W north offers vibrant Hudson River views on its way through West Point, Cornwall, and into Newburgh. Once in Newburgh, look for Route 32 around Cronomer Hill Park, a breathtaking sight in summer and fall.

Another noted scenic highway in Orange County is Hawk's Nest Drive, Route 92, near Sparrow Bush. The road runs along the Delaware River for a short distance, but you can then follow Route 209 north to the Delaware and Hudson Canal Park (see *Green Space*).

A different type of view is found along Route 17A, which cuts through the rich Black Dirt farming area around Pine Island. Kane Road near 17A in Warwick goes up Mount Peter between Warwick and Greenwood Lake, offering great views of the valley. This area is a major skyway for migrating hawks. If you follow Route 6 from Goshen to Pine Island you will travel through one of the largest onion producing areas in the country. Over 14,000 acres of vegetable farms, with several farm stands along the way, the Black Dirt region was formed from a glacial lake over 12,000 years ago. The area was once called the drowned lands before it was drained to create the farmland it is today.

WINERIES The following wineries in Orange County are open to visitors, but you might want to call ahead for operating hours, since they change depending on the season. Several special events are listed on the website www.shawangunkwinetrail.com.

Applewood Winery (845-988-9292), 82 Four Corners Road, Warwick. This small operation produces fruit wines, grape wines, and cider. Open Saturday and Sunday 11–5. The winery is a nice place to stop in the autumn, when old-fashioned, Dutch-style doughnuts are served, and you can pick your own apples and pears in the orchard.

Baldwin Vineyards (845-744-2226), 110 Hardenburgh Estate Road, Pine Bush, is open year-round for tastings, Friday through Monday 11:30–5. Hours and days expand in season, so call ahead.

Brimstone Hill Vineyard (845-744-2231), 61 Brimstone Hill Road, Pine Bush, is open Friday through Monday 11:30–5:30, with expanded hours in the summer and fall seasons. They offer a nice selection of wines.

Brotherhood Winery (845-496-9101), Route 94, Washingtonville, is open daily year-round 11–5. America's oldest winery offers visitors a tour of the wine production facility and the cellars. There is a fee, but a free tasting is included. Visitors can stroll around the grounds and enjoy the special events, including concerts and shows during the summer.

Demarest Hill Winery (845-986-4723), Grand Street, 81 Pine Island Turnpike, Warwick, is open daily year-round November through May 11–5 and June through October 11–6. The wine here is made in the Italian tradition; offerings include 36 different products.

Warwick Valley Winery (845-258-4858), 114 Little York Road, Warwick, is open year-round. The hours vary seasonally: January–Memorial Day, Thursday–Sunday 11–6; the rest of the year, open daily. Enjoy award-winning wines and ciders made from both pears (once called *perry*) and apples. They were the first to make brandy in New York State. There is a lovely vineyard, and visitors can pick their own apples and pears in season at the winery's 65-acre Friendship Farm.

WARWICK VALLEY WINERY MADE NEW YORK STATE'S FIRST BRANDY.

Orange County Tourism

✴ To Do

BALLOONING Above the Clouds (845-692-2556), P.O. Box 4816, Middletown, open May through October, offers two one-hour flights daily (one at sunrise and the other two hours before sunset) from Randall Airport. Advance reservations are a must. The price is approximately $200 per person. This is an unusual, dramatic way to see the Hudson Valley's rolling hills, forests and farmlands. Fully insured; certified pilot.

Fantasy Balloon Flights (845-856-7103), 2 Evergreen Lane, Port Jervis, offers half-hour rides, departing from Randall Airport, May through October; advance reservations necessary. FAA certified commercial pilots; fully insured. All flights include champagne and a flight certificate. Groups accommodated.

BOAT CRUISES One of the best ways to see the Hudson is from the river itself. As far back as the early days of European settlement in the region, the river catered to tourists in addition to being a major trade route. Today, a few companies offer travelers a relaxing way to take in the scenery while cruising.

Hudson Highlands Cruises (845-534-SAIL/7245), P.O. Box 355, Cornwall-on-Hudson, has daily cruises aboard the *Commander* (on the National Historic Register) leaving from Haverstraw Marina and West Point. The narrated excursion tours run daily, May through October. Snack bar.

Hudson River Adventures (845-220-2120), 26 Front Street, Newburgh, offers cruises—call for complete schedule—from May through October, Wednesdays through Sunday, on the *Pride of the Hudson,* departing from Newburgh Landing

CRUISES ON THE HUDSON DEPART FROM NEWBURGH LANDING

Orange County Tourism

(just off Route 9W near the junction of Route 84). Or from the NYS Thruway, take exit 17 and follow 17K east, which becomes Broadway; at the end of Broadway, turn left onto Colden Street and follow to the bottom of the hill. Newburgh Landing is on the opposite side of the train trestle. Bannerman's Castle, which rises from the north side of Pollepel Island like a medieval fantasy, is one of the most intriguing sights on the Hudson. Travelers can discover the mystery and history of the castle with the 40-minute narration as the tour boat approaches the island. Castle enthusiasts will love this cruise and special tours of the island via water taxi were being planned as of this writing. Snack bar.

The *River Rose* (845-562-1067), Newburgh Landing, Newburgh. This two-deck Mississippi-style paddleboat plies the Hudson May through October, Friday through Sunday, rain or shine. Particularly nice during foliage season, with magnificent views of Breakneck Ridge and Storm King Mountain. Snack bar. Call for complete schedule and special events excursions.

The Newburgh Waterfront is a wonderful place to visit, even if you aren't interested in embarking on a cruise. The paved walkway to the river offers spectacular views of Bannerman Island, Storm King Mountain, Mount Beacon, and the Newburgh Bay. Stroll past several shops, and enjoy a drink al fresco in the warm-weather months at one of the area's restaurants. (From the NYS Thruway, take I-84 east to exit 10, just before the Newburgh-Beacon Bridge. Make a right off the exit and a left at the next light. Follow to the waterfront.)

CANOEING AND KAYAKING The Delaware River may not have the same cachet as the Colorado, but it can offer a beautiful day of canoeing or kayaking. Most canoe and kayak rentals are in the western part of the county; the trips may range from drifting idylls to challenging white water in the spring. **Silver Canoe Rentals** (845-856-7055), 37 South Maple Drive, Port Jervis, also rents kayaks and rafts. Transport and pickup are included in their rates, and they are open daily, April through September, 8–7; **Wild and Scenic River Tours and Rentals** (845-557-8783, 800-836-0366) in Barryville; **Lander's Delaware River Trips** (800-252-3925), Route 97, Narrowsburg, and **Kittatinny Canoes** (1-800-FLOTA-KC), Barryville, all rent canoes, kayaks, and equipment. They will help you organize a safe, successful outing, particularly if you are a first-timer. Some of these outfitters offer guide services. For safety reasons, call and ask about river conditions before you go. (Because Orange and Sullivan Counties overlap in relation to the Delaware River, check the listings in the Sullivan County chapter, as well.)

FARM STANDS AND PICK-YOUR-OWN FARMS Few people know that Velveeta cheese was created at a factory on Mill Pond Parkway in Monroe in 1917. Because so much of Orange County is agricultural (the Black Dirt area produces half of the onions grown in New York State), you will find dozens of farm stands here. Some specialize in one particular fruit or vegetable, others offer a wide variety, but everything is as fresh as it gets. Try to plan a trip to the Orange County Onion Harvest Festival if you are visiting in August (see *Special Events* at the end of this chapter).

The Pine Island area offers several top-drawer farm stands and pick-your-own farms. A couple of my favorite stops are **Scheuermann Farms** (845-258-4221), Little York Road, off County Road 1, open May through October, a fifth-generation family farm offering top-quality flowers, fruits, and vegetables grown on the premises, and **Sudol Farms** (845-258-4260), 762 County Route 1, open September through December 9–5, which stocks a variety of local produce including apples, honey, gourds, squash, and Indian corn.

Applewood Orchards (845-986-1684), 82 Four Corners Road, Warwick, is open in September and October. They operate a roadside stand with vegetables but specialize in several varieties of pick-your-own apples and pumpkins. There are free wagon rides, puppet shows, an animal petting area, and a nature walk. A great place to take the kids.

Ace Farms (845-873-1381), County Road 105, Highland Mills, 1.5 miles west of Route 32. Open year-round, Ace has a wide selection of fruits and vegetables (some pick-your-own) and in autumn, hayrides and pumpkins. **Hodgson's Farm** (845-778-1432), 2290 Albany Post Road, Walden, is open May through Christmas, Friday through Sunday 10–5. The kids will enjoy exploring the petting zoo; in the fall there are hayrides and a haunted house. You may also enjoy a farm or greenhouse tour; ideal for group visits. **Overlook Farm Market** (845-562-5780), Route 9W, Newburgh, sells local apples, peaches, nectarines, pumpkins, and a variety of home-baked pies, cakes, and cookies.

For a different type of experience, visit **Swissette Herb Farm** (845-496-7841), 216 Clove Road, Salisbury Mills, which sells herbs and plants, dried spices, medicinal teas, and other herb-based products. Located off Route 94 outside Vails Gate, the farm is open daily May through October. **Krisco Farms** (845-294-7784), Purgatory Road (off the Sarah Wells Trail) in Campbell Hall, is a dairy farm and offers some unusual delights: chocolate milk, fresh eggs, yogurt, and ice cream in their farm store. Christmas trees may be cut at **Fox Ridge Christmas Tree Farm** (845-986-3771), Fox Hill Road, Warwick, **Maples Farm** (845-344-0330), 749 Route 17M, Middletown (their shop includes homemade fudge, baked goods, and crafts), and **Pine View Farm** (845-564-4111), 575 Jackson Avenue, New Windsor. (Here you can cut your own balsam, Canaan, and Fraser fir; and blue, white, and Norway spruce. There are candy canes, coloring books, and live animals for the children. Open weekends in December 9–4.)

Farmers markets also bloom in Orange County. The selection is often unique. The **Goshen Farmers Market** (845-294-7741) is held off Main Street in the central parking lot every Friday 10–7, May through November. The **Middletown Farmers Market** (845-343-8075) sets up Saturday 8–noon, late June through October, at the municipal lot on James and Depot Streets. The **Warwick Farmers Market** (845-986-2720) is held Sundays 10–3, July through October, at the South Street parking lot.

GOLF **Central Valley Golf Club** (845-928-6924), 206 Smith Clove Road, Central Valley, was built in 1922 and is still owned and operated by the same family.

An 18-hole challenging course set against the Ramapo Mountains, Central Valley is open daily from mid-March through November, dawn to dusk.

51

ORANGE COUNTY

Mansion Ridge Golf Club (845-782-7888), 1292 Orange Turnpike, Monroe, is New York's only Jack Nicklaus Signature Design course open to the public. At one time a 220-acre estate, this 6,889-yard championship course features stunning rock formations and great scenery. The stone-barn clubhouse has a pro shop and restaurant. Open April through November, dawn to dusk.

Scenic Farms Golf Course (845-258-4455), Glenwood Road, Pine Island. Open April through November, weekdays 7 AM–8 PM, weekends 6:30 AM–10 PM. This professionally designed nine-hole executive golf course is excellent for beginners and challenging for advanced golfers. There is a driving range as well as practice putting and chipping greens.

Stony Ford Golf Course (845-457-4949), 550 Route 416, Hamptonburgh. Located in Thomas Bull Memorial Park, just south of Montgomery, this 18-hole course is open March through November, dawn to dusk.

Wallkill Golf Club (845-361-1022), Sands Road, Fair Oaks; exit 119 off Route 17 West (845-361-1022). Open April 1–November, this 18-hole championship course is fairly challenging. Driving range and restaurant on premises.

West Point Golf Course (845-938-2435), on the outskirts of the USMA, West Point. Founded in 1948, this hilly, challenging course has a practice green with pitching and chipping areas. They suggest calling three days in advance for a tee time.

HIKING Trails range from easy to advanced and offer views of river, woodlands, and meadows. The first section of the **Appalachian Trail** was founded at Bear Mountain in 1923, and a portion of it offers spectacular views of Greenwood Lake as it weaves through the southwest section of the county; call the Palisades Interstate Parks Commission (845-786-5003) for maps and specific trail information.

Black Rock Forest, Route 9W, north of West Point in Cornwall, has marked and unmarked trails that vary in length; decent hiking skill is required. Trail maps are available in a parking lot on the southbound lane of Route 9W.

The **Heritage Trail** (845-294-8886) is a converted railbed of the Erie Railroad. One can walk or bike this scenic route, which passes through Chester, Goshen, and Monroe. All three towns have entrances to the trail.

The **Highlands Trail** is a rather rugged 35-mile trail that starts in Cornwall-on-Hudson, traverses the scenic highlands, continues over Schunnemunk Mountain, through Black Rock Forest, to the top of Storm King Mountain.

Two parks have trails of varying difficulty: **Schunnemunk,** Route 32 in Highland Mills, has six marked trails, the longest of which is 8 miles; and **Winding Hills Park,** Route 17K, Montgomery, has trails, a place to picnic, and a nature study area.

Sterling Forest State Park (845-351-5907), 115 Old Forge Road, Tuxedo has the 8-mile **Sterling Ridge Trail,** the 3-mile **Allis Trail,** the 4-mile **Indian Hill**

Loop, 7 miles of the Appalachian Trail, and 10 miles of the Highlands Trail. The information center is located at the south end of Sterling Lake.

Stewart State Forest (845-256-3076), in the town of New Windsor, has semi-paved areas for walking, running, mountain biking, and horseback riding. There are three areas along Route 207, between Drury Lane and Route 208, where one can pull off the highway and access the trailheads.

HORSEBACK RIDING **Borderland Farm** (845-986-1704), 340 State Route 94. Warwick, is a 230-acre riding facility with both indoor and outdoor rings and miles of trails. Located at the NY/NJ border, this facility also offers lessons at all levels.

Clove Acres Riding Academy (845-496-8655), 299 Mountain Lodge Road, Monroe, specializes in English riding. The family atmosphere makes this place ideal for the youngest riders.

Gardnertown Farms (845-564-6658), 822 Gardnertown Farm Road, Newburgh. There is no trail riding here, but there are indoor and outdoor facilities, polo lessons, and tournaments. Riding by appointment only.

Juckas Stables (845-361-1429), Route 302, Bullville. This establishment has been in business for nearly 40 years. There are lovely trails, and both English and Western riding are offered. Friendly, informal atmosphere.

ICE SKATING **Bear Mountain State Park** (845-786-2701), Route 9W, Bear Mountain. This outdoor rink offers public sessions of an hour and a half from mid-October to early March. There is admission, but kids under five skate free. Rentals available.

Ice Time Sports Complex (845-567-0005), 21 Lakeside Road, Newburgh, (exit 6 off Interstate 84 at Route 17K). Two Olympic-sized indoor ice rinks offer public skating and figure-skating sessions. This is a great place for family fun. Lessons, rentals, and skating camp in July and August. Lockers, snack bar, pro shop, spacious seating area for spectators.

SKIING **Mount Peter** (845-986-4940), Route 17A & Old Mt. Peter Road, Warwick, has a vertical drop of 400 feet, two double chairlifts, and eight downhill slopes for skiing and snowboarding. Open daily in-season, but it's a good idea to call for hours.

Sterling Forest Ski Area (800-843-4414), on Route 17A West, Tuxedo, is open daily, mid-December through mid-March, and offers night skiing every day. There is a vertical drop of 400 feet, four double chairlifts, and seven slopes, which will delight both skiers and snowboarders.

SWIMMING **Bear Mountain State Park Pool & Harriman State Park Beaches** (845-786-2701), Route 9W, Bear Mountain. From Memorial Day weekend through Labor Day, these swim areas will be particularly appealing to those traveling with young children. It is best to call ahead for the schedule. Admission fee.

Redwood Tennis and Swim Club (845-343-9478), 620 Van Burenville Road, Middletown. Open daily, June through Labor Day weekend. The pool is huge and is located in a 9-acre recreation area with picnic tables and outdoor and indoor clay tennis courts. Admission fee.

✳ Green Space

Delaware & Hudson Canal Park/Neversink Valley Area Museum (845-754-8870), just off Route 209 on Hoag Road, about 10 miles south of Wurtsboro in Cuddebackville; watch carefully for signs. The park is open year-round, with special events scheduled in the warmer months. The museum is open March through December, Thursday through Sunday noon–4, and by appointment. Admission fee. This 300-acre park, a registered National Historic Landmark, recalls an era when coal, lumber, and other goods were moved from Pennsylvania to New York by a combination of water, mules, and backbreaking labor. Huge barges were often run as family businesses, with the crew consisting of parents and children. And there wasn't much room for profit, since the barges moved at a leisurely 3 miles per hour. The park sponsors seasonal events that evoke life in old-time New York State. Demonstrations have included ice cutting, story evenings, nature walks, and even a silent-film festival (the park was once used by D. W. Griffith). The museum has exhibits about the canal and its people and is located in a restored blacksmith's house near the aqueduct; other buildings include a lockkeeper's house, a canal store, and a full-sized replica of a canal barge. Tours of the towpath are offered Sunday afternoons; call for a schedule.

In addition to its regular historical exhibitions, the museum now offers canal boat rides on the *Neversink Kate*. The 30-minute ride costs approximately $5 and includes a narrated history of the D&H Canal.

Indian Hill/Southfields Furnace (845-473-4440), Orange Turnpike, Tuxedo. (From exit 16, NYS Thruway, take Route 17 south. Make a right on County Route 19, also known as Orange Turnpike. After approximately 1 mile, the entrance is on the right.) The fascinating ruins of a 19th-century iron furnace can be seen at this 500-acre park. The trails include a 4-mile loop traversing hardwood forest and rock outcroppings. Panoramic views of the Ramapo River Valley and Harriman State Park.

Moodna Creek Marsh (845-473-4440), Plum Point Lane, New Windsor. (Take Route 9W to Plum Point Lane, which is north of the intersection of Routes 9W and 94.) You can travel by canoe or kayak on the Hudson River from this state-owned, 60-acre Kowawese Unique Area, managed by the NYS Department of Environmental Conservation. You may see the historic homestead of one of George Washington's lieutenants, the Squire Nicoll house, which dates back to 1735 (not open to visitors). There are wonderful views of Bannerman's Castle on Pollepel Island, Mount Beacon, and Storm King Mountain. Also see **Bear Mountain** and **Harriman State Parks** under *Green Space* ("Rockland County") and **Storm King Art Center** under *To See* in this chapter.

✳ Lodging

Bed and breakfasts have proliferated throughout Orange County in recent years. In fact, there is now an Orange County B&B Association (800-210-5565); they may also be accessed through the Internet at www.new-york-inns.com. The following selections for overnight accommodations around the county are particularly charming or special in some way:

Caldwell House B&B (845-496-2954), 25 Orrs Mills Road, Salisbury Mills 12577. ($$$) If you want a truly deluxe B&B experience, try this establishment, a renovated home that dates back to 1803. There are four rooms, all with private bath, TV, and VCR; one has a Jacuzzi. All rooms are decorated with antiques; the four-poster beds have handmade linens.

Cromwell Manor Inn (845-534-7136), Angola Road, Cornwall 12518. ($$$) This renovated inn, a historic country estate dating back to 1820, is situated on 7 acres of woodland and gardens near West Point and Stewart Airport. The 13 rooms and suites (all with private bath) are beautifully decorated with period antiques. Many

THE CROMWELL MANOR INN, CORNWALL

Orange County Tourism

rooms have a working fireplace and Jacuzzi, and all are air-conditioned. A full breakfast is served in the country dining room or on the veranda. Step back in time without sacrificing modern amenities. This inn is only a 10-minute drive from West Point and a few miles from Storm King Art Center (see *To See*). The lovely village of Cornwall, with its charming shops and variety of restaurants, is down the road. Jones Farm Country Store (see *Selective Shopping*) is next door to the inn. Open year-round.

Anthony Dobbins Stagecoach Inn (845-294-5526), 268 Main Street, Goshen 10924. ($$) A former stagecoach stop, this inn is located in the middle of a country town, a few minutes' walk from shopping, dining, and the racetrack and museum. Four rooms, all with private bath; rates include a full breakfast. Open year-round.

Eddy Farm Resort (845-858-4300, 800-336-5050), Routes 42 and 97, Sparrow Bush 12780. ($$) Open year-round (except mid-December to mid-January). Located on the banks of the Delaware River, this hotel has been taking care of guests for more than a century. When craftsmen took their logs down to Pennsylvania, they stopped at Eddy Farm; after the Civil War, families would visit from the city. This is a full-service resort, with an outdoor pool, golf course, dance floor, and restaurant (meals can be included, and a B&B plan is an option). Both private and shared bath arrangements are available. The hotel will arrange rafting trips on the Delaware River and offers entertainment throughout the season.

Glenwood House Bed and Breakfast (845-258-5066), 49 Glenwood

Road, Pine Island. ($$) Enjoy accommodations in an elegant Victorian farmhouse located only 10 minutes from the village of Warwick, in a beautiful rural area of Orange County renowned for onion growing. Five rooms, all with private bath, some with fireplace and whirlpool. There is also an outdoor hot tub, deck, and cabana. Open year-round.

Hambletonian House (845-469-6425), 19 High Street, Chester. ($$) This elegant Victorian home, built in 1850, is situated on a hill surrounded by trees and gardens. The period furnishings will transport guests back in time to an era when the pace was slower. A full breakfast is served on the porch (in season) or in the dining room. There are two air-conditioned rooms, each with a private bath.

Heritage Farm (845-778-3420), 163 Berea Road, Walden 12586. ($$) This bed & breakfast is located on a working horse farm. The 18th-century Connecticut saltbox home is situated on 21 acres, an ideal place to stay for those who ride horses or would like to do so—horse lovers will be delighted by a stay at this farm. There are three rooms—one with private bath and two that share a bath. A full country breakfast is served.

Inn at Stony Creek (845-986-3660), 34 Spankytown Road, Warwick 10990. ($$) Enjoy a historic 1860 Greek-Revival farmhouse that overlooks scenic meadows and a stream. The four rooms, all with private baths, include TV, VCR, and computer lines. There is afternoon or evening tea served by the fireplace and a continental breakfast.

Mead Tooker House B&B (845-457-5770), 136 Clinton Street, Montgomery 12549. ($$) This elegant guest house is located in the historic section of town. The house itself has an interesting facade that will delight architecture buffs. The five guest rooms are decorated with antique French furniture, and a few of the rooms have a fireplace. All have private baths. Breakfast is created according to your taste. Three restaurants are within easy walking distance of the B&B. Open year-round.

Meadowlark Farm (845-651-4286), 180 Union Corners Road, Warwick 10990. ($$) Enjoy staying in a farmhouse built in 1865. The three air-conditioned rooms all have private baths. In the summer months a full breakfast is served with fresh produce from the lovely garden. Living room with fireplace. No children. Open year-round.

Peach Grove Inn (845-986-7411), 205 Route 17A, Warwick 10990. ($$) This restored 1850 Greek-Revival home overlooks a 200-acre farm. There are four large rooms, all with private baths. The full breakfast features delicious home-baked breads and cakes. A great place to slow down and get away from everything! Open year-round.

Point of View Bed & Breakfast (845-294-6259), 253 Ridge Road, Campbell Hall 10916. ($$) Adjacent to one of Orange County's most beautiful horse farms, this Cape Cod features a cozy, informal ambience. There are two spacious modern rooms, both with private bath, telephone and cable TV. The owners, Elaine and Bill, have lived in the county for 25 years and welcome both recreational and business travelers. Open year-round.

Silent Farm (845-294-0846), 35 Axworthy Lane, Goshen 10924.

($$) This is the place for horse lovers. The four rooms and one suite overlook an 85-acre horse farm. Breakfast is served by the dining room fireplace or on the deck in the warm-weather months. Horseback riding (and lessons) are available. Open year-round.

Stockbridge Ramsdell House (845-562-9310), 158 Montgomery Street, Newburgh 12550. ($$) Overlooking the river, the Newburgh-Beacon Bridge, and the Hudson Valley, this Queen Anne Victorian offers five large rooms, four of which have magnificent river views. One room has an outdoor deck, another has a screened-in porch, two have fireplaces, and all have canopy beds. Built in 1870 for H. Stockbridge Ramsdell, president of the Erie Railroad, the house has been lovingly restored. A full gourmet breakfast is served fireside in cool-weather months, wine and cheese from 5 to 6. Open year-round.

Storm King Lodge (845-534-9421), 100 Pleasant Hill Road, Mountainville 10953. ($$) This comfortable country lodge—the converted carriage house of a former estate—has views of Storm King Mountain, and it's only minutes away from Storm King Art Center (see *To See*) and close to West Point. The four guest rooms all have private baths; two have a fireplace. The cozy ambience reflects the warmth of the family that operates the lodge. They have been in the area for years and won't steer you wrong with their suggestions. Open year-round on weekends; every day in July and August.

Sugar Loaf Village B&B (845-469-2717), Pine Hill Road, Sugar Loaf 10981. ($$) This renovated house, over 100 years old, features three antiques-filled guest rooms, each with its own bathroom complete with jet tub. A nice mix of the old and new and a great place to relax after shopping in Sugar Loaf. A country breakfast is served in the bird- and rose-filled garden. In winter the breakfast table is lit by candles and a cozy fire. Open year-round.

Thayer Hotel (845-446-4731), U.S. Military Academy, West Point 10996. ($$$) The Thayer Hotel reflects a long gone time of grandeur, with many guest rooms overlooking one of the most scenic parts of the Hudson River: the Hudson Highlands. There are 148 renovated rooms here. Breakfast is not included in the room rate; the dining room serves on the terrace, which offers an exquisite panoramic view of the Hudson Valley. The hotel is within minutes of the military academy's points of interest. Open year-round; reservations are required, especially on special-events weekends at the academy.

Victorian River View (845-446-5479), 30 Scott's Circle, Fort Montgomery 10922. ($$) There are five rooms with shared baths in this 1888 Victorian home overlooking the Hudson River and Bear Mountain Bridge. The rooms are chock-full of bric-a-brac, and all the rooms have air-conditioning, TV, and VCR. Continental breakfast is included.

Warwick Valley Bed & Breakfast (845-987-7255), 24 Maple Avenue, Warwick 10990. ($$) All four rooms have private baths in this 1900 Colonial Revival home decorated with antiques and country furniture. The living room has a fireplace, and in-season a full breakfast is served to guests on the covered porch. Open year-round.

✳ Where to Eat

DINING OUT

In Cornwall & Newburgh area (Eastern Orange County)

Beeb's (845-568-6102), 30 Plank Road, Newburgh. ($$) Open Monday through Thursday, 11:30–9:30; Friday till 10, Saturday 5–10; Sunday brunch 11:30–3, dinner 3–8. This 19th-century roadhouse has a hand-carved mahogany bar and two candlelit dining rooms that enhance the romantic atmosphere. The American-bistro menu offers an eclectic blend of choices like pan-seared crab cake with rémoulade sauce for an appetizer and slow-roasted quail stuffed with chorizo sausage, garlic, and bacon for an entrée. The service is first-rate; a great addition to the Newburgh restaurant scene. Not recommended for children.

Canterbury Brook Inn (845-534-9658), 331 Main Street, Cornwall. ($$) Open Wednesday through Sunday for dinner at 5. Hans and Kim Baumann offer up a touch of Switzerland in Cornwall. Fine Continental cuisine may be enjoyed while overlooking Canterbury Brook or dining fireside in the cooler months. Specialties of the house include roast duckling, veal langoustine, classic Wiener schnitzel, pasta with fruits de mer, New York sirloin steak, filet mignon, and an array of fresh-fish specials. The desserts are truly spectacular, and cappuccino and espresso are available.

C. D. Driscoll's (845-566-1300), 1100 Union Avenue, Newburgh. ($$) Open daily for lunch and dinner, 11:30–10:30. This establishment offers live entertainment on Friday and Saturday evenings (there is a wide range of music, including jazz and rock). The cuisine is standard American, although there are some spicy Mexican dishes that are quite popular. Not recommended for children on weekend evenings.

Cena 2000 (845-561-7676), 50 Front Street, Newburgh. ($$) Open daily for lunch noon–3; dinner 5–10 (until 11 Friday and Saturday, until 9 Sunday). Northern Italian, Tuscan cuisine is featured here; there is fresh fish, pasta, seafood, filet mignon, veal chop, grilled shrimp for entrées. Desserts include homemade gelatos, tiramisu, Italian pastries. Hudson River waterfront dining May through October. Reservations recommended. Not too child-friendly, but kids are accommodated.

Chianti (845-561-3103), 362 Broadway, Newburgh. ($$) Open for lunch Monday through Saturday 11–2:30; dinner Monday through Saturday 5–10. Dinner served Sunday 1–9. Every Wednesday evening there is live music. Northern Italian and Continental cuisines are the specialties here. The pasta is homemade, and there is an excellent wine list.

Il Cenacolo (845-564-4494), Route 52, Newburgh. ($$$) Open for lunch Wednesday through Friday and Monday noon–2:30; dinner daily at 5, Friday and Saturday at 6, Sunday at 4. Fine food from northern Italy is the byword at this excellent restaurant, based on an Italian supper room. Select from buffalo-milk mozzarella with roasted red peppers, spinach gnocchi with venison sauce, tuna steak in garlic and olive oil, and many types of pasta. Save room for the homemade desserts and excellent espresso. Not recommended for children; reservations required.

Lake View House (845-566-7100), 205 Lakeside Road, Newburgh. ($$)

Open daily for dinner except Tuesday, from 5; lunch served weekdays except Tuesday, 11:30–2:30. Watch the sun set over Orange Lake while dining at a restaurant in operation since 1899. The chef-owner specializes in traditional American fare. Hearty soups, salads, and sandwiches are served for lunch.

Machu Picchu Peruvian Restaurant (845-562-6478), 301 Broadway, Newburgh. ($) Open daily except Tuesday, 10–10 (until midnight Friday and Saturday). After traveling to Machu Picchu in 1984 and finding it one of the most amazing places on the planet, I was intrigued by the name of this restaurant. I wasn't disappointed. There are breakfast specialties here—the tacu tacu (eggs cooked with fresh garlic, diced tomatoes, onions, rice and beans) is quite tasty—as well as hearty soups and fish stews that are a meal in themselves for lunch. The entrées, served with rice and beans, include chicken, lamb, steak, and seafood. Children welcome.

Painter's Tavern (845-534-2109), Village Square, Route 218, Cornwall-on-Hudson. ($$) Open Monday through Saturday for lunch and dinner, 11:30–10; Sunday brunch 10:30–3, dinner 3–10. Perfect for any meal. There are nightly dinner specials, along with creative variations on burgers, sandwiches, and salads. The sun-dried tomatoes with cream pasta sauce is an excellent selection, and there are dozens of imported and domestic beers bottled and on tap. Children are welcome.

Nikola's (845-561-5255), Park Place, Newburgh. ($$) Open for lunch daily 11:30–4; dinner 5–10. Arrive by boat if you like at this chef-owned and -operated Hudson River establishment; you can dock in one of the slips owned by the restaurant. Relax and enjoy all kinds of fresh seafood (crab legs, shrimp scampi, lobster) in a casual atmosphere. Eclectic seasonal menu. Children welcome.

River Grill (845-561-9444), 40 Front Street, Newburgh. ($$) Open daily for lunch Monday through Saturday 11:30–3; dinner 5–9, till 10 Friday and Saturday; Sunday noon–9. Steve Melia, the chef-owner, offers an array of seafood, steaks, chops, rack of lamb, and a nice selection of pastas. The River Grill Calamari is lightly coated in their own special blend of seasoned flour and served with two sauces: a spicy fra diavolo and chive horseradish. Enjoy the wonderful river view from the bar and most parts of the restaurant.

Torches (845-568-0100), 120 Front Street (Newburgh Waterfront), Newburgh. ($$) This enormous restaurant has huge windows that offer river views. A 5,700-gallon fish tank filled with colorful tropical fish plus clamshell lampshades add to the nautical decor. There is an extensive raw bar and large mahogany bar where I have enjoyed the tricolor nachos with roasted corn jalapeño salsa and Vermont cheddar in the relaxing atmosphere. The soups, salads, sandwiches, steaks, and seafood are decent, but just about everyone goes here for the river views.

Yobo (845-564-3848), 1297 Route 300, Newburgh. ($$) Open daily for lunch and dinner 11–10. Serving Asian cuisine since 1980, this restaurant has a waterfall inside its walls, and the sound of the running water is relaxing and reminiscent of the Far East. One of my favorite dishes here is the Thai firecracker seafood, with a blend of hot-and-sweet-flavored sauce mixing scallions, cilantro, and peppers with seafood, served over a bed of vermicelli noodles. There are wonderful soups here as well as sushi and Korean and Indonesian favorites. Children welcome.

In Monroe, Montgomery, Goshen (Central Orange County)
Bull's Head Inn (845-496-6758), Sarah Wells Trail, Campbell Hall. ($$) Open for dinner Tuesday through Thursday 5–9; Friday and Saturday till 10; Sunday 3–8. Enjoy fine dining in a colonial atmosphere with many unusual American specialties. If you love garlic, make sure to order the baked garlic appetizer. Popular entrée selections include shrimp with four cheeses, filet mignon with peppercorn sauce, and pork tenderloin with fresh fruit.

Catherine's (845-294-8707), 153 West Main Street, Goshen. ($$) Open for lunch Tuesday through Friday 11:30–2:30; dinner Tuesday through Saturday 5:30–9. Contemporary American cuisine here features a variety of pasta and seafood specialties served in a comfortable country setting. The restaurant is housed in a historic building that dates back to 1869.

88 Charles Street (845-457-9850), 88 Charles Street, Montgomery. ($$) Open for lunch Monday through Friday 11:30–4; dinner 5–10, Saturday till 11, Sunday 4–10. The bar is open from 4 PM. The outstanding Northern Italian cuisine here features veal, chicken, pasta, seafood, and steaks. Large portions, reasonable prices, romantic atmosphere.

Ile de France (845-294-8373), 6 North Church Street, Goshen. ($$) Open for lunch Tuesday through Saturday 12–2; dinner starting at 5.

Reservations recommended. This French American restaurant takes its wine seriously. It is properly cellared to age well and then served at the perfect temperature. Choose from over 100 wines from every area of France to complement such meals as grilled tuna with ratatouille taponade and Angus beef filet mignon with peppercorn sauce and roasted potatoes.

Owen Murphy Inn (845-294-0182), 1700 Route 17M, Goshen. ($$) Open for lunch Wednesday through Monday noon–2:30; dinner Monday, Wednesday, and Thursday 5–9; until 10 on Friday and Saturday; Sunday brunch 11:30–3, dinner 3–8. Enjoy cuisine and imaginative daily specials from Provence and Tuscany served in a lovely greenhouse, on the outdoor deck, or in one of three dining rooms. There is also a nightclub and bar. The Culinary Institute-trained chef is continually adding wonderful creations to the menu. The Irish mixed grill includes New Zealand lamb, Irish sausage, baked tomato, and baked potato. Even crocodile is served here.

Velvet Monkey (845-781-7762), 46 Millpond Parkway, Monroe. ($$) Open daily for dinner 5–10, until 11 Friday and Saturday, until 9 Sunday. Brunch is served Saturday and Sunday noon–4. Those interested in gourmet dining will enjoy this establishment with its mix of New American and international cuisines prepared from organic meats, duck, chicken, and quail. Everything is made on the premises, including the excellent desserts. Both the chef and owner are Culinary Institute graduates—attention is paid to all the details here.

Winding Hills Clubhouse Restaurant (845-457-8133), 1847 Route

17K, Montgomery. ($$) Open for lunch daily noon–2; dinner Tuesday through Thursday 5–9, Friday and Saturday till 10; Sunday brunch 9:30–3, dinner 3–8. Enjoy international favorites, as well as steaks and seafood, in a beautiful dining room with scenic views of the golf course.

In Central Valley, Sugar Loaf, Warwick (South-central Orange County)

Chateau Hathorn (845-986-6099), 33 Hathorn Road, Warwick. ($$) Open for dinner Wednesday through Saturday 5–10, Sunday 3–8. Enjoy Continental cuisine with a French touch in a restored mansion dating back to the 1700s. The menu changes seasonally, but the rack of lamb and chateaubriand are specialties of the house. For dessert try the coupe Denmark: melted Toblerone chocolate served over homemade vanilla ice cream and topped with fresh whipped cream.

Deep Sea (845-986-7288), 25 Elm Street, Warwick. ($$) Open daily for lunch 11–4; dinner served 4–9. This casual restaurant adjoins a fish marketplace. The fresh fish and seafood varies throughout the year, depending on what's in season. When I stopped by in early October, the specials included grilled tuna Dijonaise with capers and artichokes as well as blackened mahimahi with pico de gallo and guacamole. Turf lovers will appreciate Murray's (free-range) chicken, certified Black Angus beef, and a full selection of meats. Do note that diners must bring their own wine or beer (Deep Sea does not have a liquor license), and no reservations are taken unless there are eight or more in your party. Children welcome.

Gasho of Japan (845-928-2277), Route 32, Central Valley. ($$) Open daily except Sunday for lunch at noon; dinner at 5:30. This authentic, graceful, 400-year-old farmhouse was dismantled in Japan, shipped to its present site, and reassembled. Gasho features hibachi-style fare: As you sit at heated steel-topped tables, Tokyo-trained chefs dazzle both eye and palate, preparing filet mignon with hibachi snow crab, prime beef, and lobster tail before your very eyes. Shrimp, scallops, and eel are other specialties, and all dinners include soup, salad, vegetables, rice, and tea. After dinner take a stroll through the Japanese gardens. Children welcome.

The Jolly Onion Inn (845-258-4277), Pine Island Turnpike, Pine Island. ($$) Open daily, except Monday and Tuesday, for dinner at 5, open Sunday at noon. A local tradition serving Continental cuisine, this inn is located right next to a large farm stand in the scenic Black Dirt region of Orange County. An extensive doll collection is on display at the restaurant, which will enchant many children.

Sweet Basil Restaurant (845-783-6928), Route 17M, Harriman. ($$) Open Tuesday through Friday for lunch 11:30–2; dinner 5–9 weekdays, Saturday till 11, Sunday 4–9. Continental cuisine with an Italian flair in a country-bistro atmosphere. Specialties of the house are veal Luigi, honey-roasted filet of salmon, and rack of lamb. Signature desserts include Grand Marnier cheesecake baked in a hollowed-out orange and bananas Foster.

Ten Railroad Avenue (845-986-1509), 10 Railroad Avenue, Warwick. ($$) Open for lunch Monday through

Friday 11:30–2:30; dinner Monday through Saturday 5–10, Sunday noon–8. Spanish and Italian cuisines are served here in a casual atmosphere; fish, pasta, and chicken specials daily. The chef suggests the paella if you enjoy that dish. Live music on Friday and Saturday evenings.

Warwick Inn (845-986-3666), 36 Oakland Avenue, Warwick. ($$) Open Tuesday through Saturday at 5, Sunday at 1. This 180-year-old mansion has been owned and operated by the Wilson family for the past 45 years. Original moldings, fireplaces, and antiques add to the cozy atmosphere. Roast prime rib and fresh roast turkey are served Friday through Sunday. Seafood specialties include baked stuffed shrimp, swordfish, and broiled stuffed flounder. Children welcome. Reservations suggested.

Middletown, Port Jervis (Western Orange County)

Cornucopia (845-856-5361), Route 209, Port Jervis. ($$) Open for lunch Tuesday through Friday noon–2; dinner Tuesday through Saturday 5–9, Sunday 1–8. Reasonably priced Continental cuisine is served in a casual atmosphere. The specialties are sauerbraten and Wiener schnitzel; excellent salad bar.

Flo-Jean Restaurant (845-856-6600), Routes 6 and 209, Port Jervis. ($$) Open for lunch and dinner Wednesday through Sunday noon–10. Situated on the banks of the Delaware River, this establishment has been in business since 1929. The building was formerly used to collect tolls for the bridge. On the upper level the main dining room offers scenic views of the river, while the intimate Toll House lounge on the lower

level has a more casual atmosphere. The Continental cuisine is of decent quality; children are welcome.

John's Harvest Inn (845-343-6630), 629 North Street, Middletown. ($$) Open for dinner Wednesday through Saturday from 5:30, Sunday 3–8. The Continental cuisine here is very good, and the portions are hearty. The fresh seafood and veal dishes are specialties of the house.

EATING OUT

In Newburgh and Cornwall

Cafe Pitti (845-565-1444), 40 Front Street, Newburgh. ($$) Open daily for lunch and dinner 11:30–10. This is a wonderful place to go in the warm weather to sit outside on the terrace by the waterfront and watch the boats go by on the Hudson. The interior is casual, a place to enjoy salads, personal thin-crust pizza, and paninis. For dessert there is gelato, cappuccino cake, and sorbet. Children welcome.

Commodore's (845-561-3960), 482 Broadway, Newburgh. ($) Open daily 10–6; closed Sunday during the summer. Located in an old-fashioned ice cream parlor, Commodore's has been in business and run by the same family since 1935. They are famous for their handmade chocolates and candies. There are the usual delicious classics like marzipan and truffles as well as Swedish fudge and almond bark. In late November call to find out when they start handmade candy cane demonstrations, which are held on weekends noon–4.

Cosimo's on Union (845-567-1556), Union and Orr Streets, Newburgh. ($) Open daily 11:30–10 for lunch and dinner. The specialty here is the brick-oven-baked personal-sized pizza. There are dozens of toppings. Also available is a large selection of pasta dishes. The restaurant is very close to Stewart Airport and the NYS Thruway (exit 17). If you are traveling with children, this is a good choice.

Johnny D's (845-567-1600), 909 Union Avenue, New Windsor. ($) Located just off the NYS Thruway (exit 17), and open 24 hours a day, 7 days a week. Salad lovers will be delighted with their extensive menu of "Glorious Salads." My favorite is the Mexicobb Salad, but there are nearly 20 to choose from as well as over a dozen types of enticing burgers. This is a diner with an imaginative flair, so expect the ordinary made somewhat extraordinary.

Prima Pizza (845-534-7003, 800-22-NY-PIE), 252 Main Street, Cornwall. ($) A family restaurant for over 35 years, this is a must for anyone passing through Cornwall or heading in either direction on Route 9W. The short detour is worth it. Owner Anthony Scalise regularly airmails brick-oven-cooked pizzas to places as far away as California. (He was asked to send pizza to the troops in the Middle East during Operation Desert Storm.) The finest blends of mozzarella cheese and fresh dough are made daily. All sauces and meatballs are cooked on the premises, and cholesterol-free oil is used with everything served here. My favorite slice is the fresh basil and tomato. "Sweep the Kitchen," as the name implies, has everything on it. There are calzone, subs, salads, and an array of pasta dishes for those who prefer other Italian specialties. Ask about shipping a pizza anywhere in the country; it makes a unique gift.

In Central Orange County
Daily Bean Cafe (845-469-9810), 11 Union Street, Montgomery. ($) Open Monday, Tuesday, and Thursday 9–5, Saturday till 6, Sunday noon–5. Enjoy homemade soups and sandwiches with cappuccino or espresso in a relaxed atmosphere. Try the tarragon chicken salad or eggplant with sun-dried tomato and mozzarella sandwiches, favorites with local residents. There's music here on most weekends, and it's a great place to enjoy a freshly prepared dessert like chocolate mousse cake.

Hacienda Restaurant (845-294-9795), Route 17M, Goshen. ($) Open daily 11:30–8 for lunch and dinner. This establishment is owned and operated by the chef, who turns out authentic Mexican fare—tacos, burritos, enchiladas—served in a casual atmosphere. The restaurant is housed in a restored Victorian mansion with a lovely fireplace. Children are welcome.

In Sugar Loaf & Warwick
The Barnsider Tavern (845-469-9810), King's Highway, Sugar Loaf. ($$) Open Tuesday–Sunday from 11. This tavern has a beautiful taproom with handwrought beams, country decor, and a glassed-in patio with a view of the Sugar Loaf Crafts Village (see *Selective Shopping*). A fire is always crackling on the hearth in winter, and the menu of burgers, quiche, and other fine café foods makes this a nice stop for lunch. Children welcome.

The Creamery at Bellvale Farms (845-986-3030), 75 Bellvale Lake Road, (at intersection of Route 17A and Kain Road, Mount Peter), Warwick. ($) This family farm produces and sells its own ice cream. Open for ice cream daily from noon–9; the main dairy barn is open Sunday from 3:30–4:15, when baby calves are fed and cows are milked. There are also Holstein cows, a fresh-vegetable stand open during the summer, pick-your-own pumpkins, and hayrides in the fall. This is a great stop for those traveling with children.

Jean Claude's Patisserie & Dessert Café (845-986-8900), 25 Elm Street, Warwick. ($) Open Wednesday through Sunday 8–6. Those who love fine pastries, brioche, fruit tarts, petits fours, baba au rhum, cream puffs, and handmade truffles should be sure to stop at this fantastic bakery.

✳ Selective Shopping

ANTIQUES The love of history found across Orange County extends to a love of antiques and collectibles, and many shops cater to the connoisseur. Some of my favorites are the following places:

Antique Center of Orange County (845-651-2711), 2 North Main Street, Florida. Open Wednesday through Saturday 10–5, Sunday 11–4. Explore over 6,000 square feet of collectibles and antiques as well as a large selection of toys, furniture, and kitchen items.

Arnell's Antiques & Restoration (845-477-8747), Windermere Avenue, Greenwood Lake. Open Monday through Saturday 10–5. Two floors of antique furniture are housed here, along with a large quantity of glass and silver.

Coal-Bin Antiques (845-457-5400), 20 Railroad Avenue, Montgomery. Open year-round, except the month of January, Thursday through Tuesday

10–5. There are 1,400 square feet of furniture, china, Depression glass, and a large selection of antique toys.

Country Heritage Antiques Center (845-744-3792), Route 302, Pine Bush. Open Thursday through Sunday 11–5:30 or by appointment. Furniture of all types is the specialty here. There is a good-sized collection of armoires, cupboards, desks, bookcases, china closets, dressers, beds, tables, and chairs.

A number of antique and novelty stores have clustered in the historic village of **Montgomery** in recent years, making it a great stop for those wanting to take a short break from traveling. It is a wonderful place to stroll or browse, whether you are traveling north or south.

AUCTIONS Auctions are usually held on a regular basis, whether once a month or once a week. Estate sales may provide the antiquer or junker with everything from Persian rugs to eccentric collectibles. The best way to locate what's going on where is to check the classified listings in a local newspaper. Flea markets are another treat springing up on warm weekends; look for markets that jumble together new and old rather than just offering overstock and discontinued items. Most auctions and markets will not accept out-of-state checks; they will accept credit cards (most of the time), cash, and traveler's checks.

Old Red Barn Antiques and Auctions (845-754-7122), in Cuddebackville, has weekend auctions the first Saturday of the month. It also has a line of antiques and is open weekend afternoons.

Mark Vail Auction Services (845-744-2120), at Kelly Avenue in Pine

Bush, has antiques and estate auctions approximately twice a month. Call for dates.

Also in Pine Bush is **Pine Bush Auction** (845-457-4404), 157 Ward Street, which holds auctions twice a month on Saturdays. Call for schedule.

CRAFTS Clearwaters Distinctive Gifts & Jones Farm Country Store (845-534-4445), 190 Angola Road, Cornwall. Open every day year-round, weekdays 8–6, weekends until 5. Since 1914 this fifth-generation family farm has served the Hudson Valley with home-grown produce, fresh eggs, maple syrup, honey, preserves, coffees, and many gourmet items. Grandma Phoebe's kitchen features homemade baked goods, cream and butter fudge, and wonderful apple cider doughnuts. Children are always welcome to visit the animals and enjoy the observation beehive. The second floor of the store is an enormous gift shop with books, china, novelty items, and wonderful hand-crafted goods. This store makes an interesting stop in Cornwall, a lovely village with a number of fine shops and restaurants.

Little Bit of Pine Island (845-258-7122), County Route 1, Pine Island. Open daily 10-6. There is a good selection of crafts from local artists, gift items, and dried and silk flower arrangements as well as a year-round Christmas section.

Sugar Loaf Crafts Village (845-469-9181). Take exit 16 off the NYS Thruway to Route 17, and go west for 8 miles to exit 127; follow the signs. Open daily 11–5 except Monday year-round. Named for the local mountain that is shaped the way sugar was during colonial times, Sugar Loaf—with its bare crest—has been the subject of unusual speculation. Originally the mountain was a Native American burial ground, and over the years various relics and bones have been uncovered there. Once a bustling stagecoach and river stop, the area lost its prominence when the railroads bypassed it in the mid-19th century. But over the last 25 years, Sugar Loaf has regained its spirit. Home to dozens of crafts-people who live and work in many of the buildings along King's Highway and Wood's Road, the village is a terrific place to find a special gift or add to a collection. Visitors will find hand-crafted stained glass, pottery, paintings, photography, and jewelry. As befits an art colony, there are craft fairs and art shows throughout the year as well as a fall festival and holiday caroling. The village is charming; an excellent place to spend an afternoon talking to a number of artists at work in their studios. Visitors will do lots of walking; parking is at either end of the village in well-marked lots.

FACTORY OUTLETS If you ever tire of taking in the beauty of Orange County, there is always shopping to enjoy—and plenty of it. Factory outlets have come a long way from the dingy shops of the past, and a stop at **Woodbury Common** (845-928-4000), Route 32, Central Valley (open daily year-round, except major holidays), will prove this. There are more than 200 shops in this Colonial-style mall, selling everything from shoes, clothing, sweaters, and watches to toys, wallets, crystal, and stockings. The mall sponsors special events throughout the year, and there is a large food court.

Gillinder Glass (845-856-5375), corner of Erie and Liberty Streets, Port

Jervis. Open Monday through Saturday 9:30–5, Sunday noon–4. Call ahead for tour times and group information. This site offers visitors a rare chance to watch glass being heated, molded, shaped, and cooled into fine collectibles. The factory, which has an on-site shop, has a viewing area, and the furnaces glow as the craftspeople use the same techniques employed a century ago. After a tour, stop by the **Tri-States Monument** (at the junction of the Neversink and Delaware Rivers, Laurel Grove Cemetery). Just under the Interstate 84 bridge is a rock on which you can stand in three states (New York, Pennsylvania, and New Jersey) at once; it also notes the boundary between New York and New Jersey.

TWG Fabric Outlet (845-343-3423), 15 Wisner Avenue, Middletown, specializes in decorative fabrics and is an exclusive importer of 60-inch lace. They are open daily 9–6 except Saturday, Sunday 11–4.

✴ Special Events

April: **Brigade of the American Revolution Spring Encampment** (845-561-5073), New Windsor Cantonment, Temple Hill Road, Vails Gate (see *Historic Sites*). The last encampment of the Continental Army is reenacted. Call for exact date and schedule of events at the site. Admission fee.

July–August: **Orange County Fair** (845-343-4826), Wisner Avenue fairgrounds, Middletown. Dates are usually mid-July to early August; gates open at noon. Admission fee. One of the oldest county fairs in New York State, this one started as an agricultural display between 1818 and 1825. Local interest did not really begin to build until 1841, however, when the New York State Agricultural Society entered the picture. From then on the fair was a hit. The 1841 extravaganza featured horses, cows, pigs, farm exhibits, and races; a visit to the fair today will turn up top-name entertainment, scores of food booths, thrill-a-minute rides, and some rather unique events such as pig racing, where swift-footed swine dash for the purse: a cookie. Visit the lumberjack exhibition for a display of woodsmen's skills and a log-rolling contest. Native American shows, stock-car racing, and petting zoos are also on-site, along with the finest local produce and livestock and even an old-fashioned tent circus.

July–September: **New York Renaissance Faire** (845-351-5171, after June 1st), Route 17A, Sterling Forest, Tuxedo; watch for signs. Open late July through mid-September, weekends only. Call for exact dates and hours. Admission fee. Knights and ladies, sorcerers and their apprentices, fools and varlets, bumpkins and wantons all gather on the glorious grounds of Sterling Forest to re-create the lusty days of a merry olde English fair. The festival runs for eight consecutive weekends and presents a colorful, noisy look at a misty period of time somewhere between King Arthur and Shakespeare. Falconers show off the skills of their birds, opera and Shakespeare are presented at the Globe Theatre, Maid Marian flirts with Robin Hood, ladies dance beneath a maypole, and the extensive rose gardens are open for strolling. Craftspeople display and sell their wares (many belong to the Society for Anachronisms and stock things like chain-mail shirts), and the aromas of "steak on a stake," mead, and

ANNUAL NEW YORK
RENAISSANCE FAIRE IN STERLING FOREST

Hudson Valley Tourism, Inc.

cheese pie flavor the air. There are
jugglers, knife throwers, mud fights,
and a living chess game in which the
"pieces" wander the gardens to their
squares. The actors play their roles
throughout the entire festival, so

authenticity combines with the personal touch. Kids adore the noise and
action, and there is enough to see and
do for everyone.

August: **Orange County Onion Festival** (1-877-ONION-99) is held in
Pine Island in August every year.
Admission fee. The event celebrates
Polish settlers' contribution to the
onion industry (and those of Irish,
German, and Italian immigrants, as
well) with song, dance, and plenty of
onions! **Willow Creek Bluegrass
and Old Time Music Festival** (845-
783-9054), Orange County Farmers
Museum, Route 17K, Montgomery.
Admission fee, but children under 12
are admitted free when accompanied
by an adult. Bring lawn chairs to this
three-day weekend event in mid-
August. There are hayrides, farming
demonstrations, children's activities,
and a chance to hear some of the best
bluegrass music.

November: **Crafts on the Hudson**
(845-679-8087), Mount St. Mary College, Kaplan Recreation Center,
Route 9W, Newburgh. Admission fee.
This Thanksgiving weekend (Saturday
and Sunday) craft fair includes artisans from throughout the northeast.
There's music, children's activities,
and fun for the entire family.

Sullivan County 3

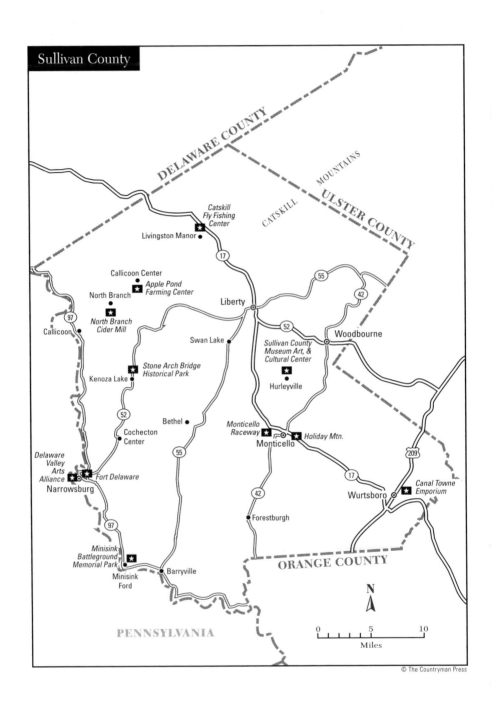

Sullivan County

DELAWARE COUNTY

CATSKILL MOUNTAINS

ULSTER COUNTY

Catskill
Fly Fishing
Center
Livingston Manor

17

55

42

Callicoon Center

Apple Pond
Farming Center

North Branch

North Branch
Cider Mill

97

Callicoon

Liberty

52

Swan Lake

Woodbourne

Sullivan County
Museum Art, &
Cultural Center

Kenoza Lake

Stone Arch Bridge
Historical Park

Hurleyville

52

Bethel

Cochecton
Center

55

Monticello
Raceway

Holiday Mtn.

Monticello

Delaware
Valley
Arts
Alliance

Fort Delaware

Narrowsburg

42

209

Canal Towne
Emporium

17

Wurtsboro

97

Forestburgh

Minisink
Battleground
Memorial Park

Minisink
Ford

Barryville

ORANGE COUNTY

N

PENNSYLVANIA

0   5   10
Miles

© The Countryman Press

SULLIVAN COUNTY

Only 90 miles northwest of New York City lies Sullivan County: 1,000 square miles of outdoor treasures. The Delaware River snakes along the county border and down into Pennsylvania, where the rugged, untamed countryside is home to bald eagles. To the north, visitors will discover the charm of tranquil, silvery lakes, lush forests, and narrow valleys where tiny villages nestle alongside bubbling streams. Sullivan also offers some of the world's best trout fishing, and on opening day of the season—rain or snow—rods and flies are taken from basements and garages across the county in pursuit of the annual dream of catching "the big one." Only a small percentage of the county is considered agricultural, but there are dairy and pick-your-own farms as well as abundant orchards. A drive through Sullivan County is a reminder that not too long ago this area was the frontier, a place where bears, bobcats, and the mysterious panther haunted the uneasy sleep of woodsmen and pioneers.

GUIDANCE **Sullivan County Visitors Association** (845-794-3000, ext. 5010, 800-882-CATS), County Government Center, 100 North Street, Monticello 12701; www.scva.net.

Liberty Chamber of Commerce (845-292-1878), P.O. Box 147, Liberty 12754; www.welcometoliberty.com.

Roscoe Chamber of Commerce (607-498-6055), P.O. Box 443, Roscoe 12776; www.roscoeny.com.

Wurtsboro Board of Trade (845-888-VISIT), P.O. Box 907, Wurtsboro 12790; www.wbot.org.

GETTING THERE *By car:* Sullivan County is accessible from Route 17 (future Route 86) and Route 209. You can pick up Route 17 at NYS Thruway exit 16 (Harriman).

By bus: **Rolling V Transportation Services** (845-434-0511, 800-999-6593), 5008 Main Street, South Fallsburg, provides bus, taxi, and limo services for the local area as well as long distance. **Short Line** (800-631-8405, ext. 111), Sturgis Road, Monticello, offers frequent express service from the Port Authority Bus Terminal in Manhattan as well as other parts of the metropolitan area.

By air: **Stewart International Airport** (845-564-2100), 1035 First Street, New Windsor, has service to major East Coast cities daily. Charter service and private aircraft can be accommodated at **Monticello Airport** (845-794-6888), **Sullivan County International Airport** in White Lake (845-791-5450), and **Wurtsboro Airport** (845-888-2791).

MEDICAL EMERGENCY **Catskill Regional Medical Center,** Bushville Road, Harris (845-794-3300) or **Grover Hermann Division,** Route 97, Callicoon (845-887-5530).

✳ To See

Bethel Woodstock Museum (845-583-4300), Bethel. Open year-round, Monday through Saturday 10–5; Sunday 10–3. Free. The first and only museum of its kind at the home of the original 1969 music festival. Photographs and articles from all over the world on events commemorating the concert over the past 35 years. Woodstock aficionados of all ages will particularly enjoy making a pilgrimage here.

The actual **Woodstock Festival Site** (845-295-2448), now part of Bethel Woods Center for the Arts, is on Hurd Road, in Bethel, not in Woodstock (Ulster County), over 50 miles away. This is where it happened: three days of peace, mud, and rock 'n' roll. A small monument marks the spot, and plenty of people stop and share stories. The area surrounding Bethel is beautiful, a good place for a leisurely drive, a walk, or a picnic.

Canal Towne Emporium (845-888-2100), located at the intersection of Sullivan and Hudson Streets in Wurtsboro. Open daily 10–5 year-round. Free. Originally opened in 1845 as a dry-goods establishment near the Delaware & Hudson Canal and now restored to its turn-of-the-20th-century charm, this country store has received awards for historic preservation. The fixtures, furnishings, and equipment are all antiques, and include the first electric coffee mill ever used in the store, advertising prints, tins, and jars. Today the emporium sells fine furniture, handcrafted items, and decorative accessories as well as books. Try the penny candy or the pickles!

Across the street is **The Potager** (845-888-4086), 116 Sullivan Street, which is open daily except Tuesday 10–5. This unusual gift and clothing shop is filled with eclectic items that will delight just about anyone. There is also a small café downstairs in the building so that when you tire of shopping, you can relax and enjoy a cold drink and snack. (See *Eating Out.*) They have a small garden center and a good selection of baskets, plants in season, and treats for gardeners; this spot is also the home of the "lasagna gardener." Pat and Mickey Lanza, the owners, will gladly explain just how that layered gardening works!

Catskill Fly Fishing Center and Museum (845-439-4810), 1031 Old Route 17 (Main Street), Livingston Manor. Open daily April through October 10–4; November through March, Tuesday–Friday 10–1, Saturdays until 4. Admission fee. Dry-fly fishing enthusiasts will certainly find a lot to do in Sullivan County, where they will discover some of the best trout streams in the nation. Visitors should not miss this museum, located on 53 acres along Willowemoc Creek.

There is a changing exhibit of fly-fishing equipment (such as rods, reels, and flies), memorabilia, a library, and a hall of fame; it also presents the story of Lee Wulff, a streamside legend, who brought elegance and science to the fly-fishing art. Special appearances by well-known anglers and craftspeople take place during the summer season, and there are special events, including workshops, seminars, and just-plan-fun get-togethers.

The Eagle Institute (845-557-6162), P.O. Box 182, Barryville. Open weekends only mid-December through March. Sullivan County attracts more bald eagles than anywhere else on the East Coast, drawn by the open waters and virgin forests. Every winter more than a hundred eagles migrate here from Canada, and in the spring they return north. The county now has an information clearinghouse for migratory and breeding eagle data, and it is open to the public. On-site interpretive programs are offered on weekends during the winter months, when the eagles are migrating. The birds are sure to intrigue just about everyone, but children who have learned in school about eagles will particularly enjoy this stop. There are workshops, slide presentations, and guided eagle watches to habitat areas. Call ahead for schedule information; this is one of the few Sullivan County attractions where winter is high season.

Sullivan County Museum and Historical Society (845-434-8044), 265 Main Street, Hurleyville. Open year-round, except January, Wednesday through Saturday 10–4:30, Sunday 1–4:30. An array of changing exhibits compliments the permanent ones that relate the history of the region. One focuses on Frederick Albert Cook, an early-20th-century explorer who, in addition to being a physician and anthropologist, was the first American to travel to both the North and South Poles. The town of Hurleyville itself is charming—a nice place to wander and enjoy art galleries, shops, and restaurants.

HISTORIC SITES **Apple Pond Farming Center** (845-482-4764), Hahn Road, Callicoon Center (call ahead for detailed directions). Open year-round Tuesday through Sunday 10–5. Admission fee. Today most farms are run with advanced technology as older agricultural methods and theories are slowly being lost in an avalanche of computer information. But there are still many farmers who cherish the old ways and believe that if the land is worked well, it will yield a bountiful harvest. At the Apple Pond Farming Center, an educational center and working farm, visitors can judge for themselves the merits of organic farming practices, wind turbines, renewable energy sources, and horse-drawn equipment. The farm is located on a rocky hillside with enchanting views of meadows, mountains, and valleys. Visitors can enjoy one of several different tours, which may include wagon rides, a sheepherding demonstration, beekeeping, and haying. Sleigh rides can be arranged in winter. The farm is stocked with sheep, draft horses, goats, and several incredible Border collies, whose obvious dedication to the task of sheepherding is alone worth the trip. Special activities like outdoor riding and driving lessons, spinning and cheese-making demonstrations and classes, and draft-horse workshops are held throughout the year, but all activities require reservations. A new addition is renewable-energy workshops. The gift shop offers products made with farm produce. Don't expect a neat little restoration, and do expect to get a little mud on your shoes.

Fort Delaware Museum of Colonial History (845-252-6660), Route 97, Narrowsburg. Open Memorial Day weekend, weekends in June, and daily from late June until Labor Day 10–5. Admission fee. Much attention is paid to the people who settled the main cities of New York, but those who decided to take on the wilderness are often forgotten. At the Fort Delaware Museum, the daily life of the backwoods settler is explored through exhibits, crafts demonstrations, and tours. The fort is a reconstruction of the original frontier settlement of Cushetunk on the Delaware River, with its stockades and stout log homes, which offered the only protection from Native Americans and, later, English troops. The fort consists of a small settlement entirely surrounded by high log walls, or stockades. During the tour, visitors see the blockhouses (where arms and ammunition were stored), settlers' cabins, a meetinghouse, a blacksmith shop, a candle shed, a loom shed, and more. Outside the fort walls you'll find a small garden planted with crops typical of the era plus the stocks, which were used to punish minor infractions of the law. Costumed guides and staff members demonstrate skills and crafts from the period, including candle making, blacksmithing, and even weaponry. Special events are scheduled throughout the season, so your visit may include a show by Revolutionary War soldiers, weavers, or cooks.

Minisink Battleground Memorial Park, Route 168, Minisink Ford. Open May through October dawn to dusk. Free. One of the unusual and forgotten Revolutionary War battlegrounds in the region, this site offers visitors a chance to walk along trails that tell stories of both nature and combat. In July 1779 the area's most important historic battle took place when a group of American rebels were defeated by Mohawks in a massacre that took almost 50 lives. In an eerie postscript, the bones of the dead were not gathered and buried until more than 40 years after the battle because the area was wilderness, and not many people visited.

Today the 56-acre park has three walking trails from which to explore its history and the surrounding natural setting. The blazed trails have descriptive markers that tell the story of the area, and written trail guides can be picked up at the interpretive center. The **Battleground Trail** depicts the tactics and strategy of a woodland skirmish and includes stops at Sentinel Rock, where the lone American defender was killed; Hospital Rock, where a rebel doctor lost his life while tending to his wounded charges; and Indian Rock, which legend says was set up to commemorate the dead. The **Woodland Trail** meanders through wetland, dense foliage, and a variety of ferns. The park map points out the trail's flora and describes some of the animal life you may encounter, such as foxes, wood frogs, raccoons, and maybe even a bald eagle. On the **Old Quarry/Rockshelter Trail,** discover the logging, quarrying and Native American histories of this section through trail markers. You may also want to plan a visit to the battleground in time for the small memorial service held each July 22nd, the anniversary of hte fight, to honor those who fell here.

Roebling's Suspension Bridge. Look for the historic marker opposite the entrance to the Minisink Battleground. Built by the designer of the Brooklyn

THE SUSPENSION BRIDGE ON THE DELAWARE RIVER WAS BUILT BY THE DESIGNER OF
THE BROOKLYN BRIDGE: JOHN ROEBLING

Joseph Puglisi

Bridge, this crossing on the Delaware River is the oldest of its kind still standing. The aqueduct was constructed because canal boats and logging rafts kept crashing into one another on the river; the aqueduct would actually carry the canal boats over the river itself. The aqueduct was turned into a bridge crossing in the late 19th century, and today it still carries traffic across to Pennsylvania.

SCENIC DRIVES With more than 1,000 square miles of countryside, just about any drive through Sullivan County will take you past exquisite views that change with the seasons: The earliest blush of spring may be enjoyed by driving along any back road or even on the Quickway (Route 17); summer is lush and lazy anywhere you turn; fall splashes the meadows and forests with color; and winter here is strikingly beautiful. Sullivan County offers detailed theme driving tours in their county literature (call 1-800-882-CATS for a copy). The following trips are my own favorites.

If you want to travel the southernmost section of Sullivan County and see some spectacular river and mountain scenery, start your tour in Monticello. From there head south on route 42 to Sackett Lake Road (you will go through a town called Squirrel Corners), and keep going south to Forestburgh Road, where you will make a right. This is the reservoir area of **Mongaup Falls,** a good spot to sight bald eagles. At Route 97 head west along the snaking river drive known as **Hawk's Nest,** with its views of New York and Pennsylvania; you will pass Minisink Battleground Park and Roebling's Suspension Bridge (see *Historic Sites*), head north on Route 52 to Liberty, where you can pick up Route 17 back to Monticello.

A second drive, which will take you past some of the few remaining **covered bridges** in the county, begins at Livingston Manor (exit 96 off Route 17). Turn onto Old Route 17 from the Vantran covered bridge, built in 1860 and one of the few existing bridges constructed in the lattice-truss and queen-post styles.

Go back to Livingston Manor and follow the signs east from town along DeBruce Road to Willowemoc, which has a covered bridge that was built in 1860 in Livingston Manor, then cut in half and moved to its present site in 1913. From Willowemoc, take Pole Road to West Branch Road, which leads into Claryville. The Halls Mills covered bridge, built in 1912, is on Claryville Road over the Neversink River. Head south from Claryville to Route 55, then west back to Liberty.

Another sight worth making time to see is **Tomasco Falls,** often called the Niagara of Sullivan County. These spectacular waterworks are a refreshing sight on a hot spring or summer's day but are particularly dramatic after heavy rains. To get there, take Route 209 to Kerhonkson. Turn onto County Route 55, and follow to Mountaindale. The falls are visible from this road.

Other roads that offer outstanding views include State Routes 209, 55, and 55A. Route 17 is the major north-south road through Sullivan County and provides access to most of the region's scenic areas and byways.

✳ To Do

CANOEING, KAYAKING, AND RAFTING Canoeists, kayakers, and rafters enjoy the Delaware River's rapids and eddies from spring to fall. Both the Upper Delaware (from Hancock to Port Jervis) and the main section of the river (from Port Jervis to the Chesapeake) are used for recreation, although there are sections that are particularly good for novices and the less adventurous. As with any other water sport, a few guidelines and suggestions will make your trip comfortable and safe. Most rental agencies require that you know how to swim and that flotation gear be worn by anyone in a canoe or raft—it may look harmless, but the Delaware can reach depths of 15 feet. For your own comfort, take along sunscreen, lightweight sneakers, extra clothing, snacks, and a hat. If you go early in the season, the water may be higher and colder than if you go in late July or the month of August. The companies listed below rent equipment, and some offer a return trip to your starting point. Although you don't need to make a reservation, on busy summer and holiday weekends it may pay to call before you go. Rates are often lower midweek. The river is now managed by the National Park Service; for information, call 845-252-3947.

Cedar Rapids Kayak and Canoe Outfitters (845-557-6158), at Cedar Rapids Inn, Barryville, has double and single kayaks, canoes, rafts, and tubes for rent; there is also a nice riverside restaurant where you can have refreshments and watch the fun.

Kittatinny Canoes (1-800-FLOAT-KC), Route 97, north of Barryville, is one of the oldest (over 60 years) operating canoe-rental companies, and it also has rafts, tubes, and kayaks. They offer camping and special discounts.

Landers River Trips (1-800-836-0366), Narrowsburg, has campgrounds and a motel for guests in addition to full river equipment (canoes, tubes, kayaks) for rent.

Upper Delaware Campgrounds (845-887-5344), Callicoon, has complete float and package trips for river lovers.

Wild and Scenic River Tours and Rentals (845-557-8783 or 1-800-836-0366), Barryville, has adventure vacations for all ages and skill levels, along with canoe, raft, tube, and kayak rentals. Fishing trips are also available.

The following companies also rent equipment: **Jerry's Three River Canoe Corporation** (845-557-6078), Pond Eddy; **Silver Canoe Rentals** (845-856-7055, 800-856-7055), Pond Eddy; **Whitewater Willie's Raft and Canoe Rentals** (845-856-2229, 800-233-7238), Pond Eddy; **Indian Head Canoes** (845-557-8777, 800-874-BOAT), Barryville.

FARMS STANDS AND PICK-YOUR-OWN Nothing tastes like fruits and vegetables that still have the blush of the sun and the mist of the morning on them. Harvesting begins in Sullivan County in late spring with asparagus and berries and ends in late fall with pumpkins and apples (although some stands stock local eggs, maple syrup, and honey year-round). Hours vary with the season and type of harvest, and not all stands are open daily, so it is suggested that you call before you make a special trip. There are also lots of small, family-run farm stands that carry only one or two items and are open for only a few weeks a year; keep an eye out for these, too. They often have unusual selections or heirloom varieties. Whether you pick the produce yourself or buy from a roadside stand, the selection and quality in Sullivan County are excellent.

Many area farmers attend the **Sullivan County Area Farmers Market** (845-292-6180) with locations in four towns: In Callicoon Creek Park in Callicoon, the market is held Sundays 11–2 mid-May through early November. In Liberty (Darbee Lane), the market is held Fridays 3–6, mid-May through mid-October. In Monticello, at 211 East Broadway, the market is open weekends year-round 8–7. In Roscoe the market is held Sundays 11–2 from mid-May through October.

Apple Pond Farming Center (845-482-4764), Hahn Road, Callicoon Center, is an organic farm that sells a variety of fruits and vegetables at its roadside stand. Since it is off the beaten track, you may want to combine a tour of the farm (see *To See—Historic Sites*) with a visit to the farm stand.

Diehl Farm (845-887-4935), Gabel Road, Callicoon, is a well-stocked stand with a full range of local crops, from apples to eggs and dairy products. Call for hours.

Fisher Farm (845-292-5777), Aden Road, Liberty, has only pick-your-own pumpkins and squash in fall. Call for hours.

Gorzynski Organic Farm (845-252-7570), Route 52, Cochecton Center, raises vegetables, apples, berries, cherries, and more, using organic methods. Call for hours.

Knaub's Farm (845-252-3781), 1168 County Route 23, Narrowsburg, is a roadside farm stand selling seasonal produce, eggs, pies, cakes, Christmas trees, cider, and candy apples. Open weekends and holidays from Memorial Day through Christmas Eve, Saturdays 9:30–7, Sundays 10–4.

Maas Farm Stand (845-985-2686), Route 55, Grahamsville, has lots of pick-your-own peppers, eggplants, and squash, among many other crops.

River Brook Farm (845-932-7952), Route 97 and C. Meyer Road, Cochecton, will provide heirloom potatoes along with beans, carrots, garlic, and lots of other greenery.

Silver Heights Farm (845-482-3572), 275 Eggler Road, Jeffersonville, has an unusual specialty: heirloom tomatoes and roses.

Walmut Mt. Nursery & Organic Farm (845-292-8172), Ferndale-Loomis Road, Liberty, has naturally grown produce in season, herbs, and transplants. Open daily 9–6 mid-May through mid-November.

Herbs are the specialty at the **Catskill Morning Farm** (845-482-3984), Youngsville, and vegetables and flowers are their other colorful crops; call for hours before you go. Eggs are extra special at **Kaplan's Egg Farm** (845-434-4519), Glen Wild Road, Woodridge.

Sullivan County hosts a **Down on the Farm Day** each summer, when self-guided driving tours of several local farms are offered to visitors. Call 845-794-3000, ext. 5010, for the schedule.

Some farms also offer visitors the chance to select and cut their own Christmas trees; you can bring your own saw or rent one for the day. Dress warmly, bring rope to tie the tree to the car, and have a nice holiday. But remember, call ahead for directions, hours, and prices: **Ted Nied Christmas Trees** (845-482-5341), Jeffersonville; **Pine Farm Christmas Trees** (845-482-4149), Livingston Manor; **Trees of the Woods** (845-482-4528), Callicoon Center.

FISHING Sullivan County is an angler's paradise. The famed Willowemoc and Beaverkill streams produce prize-winning trout each year in addition to being recognized as the cradle of American fly-fishing. The Delaware River offers its rich bounty to the patient angler, as do Mongaup Creek and Russell Brook. Then there are the icy lakes of the county with such entrancing names a Kiamesha, Kenoza, Swan, and Waneta. There are hundreds of fine fishing areas in Sullivan County, and too little space to do them all justice. The following general information, however, will assist you in finding the perfect spot to enjoy a rocky stream, a sunny sky, and, just maybe, a record catch!

SULLIVAN COUNTY IS AN ANGLER'S PARADISE.

The county's streams and rivers are famed for their brook, brown, and rainbow trout, but bass, pickerel, walleye, and shad are also plentiful. All streams on state land are open to the public; other streams often have public fishing rights through state easements, which are indicated by signs. New York State requires fishing licenses for anyone over 16 as well as special reservoir permits (call the New York City Board of Water supply for application information, 845-338-3604). There are strict fishing seasons for certain species, and you could be in for a heavy fine if you disobey the law. The brochure you receive when you get your license should answer all of your questions. Lake fishing is also popular in Sullivan, but there are separate use fees charged, and some lakes are privately owned by hotels or resorts, so check on the site before you fish.

The Beaverkill is one of the best-known trout streams in the world and may be reached from Roscoe, Livingston Manor, Lew Beach, Beaverkill, and Rockland. Fly-fishing tackle may be purchased in Roscoe at **The Beaverkill Angler** (607-498-5194), Stewart Avenue. Or call **White Cloud's Beaverkill Fly Fishing School** (607-498-4611) in Roscoe: This private school offers students a chance to learn casting, fly-tying, and moving-water fishing techniques. You can schedule lessons to meet your needs. **The Wulff School of Fly Fishing on the Beaverkill** (845-439-5020), Box 948, Livingston Manor, is located in the beautiful upper Beaverkill Valley. The school's 100 acres has a building designed to meet teaching requirements. In addition to fly-fishing, you can learn wading, streamcraft, and obstacle casting. If you have extra time, enjoy fishing in the Delaware River's main stem and its east and west branches as well as the no-kill stretches of the Beaverkill and Willowemoc Rivers. Package deals with lodging are available.

Willowemoc Creek is found between Roscoe and Livingston Manor, along Old Route 17. Mongaup Creek runs from Livingston Manor to Mongaup Pond. The Neversink River is at Claryville on County Routes 19 and 15, and you can pick up the Delaware River at East Branch on Route 17.

Among the lakes are Kenoza Lake (Route 52, Kenoza Lake Village), Swington Bridge Lake (Route 17B, Mongaup Valley), Swan Lake (Route 55, between Liberty and Kauneonga Lake), White Lake (junction of Route 17B and 55), Waneta Lake (County Route 151 in Deckertown), Cable Lake (Route 17 northwest of Roscoe, end of Russel Brook), and Kiamesha Lake (Route 42, Kiamesha).

The **Beaverkill Trout Hatchery** (845-439-4947), 22 Alder Lake Road, Livingston Manor, is a fish hatchery that will give you a tour if you call in advance. They are open April through September, Saturday and Sunday 8–5 for fish and pay pond on the premises. They also sell fresh and smoked trout.

The **New York State Fish Hatchery** in DeBruce (845-439-4328) is a great place to take young children. Open 8:30–4 weekdays, 8:30–noon weekends.

The Eldred Preserve Resort (845-557-8316, 800-557-FISH), Route 55, between Barryville and White Lake, has three stocked trout ponds and two bass lakes. There are some restrictions on fishing for nonguests, so call ahead. Trout fishing is allowed (no license required) and bass fishing with boat rental reservation only.

Paradise Lake Fishing Preserve (845-439-4618/4990), Old Route 17 West, Livingston Manor (1.5 miles west of town), offers fee fishing, and no license is necessary. The lake is stocked with trout, large-mouth bass, channel catfish, and bluegills. They are open April through October.

GOLF The beauty of Sullivan County's farm country carries over to its golf courses. Many resorts have outstanding courses that are open to the public. Well-known championship courses at Grossinger's, Kutsher's, Villa Roma, and Lochmore co-exist here with family friendly nine-hole courses like Lake View. It is best to call ahead to confirm hours and check if reservations are needed for a tee time.

Grossinger Country Club (845-292-9000, 888-448-9686), Liberty, has 27 holes of golf, a driving range and putting greens, and full facilities. Rated four and a half stars by *Golf Digest*. Call for schedule.

Island Glen Golf Course (845-583-1010), Route 17B, Bethel, has nine holes, a practice green, and a clubhouse. Open daily April through October, 8–6.

Kutsher's Country Club (845-794-6000, 800-431-1273), Kutsher Road, Monticello, has an 18-hole championship golf course designed by William F. Mitchell. Lessons, pro shop, carts, clubhouse, and driving range. Open mid-April through mid-November, 8–sunset.

Lake View Golf Course (845-557-6406), Mud Pond Road, Highland Lake, is a good nine-hole course for novice golfers.

Swan Lake Golf and Country Club (845-292-0323), Eagle Drive, Swan Lake, is an 18-hole PGA-rated course nestled high in the Catskills. Open daily April through November 7–6.

Tennanah Lake Golf & Tennis Club (607-498-5501), 100 Belle Road, Roscoe, is open April through October, 7 AM–9:30 PM. An 18-hole par-72 course, practice facility, driving range, and pro shop. They offer club rentals and lessons for novices.

Villa Roma Country Club (845-887-4880, 800-533-6767), 356 Villa Roma Road, Callicoon, has an 18-hole course, a putting green, and full facilities. Open April through mid-November. Call for hours.

Public courses include **Sullivan County Golf and Country Club** (845-292-9584), Route 52, Liberty; **Tarry Brae** (845-434-2620), South Fallsburg; and the **Lochmore Golf Course** (845-434-1257). 586 Loch Sheldrake/Hurleyville Road, Loch Sheldrake with its par-71, 18-hole course.

HARNESS RACING Monticello Raceway (845-794-4100 ext. 455), Raceway Road, Monticello. Take Route 17 to exit 104; follow signs. Open year-round, but days and hours vary, so call ahead. Admission fee. Recognized as one of the world's fastest half-mile harness tracks, Monticello Raceway is home to many famous pacers and trotters. Because it is not as large as other harness tracks, Monticello has smaller crowds and plenty of parking. But the action here is just as heart pounding, the crowds just as enthusiastic. The grandstand is glass-enclosed, and the racing goes on rain or shine. There is exotic and parimutuel wagering, and the paddock is indoors. On special-events days, meet the drivers and their horses, or enjoy a meal while watching the races from your table. Simulcasting of thoroughbred and harness races day and night.

HORSEBACK RIDING RR Stables (845-888-9712/2210), 2 Sullivan Street, Wurtsboro. Open daily 10–5; winter trail rides by appointment. There are guided horseback riding tours on scenic trails. Pony rides will enchant the kids. Three or four hour rides available to experienced riders.

Stone Wall Farms (845-482-5302), 139 County Route 127, Jeffersonville. Open year-round, Monday through Friday 8–7, Saturday 2–5. This is the place, whether you ride English or Western or want to take lessons. Classes available at all levels of ability.

SOARING Wurtsboro Airport (845-888-2791), Route 209, Wurtsboro. Open daily, weather permitting. Established in 1927, this airport is home to the oldest soaring site in the country. Soaring is done in sailplanes—motorless craft that are towed into the air and released. The pilot then sails the plane on the air currents—sometimes for hours—before gliding in for a landing. A 20-minute demonstration flight with a certified pilot can be arranged; if you enjoy the sport and want to learn how to do it, flight instruction is available.

✳ Winter Sports

CROSS-COUNTRY SKIING There are so many places to cross-country ski in Sullivan County that you would have to spend several winters here to try all the trails. Many local parks allow skiing for free, but often the trails are not groomed, and there are no nearby rentals. At the large resorts some trails are open for a fee to day visitors, but if you are uncertain of a hotel's policy, it is suggested that you call ahead; policies may also change from year to year.

DeBruce Country Inn on the Willowemoc (845-439-3900), 982 DeBruce Road, DeBruce, has miles of cross-country trails, unmapped and unmarked within the Catskill Park. It is located near Mongaup State Park and has a restaurant, lounge, and sauna.

Kutsher's Country Club (845-794-6000), Route 17 exit 105B, Monticello, has both cross-country and downhill skiing but only for guests of the hotel.

Villa Roma Country Club (845-887-4880), Callicoon, is open to the public as well as hotel guests for both cross-country and downhill skiing. They have 100 percent snowmaking.

Try the 160-acre **Town of Thompson Park** (845-796-3161), Old Liberty Road, 1.5 miles past the Monticello Post Office; the 110-acre **Hanofee (Liberty) Park** (845-292-7690), on Infirmary Road, off Route 52 east, in Liberty, where you will find rentals, a trail fee, and a heated hut on weekends; and 260-acre **Walnut Mountain (Pearson) Park** (845-292-7690), Liberty, with rentals and a heated trail hut on weekends.

DOWNHILL SKIING While downhill skiing in Sullivan County does not revolve around large resorts like Hunter or Windham, it does have a few centers that offer lots of fun for travelers of all ages. (See also *Cross-Country Skiing*.)

Holiday Mountain Ski Area (845-796-3161), 99 Holiday Mountain Road, Monticello (exit 107 off Route 17 at Bridgeville), has both day and night skiing, 15 slopes, 100 percent snowmaking, and a vertical drop of 400 feet. The longest run is 3,500 feet, and both beginners and advanced skiers will enjoy the slopes here; cross-country skiing is allowed, and so is snowboarding. A ski shop, snack bar, and parking are available. Open mid-December through mid-March.

ICE FISHING Every winter ice fishing contests are held, including an ongoing event at the **Eldred Preserve** (800-557-FISH), depending on ice conditions. Also, the **King of the Ice** contest is held every February by the Sullivan County Conservation Club. An **Ice Tee Open**, a Sunday afternoon golf outing on the ice, is sponsored by the Town of Highland Lions Club. Call the Sullivan County Visitors Association for exact dates and locations (845-794-3000, ext. 5010). Who says there isn't much to do in the winter?

✳ Green Space

Lake Superior State Park, Duggan Road, between Route 17B & 55, Bethel. Open year-round; beach area open Memorial Day weekend through Labor Day from 11–7. This state park offers swimming, boating, boat rentals, fishing, and picnic facilities. The beach is a perfect stop for families traveling with children.

Stone Arch Bridge Historical Park, Route 52, Kenoza Lake. Open year-round. Free. This three-arched stone bridge, which spans Callicoon Creek, is the only remaining one of its kind in this country. Built in 1872 by two German stonemasons, the bridge was constructed from hand-cut local stone and is supported without an outer framework. Replacing an earlier wooden span that finally collapsed from the constant weight of wagonloads of lumber, the Stone Arch Bridge gained fame not only for its graceful design and unusual construction but also for a bizarre murder that took place on or near it in 1892. A local farmer, believing that his brother-in-law had put a hex on him, convinced his son that only the brother-in-law's death could lift the curse. So the young man carried out the murder and dumped the body into the river. The case drew enormous publicity because of the witchcraft angle, and there have even been reports of a ghost appearing on the bridge. Today, visitors fish from the banks, picnic on shore, or just walk through the 9-acre landscaped park and along the nature trails. Children will enjoy the small play area.

✳ Lodging

Sullivan County is probably best known for the Catskills resorts that flourished there for nearly a century. While some of the hotels, like Kutsher's, still welcome guests, others, like the Concord, have shut their doors. But the region offers a wide variety of bungalows, resort hotels, bed & breakfasts, and inns, offering inexpensive to luxury accommodations. Be certain to call before you go; the resorts can be booked well in advance of the summer months and winter holidays.

All Breeze Guest House (845-557-6485), 1101 Haring Road, Barryville 12719. ($) This bed & breakfast offers a nice getaway for families with children. There are ponds to swim in and fields and woods to walk and explore. The guest house is close to several of the rafting outfitters. There are four rooms, and all have private bath. Open mid-April through mid-December. Pets welcome.

Bradstan Country Hotel (845-583-4114), Route 17B, White Lake 12786. ($$) This unique bed & breakfast features three cottages and five comfortable suites, all with private baths, overlooking beautiful White Lake. Also on the premises is a cabaret with live entertainment and a full bar. A gourmet breakfast is served, and special diets can be accommodated. Open year-round, except the month of March.

DeBruce Country Inn on the Willowemoc (845-439-3900), 982 DeBruce Road, off Route 17 (exit 96), DeBruce 12758. ($$) This inn, which dates from the turn of the 19th century, is located within the Catskill Forest Preserve and on the banks of Willowemoc Creek. The 14 guest rooms all have private baths. There is a sauna, exercise room, and outdoor pool. The Dry Fly lounge is the perfect place to unwind at the end of the day. Room rates include a full breakfast and choice of dinner. Prices are exceedingly reasonable. A perfect retreat for bird-watching, fly-fishing, hiking, and outdoor recreation. Art and craft gallery on the premises. Open year-round.

Fox Mountain Bed & Breakfast (845-292-0605), 628 Fox Mountain Road, White Sulphur Springs 12787. ($$) This newly renovated 1880s farmhouse is filled with hand-hewn beams and a country kitchen that reflects its rustic past. There are three charming suites with amenities that include an interior waterfall, marble hearth fireplace, mist shower, and hot tub. One single room is available. The large outside deck is perfect for breakfast in the summer months.

Gable Farm (845-252-7434), 90 Gables Road, Narrowsburg 12764. ($) Located on 106 acres of quiet meadows and woods that belong to a working farm, near where the original Woodstock concert took place, this pictur-

esque establishment offers cross-county skiing in winter and an in-ground pool in summer. The two guest rooms have private baths. There are goats and sheep here, and visitors are allowed to bring pets. Open year-round.

Griffen House (845-482-3371), 27 Maple Avenue, Jeffersonville 12748. ($$) This award-winning Victorian mansion, tucked away on a 2-acre estate in the village, once hosted FDR. All four guest rooms have private baths. There is a gourmet restaurant on the premises that serves groups by advance reservation only. Open year-round.

The Guest House (845-439-4000), 408 DeBruce Road, Livingston Manor 12758. ($$$) This luxurious 40-acre retreat is the perfect romantic getaway. There are four guest rooms with private baths in the main house and three other rooms in cottages on the premises; one has a whirlpool bath surrounded by palm trees; all have king- and queen-sized beds. A fully equipped fitness room is available, and guests can book tennis lessons or a massage. Lounge with baby grand piano and fireplace. Breakfast is served any time in the morning—or early afternoon. Located on Willowemoc Creek, with private fly-fishing. Open year-round.

The Inn at Lake Joseph (845-791-9506), County Road 108, off Route 42, Forestburgh 12777. ($$$) A 19th-century Victorian mountain retreat nestled in the Catskills and surrounded by acres of forest, this inn was built by a prosperous businessman who then sold the house to the Roman Catholic Church, which used it as a retreat for Cardinals Hayes and Spellman. A private spring-fed lake offers swimming, boating, and fishing. There are two tennis courts, as well. This is a secluded spot where every detail is attended to, one of the county's best inns. The mansion has six fireplaces, and each of the 15 guest rooms has canopied bed, Persian rugs, lacy linens, and fine antiques as well as a private bath. The carriage house is perfect for families, with its own library, TV, and stereo. Fitness center and outdoor pool. Open year-round.

Kutsher's Country Club (845-794-6000, 800-431-1273), Kutsher Road, off Route 42, Monticello 12701. ($$) Since 1907 the Kutsher family has been running this resort. Although it's large (more than 400 rooms), an informal homey atmosphere prevails. There is an 18-hole golf course on the grounds, and the indoor ice rink is open all year. The lake offers boating and fishing. Guests will enjoy indoor and outdoor pools, a health club, racquetball, tennis, and a full children's program. Rates include three meals a day. Open year-round.

Lanza's Country Inn (845-439-5070), 839 Shandelee Road, Living-ston Manor 12758. ($$) An 80-year old building with a pub and restaurant houses this family-owned and operated inn. Each one of the nine guest rooms is different—all are furnished with period pieces and have private baths; some have canopied beds. The full breakfast includes homemade breads, juice, and coffee. A lake is nearby for swimming, fishing, and boating, and there are cross-country ski trails. Children welcome. Open mid-March through mid-December.

Lazy Pond Bed & Breakfast (845-292-3362), 79 Old Loomis Road, Liberty 12754. ($$) Although this B&B is only 1.5 miles from town, a stay here makes you feel as though you are transported back in time. This three-story Victorian houses 11 rooms, 9 with private baths, and all have queen-sized beds. Enjoy breakfast in the West Wing on a wraparound porch that overlooks a beautiful pond. Open year-round.

The Lodge at Rock Hill (845-796-3100 or 1-866-RH-LODGE), 283 Rock Hill Drive, Rock Hill 12775. ($$)

THE INN AT LAKE JOSEPH

The hotel offers 78 newly renovated, beautifully appointed rooms and suites (some with Jacuzzis) on 55 acres with hiking and mountain biking and cross-country skiing in the winter. Fitness center, cable TV, air-conditioning. Children welcome. Open year-round.

Magical Land of Oz (845-439-3418), 753 Shandelee Road, Livingston Manor 12758. ($) This elegant century-old farmhouse is as eclectic as its name is unusual. You can enjoy a hot tub on the terrace, a workout in the exercise room, or a swim in the nearby lake. There are sheep, goats, and chickens on the premises and lovely gardens in-season. Five room share three bathrooms. Open year-round.

New Age Health Spa (845-985-7645 or 1-800-682-4348), Route 55, Neversink 12765. ($$) This is a quiet, casual, reasonably priced retreat that focuses on weight loss, destressing, and regenerating vitality. The approach is a combination of exercise and nutrition, helping guests develop permanent changes in their daily regimen and habits that they can take home with them. In addition to massages, mud baths, facials, and aromatherapy, classes are available throughout the day in stretching, body conditioning, yoga, and Tai Chi. The indoor pool and Jacuzzi are first-rate, and you will also find a sauna and steam room. A daily hike is organized for guests—the spa is located on the edge of a state forest, and there are many scenic trails to explore. The spa pampers guests with gourmet, healthful meals that are both low fat and delicious. This is a great place to stay for those on special diets since the menu features fresh fruits, vegetables, and juices. Most of the herbs are grown in greenhouses on the premises during warm-weather months. Good value for the money; special packages during the off-season. Open year-round.

Reynolds House Inn (607-498-4422), 1934 Old Route 17, Roscoe 12776 ($$) Built in 1902 as a tourist home, this is the county's oldest operational bed & breakfast. The three-story Victorian offers fly-fishing, hiking, golfing, and fine restaurants nearby. The seven decorative guest rooms have private baths, cable TV, and air-conditioning. The elegant Rockefeller Suite, where John D. Rockefeller was a frequent guest in the 1920s, has a king-sized bed and a claw-foot tub. A full breakfast is served in the parlor in winter or on the wraparound porch, weather permitting. Open year-round.

Rolling Marble Guest House (845-887-6016), 12 Railroad Street, Long Eddy 12760. ($) This lovely 14-room Victorian, over 100 years old, with high ceilings, French doors, and wraparound porches, is located right on the Delaware River. Built by local sawmill owner George Gould when Long Eddy was a prosperous town, thanks to the lumber and bluestone industries, the house was bought and renovated in 1985 by the current owners. There are four rooms that share two and a half baths. Open July and August only. Well-behaved children are welcome.

Roscoe Motel (607-498-5220), Old Route 17, Roscoe 12776. ($) Located near some of the most famous fishing waters in the country, this is a funky motel that is inexpensive and provides the necessary amenities. A great place to stay if you are traveling with young children. Open year-round.

Sivananda Ashram Yoga Ranch (845-434-9242), Budd Road, Woodbourne 12788. ($). The 36 rooms here on this 78-acre retreat are dormitory-style accommodations, and all share baths. A yoga vacation includes twice-daily classes and vegetarian meals. There are classes in meditation, guest lectures and workshops, cultural programs, and family yoga. There is a sauna for guests; children are welcome. Open year-round.

Stone Wall Acres (845-482-4930), 142 Eagin Road, Youngsville 12791. ($$) There is one carriage house here, furnished in original antiques—the perfect spot for those seeking a secluded getaway. You will feel transported to England, being surrounded by a country garden on 6 private acres. The carriage house has a living room/dining room, loft bedroom, and fireplace. Breakfast may be served there, in the main-house dining room, or poolside on the patio, depending on your preference. Open year-round.

Tennanah Lake Golf & Tennis Club (607-498-5502), 100 Belle Road, Roscoe 12776. ($$) There are 24 rooms with private balconies here (one is completely handicapped accessible) with all the amenities. The emphasis is on golf and tennis packages, but visitors can enjoy swimming in the lovely indoor pool or relaxing by the lake. A restaurant and coffee shop are on the premises. A good place to stay if you are traveling with older children.

Villa Roma (845-887-4880), Villa Roma Road, Callicoon 12723. ($$) There are 230 air-conditioned rooms, all with TV, telephones, and Internet access at this full-service family owned-and-operated resort that has been in business for over 40 years.

Guests can enjoy a variety of activities—fishing, swimming in the indoor and outdoor pools, golf, and horse-drawn sleigh rides in winter. The place has a decidedly Italian accent, and all room rates include terrific food. There is even a weekly Caesar's Night feast. Special events include children's programs, auctions, and rafting expeditions.

✳ Where to Eat

Sullivan, although not a large county, has few major roads and is time-consuming to navigate. Restaurants are grouped according to location in the county: southeast, southwest, northwest, and northeast.

DINING OUT

In Southeastern Sullivan (Forestburgh, Monticello, Rock Hill, Wurtsboro)

Bernie's Holiday Restaurant (845-796-3333), Route 17, Rock Hill. ($$) Open Tuesday–Sunday for dinner daily at 5. One of the largest restaurants in Sullivan County and also one of the best. The specialties here are gourmet Chinese, Continental, and American; the Cajun dishes are also first-rate. Children welcome.

Buona Fortuna (845-796-4110), 46 Forestburgh Road, Monticello. ($$) Open Tuesday through Saturday 11–10, Sunday and Monday 4–10. Enjoy Northern Italian cuisine prepared to order by the chef-owner. Children welcome.

Gaetano's (845-796-4901), Route 17B, Mongaup Valley. ($$) Open Wednesday through Sunday for dinner 5–9. Enjoy fine Northern Italian cuisine in this delightful restaurant, located only 4 miles from the Monticello Raceway. Reservations requested.

House of Lyons (845-794-0244), Jefferson Street, Monticello. ($$) Open for lunch Tuesday through Friday noon–3; dinner served Tuesday through Sunday 5–9:30. The specialties here are fresh seafood and prime rib, but the menu is huge and offers a range of Continental cuisine. There are chicken wings and burgers for children, who are welcome.

The Old Homestead Steakhouse (845-794-8973), 472 Bridgeville Road, Monticello. ($$) Open daily 4:30–10 for dinner. Hours change seasonally. This is the place to go for surf and turf. The large 24-ounce sirloin steak is a specialty of the house. You can also try steamed or stuffed lobster, grilled salmon or swordfish along with a large menu featuring an array of steak dishes.

In Southwestern Sullivan (Barryville, Eldred, Narrowsburg, White Lake)
Eldred Preserve (845-557-8316), Route 55, Eldred. ($$) Open for dinner Monday through Saturday 5–9, Sunday 1–8. The dining rooms here overlook three stream-fed ponds—stocked with rainbow, brown, brook, and golden trout—as well as 2,000 acres of unspoiled forest. Needless to say, the specialty is trout from the preserve's ponds. The fish is served many ways, including smoked, and all baking is done on the premises. There is also a 21-room motel, and two private lakes are open for boating and fishing (see *To Do: Fishing*). Guests can enjoy the tennis courts and outdoor pool in warm weather or ice fishing in winter. Children welcome.

The Front Porch (845-583-4838), 1577 Route 17B, White Lake. ($$)

Open April through December, Wednesday through Sunday, from 11:30–9 for lunch and dinner. Dine outdoors, weather permitting, and enjoy an eclectic menu featuring world fusion cuisine combining Asian, Italian, and American favorites. Chicken bouillabaisse, shrimp pad thai, and marinated tuna carpaccio are a few popular entrées here. Desserts, all baked on the premises, range from chocolate mousse and chocolate brownie torte to mango cheesecake and pumpkin banana tart.

The Lighthouse (845-583-5090), Route 17B, overlooking White Lake. ($$) Open year-round daily from 5 for dinner. A White Lake tradition, this establishment has been in business for over 50 years. The two newly renovated dining rooms each have an outdoor deck, where you can enjoy seafood, steaks, chops, rack of lamb, fresh fish, and other standard Continental specialties. Casual dining atmosphere; great for families.

The Millbrook Inn (845-856-7778), Route 97, Pond Eddy. ($$) Open for dinner Friday and Saturday 5–9:30; Sunday noon–8. Fine country dining featuring a mix of American and European favorites. The emphasis here is on freshness, and the entrées are imaginative. A few of the specialties are tidewater shrimp, maple walnut chicken, and game pie. Children are welcome.

The Narrowsburg Inn (845-252-3998), 182 Bridge Street, Narrowsburg. ($$) Open March through December Wednesday through Sunday for lunch and dinner from 11:30–9. Enjoy Continental cuisine surrounded by an historic atmosphere. There is outdoor dining overlooking the Delaware River in the warm weather. Children welcome.

Tre Alberi (845-557-6104), Route 97, Barryville. ($$) Open for dinner daily, except Wednesday 5–10; reservations suggested. This restaurant serves some of the best Northern Italian cuisine to be found in the Catskills. There are different pasta, fish, and poultry specials each day, and all are prepared to order. The desserts are made on the premises, and the chef-owner oversees their preparation. A worthwhile stop for those who appreciate fine dining.

In Northwestern Sullivan (Callicoon, Jeffersonville, Livingston Manor, Roscoe, Tennanah Lake)
The Kitchen (845-482-9332), 4879 Route 52, Jeffersonville. ($) Open Wednesday and Thursday 11–9, Friday until 10, Saturday 9 AM–10 PM, Sunday 9–9. Call for winter hours. American cuisine with a Southern flair, including shrimp and grits cake appetizer, Coca-Cola baked ham, Cajun-style catfish, burgers, steaks, and an array of soups and salads. Homemade cakes and pies for dessert. Exceptional wine list.

Matthew's on Main Street (845-887-5636), 19 Lower Main Street, Cochecton. ($$) Open daily for lunch 11–5; dinner 5–9:30, until 11 Friday and Saturday. It's hard to miss the bright-red building with green-and-tan trim that houses this chef-owned family restaurant featuring upscale fare at reasonable prices. This beautifully renovated building dates back to 1865, and outdoor dining may be enjoyed on the deck day and night in the warm weather. You can order lunch all night; the light-fare menu is always available. International cuisine—fresh fish, smoked duck, prime rib, and sesame-crusted salmon are just some of the tasty entrées.

Desserts include fruit sorbets cakes and pies, all made from scratch on the premises. This casual, comfortable spot also has a full bar with beautiful tin ceilings. Children welcome.

Michelangelo's Restaurant (845-482-3900), Main Street, Jeffersonville. ($$) Open Monday through Saturday 11–9. The southern Italian cooking here features Neapolitan specialties including the chef's favorites— eggplant parmigiana and eggplant rollotini. All sauces are fresh and homemade. I enjoyed the linguini Michelangelo: pasta topped with arugula, jumbo shrimp, a few cherry peppers, and a light tomato sauce. Desserts include cannoli, tiramisu, and sorbet . . . if you have room.

The 1906 House (845-887-1906), Main Street, Callicoon. ($$) Open daily for dinner 5–9; call for winter hours. Enjoy both traditional favorites and nouvelle cuisine specialties prepared by a Culinary Institute-trained chef. The Black Angus beef is popular, and so are the game dishes, which include venison, quail, and rabbit. All soups and desserts are made on the premises. Entertainment on weekends. Reservations suggested.

Rafael's (845-439-5121), 2 Pearl Street, Livingston Manor. ($$) Open Wednesday through Monday for lunch 11:30–3; for dinner 4:30–9. Bar remains open with light fare throughout the early-morning hours. Cuban, Italian, and American cuisine is the mix here. Some specialties of the house are the paella, rice with chicken (arroz con pollo), rice and beans, Cuban sandwiches, pasta, seafood— and, last but not least, great frozen margaritas. Live music on weekend evenings.

Ted's Restaurant (845-482-4242), 4896 Route 52, Jeffersonville. ($$) Open daily year-round 6 AM–9 PM. Turkish, Mediterranean, and American cuisine meld here. Try the mixed grill, which combines lamb, chicken, and gyro items; the shrimp kabob is excellent, as well. The Turkish appetizers are a nice way to sample, a variety of new tastes. For the less adventurous, there is the Gusburger, a half-pound bacon cheeseburger on a hard roll with fries (one of the most popular dishes here). Children's menu.

In Northeastern Sullivan (DeBruce,Hurleyville, Liberty)
Christopher's Seafood House (845-436-8749), 219 Main Street, Hurleyville, ($$). Open daily at 3; Sunday brunch noon–3; dinner 3 on. The Continental cuisine includes all of the Italian specialties. The chef's favorites are the seafood cannelloni, sautéed soft shell crabs (in season), prime rib, and zuppa di pesce. The kids will enjoy the spareribs.

Dead End Café (845-292-0202), Route 17, Parksville. ($$) Open for dinner daily at 5 during summer months; call for hours at other times of the year. All kinds of Italian fare are served here, with unusual seafood specials nightly. There is a live music charge and excellent espresso and cappuccino.

Piccolo Paese (845-292-7210), 271 Route 52, Liberty. ($$) Open for lunch Monday through Friday noon–3; dinner served daily 4:30–10. This elegant yet moderately priced Northern Italian restaurant features fresh home-made pasta, seafood, chicken, veal, and imaginative appetizers. The chef-owner creates terrific daily specials that I highly recommend.

& Restaurant (845-791-4600), Route 42 North, Monticello. ($) Open daily 11:30–10. This Italian-American restaurant specializes in pizza and calzones as well as the standard favorites: lasagna, manicotti, and an array of other pasta dishes. Children welcome.

Catskill Morning Farm (845-439-4900), 87 DeBruce Road, Livingston Manor. ($$) Open year-round, 9–5 Thursday through Tuesday. This café features a coffee and cappuccino bar, homemade baked goods, healthful lunch items, and a gourmet brunch on Saturday and Sunday. There is a gift shop and garden center with greenhouse on the premises.

Dave's Big Eddy Diner (845-252-3817), 40 Main Street, Narrowsburg. ($) Open for dinner Friday and Saturday 6–9, Wednesday through Sunday 7–3. They serve breakfast, lunch, and dinner here but hours change seasonally, so you may want to call before you go. Imaginative touches are added to the good old American favorites. This is a terrific place to stop for those traveling with kids; good value.

The Feast (845-791-0244), 334 Broadway, Monticello. ($) Open daily year-round 10–7. This combination deli/specialty shop is one of the few places in the Catskills where you will find New York Carnegie Deli corned beef and pastrami. All the great deli specialties are served here; gourmet items for sale. Outdoor dining in the warm-weather months.

Frankie & Johnnie's (845-434-8051), Main Street, Hurleyville. ($) Open daily year-round 11:30–11. This reasonable Italian-American restaurant specializes in steak, seafood, pasta, and pizza. It's a great spot for lunch or dinner if you're traveling with children.

Lanza's Country Inn (845-439-5070), 839 Shandelee Road, Livingston Manor. ($$) Open for dinner daily April through mid-December, Wednesday through Sunday from mid-December through March. You can enjoy a variety of beef, seafood, pasta, and vegetarian dishes here; There is pizza and "pub grub" (light fare) available at the bar.

Liberty Diner & Restaurant (845-292-8973), 30 Sullivan Avenue, Liberty. ($) Open daily 24 hours. You will find the standard diner fare here in this combination diner/restaurant with two large dining rooms. A local oasis.

Peez Leweez (845-439-3300), 2 Pearl Street, Livingston Manor. ($) Open daily, year-round: Monday through Thursday, 6:30–4, Friday until 10, Saturday 8 AM–10 PM, Sunday 9–3. Enjoy pastries, homemade soups, sandwiches, quiche, and salads at this coffee bar, which serves up some of the best espresso and cappuccino around. Fear not, tea drinkers, there is a good selection from which to choose!

Pete's Pub (845-932-8110), Route 52, Lake Huntington. ($) Open Wednesday through Monday noon–10. This family-style restaurant offers an array of old favorites like pot roast, beef stew, and lobster tails. On weekends there's a salad bar. The fare is simple, and the portions are hearty. There are also steaks, pasta dishes, and burgers of all kinds.

The Potager (845-888-4086), 116 Sullivan Street, Wurtsboro. ($) Open year-round 11–5. Located downstairs in a retail store, this small café serves outdoors in the warm-weather

months. It's a good place for those traveling with children to have lunch. (See also *To See.*)

✳ Entertainment

ARTS Sullivan County has a long tradition of supporting the arts, and the cultural programs and shows offered throughout the region are quite good. The **Delaware Arts Center** (845-252-7576) is headquartered in the historic Arlington Hotel in Narrowsburg, 37 Main Street, which is on the National Register of Historic Places. Its gallery is open year-round for exhibits and special events, so call for a schedule. This is also the home of the **Delaware Valley Arts Alliance**, the arts council for Sullivan County.

The **Catskill Art Society** (845-436-4227), 263 Main Street, Hurleyville, sponsors art, studio and architectural tours, workshops, and more. Call for locations and schedules of events in the county.

The Sullivan County Museum, Art and Cultural Center (845-434-8044), 265 Main Street, Hurleyville, is open year-round Wednesday through Saturday 10–4:30, Sunday 1–4:30. Closed January. They display local historical material as well as the work of local artists. (See also *To See.*)

PERFORMING ARTS A summer-stock theater housed in a 130-year-old barn can only mean fun, and that's what you'll have when you attend a performance at the **Forestburgh Playhouse** (845-794-1194), 39 Forestburgh Road, Forestburgh 12777. Drama, comedies, and musicals are all on the bill, and you can enjoy postshow cabaret and cocktails in the adjoining tavern. They are open from late June through Labor Day, closed Monday, but it is best to call for the summer schedule.

The **Arts & Cultural Team at Sullivan (ACTS)** (845-434-5750, 800-577-5243 ext. 4303), Sullivan County Community College, Loch Sheldrake, has dance, theater, and musicals as part of its series along with holiday offerings and family shows.

The **Delaware Valley Opera** (845-252-3136) is headquartered at 170 Main Street in Narrowsburg. They present two operas, one in July and one in August, each year at the **Tusten Theatre**, 210 Bridge Street, where you will also find a variety of live music concerts, including jazz, classical, and bluegrass. A few dramatic productions are scheduled during the summer months. The theater is also home to the **Delaware Valley Chamber Orchestra.**

✳ Selective Shopping

There are some delightful specialty shops to be discovered while browsing the streets of Sullivan County's quaint villages like Hurleyville, Narrowsburg, Roscoe, and Wurtsboro. One of my favorites is the **Delaware River Trading Company** (845-557-0837), 3396 Route 97 in Barryville. Open during the summer, Thursday through Tuesday 10–5, they have an eclectic collection of gifts, jewelry, local art, and Delaware River souvenirs. Have a cup of organic coffee after shopping.

ANTIQUES The search for treasures in the county can take you to a dusty little shop on a side road or into full-fledged auction barns where the prices are steep and the sales are fast. Many antiques shops are open all year, but some serve only the vacation crowds; call before you go to avoid disappointment. There are dozens of shops throughout the county, and the following is only a sampling:

Ace Trading Company (845-434-4553), Main Street, Hurleyville, has a wide selection, ranging from antiques to odds and ends.

DELAWARE VALLEY CHAMBER ORCHESTRA

Courtesy Delaware Valley Arts Alliance

The Antique Palace Emporium (845-292-2270), 300 Chestnut Street, Liberty, has more than two floors of restored furniture and original collectibles.

Cain's Antiques (607-498-4303), 174 Rockland Road, Roscoe. Open year-round, Friday through Monday 9–4:30. Located on two floors in an old country store, they specialize in refinished furniture, china, lamps, glass, mirrors, and decorative accessories for both the retail and wholesale market.

Callicoon Flea Market (845-887-5411), 43 Lower Main Street, Callicoon, has everything from furniture to collectible pottery, along with reproduction furniture and decorative items.

Ferndale Marketplace Antiques & Gardens (845-292-8701), Route 17, exit 101, 52 Ferndale Road, Ferndale. Open all year Friday through Monday, 10–5, July through Labor Day daily. Formerly home to Manion's General Store and the Ferndale Post Office, this grand multidealer shop has 13 rooms in a four-story historic Victorian building. There is a wide selection of antiques, furniture, paintings, toys, glassware, lighting, fine decorative accessories, and everything in between. The largest antiques shop in Sullivan County.

The Flea Market at Monticello Raceway (845-796-1000), Route 17B, Monticello. Up to a hundred vendors offer mostly new merchandise with lots of surprises. Last weekend in June through Labor Day weekend, Saturday and Sunday 9–5.

Hurleyville Antique Center (845-434-4553), 222 Main Street, Hurleyville. Open daily May through October 11–5. This huge store is chock-full of antiques, collectibles, paintings, and many other items of interest.

Larry's Dog House Woodstock Memorabilia (845-583-5991), corner of Route 17B and Dr. Duggan Road, White Lake. Open May through September but will open at other times with a little advance notice. This is it: the Woodstock collector's vision of paradise. Quirky but grandly local.

Memories (845-292-4270), Route 17 between exits 98 and 97 (watch for signs), near Ferndale, has a large general line and has long been a popular stop with vacationers.

Ulster County

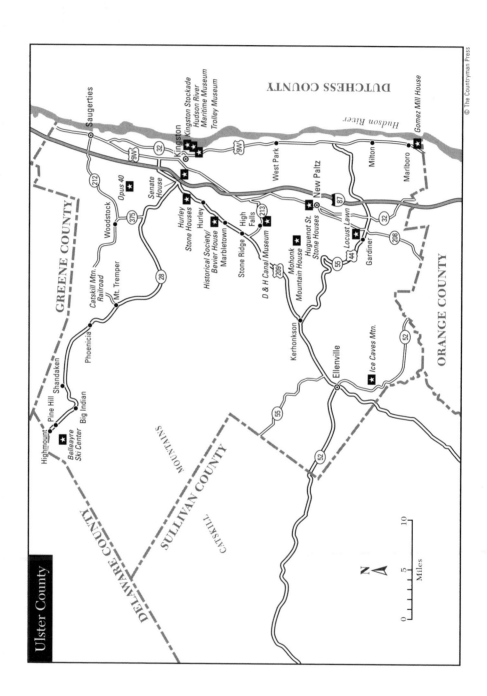

Ulster County

Saugerties

Kingston
Kingston Stockade
Hudson River
Maritime Museum
Trolley Museum

DUTCHESS COUNTY

Hudson River

Gomez Mill House

West Park

New Paltz

Milton

Marlboro

212
9W
32
9W
87
32
208

Opus 40

Woodstock

375
Senate House

Hurley
Stone Houses
Hurley
213

Historical Society/
Bevier House
Marbletown

Stone Ridge
High Falls

Huguenot St.
Stone Houses
Locust Lawn
Gardiner

Mt. Tremper

Catskill Mtn.
Railroad

28
D & H Canal Museum

Mohonk
Mountain House

205

55
44
55

ORANGE COUNTY

Phoenicia

Kerhonkson

Big Indian
Shandaken
Pine Hill
Highmount

Bellayre
Ski Center

Ellenville

Ice Caves Mtn.

52

GREENE COUNTY

DELAWARE COUNTY

SULLIVAN COUNTY

CATSKILL MOUNTAINS

55
52

N

0   5   10
Miles

ULSTER COUNTY

Both the Dutch and the English settled in Ulster County, drawn by the lush farmlands along the Hudson. Snug, well-built homes were constructed of stone, brick, and wood; many still stand and are open to the public. Ulster County was not always blessed with peace and prosperity, however; it was the scene of conflict during the American Revolution, when the city of Kingston was burned by the British, and spies were hung in the outlying orchards. But the area rebuilt itself through the years, and today Ulster is a study in contrasts. Businesses have settled alongside farms, and artist colonies thrive among boutiques. Dutch names of towns and lanes recall the past, while a thriving community of second-home owners, immigrants, and vacationers has brought different cultures to the region.

Ulster is mountainous, flat, river lined, and forested by turns, and the outdoors offers excellent fishing, skiing, and hiking. There's enough here to keep visitors busy for another century or so! The region is easy to travel, with several major roads and enough byways to please every traveler. Bring a camera when you visit because the seasonal changes in Ulster are dramatic, with spring giving way to summer overnight and winter making guest appearances as late as April.

GUIDANCE **Ulster County Tourism** (845-340-3566, 800-342-5826), 10 Westbrook Lane, Kingston 12401; www.ulstertourism.info.

Ulster County Chamber of Commerce (845-338-5100), 1 Albany Avenue, Kingston; www.ulsterchamber.org.

GETTING THERE *By car:* Ulster County is accessible from the New York State Thruway exits 18, 19, and 20, and in the southern section of the county from Routes 17 and 9W.

By bus: **Adirondack/Pine Hill Trailways** (845-331-0744, 800-858-8555), 400 Washington Avenue, Kingston, offers frequent daily service between the Port Authority in Manhattan and New Paltz, Kingston, Woodstock, and Phoenicia as well as points north and west.

By train: **Amtrak** (800-872-7245), operates trains between Manhattan and

Rhinecliff, which is a 10-minute drive over the Kingston-Rhinecliff Bridge to Ulster County.

By air: **Albany International Airport** (518-242-2200), 737 Albany Shaker Road, Loudonville, is the closest major airport to the northern part of the county. **River Aviation, Inc.** (845-336-8400), 1161 Flatbush Road, Kingston, operates Kingston Airport, located near the Kingston-Rhinecliff Bridge. **Stewart International Airport** (845-564-7200/2100), 1035 First Street, New Windsor, is the closest major airport to the southern part of the county.

MEDICAL EMERGENCY It is now possible to dial 911 anywhere in the county for emergency assistance.

Benedictine Hospital (845-338-2500), 105 St. Mary's Avenue, Kingston.

Ellenville Regional Hospital (845-647-6400), Route 209, Ellenville.

Kingston Hospital (845-331-3131), 396 Broadway, Kingston.

Emergency One Urgent Care and Diagnostic Center (845-338-5600), 40 Hurley Avenue, Kingston.

✳ To See

Delaware & Hudson Canal Museum (845-687-9311), Route 213 to High Falls, and turn right onto Mohonk Road. Open May through October, Thursday through Saturday and Monday 11–5, Sunday 1–5. Admission fee. This museum is dedicated to the history and lore of the great Delaware & Hudson Canal. Built in the early 19th century, the canal was used to ship coal from the mines in Pennsylvania to the factories of New York; later cement was shipped south to be used for bridges and skyscrapers. The canal's designer was also responsible for the Erie Canal, and the locks, basins, and dams were engineering wonders of their era. In the museum, visitors will find a miniature setup of the canal and its workings, offering a sense of what life was like on the canal boats used for the six-day trips. While you are at the museum, take the self-guided tour of the locks (located across the road); along the tour you will see examples of stonework, snubbing posts, weirs, locks, and loading slips.

Samuel Dorsky Museum of Art (845-257-3844), SUNY New Paltz, 75 South Manheim Boulevard, New Paltz. Open year-round Wednesday 1–8, Thursday through Sunday 1–5. Closed Monday, Tuesday, and holidays. Donation. A new addition to the region, opened in 2002, this is the only art museum between Manhattan and Albany on the west side of the Hudson River. There are six galleries with a total of over 9,000 square feet of space. Enjoy changing exhibits of contemporary art, which complement exhibits from the museum's permanent collection that spans more than 4,000 years. (The focus includes American and European works on paper, regional paintings, prints, sculpture, photographs, and metalwork.) There is an emphasis here on the cultural heritage of the Hudson Valley and Catskill Mountains as well as diverse world cultures.

Empire State Railway Museum (845-688-7501), Ulster & Delaware Railroad Station, Phoenicia (watch for signs from Main Street). Open weekends Memorial

Day weekend through Columbus Day 11–4. Donation. This small museum offers excellent exhibits about railroads and life in the Catskill Mountains. Past shows have included photographs and artifacts related to the building of the reservoirs, tourism history, and railroads in the Catskills. The volunteer guides all love trains and their history, and they make the tour fun for all.

Hudson River Maritime Museum & Rondout Lighthouse (845-338-0071), 50 Rondout Landing (at the foot of Broadway), Kingston. Open daily May through mid-October 11–5. Admission fee. This museum is dedicated to preserving the maritime heritage of the Hudson River. For almost 200 years the Hudson was a major water highway between New York City and Albany. One of the ports of call along the way was the Rondout Landing in Kingston, once a bustling area of boatyards and rigging lofts that echoed with steam whistles and brass ships' bells. But when shipping on the Hudson fell into decline, so did the fortunes of the Rondout. Then in 1980 the museum was opened and has since restored several riverside buildings and historic vessels; visitors can now see a working part of the Hudson's legacy. An exhibit hall features shows on marine history. Outside there is an ever-changing display of river vessels, including the 1899 steam tug *Mathilda* and the cruise boat *Indy 7*. Visitors to the landing have also included the presidential yacht *Sequoia* and the sailing ships *Clearwater* and *Woody Guthrie*. Special weekend festivals are held throughout the year, including a Harvest Festival in October, a Shad Festival in May, and sailing regattas and gatherings of antique wooden boats.

Tours to the **Rondout Lighthouse**, a satellite museum, are offered May through mid-October. During the months of May, June, September, and October: Saturday and Sunday at noon, 1, and 2 on the hour; July and August: Thursday through Monday at noon, 1, and 2. On Saturday and Sunday there is an additional boat trip at 3. This tour gives visitors a glimpse into a way of life that was once typical of Hudson River lighthouse keepers and their families.

Fred J. Johnston Museum (845-339-0720), 63 Main Street, Kingston. Open May through October, Saturday and Sunday 1–4; admission fee. For the lover of American decorative history and fine antiques, a stop here is mandatory. This extraordinary collection was assembled by Johnston, a dealer and friend of Henry du Pont, who compared Johnston's furniture and decorative items to those found in du Pont's own museum, Winterthur. The house was built around 1812 for a prominent local attorney, who counted Washington Irving and Martin Van Buren among his friends and guests. Visitors today will enjoy the fine 18th-and 19th-century examples of furniture, porcelain, and needlework that fill the house, including examples by local cabinetmakers and artists like John Vanderlyn.

RONDOUT LIGHTHOUSE, KINGSTON

Hudson Valley Tourism, Inc.

The Marketplace at Catskill Corners (845-688-5800), Route 28, Mount Tremper. Open year-round daily 10–5, extended hours in summer season. Closed Tuesdays January through June. Admission fee. Catskill Corners is one of the county's premier family destinations for fine lodging and dining, shopping, and family entertainment. This is it: **Kaleidoworld,** home of the Guinness Book of World Records-certified world's largest kaleidoscope. Visitors actually walk into the 60-foot-high, silo-shaped room, where they experience a color and sound show unlike any other. Then step into the shops; one of them offers one of the largest selections of kaleidoscopes in the country. The other boutiques feature regional books, cashmere items, antiques, furniture, and unique gifts for the home as well as children's toys. The site also has the second largest kaleidoscope in the world, along with a John Burroughs nature park, several lovely gift shops, and The Lodge, a fantasy of what everyone thinks a mountain resort should look like (see *Lodging*). A must-see for families traveling in western Ulster County.

Overlook Observatory (845-679-0785), 141 Silver Hollow Road, Willow; approximately 7 miles west of the village of Woodstock off Route 212. Hours by appointment; fee charged for classes. Both home and scientific workshop to nationally known astronomer Bob Berman, the observatory offers visitors a guided tour of the night sky, with all its mysteries, quirks, wonders, and outstanding instruments for viewing the heavens. Bob is a knowledgeable and enthusiastic guide as well as the author of three popular astronomy books that have been featured in national media.

A. J. Snyder Estate (845-658-9900), Route 213, Rosendale (watch for signs). Tours from May through October, Saturday, Sunday, and Wednesday 1–4 and by appointment. Admission fee. This estate sits directly across from the Delaware & Hudson Canal. The house is open for tours, and the carriage house, with its fine collection of more than 20 antique sleighs and carriages—some dating from the 1820s—is a must-see. Phaetons, wagons, and cutters are all here and in beautiful condition. There are also the ruins of old cement kilns on the property, the canal slip, and the Widow Jane Mine, a cave often used for special events, including concerts and plays. Call for a schedule.

Tibetan Buddhist Monastery (845-679-5906), Meads Mountain Road, Woodstock; at the village green turn onto Rock City Road, which becomes Meads Mountain Road; follow up the mountain for 2.6 miles to the top. Group tours are offered by appointment. Monastery tours for individuals leave the bookstore Saturday and Sunday 1:30–3. Karma Triyana Dharmachakra Monastery is situated high above Woodstock and is worth a trip any time of year. Founded in 1978, the monastery combines traditional Tibetan architecture and design with Western construction. The main shrine room is 2,400 square feet and features one of the largest statues of Buddha in North America, while smaller shrines are decorated with traditional art. Be sure to see the gift shop, with its wide assortment of imported items from the Himalayas in addition to books. A nice change of pace from the crowded streets of Woodstock on weekend afternoons!

FOR FAMILIES **Catskill Mountain Railroad** (845-688-7400), Route 28, Phoenicia. Open Memorial Day weekend through Labor Day weekend and holidays 11–5; September and October, weekends only noon–4; trains leave every hour on the hour. Admission fee, but children under the age of 4 ride for free. This 6-mile round trip from Mount Pleasant to Phoenicia takes about 45 minutes. The train stops at the Empire State Railway Museum on High Street in Phoenicia (see *To See*), where riders will enjoy a guided tour. Plans are underway at this writing to expand the line to Kingston for a 50 mile round-trip. This is a wonderfully relaxing way to take in the countryside if you are traveling with children; besides, just about everyone loves train rides.

Forsyth Park Children's Zoo (845-339-3053), off Lucas Avenue just beyond Millers Lane on the left, Kingston. Open daily September through April: Monday through Friday 7–3, weekends and holidays 7–11; May through August: Monday through Friday 7–7, weekends and holidays 9–5. Free. There are nine species of mammals in this small zoo, which includes llamas, deer, bulls, pygmy goats, and sheep. An aviary on the premises is filled with a variety of birds. There is a large playground in the park, and the two activities make a nice outing for those with young children.

Trolley Museum (845-331-3399), 89 East Strand, Kingston; follow Broadway south where it ends, turn left, and watch for signs. Open Memorial Day weekend through Columbus Day, weekends and holidays noon–5. Admission fee. Housed in an old trolley shed along the Rondout. For anyone who remembers the ring of a trolley bell or the rolling ride of a self-propelled car, this museum offers displays—and lots of nostalgia. Visitors may also enjoy a short ride on a restored trolley car.

Widmark Honey Farm (845-255-6400), Route 44/55, Gardiner. Open daily year-round 10–6. Admission fee (credited to any purchase). The farm offers bears and honey, but here the bears have been raised practically as family pets, and they will entertain visitors with their wrestling, climbing, and activities. A perfect outing for anyone with small children; adults will enjoy the self-guided apiary tours and honey tastings. There is a retail shop with local farm goods and, of course, many varieties of honey.

HISTORIC HOMES Bevier House and Ulster County Historical Society (845-338-5614), 6 miles south of Kingston on the right side of Route 209. Open June through September, Wednesday through Sunday 1–5. Admission fee. Built in the late 1680s, this stone house now serves as headquarters of the county historical society, and it is a treasure trove of odd collections and memorabilia. The house was once a single-story Dutch farmhouse, and much of the present structure was added during the last three centuries. Throughout the house you will see fine Hudson Valley Dutch and Victorian furniture in addition to the tool and kitchenware collections, ceramic pottery from an early factory in Poughkeepsie, portraits, and decorative accessories. The Bevier House is not a formal museum and has a great old-fashioned feel about it.

Gomez Mill House (845-236-3126), Mill House Road, Marlboro. Open April through October, Wednesday through Sunday, with tours at 10, 11:30, 1, and 2:30. You must take a tour to see the inside of the museum and home. Open off-season by appointment. Admission fee. (*Note:* This site lies in both Orange and

Ulster Counties, which is why there are entries in both sections of this book.) Visitors will see the oldest surviving Jewish homestead in North America here as well as a unique cultural landmark. Built in 1714 as a sawmill and trading post, the site was named after the Gomez family, which supplied traders roving the upstate New York wilderness. Later, owners were farmers, boatmen, members of the Continental Army, writers, and painters; Dard Hunter (who owned the place from 1913 to 1919) was a paper mill owner whose mill is still in working condition (you can buy handmade paper in the gift shop). The site has also served as a home, inn, and school, and the buildings reflect the many personalities of those who have lived and worked here.

Huguenot Street Stone Houses (845-255-1660 or 255-1889), Stone House Street, off Route 32 in New Paltz. The area is open year-round; tours are offered May through October, Tuesday through Sunday 10–4. Admission fee. The tours last one and a half hours, but those with younger children may choose to leave after an hour; the last half hour delves into more detailed history about the stone houses. The Grimm Gallery is open by appointment only.

In 1677 a group of 12 Huguenot men purchased almost 40,000 acres of land from the Esopus Indians and began the settlement that was referred to as "die Pfalz," after an area in the Rhineland Palatinate. By 1692 their original dwellings were being replaced by stone houses, several of which still stand today as a result of the efforts of the Huguenot Historical Society. A trip to New Paltz offers a unique chance to see what life was like three centuries ago in upper-middle-class homes. The walking tour begins at the Dubois Fort on Huguenot Street, near the gift shop. All the buildings are owned by the society, and many still have their original furnishings. At the Abraham Hasbrouck house (1721), the dark rooms include a cellar-kitchen, which was the heart of village social life, and a built-in Dutch bed. Other houses of the period include the Bevier-Elting House, distinguished by a long well sweep and covered walk for the convenience of the ladies; the **Freer House,** with its mow door, which made it easier to move provisions into the attic; and the **Dubois Fort,** reputed to be haunted by a headless lady. Possibly the most interesting house is the **Jean Hasbrouck House** (1678), which once served as a store and tavern. Downstairs is a bar as well as a jambless fireplace with its curtainlike decorations; upstairs is a massive brick chimney, the only one of its type in the United States. Several other buildings are also open to the public, including the reconstructed

ONE OF HUGUENOT STREET'S STONE HOUSES IN HISTORIC NEW PALTZ

Hudson Valley Tourism, Inc.

French Church, the Federal-style **LeFevre House,** and the **Deyo House,** a remodeled 17th-century home.

The **Huguenot Path** is a self-guided walking tour through the Harcourt Nature Sanctuary spanning Huguenot Street and the Wallkill River trail; ask in the gift shop for a brochure to assist in guiding you along the way.

Hurley Patentee Manor (845-331-5414), Take Route 209 south to Hurley and follow signs to Old Route 209 and the manor house. Open July 4th weekend through Labor Day, but call first. Admission fee. This National Historic Landmark is a combination of a Dutch cottage, built in 1696, and a 1745 Georgian manor house. The manor was the center of the Hurley Patent, a 96,000-acre land grant that included the land between Woodstock and New Paltz but that today has been reduced to the 5 acres surrounding the house. The house is privately owned and has been restored to its original condition. The owners display many fine antiques from the 17th to the 19th centuries. The basement has one of the few indoor animal pens still in existence and is also the display area for Hurley Patentee Lighting, a company that crafts handwrought reproduction lighting fixtures and is still operating today.

Locust Lawn and **Terwilliger House** (845-155-1660), Route 32, outside Gardiner. Open May through October, by appointment only. Admission fee. These two sites are within minutes of each other, and are administered by the Huguenot Historical Society of New Paltz. **Locust Lawn,** a Federal-style mansion, was designed by a Newburgh architect and built in 1814 for Colonel Josiah Hasbrouck, a Revolutionary War veteran. The elegant white Federal-period mansion has a magnificent three-story central hall and still houses a fine collection of 18th-and 19th-century furniture and decorative arts, as well as several portraits by the American folk painter Ammi Phillips. Since Locust Lawn remained in the Hasbrouck family until the 1950s, when it was donated to the society, many of it original furnishings remain. Also on the site are outbuildings typical of a farm of that era, and visitors can see the carriage house, smokehouse, and slaughterhouse. One rare artifact found here is the great oxcart that was used to transport supplies to the beleaguered army at Valley Forge.

Down the road from Locust Lawn stands the **Terwilliger House,** built in 1738 and left almost untouched over the last 250 years. This is a fine example of the architectural style used by the Dutch and French Huguenot settlers in the Hudson Valley. Built of stone, with a center hall and great fireplace, the house has been furnished in the style of the era.

HISTORIC SITES **Kingston Heritage Area Visitors Centers** (845-331-7517, 800-331-1518), 20 Broadway and 308 Clinton Avenue, Kingston. Open year-round Monday through Friday 9–5; May through October also open Saturday and Sunday 11–5. Free. New York State has designated Urban Cultural Parks as the interpreters of urban settings of particularly historic interest; Kingston is known for its importance in the history of transportation. The center is located in the Stockade area (once surrounded by walls of tree trunks 13 feet high) and offers orientation displays that cover Kingston from 17th-century Dutch settlement to the present. Directions for self-guided walking tours are available, and guided tours may be arranged by appointment. While uptown, you may also want to stop by the **Volunteer Firemen's Hall and Museum,** 265 Fair Street, open May through October Friday and Saturday 10–4. The museum is in an old firehouse, where antique fire apparatus, memorabilia, and period furniture are on display.

The Broadway location, on the Rondout, offers permanent exhibits on Kingston's history and architecture and offers brochures, maps, and a calendar of events for travelers.

Mohonk Mountain House (845-255-1000), 6 miles west of New Paltz; take Route 299 west over the Wallkill River, turn right at the Mohonk sign, then bear left and follow the road to the gate. Open year-round; call ahead for ice-skating, cross-country skiing, and hiking information and special events weekends. Admission fee. When Alfred and Albert Smiley built this resort in 1869, they were determined to preserve the surrounding environment and offer gracious accommodations to visitors from the city. Guests here could hike the nearby Shawangunks, take a carriage ride around the manicured grounds, or enjoy the carefully tended flower gardens. There was a lake for ice skating as well as croquet lawns; the hotel itself was furnished with the best of the Victorian era: acres of polished oak paneling and floors, hidden conversation nooks, and homey, overstuffed furniture. Mohonk has endured the last century with timeless grace, and today visitors will find many things unchanged. The resort is still dedicated to preserving the natural world, and the gardens have won awards for their beauty. Mohonk sits next to a trout-stocked lake that becomes the focus of special winter carnival weekends. A stone tower atop the mountain offers a six-state view on sunny days. Hikers, birders, horseback riders, and cross-country skiers will find Mohonk unequaled. Day visitors are welcome, but it takes more than a day to sample all of the surprises at Mohonk.

Old Dutch Church (845-338-6759), 272 Wall Street, Kingston. Open year-round Monday through Friday 10–3; tours by appointment. Free. Organized in 1659, the Reformed Protestant Dutch Church of Kingston has served the people of the area continuously ever since. The present building was constructed in 1852; its bluestone exterior is in the Renaissance Revival style, and the windows were made in the Tiffany studios. Local tradition once held that the bell was cast from silver and copper items donated by the congregation. Inside you will see bronze statues as well as artifacts from the 1600s onward. Take time to talk through the churchyard and view the fine examples of early gravestone art (Governor DeWitt Clinton's gravesite is located here). In the spring thousands of yellow and red tulips planted in honor of the Netherlands line the church walks. In addition to wonderful Christmas concerts, there are musical performances by local artists on Thursdays at 12:15 PM during the spring and fall. Call for a schedule of events; the church is a magnificent place to hear music any time of year.

Opus 40 and **The Quarryman's Museum** (845-246-3400), Fite Road, Saugerties; follow Route 212 west from Saugerties, make a left on Glasco Turnpike, then follow signs to end of Fite Road. Open Memorial Day weekend through Columbus Day Friday–Sunday, holidays, and Mondays noon–5. Admission fee. In 1938 artist Harvey Fite's bluestone quarry outside Saugerties was merely the source of material for his sculpture. But as work on the individual pieces progressed, Fite realized that the terraces and steps he had created as a backdrop for the sculpture had themselves become the focus of his work. Naming the site Opus 40 because he believed it would take 40 years to complete, Fite set about creating a vast environmental work that would eventually contain 6 acres of steps, levels, fountains, pools, and paths. Each of the hundreds of thousands of bluestone pieces was hand cut and fitted, and the 9-ton central monolith was lifted into place with a boom and winches. Today Opus 40 is open to the public as an environmental sculpture and concert site. Fite, who had studied theology and law and worked as an actor and teacher, also built a museum to house his collection of quarrymen's tools and artifacts. The museum offers a rare glimpse into a lost way of life.

Saugerties Lighthouse (845-247-0656). Lighthouse Drive, Saugerties; from the center of Saugerties, follow Main Street to the end heading north; make a right turn onto Mynderse Street, which becomes Lighthouse Drive—although there are no signs— and keep bearing to the left; the site is also accessible by boat from the Route 9W boat-launch area. Open Memorial Day weekend to Labor Day; tours given on weekends and holidays 2–5. Donation. Enjoy a walk through the Ruth Glunt Nature Preserve, and at low tide walk out to the historic lighthouse, which contains a museum with artifacts from the commercial heyday of the Saugerties waterfront. Overnight accommodations are available year-round (see *Lodging*), and a live-in lighthouse keeper resides on the premises. I spent a night here in the month of June, and it was truly a memorable experience!

Senate House (845-338-2786), 312 Fair Street, Kingston. Open mid-April through October Wednesday–Saturday 10–5, Sunday 1–5. Group tours available by appointment year-round. Admission fee. When the New York State government was forced to leave New York City during the Revolution, it sought safety upstate. The house in

THE HISTORIC OLD DUTCH CHURCH IN THE UPTOWN AREA OF KINGSTON DATES BACK TO 1659.

Joseph Puglisi

which the committee met was built in the 17th century by a Dutch settler, Wessel Ten Broeck, and was partially burned by the British in 1777. After numerous additions and changes to the building, the house has been restored to reflect its part in history. Visitors can see several rooms, including the kitchen with its kitchenware and huge fireplace and the meeting room in which the first state senate deliberated. The colonial gardens at this site are beautiful, especially in June when the roses are in full bloom. A second Colonial Revival–style building on the site, added in 1927, houses a museum with historic displays and changing exhibits that reflect the story of Kingston. One room is given over to the works of John Vanderlyn, a Kingston native who was considered one of the finest painters in 19th-century America. The Italianate-style **Loughran House** (1873) is used for site offices and serves as another venue for changing exhibits. This historic site offers a variety of special events, including concerts, videos and lectures throughout the year. Evening candlelight tours are given during the month of December.

SCENIC DRIVES Ulster County has hundreds of miles of well-maintained roads, coupled with some of the most spectacular views in the Hudson Valley. It doesn't matter if you travel in autumn, with all the riotous color, or in winter, with its icy beauty—Ulster will often surprise you with its striking scenery.

For a drive that offers history as well as scenic beauty, start at **Kingston** (exit 19 off the NYS Thruway) and go south along **Route 209.** This is one of the oldest roads in America: the Old Mine Road, which was a trading route between upstate New York and Pennsylvania in the 17th-century. As you pass by Hurley, Marbletown, and Stone Ridge, you will see acres of fields planted with sweet corn, the area's largest agricultural crop, and you will see many farm stands in summer and autumn. The architectural styles of the homes range from Dutch stone to late Victorian. At Route 213 head east through High Falls, along the old Delaware & Hudson Canal. Stop in at the High Falls Food Co-op if you like natural foods, or just continue down the road that follows the canal into Rosendale. At Route 32 you can head south into New Paltz and explore the old stone houses, or head north back to Kingston.

For a second scenic route from **Kingston,** take **Route 9W** south along the Hudson River. At West Park you may want to follow the signs to Slabsides, once the writing retreat of naturalist John Burroughs; it's on your right across the railroad tracks (park at the bottom of the hill and walk up). Back on Route 9W, continue south and take Route 299 west through New Paltz, then follow Route 44/55 west for some of the finest views and overlook sites in the Shawangunks. At Route 209 head back north past old Dutch farms and stone houses to Kingston.

From Kingston you can also follow **Route 28** to Route 28A around the **Ashokan Reservoir,** a special treat in the autumn months. Follow the signs to the pump station, and walk around the fountain or have a picnic—it is a fairly uncrowded, undiscovered area, except on weekends. However, since New York City watches its watershed area very carefully, be wary of where you park, hike, or stop. The NO PARKING and NO STOPPING signs are serious; violators are usually fined.

For an unusual drive, take the **Hudson Valley Pottery Trail** to studios in Accord, High Falls, and Stone Ridge. Call 800-331-1518 for a brochure with a detailed map and list of craftspeople who open their studios to visitors (See *Selective Shopping: Pottery and Ceramics.*)

You can also take a **self-guided driving tour** through 300 years of European settlement in the Kingston area. Call 800-331-1518 for a guide, or pick one up at the NYS Thruway (exit 19) tourism caboose, just off the roundabout (Washington Avenue).

✳ Villages

There are several beautiful villages in Ulster County. My three favorite places that are great for walking and self-guided tours are Hurley, Saugerties, and Woodstock, located near exits 19 and 20 of the NYS Thruway.

Hurley. Take Route 209 south to Hurley and follow signs. Every second Saturday in July, for one day only, the historic stone houses here are open to the public; it's called **Hurley Stone House Day.** Admission is charged for the house tours. The village of Hurley was established in 1651 by Dutch and Huguenot settlers, who built wooden homes along the Esopus Creek. After a short war with the Esopus Indians, which resulted in the burning of much of the settlement, the homes were replaced with stone structures, 25 of which are still standing. Hurley was a hotbed of activity during the Revolution, serving as the state capital when Kingston was burned, a resting place for troops, and a meeting place for spies. Later Hurley was a stop on the Underground Railroad, the escape route for slaves fleeing to Canada, as well as the home of abolitionist Sojourner Truth.

Visitors can still walk around the town and see the largest group of stone houses still in use in the country. Although the homes are open only one day each year, Hurley is worth a walk any time, and many of the buildings have historic markers that tell something of their history and lore. Along Main Street look for the **Polly Crispell Cottage** (built in 1735), which was once used as a blacksmith shop. This house was also equipped with a "witch catcher"—a set of iron spikes set into the chimney, presumably to discourage witches (and birds) from flying in. The **Jan Van Deusen House** became the temporary seat of New York's government in 1777, and a secret room was used to store important documents. The outer door is set off by the work of an early Hurley blacksmith, and a date stone is visible. There is an antiques shop in the back of the house (see *Selective Shopping: Antiques*).

Also on Main Street: the **Dumond House,** which was to confine a convicted British spy before he was hung from an apple tree across the road; the **Parsonage,** built in 1790; and the **Elmendorf House** (once the Half Moon Tavern), built in the late 1600s. A burial ground can be found between the Crispell and Elmendorf buildings. If you drive west on Main Street, follow the Hurley Avenue Extension and you will see several more stone buildings.

A corn festival, held in mid-August, celebrates the local sweet-corn industry. Held on the grounds of the Hurley Reformed Church, the festival offers crafts and corn. Fresh ears of corn by the thousands are dished up with butter. There is also corn chowder, corn bread with honey, and entertainment.

Saugerties. Once a prosperous river town, a center of the bluestone and tanning industries, Saugerties has had its ups and downs over the past 200 years. During the 1830s, the town was well situated on the Hudson River so that bluestone could be floated down to Manhattan from the docks for use in city sidewalks and streets. Today travelers will be treated to a Renaissance in Saugerties—just walk up and down Main Street and Partition Street and visit the bookstores, antiques shops, galleries, and interesting eateries. There is a strong commitment to revitalizing the community through civic projects and commercial ventures. Don't miss **Krause's Homemade Chocolates** (845-246-8377), 41 South Partition St., a fourth-generation chocolatier—the owner makes 44 types of candies on location. **The Booktrader** (845-246-7205), 252 Main Street, carries an incredibly complete collection of regional titles. The **Saugerties Lighthouse,** with its wonderful Hudson River views, is now a bed & breakfast (see *Lodging*). On Sunday mornings there is a **farmers market** (see *To Do: Farmers Markets & Pick-Your-Own Farms*). The best way to see the town is to wander and enjoy!

Woodstock. The town of Woodstock has long attracted creative people. Home to farmers and quarrymen for two centuries, the hamlet saw new changes in the spring of 1902, when Ralph Radcliffe Whitehead, an Englishman schooled in the theories of John Ruskin, was searching for a place where an arts colony could be organized. With two friends as partners, Whitehead bought seven lush farms and formed a community called Byrdcliffe (a combination of his and his wife's names). Workshops for metalworkers, potters, and weavers were soon built, and over the years the colony has continued to attract artists and craftspeople. Today the **Byrdcliffe Arts Colony,** America's first utopian arts and crafts colony, situated on 300 wooded acres with 30 picturesque buildings and listed on the National Register of Historic Places, is worth a short walking tour—brochures are available at the Woodstock Guild on Tinker Street. During the 1930s, folksingers discovered Woodstock; later the town became a haven for "beatniks," and then talents like Pete Seeger, Bob Dylan, Joan Baez, Peter, Paul, and Mary, and other musicians of the 1960s who discovered inspiration there. In 1969 an eponymous concert, actually held nearly 50 miles away on a farm in Bethel (Sullivan County), made Woodstock a legend in the world of rock music—and the world at large. (The promoters/organizers of the event lived in Woodstock, hence the name.)

Today the somewhat eccentric but never dull town is still a gathering place for talent of all types. The surrounding mountains, and the shadow of Overlook Mountain, create a dramatic backdrop for local galleries and shops. Woodstock's main thoroughfare is Mill Hill Road, which becomes Tinker Street (according to legend, a tinker's wagon sank into the spring mud here). Just about all the shops and galleries in town can be reached by an easy walk, so explore leisurely. Of special interest are **Mirabai Books, H. Houst & Son, Chez Grand'mere,** and the **Center for Photography,** all on Tinker Street. (See *Selective Shopping: Art Galleries* for an art tour of town.) **Mower's Saturday Market** (845-679-6744), Maple Lane, in the center of town has been a tradition in Woodstock for nearly

30 years. A large flea market, offering antiques, crafts, collectibles, and an array of eclectic offerings, Mower's is a must for Saturday shoppers in the village. Open mid-May through October 9–5. There are parking lots on Rock City Road or Tannery Brook Road. There is also a municipal lot near the town offices; watch for signs. Also on Tinker Street, in the old firehouse, is the **Woodstock Historical Society Museum** (845-679-7564), which will be of interest to history buffs. They have displays with artifacts and old photographs of the town's past. **The Colony Café** (845-679-5342), in the historic Colony Arts building, 22 Rock City Road, offers an eclectic mix of music nightly except Wednesday. Call for a schedule of events. The **River Rock Health Spa** (845-679-7800), 62 Ricks Road, just west of town toward Bearsville, is a great place to pamper yourself at the end of a day of sightseeing. Call in advance for an appointment to schedule a facial, massage, peel, or wrap. A variety of packages is available. And don't forget to take a drive up Rock City Road to the **Tibetan Buddhist Monastery** (see *To See*) before leaving town. And if you get tired, sit on the village green, and watch the colorful parade of people go by. (Kids will love **Woodstock Wonderworks,** an amazing playground designed by the town's kids themselves and built in 1989 under the guidance of an award-winning company by the parents, youngsters, and townspeople. So if you are traveling with children, check out this play area at Woodstock Elementary School on Route 375.)

WINERIES AND BREWERIES The Hudson Valley has become an important center of wine production in New York, and visitors are welcome to stop at Ulster County's wineries. They range in size from tiny "boutique" wineries to full-sized vineyards, complete with restaurants, bottling plants, and cellars. Wherever you go, however, you will find people who love their work and are willing to share their expertise and wines with you. Some of the vintners offer formal guided tours; others just have a showroom and tasting area. You may want to call before you go—there are special events, concerts, and tours throughout the season, and hours may change when the harvest begins. Most of the sites are free as are the tastings, but there may be admission charged to special events.

Adair Vineyards (845-255-1377), 52 Alhusen Road, New Paltz. Open daily June through October 11–6; May, November, December Friday through Sunday 11–5. The vineyard has an old Dutch barn and offers tastings, tours (by calling ahead), and picnic area. The picture-perfect Ulster County spot looks as if unchanged through the centuries. All wines here are made from estate grown grapes.

Baldwin Vineyards (845-744-2226), 176 Hardenburgh Road, Pine Bush, is located on a 200-year-old estate where more than 40 acres of pastures, vineyards, and woodlands are open for strolling. Open daily July through October 11:30–5:30, April through June and November and December Friday through Monday 11:30–5, January through March Saturday and Sunday 11:30–4:30. Their award-winning wines include chardonnay, merlot, Riesling, brut champagne, and a strawberry-flavored wine.

Benmarl Winery (845-236-4265), 156 Highland Avenue, off Route 9W, south of Marlboro (look for signs). Open daily except Tuesday January through March noon–4, April through December until 5. Visitors may enjoy a tour, tasting, and a stop at the art gallery on the premises—the founder of the winery was an illustrator—at this scenic winery situated high on a hill overlooking the orchards with magnificent views of the Hudson River and surrounding countryside.

Brimstone Hill Vineyard (845-744-2231), 61 Brimstone Hill Road, Pine Bush. Open daily July through October 11:30–5:30, May and June, Friday through Monday; January through April, Saturday and Sunday only. French-style wines are the specialty here, especially dry reds and sweet whites.

El Paso Winery (845-331-8642), 742 Broadway (Route 9W), Ulster Park. Open Wednesday through Sunday April through December 11–6. A variety of decent New York State wines are produced, bottled, and sold in this cozy barn, including a merlot and barn red (my favorite). The lovely shop on the premises has unusual gifts for the oenophile as well as a nice selection of regional books. Make sure to check it out.

Kedem Royal Winery (845-236-4281), 1519 Route 9W, Marlboro. Open year-round Sunday through Thursday 10–4:30; tours are given Wednesday, Thursday, and Sunday at 11, 1, and 3. A short video explains the background of this unusual winery, which produces a variety of kosher wines.

Keegan Ales (845-331-BREW), 20 St. James Street, Kingston. Open year-round, Thursday and Friday 3–7; Saturday and Sunday noon–7. This microbrewery features three different beers: a golden ale, a pale ale, and a milk stout. Beer lovers will enjoy relaxing in the spacious taproom. This is the only brewery in the Hudson Valley.

Magnanini Farm Winery (845-895-2767), 172 Strawridge Road, Wallkill. Open April through December weekends only: Saturday 1–5, Sunday 2–6. This small winery offers free tastings. A restaurant on the premises serves Northern Italian fare (dinner at 7 PM Saturday, lunch at 1 PM Sunday; both by reservation).

Rivendell Winery (845-255-2494), 714 Albany Post Road, New Paltz. Open year-round daily 10–6. Enjoy tours and tastings at one of the state's most renowned wineries, located on a hilltop in a beautiful, rural part of the county. The gift shop features dozens of wines from throughout the state. Special events are held on the premises year-round, so call for a schedule.

West Park Wine Cellars (845-384-6709), Burroughs Drive (off Route 9W), West Park. Open March through December Saturday and Sunday 11–5:30. They produce wonderful chardonnay here, and visitors can enjoy using the lovely picnic area overlooking the Hudson River. There are sometimes summer concerts featuring fine jazz performers. Call for a schedule.

Whitecliff Vineyard and Winery (845-255-4613), 331 McKinstry Road, Gardiner. (Take Route 299 to County Route 7; McKistry Road is off there.) Open June through December Thursday through Sunday noon–5, until 6 on Saturday. This 75-acre farm grows chardonnay, merlot, cabernet franc, and pinot noir grapes. There are phenomenal views of the Shawangunks from the winery.

Windsor Vineyards (845-236-4233)26 Western Avenue, Marlboro. Open year-round Monday through Saturday 10–5, Sunday noon–5. New York and California wines and champagnes are offered for tasting and in the gift shop.

AIRPLANE RIDES, HANG GLIDING, AND SKYDIVING **The Flight School** (845-647-3377), 150 Canal Street, Ellenville, features hang gliding, paragliding, and ultra-light instruction. Open seasonally; call ahead.

River Aviation (845-336-8400), 1161 Flatbush Road, Kingston. Open year-round by appointment for half-hour sightseeing flights—or longer—in two-seat or four-seat planes. You can fly over your home and photograph it from the air. Reasonable prices.

Skydive the Ranch (845-255-4033), 45 Sandhill Road, Gardiner. Open daily year-round, weekdays at 9:30 AM, weekends and holidays at 8 AM. Call in advance to reserve a place in class. Sky-diving instruction available; first-timers welcome. If you want to try something new, this may be the activity you've been imagining. All first jumps are in tandem—divers are attached to an instructor both in freefall and under a specially-designed parachute built for two. There is nearly a minute of freefall and several minutes under the canopy of the chute. Those who jump must be at least 18 years-old and under 225 pounds; dress comfortably, and bring sneakers. Price (approximately $200) includes training, equipment, and the jump.

ARCHERY **Robin Hood Archery** (845-626-0983), 707 Fischer Lane, Accord; off Route 209. Open year-round. They have both an indoor and outdoor range here for shooting. A great rainy-day activity for those traveling with older children.

BICYCLING **Hudson Valley Rail Trail** (845-483-0428, 691-8666), 12 Church Street, Highland. Open dawn to dusk. This 4.2-mile nature trail extends from the Mid-Hudson Bridge through the town of Lloyd. There is a 2-mile paved portion of the trail. A great spot for family bicycle outings. This trail is part of a network of a thousand rail trails that cover 10,000 miles across America. Turn-offs along the way run to overlooks and down to the banks of the river—great places to get off your bicycle for a picnic and take in the scenery.

Minnewaska State Park Preserve (845-255-0752), Route 44/55, New Paltz. Open year-round daily from 9 AM (closing time is posted each day). Admission. This preserve is located atop the dramatic Shawangunk Mountain Ridge, over 2,000 feet above sea level, and offers miles of trails and carriage roads for bicyclists of all abilities.

Mohonk Preserve (845-255-0919), 3197 Route 44/55, Gardiner 12525. Open daily from sunrise to sunset. Day use fee for nonmembers. There are over 100 miles of trails and carriage roads for use by bicyclists. Visitors center is open daily 9–5 and offers exhibits.

Shawangunk Rail Trail (845-895-2611), 14 Central Avenue, Wallkill 12589. This 3-mile section of unpaved rail trail with views of the Shawangunk Mountains provides easy access to the Wallkill River and village of Wallkill. A nice ride for mountain bikers.

Wallkill Valley Rail Trail, P.O. Box 1048, New Paltz 12561. Open dawn to dusk. This 12.2-mile linear park between the New Paltz–Rosendale and Gardiner-Shawangunk town lines was where a busy railroad line existed in the late

19th century, transporting produce and dairy products from Ulster County to New York City. It also served as a commuter railroad. In 1977 the railroad took its last freight run. And in 1983, all the ties and rails were removed, and community volunteers cleared the trail. The rail trail officially opened to the public for recreational use in 1993. Enjoy a walk, jog, or bike ride along this scenic trail, maintained and managed by volunteers. Motorized vehicles are prohibited, except for those used by handicapped people. A detailed brochure is available (see address).

The following Ulster County shops rent both mountain bikes and road bikes: **Bicycle Depot** (845-255-3859), 15 Main Street, New Paltz; **Bistro Mountain Store** (845-255-3424), 3124 Route 44/55, Gardiner; **Cycle Path** (845-255-8723), 138 Main Street, New Paltz; **Overlook Mountain Bikes** (845-679-2122), 93 Tinker Street, Woodstock; **Table Rock Tours & Bicycle Shop** (845-658-7832), 292 Main Street, Rosendale.

BOAT CRUISES The Hudson runs the length of Ulster County, and visitors can select from several companies that cruise the river. Even if you don't know port from starboard, there are tours that take all the work—but none of the fun—out of a river trip. One warning: It can be very breezy and cool yet sunny out on the river; bring a hat, scarf, sweater, and sunscreen.

Great Hudson Sailing Center (845-429-1557), Dock Street, Kingston, offers sailing lessons from April through October. If you want to try your hand at sailing, this is a good place to go.

Hudson River Cruises (845-340-4700, 800-843-7472), Rondout Landing, Kingston. Open daily Tuesday through Sunday July and August with cruises at 11 and 2 and Friday evenings at 8, May, June, September, and October weekends only 11 and 2. They offer two-hour cruises heading south of Kingston for one hour toward the Hyde Park area, passing both the Kingston and Esopus Meadows lighthouses. Enjoy the roomy ship *Rip Van Winkle*, which features plenty of seating, rest rooms, and a snack bar. Because the river tends to be less choppy than the ocean, the ride is smooth and pleasant. Music is provided on some trips.

North River Cruises (845-339-1050 or 679-8205), 24 Cutten Drive, Saugerties. The *Teal*, a medium-sized boat docked at Rondout Landing in Kingston, is run by Captain John Cutten. The boat is fitted with rich wood and brass, and the atmosphere aboard takes you back to a time of genteel river travel, yet there are all the modern amenities. Available for private excursions and corporate sightseeing charters.

CANOEING AND KAYAKING **Atlantic Kayak Tours** (845-246-2187), 320 West Saugerties Road, Saugerties. Open April through mid-November for kayak trips on the Hudson River, Esopus, and other local waterways, this outfitter will make an excursion fun; a particularly good choice for first-timers.

FARMERS MARKETS AND PICK-YOUR-OWN FARMS Since the earliest colonists arrived, fruit farming has been important to Ulster County's economy. The first commercial orchard in the country was established here in 1820. At that time, Robert Pell of Esopus began growing Newton Pippin apples for export to England. Apples are still the leading fruit crop, with over 8,000 acres planted and about 3 million bushels produced annually. Notice that many orchards are located on the sides or top of hills, which reduces the likelihood of crop losses due to late-spring frost.

Some Ulster County farms are still owned by the families that founded them; others have been cultivating the same site for centuries. The harvest season here stretches from early-summer strawberries to late-fall pumpkins and holiday greenery. Some farm stands offer freshly baked pies and cakes, while others have recipes for you to take home, along with food and other local goodies. Pick-your-own farms let you do the work as well as giving you the choice of what you want in the basket. Most growers provide containers, but if you bring your own, the price is usually lower. However you decide to gather in the harvest, the following is just a sampling of places to try. Because weather conditions make it difficult to predict exact harvest dates, do call ahead for information about the crops available when you intend to go.

Farmers Markets
The Kingston Farmers Market (845-331-3659), Wall Street between North Front and John Streets, in uptown, close to exit 19 off the NYS Thruway. Open June through October Saturday 9–2. You will find fruits and vegetables, fresh-cut flowers, cheeses, breads, smoked meats, organic chicken, meats and game, honey, pies, and more.

New Paltz Farmers Market (845-255-3538), North Front Street in the Elting Library parking lot. Open mid-June through October Sunday 10:30–3. Local produce, breads, soaps, flowers, mustard, and jellies.

Saugerties Farmers Market (845-246-9371), corner of Market and Main Streets. Open mid-June through October Saturday 9–2. Produce, fruit, flowers, breads, and more. There is often music here, as well.

Pick-Your-Own & Farm Stands
Davenport Farms Market (845-687-0051), Route 209, Stone Ridge. Open March through December. An extensive selection of local produce, including raspberries, grapes, corn, apples, pumpkins, and melons. There is a second market off the Kingston roundabout, Washington Avenue Extension, **Davenport's Farm Market,** which specializes in flowers and fresh produce, fruits and vegetables. They are open 6:30 AM–7 PM and have beautiful hanging baskets, cider, and plants of all kinds.

Dressel Farms (845-255-0693), 271 Route 208, New Paltz. Open September through June, closed Sunday and holidays. You can pick your own strawberries, apples, and pumpkins here in season, surrounded by magnificent views of the Shawangunk Mountains.

Barthels Farm Market (845-647-6941), farther south on Route 209 in Ellenville. Open April through December. They offer an array of vegetables at this bountiful stand.

Four Winds Farm (845-255-3088), 158 Marabac Road, Gardiner, has certified organic vegetables, grass-fed lamb and beef, poultry, turkey and pork, as well as eggs and herbs. Do call ahead for directions and to make sure someone will be there. This place is a real find; stock up if you are on the way home. **The Gippert Farm** (845-247-9479), an organic farm in Saugerties, offers eggs, chicken, turkey, and, at times, lamb. Two other places with certified organic produce are **Swenson's** (845-626-3915), Route 209, 0.5 mile east of Accord, with an array of fruits and vegetables, and **White Feather Organic Farm** (845-744-2422), Route 52 and Sinsabaugh Road, Pine Bush, with a working organic vegetable farm and roadside stand. Open June through October weekends only 10–6.

Jenkins-Leuken Orchards (845-255-0999), Route 299 West, 4 miles west of the village of New Paltz. Open daily August through May 9–6. Pick-your-own apples and pumpkins. They have a large variety of apples, including Macouns. Pears, peaches, tomatoes, and vegetables are available in season. Honey and cider are produced on the farm, as well.

The Apple Bin, Route 9W, Ulster Park. Open daily year-round except the months of January and February. Many varieties of apples, vegetables, gourmet take-out items, great baked goods, although no pick-your-own.

Alyce & Roger's Fruit Stand (845-688-2114), Route 28, Mt. Tremper, offers a dazzling array of local produce, and there are lots of jack-o'-lanterns come October.

Wilklow Orchards (845-691-2339), Pancake Hollow Road, Highland; from exit 18 off the NYS Thruway, turn right on Route 299, go 2.3 miles, turn right on New Paltz Road, go about 1 mile, and make a right onto Pancake Hollow Road for another mile to the orchard. One of the oldest family-run pick-your-own farms, in business for more than 100 years, open daily Labor Day through October for pick-your-own apples (there are 10 varieties here) and pumpkins. The stand sells homegrown vegetables, fruitsm and cider. Kids will enjoy the farm animals on the premises.

Stone Ridge Orchard (845-687-0447), 3120 Route 213. Open from mid-August through October daily 9–5 for pick-your-own apples, pumpkins, and raspberries. They have over a dozen varieties of apples here, and the orchard is surrounded by hundreds of acres of forest and farmland. There are hayrides for the kids, picnic benches, and fresh cider. The shop on the premises offers maple syrup, home-baked pies, and other treats. This spot is easy to find, right on Route 213 off Route 209, and it's a beautiful place to spend a couple of hours on an autumn afternoon.

One of my favorite places to pick strawberries, blueberries, and pumpkins in Ulster County is **Saunderskill Farms** (845-626-2676), 5100 Route 209, Accord. Open daily except Monday April through December, 9–6. This beautiful family-owned-and-operated farm and store, named for the tributary of the Rondout Creek that flows through the farm, offers homegrown vegetables (excellent corn and tomatoes), fruits, flowering annuals, perennials, and herbs. The on-site bakery makes fine fruit pies, cookies, brownies, and cider doughnuts. There is local maple syrup, honey, and jams. In autumn children will enjoy the horse-drawn hayrides. There are special events throughout the year, including an antique tractor pull, a corn festival, and winter holiday festivities, so call ahead to see what's happening before you go. Originally granted to Hendrick Schoonmaker by Peter Stuyvesant in 1663, the family's original 300 acres have been continuously farmed since 1680, making Saunderskill Farms the second-oldest family farm in the country. (It now includes more than 800 acres.) The stone manor house, built in 1787, still stands on the property. Jack, Dan, Dave, and Kathy Schoonmaker are on the premises every day.

Some local fruit farms that specialize in pick-your-own fruits include: **Kelder's Farm & U-Pick** (845-626-7137), 5575 Route 209, Kerhonkson, with berries and pumpkins as well as a petting zoo and hayrides. They are open April through October 10–6. **Mr. Apples Low-Spray Orchard** (845-687-9498 or 687-0005), Route 213, High Falls, with several varieties of apples, pears, and cider. Open August through November daily 11–5:30, 9–6:30 on weekends. **Minard Farms** (845-883-7102), off Ohioville Road, Clintondale, with apples, cider, picnic areas, and hayrides in season; **Tantillo's Farm Market** (845-255-6196), 730 Route 208, Gardiner, for picking cherries, apples, peas, peaches, tomatoes, and pumpkins. Also in Gardiner is **Wright Farms** (845-255-5300), Route 208, for apple and cherry picking; they are open year-round, and the Wright family has been farming here for over 100 years. In Milton: **Clarke Westervelt Fruit Farm** (845-795-2270), 182 Clarke's Lane, with apples; **Locust Grove Farm** (845-795-5194), North Road with berries, cherries, peaches, apples, plums, and pumpkins in-season; and **Prospect Hill Orchards** (845-795-2383), 40 Clark's Lane, with cherries, peaches, apples, pears, and pumpkins; open in-season, weekends only 9–4.

A couple of larger farm markets worth stopping at: **Adam's Fairacre Farm** (845-336-6300), on Route 9W in Lake Katrine; and **Wallkill View Farm** (845-255-8050), on Route 299 just outside of New Paltz. The produce and baked goods here are first-rate. You can also pick your own pumpkins in-season.

Maple Syrup Farms

The time for maple syrup tastings and tours is mid-Feburary to mid-April. The following places will be glad to show you around and sell you their delicious syrup, maple cream, and honey. It's a good idea, however, to call before you go, since erratic weather will often affect the season. **Arrowhead Farm** (845-626-7293), 5941 Route 209, Kerhonkson, has tours during the season. **Long Year Farm** (845-679-7564), 42 Schoonmaker Lane, Woodstock, is open year-round for sales. **Lyonsville Sugarhouse** (845-687-2518), 591 County Route 2, Accord, offers tours. **Mountain Dew Maple Products** (845-626-3466), 351 Samsonville Road, Kerhonkson, has wonderful tours and is open year-round for sales. **Oliverea Schoolhouse Maple Syrup** (845-254-5296), 609 Oliverea Road, Oliverea, is open year-round. **Swenson's Maple Syrup** (845-657-2547), 12 Markle Road, Shokan, is open during sap season only.

FISHING Ulster County offers fishing enthusiasts a chance to try their luck in scores of streams, a reservoir, and the great Hudson River. The waters are well stocked with a variety of fish—trout, bass, pike, pickerel, and perch, are just some of the more popular catches. Fishing areas are well marked, and New York

State licenses are required as are reservoir permits. Call the **Department of Environmental Conservation Department of Fisheries** (845-256-3161), New Paltz, for detailed information.

There are very few fishing guide services due to the fact that the Esopus Creek and other waterways are very accessible. Just about anyone can get to many terrific fishing spots in the county with ease. Some of the better-known fishing streams include the renowned Esopus Creek (access points along Route 28, west of Kingston), Rondout Creek (access points on Route 209, south of Kingston), Plattekill Creek (access near Route 32 in Saugerties), and the Sawkill Creek (access along Route 212 in Woodstock). Most of the main access points are indicated by brown-and-yellow state signs; many also have designated parking areas. If you are uncertain about the stream, ask; otherwise you may find yourself on the receiving end of a heavy fine. Holders of reservoir permits will want to try the Ashokan Reservoir (Route 28A, west of Kingston), with 40 miles of shoreline and trout, walleye, and bass lurking beneath the surface. The Kingston City Reservoir requires a city permit for fishing, but it is worth the extra effort to obtain.

GOLF Ulster County golf courses can be by turns dramatic, relaxing, and colorful, and the areas that offer golf cater to a wide range of skills and interests. Hotel courses are usually open to the public, but it is recommended that you call in advance, since they schedule special events and competitions.

In the Kingston and Saugerties area:
Alapaha Golf Links (845-331-2334), 180 Sawkill Road, Kingston. Open daily 7–dusk. This nine-hole course, par 30, is 1,800 yards long and a great place for novices. Driving range and putting green.

Green Acres Golf Club (845-331-2283), end of Harwich Street, Kingston. Open daily 7–dark. This nine-hole, par-36 course is 2,774 yards long. There is a driving range here but not much else. A popular place with local residents.

Kaatsbaan Golf Club (845-246-8182), 1754 Old Kings Highway, Saugerties. Open 8–dark. There are nine holes and a par 35 at this 3,100-yard-long course. There is a clubhouse restaurant on the premises; pro shop and lessons are available.

In the New Paltz area:
Apple Greens Golf Course (845-883-5500), 161 South Street, Highland. Open weekdays 7–dusk, weekends 6 until dusk. This 18-hole course, par 71, is 6,500 yards in length and there is a driving range, putting green, clubhouse restaurant, pro shop, and lessons as well as a twilight rate.

Mohonk Mountain House (845-256-2143), 1000 Mountain Rest Road, New Paltz. Open dawn to dusk. There are nine holes, par 35, at this scenic course. Driving range, putting green, and lessons available.

New Paltz Golf Course (845-255-8282), 215 Huguenot Street, New Paltz. Open March through November dawn to dusk. There are nine holes at this par-36 course with all the amenities: driving range, putting green, restaurant, pro shop, lessons.

Walker Valley Golf Club (845-744-2714), Route 52, Walker Valley. Open daily 7–7. This nine-hole course is 1,700 yards long, par 32. There are a restaurant and pro shop on the premises.

In Accord, Kerhonkson, and Ellenville:

Hudson Valley Resort (845-626-2972), 400 Granite Road, Kerhonkson. Open daily 7–6. This 18-hole, 6,700-yard course where par is 71 is beautiful; it is on the grounds of a full-service resort, and you will find all the amenities here: driving range, putting green, restaurants, hotel facilities, pro shop, lessons, golf school, group packages. Make sure to make a reservation to tee off in advance, especially on weekends.

Nevele Grand Resort (845-647-6000), Nevele Road, Ellenville. Open 7–dusk. There are 27 holes on this magnificent course where par is 35. Since the Nevele is a full-service hotel, there is a restaurant, snack bar, lodging, driving range, putting green, pro shop, lessons, golf packages, and group rates. This is one of the most challenging courses in the area, and it's quite popular, so make advance reservations if you want to be assured of getting in.

Rondout Golf Club (845-626-2513), Whitefield Road, Accord. Open daily 6 AM–7 PM. This 18-hole, par-72 course has a driving range, putting green, restaurant, pro shop, lessons, golf packages, and twilight rate.

Shawangunk Country Club (845-647-6090), 14 Nevele Road, Ellenville. Open March through November 7–7. This nine-hole, par-34 course has a putting green and restaurant; pro shop and golf packages available. It's just down the road from the Nevele Grand Resort.

Stone Dock Golf Course (845-687-9944), 112 Stone Dock Road, High Falls. Open 7–dusk. This nine-hole, par 36, 3,315-yard course is pleasant to play. There is a driving range and a restaurant on the premises. You can register for lessons if you desire at the pro shop. They also offer group packages and a twilight rate.

HIKING Ulster County has some of the best hiking in the Hudson Valley, with views that go on for miles and trails that range from an easy walk to a hard day's climb. The following suggestions for afternoon or day hikes provide magnificent vistas, but it is

ULSTER COUNTY GOLF COURSES CATER TO A WIDE RANGE OF SKILLS AND INTERESTS.

Hudson Valley Tourism, Inc.

recommended that you use maps available locally to make your hike as much fun and as safe as possible. And remember to dress appropriately; Lyme disease is prevalent in many areas.

Belleayre Mountain (845-254-5600), Route 28, Highmount, offers excellent hiking in the Catskill Forest Preserve. There are marked cross-country ski trails that provide a nice walk in the woods, and a hike to the summit of Belleayre reveals sweeping views of the mountains below. Elevations range from 600 to 4,200 feet, and much of the area is rugged, steep terrain. A more moderate walk is the hike to Pine Hill Lake, which is part of the state preserve. In the summer months you can stop for a swim there.

Black Creek Forest Preserve (845-473-4440), intersection of Route 9W and Winding Brook Acres Road, Esopus. This 130-acre forest preserve lies along a major Hudson River tributary. Walkers will cross a suspension footbridge over the Black Creek and pass through forest woodlands with vernal pools on the three hiking trails (a total of 2.5 miles) that have direct access to the Hudson River. This is a lovely place for a short hike; a good choice on a hot day, since it always seems a bit cooler here with much of the trail area being shaded.

Esopus Meadows Point Preserve (845-454-7673), located 1 mile from the intersection of Route 9W and River Road, Port Ewen. There are 3,500 feet of Hudson River shoreline in this 100-acre site that offers great views of the Esopus Meadows Lighthouse, 3 trails, and an environmental center. The trails go through lovely woodlands and in some places along the river. This is a fine place to take a hike for an hour or two on gently sloping terrain.

Frost Valley YMCA (845-985-2291), County Route 47 off Route 28, Big Indian, has hundreds of acres to explore on several different trails. Stop in and get a map before you start out. (See *Cross-Country Skiing* for directions.)

Mohonk Mountain House (845-255-1000), Mountain Rest Road, New Paltz; **Mohonk Preserve** (845-255-0919), 3197 Route 44/55, Gardiner; and **Minnewaska State Park** (845-255-0752), Route 44/55, New Paltz. These three areas are for day use only and charge a fee. The Shawangunk trails found at these sites are excellent (see *Green Space*), although somewhat crowded on summer weekends. Mohonk Mountain House has 128 miles of paths and carriage roads to hike, and there are several first-rate spots for rock climbing in this area, as well.

Overlook Mountain, Meads Mountain Road, Woodstock, is a moderate walk up a graded roadbed. From Tinker Street at the village green, take Rock City Road to Meads Mountain Road, which leads straight to the trailhead, across from the Tibetan monastery on the right side of the road (see *To See*). The summit takes about an hour to reach, depending on how fast you travel the 2-mile ascent. You will pass the ruins of the Overlook Mountain House on the way up; a lookout tower and picnic tables are at the top. The view of the valley and river is incomparable.

Shaupeneak Ridge Cooperative Recreation Area (845-473-4440), Old Post Road, Esopus (a parking lot is located 0.2 mile from the intersection of Route 9W and Old Post Road). There are 3.5 miles of trails that wend their way through this 561-acre wildlife conservation area owned by Scenic Hudson. You will see wetlands and Louisa Pond, which was carved out by glaciers thousands of years ago. This is a good place to go for a hike of moderate difficulty that is easily accessible from a main road. This site is used for several environmental education programs.

Vernooy Kill Falls in Kerhonkson can be reached by taking Route 209 to Lower Cherrytown Road, then bearing right and continuing 5 miles to Upper Cherrytown Road. In another 3 miles you will see the parking lot on the right and the trailhead on the left. The trail is just over 3.5 miles up and back.

The Wallkill Valley Rail Trail, 12.2 miles of linear park, on a former railroad track, between New Paltz and Gardiner. Good places to pick up the trail: in the historic Huguenot Street area or downtown New Paltz (across the street from the parking lot at the Water Street Market is one easy access area). Since October 1993 this valuable community resource has attracted visitors from around the Hudson Valley and beyond. (See *Bicycling*).

ROCK CLIMBING The Shawangunk mountain range in Ulster County is renowned nationally for rock climbing. Those want to learn should contact one of the outfitters that specialize in instruction.

Diamond Sports Rock Climbing School (845-255-1897, 800-776-2577), Gardiner.

Eastern Mountain Sports Climbing School (845-255-3280, 800-310-4504), 3124 Route 44/55, Gardiner.

High Angle Adventures (845-658-9811, 800-777-2546), 178 Hardenburgh Road, Ulster Park. Open for full-day instruction with some of the best climbers in the East.

Mountain Skills (845-687-9643), Stone Ridge. Jim Munson, the owner of this company, provides instruction and guided climbs for either ice or rock climbing, depending on the season.

The Inner Wall (845-2255-ROCK), 234 Main Street (Eckerd's Plaza), New Paltz. This indoor rock climbing gym is open year-round and provides a great place to practice—even in the pouring rain or a snowstorm.

Sundance Rappel Tower (845-688-5640), 64 Route 214, Phoenicia. Open year-round on weekends or by appointment. Here you can practice rope-descent technique and rappelling.

SWIMMING Many of the best places to swim in Ulster County are reservoirs; naturally, they strictly forbid swimming. In recent years, community swimming holes are quietly fading away due to owners expecting privacy on their land and a fear (a realistic one) of being sued in the event of an accident. However, there are rivers and creeks with access in several places along main roads that are not on private property; they are pleasant places to stop and cool off on a hot day. While driving through the county, you will discover such places.

The following are some scenic places to swim; all have lifeguards, a beach, and picnic areas:

Kenneth L. Wilson State Park (845-679-7020), 857 Wittenberg Road, Mount Tremper. Open daily Memorial Day weekend through Labor Day 9–6. This lake with a clean, sandy beach surrounded by mountains offers a wonderful place to go for those traveling with young children. There are picnic tables, but there isn't much shade here, so bring an umbrella. There are walking trails if you tire of sunbathing and swimming.

Kingston Point Beach (845-331-1682), Kingston Point Beach, Kingston. Take Broadway to the end, turn left, and follow East Strand (which becomes North Street) 1 mile to the park. The beach is open year-round, dawn to dusk. Free. Open mid-June through Labor Day for swimming. This small beach on the Hudson River is run by the city. There are no services here, and it isn't advisable to swim in the Hudson River even now, but it is still a beautiful spot to sunbathe and enjoy the river views. Kids will love the sandy beach and small playground as well as watching the sailboats pass by.

Minnewaska State Park (845-255-0752), Route 44/55, New Paltz. Admission. Open mid-June through Labor Day 11–5:30 for swimming in Lake Awosting at the designated beach area only. This is a great place to be since there is also great hiking in the park; being high up in the Shawangunks, the weather is always a few degrees cooler than in town below.

Pine Hill Lake Day Use Area (845-254-5600, 254-5202), Route 28, Highmount. Open daily mid-June through Labor Day. Admission. This lovely lake offers swimming, boating, and fishing with a beach area, picnic pavilions, and snack bar. Bring your own canoe, or rent a kayak, pedal-, or rowboat. Run by the state, admission is by the car. Reasonable boat-rental rates. The beach is roped off into different sections; there is a diving section and an area for toddlers.

Ulster Landing Park (845-336-8484), Ulster Landing Road (off Route 32), Kingston. Open daily Memorial Day weekend through Labor Day 10-8. This county-owned and run park, offers a small, quiet, sandy beach area just north of the Rhinecliff Bridge with swimming in the Hudson River—although, as with Kinston Point Beach, swimming in the Hudson is still not advisable. Rest rooms and picnic pavilion. This spot is less frequented by people since it is a little off-the-beaten-track.

TUBING Very popular in the area, tubing isn't so much a sport as it is a leisurely pursuit. It doesn't take any special skills and can be done by just about anyone. All you do is rent a huge, black inner tube, put it in the water, and hop on for rides that last anywhere from one to three hours. Maneuvering can be done with your hands, and proper tubing attire consists of shorts and a T-shirt, or a bathing suit, with old sneakers. A life jacket is recommended for those who are not strong swimmers. Although most of the waters are not very deep, they are cold, and the currents can be swift. The tubing season runs from the first warm weather until the last—somewhere between late May and early September—but the best time to go is the dog days of August. You will have to leave a security deposit for the tubes, and rental does not include extras like life jackets or "tube seats," which keep you from bumping along the rocky bottom; some sites will arrange to transport you back after the trip.

Tubes and gear, including helmets, can be rented at **F-S Tube and Raft Rental** (845-688-7633, 866-4FS-TUBE), 4 Church Street (behind Phoenicia Pharmacy), Phoenicia. **Town Tinker Tube Rental** (845-688-5553), Bridge Street, Phoenicia, is the grandfather of tubing services, with a well-stocked headquarters, having been in business for many years.

✳ Winter Sports

CROSS-COUNTRY SKIING Ulster County is a good place for cross-country enthusiasts. When valleys, meadows, and fields receive a cover of snow, new trails are broken, and old ones are rediscovered.

Belleayre Mountain (845-254-5600; see *Downhill Skiing*) in Highmount, has several marked, groomed trails that cover 5.5 miles; they follow the old Ulster and Delaware Turnpike, and even pass an old family cemetery. Some are mogul trails—for those who want a particularly challenging experience. Lessons are available, but call in advance to schedule; rentals are offered just across the road from the trails. There is no fee for skiing, and no charge for parking or use of the lodges on the premises.

Frost Valley YMCA (845-985-2291), Frost Valley Road, Claryville. Take Route 28 west to Oliverea (County Route 47). Go 15 miles and you will see Frost Valley. Admission fee. There are 20 miles of groomed trails that wind in and out of lovely forest and alongside streams. The trails are color coded, and there is a warming hut. A small use fee is charged; call for lesson and rental information.

Kenneth L. Wilson State Park (845-679-7020), Wittenberg Road, Mt. Tremper. Free. Enjoy approximately 5 miles of color-coded trails that wind through woodland forest, wetlands, and along a lake. Great for beginners. No services; you must have your own equipment.

Minnewaska State Park (845-255-0752), Route 44/55, New Paltz. Free. There are 150 miles of cross-country trails for every ability here, from novice to advanced.

Mohonk Mountain House & Mohonk Preserve (845-255-1000, 800-772-6646; Preserve 845-255-0919), Mountain Rest Road, New Paltz, Preserve: 3197 Route 44/55, Gardiner. Admission fee. The hotel offers 35 miles of carriage-road trails opening onto views of distant mountain ridges, glens, and valleys. Trails are color coded and mapped, and

DOWNHILL SKIING AT BELLEAYRE MOUNTAIN, THE LARGEST DOWNHILL SKI AREA IN ULSTER

Hudson Valley Tourism, Inc.

there is a use fee. Rentals and refreshment sites available. The preserve also has many miles of cross-country ski trails; a map is available at the visitors center.

Williams Lake Hotel (845-658-3101, 800-382-3818), Binnewater Road, Rosendale, has excellent cross-country skiing for the beginner and for skiers with young children. Great lake views. Fee charged.

DOWNHILL SKIING Downhill skiing in Ulster County offers the best of all worlds: country surroundings and challenging slopes convenient to several cities, including Albany and New York.

Belleayre Mountain (845-254-5600), Route 28, Highmount, is the largest downhill ski area in Ulster County, with the longest ski trail in the Catskills (the Deer Trail at 12,024 feet). Open daily mid-November through mid-April 9–4. Owned by New York State, Belleayre has a top elevation of 3,429 feet, the highest peak in any Catskill ski area. It is the only ski area in the state with a natural divison: The upper mountain is for intermediate and expert skiers; the lower mountain is for beginners and novices. There is plenty of free parking, and a courtesy shuttle runs throughout the parking area all day. At the upper mountain 38 trails are serviced by snowmaking equipment. There are eight lifts: a quad as well as double and triple chairlifts. New equipment makes the wait shorter and gets you up the slopes quickly. Runs range from novice and intermediate to extreme expert. For those who want even more of a challenge, there is a complete racing program for both adults and children. The ski school at Belleayre is outstanding, with patient, capable instructors who can teach the youngest beginner or help advanced experts polish their skills. Snowboards are allowed (with rentals, sales, and instruction available), and there is a terrain park and half pipe. The Overlook Lodge (upper lodge), is a huge, welcoming log building with a fieldstone fireplace, bar, ski shop, cafeteria, lounge area and outside deck. The Discovery Lodge (lower lodge), has a cafeteria and ski shop. Both offer rental equipment, rest rooms, and locker areas. Belleayre has great children's programs (including the KidsCamp) and a fully equipped nursery; call for reservations before you go. Beginners get their first lesson for free; they should check out the "Learn to Ski 1, 2, 3" program, which *Skiing* magazine called the best learn-to-ski program in the East. There are music festivals and other activities in summer and fall (see *Special Events*). Belleayre is very family and service oriented. The old-fashioned feeling about this ski center reminds me of the place I learned to ski in the early 1960s. It's a favorite of many local residents, offering good value for the money and a variety of package deals. I shouldn't neglect to mention that you get to ski free on your birthday.

Sawkill Family Ski Center (845-336-6977), 167 Hill Road, Kingston (located off Sawkill and Jockey Hill Roads). Open from late December through mid-March on weekends and holidays only; Friday nights 5–8 tubing only. This is the smallest ski area in the East, with one rope tow and a snow tubing run with its own lift. There are three ski trails and a nice terrain park for snowboarding; they make lots of snow here and keep the area in great condition. This is an ideal place for families with young children. Inexpensive lift tickets. Snowboard and ski rentals available.

ICE SKATING Kiwanis Ice Arena (845-247-2590), Washington Avenue Extension and Small World Way, Saugerties. Open daily October through March. Call for schedule. This enclosed ice skating rink, while not heated, is a great place to skate any day from approximately 10–6. There is a series of one-and-a-half-hour sessions, and the cost is minimal. Children under the age of five skate free. Skate rentals are available. There are rest rooms and a snack bar.

Nevele Grande Ice Rink (845-647-6000, 800-647-6000), off Route 209, Ellenville. This rink is open to the public from Thanksgiving through March. Admission. For those who love skating outdoors, this covered rink is the place to go. Hours and days vary depending on the hotel schedule, so make sure to call ahead. There are usually two sessions: 10–1 and 2–5. The cost is $7.00, but if you take a lesson with Heidi Graf, an excellent instructor and a former Swiss Olympic skating champion who has worked at the hotel for decades, the admission fee is waived. Rental skates are available.

Williams Lake Hotel (845-658-3101, 800-382-3818), Binnewater Road, Rosendale. Open weather permitting; always call the hotel before you go. There is a charge for skating on the lake here, but it is well worth it, especially for those who love lake skating. Rentals are available. There is also cross-country skiing on lovely wooded trails (and rentals), so it makes a good place for a family outing—offering a winter sport to please just about everyone.

✳ Green Space

Catskill Forest Preserve (845-256-3000). This state-owned and maintained land within the Catskill Park—300,000 acres of forests, lakes, springs, cliffs, teeming with birds and other wildlife—serves as a watershed, recreational area, and ecological reserve. There are seven mountainous areas, each with hiking trails ranging from easy to difficult (see *To Do—Hiking*).

Minnewaska State Park (845-255-0752), Route 44/55, New Paltz. Open daily from 9 to dusk most of the year. Hours change seasonally and are posted daily at the entrance. Located on the dramatic Shawangunk Mountain Ridge, this park offers spectacular mountain views, waterfalls, and meadows. Lake Minnewaska itself is surrounded by a network of woodland trails and carriageways that are excellent for hiking, horseback riding, and cross-country skiing. The paved carriageways make for fine biking. You can take a leisurely 2-mile walk around Lake Awosting, a nice way to get oriented in this large park. Swimming is permitted at the sandy beach area, and there is a lifeguard on duty. The lake is about a 3-mile walk from the entrance if you decide to hike in. Minnewaska is a day-use area only; no camping is permitted. There are several places to picnic, however, some with raised portable grills. Those who visit in November and December should be aware that hunting is permitted in certain outlying areas of the park.

The Mohonk Mountain House (845-255-1000), Mountain Rest Road, New Paltz. Open daily year-round dawn to dusk. Admission fee. This 2,000-acre natural paradise surrounding the Mohonk Mountain House resort is filled with miles of hiking trails and carriage roads stretching out in all directions. The trails are ideal for cross-country skiing and walking. From the tower at Sky Top, the highest point along the trails (1,500 feet above sea level), you can see six states on a clear day (New York, New Jersey, Pennsylvania, Connecticut, Massachusetts, and Vermont). Sky Top was built in 1920 as a memorial to Albert Smiley, one of the founders of Mohonk Mountain House, which opened in 1870. The panoramic vistas from some of the trails here are some of the most scenic views in the Hudson Valley.

The Mohonk Preserve (845-255-0919), Route 44/55, Gardiner. (Not far from the junction of Routes 44/55 and 299: if you are traveling from New Paltz on Route 299, turn right and look for signs on the right about 1 mile up 44/55.) Visitors center is open daily 9–5; preserve is open from dawn to dusk. Day-use fee for nonmembers. There are over 100 miles of trails and carriage roads to explore in this preserve, which consists of over 3,000 acres. Pick up a map at the visitors center.

Sam's Point Preserve (845-647-7989), 400 Sam's Point Road, Cragsmoor (off Route 52, near Ellenville). Open year-round dawn to dusk. Visitors center open weekends May through October. This 5,000-acre preserve in the northern Shawangunk Mountains—known to locals as "the Gunks"—is now owned by the Open Space Institute and managed by the Nature Conservancy. You will find one of the best examples of ridgetop dwarf-pine barrens in the world here. The views are magnificent, and the hiking trails are excellent, leading to Sam's Point, Verkeerderkill Falls, the Ice Caves, and Indian Rock. This is an environmentally sensitive area, and it is important that visitors stay on the marked trails. To reduce potentially damaging impact to the trail area, particularly to the delicate mosses, hike in early spring when there is still a protective snowpack. Formed by glaciers, the point is a little less than 0.5 mile above sea level, and offers a flat viewing area from which you can see five states on a clear day. There are safety walls, but you will feel suspended over the valley below; if you don't like heights, don't stop here. Sam's Point supposedly got its name from a trapper who, fleeing a Native American war party, jumped over the edge and landed safely in some trees. Nature trails lead to a dwarf-pine bar-

THE MOHONK PRESERVE OFFERS SOME OF THE MOST BEAUTIFUL HIKING IN THE REGION.

Dale Evva Gelfand

ren. Trails are well marked, and tours are self-guided with signs. A walk will take you past chasms and tunnels and around incredible balanced rocks. Explore at your own pace.

✳ Lodging

Many of the bed & breakfasts in Ulster County are tucked away down private roads or are off the beaten path and in private homes. They are sometimes difficult to contact since they may not always have a separate listing in the local telephone directory. The most up-to-date listings can be obtained by called Ulster County Tourism (800-DIAL-UCO). The following list is not comprehensive but is what I consider the best places in their class; they are organized by area of the county.

Northeastern Ulster County (Kingston, Saugerties, Woodstock)
Bed by the Stream (845-246-2979), 7531 George Sickle Road, Saugerties 12477. ($$) This peaceful lodging in a private home is located on 5 acres of streamside property and offers an in-ground pool and creek swimming. Marked hiking trails are available nearby and Hunter Mountain and Ski Windham are only a short drive away (see To Do—Downhill Skiing in "Greene County"). Bed by the Stream offers one master suite, two rooms with private bath, and two rooms that share a bath; all have queen-sized beds, cable TV, and views of Blue Mountain. A country breakfast is served on the porch overlooking the stream; children are welcome.

Black Lion Mansion Bed and Breakfast (845-338-0410), 124 West Chestnut Street, Kingston 12401. ($$$) This Kingston landmark has been magnificently restored to its former Victorian splendor. The spectacular views of the Hudson River will delight visitors as will the gracious, beautifully appointed bedrooms filled with fine antiques. Enjoy afternoon tea on the terrace or in the parlor by the fireplace in cooler weather. Choose a two-room suite or one of six large bedrooms, all with private bath and cable TV. Special and luxurious; near the Rondout section of the city.

Bluestone Country Manor (845-246-3060), P.O. Box 144, West Camp, 12490. ($$) Built in the 1930s, on a hilltop in the Catskills, this meticulously restored and maintained estate features an imported brick exterior, hardwood floors inlaid with teak, a gracious stairway, and a screened-in front porch. Guests begin their day with a full country breakfast served in the main dining room or in an intimate setting by the fireplace. Four rooms all have private bath, and there is a carriage house with kitchenette.

Café Tamayo Bed & Breakfast (845-246-9371), 89 Partition Street, Saugerties 12477. ($$) The official name of this establishment is Upstairs at Café Tamayo, Bed and Gourmet Breakfast, and that about says it all. Located above the Café Tamayo, an outstanding dining spot (see Dining Out), the bed & breakfast features one suite and two rooms, all with private baths. A gourmet breakfast is prepared by chef-owner James Tamayo. The café/B&B is in the midst of the antiques shops and boutiques of the village and only a short drive from Woodstock, Kingston, and the major ski areas.

Emerson Inn and Spa (845-688-7900), 146 Mount Pleasant Road, Mt.

Tremper 12457. ($$$) This luxurious establishment—with 23 individually and lavishly decorated rooms and suites—is reminiscent of a European country manor hotel. You will find a full-treatment spa (facials, massages, body wraps, ayurvedic treatments), sauna, indoor pool, and fitness facilities. The outstanding service (the staff is European), personal amenities, and attention to detail will please the most discerning guests. Gourmet restaurant on the premises serves first-rate fare (see *Dining Out*), and rates include use of spa facilities, dinner, full breakfast, and afternoon tea at 4 (a wonderful repast after hiking or biking in the nearby mountains). This establishment is very special, the perfect place to celebrate a birthday or anniversary; featured in several prominent national magazines. Open year-round.

The Lodge at Catskill Corners (845-688-2828, 877-688-2828), 5368 Route 28, Mt. Tremper 12457. ($$$) Located minutes away from Belleayre Mountain and the town of Woodstock, this luxurious lodge, opened in 1997, features contemporary Adirondack-style decor in all 27 rooms. The spacious private suites offer wet bar, refrigerator, and whirlpool bath, and all accommodations have air-conditioning, cable TV, telephones and data ports for computers. Many rooms have decks overlooking the scenic Esopus Creek. Guests can enjoy streamside dining at the Catamount Café next door (see *Dining Out*). Great for families. Children and pets welcome. Open year-round.

Maverick Cottage B&B (845-679-3845), 9 Jones Quarry Road, Woodstock 12498. ($$) The original cottage section of the house was built in the 1920s as part of an artist colony, along with the renowned Maverick Concert Hall. There are three guest rooms,

THE EMERSON INN.

one with private bath. All have views of the surrounding woodlands. Enjoy a hearty organic breakfast between 8 and 10, at your convenience. Located a mile from the village of Woodstock. Open year-round.

Onteora: The Mountain House (845-657-6233), Pine Point Road, Boiceville 12412. ($$) Onteora has the most spectacular mountain views of any B&B in the Catskills. Located 1 mile off Route 28, it was the estate of Richard Hellman, the mayonnaise mogul. There are five bedrooms, all with cathedral ceilings and private baths. Breakfasts are made to order, with requests taken the evening before. Children over the age of 12 are welcome. Open year-round.

Rondout Bed and Breakfast (845-331-8144), 88 West Chester Street, Kingston 12401. ($$) This late-19th-century house is close to Kingston's restaurants, museums, and river landing, and guests will enjoy personal attention as well as the location's convenience. Hearty breakfasts may include waffles and homemade maple syrup, and evening refreshments are served by the fireplace. Well-behaved children welcome. Four rooms, two with private bath. Open year-round.

Saugerties Lighthouse Bed & Breakfast (845-247-0656), 168 Lighthouse Drive, Saugerties 12477. ($$) Treat yourself to a unique, romantic experience: Sleep in a renovated lighthouse. Watch the boats pass by, and see the stars from the bedroom window. The lighthouse keeper will prepare a hearty breakfast in the morning. Two upstairs rooms share a bathroom downstairs. Travel light since it's a 10-minute walk from the parking area. Open year-round.

ENJOY SPECTACULAR MOUNTAIN VIEWS FROM ONTEORA: THE MOUNTAIN HOUSE

Twin Gables: A Guest House (845-679-9479), 73 Tinker Street, Woodstock 12498. ($$) The architecture and furnishings of the 1930s create a relaxed, easy ambience at this guest house; its service and hospitality have earned it a reputation for comfort and affordability. There are nine guest rooms, and a living room and refrigerator are available to visitors. Twin Gables is only a short walk from restaurants, shopping, galleries, and entertainment. The New York bus line stops nearby, so it's a great spot for those traveling to Woodstock without a car. Rooms are all air-conditioned; three have private baths; six share three baths. Children are welcome at the owner's discretion. Open year-round.

Vly Yonders Nature Retreat, 165 Hollow Road, Glenford. ($$) In the 1800s, the lands east of Yankeetown Pond in the Woodstock area were known as "the Vly," and those who lived there were known as "vly Yonders"—people of the valley. At one time this 78-acre property with 20 units (10 one-bedroom cabins, 3 two-bedroom cabins, and 7 wooden yurts, all with either mountain or pond views) was a children's naval sea scout camp known as Camp Alert. The retreat adjoins 600 acres of protected lands and is a perfect getaway for travelers interested in hiking and walking trails through peaceful woodlands or to old stone quarries. Filled with wetlands, this area provides a rich habitat for wildlife. Geothermal heating and cooling and energy-saving lighting were combined with energy-efficient construction techniques. At press time there was no listed telephone; try their web site for updated information: www.vlyyonders.com.

Wild Rose Inn Bed & Breakfast (845-679-5387), 66 Rock City Road, Woodstock 12498. ($$$) Enjoy an elegant Victorian ambience in the heart of town. The five rooms are all beautifully furnished with antiques, and all have air-conditioning, cable television, and whirlpool baths. A gourmet continental breakfast is served. Children are welcome, and a portacrib is available. Open year-round.

Woodstock Country Inn (845-679-9380), 27 Cooper Lake Road, Woodstock 12498. ($$) This quiet, elegant inn is located in the countryside outside the village of Woodstock, yet it is near enough that a short drive will bring you to all the cultural action the town is famous for. The inn—which once belonged to artist Jo Cantine, whose work is in the permanent collection of the Metropolitan Museum of Art—has been restored and is filled with antiques. There are charming nooks throughout the place to relax or dream in. Several of Cantine's paintings and some of her hand-painted furniture are displayed in the common room. Accommodations include five rooms, all with private bath, air-

conditioning, and private deck or porch; there is a lovely heated in-ground pool with magnificent mountain views. Special midseason rates. Open year-round.

Woodstock Inn on the Millstream (845-679-8211), 38 Tannery Brook Road, Woodstock 12498. ($$) This is almost a motel—efficiency units are available—but it has its own special charm. Set right on a brook, there are 18 separate rooms here. The innkeeper gives you the option of enjoying an elaborate continental breakfast buffet waterside or in the sunroom. There is a porch for rocking, and a short walk brings you to the village green. All rooms are air-conditioned, with cable TV and wireless Internet access. Children are welcome. Open year-round.

Southeastern Ulster County (New Paltz, Gardiner, Stone Ridge)

Audrey's Farmhouse Bed & Breakfast (845-895-3440), 2188 Brunswyck Road, Wallkill 12589. ($$) This pastoral spot offers visitors a relaxing getaway. There are five guest rooms (three with private bath, two share a bath), each with air-conditioning and magnificent mountain views. Guests can use the in-ground pool in the warm-weather months and enjoy an outdoor Jacuzzi and fireplace in the main room. A gourmet breakfast is served. Pets welcome. Open year-round.

Captain Schoonmaker's Bed & Breakfast (845-687-7946), Route 213, High Falls 12440. ($$$) A fine spot for antiques lovers, this 18th-century house will make you feel as if you are stepping back into an earlier time. Schoonmaker's has been featured in many publications, and the hostess serves a seven-course breakfast that should hold you until dinner. Four rooms have private bath. All rooms have a private balcony, air-conditioning, and Jacuzzi and overlook a stream. Children under the age of 10 permitted weekdays only. Open year-round.

Deerfield (845-687-9807), RD #1, The Vly, Stone Ridge 12484. ($$) Once a boardinghouse, this turn-of-the-19th-century building has been renovated for modern overnight guests. The rooms are airy and light, and there is a nice mix of antiques and country throughout the inn. You will find more than 30 acres to explore, with shops and points of interest a short drive away. Guests can enjoy an in-ground pool, a Steinway piano, and a large gourmet breakfast. Two of the six guest rooms have private bath; the other rooms share two baths.

Fox Hill Bed and Breakfast (845-691-8151), 55 South Chodikee Lake Road, Highland 12528. ($$) This B&B is located about 5 miles from exit 18 off the NYS Thruway. Wander through the woods, sit by the garden pool and feed the colorful koi, or just relax in your room. There are three suites, all with private bath, air-conditioning, TV, and VCR; one with a fireplace. There is a whirlpool spa, fitness center, and heated in-ground pool. Open year-round.

The Guesthouse at Holy Cross Monastery (845-384-6660), Route 9W, P.O. Box 99, West Park 12493. ($) This monastery has spectacular views of the Hudson River and provides a rather unique bed & breakfast experience. The reasonable per-person donation (they ask $70 per night), includes a room and three meals served in a large dining room with the monks. On some weekends special educational programs are offered; you can call for a schedule of events. Open year-round except the month of August.

The Inn at Applewood (845-691-2516), 120 North Road, Highland 12528. ($$) There are four rooms (actually they are efficiencies), all with private bath, refrigerator, and microwave, in the same building as the excellent restaurant, The Would (see *Dining Out*). Full breakfast is served on weekends; continental during the week. Approximately 8 miles from NYS Thruway exit 18. Children over the age of 13 only. Open year-round.

Inn at Stone Ridge (845-687-0736), Route 209, Stone Ridge 12484. ($$$) For a romantic getaway, this gem should be at the top of your list. It's a fantastic place to go year-round but particularly so in spring, when the flowers around the stone swimming pool (one of the most beautiful pools I have ever swum in) are in bloom. The former Hasbrouck House is an 18th-century stone mansion set on 40 acres amid magnificent gardens. There are five beautifully renovated suites. Listed on the National Register of Historic Places, the inn is open all year; a first-rate restaurant, Milliways, is on the first floor of this stunning spot (see *Dining Out*).

Locktender's Cottage/DePuy Canal House Inn (845-687-7700), Route 213, High Falls 12440. ($$$) The Locktender's Cottage is a romantic getaway situated alongside the Delaware & Hudson Canal in the center of picturesque High Falls. The Victorian cottage once served as a lodging for the canallers, the sturdy men who manned the barges; today it

THE INN AT STONE RIDGE

is owned by John Novi, the chef and proprietor of the DePuy Canal House and Chefs on Fire right across the road (see *Dining Out*). The upstairs suite has a kitchenette, Jacuzzi, and air-conditioning; the bedrooms on the lower floor have private baths and air-conditioning. The Schneider House (DePuy Canal House Inn) has two suites, both with private bath and kitchenette. The two buildings are within minutes of many local activities, and, of course, there are John Novi's culinary gems—(DePuy Canal House (see *Dining Out*), Chefs on Fire, and The New York Store—(see *Eating Out*)—on the premises. Open year-round.

Minnewaska Lodge (845-255-1206), at the intersection of Routes 299 and 44/55, Gardiner 12525. ($$$) This contemporary 26-room mountain lodge is nestled on 17 acres at the base of the spectacular Shawangunk Ridge. The lodge successfully combines the ambience of a bed & breakfast with the conveniences of a fine hotel. All rooms have private decks and mountain views. Guests may enjoy the fitness center on the premises as well as hiking in the nearby Mohonk Preserve and Minnewaska State Park. A full buffet breakfast is included in the price. Children are welcome. Open year-round.

Mohonk Mountain House (845-255-1000), Mohonk Lake, New Paltz 12561. ($$$) This National Historic Landmark is a mountaintop Victorian castle that stands in the heart of 22,000 unspoiled acres. Dazzling views are everywhere, and serene Mohonk Lake adds to the dramatic setting. Although the hotel offers a museum, golf, boating, tennis, spa services, a stable, modern sports facilities, and wonderful hiking on 85 miles of trails and carriage roads, the place is still very much the way it was more than 100 years ago (it is still managed by the Smiley family, who founded the hotel). During the winter the trails become a cross-country-skiers paradise; there's an ice rink in a Victorian open-air pavilion and snowshoeing with equipment available for guests. Midweek packages are available, and special events weekends are held throughout the year (see *To See—Historic Sites*). Activities are offered for children ages 2–12. Of the 251 rooms, over 100 have working fireplaces and nearly 200 have a balcony; all have private bath. Rates include three meals a day; men must wear jackets for the evening meal. Open year-round.

Mountain Meadows Bed and Breakfast (845-255-6144), 542 Albany Post Road, New Paltz 12561. ($$) This lovely country home nestled in the foothills of the Catskills is a fine place for people who enjoy a casual atmosphere, lounging by an in-ground pool, relaxing by a fireplace, or playing a game in a recreation room. The spacious landscaped grounds offer croquet, badminton, and horseshoes. All four rooms have private bath, central air-conditioning and a king- or queen-sized bed. Located only 4.5 miles from the NYS Thruway exit 18. Open year-round.

Nieuw Country Lloft (845-255-6533), 41 Alhusen Road, New Paltz 12561. ($$) This cozy, 18th-century Dutch stone house has six fireplaces, beamed ceilings, and wide-plank floors. Three bedrooms (one with fireplace) are dressed up with period furniture and quilts, and the country breakfast is a hearty way to begin a day. Locally produced wines are offered in the evening. Walkers will enjoy the on-site nature trails; many outdoor activities are located a few minutes' drive from the inn. There is one room here with private bath. Children not permitted. Open year-round.

The 1712 House (845-687-7167), 93 Mill Dam Road, Stone Ridge 12484. (Take Route 209 south toward Ellenville from NYS Thruway exit 19; about 10 miles along, just before the first traffic light you see, make a right onto Mill Dam Road. The house is down the hill, past the pond on the left.) When the King of England and a local Native American chieftain granted the Hardenbergh family a tract of land that encompassed about 250 square miles, the 1712 House was part of their original farm. Built in the

THE 1712 HOUSE IN STONE RIDGE

style of the 1700s, its features include custom-made colonial furniture (all crafted from trees cut on the land and all pieces replicas of 18th-century items). Set on 80 acres, this majestic bluestone-and-wood structure offers guests a 6-acre front lawn, winding streams, sprawling hills, mountains and meadows—as well as all the modern amenities. The spacious living and dining rooms are complete with an enormous fireplace, wide-board floors, and beamed ceilings. The six bedroom suites each offer private bath, whirlpool or claw-foot bathtub, air-conditioning, telephone, cable TV, VCR, and high-speed Internet access. Each one has a beautiful view of the grounds, sitting chairs, and table and chairs for in-room dining. A full gourmet breakfast will be made to your order: Enjoy it on the deck, the bluestone patio, or in your room. A place to celebrate a special occasion. Not recommended for children. Open year-round.

Sparrow Hawk Bed and Breakfast (845-687-4492), 4496 Route 209, Stone Ridge 12484. ($$) This recently renovated brick Colonial, originally a 1770 farmhouse, features five unique air-conditioned guest rooms, all with private bath. A full gourmet breakfast is served fireside in the dining room or on the outdoor patio. Enjoy afternoon tea in the spacious great room, with its cathedral ceiling, beautiful concert piano, and balcony library. Open year-round.

Whispering Pines Bed & Breakfast (845-687-2419), 60 Cedar Hill Road, High Falls 12440. ($$) This secluded contemporary B&B has skylights and is surrounded by 50 acres of private woods. There are four plush bedrooms, all with private bath,

two with Jacuzzis. There is a large video library as well as a reading library. The huge outdoor deck has a Jacuzzi that may be used any time of year by guests. Open year-round.

Northwestern Ulster County (Big Indian, Highmount, Pine Hill)
The Alpine Inn (845-254-5026), Alpine Road, Oliverea 12410. ($$) A pristine mountain lodge nestled on a hillside near the base of one of the tallest peaks in the Catskills, this inn will appeal to those who enjoy exploring the outdoors. Twenty-five rooms with private bath, private balcony, air-conditioning, and cable. Complete with an Olympic-sized pool. Breakfast and dinner are served. Children are welcome. Open year-round.

Auberge du Canard Bed & Breakfast (845-254-4646), Route 28, Big Indian 12410. ($$) This inn has lovely mountain views. Bus travelers can disembark just outside the inn's doors, so it's an excellent choice for people who want to get away but don't have a car. Fishing, hiking, and skiing are nearby; full breakfast is served, and the Luke's Grill offers fine French country dinners (see *Dining Out*). There are three rooms, each with private bath (though one room has a bath across the hall). Children are welcome. Open year-round.

Beaverkill Valley Inn (845-439-4844), Beaverkill Road, Lew Beach 12753. ($$$) This National Historic Site, built in 1893 and restored in recent years by Laurance Rockefeller, offers a perfect retreat for those who love the outdoors. Located within the Catskill Forest Preserve, near hiking trails and some of the best fishing anywhere, the inn also has tennis courts and a lovely indoor pool. During the summer you can bike, hike, swim, and fish; in winter, cross-country ski—and swim. There are a total of 20 rooms, and all have private bath. Children welcome. Open year-round.

Birchcreek Inn (845-254-5222), Birchcreek Road, Pine Hill 12465. ($$) This inn is in a secluded but wonderful spot, with a sign indicating its location just off Route 28. More than 100 years old, on 23 private acres, the estate combines the rustic and the refined for an informal yet elegant ambience. Every guest room has a private bath. Check out the Champagne Room for a birthday, anniversary, or other special occasion: It's huge—as is its luxurious bathroom. There is also a lovely cottage outside the main house with a fireplace and kitchenette. The heated outdoor pool is a great place to relax in the warm weather. Spa facilities available. Children over the age of 12.

Copper Hood Inn and Spa (845-688-2460), Route 28, Shandaken 12480. ($$) Tucked away alongside a well-known fishing stream, the Copper Hood is a full-service spa, offering one of the few Olympic-sized indoor heated pools in the region: Jacuzzi, massage, and herbal wraps are part of the various spa packages, which include meals, lessons, and an array of treatments. There are hiking trails and fishing on the premises, as well. All 20 rooms have private bath. Open year-round.

Full Moon (845-254-5117), Valley View Road, Oliverea 12410. ($$) This newly established mountain resort and performance venue is dedicated to the celebration of nature, music, and the arts. The rustic accommodations are located on a 100-acre wonderland of fields and streams surrounded by the Catskills. The Esopus Creek gently wends its way through the property, and a variety of affordable lodges and cottages are available, including accommodations in a turn-of-the-20th-century country inn with simple, charming guest rooms. The main building has a

SPARROW HAWK BED & BREAKFAST

wraparound sunporch, library, outdoor pool, and dining room/café. Tent camping is permitted on the fields and meadows. A full breakfast is included. Music is always in the air with concerts, dances, and acoustic shows in the smoke-free performance space with a full bar. Guests are encouraged to bring instruments of their own. Three state trailheads are located within 5 miles of the front door, as the resort is located in the Catskill Mountain Forest Preserve. Buffet dinners and breakfasts are served in the café on weekends. Children welcome. Open year-round.

Southwestern Ulster County (Kerhonkson, Ellenville area)

Hudson Valley Resort (1-888-9HUDSON), 400 Granite Road, Kerhonkson 12446. ($$$) Set on 400 acres between the Catskills and Shawangunk Mountains, this newly renovated 300-room luxury resort features magnificent views, a European-style health spa, indoor and outdoor pools, exercise equipment, tennis courts, and a Jacuzzi as well as an 18-hole golf course. Travelers will discover a balance between modern comfort and charm during a stay here. The spa offers massages, facials, acid peels, seaweed-clay body treatments, and a fitness center. (It is open to the public as well as hotel guests.) Minnewaska State Park with its world-famous hiking and rock climbing is close by. A fine restaurant on the premises, Bentley's American Grill, offers American regional cuisine. Open year-round.

Nevele Grand Resort (845-647-6000, 800-647-6000), Nevele Road, off Route 209, Ellenville. 12428. ($$$) This beautifully maintained, full-service resort with nearly 700 rooms has

been in business since 1901. The facilities are first-rate, particularly the par-70, 18-hole golf course, Olympic-sized ice rink (open November through March), indoor and outdoor pool complex and fitness center, tennis courts, and horseback-riding trails. During the winter there is a downhill ski slope with snowmaking and lift as well as cross-country trails. There are always scheduled activities for children; from late June through Labor Day there is a day camp program for kids 3–10. Open year-round.

✳ Where to Eat

DINING OUT

Northeastern Ulster County

Armadillo (845-339-1550), 97 Abeel Street, Kingston. ($$) Open Wednesday through Sunday for dinner 5–10. Tex-Mex Southwest cuisine from an enormous menu includes great ribs, fajitas, and chicken specialties; make sure you try the grilled tuna with lime marinade and wasabi mustard. Outdoor dining in the warm-weather months in a charming patio area. A nice touch: Crayons are provided so that you—or the kids—can draw on the paper tablecloths.

Bear Café (845-679-5555), Route 212, Bearsville (2 miles west of Woodstock). ($$) Open daily, except Tuesday, for dinner from 5. This is a French-American bistro that serves a range of imaginative entrées from grilled fish and chicken to steaks and unusual pasta dishes. The appetizers, salads, and daily specials are consistently excellent. My favorite dishes are the salmon, shrimp Caesar, and portobello burger with homemade French fries; the steaks are superb, as well. (I eat hamburgers and fries a few times a year; this is where I go.) There is a nice view of the Sawkill Creek from the dining area. Be sure to make a reservation, especially on weekends and any evening during the summer; this is one of the best restaurants in the county, and it's busy year-round.

Blue Mountain Bistro (845-679-8519), Route 212 and Glasco Turnpike, Woodstock ($$) Open for dinner Tuesday through Sunday 5–10. This cozy spot is located in a renovated 18th-century barn and offers diners a romantic setting with fine French-Mediterranean cuisine drawing from Italy, France, Spain, and Greece; garlic, olives, and herbs are the featured ingredients. There is salmon in parchment paper (my favorite here) and leg of lamb with red wine, garlic, and fresh rosemary. The freshest local produce is used, and they have their own salad and herb garden during the summer months. Children welcome.

Bois D'Arc (845-679-5995), Zena & Sawkill Roads, Woodstock. ($$) Open for dinner Thursday through Sunday, 5:30–9:30. Pronounced "Bo Dark," this restaurant features superb American regional cuisine, and was originally located (10 years ago) in the town of Red Hook. The chef hails from the southern part of the country and the pork ribs appetizer is excellent (it's even smoked on the premises). The lamb chops, fresh fish dishes, and vegetarian choices are all imaginatively and meticulously prepared—without being fussy; however, portions here are not oversized. Housed in an 18th-century stone house, the place lends itself to a romantic, intimate dining experience. I wouldn't recommend this establishment for those traveling with children.

Café Nouba (845-340-4770), 288 Fair Street, Kingston ($$) Open

for dinner Tuesday through Sunday 5–11. First-rate Asian cuisine—including Thai, Japanese, and Vietnamese dishes—in a setting reminiscent of restaurants in South Beach, Miami. The flavors of the Pacific Rim highlight the fare here: I highly recommend the tamarind-lacquered salmon, which is served with marinated vegetable spaghetti. The tuna tatki with tamarind-ginger sauce and soba noodles is also quite good. The ambience is wonderful—you feel far from Kingston, New York, here! Not recommended for children. Call for reservations, particularly during the summer months and on weekends.

Café S (845-679-3434), at the Woodstock Golf Club, junction of Routes 212 and 375, Woodstock. ($$) Open daily for breakfast 8–11; lunch 11–3; bar menu 3–5; dinner 5–9:30; Sunday brunch 10–2:30. During the winter hours vary, so call ahead. Creative international cuisine with a large variety of entrées, including steaks, seafood, pasta, and salads; a wide selection of side dishes, as well. A great place to stop for lunch away from the hectic pace in the center of town; there are wraps, sandwiches, and salads at reasonable prices. In the warm-weather months, enjoy dining on the terrace overlooking the Sawkill Creek and golf course. In the winter, there's cozy fireside dining. Children's menu.

Café Tamayo & Mediterranean Kitchen (845-246-9371), 89–91 Partition Street, Saugerties. ($$) Open for dinner Thursday through Sunday 5–10. A popular bistro housed in a renovated 1864 landmark building, Café Tamayo serves home-style American and international cuisine and features such specialties as country pâté with spicy red cabbage and green chili, braised duck legs with mole sauce, and cassoulet. The latest addition, attached to Café Tamayo, is Mediterranean Kitchen (open daily for dinner from 5; Sunday brunch 11:30–3), which serves grilled pizza, fresh seafood, and several vegetarian options. They offer outdoor dining on the patio in the warm weather and an open design cooking space so that patrons can sit at copper-topped counters and watch their meals being prepared. Children are welcome at both restaurants; under the age of 9 they eat free from the children's menu at the Mediterranean Kitchen.

Carmine's (845-334-9383), 14 Thomas Street, Kingston. ($$) Open daily from 11–11 for lunch and dinner. Italian family-style cooking with enormous portions. This is a great place to go with a large group, although I have eaten here alone, and they have recently instituted a single-serving Northern Italian trattoria-style menu. The zuppa di pesce is excellent and contains a whole Maine lobster; another of my favorites is the eggplant parmigiana. The upstairs dining room can be somewhat noisy on weekend evenings when the restaurant is crowded, but that's part of the lively, upbeat atmosphere of the place. Live music (usually piano) Friday through Sunday nights. Children are welcome.

Catamount Café (845-688-2828), Route 28, Mount Tremper. ($$) Open daily for dinner 5–10; after Labor Day until Memorial Day, closed Monday. Savor contemporary Hudson Valley and American cuisine, featuring fresh meat and fish as well as game. Dine in a Catskill Forest Preserve setting, in a cozy lodge with a casual atmosphere situated on the banks of the Esopus River. A few house specialties are salmon, filet mignon, trout, and an array of vegetarian dishes. Children welcome.

Downtown Café (845-331-5904), 1 West Strand, Kingston. ($$). Open daily for lunch 11–3:30; dinner 6–10, until 11 on Friday and Saturday. Sunday brunch 9–noon. This friendly, casual restaurant with sidewalk-café tables in the warm-weather months is located in the Rondout section of Kingston, at the foot of Broadway by the waterfront. The owner hails from Venice but offers an international menu. The sumptuous, creative fare includes entrées like basil gorgonzola and spinach tart, soft-shell crabs with mango sauce puree, grilled swordfish, and tuna tartare with watercress and pignoli vinaigrette. Don't skip dessert here; my favorite is the raspberry cheesecake. Children welcome, but they probably should be somewhat adventurous eaters!

Emerson Inn (845-688-7900), 146 Mount Pleasant Road, Mount Tremper. ($$$) Open daily for breakfast 8–10:30; lunch 12:30–2; dinner 6:30–9:30; hours may vary slightly with the season, so call ahead. The chef here, Ross Fraser, has worked in Europe for many years as senior sous chef to the Duke and Duchess of Roxburghe Castle at their award-winning Rosburghe Country House Hotel and as senior chef at the Kinnaird Country House, a Michelin-rated, Relais & Châteaux property in Scotland. Typical winter entrées may include roasted loin of lamb with parsnip puree, port-glazed white asparagus, chanterelles, black trumpet mushrooms, dried figs and truffles, or grilled Hudson Valley duck breast served with toasted coconut and almond pilaf, sautéed bok choy and a soy-ginger sauce. The fare at the Emerson Inn and Spa has been lauded by *Gourmet* and *Wine Spectator* magazines (the wine list is truly exceptional). Dinner reservations required. There is a wonderful Afternoon Tea served daily between 3 and 5 for $20 per person. Not recommended for children.

Emiliani Ristorante (845-246-6169), 147 Ulster Avenue, Saugerties. ($$) Open daily for dinner from 5. Some of the finest Northern-Italian cuisine you will find anywhere in the Catskills is served in this informal yet elegant establishment. The pastas are made on the premises, and all dishes are made to order. Children welcome.

The Golden Ginza (845-339-8132), 24 Broadway, Kingston. ($$) Open daily for lunch Monday through Friday 11–2:30; dinner is served daily 3–10. Enjoy all types of Japanese cuisine, including tempura, teriyaki, sushi, and sashimi. Children will love watching the flames rising from the grill at the center of the table if you order hibachi dinners; they are prepared Benihana style. There is a sushi bar for those who enjoy this delicacy; everything is prepared fresh.

Kyoto Sushi (845-339-1128), 337 Washington Avenue, Kingston. ($$) Open Monday through Thursday 11:30–9:30, Friday and Saturday until 10, Sunday 3–9. Enjoy the artistry of Chef Chun Chao Chen from Manhattan, now in uptown Kingston, and dine on meticulously prepared sushi and sashimi. For those who prefer cooked to raw cuisine, there's chicken or beef teriyaki on the bill of fare. A new, lively addition to the city's

restaurant scene, Kyoto Sushi opened in the latter part of 2003. A must for sushi aficionados while visiting Ulster County.

Le Canard-Enchaine (845-339-2003), 276 Fair Street, Kingston. ($$) Open daily for lunch 11:30–3:30 and dinner from 5 on. Enjoy a classic French meal in a casual bistro atmosphere, a touch of Paris in Kingston. A variety of the freshest fish is available daily, or choose from four classic duck entrées. The freshly baked pastries are excellent, and so is the café au lait and cappuccino. A good choice for lunch—there is a fixed price lunch daily that includes soup or salad, entrée, and dessert and coffee or tea. It's a bargain—and a great choice when you want a leisurely afternoon repast.

Little Bear Chinese Restaurant (845-679-8899), Route 212, Bearsville (2 miles west of Woodstock). Open daily for lunch and dinner noon–10:30. Sit along the Sawkill Creek in the warm-weather months, and enjoy fine Chinese cuisine. They offer an array of vegetarian dishes here as well as imaginative entrées that are quite different than the usual Chinese-restaurant fare. The setting is lovely, and the service is excellent; great take-out, as well. Children welcome.

Mariner's Harbor (845-340-8051), 1 Broadway, Kingston. ($$) Open Monday 4–10, Tuesday through Saturday 11:30–10, Sunday noon–9. Live Maine lobster, Black Angus beef, and fresh seafood are the specialties of the house. Enjoy waterfront dining in the historic Rondout district of Kingston. Even if you aren't interested in eating a full meal, this is a wonderful place to relax with drinks and appetizers (try the fried calamari) while watching the boats pass by. Children are welcome.

Milliways (845-687-0736), Route 209, Stone Ridge. ($$) Open Wednesday through Sunday for dinner from 5. Enjoy fine regional American cuisine in this stone house that dates back to the 18th century (see *Lodging*). The owner, Dan Hauspurg, and his first-rate chef change the menu every two weeks to include items from the Pacific Rim, Mississippi Delta, and Hudson Valley. My favorite is the Chesapeake crabcakes. This is one of the most romantic, elegant restaurants you will find anywhere, and the food and service are consistently excellent.

New World Home Cooking (845-246-0900), 1411 Route 212, Saugerties. ($$) Open daily for dinner 5–11; lunch Monday through Friday noon-2:30. Eating here is like taking a tour of America's finest and funkiest restaurants. The house specialties are Jamaican jerk chicken, Thai mussel stew, and black-sesame-seared salmon (my favorite). Try the phenomenal blackened string beans with rémoulade appetizer—it's wonderful. According to chef-owner Ric Orlando, the emphasis is on peasant flavors, and the colorful, casual ambience reflects the many cultures represented on New World's menu. This is a marvelous, lively, fun place to eat, and there is often live music after 9, so call ahead to see what's happening. Children welcome.

The Red Onion Restaurant & Bar (845-679-1223), 1654 Route 212, Saugerties. ($$) Open daily for dinner except Wednesday 5–10, Friday and Saturday until 11; Sunday brunch 11–3. This was one of the only places in Ulster County with a

smoke-free bar long before it was required by law. The creative international bistro cuisine is first-rate, and so is the service. Enjoy such appetizers as spicy shrimp ragout with garlic chilies and lemon. Entrées include wild striped bass on herbed risotto with lobster mushrooms—although the shallot- and herb-marinated New Zealand lamb chops over mashed potatoes with black-olive sauce and grilled asparagus is my favorite. Desserts range from crème caramel with fresh berries to tricolor chocolate mousse, with white, milk, and dark chocolate. An all-around wonderful place to dine. Children welcome.

Reginato Ristorante (845-336-6968), Leggs Mill Road, Lake Katrine. ($$) Open for lunch Monday through Friday 11:30–2:30; dinner Monday through Saturday 5–10, Sunday 1–10. Enjoy homemade Northern Italian specialties in a relaxed atmosphere. Children are welcome.

Reservoir Inn (845-331-9806), County Route 1 and Dike Road, West Hurley. ($$) Lunch Tuesday through Saturday 11:30–2; dinner Tuesday through Sunday 5–11. Consistently good family fare at reasonable prices is offered in a cozy atmosphere. Italian specialties include terrific pizza; there are many pasta dishes, as well as early-bird specials from 5–7 on Wednesday and Thursday, 5–6 on Friday, 1–5 on Sunday. Children welcome.

Ship to Shore Restaurant (845-334-8887), 15 West Strand, Kingston. ($$) Open daily for lunch and dinner from noon until closing. The specialties here are steaks and seafood. One of my favorite dinner entrées is the 16-ounce boneless New York sirloin with peppercorn butter. For lunch there's the salmon club or grilled portobello mushroom burger with roasted red peppers and fresh mozzarella. Take a walk after your meal along the Rondout. There is live music on Friday and Saturday night, so call ahead to see what's going on. Not recommended for children.

Stella's (845-331-2210), 44 North Front Street, Kingston. ($) Open Wednesday through Saturday 5–10 for dinner only. For some of the best traditional Italian home cooking, including baked lasagna, eggplant parmigiana, or spaghetti and meatballs, this is the place to go. The casual atmosphere and good-sized portions make this a local favorite. Stella's has been open for many years (there's a popular local bar next door owned by the same people), and they offer a child-friendly menu.

Twenty Three Broadway (845-339-2322), 23 Broadway, Kingston. ($$) Open daily except Tuesday, for lunch noon–5; dinner 5–10; late-night menu 10–midnight. One of the most exciting additions to the burgeoning restaurant scene in Kingston, this establishment serves up the best onion soup and grilled tuna salad I've had just about anywhere in the upper Hudson Valley. Their rack of lamb, pasta Mediterranean, and bistro fare are also first-rate. Elegant, romantic ambience; excellent wine list. Just a block from the Rondout Creek in the scenic waterfront area. Not recommended for children.

Ugly Gus Café (845-331-5100 or 334-UGLY), 11 Main Street, Kingston. ($$) Open Monday through Friday for lunch from 11:30–4; dinner daily except Sunday 5–10. The American cuisine here is hearty and satisfy-

ing, with turkey pot pie, ravioli of the day, Buffalo chicken salad, and Maryland-style crabcake sandwiches, just some of my favorite choices for lunch—and, of course, there are big ugly burgers with at least a dozen mouthwatering toppings. For dinner, try the grilled swordfish, roasted salmon, filet mignon, steak *au poivre* or barbecued ribs. All entrées include family-style salad, vegetable, and choice of potato or rice. The children's menu (must have two forms of ID, claims the menu) lists their #1 best-seller—liver and onions with lima beans and rutabaga—all you can eat for free!

Violette (845-679-5300), 85 Mill Hill Road, Woodstock. ($$) Open Monday through Thursday noon–10, Friday until 11, Saturday until midnight; Sunday brunch 11–5; Sunday dinner 5–10. This new addition to the Woodstock restaurant scene is a welcome one, and diners may enjoy country French cuisine in a cozy atmosphere here. The taproom adjoining the restaurant is a great place to stop for a drink and enjoy bistro fare. A fixed price three-course dinner for $25 per person is an excellent value.

Southeastern Ulster County

Benson's (845-255-9783), at the junction of Routes 208 & 44/55, Gardiner. ($$) Open daily for dinner at 5. Blessed with a panoramic view of the Shawangunk Mountains, the building that houses this restaurant dates back to the early 1860s, when it was used by farmers for cattle auctions. Since 1974 it has been an elegant restaurant owned by the Benson family. It specializes in fine Continental cuisine. I strongly recommend the duck or steak.

Brickhouse Restaurant (845-236-3765), 1 King Street, Marlboro. ($$)

Open Tuesday through Saturday for dinner 5–10; lunch Friday only 11:30–2:30; Sunday brunch 10:30–3, dinner 4–9. Located in a historic building, this restaurant offers a romantic atmosphere, with beautiful dark-wooden walls and floors, velvet-covered chairs, and antique furnishings. The New American cuisine includes popular dishes like jumbo curried-chicken dumplings as an appetizer and shrimp over fettuccine with garden vegetables for an entrée. On weekday evenings there's a fixed-price three-course dinner that includes a glass of wine. Live jazz on Saturday night.

Clove Café (845-687-7911), Route 213, High Falls. ($$) Open for breakfast and lunch Monday through Friday 7–3; brunch Saturday and Sunday 9–4; dinner Wednesday through Monday from 5. Serving American cuisine with a European touch. Excellent steaks, hamburgers, fish, and pasta. Breads are baked fresh on the premises daily. Children welcome.

The Country Inn (845-657-8956), County Route 2, Krumville. ($$) Open for dinner Wednesday through Sunday 5–9, until 11 Saturday. (From Route 209, take Krumville Road/County Route 2 for 6 miles; restaurant is on the right.) The road twists and turns as you approach this rustic oasis in the woods of Ulster County that has been a renowned local spot for decades. John, the new chef-owner (Larry retired), is a graduate of the Culinary Institute. There are still 350 types of beer available with 10 on tap, but the food has undergone a transformation (the prices have not). To start, or as a snack, don't pass up the calamari with roasted red pepper sauce for dipping—it's some of the best I've ever had. I thoroughly enjoyed the duck, which was cooked to perfection and served over white beans accompanied by string beans. The steak is excellent and is served with irresistible home-made fries. An unusual dining experience with a unique ambience.

DePuy Canal House (845-687-7700), Route 213, High Falls. ($$$) Open Thursday through Saturday for dinner at 5; Sunday brunch 11:30–2, dinner 4–9. If you want a spectacular meal on a special occasion, make certain you dine at this establishment, which is housed in an 18th-century stone house, formerly a tavern, with each dining room decorated differently. The amazingly creative American regional cuisine blends an array of fascinating flavors. Owner John Novi, a master of culinary innovation, has been delighting diners in this venue for over 30 years and has been written up internationally. Some wonderfully original dishes to try: the scallop soufflé in a garlic-saffron sauce with Pernod, artichoke heart stuffed with lump crab meat, eggplant tart stuffed with ratatouille and goat cheese, lamb tenderloins with fine herbes. Dinner is a prix fixe leisurely repast: four courses $60; seven courses $75; however, there is an à la carte menu every night. Excellent service and terrific wine list. Not for children.

The Loft (845-255-1426), 46 Main Street, New Paltz. ($$) Open daily 11:30–11:30. The regional American fare here is quite good. Try the grilled marinated Gulf shrimp for an appetizer and the Loft island duck (duck breast marinated and topped with an orange and ginger brandy glaze, served with wild rice and an array of steamed vegetables). The lunch menu includes pasta dishes, salads, excellent soups, and sandwiches. Fine food at reasonable prices. Children welcome.

Mariner's-on-the-Hudson (845-691-6011), 46 River Road, Highland. ($$) Open daily from 11 AM for lunch and dinner; Sunday brunch 11–2. This is the place to go to enjoy waterfront dining right by the Mid-Hudson Bridge. The outdoor deck seats 200, and you can watch the boats pass by as you enjoy steamed clams, calamari, mussels, or the Mariner's renowned lobsters (served steamed, broiled, or stuffed). My favorite dinner entrée is the stuffed shrimp scampi. Wednesday and Thursday nights offers an all-you-can-eat seafood buffet—an incredible bargain. Children welcome.

Northern Spy Café (845-687-7298), Route 213, High Falls. ($$) Open daily (except Wednesday) for dinner 5–10; Sunday brunch 11–3. Creative American cuisine is how the chef, a Culinary Institute graduate, describes the fare in this informal yet elegant restaurant, serving grilled fish, steaks, pasta, and vegetarian dishes. He also takes pleasure in adding interesting touches to traditional favorites from around the world. One popular entrée is the Moroccan-style chicken with ginger and cilantro. Desserts include a Northern Spy pie named after the apples from the orchard in back of the restaurant. You can enjoy dinner at the bar or on the terrace in the warm weather. Children welcome.

Ristorante Locust Tree (845-255-7888), 215 Huguenot Street, New Paltz. ($$$) Open for dinner Wednesday through Sunday from 5:30. Reservations recommended. Enjoy fine Euopean-Italian cuisine, by the fireside in the winter months or on the lovely patio during the summer. The

menu changes daily and features the freshest ingredients available—they use only local, organic, pasture-raised meats, dairy, and produce. Sophisticated service in an elegant, intimate atmosphere. Not recommended for children.

The Rosendale Cement Company (845-658-3210), 419 Main Street, Rosendale. ($$) Open Thursday through Monday for dinner 5:30–10, until 11 Friday and Saturday; Sunday brunch 11–3. Lunch is served outdoors in the garden, May through September only, 11–3. Rosendale was known for its cement in the early 1900s, when the natural limestone deposits were discovered in town. The cement could harden underwater, which made it the best choice for landmarks like the Statue of Liberty and the Brooklyn Bridge. The motto at this establishment—housed in a former saloon and brothel that date back 150 years—is "Eat, drink, and bond." The contemporary eclectic cuisine is excellent, and includes comfort foods like meat loaf and macaroni and cheese, although the restaurant is known for its wonderful fish entrées. The menu changes seasonally, reflecting what's freshest year-round. In the summer months enjoy grilled tuna with lentil salad and spicy green beans or baked trout. There are enticing steak and chicken entrées in addition to vegetarian selections like gnocchi with basil and tomato. Desserts are phenomenal and include a nutty buddy (homemade ice cream topped with pecans inside a sugar cone), a mini chocolate cake, lime tartlet, and banana crème brûlée. Children welcome.

Ship Lantern Inn (845-795-5400), Route 9W, Milton. ($$). Open for lunch Tuesday through Friday noon–2; dinner Tuesday through Saturday 5–10, Sunday 1–8. This charming restaurant has nautical decor and serves fine Continental cuisine. The food and service are consistently excellent. House specialties include fresh fish, mignonette of beef Bordelaise, and Saltimbuca Romana. Children are welcome.

Swiss Country Inn (845-255-9772), Route 44/55, Gardiner. ($$) Open daily except Wednesday; lunch 11:30–3; dinner 5–9. Closed for vacation the last week in February and first two weeks of March. Winter hours (January through April) may vary, so call ahead. For a touch of Switzerland in the Shawangunks, head here. Enjoy a fondue (served from October through March), accompanied by one of 57 types of beer, in a dining room with white lace curtains, lots of wood (including a cuckoo clock), and an alpenhorn. If you have never tried raclette (sliced, boiled potatoes topped with melted Swiss mountain cheese), it's a great wintertime treat, particularly after a day of skiing. Entrées all come with bread, salad, and vegetables—or a choice of spaetzle or potatoes. There are seven different fondues from which to choose as well as an extensive menu, including German and Italian dishes (the mix, like Switzerland itself!). Children welcome.

The Would Restaurant (845-691-2516), 120 North Road, Highland. ($$) Open for lunch Monday through Friday 11:30–2; dinner daily 5–10. A former gin mill once known as the Applewood Bar, this informal restaurant is becoming renowned for its high-quality creative cooking. There is a mix of international and New American cuisine, with several unique touches. The Oriental chicken salad with roasted almonds and Chinese noodles is popular for lunch. The dinner menu includes grilled lamb chops on roasted walnut-mint pesto with Mediterranean vegetable compote. The pastry chef bakes focaccia and pesto bread as well as great desserts. Try the flaky apple pie spiced with cinnamon, or the raspberry-chocolate brûlée.

Northwestern Ulster County
Loretta Charles (845-688-2550), 7159 Route 28, Shandaken. ($$) Open for dinner daily except Monday from 5. Saturday and Sunday lunch is served noon–2:30. Contemporary American cuisine featuring wood grilled steaks and seafood.

Luke's Grill (845-254-4646), Route 28, Big Indian. ($$) Open daily except Wednesday at 5 for dinner. Specialties at this casual French restaurant are excellent pâtés and baby rack of lamb, and for dessert the chocolate mousse with hazelnuts is a treat. The food is consistently first-rate, and so is the service. Children are welcome.

Ricciardella's Restaurant (845-688-7800), Main Street, Phoenicia. ($$) Open Wednesday through Saturday 4:30–10, Sunday 2–10. This restaurant offers diners standard Italian fare and decent seafood in an informal atmosphere at reasonable prices. Check out the early-bird specials. Live lobster tank. Children welcome.

EATING OUT

Northeastern Ulster County
The Alternative Baker (845-331-5517), 35 Broadway, Kingston. ($) Open Thursday through Monday 8–6, Sunday until 4. You will find dairy-free, sugar-free, wheat-free, and

organic baked goods here in addition to standard favorites like brownie fudge cake. The focacce, buttermilk scones, and muffins are popular and delicious. There are only a few tables, but this is a great stop if you want to pick up a snack or pack a picnic lunch.

Ann Marie's Gourmet Market-place (845-246-5542), 216 Main Street, Saugerties. ($) Open daily (closed Tuesdays during the winter months), 7–7. This bustling café-bistro is known for hearty fare—homemade wraps, burritos, lasagna, frittatas, and potato pancakes—and they are all displayed before you, making it even more difficult to choose. They roast their own turkey and roast beef and have an array of coffees, teas, and excellent baked goods. Wonderful for breakfast, lunch, or an early dinner.

Catskill Mountain Coffee (845-334-8455), 906 Route 28, Kingston. ($) Open daily 8–4. Enjoy organic coffee, homemade desserts, and soups in this "coffeehouse." Don't forget to purchase coffee beans before you leave—their product is some of the best you will find in the region.

China Rose to Go (845-338-7443), 608 Ulster Avenue, Kingston. ($$) Open Monday through Friday 11:30–9, Saturday 3-10. The Chinese food is first-rate at this small eatery with counter service and a few tables.

Coffee Beanery (845-336-8146), 1090 Morton Boulevard, Kingston. ($) Open Monday through Friday 7 AM–10 PM, Saturday 8 AM–10 PM, Sunday 10–10. Hours vary slightly in the winter. This spacious, immaculate café has an array of desserts (pies, pastries, frozen drinks), coffees, teas, yogurt, ice cream (waffle-cone sundaes, parfaits, banana splits, hot-fudge

brownies), bagels, and muffins. This is a mom-and-pop operation, and all baked goods are made on the premises. Children will love it.

Deising's Bakery & Coffee Shop (845-338-7503), 111 North Front Street, Kingston. ($) Open Monday through Friday 6–6, Saturday until 5, Sunday until 2, for breakfast, lunch, and dessert. Deising's has quality pastries, breads, and other baked items (try the napoleons and butter cookies). The coffee shop offers large, overstuffed sandwiches, fresh quiches, and hearty soups—all made fresh daily. Breakfast is a bargain. Children welcome.

The Dutch Tavern (845-246-0073), 253 Main Street, Saugerties. ($) Open daily except Monday for lunch and dinner 11–9, until 10 on Friday and Saturday. Call before you go on Sunday since they are closed at certain times of the year. Hearty American favorites in a tavern atmosphere. Try the stuffed garlic cheeseburger, a specialty of the house, or the Pilgrim (thinly sliced turkey breast, homemade stuffing, and provolone sandwiched between two slices of fresh rye bread and grilled). The sandwiches, salads, soups, and chili are very good, the portions are generous, and the price is right. Along with carnivorous fare, there's veggie-bean chili, veggie burgers, and veggie pitas.

El Coqui Latin Jazz Café (845-340-1106), 21 Broadway, Kingston. ($) Open for lunch and dinner noon–10. Authentic Puerto Rican cuisine in an informal atmosphere. Enjoy salads (including conch), red snapper with Creole sauce, island-style cassava and vegetables as well as roast pork, beef, shrimp, or veggie wraps. Live entertainment Friday nights. Children welcome.

El Danzante (845-331-7070), 720 Broadway, Kingston. ($) Open daily 11:30–9 for lunch and dinner. This colorful, informal Mexcan-American restaurant offers steaks and seafood along with flautas, chimichangas, soft tacos, burritos, quesadillas, fajitas, and salads. The menu is huge, and everything is prepared to order. The tacos are made with double corn tortillas topped with chopped onions and cilantro and served with homemade guacamole and salsa—my favorite item on the menu here. The chiles rellenos (stuffed peppers Mexican style with chicken, fresh herbs, and spices) served with rice and beans is first-rate. Children welcome.

Eddy's Restaurant (845-338-9793), 742 Broadway, Kingston. ($) Open Monday through Friday 5–4, Saturday 6–3, Sunday 6–1. Watch your breakfast prepared before you in this small, unpretentious restaurant at the upper tip of Broadway. The atmosphere—and prices—are something out of another era, and it's worth a stop. They cook their own turkey, roast beef, corned beef, and ham here: Those are the best sandwiches to order for lunch—they're fresh and delicious. Many local folks have no idea this place exists, which is what I like best about it! Kids are welcome.

Gabriel's Café & Bakery (845-338-7161), 50 John Street, Kingston. ($) Open Monday through Friday 8–4:30, Saturday 9–3:30. All the excellent baked goods here are made on the premises: scones, muffins, challah, pita bread, croissants. The eggs served are from free-range chickens. You can enjoy breakfast all day. Try the French toast topped with Lyonsville Sugarhouse (Ulster County) maple syrup. For lunch there's grilled chicken or salmon Caesar, falafel, hot and cold soups, burrito of the day, and an array of fruit and vegetable juices from the juice bar. They even offer quite a few vegan and vegetarian selections, which is somewhat uncommon in Kingston. Healthful, gourmet choices at reasonable prices in an informal café atmosphere. Children welcome.

Gilded Otter Restaurant & Brewery (845-256-1700), 3 Main Street, New Paltz. ($$) Open daily noon–midnight. The dining room and pub here overlook the Wallkill River and offer views of the Shawangunks, as well. This is a place beer lovers should not miss; do try some of brewmaster Darren Cuirrier's award-winning creations.

Gypsy Wolf Cantina (845-679-9563), Route 212, Woodstock. ($) Open daily except Monday for dinner from 5. This is an authentic Mexican cantina with colorful decor and a festive atmosphere. The chips and salsa are first-rate, and the Gypsy Wolf platter includes a little of everything to put in your tortillas. Wonderful margaritas. Children welcome.

Hansen Caviar Company (845-331-5622), 881 Route 28, Kingston. (It's located on the right side of the highway if you are heading east toward Kingston, about a half mile from the traffic light at Zena Road.) ($$) Open Monday through Thursday 9:30–5:30, Friday until 7, Saturday 10–4; closed Sunday. Several kinds of Russian and American caviars, including fresh American sturgeon caviar, are offered here; there is also goose foie gras, Scottish and Norwegian smoked salmon, truffles, and more. Although not a traditional eatery, this is a great stop for a gourmet picnic.

Jane's Homemade Ice Cream (845-338-8315), 305 Wall Street, Kingston. ($) Open Monday through Friday 9–6, Saturday 10–5. Homemade ice cream is the specialty, along with cakes, cookies, and scones. Breakfast and lunch are served, and there is a variety of soups, salads, wraps, sandwiches, and vegetarian dishes, all freshly prepared before you.

The Joyous Café (845-334-9441), 608 Broadway, Kingston. ($) Open Monday through Friday 11–7; evenings when there are shows at UPAC, starting at 5. Upscale gourmet fare for eat-in or take-out. Choose from California cobb salad, roasted chicken salad, turkey pastrami Reuben, or roast beef with horseradish sauce on a hard roll. Try the joyous frites: a French fry–filled cone topped with a choice of garlic or pesto aioli, horseradish, or Asian BBQ sauce. You can get take-out, or ask for a boxed lunch; wine and beer available. The ordinary is made more exciting at this midtown eatery across the street from Ulster Performing Arts Center.

La Florentina (845-339-2455), 604 Ulster Avenue, Kingston. ($) Open weekdays 11:30–10, weekends 4–11. Excellent pizza, calzone, and other baked specialties. A traditional wood-fired oven is used. Even the cheeses are homemade, and there are outstanding dishes such as pizza with veal and broccoli (the dough is yeast-free). Great Sicilian (and other Italian) desserts, including cannoli, ices, and layer cake. Children welcome.

Maria's Bazar (845-679-5434), Tinker Street, Woodstock. ($) Open daily 6:30 AM–8 PM, Sunday until 7:30. Maria is well-known in town for her home-cooked Italian specialties; her renowned vegetarian lasagna is wonderful. A variety of salad creations, fresh pastas, homemade soups, and baked goods are to be found here; vegetarians will find many selections from which to choose. This is one of the few places in Woodstock where you can dine outdoors—they have a lovely, large open-air patio, and it's off the street. Children welcome.

Monkey Joe's Roasting Company & Coffee Bar (845-331-4598), 478 Broadway, Kingston. ($) Open Monday through Friday 6:30–6:30, Saturday 7:30–6. This delightful café is housed in the Hutton building (1906), formerly an oyster house. The original tin ceiling, tile floor, schoolhouse lights, wainscoting, and fireplace make this charming renovated space relatively unchanged for close to 100 years. It's a wonderful spot to enjoy organic coffee—espresso, cappuccino, latte, café au lait, caffè mocha, or a monkey frost (a flavored frozen drink). Other offerings are chai frost, iced chai, raspberry tea frost, and several types of tea (black, green, and herbal varieties). For those who prefer hot chocolate, theirs is first-rate; so is the chocolate egg cream. Baked goods include bagels, muffins, scones, cakes, cookies, and biscotti. Children are welcome.

Nekos Luncheonette (845-338-8227), 309 Wall Street, Kingston. ($) Open daily except Sunday 7–3. This family-owned and -operated all-American luncheonette could be right out of a Norman Rockwell painting. They offer a huge menu of classic favorites, including home-cooked pastrami, hot turkey with French fries and gravy, and first-rate chicken-salad sandwiches. I love the Greek salad—and the dark-chocolate bars that are made on the premises (the other family business is hand-dipped chocolates). The portions are generous and the prices are reasonable. This is a popular local haunt. Eddy, the chef-owner, cooks every day, and the same wait staff has been working there for years, providing excellent service. Children welcome.

Pine View Bakery (845-657-8925), 3374 Route 28, Shokan. ($) Open daily 6:30–3. This breakfast-and-lunch eatery offers simple, straightforward food at amazingly reasonable prices. It's an old-fashioned place with a counter and six or seven tables at most. The place has a large loyal customer base, almost all locals. I enjoy having breakfast on the terrace during the summer and always order the egg sandwich on their fresh eight-grain bread, which is excellent. Children are welcome, but it's a small place, so they can't run around here without getting underfoot.

The Spotted Dog (845-688-7700), at Catskill Corners, Route 28, Mount Pleasant. ($) Open Monday, Wednesday, and Thursday noon–7; Friday, Saturday, and Sunday until 9:30. Located about 20 miles west of the NYS Thruway exit 19, this place is built like a Victorian firehouse. Children especially will enjoy dining inside a real fire truck and with fire equipment all around. Reasonable prices for quality family fare, including burgers, salads, sandwiches, wraps, and hearty soups.

West Strand Grill (845-340-4272), 50 Abeel Street, Kingston. ($$) Open daily except Monday from 3 PM. This restaurant, located in a renovated building that was once a synagogue

dating back to 1892, serves contemporary American favorites such as herb-grilled rack of lamb, ginger pan-fried sea bass, and West Strand grilled primavera pasta. There's patio dining overlooking the Rondout waterfront. Live music every weekend and a beautiful bar.

Southeastern Ulster County
The Bakery (845-255-8840), 13A North Front Street, New Paltz. ($) Open 7 AM–8 PM (until 6 November through March). The bagels, rugelach, and butter cookies are first-rate at this place popular with students and local residents. The outdoor café is surrounded by gardens and provides a pleasant ambience for those who want to relax and enjoy a treat from the coffee bar. Overstuffed sandwiches, salads, and intriguing pasta dishes are a few of the lunch options.

The Egg's Nest (845-687-7255), Route 213, High Falls. ($) Open daily 11 AM–2 AM. Located in a former parsonage, this cozy restaurant with funky, fun decor has homemade soups, great sandwiches, and chili, and they're known for crispy-crusted praeseaus, a pizzalike creation that's delicious. The place is an original, and it's worth a stop for lunch, early dinner, or an afternoon snack. The nachos are wonderful; the prices are great. Children welcome.

Chefs on Fire Bistro (in the basement of the DePuy Canal House) (845-687-7778), 1315 Route 213, High Falls. ($$) Open Wednesday through Sunday for lunch or dinner 11–9; breakfast Saturday and Sunday only 9–noon. There are wonderfully creative soups, salads, and appetizers here. Some of the tantalizing possibilities include: grilled chicken and

SPOTTED DOG RESTAURANT AT CATSKILL CORNERS

roasted red pepper quesadilla, fish of the day with garlic and lemon aioli, hazelnut pesto gnocchi with grilled chicken breast and tomato, a variety of panini sandwiches, frittatas, and wood-fired oven baked pizzas. I can't wait to try the shrimp scampi pizza topped with roasted smoked tomato, garlic, and parsley. They even have a calamari pizza. For dessert, stop in at **The New York Store** (Wednesday through Sunday 8 AM–7 PM), next door in the Thomas Snyder House (1860), which features wonderful gourmet baked goods (pastries, breads, desserts, chocolates, and more).

Gadaleto's Seafood Market & Restaurant (845-255-1717), 246 Main Street, Cherry Hill Shopping Center, New Paltz. ($$) Open daily except Sunday 8 AM–9 PM. Enjoy fresh fish, shrimp, clams, crabs, or lobster in this informal eatery. A great place to get takeout, as well. Children welcome.

Harvest Café (845-255-4205), 10 Main Street, Water Street Market,

New Paltz. ($$) Open daily except Tuesday 11–8. Organic American and vegetarian cuisine with imaginative specialties, including a salmon BLT with herb mayonnaise on a fresh-baked roll, Asian soba-noodle salad with soy ginger vinaigrette, and a barbecued pork burrito with chive sour cream and carrot slaw. Outdoor patio dining in the warm-weather months. Children welcome.

Highland Café (845-691-6913), 329 Main Street, Highland. ($) Open Monday through Friday 7–2:30, Saturday 8–2. Homestyle breakfast (served until 11 AM) and lunch in pleasant, spacious surroundings where tables have plenty of privacy. The eggs and omelettes are quite good, and for lunch try one of my favorites: grilled Cajun chicken in an herb wrap with Creole mayo, lettuce, and tomato. There's a pasta selection daily, a low-fat menu choice that continually changes, and an array of soups, sandwiches, wraps, and salads. Prices are exceedingly reasonable, and portions are generous. Travelers may rarely find themselves driving through Main Street in Highland and often pass on this café; it's a real find—worth getting off 9W for and going into the village! Children welcome.

Main Course (845-255-2600), 232 Main Street, New Paltz. ($) Open daily except Monday for lunch and dinner 11:30–10. Fresh, delicious spa cuisine, featuring contemporary American dishes with grilled fish specials, homemade pasta, imaginative salad creations (you can make your own entrée by choosing two, three, or four different salads). Casual and relaxing, with healthful—and tasty—choices.

Raccoon Saloon (845-236-7872), Main Street, Marlboro. ($) Lunch served daily 11:30–2:30; dinner Tuesday through Sunday 5–9. Some of the best burgers in the region, along with excellent fries, chicken, ribs, soups, and salads have been prepared here for decades. This renowned local eatery, a popular casual stop for lunch or dinner, also has a cozy bar with great views. Children are welcome.

Rosendale Café (845-658-9048), 434 Main Street, Rosendale. ($) Open Monday 5–11, Tuesday through Sunday 11–11. This vegetarian restaurant offers a variety of soups, salads, sandwiches, and pasta dishes. Try the Fakin' Bacon FLT. The nachos and burritos are also tasty. Their meatless black-bean chili over brown rice is excellent. Organic coffees and homemade desserts. There's music on most weekend evenings, and it's usually quality entertainment.

Yanni Restaurant & Café (845-256-0988), 51 Main Street, New Paltz. ($) Open daily noon–11. Enjoy Greek specialties (gyros, Greek salad, souvlaki sandwich, spinach pie, and kebobs) and American favorites (chicken parmigiana sandwich, eight types of burgers, salads) in an informal atmosphere. Everything here is fresh and prepared to order. Great vegetarian specialties (falafel, veggie platter, wraps). Prices, too, are great. Children welcome.

Northwestern Ulster County

Bread Alone (845-657-2108), Route 28, Boiceville; also located on Tinker Street, Woodstock; North Front Street, Kingston. ($) Don't miss this bakery, renowned for its fantastic bread—Norwegian farm, mixed grain, Swiss peasant, Finnish sour rye, and others—all baked in a wood-fired oven. Have a cup of tea or coffee, and satisfy your craving for something sweet and rich from the array of tempting desserts so beautifully displayed. Their soups and chilies are quite good, served with your choice of bread or a roll.

Brio's (845-688-5370), Main Street, Phoenicia. ($) Open daily 7 AM–10 PM. This luncheonette is a good place to stop for an overstuffed sandwich, hearty chili, or a snack. The breakfasts are terrific, and there are 10 kinds of pancakes served. A popular place with local residents. Kids will love the spaghetti and meatballs.

Railroad Pizza (845-254-4500), Route 28 (1 mile east of Pine Hill), Big Indian. ($) Open daily except Tuesday 10 AM–9 PM. This pizzeria with a full deli features 26 soft and hard ice cream flavors, as well. Excellent quality full dinners are also served Thursday though Sunday, featuring pasta, fresh seafood, and chicken. Jon and Ron, the two brothers who run this eatery, have no processed food on the premises—everything is homemade. Great value and a perfect stop for those traveling with children.

Sweet Sue's (845-688-7852), Main Street, Phoenicia. ($) Open Thursday–Tuesday 7–3. This is a great breakfast-and-lunch place, with more than a dozen types of spectacular pancakes (including fruited oatmeal) and French toast (including walnut crunch). Everything from muffins to soups and all desserts is homemade here. A casual café with an outstanding reputation. Get there early on weekend mornings; there's usually a line out the door. Great for children.

Winchell's Pizza (845-657-3352), Reservoir Road and Route 28, Shokan. ($) Open daily 11:30–9:30. Hearty soups and unusually tempting pizzas with a thick crust; enjoy creamy homemade ice cream for dessert. This is a great stop for people traveling with children.

✳ Entertainment

PERFORMING ARTS **Backstage Studio Productions** (845-338-8700), 323 Wall Street, Kingston. This is the center of an arts-and-entertainment complex with 75,000 square feet of space, a 2,000-seat concert hall, dance studio, and art gallery with changing exhibits. Open year-round daily 10–6. Call for a schedule of events.

Kleinert/James Arts Center of the Woodstock Guild (845-679-2079), 34 Tinker Street, Woodstock, offers a series of musical performances year-round. Call for a schedule.

Maverick Concerts (845-679-8217), Maverick Road, Woodstock (just off Route 375), features chamber-music concerts on Sunday afternoons at 3 during July and August. Admission fee. Founded in 1916 by author Harvey White, the Maverick Concerts were to be a blend of the best that chamber music and the natural world had to offer. White wanted to encourage other "maverick" artists, and he attracted some of the premier string and wind players of the time to this glass-and-wood concert hall. The small building seats only 400, but many people enjoy hearing the concerts from the surrounding hillside—a setting that was White's idea of perfection. The concerts are known as the oldest chamber-music series in the country, and they are still attracting the best groups in the world, among them the Tokyo, Shanghai, Miami, and Emerson String Quartets. They also offer free children's concerts on Saturday mornings in July and August at 11.

Stone Ridge Center for the Arts (845-687-8890), 3588 Route 209 (Main Street), Stone Ridge, offers dance performances, music, and poetry. Open year-round 9–6; call for schedule of events.

Unison Arts and Learning Center (845-255-1559), 68 Mountain Rest Road, New Paltz, is a multiarts center with performances of jazz, folk, world music, and dance. There are also poetry readings, children's theater, workshops, and monthly art gallery exhibits. Outdoor sculpture garden. Open year-round, Monday through Saturday 10–5; call, and get on their mailing list—the quarterly catalog is large and includes something of interest to just about everyone.

Ulster Performing Arts Center (845-331-1613), 601 Broadway, Kingston, is on the National Register of Historic Places. The renovated Broadway Theatre is the largest arts showcase in the county, offering a variety of theater productions and concert performances from March through December. Call for a schedule.

The Uptown: A Gathering Place (845-339-8440), 33 North Front Street, Kingston, is a performance space with theater seating. They offer jazz, bluegrass, theater performances, literary readings, and lectures by renowned writers. Open year-round Tuesday through Saturday 5–11.

Woodstock Playhouse (845-679-2764), Routes 212 and 375, Woodstock, is a summer performing arts venue featuring a variety of events in music and theater. Children's performances are also offered from Memorial Day weekend through Labor Day at 11 AM.

THEATER **Bird-On-A-Cliff Theatre Company** (845-247-4007), produces a Shakespeare Festival on the grounds of the Comeau property (by the town offices) in Woodstock every July and August. They also feature dramatic productions. This is a wonderful place to enjoy a picnic dinner and take in some theater at the right price ($5 suggested donation per person). Performances begin at 5 PM; call for a schedule.

Coach House Players (845-331-2476), 12 Augusta Street, Kingston. This community theater group performs four times a year in its venue, an original coach house. Call for a schedule.

Community Playback Theatre (845-691-4118), Boughton Place 150 Kisor Road, Highland. An improvisational theater company that weaves the stories told by audience members into scenes that are then "played back" on the spot. Performances at

8 PM the first Friday of the month year-round.

New Paltz Summer Repertory Theater (845-257-3880), SUNY New Paltz, 75 South Manheim Boulevard, New Paltz. Several plays are presented each summer in theaters on the campus. Presenting a variety of productions for over 30 years, the 2003 season included *The Laramie Project* by Moises Kaufman and *Light Up the Sky* by Moss Hart. Call for current schedule. SUNY also hosts the renowned **PianoSummer at New Paltz Festival-Institute** (845-257-3860) under the aegis of internationally acclaimed pianist Vladimir Feltsman; there are master classes (some may be audited by the public) as well as concerts during the month of July. Call for a complete schedule.

Shadowland Theatre (845-647-5511), 157 Canal Street, Ellenville. This is the county's only professional nonprofit theater company, featuring a five-play main-stage season from May through September. Offerings include contemporary dramas, comedies, classics, and new plays. The theater first opened on July 3, 1920, as an art-deco movie and vaudeville house. Substantial renovations have rebuilt the interior, retaining the charm of the past and creating a tiered 148-seat intimate venue for theater. All seats are within 25 feet of the stage. Call for a complete schedule.

Shandaken Theatrical Society (845-688-2279), Church Street, Phoenicia, is a community-theater organization that produces a musical in the spring, a drama or comedy in the fall, and a summer production.

✳ Selective Shopping

Ulster County has a number of interesting villages filled with boutiques, galleries, bookshops, and stores that sell everything from teapots and hand-blown glass to soaps and chocolates. Uptown Kingston and the Rondout area of the city have an array of intriguing shops; so do Woodstock, Phoenicia, Saugerties, and New Paltz (don't forget to visit the **Water Street Market,** a village within the village of New Paltz with over 30 shops, cafés, and galleries). And wonderful eateries abound so that when you tire of shopping, you can relax and imbibe! (See *Eating Out.*)

ANTIQUES Ever since the 17th century, people in Ulster County have been accumulating things, which now turn up as valuable antiques. But even if you don't collect rare furniture, you can enjoy hunting down that special collectible vase or colorful quilt. Auctions are listed in the local newspapers, and yard sales pop up every weekend during the spring and summer. There are numerous antiques shops throughout the county, but the following places include several centers that offer many dealers under one roof and give browsers a wide selection. And since no listing of a center's stock is ever comprehensive, visitors will never know what treasures they may find while exploring on their own.

Acorn Antiques/Craftsmen's Gallery, (845-688-2100), 48 Route 214, Phoenicia, has Mission and Mission-style collectibles and antiques. In nearby Shandaken, the **Blue Barn** (845-688-2161) on Route 28 is a good place to stop for a variety of furniture items and decorative accessories.

Winchell's Corners Antiques (845-657-2177), on Route 28 in Shokan, has a wonderful collection of collectibles (and a terrific eatery next door with good pizza).

In High Falls, **Barking Dog Antiques** (845-687-4834), 7 Second Avenue and Firehouse Road, and **Cat House Antiques** (845-687-0457), 136 Bruceville Road, are fun places to browse and they are both open year-round. Do stop in at **Green Cottage** (845-687-4810), 1204 Route 213, with all kinds of unusual items of interest for the home and garden. In Gardiner, **The Country Store Antique Center** (845-255-1123), Route 44/55, has furniture and country collectibles.

In the New Paltz area, make sure to check out the **New Paltz Antiques Center** (845-255-1880) at 256 Main Street, the **Water Street Antiques Center** (845-255-2043), 10 Main Street at the Water Street Market, and **Jenkinstown Antiques** (845-255-8135), 520 Route 32 South. All have interesting collections of furniture and collectibles.

Van Deusen House Antiques (845-331-8852), 59 Main Street, Hurley, has a nice selection of furniture and collectibles. **Catskill Mountain Antiques Center** (845-331-0880), Route 28, Kingston, has all types of furniture, collectibles, and textiles. Open year-round. **Skillypot Antique Center** (845-338-6779), 41 Broadway, Kingston, is a co-op of 25 dealers who offer lamps, furniture, glassware, and collectibles. Open year-round. The **Saugerties Antiques Center** (845-246-8234/3227), 220 Main Street, is located in the antiques district of town. They are a co-op and are open daily year-round. Check out the many other smaller shops in Saugerties on both Main and Partition Streets.

If you are interested in attending an auction, **George Cole Auctioneers** (845-338-2367) holds Saturday auctions year-round. Call for more information. **JMW Auction Service** (845-339-4133), 592 Broadway, Kingston, and Route 32, Rosendale, specializes in fast-paced, fun sales.

ART GALLERIES Anyone interested in the arts should leave a couple of hours free (in the afternoon since most are closed in the morning) to drive to the following galleries and points of interest in Kingston and Woodstock; both towns are filled with wonderful paintings, photography and sculpture in an array of places, some off the beaten path. The **Art Society of Kingston** coordinates the **First Saturday Art Openings** at galleries throughout the city on the first Saturday of the month.

In the uptown area of Kingston, don't miss the **Coffey Gallery** (845-339-1350), 330 Wall Street, with its spacious, inviting ambience. It is open Tuesday and Wednesday 11–5, Thursday through Saturday 11–8, Sunday 1:30–4:30. There are changing exhibits of paintings or sculpture every month here. Owner Katharine McKenna, herself a painter, features a variety of work from both local and international artists. Also on North Front Street in the uptown section of the city is **A.S.K. Gallery** (the Art Society of Kingston) (845-338-0331), 37 North Front Street, 2nd floor, which features the work of local artists and is open Friday and Saturday 1–5 or by appointment. **The Wright Gallery**

(845-331-8217), 50 North Front Street, is open Wednesday through Saturday noon–5:30 and Friday and Saturday 7–9 PM. **The Uptown** (845-339-8480), 33 North Front Street, is open Thursday through Saturday 7–11 PM, and **The Living Room** (845-338-8353), 45 North Front Street, presents the work of contemporary regional artists and contains fine furniture handcrafted by local artisans. Open Thursday through Saturday noon–6, and by appointment.

In the Rondout area of the city, make sure to call the **Donskoj & Company Gallery** (845-338-8473), 93 Broadway, which is open by appointment only and features artists from throughout the Hudson Valley. A couple of doors down is the **Artist's Gallery** (845-340-1006), 89 Broadway, open Friday through Sunday 1–4 (longer hours in the summer months), which exhibits local artists in a range of mediums. There is a nice backyard with tables for people to relax in the warm weather.

Continue down lower Broadway to **The Gallery at Deep Listening Space** (845-339-5984), 75 Broadway, which is open on weekends 1–5 or by appointment on weekdays. On Abeel Street visit the **Watermark Cargo Gallery** (845-338-8623), 111 Abeel Street, with its ongoing exhibits of African art and artifacts; hours are by appointment.

Before you leave Kingston, if you are visiting on a weekend afternoon, stop in "midtown" at the **Mid-City Art Gallery** (845-338-2108), 572 Broadway, 2nd floor, which is open Saturday and Sunday noon–4. They show the work of local, regional and national artists; openings are the first Saturday of the month from 6–10 PM. Also in this area of the city, at 506 Broadway, are two galleries worth a stop: **The Gallery at R&F Encaustics** (845-331-3112), 2nd floor, open Monday through Saturday 10–5, which offers an array of workshops, including one on pigment sticks, in addition to changing exhibits; **Studio 8** (914-388-1919), also on the 2nd floor, is open Saturdays noon–4 and features the work of local artists, as well as others. Live music and openings every first Saturday of the month from noon–7.

West of Kingston is the perpetual art colony of Woodstock. Don't miss **The Center for Photography at Woodstock** (845-679-9957), 59 Tinker Street, open year-round, Wednesday through Sunday noon–5, which offers a changing selection of photography exhibits throughout the year. Participants include some of the most innovative photographers in the world, both established and new. Past shows have focused on local scenes, the nude, and videos. There are workshops, lectures, a library, and archives here. The **Woodstock Guild & Byrdcliffe Arts Colony** (845-679-2079), 34 Tinker Street, is open year-round Friday through Sunday 10–5. There are art exhibits, concerts, readings, and classes. A few doors away is the **Woodstock Artists' Association** (845-679-2940), 28 Tinker Street, open year-round Thursday through Monday noon–5, which offers a variety of work by local artists as well as being a museum representing artists of the original Woodstock Art Colony of the past. **Woodstock Framing Gallery** (845-679-6003), 31 Mill Hill Road, is open daily 11–5. The emphasis in this beautiful gallery, owned by longtime Woodstock resident Alice Hoffman, is on contemporary art, and the majority of exhibitors are Hudson Valley artists. Nationally renowned painter Richard Segalman, whose work is in several museums as well as galleries in New York City, Santa Fe, New Mexico, and Naples, Florida, shows his work in this gallery.

Diagonally across the street is the **Fletcher Gallery** (845-679-4411), 40 Mill Hill Road, with its focus on 20th-century American artists. The work of Peter Max, among others, has been shown here. Open Thursday through Sunday noon–5 and by appointment.

The **Art & Soul Gallery** (845-679-0027), 12 Tannery Brook Road, offers hand-painted photographs and changing shows by guest artists. They are open May through February, Thursday through Monday 11–6. Another interesting gallery is the **Hawthorn Gallery** (845-679-2711), 34 Elwyn Lane, which offers furniture, design, and architectural accessories from Asia. Open Friday through Sunday noon–6 or by appointment.

If you travel west out of the village of Woodstock toward Bearsville and make a right, staying on Route 212 when the road forks, you will come to the **Elena Zang Gallery** (845-679-5432), 3671 Route 212, Shady, just 4 miles outside of town. They are open daily year-round 11–5. This on-site pottery features handmade porcelain and stoneware along with contemporary painting and the sculpture of many internationally known artists, including Mary Frank, Joan Snyder, and Judy Pfaff. There is an outdoor sculpture show year-round in a beautiful garden setting. Visitors may walk around the grounds and enjoy the stream that runs through the property. Children are welcome.

A little farther along on Route 212 on the right is Harmati Lane; at this junction is where the **Genesis Studio/ Gallery** (845-679-4542) is located. The gallery, open May through December daily noon–5 or by appointment, features exotic creations inspired by the Middle East. Paintings and prints of the Holy Land, silver miniatures, Yemenite and Bedouin jewelry, replicas of ancient pottery, and ceramic dolls may be found here. Marble, stone, and steel sculptures are displayed along a path that encircles a pond. Visitors can take this walk and enjoy art in the outdoors.

If you continue west on Route 212, you will come to the **James Cox Gallery** (845-679-4265), 4666 Route 212, Willow, which is open year-round Monday through Friday 10–5 and on weekends by appointment. Cox is a veteran art dealer who relocated to Woodstock from Manhattan in 1990, and his gallery has changing exhibits of painting and sculpture in a beautiful garden setting. His wife, Marianna Goetz, exhibits her lovely paintings here, as well.

Farther south it's worth stopping in at the **Mark Gruber Gallery** (845-255-1241), New Paltz Plaza, New Paltz, close to the NYS Thruway exit 18, which specializes in Hudson Valley artists (primarily painters and photographers), with exhibits changing every six weeks. They are open Monday 11–5:30, Tuesday through Saturday 10–5:30. The **Highland Cultural Center** (845-691-6008), 54 Vineyard Avenue, Highland, has a gallery that is open Friday and Saturday 2–5 or by appointment, featuring changing exhibits with artists from throughout the United States. **The Women's Studio Workshop** (845-658-9133),

Binnewater Road, Rosendale, is open to the public, but call before you go; this is a working studio space. Changing exhibits year-round featuring artists from throughout the world.

POTTERY & CERAMICS Ulster County is home to the studios of several nationally renowned potters. For those travelers interested in visiting the artists' studios, 10 potteries are open to the public. They are located in High Falls, Stone Ridge, Accord, West Park, Bloomington, and West Hurley. The web site www.pottery-trail.com contains detailed directions and visuals of the work; or you can call Ulster County Tourism for the *Hudson Valley Pottery Trail* brochure (800-331-1518). A detailed map is included along with the hours that each studio is open.

✳ Special Events

February through March: Maple tours take place in late winter when the sap begins to run. There is absolutely nothing to match the fragrance of steamy maple syrup. At **Arrowhead Maple Syrup Farm** (845-626-7293), Route 209, Kerhonkson, tours are offered daily noon–5, but call before you go. **Lyonsville Sugarhouse and Farm** (845-687-2518), County Route 9, also offers tours, but call ahead for the schedule in season. **St. Patrick's Day Parade** (845-331-7517, 800-331-1518), Broadway, Kingston. Numerous bands and floats celebrate the wearing of the green with this annual, colorful celebration.

May: **Shad Festival** (845-338-0071), at the Rondout waterfront, by the Hudson River Maritime Museum. Admission fee. Enjoy shad roe dinners, demonstrations, crafts, trolley rides, and boat excursions at this annual celebration of the shad running up the Hudson River. Great for young children.

Memorial Day Weekend (and Labor Day Weekend): **Woodstock/New Paltz Art and Crafts Fair** (845-679-8087), Ulster County Fairgrounds, off Libertyville Road; follow Route 299 to the turnoff and signs. Shows are held Saturday and Sunday 10–6, Monday 10–5. Admission fee. This huge fair offers more than just booths of crafts; some of the region's finest artisans are on hand each year to exhibit their works. The craftspeople demonstrate their skills, which include quilting, scrimshaw, weaving, etching, pottery and broom making. There is a children's center with art projects for young fairgoers; face-painting is a popular activity. Furniture and architectural crafts, regionally produced foods, entertainment, wine, and dozens of food vendors are all there. The large tents will shield you from the sun, but dress appropriately for the weather—it can get very hot, both inside and outside the tents (and if it rains, make sure to wear heavy shoes . . . it does get muddy).

June: **Independence Day Celebration in Kingston** (845-331-7517), Rondout Waterfront. They always celebrate the weekend *before* July 4th in Kingston. Enjoy music, food, games, and fireworks after sunset.

July through Labor Day: **Belleayre Music Festival** (845-254-5600), Belleayre Ski Center, Route 28, Highmount. Admission fee. Call for ticket information. This wonderful outdoor music festival attracts outstanding performers to its mountaintop setting. The likes of Ray Charles, Linda Eder,

Wynton Marsalis, and Ricky Skaggs have entertained thousands, and the festival continues to grow with each passing season. There are seats under a tent as well as lawn seating, and the evening concerts offer a cool summer's night's entertainment. Get there early if you intend to sit on the lawn. There's plenty of parking, and the events are well organized. **July 4th Celebrations** (SUNY New Paltz campus, 845-255-0604), the music food and festivities start at 5, and fireworks begin at dusk. In Saugerties (Cantine Field, 945-246-3090), there is a parade at 11 AM and bands and vendors during the day. The fireworks begin at 9 PM. Free. **Hurley Stone House Day** (845-338-2283, 331-4121), Visit eight of America's oldest private homes (and a cemetery) that date back to the 17th and 18th centuries in this National Historic Landmark Dutch village on the second Saturday in July. There are costumed guides, a 1777 militia encampment, and colonial demonstrations. For those interested in history, this is a fascinating outing.

August: **Annual Catskill Heritage Festival** (845-688-2451), Catskill Corners, Mt. Tremper. Free. The Marketplace at Catskill Corners celebrates the region's cultural legacy with falconry, quilt exhibits, fly-tying demonstrations, mountain music, children's activities, and regional food tastings. Usually the first Sunday in August. **Ulster County Fair** (845-255-1380), Ulster County Fairgrounds, Libertyville Road, New Paltz. Admission fee. This annual country fair is a bargain since one-price admission includes all entertainment, shows, parking, exhibits, and the midway. If you have a bunch of kids with you, it's a great place to go the first weekend of the month. **Woodstock Poetry Festival** (845-679-0216), P.O. Box 450, Woodstock, NY 12498. The festival takes place in different venues throughout the town and is held the weekend before Labor Day weekend. Billy Collins (U.S. Poet Laureate), Lawrence Ferlinghetti, Sharon Olds, Michael McClure, and Ed Sanders are just some of the poets who read from their work and sign their books. There are dozens of events throughout the weekend. Separate admission to each event. **Annual Artists' Soapbox Derby** (845-331-7517), Rondout Waterfront, Kingston. Free. The car-like creations that ride down lower Broadway in the Rondout area are something to behold. If you are in town at this time, make sure to see this event. **Wild Blueberry & Huckleberry Festival** (845-647-7222), Ellenville. A celebration of the Shawangunk Mountains, with folk music, barbecue, all-blueberry bake sale, pie-judging contest, crafts, and exhibits. Free.

September: **Headless Horseman Hayrides** (845-339-2666), Route 9W, Ulster Park (last two weekends in September and every Friday, Saturday and Sunday in October). Admission fee. There are spectacular illusions, special effects, acres of thrills and chills, and a cast of over 100 performers to entertain you. Children will love this experience. **Woodstock Film Festival** (845-679-4265). Separate admission to each film or seminar. Screenings are offered in different venues throughout Woodstock and surrounding communities. Since 2000 the five-day program featuring more than 100 films—along with celebrity-led seminars, workshops, parties, and an awards ceremony—has grown in stature in the film industry. Book early to secure tickets. Tim Robbins, Ethan Hawke, Benjamin Bratt, Aidan Quinn, Marcia Gay Harden, Patricia Clarkson, Woody Harrelson, and Lili Taylor are just some of the featured speakers whose forthcoming films were screened here. Check the web site, www.woodstockfilmfestival.com, which is continually updated; tickets available on-line. **Hudson Valley Garlic Festival** (845-246-3090), Cantine Field, Saugerties, last weekend of the month. Admission fee. Visitors won't have to use a map to find this festival; the nutty fragrance of garlic attracts tens of thousands to this weekend celebration, where garlic-flavored foods—from pizza to ice cream—await the connoisseur. Craftspeople and entertainment enliven the daily activities, and there are dozens of garlic vendors and culinary information on hand. An unusual and fun weekend, regardless of how much garlic means to you!

October: **Reenactment of the Burning of Kingston** (845-331-7517). In 1777 the British invaded and burned the city of Kingston. Now the city reenacts the battle, complete with British and American troops and period music, crafts, food, and entertainment, including a colonial dance. The battle takes place the first weekend in October, but call for specific times and events. **Belleayre Mountain Fall Festival and Concerts** (845-254-5600), Highmount (just off Route 28, about 30 miles west of Kingston; watch for signs to the upper lodge. Open 10–5. Free (there is a charge for the ski lift). Held Saturday and Sunday of

Columbus Day weekend, this festival attracts thousands of leaf-peeping visitors. The fun goes on all day and includes bands, crafts, entertainment, German food, beer, chicken barbecue, and ski equipment sales. The festival is well run, and the site offers magnificent views of the mountains. Wear appropriate clothing, and get there early; the festival goes on rain or shine. (Keep in mind that the weather at Belleayre is always much cooler than you may expect, due to the high elevation.) **Mum Festival** (845-246-2809), Seamon Park, Route 9W, just south of the village of Saugerties. Open dawn to dusk. The park is free; admission fee to festival. For the entire month of October, Seamon Park is one big chrysanthemum celebration. Thousands of mums bloom throughout the 17–acre park at this time, and the display of yellow, lavender, and rust-colored flowers in shaped beds is breathtaking. Weekend festivals offer music, entertainment, and food, and there is a parade on opening day.

November: **Greek Festival** (845-331-3522), St. George Greek Orthodox Church, 294 Greenkill Avenue, Kingston. Free. Enjoy all the Greek culinary specialties here along with a holiday boutique. Held the weekend before Thanksgiving, Friday 5–10, Saturday 10–10, and Sunday 11–8.

International Pickle Festival (845-658-9649), Recreation Center, Route 32, Rosendale. Small admission fee. This unusual, fun festival is held the Sunday before Thanksgiving. There are dozens of food booths with wares from Germany, Romania, and Japan as well as throughout the U.S. Enjoy free samples, live music, and discover great holiday gifts. You can enter your pickled goods in the contests. There is even a pickle toss and pickle juice drinking contest. Kids of all ages will love this one.

December: **Victorian Tea** (845-647-5530), Terwilliger House Museum, Ellenville. Enjoy afternoon tea accompanied by homemade delicacies at this Queen Anne Victorian home decorated with seasonal greens and garlands. Music by the Ellenville High School chorus. Held the first Saturday in December, 1–3. **Wreath Fineries at 9 Wineries** (845-255-2494). Follow the Shawangunk Wine Trail and receive a handmade grapevine wreath at the first winery on the itinerary. At each of the nine wineries, receive an ornament to decorate your wreath, along with tastings of special holiday wines and foods. One ticket admission price admits you to all nine wineries. Oenophiles will not want to miss this seasonal event.

Delaware County

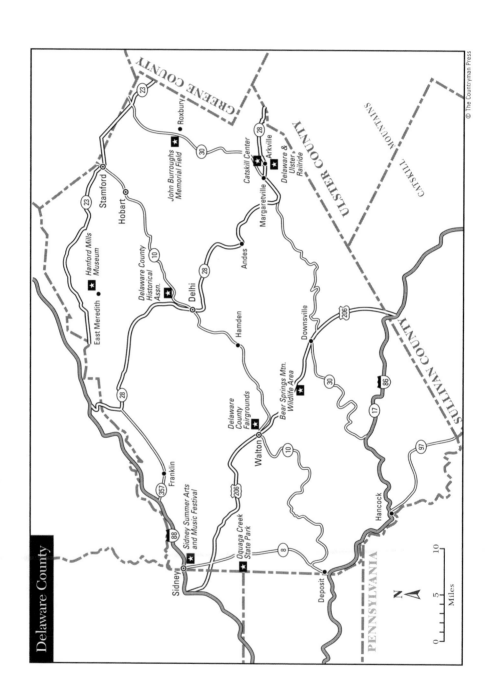

Delaware County

© The Countryman Press

DELAWARE COUNTY

One of the largest counties in New York (about the size of Rhode Island), Delaware County is a region of rolling meadows, curious cows, and small villages that look as if they were plucked from a 19th-century picture book. More than 64,000 acres are state owned and have been proclaimed "forever wild." This foresight has resulted in an area that is a paradise for anglers, canoeists, kayakers, hikers, bikers, walkers, and those who just enjoy rural charm and an old-fashioned way of life coupled with modern convenience and an easy drive.

Much of the charm of Delaware County comes from the strong influence of the 19th century, which turns up in local architecture and community get-togethers. Towns throughout the county are filled with homes and commercial buildings of Federal, Queen Anne, Greek Revival, Italianate and other styles; drive along the back roads, and you will find dairy farms and mountain views nearly unchanged for over a century. From winter pancake breakfasts to holiday open houses, from county fairs to summer auctions, the region brings back a sense of community celebration that has been lost in much of modern life.

GUIDANCE **Delaware County Chamber of Commerce** (607-746-2281, 800-642-4443), 114 Main Street, Delhi 13753; wwwdelawarecounty.org.

GETTING THERE *By car:* Delaware County is most easily reached by taking the New York State (NYS) Thruway, exit 19 at Kingston, to Route 28 west (toward Pine Hill), and following Route 28 into the county. Route 30 intersects with Route 28 in Margaretville.

By bus: **Adirondack Trailways** (800-858-8555) operates daily bus service from New York City to several towns in Delaware County. Call for information on tours and charters as well as schedules and fares if you are traveling on your own.

MEDICAL EMERGENCY Be aware that public telephones are scarce in the county, and cellular service is limited. In the event of an emergency, call 911, the **Delaware County Sheriff** (607-746-2336) or the **New York State Police** (607-432-3211).

Delaware Valley Hospital has four family health centers in the county that have 24-hour emergency care: **Walton** (607-865-2400), 2 Titus Place; **Downsville** (607-363-2517), Main Street; **Hancock** (607-637-4715), 46 East Front Street; **Roscoe** (607-498-4800), East Main Street.

Margaretville Memorial Hospital (845-586-2631), Route 28, Margaretville.

O'Connor Hospital (607- 746-0300), Andes Road, Delhi.

✳ To See

Gideon Frisbee Homestead at the Delaware County Historical Association (607-746-3849), Route 10, 2 miles north of Delhi. Open May through October Tuesday through Sunday 11–4. Admission fee. A fascinating site comprised of historic buildings that have been donated, purchased, or just rescued from neglect, where visitors can get a taste of life in rural America during the 19th century. The main building houses a library and exhibit hall, where changing displays of farm tools, household goods, folk art, and crafts are offered each season. Additional interpretive exhibits focus on different aspects of farm life in several of the other buildings. The Gideon Frisbee House, a 1797 example of Federal-style architecture, once served as a tavern, county meeting room, post office, and the private home of a local judge. The interior has been restored to reflect the changes in life from pioneer days to the period just before World War I. Decorative arts and furniture collections include Belter chairs, woven rugs, souvenir glassware, and a chair that tradition holds was used at the Constitutional Convention. The Frisbee barn houses a collection of farm implements and a permanent exhibit titled "It's a Fine Growing Time," which guides the visitor through the joys and hard work of a farmer's year. Other buildings include the gunsmith's and blacksmith's shops, the schoolhouse (still in use for educational programs), a tollhouse, a farm lane, and even a family cemetery. Special events include a farm festival at which you can enjoy demonstrations of old-fashioned rural skills.

Hanford Mills Museum (607-278-5744) Take Route 28 to the intersection of Routes 10 and 12 in East Meredith; follow the signs. Open daily May through October 10–5, with some special events in the off-season. Admission fee. Once the industrial center of the surrounding farm country, the mill has today been restored to its clanking and chugging past. Flour, lumber, wooden goods (like butter tubs and porch posts), and electricity (courtesy of nearby Kortright Creek) were all produced at Hanford Mills, one of the few remaining industrial mills of the last century still in use. Visitors will see lathes, jigsaws, and other machines used to produce woodenware, along with the pulleys and belts that were once the staples of manufacturing. Inside the mill itself, a series of catwalks and walkways wind through the workrooms where museum interpreters are hard at work; downstairs, the enormous metal reconstruction of the original wooden waterwheel is turned by the millpond waters. Throughout the site, water-generated electricity powers lightbulbs and machines, a reminder of the time when light didn't come with the simple flick of a switch. Also on the site is the Gray Barn, in which there are agricultural and farm equipment displays, a shingle mill, the millpond, and the mill store, where local crafts are sold. Hanford Mills hosts several special events each year, including fly-fishing clinics at the millpond, Independence Day complete with ice cream and speeches, and late-winter's Ice Harvest Day (when the ice is cut and stored for the summer ice cream social).

Healing Waters Farm and Carriage Museum (607-865-4420), Route 206, Walton (1 mile west of town). Open April through December, Wednesday and Thursday 11–6, Friday 10–4, Saturday and Sunday 11–4. The beautiful, restored, huge red barn here holds a collection of antique carriages from New York State and Pennsylvania, while the petting zoo includes a baby camel, buffalo, zebra, emus, llamas, sheep, goats, pheasants, and a variety of exotic pets. This is a working farm; in addition to raising horses, owner Ken Schrider has chickens for eggs, sheep for shearing, bees for honey, and free-range turkeys. The carriages seem as though they have just been unhitched from a team of horses. An Amish man in Pennsylvania, who still drives and builds horse-drawn buggies today, restores and repairs these carriages, which include double-benched covered carriages, winter sleighs, speed wagons, a doctor's buggy, and a rare hearse. All were in use during the 19th and early 20th century. Hayrides and special-themed group and educational tours are available. There are four shops on the premises: one for antiques, another for herbs (it was once the chicken coop), a toy shop, and a tack shop. Children will especially enjoy themselves here.

HISTORIC SITES Delaware and Ulster Railride (845-586-DURR), Route 28, Arkville. Open late May through October; schedules vary. Entrance to the site and depot is free, but admission is charged for the ride. The Catskill Mountains were once a daily stop for tourist and milk trains from New York City, but when the service stopped in the 1960s, many believed the echo of a train whistle was

HANFORD MILLS MUSEUM, A RESTORED INDUSTRIAL CENTER

Peter Finger

gone forever from the valleys. The Railride has resurrected some of the favorite trains that rattled along the tracks, and there is no better way to sample the fun of old-time travel than to hop aboard any of the vintage propelled trains still at work. Or take some photos of the farms and homes; many tell a tale or two about train history. Special events, held throughout the summer and fall, include a costumed train robbery, a fiddler's get-together, Halloween ghost trains, foliage runs, and more. All the tours begin at the restored Arkville Depot, and you'll find a gift shop, snack caboose, and rest rooms on-site. Wheelchair accessible.

John Burroughs Homestead & Woodchuck Lodge Historic Site (607-326-3722), John Burroughs Memorial Road, Roxbury. Take Route 30 north through Roxbury and follow signs. Open June through September weekends only 10–5 or by appointment year-round. Free. Although this is not an "active" site, the former writing studio and grave of nature writer John Burroughs is worth a stop. A friend of Teddy Roosevelt, Henry Ford, and Thomas Edison, Burroughs is a respected American nature writer whose many essays spoke of Delaware County, the Catskills, and the Hudson Valley. Today his writing nook, Woodchuck Lodge, is maintained by his family (although open on a limited basis, you can view the site from the road). Just up the road is Memorial Field—which contains Boyhood Rock, where Burroughs spent many hours observing the natural world—and the Burroughs gravesite. This is a quiet spot with a breathtaking view of the Catskills, a lovely place to sit and enjoy the same scene that inspired a great author.

SAMPLE OLD-TIME TRAVEL AT THE DELAWARE AND ULSTER RAILRIDE.

Peter Finger

SCENIC DRIVES Delaware County offers the driver many lovely views and well-maintained main roads, but—as in any other rural area—some of the back roads can be tricky in bad weather, four-wheel drive or not. Snow and ice can make the steeper stretches of both paved and dirt roads treacherous. And once off state or county routes (town roads), there are often no signs with road names, and it's easy to get lost unless you have a county road map. Deer and other wildlife are also a problem, especially at night, so be aware and don't speed.

If you want to see dairy farms, cornfields, the county seat, and the Pepacton Reservoir, start in

A COVERED BRIDGE NEAR HAMDEN

Peter Finger

Margaretville and follow Route 28 to Delhi. The town square in Delhi was painted by Norman Rockwell about 50 years ago and appeared on the cover of the *Saturday Evening Post*. The town square still looks very much as it did back then, and the gazebo was recently restored. Pick up Route 10 and take it south to Walton; pick up Route 206 and go east to Downsville. Then take Route 30 back to Margaretville. The roads are well marked, and you will pass two covered bridges along the way, one near Hamden, the other outside of Downsville. This drive also takes you past farm stands (some on the honor system: choose your produce, and put your money in a box), including Octagon Farms near Walton, where an eight-sided house has been made into a bed & breakfast (see *Lodging*). Legend has it that the ghost of a young woman killed in a carriage accident roams the road at night. If you have the time, you can detour through Delhi and follow the signs west to Franklin on the Franklin Turnpike, a winding road that offers beautiful vistas in summer.

A second county drive follows part of the old turnpike which was a major stage-coach route through the area. From **Margaretville,** follow Route 28 west to Andes and then to Delhi, then take Route 10 north to Stamford, make a right onto Route 23 and drive to Grand Gorge, and finally, turn right onto Route 30 and head south back to Margaretville. If you have a chance, stop in Stamford and look at some of the grand homes that made this village a popular turn-of-the-20th-century resort area and gave it the name "Queen of the Catskills."

If you wish to drive up **Mount Utsayantha,** follow Route 23 east to Mountain Avenue; the twisty road is accessible in spring, summer, and fall, and the views are beautiful. Call the **Department of Environmental Conservation** in Stamford (607-652-7365) for more information about this drive or hike. The headwaters of the Delaware River East Branch rise alongside Route 30 between Grand Gorge and Roxbury, and the road back to Margaretville passes through farm country.

The Catskill (Susquehanna) Turnpike once ran from the village of Catskill in Greene County to the village of **Unadilla** on the Susquehanna River. In Delaware County, the turnpike is now followed by town roads from Stamford west to Franklin, then along Route 357 to Unadilla. Some of the original stone mileage markers for the turnpike can still be seen along this route. There are hilltop views for miles along the turnpike near where it crosses Route 28.

A lovely drive follows along the shores of the two reservoirs: Pepacton and Cannonsville. From **Margaretville** head southwest along Route 30, which follows the Pepacton Reservoir to Downsville; then go northwest to Walton on Route 206, and head southwest again along Route 10 to Deposit. There are a few crossings over the reservoirs and both dams are in view.

✷ To Do

AUCTIONS It may seem that everything is auctioned off in Delaware County: Don't be surprised—it is. Cows, puppies, cabbages, eggs, Shaker chairs, Irish pewter, even antique coffins have all shown up in the hands of auctioneers. Auction lovers don't need to plan ahead; just pick up a copy of the local newspaper and look for a sale. (Local newspapers include the *Delaware County Times,* the *Mountain Eagle,* and the *Walton Reporter.*) Some auctions are weekly institutions, attended by locals and weekenders alike; others are specialty sales for real estate or farm equipment, and still others are one-time-only house sales, where the contents of a home can include some surprises.

Country auctions are fun, but there are some helpful tips to follow. Get there early: carefully examine the goods before the sale, and sign up for a card or paddle. Bring a chair for outdoor auctions plus a hat or umbrella, depending on the weather. Most auctions advertise that they accept "cash or good checks"—but in the latter case, this can be tricky if you are from out of state or not known to the auctioneer; call ahead for information. Don't buy anything you can't carry, unless you plan to make shipping arrangements. And, finally, know what you're bidding on: Don't get stuck with the overstuffed armchair because you thought you were getting the Tiffany lamp.

Roberts' Auction (845-254-4490), Main Street, Fleischmanns (park in the lot or along the street), has an auction every Saturday night at 7, year-round. You will find everything here from fine antiques to a better grade of junk. Auctioneer Eddie Roberts keeps the sale moving, and you will never be bored. The crowd is often a lively mix of locals and visitors; there are rest rooms and a snack bar. Get there early since many seats are reserved and the others go fast.

McIntosh Auction Service (607-832-4241), junction of Routes 28 & 30, Margaretville, has Saturday night auctions at 6:30 year-round. There is plenty of parking here. Seats go fast, and auctioneer Chuck McIntosh keeps everyone happy with quick sales and good humor. Everything from furniture to blackberries to fine antiques is sold here. They also do many on-site auctions throughout the summer.

BICYCLING Delaware County offers a range of terrain that will appeal to downhill racers as well as those seeking a scenic tour by bike. For those seeking on-road routes, the **Delaware County Chamber of Commerce** has developed a series of bike tours that range in length from 15 to 100 miles and are graded according to terrain. The tours are posted on their web site or you can request a printed version (see *Guidance*).

For **off-road trips,** there is the **Catskill Scenic Trail** (607-652-2281), a 19-mile Rails-to-Trails corridor. The CST can be accessed at various points, and there are designated parking areas: one is at the historic Stamford Depot at the intersection of Railroad Avenue and South Street in the village of Stamford. There is also a parking lot north of Route 10, just east of the village of Bloomville. The CST is marked with octagonal signs that show the distance to the trailhead in the direction you are facing. There is only a 400 foot change in elevation over the entire 19 miles. Stamford is the peak, and it is downhill in both directions from that point, so I suggest you begin the tour there!

Bike Plattekill Mountain Resort (1-800-GOTTA BIKE, 607-326-3500), Plattekill Mountain Road, Roxbury. Open April through November on weekends and holidays, July through Labor Day on Friday, weekends, and holidays. Admission fee. This outstanding mountain bike area offers equipment rentals, a chairlift ride to the summit, and more than 60 miles of trails. Beginners shouldn't be wary of trying mountain biking here since a package deal provides a bike, lift ticket, helmet, and one-hour lesson with a guide; riders can then enjoy the exercise all day. There are also guided road tours available, including an historical biking tour of the village of Roxbury. Sanctioned races (N.O.R.B.A.) are held throughout the season, and the site has dining and camping facilities. This is a great weekend stop any time of year.

CANOEING & KAYAKING The East and West Branches of the Delaware River as well as the Susquehanna offer spectacular opportunities for canoeists and kayakers. Some of the best canoeing in the county may be found along the western border near Pennsylvania. A word of caution: Like all water sports, don't attempt to canoe or kayak unless you are familiar with the rivers. Both the Delaware and Susquehanna can be treacherous, especially in spring or after a heavy rain. Your best bet is to use one of the canoe outfitting services, which will provide the right equipment, maps, and even a shuttle service.

Al's Sport Store (607-363-7740), junction of Routes 30 & 206, Downsville, is a clearinghouse for canoe, kayak, and fishing information. They rent equipment and have tours in season.

Catskill Outfitters (1-800-631-0105), Delaware & North Streets, Walton, can supply everything you need for an outing.

Peaceful Valley Campground (607-363-2211), Route 30, Shinhopple, offers limited outfitting services: you will find the basic equipment here, no extras.

Smith's Canoe & Drift Boat Rental (607-637-2989), Route 97, Hancock, rents canoes and kayaks for day trips.

Car top boat launches are permitted at **Big Pond,** Andes (607-652-7365), **Little Pond,** Little Pond Campground (845-439-5480), **Trout Pond and Mud Pond,** Cherry Ridge Wild Forest, Colchester (607-652-7365), **Huggins Lake,** Middle

Mountain Wild Forest (607-652-7365), and **Bear Spring Mountain Public Campground,** East Trout Brook Road, Walton (607-865-6989).

FARM STANDS When the harvest begins in early summer with strawberries and flowers, farm stands begin to blossom along the roadsides, as well. In Delaware County there are many farm stands where you can pick out the produce, bag it, and leave the money for the owner. Other stands are a bit more formal, but they all stock the best local fruits, vegetables, maple syrup, and honey. Days and hours of operation vary widely with the season and the stock, and some crops, including strawberries, seem to disappear after only a few days, so the best way to find local produce is to watch for roadside stands or stop and ask at the nearest town. This is also savvy farm country; in the past few years, county agriculture has "grown" to include such specialty crops as blue potatoes and garlic, which often turn up in Manhattan's trendiest restaurants.

The largest and best produce market in the county is the **Pakatakan Farmers Market,** at the Kelly Round Barn, Route 30, Halcottsville (north of Margaretville). Open May through October Saturdays 9–3. Vendors offer everything from fresh trout, organic produce, and bouquets of wildflowers to fine crafts and home-baked pies. Selections change with the seasons, and there is plenty of food to sample, so have a light breakfast or lunch!

Other county farmers markets include: **Andes Farmers Market,** Main Street, Andes, open June through October Saturdays 9–3; **Delhi Farmers Market**, Courthouse Square, Main Street, Delhi, open June through September Wednesdays 11–2; **Koo Koose Farmers Market,** Main Street, Deposit, open June through October Saturdays 9–1.

Mac's Farm Stand is located on Route 28 near Delhi, just before the turn into town. The stand stocks a wide variety of produce throughout the summer and into apple season.

Roxbury Gardens Stand can be found roadside on Route 30, just south of Roxbury Village. Choose your produce and leave your payment. Selections vary with the season, although you will generally find great corn, melons, squash, apples, and tomatoes.

Quarltere's Garden and Marketplace (607-326-4282), Route 30, Roxbury, has a fine selection of plants and produce.

Octagon Farm Market (607-865-7416), 34055 State Highway 10, Walton, sells its own fruits and vegetables along with lots of other local offerings and has a large selection of apples and excellent cider in the autumn.

Honey lovers may want to check out **Herklotz Apiaries** (607-829-8687), Merrickville Road, Franklin (open year-round), for its selection of sweets, candies, and other honey-related items. **Crescent Valley Apiaries,** New Kingston Road, Bovina (watch for signs), also stocks honey from its hives, as does **Ballard Honey,** Main Street, Roxbury.

Because the tree-tapping season is so changeable, maple syrup lovers should call the **Delaware County Chamber of Commerce** (607-746-2281) for up-to-date information on farms that offer sap-season tours; the chamber also publishes a farm bounty map.

FISHING Delaware County is home to the East and West Branches of the Delaware River, the Susquehanna River, and the Beaverkill Creek; it is served by the Cannonsville, Pepacton, and Schoharie Reservoirs, making fishing a popular sport in this region. The Beaverkill is probably the most famous trout fishing stream in America, the birthplace of fly-fishing, so if you want to try the sport, this is one of the best places anywhere to start. New York State fishing licenses are required. They are easy to purchase in most towns; check with the town clerk or at the village offices. For reservoir fishing, special permits are required—call the **Department of Environmental Conservation** regional office (607-652-7366) for information on permits and maps. Stream fishing areas that are open to the public are indicated by brown-and-yellow wooden signs along the streams and rivers; most areas offer off-road parking, as well. Detailed maps are available where you purchase your fishing license and at town offices. Riverfront property may be posted or off-limits as part of the New York City watershed, so the maps should be consulted; heavy fines could result from illegal fishing. Further information on specific fishing areas can be obtained by calling 800-642-4443.

GOLF Golf enthusiasts will appreciate the courses in Delaware County, where the lush greens of summer and the blazing trees of autumn provide everyone—duffer and hacker alike—a lovely setting in which to play. Greens fees vary depending on the season and the length of the membership, so call for specific information.

Delhi College Golf Course (607-746-GOLF), Scotch Mountain Road (off Route 28), Delhi, has a course that is used as a training area for students in the turf management program. It's a small gem—though it's a full 18 holes—and rarely overcrowded.

French Woods Golf & Country Club (845-887-5000), Hancock. This 18-hole, par-72 course is a challenging one in a beautiful country setting.

Hanah Golf & Country Club (845-586-4849), Route 30, Margaretville, has an 18-hole course, practice greens, and a driving range. There is also a golf school on the premises.

Hancock Golf Course (607-637-2480), Golf Course Road, Hancock, is a nine-hole, par-36 course that is a good choice for novices.

Hardwood Hills Golf Course (607-467-2347), Route 8, Masonville, is a nine-hole, par-36 course.

Meadows Golf Center (845-586-4104), Route 28, Margaretville, has a nine-hole, par-27 course, miniature golf, lessons, night golf, and a driving range. Those who just want to practice their techniques should head here, where young golfers will enjoy themselves, as well.

Sheperd Hills Golf Course (607-326-7121), Golf Course Road, Roxbury, has a hilly 18-hole course with beautiful views of the countryside.

Stamford Golf Club (607-652-7398), Taylor Road (off Route 10), Stamford. Complete facilities, 18 holes, and a driving range.

HIKING A large part of Delaware County is part of the "forever wild" park system in New York State. A number of the existing hiking trails are for experienced hikers only, and some require overnight stays in simple trail huts; those who would like detailed trail information should contact the **Catskill Forest Preserve** regional office in Stamford (607-652-7366). However, the preserve does contain more than 300 miles of trails that vary in length from a half mile to almost 100 miles, so even novice hikers will find something that they are comfortable taking on, whether for a day or an overnight. Trail brochures are available.

Americorps Outdoor Education Center (607-746-4051), Route 28, Delhi, offers woods walks, educational excursions, and a nature preserve with marked trails. A good place to introduce children to hiking.

The Catskill Center for Conservation and Development (845-586-2611), Route 28 Arkville, has special events including guided hikes, bird walks, and snowshoe excursions. Call for a schedule and to find out about membership.

Catskill Scenic Trail (CST) (607-652-2821), Railroad Avenue, Stamford (see *Bicycling*), has a marked 19-mile Rails-to-Trails area that offers a hard-packed surface and gentle grade perfect for hiking, biking, horseback riding, and cross-country skiing. An excellent choice for families with young children.

Oquaga Creek State Park (607-467-4160), Route 20, Masonville. Open year-round. There are 6.5 miles of marked hiking trails that will delight people of all abilities. The park is in three counties: Delaware, Broome, and Chenango.

Utsayantha Trail System (607-652-7581), Stamford. This marked trail system takes hikers through scenic mountaintops and serene valleys. Call in advance for trail map.

West Branch Preserve (518-272-0195), Hamden. This 446-acre preserve features a 0.7-mile moderate trail and a strenuous 2-mile mountainside trail for experienced hikers.

HORSEBACK RIDING There are miles of trails to ride on in Delaware County as well as private stables where beginners can go on a guided ride or take lessons.

Bear Spring Mountain State Park (607-865-6989, 1-800-456-CAMP), Route 206, Walton. This is the only campground in New York State specifically designed for use by horseback riders. Specially designed campsites accommodate horse trailers and provide horse lodging facilities. They have miles of trails here that will delight those who like to travel with their horses.

Catskill Scenic Trail (607-652-2821) The CST may be picked up in Bloomville, Stamford, Grand Gorge, or Hobart by those who are looking for wooded trails. There are 19 miles of gently graded trails here (see *Bicycling* and *Hiking*).

For those seeking trail rides and riding lessons: **Harper Hill Farm** (607-278-5224), Harpersfield; **Hilltop Stables** (607-832-4342), Bovina Center;

Sagamore Stables (607-865-8775), Colchester; **Sanfords Horse Farm** (845-586-2985), Margaretville; **Stone Tavern Farm** (607-326-2973), Roxbury; **Willowview Hill Farm** (607-652-2917), Stamford; and **Windswept Acres Appaloosas** (607-746-6990), DeLancey.

The Night Pasture Horse Farm (607-588-6926), Route 23, 2 miles west of the center of Grand Gorge. This 56-acre horse farms boasts a large indoor arena, a tack room, lessons, and quality horses for sale at reasonable prices. The Horseplay Tack Shop (on the premises) offers the horse enthusiast everything from bridles and saddles to a variety of gifts. Both new and used equipment are also for sale. The Catskill Scenic Trail may be accessed from the parking area.

Mountain Breeze Miniature Horse Farm (607-588-6208). Route 23, Grand Gorge, breeds little horses as well as the larger minis. The owners, Glenda and Earl Krom, offer a variety of horses for sale year-round. (The animals are handled regularly, which makes them friendly.) Stop by this lovely farm if you are considering a miniature horse as a potential pet. The kids will love petting the miniature donkeys and newborn horses.

SKIING

Downhill
Bobcat Ski Center (845-676-3143), Route 28, Andes. Open December through March, Friday through Sunday and holidays 9–4. There are 19 trails and slopes, and a 1,050-foot drop at this old-fashioned family ski area, which has been in business for over 40 years. Rentals (snowboards and skis), restaurant, and full services. A nice place for beginners; there is still a T-bar lift operating here.

Ski Plattekill (1-800-NEED 2 SKI), Plattekill Mountain Road, Roxbury. Open December through March, Friday through Sunday and during the week on

ENJOY OLD-FASHIONED FAMILY SKIING AT BOBCAT SKI CENTER.

Peter Finger

school holidays 9–4. There is a vertical drop of 1,100 feet and 35 trails, 4 lifts, including the Northface Express double chairlift. They make snow here, and snowboarders are welcome. There is a snowtubing park, along with rentals, lessons, and a snack bar. Shuttle service via bus direct from New York City and New Jersey; call for schedule.

Cross Country and Snowshoeing

Catskill Outdoor Education Center (607-746-4112), Route 28, Delhi. There are marked trails here for cross-country skiing and guided snowshoe walks for groups of six or more by advance reservation.

Kirkside Park (607-326-3722), Main Street, Roxbury. Free. This historic 11-acre treasure was formerly the estate of Helen Gould-Shepard, daughter of railroad magnate and Roxbury native son Jay Gould. Rich in natural beauty and history, and recently restored to its glorious splendor, Kirkside has rustic Adirondack-style bridges, graceful paths along the East Branch of the Delaware River, and lush plantings to admire in the warm weather months. During the winter, however, this is a wonderful place to cross-country ski. A good bet for those with young children. There are a variety of special events held here year-round (see *Special Events*).

Ski Plattekill Mountain Resort (607-326-3500), Plattekill Mountain Road, Roxbury. There are over 12 miles of cross-country ski trails (beginner to advanced); open to the public for a fee if you are not a guest of the hotel. Maps of the trails are provided. Lessons and guided snowshoe tours available by reservation.

✳ Lodging

Bed & breakfasts provide a special way to see Delaware County, and most are moderately priced; some offer package rates or special discounts during the midweek period. Make reservations since many book up over holiday weekends and when there are special events. For further information call the **Delaware County B&B Association,** P.O. Box 41, Delhi 13753 (800-335-4667); www.delinns.com. Since Delaware County is the second largest county in New York State, all entries are listed by village for your convenience.

Andes
Padrino's Bed & Breakfast (845-676-4542), Main Street, Andes. ($) There are only three rooms, all with private bath, upstairs from their restaurant (see *Dining Out*), but the breakfast is hearty, and the price is right. Make sure to have dinner here during your stay. This is a good choice for those who prefer the activity of a village rather than a more secluded establishment.

Bovina Center
The Country House at Bramley Mountain Farm (607-832-4371), Box 109, Bramley Mountain Road, Bovina Center 13740. ($) Built circa 1840, this 600-acre working farm features hand-stenciled walls and lovely wooden floors. Hiking, fishing, and swimming are available on the property, and guests can enjoy a full breakfast on the front porch or in the gazebo, weather permitting. Three guest rooms, all with private bath. Open year-round.

The Mountain Brook Inn (1-877-MYBROOK), 5333 County Route 6, Bovina Center 13740. When you walk across the brook to the inn, you will hear the brook and see the garden. This 36-acre miniparadise with an 18th-century stone bridge will be particularly appreciated by those who love seclusion. Eight suites, all with private bath, living room, and kitchen. It's like having your own place in the country, with acres of hiking trails and places to fish (there are two waterways on the property). Enjoy playing croquet, badminton, and horseshoes. Continental breakfast, custom made to your taste, arrives at your door at 8. A 15-minute drive to Margaretville, Andes, Delhi; 45 minutes to Cooperstown. Open year-round.

Stoneflower B&B (607-832-4805), 1783 Crescent Valley Road, Bovina Center 13740. ($$) Country decor and furnishings adorn this cozy home with barn beams and lovely views. Three suites all with private bath, one with a Jacuzzi. Open year-round. Children welcome.

Swallows Nest B&B (607-832-4547), 159 Miller Avenue, Bovina Center 13740. ($$) Set in the midst of the Catskills, this 1840 farmhouse tastefully blends the past and present. Relax on the porch by the pond or brook. Full gourmet breakfast. Hiking, fishing, horseback riding, and skiing are all nearby. Two rooms have private baths; two have their own bath, but it is located outside the room. Open year-round.

Delhi and Grand Gorge
The Colonial Motel (607-588-6122), 37283 Lower Main Street (a few hundred feet east of the junction of Routes 30 and 23), Grand Gorge 12434. ($) Calling this establishment a motel is really a misnomer. Several rooms are located in a large Victorian house adjacent to the motel. All have private bath. Reasonable prices; a good bet for those traveling with children. Many rooms have microwave ovens and refrigerators; some have small kitchens. Open year-round.

Matthew's Pond B&B (607-829-5222), 7051 County Highway 14 (intersection of Turnpike Road), Delhi. ($) A 200-year-old Federal-style home that is steeped in history—a former stop on the stagecoach line, a general store, and at one time, the only post office in the area. It has also been a funeral parlor! Three rooms share one bath. Open year-round.

Deposit
Chestnut Inn on Oquaga Lake (607-467-2500), 498 Oquaga Lake Road, Deposit 13754. ($$) This 30-room inn (10 suites with private baths; for remaining rooms, every two rooms share one bath) also has two private lakeside cottages. A quaint, well-appointed building, entirely chestnut inside, that has been restored to its original 1920s splendor. The owner will let you borrow a book or two about the inn's history (so inquire if you're interested). Continental breakfast is served in the restaurant on the premises (see *Dining Out*). Open April through December. Children welcome.

Scotts Oquaga Lake House (607-467-3094), P.O. Box 47, Oquqaga Lake, Deposit 13754. ($$) This family vacation resort on 1,100 acres offers evening entertainment (cabaret show) as well as an array of daytime activities, including golf, tennis, waterskiing, fishing, biking, and hiking. Three meals daily are included with the price of the room. Good value.

Downsville

Victoria Rose B&B (607-363-7838), Main Street, Downsville 13755. ($$) A lovely Queen Anne home, filled with antiques and country touches, where guests enjoy breakfast, tea, and evening snacks. Four rooms, each with private bath. Open year-round.

Adams' Farmhouse B&B (607-363-2757), Main Street, Downsville 13755. ($) Old farmhouse converted into a gingerbread Victorian and furnished with antiques. Two rooms, each with a double bed, share one bathroom. A separate trailer in the back of the house, right by a brook, accommodates those traveling with children or pets. Open May through November.

Fleischmanns, Halcottsville, Margaretville

The Carriage House Inn (607-326-7992), Main Street, Halcottsville 12438. ($) This Victorian house, more than 100 years old, still has many of its original furnishings; it is run by the builder's granddaughter, whose homemade breakfast breads and muffins are local favorites. Sherry and herbal tea are offered to guests in the afternoon. The house is set in a tiny hamlet that lies along the Delaware River, and there are many places to stroll the country lanes. Four rooms share two baths. Children welcome. Open year-round.

Hanah Country Inn & Resort (845-586-2100), Route 30, Margaretville 12455. ($$$) A recent renovation has expanded this inn into a full-service resort and conference center. There is a championship 18-hole golf course (see To Do—Golf), health club, tennis courts, indoor and outdoor swimming pools, fishing stream, and restaurant. (Golfers may want to note that a nationally recognized school is held at the inn every summer.) The lovely rooms have private bath and all the amenities one would expect at a fine hotel. Children welcome. Open year-round.

Margaretville Mountain Inn (845-586-3933), Margaretville Mountain Road, Margaretville 12455. ($$$) This restored 11-bedroom Victorian home was built as a boardinghouse and functioned as a working farm. It offers a spectacular view of the New Kingston Valley from the old-fashioned veranda. It's just a short drive from town. A full breakfast is served in an elegant dining room; outdoors on the veranda, if you like, in summer. Six rooms, all with private bath. There are limited facilities available for children and pets; call ahead for information. Open year-round.

River Run (845-254-4884), 882 Main Street, Fleischmanns 12430. ($$) This restored 20-room house has a two-bedroom suite and eight guest rooms with either private or shared bath. The yard slopes down to the river, and guests can easily walk into the center of town. (There is a great country auction only minutes away every Saturday night; see To Do—Auctions). The unusual aspect of this inn is that it welcomes both children and pets (just give the innkeepers some notice about the four-footed family members). Breakfast is hearty and healthy, and the inn has lots of antiques, stained glass, and old-fashioned comfort to offer visitors. There is a labyrinth with a stone path in the backyard, at the foot of the garden, by the water—the owners created this for fun; I am told that it intrigues many guests.

Susan's Pleasant Pheasant Farm (607-326-4266), 1 Bragg Hollow Road on Lake Wawaka, Halcottsville 12438. ($$) This is a terrific place to go if you want to kayak or canoe when you wake up in the morning. There are four rooms, all with private baths. Open year-round.

Meridale
The Old Stageline Stop B&B (607-746-6856), Turnpike Road, Meridale 13806. ($$) Enjoy a carefree stay in a 1900s farmhouse that was formerly a dairy farm and is set high on a hill with magnificent views. The rooms are decorated with country furnishings. A full breakfast is served in the sun-filled dining room or on the porch, weather permitting. Four rooms, all with private bath. Open year-round.

Walton
Octagon Bed & Breakfast (607-865-7416), Route 10, Walton 13856. ($) This bed & breakfast is housed in a historic octagonal house dating back to 1855; it is across the street from a farm stand also run by the owners. This is one of only eight brick octagonal houses in America. Enjoy a traditional farmer's breakfast in the morning: it may include pancakes and sausage in the winter months or eggs and waffles in the summer. Four rooms share one and a half baths. There are also additional accommodations: a private cottage and a creek-side house, an excellent choice for families. Make sure to inquire about the variety of possibilities here. Children welcome. Open year-round.

✳ Where to Eat
Casual is the word for Delaware County restaurants, where moderate prices are the rule, even at dinner. Hours and days of operation may vary

with the seasons, so it is wise to call ahead if you are making a long trip. In general, reservations are not necessary, except on holiday weekends.

DINING OUT
Andes/Delhi
Andes Hotel (845-676-4408), Main Street, Andes. ($$) Open daily for lunch noon–3; dinner 5–9. Housed in a historic building, this bustling restaurant and tavern features mouthwatering American favorites at reasonable prices. The prime rib, steak *au poivre*, house-cut fries, twice-baked horseradish potato, and garlic spinach are some of my favorites from the imaginative menu. Children are welcome.

Old Caledonia Tea Room (607-746-9590), 106 Main Street, Delhi. ($$) Open for lunch, Tuesday through Saturday, 11:30–3; dinner 5–9; High Tea is served June through October 3:30–5. This tearoom/restaurant is absolutely charming. It is furnished with antiques, and the food is quite good and nicely presented.

Padrino's (845-676-4542), Main Street, Andes. ($$) Open Monday, Tuesday, Thursday, Friday, and Saturday for dinner 4–10. Irene, the chef-owner, makes escarole soup that brought tears to the eyes of one diner: "I haven't had soup like that since my mother died," he said. The mouthwatering Italian-American specialties here include veal scaloppini, chicken a la Ella (sautéed chicken breasts, artichoke hearts, and mushrooms with fresh mozzarella cheese), a 16-ounce T-bone steak, shrimp Roma (sautéed shrimp with tomatoes and onions and a splash of sambuca). The homemade tiramisu, cheesecake, and cream puffs are superb. There are also three rooms upstairs over the restaurant—all with private bath—available for bed & breakfast at a reasonable price (see *Lodging*). The relaxed, informal atmosphere and terrific food make this fairly new addition to the Andes restaurant scene a must.

Arkville, Margaretville, Fleischmanns

Antonio's (845-586-1507), Route 28, Arkville. ($$) Open every day except Tuesday, serving lunch 11–2; dinner all day, until 11 PM. During the winter, the hours are more limited, so call before you go. There are over 150 entrées at this fine Italian restaurant, which is chef-owned. Everything is prepared to order. Where can you find fettuccine Alfredo prepared 12 different ways? This is the place. A wide variety of dishes at reasonable prices. Mangia. . . .

Inn Between (845-586-4265), Route 28, Margaretville. ($$) Open Wednesday through Friday for dinner 4–9:30; Saturday and Sunday, for breakfast, lunch, and dinner, 8 AM–9:30 PM. As the name implies, this is the inn between, offering a full spectrum of culinary possibilities. There is everything from fajitas, wraps, and burgers to Danish-crusted filet mignon, salmon Dijon, and rack of lamb. The chef worked for several years at LaGriglia in Windham (one of my favorite restaurants in the Catskills) and recently took over this establishment. Casual atmosphere. Children welcome.

Oakley's Tavern (845-586-3474), Route 28, Arkville. ($$) Open daily for lunch 11–3; dinner Thursday and Sunday 5–10, until 1 AM Friday and Saturday. This is a good choice for casual dining at moderate prices. They offer burgers, salads, and sand-wiches for lunch; the dinner entrées include steaks, grilled salmon, mahimahi, and ribs. Children are welcome.

The Square Restaurant (845-586-4884), Binnekill Square, Main Street, Margaretville. ($$) Open for dinner Tuesday, Thursday, Friday, Saturday, and Sunday 5–9. A casual, relaxing restaurant, The Square has windows and a dining deck overlooking a small stream. The food has a Swiss touch, and the veal dishes are particularly good. Venison is served in-season, and there are excellent daily specials. Everything is prepared to order. Children are welcome.

Deposit

Chestnut Inn on Oquaga Lake (607-467-2500) Open daily for lunch 11–2:30; dinner 4–9; Sunday brunch 11–3, dinner 1–9. ($$) The Continental fare here is hearty and plentiful. There are several seafood and fresh fish dishes from which to choose; a house special is Caribbean chicken (charbroiled breast of chicken topped with mango, salsa, and banana). I enjoyed the rack of lamb on a visit here; the breast of duck and filet mignon are also quite good. Tavern menu available. Children welcome.

Downsville

Old Schoolhouse Inn (607-363-7814), Upper Main Street, Downville. ($$) Open daily except Monday for lunch 11:30–5; dinner 5–9. Sunday brunch 10–2. This restaurant is housed in a renovated schoolhouse that dates back to 1903. In a Victorian-style dining room, hearty portions of standard American favorites are the mainstay. The lobster, prime rib, and seafood medley are the most popular entrées, and a shrimp and salad bar is included with all dinners. Desserts are homemade and are excellent. Thanks to a local taxidermist, a grizzly bear, a bison, and a deer decorate the bar.

Hamden

Hamden Inn (607-746-6800), Route 10, Hamden. ($$) Open for dinner Tuesday through Saturday 4:30–9; until 11 on Friday and Saturday. Eclectic international cuisine is served in a 160-year-old inn. The imaginative dishes range from Italian, French, and Tex-Mex to the standard American favorites. Children are welcome.

Sidney

Toddie's Restaurant & Tavern (607-563-8465), 64 Main Street, Sidney. ($$) Open for lunch and dinner Tuesday through Thursday 11–8, Friday and Saturday till 8:30. This informal family-owned and -operated establishment with Catskill Mountain decor started out as a bakery but has been a popular local restaurant for over 20 years. Of course, all desserts are made in-house as are all bread and rolls. They feature "an Americana menu," according to the owner, Toddie, who says steaks and seafood are the specialties of the house. "Everything is done from scratch, old-style."

Stamford

Belvedere Country Inn (607-652-6121),10 Academy Street, Stamford. ($$) Open for dinner Thursday through Saturday 5–9, Sunday 3–9. Eclectic cuisine with five interesting specials nightly. The Continental fare features fish, beef, chicken, and pasta dishes. Children welcome; they will enjoy the game room downstairs.

Mama Maria's Restaurant (607-652-2372), Route 23, Stamford. ($) Open Tuesday through Sunday noon–10. Eat lunch or dinner at this authentic Southern Italian restaurant in a country setting that offers home-cooked (by Mama Maria!) lasagna and manicotti as well as steaks, chops, fresh fish, and salads. A great place for the entire family.

South Kortright

Hidden Inn (607-538-9259), Main Street, South Kortright. ($) Open for dinner Tuesday through Saturday 5–9, Sunday noon–7. This quiet country inn in a pastoral setting features an international menu. The specialty of the house is prime rib, but you will also find that the lamb, duck, and seafood entrées are tasty.

Walton

Aiello's (607-865-6707), 5 Bridge Street, Walton. ($) Open daily for lunch and dinner 11–9. This Italian-American establishment is renowned for serving the best pizza and prime rib around and is a favorite with local residents. Everything here is home-made. The owner tells us that this is one of the few places in Delaware County where the eggplant is fresh, not frozen!

EATING OUT

Andes/Delhi

Cassie's Kitchen (845-676-4500), Main Street, Andes. ($) Open daily in summer 7–4 for breakfast and lunch; 4–9 for desserts only. Bacon and eggs, waffles, French toast, grilled chicken sandwiches, salads . . . everything is homemade, including desserts. The meat chili is phenomenal; soups are low salt and are excellent. Save room for the pies, some of the best anywhere.

Cross Roads Café (607-746-7007), Main Street, Delhi. ($) Open Monday and Tuesday 7–5, Wednesday through Saturday 7–8 PM. Closed Sunday. Healthful, great-tasting fare is what you will enjoy here. Everything is made fresh on the premises: salads, desserts, breads, and an array of fruit smoothies. Vegetarian and vegan dishes are also noted on the menu. There is a coffee bar with gourmet coffees. Live music in the evenings.

Quartermoon Café (607-746-8886), 53 Main Street, Delhi. ($$) Open daily for lunch 11:30–3; Sunday brunch 11:30–2, dinner 6–10. Call for dinner reservations. Locally grown produce and seasonal ingredients are the mainstay at this restaurant, where many of the superb creations have a French accent. Seafood and local trout are popular, but there are also entrées with Caribbean, Asian, and Latin influence. A full bar features organic vodkas and gins; the moderately priced wine list offers a number of northern Californian and Chilean selections from boutique wineries. (Adjoining the restaurant is **Good Cheap Food,** a wonderful, well-stocked health-food store that is definitely worth a visit.)

Slow Down Food Company (845-676-4488), Lee Lane, Andes. ($) Open Thursday and Friday for lunch 11–3; Saturday and Sunday for breakfast 9–11:30, for dinner 11:30–4. This is a great place to enjoy American favorites; everything is homemade, and the atmosphere is relaxing—just like the name!

Vasta's Pasteria (607-746-9851), Main Street, Delhi. ($) Open daily Monday through Friday 11–10, Saturday 12–11, Sunday 4:30–10. All kinds of pasta entrées, steaks, seafood, burgers, hero sandwiches, and pizzas at exceedingly reasonable prices.

Good-sized portions. Children welcome.

Bovina
Russell's Store (607-832-4242), Main Street, Bovina Center. ($). Open daily except Sunday 9–6. Serving breakfast, lunch, and early dinner, either at the counter or tables, in this marvelous general store (see *Selective Shopping*). For breakfast there are first-rate pancakes and French toast; for lunch, enjoy wraps, soups, and sandwiches; for dinner I always end up ordering the chicken or eggplant parmigiana—it's great!

Downsville
Downsville Diner (607-363-7678), Main Street, Downsville. ($) Open daily 5 AM–9:30 PM. All the diner favorites are served here, along with daily specials and pizza. All baking is done on the premises, and there is even a full line of sugar-free desserts.

Grand Gorge/Hobart
Americana Diner (607-588-8960), Route 23, Grand Gorge. ($) Open Wednesday through Monday 6–3. Closed Tuesday and from Christmas through February 15th. If you enjoy authentic home cooking, you will want to stop here for breakfast or lunch. My favorites on the extensive menu are the blueberry pancakes and French toast. If you have room for dessert, all are made from scratch. Daily lunch specials. Children will love it.

Leo's (607-538-1611), Route 10 (Main Street), Hobart. ($) Open Monday through Saturday for lunch and dinner 11–10. The Continental cuisine here is varied, and the pizza is quite good. A local haunt that offers a little bit of everything.

Sundae's (607- 588-8800), Route 23 (just outside of town), Grand Gorge.

($) Open daily for lunch 11:30–3, dinner 4–9. If you remember poodle skirts and chocolate egg creams, then you will enjoy this 1950s theme restaurant; in fact, the ambience will bring you back to the *Happy Days* era of thick, juicy hamburgers with a dairy freeze for dessert. There is '50s music playing, and for those who would love to own a car from that period, the large parking area hosts antique car shows every Wednesday, May through October. Sandwiches, wraps, and all the American standards are prepared to order.

Margaretville Area

Café on Main (845-586-2343), located in the Commons, Main Street, Margaretville. ($) Open daily for lunch 11:30–3, dinner 5–9. A relaxed place to watch the world go by on Main Street (or shop between courses), this café serves excellent light fare and many regional Italian specialties. Dinner reservations are recommended, and you can arrange to take out any of the delightful meals.

The Cheese Barrel (845-586-4666), Main Street, Margaretville. ($) Open daily 9–5. An excellent selection of snacks and cheese is found in this shop, and the dishes are great for takeout and picnics. Try the homemade soups. There is a small, close dining area, so if you want quiet and privacy, this isn't the place to go.

The Flour Patch (845-586-1919), Bridge Street, Margaretville. Open Tuesday through Sunday 7–2. Here you will find the best "made from scratch" muffins in the Catskills—plain, simple, hearty—along with great bagels and sandwiches

Monster Grill (845-254-6300), Main Street, Fleischmanns. ($$) Open

Wednesday through Sunday 6–2 for breakfast and lunch; dinner is served in the winter months, but call to check first. A huge red monster stands out front of this casual eatery. The name came naturally since everything here served is big, according to the chef-owner. There are enormous Monster Burgers, a house specialty, made with a half-pound of beef; there is an array of huge omelettes (breakfast is served all day) and grilled-chicken sandwiches. Children will enjoy the "kid room" adjoining the restaurant, which is chock-full of toys and games, enabling parents to dine in peace and quiet—if only for a short while.

Walton

T.A.'s Place (607-865-7745), 249 Delaware Avenue, Walton. ($) Open daily for breakfast, lunch, and early supper 6 AM–7 PM. Old-fashioned American favorites like meat loaf and mashed potatoes, grilled pork chops, and marinated chicken breasts are the specialties here. Everything is homemade.

✳ Entertainment

The Open Eye Theater (845-586-1660/2727), Dry Brook Community Center, Route 28, Arkville. Enjoy new plays and classics, including Shakespeare, by the company that has been performing in town for over a decade. Productions run from May through Labor Day, but call for current schedule.

Stamford Performing Arts Center (607-652-3121), 76 Main Street, Stamford. There is the full range of performance art here—plays, concerts, mime, children's theater—year-round. Stamford is also home to

Friends of Music (607-652-7865), where lovers of classical music can hear concerts from May through December at the Frank W. Cyr Center on West Main Street.

West Kortright Centre (607-278-5454), Turnpike Road, West Kortright (write: P.O. Box 100, East Meredith 13757). Take Route 28 to East Meredith, then follow signs to the center, which is in West Kortright; or follow signs from Route 10, 2 miles north of Delhi near Elk Creek Road. Open July through September, performance schedules vary. Admission fee. Nestled in a hidden valley, the West Kortright Centre is housed in a charming white-clapboard 1850s church that was rescued from neglect by dedicated volunteers. Stained-glass windows and kerosene chandeliers glow in the twilight. The center offers unique performances throughout the summer, with concerts and special events for every taste, from bluegrass to zydeco, performance art to dance. Concerts are held both outdoors, in the green fields, and inside, where guests are seated in unique rounded pews; the lawn is often dotted with preconcert picnickers. The intimate setting makes all events a delight, and you may just bump into the evening's featured performer as he or she warms up in the churchyard.

❋ Selective Shopping

Delaware County has several unique gift and antiques shops. Villages like Andes, Bovina, Margaretville, and Walton are fun to walk through; there is a variety of stores; antiques emporiums abound, and the best way to see everything is to wander. Although you can find good shopping in just about every village, Arkville is home to a lively flea market on Route 28 every Saturday and Sunday from spring through autumn, weather permitting; it begins at 9 AM. The following shops are just some of my favorites, but enjoy exploring on your own and discovering new places.

Paisley's Country Gallery (845-676-3533), Route 28, Andes, has an amazing collection of baskets from all over the world. All kinds of ordinary items and some extraordinary ones may be found at **Stewart's Department Store** (607-746-2254), 85 Main Street, Delhi.

Russell's Store (607-832-4300), Main Street, Bovina, is a don't-miss experience; they still tie up packages with string from a dispenser, the old-fashioned way. There is delicious comfort food, groceries, gifts, local crafts, homemade baked goods, maple syrup, eggs, produce, and more. They are open daily except Sunday 9–6.

In Delhi, **Dee's Tiques & Train Shop** (607-746-6900), 1260 Peaks Brook Road, 0.33 mile off Route 10, is one of the region's most complete train stores with accessories, paint, tools, books, Aladdin Lamps, and parts. **Parker House** (607-746-3141), 74 Main Street, offers a wide variety of pottery, glassware, jewelry, clocks, china, picture frames, and classical gifts. **The Yarn Shop at Highland Springs Farm,** 3.5 miles off Route 10, at 3428 Peakes Brook Road outside Delhi, features their own 100 percent Merino wool and a unique collection of vintage buttons and fabrics. Another fun stop in the area is **Meredith Mountain Farms** (607-746-3857) on Honest Brook Road, which offers all kinds of cheeses and gourmet items.

In the Hancock area: **Delaware Delicacies Smokehouse** (607-637-

4443), Greenflats Road, has all kinds of smoked delicacies—trout, salmon, turkey, Cornish hens, even shrimp—and they will be glad to mail them anywhere. The **Ultimate Fly Fishing Store** (607-637-4296), 159 East Front Street, will delight anglers, but I like looking around in there myself, and I am not into fishing at all. **Karcher's Country Kottage** (607-637-2555), 156 Leonard Street, and **City Mouse, Country Mouse** (607-637-2951), 67 Apex Road (Route 268), both have a good selection of antiques and collectibles. But call first since both are open more or less by chance or by appointment.

In Margaretville: On Main Street in the **Commons,** which houses a number of specialty shops, you will find **Home Goods** (845-586-4177), one of the best kitchenware and specialty shops in the Catskills; **Franklin Footwear and Clothing** (845-586-1633), which features country clothing at reasonable prices; and **Kicking Stones** (845-586-1844), with its fine antiques and quirky collectibles. Antiques lovers will also want to poke around **Margaretville Antique Center** (845-586-2424) on Main Street.

In Walton: **The Country Emporium, Ltd.** (607-865-8440), 134 Delaware Street, will intrigue all kinds of shoppers with an interesting variety of gifts, gourmet food items, clothing; it would be difficult to list everything carried in this wonderful place.

✳ Special Events

Since Delaware County is still a rural area, the special events here tend to take place during the "better-weather" months, from late spring through summer. For specific dates and times,

contact the **Delaware County Chamber of Commerce** (607-746-2281) or visit their web site (see *Guidance*).

June: **Meredith Dairy Fest** (1-888-290-9415),Catskill Turnpike Road (7 miles north of Delhi; 12 miles south of Oneonta, just off Route 28), Meredith, is held for an entire weekend in the middle of the month, complete with exhibits, games, tractor pulls, music, crafts, hay rides, butter making, milk shakes, ice cream, and all things dairy.

July: The week of July Fourth ushers in the **Firemen's Field Days** at the village park in Margaretville, where a carnival, rides, entertainment, games of skill (and chance), and food concessions keep everyone busy. At the Andes Presbyterian Church, Route 28, Andes, the **Strawberry Festival** is celebrated each July Fourth weekend. July also brings the four-day **Lumberjack Festival,** Riverside Park, Deposit, which includes fireworks, an art show, antique cars, raft races on the Delaware River, a walking tour of historic homes, a carnival, and lots of food, along with demonstrations of lumberjack skills. The **Peaceful Valley Bluegrass Festival,** Downsville, features some of the best in traditional music. Dozens of bands perform all weekend, and there are square dances, jam sessions, and food concessions. Held on a 500-acre farm, the festival is great for families or anyone who wants to bring along a banjo, guitar, or mandolin. There are overnight camping facilities, but spaces are limited, so call ahead.

August: The charming village of Franklin hosts **Old Franklin Day** on Main Street, with sales, open houses, displays, and special events. Call the

PARADE PARTICIPANT AT THE ARKVILLE FAIR.

Peter Finger

Delaware County Chamber of Commerce for dates and times. **Turn of the Century Day** "Vintage Baseball" in Kirkside Park, Roxbury, is celebrated on the Sunday of Labor Day weekend. Free admission. Roxbury turns the clock back to 1898, and offers the public all the pursuits of Victorian times. There is period dress, croquet, sack races, horseshoes, a barbershop quartet, chicken barbeque, and a pie social to enjoy. These are just some of the activities at this day-long event highlighting the renowned Roxbury Nine's last baseball game of the season. **The Delaware County Fair**, at the fairgrounds off Route 10 in Walton (follow signs), runs the second week of August. Open daily 9 AM–10 PM. Admission fee. Part of the agricultural and social life of Delaware County for more than a century, this is one of the last of the truly agricultural county fairs in New

York State. Each year hundreds of 4-H members gather to show off their prize goods, including sheep, pigs, cows, horses, and rabbits. The finest local produce is displayed and sold, and the handiwork building bursts with the colors of hundreds of quilts. The celebration begins on Main Street with a parade, and visitors will enjoy the show of the best livestock and the latest farm equipment and agricultural news, demonstrations, and other "country stuff." Sample milk punch served by the Delaware Dairy Princess and her court; try your hand at games of skill and chance; let the kids have fun on the carousel. You may not bid on the livestock, but you will enjoy the demolition derby, tractor pulls, horse shows, and animal dress-up days. Don't worry about going hungry here. The pancake and pie tents, the sausage sandwiches, and the antique popcorn wagon—on the National Register of Historic Places—will take care of the greatest appetite. **Sidney Summer Arts and Music Festival**, downtown Sidney (exit 9 off I-88; near Routes 7 & 8). Free. Enjoy over 15 bands, a craft fair, classic car cruise, children's carnival, games of chance, and more. This celebration is usually held the first Saturday of the month of August, but check with the Sidney Chamber of Commerce for exact date and time of events (www.sidneyonline.com/festival).

Greene County

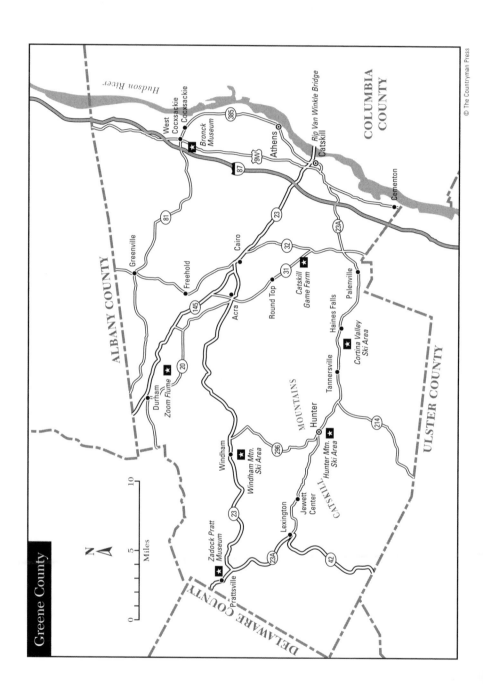
Greene County

© The Countryman Press

GREENE COUNTY

Greene County offers the perfect outdoor experience any time of year. In winter dramatic, snow-filled gorges yield to gray-and-white fields, and cross-country skiers may come across bear tracks; others can fly down the slopes at Hunter or Ski Windham, which provide some of the best downhill skiing in the East. In spring bright wildflowers cling to wind-scraped rocks, and visitors to the county can watch (or join in) the Spring Rush, a running, biking, and canoeing competition. Each June a tour of homes, farms, and estates is held to benefit the county historical society. Summer celebrates its warmth with the gifts of icy brooks for tired feet and a flood of cultural festivals. This is a fine time of year to visit North and South Lakes and Kaaterskill Falls. Autumn is a season to wonder at the colors that transform the hills and villages into paint pots full of orange and red—the magic that drew Rip Van Winkle to Catskill still enchants visitors today. Or stop by Thomas Cole's house, the place where the Hudson River School of landscape painting began. You will find both an Irish Cultural and Sports Center and a tiny Butterfly Museum in the same town: East Durham. There are also hiking trails, museums, country auctions, breathtaking waterfalls, waterfront villages, festivals, and fine restaurants to enjoy.

GUIDANCE **Greene County Promotion Department** (518-943-3223, 800-355-CATS), P.O. Box 527, Catskill 12414; www.greene-ny.com.

GETTING THERE *By car:* Greene County is off exit 21 of the New York State (NYS) Thruway. Routes 23 and 23A run east-west across the county; Route 32 runs north-south. Almost all sites in this chapter can be accessed from these roads.

By train: There are frequent daily **Amtrak** trains between New York City and Hudson (8 miles from Catskill across the Rip Van Winkle Bridge). Call 800-872-7245 for information and schedules.

By bus: **Adirondack Trailways** (800-858-8555) has daily bus service from Port Authority Terminal in New York City to Catskill, Palenville, Hunter, and Windham.

By air: **Albany International Airport** (518-869-3021) is approximately 35 miles north of the county.

MEDICAL EMERGENCY Greene County is a 911 community; dial 911 in the event of an emergency. The **Greene County Sheriff's office** (518-943-3300) and **New York State Police** (518-622-8600) may also be called directly.

Columbia Memorial Hospital (518-828-7601), 71 Prospect Avenue, Hudson 12534 (only 8 miles from Catskill, across the Rip Van Winkle Bridge).

✳ To See

Bronck Museum and Green County Historical Society (518-731-6490), off Route 9W on Pieter Bronck Road, Coxsackie. Open Memorial Day through October 15; Wednesday through Friday 12–4, Saturday and holidays 10–4, Sunday 1–4. Admission fee. The **Vedder Memorial Library** (518-731-1033/6822) is open Tuesday and Wednesday 10–4, the first Thursday of the month 7–9 PM, and the first Saturday of the month 9–noon. Once home to nine generations of the Bronck family (which also gave its name to the Bronx), the museum's collection traces the history of the Upper Hudson Valley. Visitors should begin with the original structure, a 1663 stone house that contains an Indian lookout loft— from a time when settlers were not welcome. The house was remodeled in the late 18th century, when a wing was added along with fine paneling and fireplaces. Displays include an impressive exhibit of local textiles, looms, and spinning wheels that chronicle the production of Bronck cloth and clothing. The 1738 Brick House was connected to the stone house through the hyphen-hall. This part of the family home is now used to display, among other things, a fine collection of paintings by 18th- and 19th-century artists, including Ammi

THE 13-SIDED LIBERTY BARN AT THE BRONCK MUSEUM, THE OLDEST DOCUMENTED MULTISIDED BARN IN NEW YORK

Hudson Valley Tourism, Inc.

Phillips, John Frederick Kensett, Nehemiah Partridge, Ezra Ames, Benjamin Stone, and Thomas Cole. Outside is a kitchen, a charming tiny house itself, set apart from the main house in the style of plantations. The displays here consist of furniture and kitchen tools. Farm buffs will enjoy the three barns that are found at the complex, each representing a different era. The Dutch barn, with its huge beams; the center-pole-supported, 13-sided Liberty Barn, once the storage area for the wheat harvest, now the oldest documented multisided barn in New York; and the Victorian horse barn (called the Antiquarium) each offers the visitor a look at the tolls, carriages, and wagons of the day. A walk through the family and slave cemeteries will bring you even closer to the people who made the Bronck complex a working and living farm. The Bronck Museum sponsors a Greene County house tour each June (see *Special Events*), when a different area of the county offers a look into the region's many historic homes. Researchers into local history and genealogy will want to stop at the Vedder Memorial Library, with its extensive collections of Greene County and New York State history and records.

Cedar Grove (Thomas Cole House) (518-943-7465), 218 Spring Street, Catskill. Open mid-May through October Friday and Saturday 10–4, Sunday 1–5. Groups by special appointment. Admission fee. The grounds are open at no charge daily 8–sunset. Thomas Cole, a painter, poet, and essayist, played a significant role in determining how America viewed its landscapes and vistas; his 19th-century paintings helped inspire the land conservation movement, and tourism became an industry as visitors trooped to the Catskills in search of the sites Cole depicted. His family home, Cedar Grove, is open to the public and presents an unusual look into the daily life of a Hudson River painter (in fact, Cole is credited with founding the Hudson River School of landscape art). The graceful Federal-style house and gardens still look off to the Catskill Mountains, and a locust tree that Cole mentioned in his writings remains outside the front entrance. Inside, interpretive exhibits introduce the visitor to Cole and his family, the Catskills region, artists such as Asher B. Durand and Frederic Church, and the Hudson River School. Several small oils and sketches by Cole are on display, along with family heirlooms, including his aeolian harp (a wind-powered musical instrument), sketching stool, paint box, and Bible; you'll also see leaves from his journal and his traveling trunk. Outside on the grounds, you can stop and see the family's Greek-Revival privy (with a front door for family and a back door for servants), and Cole's "Old Studio," which once served as slave quarters. There are lectures and events scheduled throughout the summer, and visitors can take a short walk to the Cole family gravesite.

Hudson-Athens Lighthouse (518-828-5294). Built in 1874, this architectural gem visible from Riverfront Park in Athens was designed in the Second Empire style. If you are interested in taking a tour, they are held June through October by appointment, so make sure to call ahead.

Irish American Heritage Museum (518-634-7497), 2267 Route 145, East Durham. Open Memorial Day weekend through Labor Day, Thursday through Sunday noon–4. Tours may be arranged any time by appointment. Small admission. The many exhibits here reveal the impact of Irish heritage in America.

There are also films, lectures educational programs, and special events through-out the summer season, so if you are interested, call ahead for a schedule.

Zadock Pratt Museum (Homestead) and Pratt's Rocks (518-299-3395), Route 23, Prattsville. Open Memorial Day weekend through Columbus Day, Thursday through Monday 1–4. School and group tours may be arranged year-round by appointment. Born in 1790, genius businessman Zadock Pratt started out as a harness maker and soon went into the leather-tanning business. He became such a prominent community leader that the town of Prattsville was named in his honor. His tanning facilities were among the largest in the state, and he built many of Prattsville's homes for his workers (more than 90 percent still stand). In later years Pratt served in both the state and federal governments. Today his home is a museum that shows what life in New York was like in the 1850s. Exhibits focus on the tanning industry as well as the story of Greene County, with rooms displaying period furniture and decorative arts. In a separate gallery the work of local artists is shown, and special events like the holiday dec-orating show are held. When your visit to the museum is completed, you can stop just outside Prattsville (on Route 23—there is a sign) at Pratt's Rocks, a memorial carved by an itinerant stonemason. Free and open year-round, the huge stone reliefs show Pratt's son, a favorite horse, and Pratt himself. A small picnic area overlooks Schoharie Creek, and there are great views from the summit.

FOR FAMILIES Armstrong's Elk Farm (518-622-8452), 936 Hervey Sunside Road, Cornwallville. Take the NYS Thruway to exit 21, pick up Route 23 west for 12 miles, and make a right on Hervey Sunside Road. Open year-round by appointment. Free. This is a fascinating educational detour for just about any-one. There are over 40 Rocky Mountain Elk in their own environment; spring is when the baby elk are born. Learn how the velvet antlers are harvested and used for a variety of drugs and natural remedies that prevent bone deterioration. The farm is also an excellent place for birdwatchers—you will see orioles, finches, bluebirds, and many more species. Les Armstrong, the owner, loves to enlighten visitors about his farm and the business of raising elk. He is an interesting char-acter and makes this a special stop.

Bear Creek Landing Family Sport Complex (518-263-3839), at the junction of Route 214 and 23A, Hunter. Open year-round Monday through Thursday 10–10, Friday and Saturday until 11, Sunday 9 AM–10 PM. Call for winter hours, which vary. Admission fee for activities. This licensed NYS fishing preserve, with rainbow, brown, and golden trout, also has a challenging sport-putting course featuring 18 holes of dramatic rock waterfalls, sand traps, and great views. There is a 400-yard golf driving range, and lessons are available in-season. In the winter months a small outdoor ice skating rink will delight children of all ages (with rentals and lessons available); there is also snowmobiling. The restaurant and pub on the premises is a delightful place to relax and enjoy a drink or lunch. An oasis of activities—all under one roof!

Catskill Game Farm (518-678-9595), Game Farm Road, off Route 32, Catskill. Open daily May through October. Admission fee. One of the oldest game farms in the country, the Catskill Game Farm is also the most popular in the East. With more than 2,000 animals such as lions, tigers, and bears to see and enjoy, a visit here should take several hours. Special shows introduce the audience to animal friends, and the petting zoo is still one of the most popular places for children. There is a small train/tram that transports visitors from one section of the zoo to another (at an additional charge) and an amusement park and picnic and play areas. It's best not to leave young children alone in the petting area since they may feel overwhelmed by all the friendly deer.

Catskill Mountain Wolf Center (518-622-8013), Route 32 (3 miles north of the Catskill Game Farm and 2 miles south of Cairo), Cairo. Open Memorial Day weekend through Labor Day weekend Thursday through Tuesday 10:30–4:30. Admission fee. This nonprofit organization is dedicated to the preservation of the wolf population through education. It offers an opportunity to see the gray wolf in a forest setting and to learn about wolves in the wild. A 20-minute film will be of interest to older children; kids will also enjoy the room with computer stations that feature wolf games. The theme here is that education is essential for future preservation.

Zoom Flume Water Park (518-239-4559), just off Route 145, Shady Glen Road, 2 miles north of East Durham. Open daily Father's Day weekend (mid-June) through Labor Day, Monday through Friday 10–6, Saturday and Sunday until 7. Admission fee. This aquamusement park is set into the Shady Glen canyon, a natural formation of steep walls and running water, so the site itself is beautiful, even if you are going to observe rather than participate in the array of water activities. The Raging River Ride and Zoom Flume let you slosh and slide your way down the canyon; there's an enormous activity pool with several slides of all sizes, a game area, and a Toddler Section for one- and two-year-olds. The Black Vortex Speed Slide takes three at a time through an exciting water adventure that older kids will love. There are nature trails, scenic overlooks, and waterfalls, and a restaurant with an observation deck for drying out in addition to a good-sized outdoor food court and picnic area. A wonderfully unique and scenic water park that is sure to make everyone in the family happy.

ZOOM FLUME WATER PARK

Hudson Valley Tourism, Inc.

SCENIC DRIVES Mountains, deep gorges, valleys, and waterfalls can all be seen during a leisurely drive through Greene County, and a tour can take all day or only a few hours, depending on the number of stops you want to make. Some of the roads are narrow and winding, though, so use the designated parking areas to take in scenic views. And be careful to check driving conditions if you take a ride in winter or early spring.

Some lovely parts of the county can be seen by taking Route 42 north over the **Deep Notch,** which is cool even on the hottest days. At Route 23A head east through Hunter, Haines Falls, and Palenville. Along the road you will see Hunter Mountain, breathtaking waterfalls, winding streams, and the **Amphitheatre,** a natural, bowl-shaped rock formation. Follow Route 23 into Catskill, where you can pick up the NYS Thruway at exit 21.

Another tour starts at the junction of Routes 23A and 23C; follow 23C east to **Jewett.** The large and elegant homes lining the roads and tucked into the hills were part of Onteora Park, a "cottage" colony where many wealthy families summered during the 19th century. The junction of Routes 25 and 23C shelters the **Old Stone Church,** in which there are some lovely murals. (The church is closed in winter.) At County Route 17 head south to Route 23A, where you can pick up the scenic drive detailed above into Catskill.

To see some exceptional churches, begin on Route 23A in **Jewett Center.** Here you will see the **St. John the Baptist Ukrainian Church** and **the Grazhda,** which were constructed in the traditional style, using large beams and wooden pins instead of nails. The interior of the church is decorated with wood carvings and panels, and the education building has displays relating to Ukrainian history. There are concerts and art shows held in the Grazhda (518-263-3862). On Route 23A in Hunter you will find **Our Lady of the Snows,** one of the oldest Catholic churches in the Mountaintop region. Continue on Route 23A to Haines Falls, where you will find the **Grotto of Our Lady of the Mountain.** This shrine was constructed in the 1920s and recalls the miracle at Lourdes. The grotto is open to the public. Continue on 23A to Palenville, where the **Gloria Dei Episcopal Church** is open for tours on Saturday. Then take Route 23A to Route 32 north into Cairo, then Route 24 to South Cairo. There you will find the **Mahayana Buddhist Temple** (518-622-3619), a retreat complex complete with Chinese temple, dragon decorations, and fine artwork. The walkways are open to the public year-round. From South Cairo, you can take Route 23B east to the NYS Thruway.

✳ To Do

AIRPLANE TOURS With its rolling meadows and steep mountain heights, Greene County is a wonderful place to see from the window of an airplane. Recreational flights add some excitement to a vacation or weekend getaway, and a call to the **Freehold Airport** (518-634-7626) in Freehold will put you in touch with someone who can arrange your excursion. Open April through November Saturday through Tuesday and Thursday; call in advance for an appointment. Most flights are approximately 15 minutes, but you can make arrangements for a longer trip. This full-service airport, right next to acres of cornfields, offers pleasure flights, lessons, and a chance to view antique aircraft. There is a small art gallery on the premises, as well.

BIKING The **Tannersville Bike Path** (518-589-5850) runs from Clum Hill Road across from Cortina Valley, down around Tannersville Lake, to Bloomer Road. This path covers about 2 miles, and walkers, hikers, and cross-country skiers are all welcome to use it. The path is marked well and is easily found.

The **Twilight General Store** (518-589-6480), North Lake Road, Haines Falls, rents mountain bikes (see *Green Space*); they are located 2 miles from the entrance of North Lake.

Enthusiasts looking for an interesting way to spend a summer or autumn day may want to make tracks to **The Bike Shop at Windham Mountain Outfitters** (518-734-4700), Route 296 and South Street, Windham, where you can hire a guide—or purchase trail maps and rent a mountain bike to ride the trails on your own. They also have guided group mountain bike rides, and there are excursions for all abilities. Then head down the road to **Windham Mountain** (518-734-4300), Route 23, Windham, for a chairlift ride and views that are magnificent, a great way to begin an autumn bike tour. The mountain maintains a network of trails for bikers. (The lift operates on weekends in September and October, during fall foliage season, 11–3.)

BOATING **North-South Lake State Park** (518-589-5058), County Route 18, Haines Falls. This is the place to go if you want to rent a canoe, kayak or rowboat, and relax on a couple of the most beautiful lakes in the county.

Riverview Marine Services, Inc. (518-943-5311), 103 Main Street, Catskill, is a full-service marine facility with a store, motorboat service, and accessories. However, they do rent kayaks, canoes, and motorboats. If you are interested in motoring on the Hudson River, this is one of the only places that offers rentals.

FARM STANDS AND PICK-YOUR-OWN FARMS Greene County is filled with farm stands: big ones, little ones, and specialty stands that carry everything from

BOATING AT NORTH-SOUTH LAKE STATE PARK IN HAINES FALLS.

Hudson Valley Tourism, Inc.

maple syrup to mushrooms. The **Catskill Region Farmers Market** (518-622-9820), at Catskill Point (end of Main Street), Catskill, is held every Saturday June through October, 9:30–1:30. A great place to see what farmers throughout the county are offering, this riverside market, on the bank of the Hudson River, usually has several different activities going on, in addition to the market (see *Entertainment*). For those who want to explore on their own, the following are some of my favorite places to discover the bounty of Greene County:

Bennett's Berry Patch (518-756-9472), Independence Lane (off Route 144), Hannacroix, has seasonal offerings of vegetables, berries, flowers, and pumpkins. Pick your own strawberries in June and July. Call for dates and times, which vary.

Black Horse Farms (518-943-9324), Route 9W, Athens, is open daily April through December 9–6 and stocks everything from vegetables, herbs, eggs, plants, and pumpkins to maple products, flowers, Christmas trees, and honey.

Black Walnut Farm (518-239-6987), Cornwallville Road, Cornwallville, is open seasonally; call for hours. This farm stand features organically produced vegetables, corn, honey, maple products, and pumpkins.

Boehm Farm (518-731-6196), 233 County Route 26, Climax, is open mid-August to mid-December daily 9–5. At this farm you can pick your own apples (several varieties are available) and peaches. They also sell sweet cider, plums, jams, and jellies.

Catskill Mountain Country Store (518-734-3387), Route 23 (Main Street), Windham. Open daily 9–6. This unique country market, bakery, café (see *Eating Out*). and gift shop specializes in organic produce in-season, local maple syrup and honey, plants, Christmas trees, and even has a small petting zoo on the premises for the young ones. A terrific oasis for travelers and local residents alike.

Catskill Mountain Foundation Green Market (518-263-4908), Route 23A (Main Street), Hunter, open daily 10–6. An enormous array of seasonal produce, both organic and nonorganic.

Duncan's Farmstand (518-622-8400), Route 23B at Silver Spur Road, Cairo, is open mid-August through December and has local goodies and produce to take home to dinner, including apples, cider, vegetables, eggs, maple products, honey, and pumpkins.

Hull-O Farms (518-239-6950), 3739 County Route 20, Durham. Open year-round; call for hours. There is a corn maze as well as pumpkins to be picked in-season at this seventh-generation working dairy farm. Families can stay overnight in private guest houses and have a chance to milk cows, feed baby calves, and collect eggs from the chickens. So if you like picking pumpkins, you might want to stay overnight, and see what a working farm is all about (see *Lodging*). Great for families.

Maple Hill Farms (518-299-3604), Route 23A, 9 miles west of Hunter, is open daily but call first. They have maple cream, sugar, and syrup, pure honey, and farm-fresh preserves.

Pathfinder Farms (518-943-7096), 2433 Old Kings Road, Catskill. Do call before going to this farm, which features organically grown produce: vegetables, fruit, beef, pork, chicken, herbs and honey.

Traphagen's Honey (518-263-4150), Route 23A, Hunter, is open daily year-round 10–5 and sells all kinds of honey and honey products, as well as maple products and gourmet foods.

FISHING Fishing in Greene County can mean a lazy day spent pondside or an exciting, nerve-ripping hour fighting a sturgeon in the Hudson. There are more than 58 streams that shelter wild trout here as well as lakes, ponds, and, of course, the Hudson River. A state fishing license is required in Greene County, and town permits are also needed for the Potuck Reservoir in Catskill and the Medway Reservoir in Coxsackie. Permits and licenses can be obtained at many of the bait and tackle and sports shops across the county as well as in town clerks' offices and the county clerk's office in Catskill. Seasons and limits vary with the species of fish; check with the **Department of Environmental Conservation** (845-256-3000) for specifics. In Greene County, public fishing areas are marked by yellow signs; parking spaces are available, although they're sometimes limited. If you want to catch one of the more than 150 species of fish that are found in the Hudson River—shad, perch, herring, and sturgeon among them—you may want to use the public boat ramps that can be found in Athens, Coxsackie, and Catskill. Route 23A will take you past Rip Van Winkle Lake in Tannersville, Schoharie Creek, and the Schoharie Reservoir, all of which are great fishing areas. Route 145 leads to Lower Catskill Creek, Upper Catskill Creek, and Ten Mile Creek, while Route 296 provides access to the Batavia Kill boat launch and the East Kill Trout Preserve. BASSmaster invitational fishing tournaments have been held in Greene County; information may be obtained by calling the **Greene County Tourism Promotion Department** (518-943-3223).

Fins and Grins (518-943-3407), 5571 Cauterskill Road, Catskill, offers fishing charters as well as scenic rides on the Hudson River. Captain Bob Lewis even supplies all the equipment you will need for the excursion. **Reel Happy Charters** (518-622-8670) in Cairo, specializes in light tackle and fly-fishing for striped bass on the Hudson River.

GOLF The greens of Greene County require widely varying levels of skill, but no one who picks up a club will leave the region disappointed. The following establishments are open to the public. It is suggested that you call before you go to determine hours and available tee times.

Blackhead Mountain Lodge & Country Club (518-622-3157), Round Top has an 18-hole, par-72 championship course that is quite challenging. There is a pro shop, lessons (home of Blackhead Golf Academy), restaurant, and bar on the premises.

Catskill Golf Club (518-943-7199), 27 Brooks Lane, Catskill, has an 18-hole, 6,382-yard course. There is a pro shop, club rentals, and restaurant, all in a beautiful country atmosphere.

Christman's Windham House Country Inn and Golf Resort (518-734-4230, 888-294-4053), 5742 Route 23, Windham, one of the oldest inns in the region, offers an 18-hole, 7,072-yard Mountain Course. With four sets of tees, this forest links layout is fun to play at any skill level. There is also a nine-hole Valley Course that will please walkers and beginners. Cart and club rentals, pro shop, snack bar, driving range. There is a Roland Stafford Golf School that offers lessons, and overnight packages are available for golfers. (See *Lodging.*)

Colonial Golf Club (518-589-9807), Main Street, Tannersville, has a nine-hole course, par 35, 2,718 yards. There are carts, a pro shop, snack bar, club rentals, and lessons. A good place for novices. Gorgeous views.

Rainbow Golf Club (518-966-5343), 3822 Route 26, Greenville, offers an 18-hole, USGA-regulation championship course, driving range, carts, restaurant, bar, rentals, and golf packages in vacation apartments just off the course.

Rip Van Winkle Country Club (518-678-9779), 3200 Route 23A, Palenville, has a nine-hole Donald Ross–designed course with alternate tees, par 36, 3,120 yards. A restaurant and bar are on the premises. Nice for beginners.

Sunny Hill Resort & Golf Course (518-634-7642), Sunny Hill Road, Greenville, has a challenging 18-hole, par-66 course that overlooks a beautiful lake; clubhouse with pro shop and snack bar. Gas and hand cart rentals.

Thunderhart Golf Club (518-634-7816), 2740 County Route 67, Freehold, offers an 18-hole championship course, par 74, 6,863 yards; driving range and pavilion for outings. An informal atmosphere prevails here.

Windham Country Club (518-734-9910), 36 South Street, Windham, has an 18-hole, par-71, 6,005-yard championship course, pro shop, lessons, and new driving range. They were awarded three and a half stars by *Golf Digest* magazine.

HIKING Greene County provides some of the best hiking and views in the Catskill region. You don't have to be a seasoned hiker to enjoy a day walking on the clearly marked trails. The magnificent vistas have inspired Thomas Cole and other Hudson River painters.

Although the **Escarpment Trail** runs from Kaaterskill Creek on Route 23A to East Windham on Route 23 (24 miles in all), there are several short hikes along the path to Kaaterskill High Peak, North Point, and Mary's Glen. The trails in the North Lake area are renowned for their waterfalls and fantastic views of the entire Hudson Valley. **Kaaterskill Falls** and the **Catskill Mountain House** are particularly noteworthy sites. The easy-to-find entry point for these trails is at the junction of Route 23A and Kaaterskill Creek on the north side of the highway. These hikes are usually very popular on summer weekends, so you might want to go during the week to avoid the crowds. North Lake and decent campgrounds are nearby for those who want to take a swim or stay overnight.

For more experienced and adventurous hikers, there is the **Devil's Path,** named for its steepness and relative isolation. The path passes over much rugged terrain, particularly Indian Head Mountain, and includes the Hunter Mountain Trail and West Kill Mountain Range Trail. To reach the trailhead, turn south off

Route 23A at the only light in Tannersville. Continue 1.5 miles to the road's intersection with Bloomer Road. Turn left, and after a short distance bear left onto Platte Clove Mountain Road. Stay on this road for 1 mile to Prediger Road, then go about 0.5 mile farther to find the trail. Each single mountain on the Devil's Path can be hiked in a day or less.

At 4,040 feet, **Hunter Mountain** is the second highest peak in the Catskills and is best hiked on the trail that starts on Spruceton Road. To get there, take Route 42 north from Lexington and go 4 miles to Spruceton Road. The trailhead and trail are well defined.

Another pleasant day hike takes you to **Diamond Notch** and **West Kill Falls.** Located 5 miles north of Phoenicia, near Route 214, it is also easy to find. From Route 214, take Diamond Notch Road about 1 mile to a bridge, cross it, and park. The hike is about 4.5 miles and should take approximately three and a half to four hours.

The **Cohotate Preserve** (518-622-3620), Route 385, Athens is a nature preserve with a self-guided tour on nature trails that run along the Hudson River. You can see the sign for the preserve on the right side of the highway if you are heading from Catskill toward Athens. This is an easy walk and is a good choice for those traveling with children.

KAATERSKILL FALLS, A POPULAR SUBJECT FOR HUDSON RIVER SCHOOL ARTISTS

Hudson Valley Tourism, Inc.

The **Four Mile Point Preserve** in Coxsackie may be reached by taking Route 385; it is located 8 miles from the Rip Van Winkle Bridge. A 7.6-acre riverfront preserve that offers picturesque shoreline vistas and a tranquil inland pond. There are nature trails, and this is a wonderful place to observe all kinds of birds.

The **Rams Horn-Livingston Sanctuary** in Catskill may be reached by following Route 9W south from the Rip Van Winkle Bridge for 2.5 miles. Make a left onto Grandview Avenue. Follow for 0.5 mile to a parking area. There are 480 acres of the Hudson's largest tidal swamp forest here, a breeding ground for American shad and bass. There are more than 3 miles of trails. Following a 0.5-mile walk, you can canoe from the tidal marsh out to the Hudson River.

Shinglekill Falls, on the Catskills' eastern fringe, are only a few hundred feet from the road. From Cairo, head south, then west on County Route 24. After passing South Road, the falls are about 500 feet farther along on the right side. Shinglekill Grist Mill, a small store, once an old mill, provides access to the falls. For those who want to enjoy a few hours by a cool stream or are looking for an easy walk to a waterfall, this is the perfect spot.

HORSEBACK RIDING Bailiwick Ranch/Catskill Equestrian Center (518-678-5665), Castle Road, next to the Catskill Game Farm, Catskill. Open year-round. In business for over 40 years, there is riding here for all ages and abilities. Scenic mountain trail rides are offered for either one or two hours. For those who would like something more intensive, there are all-day mountain trips and overnight camping excursions. The youngest children will enjoy pony rides and the petting zoo. For those interested in lessons, both English and Western riding instruction are offered in the indoor and outdoor riding arenas.

K&K Equestrian Center (518-966-4829), Route 67, East Durham. Open May through October. This establishment has been owned and operated by the Phillips family for over 30 years. They offer guided scenic trail rides, pony rides, lessons, and overnight trips. Nice, informal atmosphere.

Rough Riders Ranch (518-589-9159), Route 23C, East Jewett. Open year-round. Ride with a cavalry sergeant and experience the spirit of the Old West on one of the theme rides here. Trail rides, pony rides, petting zoo, and overnight riding adventures are also available. Lessons are offered, as well (both Western and English).

Silver Springs Ranch (518-589-5559), Route 25, off Route 23A, Haines Falls. Open year-round. This dude ranch offers riding packages as well as daily trail riding. A good place for groups; overnight adventures are a specialty here.

Tanglewood Ranch (518-622-9531), Cornwallville. Open year-round. Trail rides here offer a five-state view. There are pony rides and horse-drawn hayrides as well as overnight trips. Western and English riding lessons available.

✳ Winter Sports

CROSS-COUNTRY SKIING Greene County is home to some of the best cross-country skiing to be found in New York State. Well over 1,000 acres of groomed and ungroomed trails snake their way through the county's forests and fields, and many of the areas are patrolled by Nordic Ski Patrol members.

Mountain Trails X-C Ski Center (518-589-5361), Route 23A, Tannersville, offers 20 miles of woodland trails that are groomed, track-set, and marked. After skiing, enjoy hot chocolate in the snack bar or the warming hut, which has a wonderfully welcome fireplace. Ski and snowshoe rentals; ski lessons available.

North-South Lake (518-357-2234), County Route 18, Haines Falls. There are no services, only open trails here on old carriage roads. The scenic overlooks are magnificent. Ski and snowshoe rentals are available at a nearby general store. A great place for more experienced cross-country skiers.

DOWNHILL SKIING Skiers from beginner to expert will enjoy excellent snow conditions, modern facilities, and some of the best skiing and most spectacular views anywhere in Greene County, which lies in New York's snow belt. Here, sudden storms can dump several inches of powder in an hour, and the ski season usually lasts six months. In addition to their specialty offerings, the following slopes have rentals, child-care services, dining facilities, picnic areas and ski shops.

Hunter Mountain (518-263-4223), Route 23A, Hunter. (From exit 21, NYS Thruway, the trip is approximately 24 miles, taking Route 23 east to Route 9W south, then 23A west; or 18 miles from exit 20, taking 32 north to 32A north to 23A west). Open 8:30–4; Hunter West 9:30–3:30. Hunter Mountain's reputation as the snowmaking capital of the East is well-deserved. The three different mountains—Hunter One, Hunter West, and Hunter Mountain—offer skiers of all skill levels a chance to test themselves on over 50 trails. Runs at Hunter can extend more than 2 miles, with a 3,200 foot summit elevation and vertical drops of 1,600 feet, and there are some extremely difficult areas, even for the expert. Double, triple, and even quadruple chairlifts (there are now 11 lifts) cut some of the lines down to size, but this is such a popular area that you should be prepared for crowds on holidays and weekends. There are special discounts during the week and no lift lines.

Hunter offers ski and snowboard lessons for all levels, and a wide variety of amateur and professional races are held during the season, including one for chefs, firemen, and nurses. There is a Terrain Park for snowboarders with a 1,000-watt stereo system that blasts motivational music while a hot dog stand at the base of the halfpipe brings a new meaning to the term "fast food." Two-slopes wide, the Terrain Park offers a dozen features and several rails for jibbing, jumping, and pumping action. (There are also snowshoeing and snow-tubing areas.) Hunter also offers 100 percent snowmaking capability, so the season sometimes begins as early as November and lasts into May. There are complete facilities here, including baby-sitting, cafeterias, a lodge, a ski shop, an art gallery, and plenty of parking.

Windham Mountain (518-734-4300, 800-SKI-WINDHAM), Route 23, Windham. Open Monday through Friday 9–4, weekends and holidays 8–4; Night skiing and snowboarding Thursday through Sunday 4–10, mid-December through early March, depending on weather conditions. This is my favorite place to ski in the Catskills; it also has one the nicest lounge areas—and bar—with a panoramic view of the mountain. The atmosphere here is friendly and relaxed. Diversity is a hallmark of Windham Mountain: it's a wonderful place for either a family excursion or a romantic escape. There are 39 trails and elevations of 1,600 feet at the base and 3,100 feet at the summit. Trail difficulty ranges from easy to expert, and the longest trail is more than 2 miles long. The Wannabe Wild Snowboard Park offers a 400-foot halfpipe, a 5-acre-plus area for boarders and tubers (with music and lights on Friday and Saturday night). A mountaintop adventure park has a total of three snow-tubing lifts and several tubes for sliding. "The First Class Skier" is a new program specifically designed for the first-time skier. It's a full-day package that puts the neophyte skier with one instructor for the entire day. A conveyer lift on the beginner slope makes learning to ski and snowboard easier than ever. The Children's Learning Center offers fun for young nonskiers (or tired kids). Windham has won awards for its courtesy services, including valet parking, rooms with computers, and excellent dining facilities, along with a senior-skier development program and lessons in racing, freestyle skiing, and snowboarding. The area is renowned for its work with disabled skiers. Also note: Mountain bike lovers may wish to inquire about the autumn special events at Windham Mountain, when bike rentals are offered and trails are open for adventurers on wheels. (See *To Do—Bicycling.*)

Cortina Mountain Resort (518-589-6500), Route 23A, Haines Falls, has a new owner and a new look. Open daily 9–4 in-season. The resort sits on 280 acres and has a base elevation of 1,925 feet and a summit elevation of 2,650 feet. There are 11 slopes and 4 lifts. A refurbished 20-room inn and snow-tubing park opened in 2002. This is a good place to go for families with young children and novice skiers.

❋ Green Space

Mountaintop Arboretum (518-589-3903), Route 23C, Tannersville. Free. Open year-round, but call about guided tours, offered by appointment. A nonprofit organization that features a living collection of both exotic and native trees and shrubs on a 10-acre site. Some are indigenous to the Catskills, others are not. Each season brings delights, from the flowering height of spring to the brightly colored autumn foliage. Many of the plants have identification markers, and there are workshops throughout the year. Horticulturalists and those who just want to know "What is that tree?" will enjoy this stop. This center serves as a botanical research facility and a place for educational programs on a variety of horticultural topics.

North and South Lakes (518-589-5058 or 943-4030). Take Route 23A to County Route 18, Haines Falls. Open daily late May through early December 9 AM–dusk. Admission fee, with an extra charge for campsites. This recreational area offers breathtaking scenery and a multitude of activities. Visitors can swim in a mountain lake with a clean, sandy beach. Boat rentals and fishing are also available. An ideal spot for a family outing.

A short hike from the North Lake is Kaaterskill Falls, one of the highest falls on the East Coast and a popular subject for Hudson River School artists. The area also has a multiuse campground with hookups for recreational vehicles; it is advisable to make reservations early in the season since this is a popular site, and it gets busy on summer weekends.

A true oasis in the wilderness (selling soft drinks, toys, t-shirts and groceries) is the **Twilight General Store** (518-589-6480), North Lake Road, Haines Falls, on the left side of the road, 2 miles before you get to the entrance of the park. They stock all kinds of camping supplies (in case you forgot something) and rent mountain bikes (see *Bicycling*). The gift shop is also filled with dozens of regional history books and guides to the Catskill Mountains.

Point Lookout Mountain Inn Gardens (518-734-3381), Route 23, East Windham. Open Thursday through Monday year-round. Free. There are perennial and herb gardens on the mountainside next to this historic inn and restaurant (see both *Lodging* and *Dining Out*) and seating areas to enjoy. But it's the view that really counts: five states, 180 miles, and 270 degrees. Breathtaking all around.

✳ Lodging

Greene County is an extremely popular resort area, and there are hundreds of B&Bs, inns, motels, and campgrounds. Some of the establishments cater to lovers of Irish, Italian, or Scandinavian heritage; others offer a full range of camping facilities on lakes and rivers. The following list is only a quality sampling of what can be discovered throughout the county.

Catskill Area (Leeds, Round Top, Purling)

Caleb Street's Inn (518-943-0246), 251 Main Street, Catskill 12414. ($$) This beautiful, elegant home is filled with antiques and has a large veranda that overlooks the Catskill Marina. There are four rooms here, all with private bath, including two large suites. It's a nice place to stay for those who want to walk to shops and restaurants and prefer to stay in town. Open year-round.

Carl's Rip Van Winkle Motor Lodge (518-943-3303), 810 Route 23B, Leeds 12451. ($$) There are 27 log cabins and 14 motel rooms here. I recommend staying in one of the log cabins, which have been renovated and are charming. Facilities include a restaurant, an outdoor pool, air-conditioning, phones, and cable TV. There are hiking trails on the premises and fishing, as well. Open mid-April through November.

Tumblin' Falls House (518-622-3981), County Route 24, Purling 12473. ($$) There are four guest rooms, and most have gorgeous views. The Falls View Suite makes for an especially romantic experience. You can wander the gardens and trails, or relax listening to the sound of "tumblin'" water on the multilevel deck (with spa) overlooking the Shinglekill Falls (see *Hiking*). Open year-round.

Winter Clove Inn (518-622-3267), Winter Clove Road, Round Top 12473. ($$) Located on 400 acres adjoining the Catskill Forest Preserve, this inn opened in 1830 and is still run by the same family. There are swimming pools, tennis courts, a golf

WINTER CLOVE INN, ROUND TOP

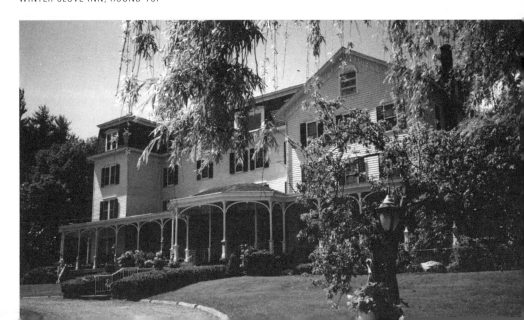

course, cross-country skiing, hayrides in autumn, and even a bowling alley on the premises. All baked goods are homemade, and many of the recipes have been passed down in the family for generations. Children are welcome. All meals are included in the rates, unless special arrangements are made in advance. The 51 rooms all have private baths. Open year-round.

Earlton/Greenville

Greenville Arms 1889 Inn (518-966-5219), South Street (Route 32), Greenville 12083. ($$$) Special care is taken to provide a quiet retreat for guests at this gem of a Queen Anne Victorian home built by William Vanderbilt in the late 19th century. Each room is decorated with antiques, and the 7 acres of lush lawns and gardens are a riot of color each spring and summer. Old-fashioned country cooking is served at the full breakfast; dinner is by reservation only. There are 15 rooms in three buildings, all with private bath. Some have private porches, fireplaces, and double Jacuzzis. There is a 50-foot outdoor pool. Older children are welcome. Open mid-May through November.

Nightingale Inn B&B (518-634-2507/7305), Route 81 & Peat Beds Road, Earlton 12058. ($$) This 1912 inn has four rooms, all with featherbeds and private bath, some with a lake views. Full country breakfast. Lovely porch and gardens. No children under the age of 16; pets allowed. Open year-round.

Hunter Area (Haines Falls, Tannersville)

Deer Mountain Inn (518-589-6268), Route 25, Tannersville 12485. ($$) This gracious, elegant turn-of-the-century country estate has seven beautiful guestrooms. All have private bath and TV, some have working fireplaces and sitting areas. Fine restaurant on the premises (see *Dining Out*). Open year-round.

Greene Mountain View Inn (518-589-9886), 132 South Main Street, Tannersville 12485. ($$) The 12 rooms all have private bath, cable TV, telephone, and air-conditioning. There is a bar, cocktail lounge, and game room on the premises. A Continental breakfast buffet is served in the morning. This place is right in town and might be a good bet for those traveling with older children who won't be bored here. Open year-round.

Eggery Inn (518-589-5363), County Road 16, Tannersville 12485. ($$) Nestled amid the majestic ridges of the Catskill Mountains at an altitude of 2,200 feet, this rustic inn offers sweeping views. The wood-burning Franklin stove and antique player piano make for a cozy atmosphere, and the dining room has a hand-crafted oak bar and an abundance of plants. During your hearty breakfast, you will enjoy an unobstructed view of Hunter Mountain. Dinner is served to groups by prior arrangement only. The 15 rooms all have private bath, telephone, and cable TV. Most rooms have air-conditioning. Open year-round.

Fairlawn Inn (518-263-5025), 7872 Main Street, Hunter 12442. ($$) This inn is the epitome of Victorian charm, from the three-story corner turret and wraparound porches to the elaborately designed wallpapered ceilings and cozy brass beds. A stunning grand staircase and antiques-filled lobby are only a preview for the inn's several large common rooms, which provide a variety of settings for quiet contemplation or socializing. Each of the nine bedrooms has a queen-sized bed and private bath. A breakfast feast here may include a spinach quiche or stuffed French toast. Special midweek rates. Open year-round.

Mountain Valley Spa (also known as **Vatra,** 518-263-4919, 800-232-2772), Route 214, Hunter 12442. ($$) This 15-acre resort at the base of Hunter Mountain is an informal, somewhat rustic retreat with all the amenities of a full-service spa. Located in the midst of the Catskill Forest Preserve, the spa provides a fitness room, sauna, indoor and outdoor swimming pools, tennis courts, and basketball and volleyball courts. Daily exercise options include aerobics, yoga, hiking, Tai Chi, dance, and water activities. The daily price is reasonable and includes three diet gourmet meals (vegan, vegetarian, and kosher meals available) as well as use of all facilities. Some packages include a free massage. Other services are available for an additional fee (facials, body wraps, manicures, and pedicures). Open year-round.

Redcoat's Return (518-589-9858), Dale Lane, Elka Park 12427. ($$) The picturesque locale of this 1850s farmhouse will delight those who love the outdoors. There are 14 rooms; half have private baths. Guests will enjoy fishing in nearby Schoharie Creek and skiing at nearby Hunter Mountain. Open year-round.

Scribner Hollow Lodge (518-263-4211), Route 23A, Hunter 12442. ($$) For people who enjoy a full-service lodge; the main building offers 37 private rooms, and town houses can also be rented. Every room is different, and the lodge has a sauna, a whirlpool, and an unusual grotto

swimming pool. The Prospect Restaurant (see *Dining Out*) is on the premises. Children welcome. Open year-round.

Washington Irving Inn (518-589-5560), Route 23A, Hunter 12442. ($$) Set back off the road, this Old-World Victorian bed & breakfast may have 50 rooms, but every one has its own distinctive charm. The beautifully renovated building, over a century old and listed on the National Register of Historic Places, is covered in cedar siding that blends nicely with the lush landscape. All rooms have renovated baths, a few with Jacuzzis, and many have fireplaces. There is also an outdoor swimming pool. Owner Stefania Jozic combines country hospitality and European elegance: guests will feel at ease from the moment they arrive. A unique feature here is the Afternoon Tea, served the first two weekends of the month from 2–5 (see *Eating Out*)—I had not tasted freshly made scones, pastries, and canapés like this since visiting tearooms in Vienna. This is the perfect way to spend a Sunday afternoon if the weather is too hot or too cold; the tearoom offers a relaxing, romantic ambience. Children are welcome; a good choice for a family reunion.

New Baltimore
River Hill (518-756-3313) P.O. Box 254, New Baltimore 12124. ($$) Away from it all—but not too far away—this restored historic home has spacious grounds, and there are spectacular Hudson River views from its rooms. Guests are welcome to enjoy the downstairs, which includes a living room with fireplace and grand piano. Breakfast is served on the terrace or in front of the fireplace in the dining room. Two rooms, each with private

bath, air-conditioning, and four-poster beds. Open year-round.

West Kill/Lexington

West Kill Mountain Bed & Breakfast (518-989-6500), 2080 Spruceton Road, Westkill 12492. ($) This is a family place, tucked into a beautiful, secluded part of the Catskills. There are 18 rooms, an outdoor pool, in-room phones, private bath, and TV. A hearty home-cooked breakfast is served in the morning. The hiking trails and trout stream on the premises make this ideal for those who love the outdoors. Groups and children welcome.

Windham Area (Durham, East Windham)

Albergo Allegria Bed and Breakfast (518-734-5560/4499), Route 296, Windham 12496 ($$$) Step up on the wicker-furnished porch here, and feel the grace and beauty of days gone by. The Victorian theme is continued throughout this bed & breakfast with antique furnishings and period wallpaper and decorations. A full breakfast of fresh fruit, home-baked muffins, croissants, omelettes, and local honey and jams is served daily. In summer enjoy breakfast on the porch. The main lounge, with its overstuffed couches and fireplace, and the library are especially warm and inviting. Seven suites and 14 rooms, all with private bath; the Jacuzzi Room is the perfect place to celebrate a special occasion. There are several fine restaurants within walking distance of this B&B.

Ashland Farmhouse B&B (518-734-3358), West Settlement Road, Ashland 12407. ($$) A farmhouse dating back to 1860 houses this B&B with five large rooms, all with private bath, nestled in the woods with views of the mountains. A full breakfast is served in the morning. No smoking is allowed on the premises. Adults only. Open year-round.

Country Suite Bed and Breakfast (518-734-4079), Route 23, Windham 12496. ($$) This restored farmhouse is only minutes from skiing, shopping, and festivals, and guests will enjoy the country furnishings and antiques. There are five rooms, each with private bath. Reservations suggested. Open year-round.

Christman's Windham House Country Inn & Golf Resort (518-734-4230), 5742 Route 23, Windham 12496 ($$) There are 49 rooms, all with private baths, at this beautifully located inn with two golf courses, an outdoor heated pool, fishing, tennis courts, hiking, a library, and a first-rate restaurant on the premises, **Messina's La Griglia** (see *Dining Out*). Children welcome. Open year-round except for the months of April and November.

Danske Hus (518-734-6335), 361 South Street, Windham 12496. ($$) Walk to the slopes at Windham from your room (there are five here, all with private baths, air-conditioning, and cable TV). The large, comfortable living room has a cozy fireplace and piano. Outside, a large deck offers panoramic views of the mountains. Breakfast is served in an heirloom-filled dining room. Your hosts provide an afternoon snack after skiing or hiking. Children and dogs welcome. Open year-round.

Golden Harvest (518-634-2305), 356 Golden Hill Road, East Durham 12423. ($$) A nice family place, this inn is located on 24 acres and was once an orchard, hence the name.

The extensive grounds include a duck pond and gazebo. There is a separate two-bedroom apartment for guests, complete with TV, VCR, and screened-in porch. A full breakfast is served on weekends; Continental only during midweek. Children and pets welcome. Open year-round.

Hull-O Farms (518-239-6950), Durham 12422. For those traveling with children, this is a homespun experience that will be long remembered. You can live the country life on this 300-acre working dairy farm that has been in the same family for seven generations. Milk a cow, collect chicken eggs, feed pigs and baby calves, fish, or go on a nature walk. The hands-on experience is unusual and fun for everyone. Hayrides and barbecues. Extremely comfortable guest houses (there are three), with home-cooked meals served in the homestead. Rates include breakfast and dinner. Children under 2 are free; ages 2–12 less than half price. There is a two-night minimum stay.

Olympia Hotel (518-734-9510), 39 Goshen Road, Hensonville 12439. ($$) This hotel is nestled in the Catskills, housed in a structure built in the late 1800s. They have been in business for over 40 years. There are 14 guest rooms, most with private bath. All have TV and air-conditioning. A full buffet breakfast is included in the price. Bar/lounge and game room on the premises.

Point Lookout Mountain Inn (518-734-3381), Route 23, East Windham 12439. ($$) This full-service inn has a spectacular 180-mile panoramic view of five states. The 14 guest rooms, all with private bath and cable TV, are housed in a building adjoining the restaurant of the same name (see

Dining Out). Other facilities include hot tub, game room, gardens, decks, and fireplace. Continental breakfast included. Open year-round.

Windham Arms Hotel (518-734-3000), Route 23, Windham 12496. ($$) Take the NYS Thruway to exit 21, and then pick up Route 23 west; it's 25 miles to the hotel. Only 0.5 mile from Windham Mountain, and the ski center's own hotel, this establishment combines a country setting with comfortable rooms and spectacular mountain views. It is ideal for families, with a dining room, coffee shop, tennis court, indoor recreation center, and outdoor pool on the premises. It combines the convenience of a hotel with the warmth of a country inn. The 55 rooms range from standard doubles to deluxe suites and have TV, telephone, and private bath. Vines Bistro & Wine Bar is on the premises. Ask about the Kids Stay Free policy here. Open year-round.

✳ Where to Eat

DINING OUT The Basement Bistro (518-634-2338), County Route 45, Earlton. ($$) Open for dinner Thursday through Sunday 5–8. Brunch served December through May 11–2. Reservations required. Closed the month of January. This unique restaurant gives diners the opportunity to try everything offered. There is a prix-fixe menu made up of a dozen courses that change daily, depending on seasonal produce available. Located on a pastoral country road in the basement of a house hand-built by the chef-owner who lives with his family upstairs, there are only 26 seats in the restaurant. Most dishes are served on one plate, creating a communal dining experience that is particularly enjoyable when there is a large group. The kitchen specializes in a healthful, imaginative style of cooking that uses purees and infused oils instead of butter and cream. Adventurous diners shouldn't pass up this restaurant.

Brandywine (518-734-3838), Route 23, Windham. ($$) Open for lunch Wednesday through Sunday 11:30–2:30; dinner served daily from 5:30. An excellent informal dining spot; the Italian specialties here are superb. Try the rich fettuccine Alfredo, the shrimp Brandywine, or the chicken Scarpariello. Desserts include fantastic cheesecake. There is a bright greenhouse room for dining and cozy booths in the main area. Children are welcome.

Chalet Fondue (518-734-4650), South Street, Windham. ($$) Open for dinner Thursday through Saturday from 5, Sunday from 2. The Swiss, Austrian, and German dishes are excellent, and the atmosphere is elegant yet relaxed. The specialties include veal entrées (I thought the Wiener schnitzel was first-rate) and a full line of fondues. They make a wonderful salad with excellent honey-lemon dressing. Children are welcome.

Chateau Belleview (518-589-5525), Route 23A, Tannersville. ($$) Open daily except Tuesday at 5. Fine Continental cuisine and spectacular mountain views are found here, along with candlelight and fine service. Not recommended for children.

Deer Mountain Inn (518-589-6268), County Road 25, Tannersville. ($$) Open daily except Tuesday for dinner from 6. Enjoy eclectic international cuisine in a romantic, quiet atmosphere where steaks, seafood, duck, and lamb (a specialty of the house) are quite popular with diners. There are also seven rooms in the adjoining inn, all with private bath (see *Lodging*). Not recommended for children.

Diamanti's Restaurant (518-678-3173), Route 32A, Palenville. ($$) Open Thursday through Monday for dinner 4:30–9. The reasonably priced Italian cuisine in this establishment attracts travelers and local residents alike. The emphasis is on seafood entrées like zuppa di pesce. Both the chicken and veal parmigiana are popular, but we recommend ordering one of the daily seafood specials. All entrées are prepared to order. Children are welcome.

The Fernwood (518-678-9332), Malden Avenue, Palenville. ($$) Open for dinner daily at 5. Standard American favorites are the specialty here. Try the steak, ribs, or one of the fine salads. They are known for their excellent margaritas.

Freehold Country Inn (518-634-2705), junction of County Routes 32 and 67, Freehold. ($$) Open daily for lunch noon–3; dinner 4–9. The American cuisine here offers something for everyone with a variety of steak, chicken, pasta, and vegetarian dishes. We suggest that seafood lovers try the fisherman's casserole, a combination of poached salmon, lobster tail, and scallops in a fennel-saffron broth, served over pasta.

Gerardo's Cafe (518-945-2720), Route 385, Athens. ($) Open for dinner Tuesday through Sunday 4–9. The Italian-American cuisine here includes a range of fresh pasta, seafood, and veal dishes. The chef's favorite is the Southern Italian chicken, which is served over pasta in a sauce with sun-dried tomatoes and capers. All desserts are homemade on the premises; we suggest sampling the chocolate mousse cake or cream puffs.

La Conca D'Oro (518-943-3549), 440 Main Street, Catskill. ($$) Open weekdays except Tuesday for lunch 11:30–2:30 and dinner 5–10; open Saturday 3–10 and Sunday 2–10. The name means "the golden bay," and this unpretentious Italian restaurant serves fine food at exceedingly reasonable prices. The veal entrées, chicken dishes, and homemade mozzarella are house specialties. For dessert there are excellent cannoli. Children are welcome.

Messina's La Griglia Restaurant at Christman's Windham House (518-734-4499), Route 23, Windham. Open May through Columbus Day and November through St. Patrick's Day, daily for dinner from 5 PM. Ed Messina worked at La Griglia for many years; he's now the proprietor. A graduate of the Culinary Institute of America, his elegant restaurant serves excellent Northern Italian cuisine, featuring some of the best fresh seafood around. House specialties include osso buco Milanese, roast duck, all kinds of fresh fish entrées, and pasta (made on the premises). Desserts are prepared by the restaurant's bakery and include chocolate specialties to die for. **Christman's Windham House,** where the restaurant is located, has two golf courses on the premises and a 49-room inn (see *Lodging*). Children welcome. Reservations suggested.

Millrock Restaurant (518-734-9719), 5398 Main Street, Windham. ($$) Open year-round Thursday through Monday for dinner 5–10. This Italian-American family restau-

rant features an open kitchen and wood-burning oven that turns out an array of gourmet pizzas. A specialty of the house is seafood, and I enjoy the seafood Lovers for Two entrée: a mix of mussels, clams, calamari, and shrimp topped with a zesty red sauce over pasta. Most desserts are homemade on the premises, and all are first-rate. Try the cannoli, crème brûlée, imported sorbets, or pumpkin cheesecake. Children are welcome.

Mountain Brook Dining & Spirits (518-263-5351), Main Street, Hunter. ($$) Open for dinner during the summer months Wednesday through Sunday from 5:30; winter hours are extended, so call to check. Enjoy contemporary American dishes with an innovative touch. Some of the house specialties are Chilean sea bass with plum wine sauce and jasmine rice or grilled filet of yellowfin tuna with red onion nectarine relish and wasabi horseradish. On Wednesdays there is a pasta special for approximately $10.

The Prospect Restaurant (518-263-4211 or 1-800-395-4683), at Scribner Hollow Lodge, Route 23A, Hunter. ($$) Open for dinner Friday through Sunday from 5; breakfast served Saturday and Sunday from 8 AM. Dinner served during the week from Thanksgiving through the end of ski season. Call for hours. Enjoy breathtaking views of Hunter Mountain and the Catskills from just about every table in the dining room. The fusion of American regional and New York State dishes include tantalizing choices like wild game mixed grill with acorn juniper sauce, apple-braised free-range chicken, and chocolate tartlet with ripe pears for dessert. Fireplace lounge with live jazz on weekends. There are several Wine Dinners throughout the year, featuring some of California's most elegant varietals, as well as other wines that compliment the regionally inspired cuisine.

Redcoat's Return (518-589-9858), Dale Lane, Elka Park. ($$) Open Thursday through Saturday for dinner at 6 by reservation. This inn, housed in a historic structure, serves up fine country-style dishes which include a nice selection of steaks, seafood, and pasta entrées. The surroundings are Old World elegant, and dinner is served in a cozy librarylike dining room with book-lined walls. Children are welcome.

Vesuvio (518-734-3663), Goshen Road, Hensonville. ($$) Open daily at 4:30. The warm atmosphere and provincial charm make this Italian restaurant a popular stop. Candlelight makes dining elegant, and the specialties include veal and fish, along with outstanding desserts like tortoni and spumoni. Children are welcome.

Victorian Rose Restaurant at Point Lookout Inn (518-734-3381), Route 23, East Windham. ($$) Open for lunch Thursday, Friday, and Monday noon–4; for dinner Saturday 4–10; Sunday 10–10. Hours vary depending on the season, so call first. Eat here on a clear day, and you can see five states from your dining booth. The Culinary Institute–trained chef hails from France yet prepares a variety of American favorites including, steaks, seafood, and pasta dishes. There are new and tempting seasonal creations like fresh salmon baked in white wine, olive oil, garlic, and lemon, topped with fresh tomato salsa; or try the blackened Black Angus strip steak seared in spicy seasonings topped with citrus butter. For lunch there are sandwiches, salads,

and wraps. Children are welcome; casual family atmosphere and fine dining are combined. Overnight accommodations available (14 rooms with private baths; see *Lodging*).

Wasana's Thai Restaurant (518-943-9134), 336 Main Street, Catskill. ($) Open Monday, Tuesday, Thursday through Saturday 11–10, Sunday 2–8. Enjoy authentic Thai food with over 40 items to choose from as well as several daily dinner specials. All items are made to order, and just about every offering can be made for vegetarians. Catskill's best-kept secret!

EATING OUT Bear Creek Café (518-263-3839), Route 214, Hunter. ($) Open daily for lunch and dinner during the summer months from 11 AM; call for hours during the winter. Enjoy hearty soups, sandwiches, burgers, and fries here while overlooking the ice rink in winter or the array of summer activities in the warm weather months. Wine and beer available. (See *To See—For Families*.)

Bell's Coffee Shop (518-943-4070), 387 Main Street, Catskill. ($) Open Monday through Friday 8–3 for breakfast and lunch. This is an old-fashioned luncheonette with large portions and low prices. The home-cooked turkey sandwich is a favorite among local residents.

Catskill Mountain Country Store & Restaurant (518-734-3387), 5510 Route 23, Windham. ($) Open Monday, Thursday, and Friday 9–3, Saturday 8–4, Sunday 8–3 (the store itself is open until 6 PM daily). This charming country store/café has a bakery, small petting zoo, and an array of produce and gourmet items on the premises. Enjoy fantastic muffins, breads, pastries, pancakes, omelettes, wraps, hearty soups, and all kinds of wonderful treats. My favorite here is the chocolate-cherry French toast. The kids will love this bustling eatery, and if they get impatient waiting for the food to arrive, you can always walk around and visit the animals.

Last Chance Antiques and Cheese Café (518-589-6424), Main Street, Tannersville. ($) Open daily at 10 AM, but hours vary seasonally. This retail gourmet store, antiques shop, and café all in one offers up some of the best homemade soups you will find in the county. There are cheeses, chocolates, quiche, huge sandwiches, and salads that make this a wonderful place to go for a meal or takeout. Children welcome.

Mariner's Point (518-943-5352), 7 Main Street, Catskill. ($) Open daily for lunch and dinner noon–11. Located on the Hudson River, this is a great spot to enjoy drinks outdoors in the warm-weather months.

Mayflower Café (518-943-7903), 355 Main Street, Catskill. ($) This antiques shop, art gallery, and café combined has a delightful ambience and is one of the most memorable stops in the town of Catskill. Just about every square inch of space is filled with something interesting to ponder. The perfect place to enjoy a cappuccino or an iced tea accompanied by one of the many mouthwatering desserts.

Washington Irving Inn (518-589-5560), Route 23A, Hunter. ($) Open for breakfast daily 8–10, for afternoon tea the first two weekends of the month 2–4. A fantastic full breakfast is served here, complete with homemade breads, pastries, and croissants. Diners can enjoy buttermilk pancakes

topped with locally produced maple syrup, fluffy French toast, or sizzling bacon and eggs prepared to your taste. Owner/chef Stephanie Jozic has restored the mansion housing the restaurant to its turn-of-the-20th-century splendor. The dining room is filled with fine silver and china collected from antiques shops throughout the Catskills. An eclectic mix of china fits in nicely with the Victorian motif. The large variety of teas is sure to please every taste, and the mélange of treats that accompanies the soothing beverage will provide sustenance for a relaxing afternoon repast with an old friend or a new lover.

✳ Entertainment

The Catskill Mountain Foundation (518-263-4908, ext. 202, weekdays; 518-263-5157, weekends), Route 23A (Main Street), Hunter 12442. This nonprofit organization has revitalized the town of Hunter. Stop in at the film and performing arts center, bookstore, and gallery on Main Street and pick up a current schedule of events that include classical, folk and jazz concerts, dance performances, a film series, art exhibits, poetry readings, festivals (see *Special Events*) and more. There is also a green market year-round, daily 10–6, featuring local organic produce, pasta, grains, eggs, cheeses, and other gourmet specialty foods, held in a beautifully restored red country barn at the foot of Hunter Mountain. This is the center to find out what is happening culturally in the mountaintop region. It's a good idea to check their web site if you're planning a visit and want to include some cultural events (www.catskillmtn.org).

Dutchman's Landing (518-943-3223),. Catskill Point, Main Street, Catskill. This area once served as a boat landing for the Hudson River craft, and today visitors can enjoy spectacular views of the river and eastern shore. You will find a farmers market and crafts market weekends from summer through fall, displays of the river and cultural history of the Catskills, travel information, a picnic and dining area, and entertainment. A great place to start a tour of Greene County and one of the easiest access areas to the Hudson River for non-boaters who just want to enjoy the area.

Ensemble Studio Theatre (518-989-6043, 212-247-4982), Lexington Center for the Arts, Route 42, Lexington 12452. Here you may enjoy music and dance performances by a

ROBERT MANNO AND MAGDALENA GOLCZEWSKI OF THE WINDHAM CHAMBER MUSIC FESTIVAL

Susumu Sato

nationally renowned theater company. They present free readings of new American plays on Saturday evenings. Master classes are offered throughout July and August. An art gallery is on the premises as well, with exhibits during the spring and fall months. Call for a schedule of events.

Greene Room Players (518-263-4233, 589-6297), P.O. Box 535, Hunter 12442. This theater group has been presenting professional musicals, revues, children's shows, comedies, and drama for over 10 years now. The performances are given year-round. There are play readings, stand-up comedy, cabaret, and musical events at the Dancing Bear Theater in the village.

Impulse Theatre & Dance (518-797-3684, 678-3205), Woodstock Avenue, Palenville 12463. Performances take place May through August in Palenville. This quality summer theater puts on contemporary dramas, comedies and musicals. There is an internship program that culminates in two showcase performances that run from June through August. From September through April this company moves to Rensselaerville, New York (Albany County). If you are interested in receiving their newsletter, which contains the annual schedule, call, and it will be sent to you.

Windham Chamber Music Festival (518-734-3868), 740 County Route 32C, Windham 12496. The former Presbyterian Church on Main Street in Windham (built in 1826) is the perfect venue for this series of chamber music performances; the acoustics are superb. The directors of this festival, Robert Manno and Magdalena Golczewski, were both musicians with the Metropolitan Opera for many years. Manno is also a composer and has written more than 30 chamber works. The festival features top-notch soloists (including a variety of musicians and opera singers), and the ticket prices are exceedingly reasonable. Performances take place throughout the year, so call for a schedule.

✳ Selective Shopping

ANTIQUES Greene County offers the antiques lover everything from the funky to the fabulous, although with a small range of shops, auctions, and flea markets. Some establishments are open year-round, but most tend to have limited hours in the off-season, so call before you go.

American Gothic Antiques (518-263-4836), Route 23A, Hunter, stocks a wonderful array of antique lamps and accessories as well as many other items. They are open Thursday through Sunday 11–5.

The Blue Pearl (518-734-6525), Route 23, East Windham, offers an array of antiques, sconces, lamps, and some of the finest reverse-painted glass in the world. Located almost at the top of Windham Mountain, this shop offers three floors of fine jewelry, clothing, and glassware. Ulla Darni's exquisite reverse-painted lamps are here, with their hand-forged iron-and-bronze chandelier bases, as well as finds from around the world. A small café on the premises offers healthy snacks and desserts, and the views outside go on forever. (After you leave the Blue Pearl, continue up the mountain to the Five State Overlook: New York, Vermont, Massachusetts, Connecticut, and New Hampshire are all in view on a clear day. Even if it's not clear,

you can watch the clouds roll in from across the country!) Open daily 10–6.

Country Hut Antiques Center (518-299-3650), Main Street (Route 23), Prattsville, is a multidealer store with 15 rooms and a barn chock-full of thousands of items to suit every taste and budget. Antiques, sports memorabilia, attic treasures, furniture, vintage clothing, collectibles, and books are just some of the things you will find. Open Friday through Monday 10–5.

The Coxsackie Antique Center (518-731-8888), Routes 9W and 81, West Coxsackie, is open daily, with wares ranging from glass and lamps to books and postcards.

Mooney's Antiques (518-634-2300), Route 145, East Durham, runs auctions year-round, so call there if you want to find out what's happening in the county auction-wise.

And, if all this shopping makes you hungry, stop in at the **Last Chance Antiques and Cheese Café** (518-589-6424), Main Street, Tannersville, where you can enjoy a gourmet snack . . . and then buy the furniture out from under the other diners (see *Eating Out*).

ART GALLERIES Greene County has a wealth of artists and art galleries, but many places are open only by chance or by appointment. For further information on their offerings, contact the **Greene County Council on the Arts** (518-943-3400), 398 Main Street, Catskill 12414. The council also operates two crafts galleries that represent regional artists, so ask for a calendar of exhibits and events or go to their web site (www.greene-arts.org).

All Arts Matter (518-966-4038), P.O. Box 513, Greenville 12083, is a non-profit organization that sponsors a diversity of programming that includes all the arts. There are exhibits, lectures, seminars, workshops, theatrical programs, musical recitals, concerts, dance events, and craft courses (www.allartsmatter.com).

Two of my own favorite galleries in Greene County are: **Stanley Maltzman's Four Corners Art Gallery** (518-634-7386), 3392 Gayhead Road, Freehold 12431. Stanley is a nationally renowned, award-winning artist who works in the Hudson River Valley tradition. He has drawings, pastels, watercolors, and lithographs for sale at his studio, but call in advance for an appointment. The other is **Windham Fine Arts** (518-734-6850), 5380 Main Street, Windham. This traditional fine-arts gallery has exhibits of local and regional artists that change every month. Open Friday through Sunday noon–5.

✳ Special Events

From spring through autumn, fairs and festivals abound throughout Greene County. Greene County Tourism Department (800-355-CATS; www.discovergreene.com) can supply you with a complete calendar of special events to coincide with your stay there. The following are just some of my favorite celebrations held annually in the county.

May: **East Durham Annual Irish Music Festival** (518-634-2286/2319), Michael J. Quill Irish Cultural & Sports Centre, 2119 Route 145, East Durham. Enjoy three days of Ireland in America with musical entertainment and activities for all ages. **Annual Hudson River Striped Bass Derby** (845-297-9308), Historic Catskill Point, Catskill. The derby is open to everyone 12 and older. Come down to the river and compete: 10–7 on Saturday; until 5 on Sunday. **Hudson River Shad Festival** (518-622-9820), 1 Main Street, Catskill. A celebration of spring and the bounty of the Hudson River with music, food, and a shad bake. The sloop *Clearwater* will even take you for a sail.

June: **Greene County Historical Society Tour of Homes** (518-756-8805), the location changes every year, so call ahead. Picnic lunches are offered for sale and tickets usually cost about $20. It's a wonderful opportunity to visit a dozen or so historic homes and support the county historical society.

July: **Mountain Culture Festival** (518-263-4908, ext. 202), Catskill Mountain Foundation Red Barn, Main Street, Hunter. Saturday and Sunday 10–5. This celebration of regional arts, crafts and culture, includes about 100 vendors who display and sell their wares. Music, food, demonstrations, bike races, and more. **Greene County Fair** (518-943-4222), Catskill Event Center, Route 32, Catskill; Wednesday through Sunday, hours vary. Concerts, amusement rides, vendors, informational booths, lawn mower races, and a farmers market are all part of the fun at this July county fair. The kids will love it. **Athens Street Festival** (518-945-1551), Riverfront Park, Athens. This day-long festival on the Hudson River includes vendors, food, and entertainment. A great family outing

August: **Hudson River Regional Festival** (800-355-2287). This two-week celebration of art, history, and music along the Hudson sponsors events in Athens, Catskill, Coxsackie, and other river towns. There is a gallery trail with over 50 art exhibits as well as historic walks showcasing unique architecture, lighthouse tours, jazz, classical music concerts, and more. **Great Northern Catskills Balloon Festival** (518-966-5050), Balsam Shade Resort, 6944 Route 32, Greenville. This annual event offers crafts, food, vendors, entertainment, and, of course hot-air balloons and balloon flights (in the early-morning and evening hours). If you have always wanted to try ballooning, this is a good opportunity. **International Celtic Festival** (888-HUNTER-MTN), Hunter Ski Bowl, Route 23A, Hunter. Admission fee. This celebration of Celtic spirit transforms Hunter Mountain into the Emerald Isle. The weekend is filled with caber tosses, border collie sheep-herding demon-strations, entertainment, food, crafts, and a pipe and band competition. **Leeds Irish Festival** (518-943-6451), Leeds Festival Fair Grounds, Route 23B, Leeds. Enjoy Irish music and dancing with bands from Ireland. For those who enjoy Irish traditional music.

September: **Catskill Mountain Thunder Motorcycle Festival** (518-634-2541), Blackthorne Resort, 348 Sunside Road, East Durham. Admission fee. This shindig lasts from 9 AM until the wee hours of the morning. All bike brands are welcome at the vendor expo. There are fireworks, an antique bicycle exhibit, fashion show, parade, and rodeo games. **Annual Autumn A-Fair** (518-734-3852), on Main Street, Windham. This town-wide fall festival includes regional foods from local restaurants, vendors galore, entertainment, music, and all-around great family fun.

Albany

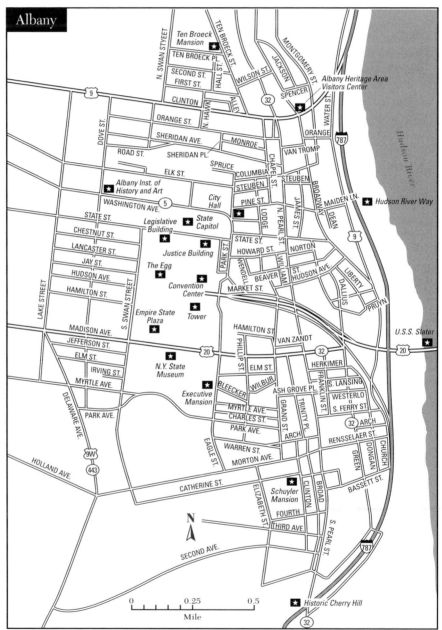

Albany

Ten Broeck Mansion ⭐

TEN BROECK PL.

SECOND ST.

FIRST ST.

N. SWAN STYEET

HALL ST.

WILSON ST.

JACKSON

MONTGOMERY ST.

SPENCER

Albany Heritage Area Visitors Center ⭐

WATER ST

CLINTON

9

ORANGE ST.

SHERIDAN AVE.

DOVE ST.

N. HAWK

ALLEY

32

MONROE

ORANGE

VAN TROMP

787

ROAD ST.

SHERIDAN PL.

SPRUCE

COLUMBIA

Hudson River

Albany Inst. of History and Art ⭐

ELK ST.

STEUBEN

STEUBEN

CHAPEL ST.

BROADWAY

WASHINGTON AVE.

5

City Hall ⭐

PINE ST.

LODGE

N. PEARL ST.

JAMES ST.

DEAN

MAIDEN LN.

Hudson River Way ⭐

STATE ST.

Legislative Building ⭐

State Capitol ⭐

STATE ST.

9

CHESTNUT ST.

HOWARD ST.

NORTON

LANCASTER ST.

Justice Building ⭐

PARK ST.

WENDELL

WILLIAM

ST.

LIBERTY

JAY ST.

The Egg ⭐

BEAVER

HUDSON AVE.

DALLIUS

HUDSON AVE.

MARKET ST.

PRUYN

HAMILTON ST.

Convention Center ⭐

LAKE STREET

S. SWAN STREET

Empire State Plaza ⭐

Tower ⭐

HAMILTON ST

VAN ZANDT

U.S.S. Slater ⭐

MADISON AVE.

JEFFERSON ST.

20

32

20

ELM ST.

PHILLIP ST

ELM ST.

HERKIMER

IRVING ST.

N.Y. State Museum ⭐

WILBUR

ASH GROVE PL.

FRANKLIN ST.

S. LANSING

MYRTLE AVE.

BLEECKER

WESTERLO

DELAWARE AVE.

Executive Mansion ⭐

MYRTLE AVE.

GRAND ST.

TRINITY PL.

S. FERRY ST.

PARK AVE.

CHARLES ST.

PARK AVE.

ARCH

32 ARCH

RENSSELAER ST.

GREEN

DONGAN

CHURCH

HOLLAND AVE.

9W

443

WARREN ST.

MORTON AVE.

EAGLE ST.

BASSETT ST.

CATHERINE ST.

ELIZABETH ST.

Schuyler Mansion ⭐

CLINTON

BROAD

S. PEARL ST.

N
↑

FOURTH

THIRD AVE.

787

SECOND AVE.

0   0.25   0.5

Mile

Historic Cherry Hill ⭐

32

© The Countryman Press

ALBANY

Albany is the oldest chartered city in the United States. It is also the second oldest continually inhabited settlement in the country. Long before Albany received its city charter, granted July 22, 1686, by Governor Thomas Duggan, the settlement was an important river stop and trading center. After Henry Hudson visited the region in 1609, Albany's fertile valleys and abundant game attracted Dutch settlers. Albany was to become a city of tremendous contrast—stagecoaches and steamboats, muddy roads and medical colleges, farmers and politicians. But through a combination of pride, pluck, and foresight, Albany has made the best of it all. A visit to the city today can focus on many things—history, politics, art, architecture—and can be made at any time of year. Spring brings the blossoming of thousands of tulips, pools of color that reflect Albany's Dutch origins. The Pinksterfest, a weekend celebration in May, welcomes the warm weather in the Dutch tradition, and the city parks come alive with fairs and shows. In summer the great Empire State Plaza becomes a unique combination of outdoor park, art gallery, and seat of government, and autumn turns out to be a perfect time to explore the city on foot and discover the tiny side streets that still remain from three centuries ago. Winter ushers in Victorian greenery displays, snow festivals, and the lighting of the state Christmas tree. Whatever the season, be prepared to discover an area where the past and future coexist.

GUIDANCE Albany County Convention and Visitors Bureau (518-434-1217), 25 Quackenbush Square, Albany 12207; www.albany.org.

GETTING THERE *By car:* The city is located off exits 23 and 24 of I-87 (NYS Thruway); watch for signs.

By bus: **Adirondack Trailways** (800-858-8555), runs several buses daily to the city of Albany from the Port Authority Bus Terminal in Manhattan.

By air: **Albany International Airport** (518-242-2299), 737 Albany Shaker Road, is located at exit 4 off the Northway (take the NYS Thruway to exit 24; pick up the Northway there at exit 1N just after passing through the toll booth).

By train: **Amtrak** (518-462-5763, 800-872-7245) service is available to 525 East Street in Rensselaer, just across the river from Albany. Trains leave from Penn Station in Manhattan.

MEDICAL EMERGENCY **Albany Medical Center** (518-262-3131), 43 New Scotland Avenue.

Albany Memorial Hospital (518-471-3111), 600 Northern Boulevard.

St. Peter's Hospital (518-525-1324), 315 South Manning Boulevard.

✳ To See

The Albany Institute of History and Art (518-463-4478), 125 Washington Avenue. Admission fee. Open year-round; Wednesday through Saturday 10–5, Sunday noon–5. Founded in 1791, this exceptional museum is one of the oldest in the country, and it is still providing visitors with a chance to see varied, changing exhibits that focus on the Hudson Valley's cultural history. The building is a graceful collection of individual galleries and sweeping staircases, and there is even a small display area in the entrance hall. The institute's collections include fine European porcelain and glass; Dutch furniture, paintings, and decorative arts from the early settlement period in Albany; pewter and silver produced by local smiths in the 18th century; and breathtaking examples of the Hudson River School of painting. The Dutch Room offers an interesting look into early Albany family life. Be sure to see the Egyptian Room on the lower level, where human and animal mummies rest along with some of their prized belongings. Changing exhibits are featured throughout the year, and special events include noontime arts talks, a lecture and slide series, an antiquarian book show, and the colorful holiday Festival of Trees. The gift shop stocks many books about New York State history.

Albany Heritage Area Visitors Center and Henry Hudson Planetarium (518-434-1217, 800-258-3582), 25 Quackenbush Square. Open daily 10–4. Free. This site offers guests a series of changing exhibits, interactive displays that highlight history and culture in the capital city and provide an overview of the region. The planetarium (518-434-0405) features star shows on Saturday mornings at 11:30 for children and at 12:30 for adults; there are special programs during school vacation periods throughout the year, as well.

The Albany Trolley (518-434-0405), Visitors Center, 25 Quackenbush Square. Open July and August only; reservations recommended. Free parking. This is a great way to see the historic sites of the city during the summer months and to get oriented upon arrival. A narrated tour tells the story of the city and the legends behind several stately landmarks and important attractions. All tours begin with a film, *Albany: A Cultural Crossroads.*

New York State Museum (518-474-5877), Madison Avenue, Empire State Plaza. To reach the plaza, take exit 23 off the NYS Thruway. Pick up I-787, and get off at the Empire State Plaza exit. Open year-round (except national holidays) 10–5. Free. Today it anchors one end of the Empire State Plaza, but the museum has been a part of the state's history since 1836, making it one of the oldest state museums in the country. It is not, however, a dusty old repository with outdated displays of rocks and unidentified bones. This museum is alive with multimedia presentations that allow visitors to experience everything from a thunderstorm to a Lower East Side pushcart alley of the 1920s. The permanent exhibits include "Adirondack Wilderness," which explores the natural history of that region; "New York Metropolis," which focuses on New York City and the surrounding counties (here you will find a Duke Ellington–era A train and a set from *Sesame Street*); and displays that focus on Native American life and the Ice Age in the Empire State. A moving September 11th exhibit was installed in 2002. Another relatively recent addition is the second-floor exhibit that has a huge carousel and an old-fashioned soda fountain, depicting life in an era long past. Changing exhibits may feature folk art, dinosaurs, giant insects, or contemporary art and fine crafts, and shows are given in the museum's theater. Special events are scheduled all year; you may get to enjoy a Victorian holiday, a children's sleepover in the museum, or even a visit with an American artist. The gift shop is worth checking out.

USS *Slater* Destroyer Escort-766 (518-431-1943), the Snowdock at Broadway & Quay, at the foot of Madison Avenue. Exit 3B off Route I-787 South. Open Wednesday through Sunday 10–4. Admission fee. Step back in time aboard the last Destroyer Escort warship still in World War II battle configuration. See how the crew lived and carried out its mission of antisubmarine warfare. Armament, combat-information and radio rooms, pilot house, galley, mess, officer's quarters, and crew's sleeping area are authentically restored. Military history buffs will enjoy this stop.

HISTORIC HOMES Historic Cherry Hill (518-434-4791), 523½ South Pearl Street. Open April through December; call for times of tours, which are on the hour but change seasonally. Admission fee. Built in 1787 by Philip Van Rensselaer to replace what was called the Old Mansion, this Georgian house was the centerpiece of a 900-acre farm. Cherry Hill remained in the family for five generations, until 1963, and provides the visitor with a rare picture of the growth and care of a home over 176 years. The farm has, of course, disappeared under Albany streets, and the view across the road is now of oil tanks instead of orchards, but the house itself still offers a sense of grace and elegance. A visit begins in the basement orientation center, where a wall chart untangles the complicated series of marriages and relationships that kept Cherry Hill in the family. Upstairs, many of the 31 rooms have not been restored to match one particular period but contain the designs, belongings, and personal touches of their inhabitants. The collections found here are irreplaceable as a record of America's social history. There are more than 150 chairs, more than 30 tables, and thousands (20,000 at last count) of decorative objects, which include 18th-century paintings, 19th-century Oriental export ware, and even 20th-century clothing. Although the house was modernized over the years, things such as heating ducts and plumbing are carefully hidden away. Cherry Hill is a special place, chock-full of New York history and spirit. A holiday tour is offered in December and often features rarely exhibited toys from the museum's collection.

Schuyler Mansion (518-434-0834), 32 Catherine Street. Open April through October, Wednesday through Sunday 10–5. Admission fee. Once home to Philip Schuyler, a general in the Revolutionary War, the Schuyler Mansion was completed in 1764 on a rolling plot of land known as the Dutch Church Pasture. Schuyler was an important figure during the war, and many well-known statesmen, including Washington, Franklin, and the defeated English general John Burgoyne, visited the mansion over the years. During the war, Schuyler's daughter married Alexander Hamilton here, and a kidnap attempt was later made against her by the Tories; a gash on the wooden banister is said to have been made by a kidnapper's tomahawk. The house did not remain in the family after Schuyler's death but passed through a succession of owners before being purchased by New York State in 1912. Although numerous changes have been made to the exterior of the house over the years, including the removal of all the outbuildings, visitors can still see many examples of 18th-century furniture, glassware, pottery, and art as well as Schuyler family possessions. The interior restoration has been ongoing over the years.

Ten Broeck Mansion (518-436-9826), 9 Ten Broeck Place. Open April through December Thursday and Friday 10–4, Saturday and Sunday 1–4; closed holidays. Admission fee. Home of the Albany County Historical Association, this Federal mansion was built in 1798 for General Abraham Ten Broeck, who was a member of the Continental Congress and fought in the nearby battle of Saratoga. Once called Arbor Hill, the house now offers a look at the lifestyle of Albany's upper class during the last two centuries. Exhibits include period furniture and decorative items, and the house also contains a wine cellar, which when

SCHUYLER MANSION, ONCE HOME TO REVOLUTIONARY WAR
GENERAL PHILIP SCHUYLER

Albany County Convention and Visitors Bureau

NEW YORK STATE'S CAPITOL.

rediscovered during renovations was found to have a valuable collection of very aged wines!

HISTORIC SITES **State Capitol** (518-474-2418), located at the State Street end of the Empire State Plaza. Open daily, except holidays, year-round, Monday through Friday for tours at 10 AM, noon, 2 and 3; Saturday and Sunday at 11 AM, 1 and 3. Tours leave from the Empire State Plaza visitors center courtyard. This fairy-tale building, with its red towers and hundreds of arched windows, is one of the few state capitols not topped by a dome. Construction, completed in 1899, took more than 30 years and cost the then-unheard-of sum of $25 million. This is where the state senate and assembly meet and where you will find the governor's offices once used by Theodore Roosevelt, Nelson Rockefeller, and Franklin D. Roosevelt. Throughout the building are thousands of fine stone carvings, a tradition that can be traced back to the great churches of the Middle Ages. Many were caricatures of famous politicians and writers; others were of the families and relatives of the artisans; still others were self-portraits of the stone carvers themselves. But the most compelling carvings are the ones that form the **Million Dollar Staircase,** which took years to complete and is the best known of all the capitol's embellishments. Another unusual architectural feature is the senate fireplaces: The huge chimneys did not draw well, so the fireplaces' original function was abandoned in favor of using them as private "discussion nooks." And if you enjoy military history, don't miss the small military museum here; it traces the history of the state militia and National Guard. Flower lovers should make a special point of visiting the Capitol Park in spring, when thousands of tulips blaze into red and yellow bloom.

Executive Mansion (518-473-7521), 138 Eagle Street, Albany. Tours are offered Thursday 10–2, but call at least two weeks in advance for reservations during the busy summer and autumn months. Closed the month of July. This mansion is tucked down a side street just around the block from the Empire State Plaza. Built in 1850 as a private home, it now serves as the governor's residence. The tour covers the public rooms, which are filled with art from the 18th through the 20th centuries.

WALKING TOURS There is so much to see in this historic city that a walk down just about any street will give you a glimpse into Albany's colorful past.

The **Hudson River Way** opened for all to enjoy on August 10, 2002, extending from Broadway at Maiden Lane, over I-787, to the **Corning Riverfront Park** and amphitheater (see *Green Space*). This magnificent pedestrian walkway was designed to connect downtown Albany to the shores of the historic Hudson River, and also to tell the story of Albany through a series of paintings depicting historical artifacts. Created by mural principal artist Jan Marie Spanard and her talented crew, the paintings adorn the two staircase landings and the 30 lampposts that line both sides of the bridge. The story begins hundreds of millions of years ago when Albany was at the bottom of a prehistoric sea. As you progress over the bridge, the story continues through time, and includes the early Dutch merchants and other scenes of historic importance. There are two large murals on the landings that divide the three flights of the grand staircase. The paintings are done in a permanent liquid stone paint called "keim" that will not fade, peel or change for decades. Although this isn't a tour for people with young children, I recommend a walk over the pedestrian bridge for visitors to the capital who can walk stairs and don't mind the river breezes (beware that they can be quite brisk in the cool-weather months).

GATHERING ON A SUMMER'S EVENING AT THE EMPIRE STATE PLAZA

Albany County Convention and Visitors Bureau

The following are not specific city tours but rather suggestions for starting points on an Albany exploration:

An example of a 19th-century row-house community, the **Pastures Historic District,** is bounded roughly by Morton and Second Avenues and Elizabeth and Pearl Streets. Here you will also find the Schuyler Mansion (see *Historic Homes*) as well as many impressive private homes. The **Mansion Historic District,** bounded by Eagle, Dongan, Hamilton, and Ferry Streets, is a kaleidoscope of building styles, Italianate, Federal, and Greek Revival being only a few. Although the area became run-down earlier in this century, people have been rediscovering the richness of the district, and there is a sense of renewal here. The **Center Square–Hudson Park Historic District,** bounded by South Swan Street, Madison Avenue, South Lake Street, and Spring Street, is the largest historic district. Its centerpiece is **Washington Park,** a 90-acre area that once served as parade grounds and cemetery. Throughout the park you will find statues, lovely flower beds, and a lake (see *Green Space*). The district itself has scores of restored houses and commercial buildings.

For a schedule of walking tours of **Underground Railroad sites** in the downtown area, call 518-432-4432. There are some fascinating ones, and they are located throughout the city.

✳ Green Space

Corning Riverfront Park (800-258-3582). This section of the Corning Preserve lies along the west bank of the Hudson River. (To get there, take exit 23 off the NYS Thruway; pick up I-787, and get off at exit 4. Follow signs for Colonie Street.) This is a delightful park where strollers will enjoy walking along the river. Rollerskaters and bikers can pick up the Hudson-Mohawk Bikeway here and enjoy miles of paths (see *Bicycling*).

Governor Nelson A. Rockefeller Empire State Plaza (518-474-0559) is located off exit 23 of the NYS Thruway (go through the tollbooth to I-787 and take the Empire State Plaza exit) and bounded by Swan, Madison, State, and Eagle Streets. Open daily year-round. Free. Popularly called the Plaza, this is really a government complex that includes office buildings, a convention center, a performing arts center known as **the Egg** (see *Entertainment*), a concourse, and the state museum (see *To See*). Built at a cost of more than $2 billion and finished in 1978, the Plaza has fulfilled then-Governor Nelson Rockefeller's dream of a government center that would

WASHINGTON PARK, A 90-ACRE HAVEN IN THE MIDDLE OF ALBANY

Albany County Convention and Visitors Bureau

draw visitors and allow them to feel in touch with their state government. Tours of the Plaza are offered several times a day, but you may enjoy walking it yourself. The esplanade area is wonderful to explore, with tranquil reflecting pools, plantings, modern sculpture by such artists as David Smith, and even a play area known as the Children's Place. An environmental sculpture called *The Labyrinth* offers benches to the weary. Lining the interior halls of the concourse are fine examples of modern art on permanent display—the largest publicly owned and displayed art collection in the country, and they are all the work of New York artists. More than 92 sculptures, tapestries, paintings, and constructions are displayed, among them works by such artists as Calder, Nevelson, Frankenthaler, and Noguchi. Special art tours are offered (call for hours), or stop at any of the tourist booths and ask for the tour brochure.

There are a series of **12 memorial statues and sculptures** that provide an interesting walking tour through the plaza. In addition to the New York State Vietnam Veterans Memorial there are memorials honoring fallen firefighters, George Washington After Houdon, General Philip Henry Sheridan, police officers, women war veterans, those from New York State who fought in World War II and the Korean War, Dr. Martin Luther King Jr., children who died at the hands of abusers, parole officers who were killed in the line of duty, and crime victims.

For an above-the-clouds view of the entire mall, take the elevator to the 42nd floor of the **Corning Tower Observation Deck** at Empire State Plaza. Open daily except holidays 10–2:30. *Note:* For security purposes, anyone over the age of 16 must present photo ID before being allowed to enter the elevator. From the observation deck, one can see a magnificent 270-degree view looking southeast toward the Taconics and Berkshires, west to the Catskills, and northeast toward the Adirondacks. A great stop on a clear day.

Outside, near the wide stairway to the New York State Museum, special events are held throughout the summer, among them an Independence Day celebration, concerts, ethnic celebrations, a Blues Fest, and the Empire State Plaza Farmers Market. (see *To Do—Farm Markets*). First Night Albany, a citywide New Year's Eve celebration, may be enjoyed at the Plaza, as well (see *Special Events*). Children who like to walk will enjoy the activities on the mall.

Washington Park (518-434-5412), State & Willett Streets, Madison & Lake Avenues. This 90-acre park in the center of Albany is the site of several interesting and enjoyable special events throughout the year (see *Special Events*).

✳ To Do

BICYCLING **The Hudson-Mohawk Bikeway** (800-258-3582). This 41-mile bike path is one of the area's most popular recreational features, traveling along the Hudson and Mohawk rivers and connecting the areas of Albany, Schenectady, and Troy. For those who prefer other means of travel, Rollerblading is also permitted here. To access the Bikeway, head to the **Corning Preserve,** along the west bank of the Hudson River. (Take exit 23 off the NYS Thruway and pick up I-787 north to exit 4. Follow the signs for Colonie Street.) The Bikeway also includes the **Colonie Riverfront Bike-Hike Trail** (518-783-2760), a 5.5 mile trail that runs along the Mohawk River; the **Niskayuna Riverfront Bike-Hike Trail** (518-372-2519), a 7-mile paved path built on an old railroad bed along the Mohawk River; and the **Rotterdam Riverfront Hike-Bike Trail** (518-356-5344), a 7-mile paved path.

BOAT CRUISES **Dutch Apple Cruises, Inc.** (518-463-0220), 141 Broadway. River tours daily, April through October; there are two-hour sightseeing cruises or three-hour dinner cruises available on a tour boat that holds 145 people. Reasonable prices; discounts for children and seniors.

FARM MARKETS **Empire State Farmers Market** (518-457-7076), Empire State Plaza. Open July through October Wednesday and Friday 11–2. Approximately 20 vendors gather on the plaza to sell fruits, vegetables, baked goods, honey, maple syrup, and other local produce in-season.

Engels Farm Market (518-869-5653), 667 Albany Shaker Road. (Take the NYS Thruway to exit 24; pick up the Northway to exit 4. Make a left off the exit and another left at the next light. The market is right there.) This farm market is first-rate and is located across the street from the Desmond Hotel (see *Lodging*).You will find all kinds of produce in-season: fresh fruits and vegetables as well as local honey and maple products.

Goold Orchards (518-732-7317), 1297 Brookview Station Road, Castleton. Head across the Route 9 & 20 Bridge into Rensselaer County and down Route 9 (follow the Goold Orchards signs) for pick-your-own strawberries in June, apples and raspberries in September. The farm store and bakery offer homemade cider doughnuts and fresh-pressed cider, an array of fruit pies and cookies, all made fresh on the premises. The bakery is open Labor Day through November. The store is open year-round for apples and cider.

Lansing's Farm Market (518-464-0889), 204 Lishakill Road, Colonie. Open April through Christmas. (Take NYS Thruway to exit 24, then pick up Route 5 west to Lishakill Road). Pick your own strawberries here in June. Other goodies on sale in the market include tomatoes, corn, peppers, squash, and all other fruits and vegetables grown on the Lansing farm in-season.

Shaker Shed Farm Market (518-869-3662), junction Sand Creek Road and Route 155, Colonie. Open Easter through Christmas. (Take the NYS Thruway to exit 24; pick up the Northway to exit 4, make a left off the exit and another left onto Albany-Shaker Road—staying to the left. You will pass the airport. At the stop sign, make a left. The market is over the hill on the left side of the road.) Pick your own tomatoes here in late August. The market offers home-grown produce, crafts, candles, and fresh pies. Enjoy a drink and dessert in the café. During the spring months there are plants galore; at Christmas, a nice selection of wreaths and trees.

GOLF **Capital Hills at Albany** (518-438-2208), 65 O'Neil Road, Albany. This 18-hole, par-71 public course, owned by the city of Albany, is the only place to golf in the capital. For walkers who accompany golfers to this course, there is a

2.6 mile trail that wends its way through wooded areas. Open April to November, weather permitting. Call in advance for tee time. Restaurant, full bar, driving range.

Mill Road Acres (518-783-7244), 30 Mill Road, Latham. This 18-hole, par-58 public course is open April through October. There is equipment rental and senior discounts. Full bar and snack bar on the premises.

Town of Colonie Golf Course (518-374-4181). 418 Consaul Road, Colonie. This 36-hole, par-72 course is open April through October. Call two days ahead to insure a tee time if you are a resident of Colonie; otherwise, there are no reservations. There is equipment rental and a driving range. Restaurant, full bar, snack bar on the premises.

ICE SKATING **Albany County Hockey Training Facility** (518-452-7396). Albany-Shaker Road, Albany. Open year-round except the month of June for both figure skating and hockey. There are both free-style and public sessions for figure skating. Snack bar on premises.

Empire State Plaza (518-474-2418), Outdoor Plaza, Albany. Outdoor skating in the winter months, weather permitting.

Swinburne Rink and Recreation Center (518-438-2406), Clinton Avenue below Manning Boulevard, Albany. Outdoor skating rink, but call before you go for time of sessions; keep in mind that the schedule is weather-dependent here.

SHOPPING MALLS The Albany area is known for its excellent shopping, and the majority of shops may be found in the city's malls. The following three shopping districts are all different in style and provide enough variety for just about any visitor.

Colonie Center (518-459-9020), 131 Colonie Center, Wolf Road and Central Avenue, Albany. (Take the NYS Thruway to exit 24, go through tollbooth and head to exit 1N—the Northway. Get off at exit 2, Wolf Road.) Macy's and Sears are the anchor stores in this huge mall, which is filled with shops as varied as the Christmas Tree Shop and Victoria's Secret. The mall is also surrounded by stores: across the street are Bed Bath & Beyond and Barnes & Noble; just next door is Borders Books & Music.

Crossgates Mall (518-869-9565), 1 Crossgates Mall Road, Albany. (Take NYS Thruway to exit 24; go to the farthest right toll booth. Make a right onto Western Avenue. Crossgates Mall Road is less than a mile ahead on the right.) This enormous mall has over 250 stores, including Eastern Mountain Sports, Chico's, Eddie Bauer, Filene's, and JC Penney as well as an 18-theater (stadium seating) and a 12-theater cineplex.

Stuyvesant Plaza (518-482-8986), Western Avenue & Fuller Road, Albany. (Take the NYS Thruway to exit 24. Go south on Route 87, the Northway, to Western Avenue. Make a left turn. Approximately 1,500 feet ahead of you, on the left, is Stuyvesant Plaza. Look for sign.) What I like best about this shopping area is that the upscale stores are not enclosed in a mall; the set-up is rather old-fashioned, and you must walk outdoors along a sidewalk from store to store.

However, the shops (and restaurants) are first-rate and include the Book House, one of the best independent bookstores you will find anywhere. Unless it's raining, I'd head here first—especially if you are looking for something a little different.

SPECTATOR SPORTS **Albany Attack** (518-427-8145), National Lacrosse League, Pepsi Arena, 51 South Pearl Street, Albany. The season for lacrosse here runs from January through April.

Albany Conquest (518-427-8145), Arena Football 2 League-AF2-Pepsi Arena, 51 South Pearl Street, Albany. You can catch a game from April through July.

Albany River Rats (518-487-2244), American Hockey League—New Jersey Devils affiliate, Pepsi Arena, 51 South Pearl Street, Albany. The season runs from October through April for hockey.

Siena Saints Basketball (518-487-2000), Division 1 College Basketball, Pepsi Arena, 51 South Pearl Street, Albany. Call for schedule.

✳ Entertainment

Albany Civic Theatre (518-462-1297), 235 Second Avenue. Admission fee. Musicals and dramas are offered throughout the year. There is also a playwright's showcase, an annual spring event, that is offered free of charge.

Albany Symphony Orchestra (518-465-4755), 19 Clinton Avenue. Admission fee. The season runs from September through May, and performances are given at the newly renovated Palace Theatre in Albany and the acoustically renowned Troy Savings Bank Music Hall across the Hudson River in the city of Troy. There is a varied mix of concerts as well as a series of children's musical performances. Every March the American Music Festival delights local residents and visitors alike. Call for schedule.

Capital Repertory Theatre (518-462-4531, 445-SHOW), 111 North Pearl Street. Admission fee. Theater lovers will enjoy the year-round performances here; Capital Rep has been offering first-rate entertainment for nearly 25 years. The company employs professional equity actors and designers from New York City. There are usually six productions over the course of the year; they include musicals, comedies, dramas, and family-oriented productions. Several student matinees are also offered in conjunction with the educational department.

eba Dance Theatre (518-465-9916), 351 Hudson Avenue. Once known as electronic body arts, this company offers dance performances throughout the year. The emphasis is on modern dance, but there is an Arts in Education program that takes a variety of works into the city schools. Call for schedule.

The Egg (518-473-1061), Empire State Plaza. This marvelous venue includes year-round ballet, modern dance, theater, rock concerts and other musical performances, even storytellers and monologists. Visitors may enjoy a virtual cornucopia of entertainment here. Call for a complete schedule.

Pepsi Arena (518-487-2000), 51 South Pearl Street. (Take NYS Thruway to exit 23. Pick up I-787 north and go to the downtown Albany exit—Routes 9 & 20

West. At the light, make a left onto Broadway, and go under the bridge. At the next light, make a left, and then at the following light make a right onto Madison Avenue. Go two more lights and make a right onto South Pearl Street. Follow signs into arena.) This sports and entertainment complex is home to several athletic teams (see *Spectator Sports*); it's also where you can see a range of entertainment: from Cher, Stars on Ice, and Yanni to Bon Jovi, Nelli, and Sesame Street. There are car and motorcycle shows, regional basketball playoffs, and more. Call for schedule or see their web site: www.pepsiarena.com.

✳ Lodging

Albany Marriott Hotel (518-458-8444, 800-443-8952), 189 Wolf Road, Albany 12205. ($$$) This hotel is near four major shopping malls, a 5-minute drive from the airport, and less than 20 minutes from downtown. Each room in this luxury hotel is equipped with cable TV (including HBO) and other modern amenities. There are indoor and outdoor pools, sauna, whirlpool, and exercise rooms. A continental breakfast is served, and there are restaurants on site. Open year-round.

Clarion Inn & Suites (518-785-5891, 800-830-5205), 611 Troy-Schenectady Road, Latham. ($$) There are 132 rooms in this moderately-priced establishment, where you will find an outdoor pool and exercise room. Close to the airport. Open year-round.

Courtyard by Marriott (518-482-8800, 800-321-2211), 168 Wolf Road, Albany. ($$$) Enjoy swimming in the indoor pool at this 80-room hotel with all the amenities, including a restaurant, exercise room, and free transportation to the airport.

Crowne Plaza (518-462-6611, 800-227-6963), Ten Eyck Plaza, Albany 12210. ($$$) Located in the heart of downtown near the capitol and Empire State Plaza, this luxury hotel has 384 guest rooms and 18 suites. You will find an exercise, room,

indoor heated pool, and whirlpool. Complimentary airport transportation and free parking are provided; a gift shop, auto-rental facilities, and an airline office are on-site. The hotel's restaurant, **Webster's Corner,** has an excellent and reasonably priced lunch buffet Monday through Friday 11:30–2.

The Desmond (518-869-8100, 800-448-3500), 660 Albany Shaker Road, Albany 12211. ($$$) The best features of an inn and a hotel are combined at the Desmond, with its period reproduction furniture, paintings, handsome wood paneling, and courtyards that bloom with flowers and plants all year. All rooms have custom-made furniture, and guests can use two heated pools, a health club, saunas, exercise rooms, and a billiard room. **The Scrimshaw Restaurant** in the hotel has fine food. Open year-round.

Holiday Inn Turf (518-458-7250, 800-HOLIDAY), 205 Wolf Road, Albany. ($$$) There are over 300 rooms in this luxurious hotel, with both indoor and outdoor pools, exercise room, and restaurant on the premises. Open year-round.

Kittleman House (518-432-3979), 70 Willett Street, Albany. ($$) This charming B&B is housed in a three-story brownstone built in 1867 and located on Washington Park's fashionable Willett Street, minutes away from the Empire State Plaza. There are two reasonably priced rooms here, both with private bath, and you can opt for the breakfast of the day (which changes every morning), or order a continental breakfast custom-made to your taste. The owner lives on the premises, and the hospitality and cozy atmosphere offer a change from the usual city hotel scene. Children over the age of 10 only. Open year-round.

Mansion Hill Inn (518-465-2038, 888-299-0455), 115 Phillip Street, Albany. ($$) This bed & breakfast is within walking distance of the state capitol and the downtown business district. Winner of a preservation award, the inn has eight rooms, each with private bath. Choose from a wide variety of dishes on the breakfast menu. Children welcome. Open year-round.

Morgan State House (518-427-6063, 888-427-6063), 393 State Street, Albany. ($$$) This luxury inn on Washington Park offers 16 rooms, all with private bath; 6 are located in the 19th-century main house, and 10 are in the condominium suites that date back to the early 20th century. Full breakfast served. Children over the age of 16 only. Open year-round.

Ramada Inn Albany-Downtown (518-434-4111, 800-272-6232), 300 Broadway, Albany. ($$) This economy motel has an outdoor pool, a small restaurant and exercise room, and it's not far from several of the city's attractions. Open year-round.

State Street Mansion Bed & Breakfast (518-462-6780, 800-673-5750), 281 State Street, Albany. ($$) This B&B is located in the center of the city's Center Square Historic District, only one block away from the capitol and the Empire State Plaza. One of the oldest B&Bs in Albany, in business for nearly 85 years, it offers

readily accessible cultural activities, entertainment, and dining, making it a popular stop with business people. The brownstone dates back to 1889; the12 rooms all have private baths. A continental breakfast is served. **The Bleecker Café** on the premises serves lunch and dinner daily. Parking is available and included in the room charge.

Suisse Chalet (518-459-5670), 44 Wolf Road, Albany. ($) There are approximately 100 rooms in this budget motel, which offers exercise facilities and a continental breakfast. Open year-round.

THE MORGAN STATE HOUSE BED & BREAKFAST

✳ Where to Eat

Albany offers a wealth of restaurants to choose from, and they offer a range of culinary traditions—from fusion cuisine to Indonesian—for both the adventurous and the less daring diner alike. The following establishments were selected for their particularly good quality food or interesting offerings and atmosphere; they provide only a hint of the culinary treasures in the capital city.

DINING OUT The Barnsider (518-869-2448), 480 Sand Creek Road. ($$) Open for dinner Monday through Saturday 5–10, Sunday 4–9. The specialties here are the hand-cut steaks and fresh seafood, which include entrées like prime rib of beef and baked stuffed shrimp. Light fare is also available, and there is a full bar. Children are welcome.

Bongiorno's (518-462-9176), 23 Dove Street. ($$) Open for lunch Monday through Friday 11:30–2; for dinner 5–9, Saturday 5–10. The seafood and veal dishes are superb at this excellent Italian restaurant. The clams marinara, seafood fra diavolo, and veal Francese are a few of my favorites. There are always lunch specials during the week. Mangia, and feel like you escaped to Italy for a repast!

Caffè Italia (518-482-9433), 662 Central Avenue. ($$$) Open daily for dinner 5–11. This family-run Italian restaurant is a popular spot with members of the state legislature (a dish or two are even named after lawmakers). Everything is prepared to order, and the veal and pasta specialties are worth the trip. Reservations required. Not recommended for children.

Clayton's Caribbean American Cuisine (518-426-4360), 244 Washington Avenue. ($) Open daily 11–11. Authentic Caribbean and Spanish food, with entrées like arroz con pollo, curried chicken, jerk chicken, veggie fajitas, and a wide variety of fresh seafood and vegetarian dishes. Wine and beer served. Children welcome.

Daniel's Café (518-694-5320), 144 Washington Avenue. ($$) Open for lunch Monday through Friday 11–3; dinner daily 5–10. Enjoy an imaginative melding of continental and Israeli fare, with interesting flavor combinations. The Greek baked salmon in phyllo is wonderful.

El Mariachi (518-432-7580), 289 Hamilton Street; also (465-2568) 62 Central Avenue. ($) Open Monday through Friday 11–10, Saturday and Sunday 1–10. Authentic homestyle Mexican and Spanish regional dishes, including paella. There is a full bar with over 45 fine tequilas to make those margaritas special. For those like me who prefer the homemade sangria, they offer both white and red. Enjoy lunch specials during the week; they're good value for the money.

Jack's Oyster House (518-465-8854), 42 State Street. ($$) Open daily for lunch and dinner 11:30–10, until 11 on Friday and Saturday. This is Albany's oldest restaurant, and for 80 years it has been run by the same family. The steak and seafood are traditions, and the specialties are consistently good. Reservations suggested. Children are welcome.

Justin's (518-436-7008), 301 Lark Street. ($$) Open daily for lunch 11:30–2:30; dinner served from 5; late-night menu available until 1 AM. Located in Albany's answer to Greenwich Village, part of this restaurant dates back to the 1700s, and there has been a tavern or inn on this site ever since. All soups are made fresh every day—the Provincetown seafood chowder is a favorite of mine. For appetizers, try the risotto ravioli filled with sun-dried tomato, prosciutto, basil, and risotto. The entrées range from fresh seared tuna steak on a bed of warm French lentils, bacon, and sun-dried tomatoes to char-grilled double-cut pork chop served with corn bread, house baked beans, and picnic slaw. There are always daily specials, and the café menu has unusually enticing gourmet sandwiches. Jazz is featured on some evenings; call in advance for the schedule. Reservations suggested. Not appropriate for children.

La Serre Restaurant (518-463-6056), 14 Green Street. ($$$) Open Monday through Friday for lunch 11:30–2; dinner served Monday through Saturday from 5. This elegant continental restaurant is housed in historic building complete with bright awnings and window boxes full of flowers. The service is superb, and specialties include an award-winning onion soup, bouillabaisse Marseillaise, loin of veal with béarnaise sauce, and steak *au poivre*. Sumptuous desserts are made fresh daily.

McGuire's (518-463-2100), 353 State Street, near Lark Street, close to the capitol. ($$$) Open Monday through Saturday from 5–10. Housed in a restored, historic structure that was once an ice-cream parlor, this intimate, elegant establishment, which seats about 60, features some of the finest Continental cuisine to be found in Albany—or anywhere in the Hudson Valley. A relatively new addition to the capi-

tal's restaurant scene (they opened in August 2002), and Chef Andrew Plummer's Delmonico steak attracts a loyal following. For those interested in surf, the lobster risotto appetizer and red snapper are favorites of mine. The sea bass, which combines Caribbean and Japanese flavors, is one of several fish entrées from which to choose. And save room for the beautifully presented, imaginative desserts. The service is first-rate; the wait staff is particularly knowledgeable about the offerings. Advance reservations necessary, even during the week. Valet parking. Not recommended for children.

Miyako (518-482-1080), 192 North Allen Street. ($) Open Tuesday through Sunday for lunch noon–2; for dinner 5–10. At this informal Japanese restaurant you can watch the chef make your meal on the hibachi table, or enjoy the creative, freshly prepared fare from the sushi bar. Children welcome.

My Linh (518-465-8899), 272 Delaware Avenue. ($$) Open Tuesday through Thursday and Sunday 5–9:30, Friday and Saturday until 10. Albany's first Vietnamese restaurant, it opened in 1993 and is still a popular restaurant among local residents. Dinner is served in a casual, comfortable atmosphere. One of my favorite dishes is the shrimp summer rolls. The crispy pan-fried boneless duck is tender and served perfectly. And the crepes filled with chicken or sliced beef sauté in a spicy curry sauce is quite good. Vegetarians will have an array of items to choose from, like grilled tofu topped with spicy bean curd sauce. Children welcome.

Nicole's Bistro at the Quackenbush House (518-465-1111),

25 Quackenbush Square. ($$) Open Monday through Friday for lunch 11:30–2:30; for dinner 5–10. This restaurant is located in the oldest building in Albany and dates back to the late 17th century. Once a private home, the brick structure is now a gathering place with gorgeous gardens in the heart of downtown Albany. Enjoy fine French cuisine, including duck with pear sauce. The food is first-rate, and the building—with its towers and curves—is intriguing. Outdoor dining in the warm-weather months.

Ogden's (518-463-6605), Lodge and Howard Streets. ($$) Open for lunch Monday through Friday 11:30–3; for dinner Monday through Saturday from 5:30. Enjoy Continental and New American cuisine, with such specialties as aged Angus beef with Roquefort sauce and grilled Norwegian salmon with ginger tamari beurre blanc. Salads and sandwiches predominate at lunchtime. The black bean soup has been on the menu for over 25 years, and Ogden's is well-known throughout Albany for this Cuban-style treat. All breads and desserts are made on the premises, and every dish is prepared to order. An elegant, yet casual, spot located in a restored turn-of-the-19th-century building, with food that is consistently excellent. This is one of the best establishments in the capital.

Real Seafood Company (518-458-2068), 195 Wolf Road, Colonie. ($$) Open Monday through Thursday 11 AM–11:30 PM, Friday and Saturday 3–11:30, Sunday 3–9:30. This popular seafood emporium has an impressive raw bar. The menu features such entrées as char-grilled Block Island swordfish, tuna medallions in white wine and herbs, and a blue-plate combination special of the day that changes seasonally. Children welcome.

Sitar (518-456-6670), 1929 Central Avenue. ($$) Open daily for lunch 11:30–2:30 and Monday through Saturday for dinner 5–10. Indian specialties are prepared to your taste, among them tandoori or curry dishes, chicken and vegetarian entrées. This is one of the best Indian restaurants in the Hudson Valley; it's reasonably priced, as well. Children are welcome.

Taste of Greece (518-426-9000), 193 Lark Street. ($$) Open Monday through Friday 11–10, Saturday 2–10. Enjoy all the Greek favorites in a relaxed bistro setting. There is spanakopita (spinach pie), Greek salad, gyros, souvlaki, kebabs, moussaka, and more. Extensive vegetarian menu; wine and beer served. Children are welcome.

Yono's (518-436-7747), 64 Colvin Avenue. ($$) Open Tuesday through Saturday for dinner 5:30–10. Indonesian cuisine is found here, along with Continental specialties. Chicken, vegetarian dishes, and excellent steaks coexist on the eclectic menu with Far Eastern specialties. In summer the garden patio is open for dining. Reservations are strongly suggested since this is one of the most popular restaurants in the city.

EATING OUT Aromi D'Italia (518-452-9200), 2050 Western Avenue, Guilderland. ($$) Open daily for lunch and dinner 10 AM–11 PM. The freshest ingredients and quality products enhance the menu at this contemporary Italian café. In addition to world famous gelato (made fresh daily on the premises), diners will savor pasta entrées, gourmet pizzas, huge salads, paninis (served on homemade focaccia bread), rich desserts, espresso, and coffee drinks. Children are welcome.

Albany Pump Station (518-447-9000), 19 Quackenbush Square. ($) Open daily 11:30–10, until 11 Friday and Saturday, Sunday noon–8. This downtown city brew pub offers a wide variety of American favorites. The menu includes everything from meat loaf, burgers, and calamari to mango salmon, dinner salads, and overstuffed sandwiches. There is a full bar, and the place is a popular spot for drinks and a light dinner with a younger crowd after the workday. Not recommended for children.

Big House Brewing Company (518-445-2739), 90 North Pearl Street. ($) Open Tuesday through Saturday from 4 PM. Dozens of beers and ales are offered in this lively spot, from Ale Capone Amber to Ma Barker Light. The hearty food includes burgers, sandwiches, steaks and salads. Tuesdays there are $2 pints all night.

Daily Grind (518-427-0464), 204 Lark Street. ($) Open daily 7 AM–10 PM except Sunday, when they close at 8 PM. There is more than coffee here; upstairs is a retail store specializing in fresh-roasted coffee beans, while downstairs a European-style café offers an eclectic variety of light fare (soups, sandwiches, wraps, desserts, biscotti, cookies). There is a decent selection of teas for those who don't indulge in coffee in the daily grind!

Debbie's Kitchen (518-463-3829),456 Madison Avenue. ($) Open Monday through Friday 10–9; Saturday 11–6. This is the downtown

Albany place to go for homemade soups and sandwiches with a creative flair. Chef Debbie Lauber weaves a touch of color and crunch into the ordinary. Her smoked turkey-breast sandwich with garlic mayo, sliced pears, sunflower seeds, roasted onions and cheddar cheese is a wonderful variation on the usual turkey sandwich. Vegetarian combos and fresh salads are available, and a wide variety of freshly baked cakes and cookies are difficult to pass up for dessert. Debbie's chocolate brownies are some of the best in the city. Children are welcome.

El Loco Café (518-436-1855), 465 Madison Avenue. ($) Open Tuesday through Saturday for lunch and dinner 11:30–10. This lively café specializes in Tex-Mex fare and is located in a restored 19th-century building. El Loco is well known for its chili (the heat is up to you) and its large selection of Mexican beer. Even after all the chili and beer you can down, the desserts are still tempting. Children are welcome.

Mamoun's Mideast Café (518-434-3901), 206 Washington Avenue. ($) Open daily 11:30–10. In addition to the vegetarian fare at this Middle Eastern restaurant, there is a variety of chicken and lamb dishes. Try the shish kebob—it's a house specialty. The food is prepared to order and will appeal to everyone. Mamoun's is a family-run business; once when I arrived with a friend, the restaurant was closed. However, someone came to the door, invited us in, and within minutes, we were seated and ordering a meal.

Organic Café (518-482-3749), 64 Colvin Avenue, within Armory Center. ($) Open for breakfast and lunch Monday through Friday 6–2. As the name implies, they specialize in organic and natural foods. The omelettes, French toast, personal pan pizzas, sandwiches, homemade soups, and fruit and vegetable drinks—all made fresh—are first-rate. A great place to stop for a healthful meal or snack that tastes great. Children welcome.

Peaches Café (518-482-3677), Stuyvesant Plaza. ($) Open Monday through Thursday 8 AM–9:30 PM, Friday and Saturday until 11 PM, Sunday 8–8. Enjoy breakfast all day, every day, in a relaxing atmosphere; Belgian waffles and specialty omelettes are what they are known for here. At lunchtime, the soups, salads, sandwiches, and wonderful wraps are the perfect antidote to the hectic pace of shopping. Children welcome.

Quintessence (518-434-8186), 11 New Scotland Avenue. ($) Open daily for breakfast, lunch, and dinner 8 AM–midnight. This art-deco diner bustles with good food and special theme nights, including Italian, seafood, and German dinners. The large menu has an international flair; something to please every taste. Children are welcome.

Shades of Green (518-434-1830), 187 Lark Street. ($) Open Monday through Saturday 11–9. Closed Sunday (and on Saturday during the winter months). Gourmet vegetarian cuisine with international influences is what you will find in this delightful eatery. Enjoy homemade soups, fresh-squeezed fruit and vegetable juices, tasty shakes, inventive salads, and more. There are many options for vegans. This is certainly the healthy choice, but the food is both good for you *and* tasty !

✳ Special Events

Seasonal events abound in the capital city, and enhance any vacation stay. So if you are planning a trip to Albany, call 800-258-3582 for a complete listing, or check out what's happening when you will be there online at www.albany.org.

February: **Albany American Wine Festival** (518-464-WINE). This festival is held at the Desmond Hotel, 660 Albany Shaker Road, the first weekend in February every year. There are tastings, seminars, and dinners, featuring wines from all over the country. A one-day pass can be purchased. The lectures are designed to appeal to oenophiles as well as those who want to learn more about wines.

March: **The Capital District Garden & Flower Show** (518-356-6410), deemed one of the top 100 events in America by a national tour organization, is held across the Hudson River at Hudson Valley Community College in Troy. Learn more about the art of gardening with vendors, workshops, lectures, floral designers, and more.

May: The **Annual Tulip Festival,** also known as Pinksterfest (518-434-2032), is usually held the second weekend in May and includes outdoor crafts and food fairs in Washington Park, entertainment, the crowning of the Tulip Queen, scrubbing down State Street, and a dance. The celebrations are colorful and peopled with costumed performers—and, of course, over 100,000 tulips.

June: The **Lobster Fest** (518-434-5412) is held in Washington Park on the third Sunday of the month (Father's Day), complete with fresh lobster, grilled steak, music, and more. A great way to spend the day with Dad.

July: **Cross State Bicycle Tour** (518-434-1583) is a 400-mile bicycle tour from Buffalo to Albany along the historic Erie Canal. Half the ride is off-road, on the traffic-free Canalway Trail; the rest is on rural roads. The race draws participants from many states, and it takes eight days. Sponsored and organized by the New York Parks and Conservation Association, the tour usually begins the first Monday after July 4th. The **Fleet Blues Fest** (518-473-0559) at the Empire State Plaza is fun for the entire family, featuring the hottest in contemporary and traditional blues performances. **A Taste of Lark** (518-434-3861), held on Lark Street in the city, offers an opportunity to taste the variety of cuisine that this neighborhood has to offer. One ticket allows you to sample food and drink from over 25 different restaurants. **Shaker Craft & Herb Festival** (518-456-7890), Shaker Heritage Society, Shaker Meeting House, Albany Shaker Road. Several vendors exhibit their wares, offering the crafts and herb traditions of this fascinating group.

August: **Riverfest** (518-434-2032) on the bank of the Hudson River. This all-day event offers a wide variety of entertainment in the Riverfront Amphitheater, activities for children, fantastic food, water activities, and fireworks over the river at dusk. **Latin Fest** (518-434-2032), Washington Park, offers the best in Latin music, food, and crafts. Children's rides will delight the young ones and make this a festive family outing.

September: **JazzFest** (518-434-2032), is held in downtown Albany in Riverfront Park. Right by the water,

EVERY SPRING ALBANY CELEBRATES ITS DUTCH HERITAGE WITH PINKSTERFEST, THE TULIP FESTIVAL.

Albany County Convention and Visitors Bureau

listen to jazz in the Riverfront Amphitheater.

October: The **Columbus Day Parade and Italian Festival** (518-434-2032), extends from Western Avenue to Washington Park and includes such traditional street fair foods as fried dough, cannoli, sausage and peppers, pizza, pasta, and more.

November: **Symphony of Lights** (518-465-2143) is a magnificent three-dimensional illuminated holiday display glowing with over 10,000 lights on State and Pearl Streets. Shining brilliantly as the centerpiece of downtown is a 17-foot animated gold-glittered trumpet. From mid-November to January 2nd. **Capital Holiday Lights in the Park** (518-258-3582), Washington Park, is a dazzling drive-through holiday light display with more than 40 illuminated scenes and characters. At the end, there are surprises and holiday treats in the park's Lakehouse. Thanksgiving through January 5th. Admission fee.

December: **First Night Albany** (518-434-2032) is held at various locations throughout downtown. A celebration of the arts, with fun for the entire family. There are dozens of entertainers, activities for the children, and fireworks.

Saratoga Springs and Environs

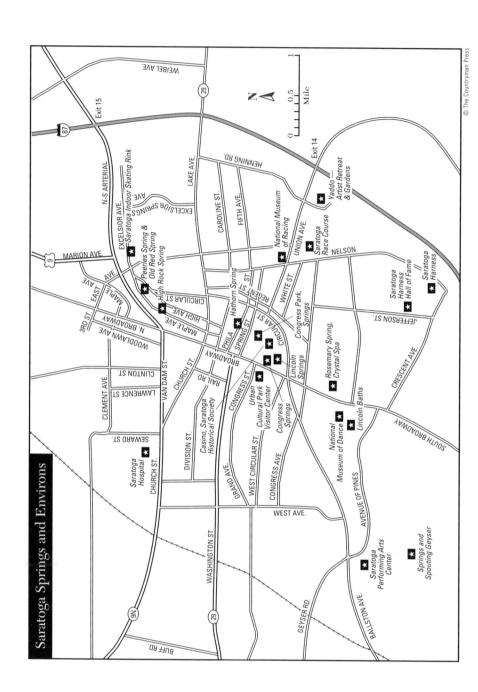

Saratoga Springs and Environs

© The Countryman Press

SARATOGA SPRINGS AND ENVIRONS

I t is nearly impossible to describe Saratoga Springs—elegant, gracious, exciting, mysterious, and eccentric are only some of the words that come to mind. Since the 18th century, when natural medicinal springs were discovered in the region, Saratoga Springs has played host to visitors from around the world. There are 15 outstanding public golf courses in the area. Parks and nature preserves abound for hiking and biking. Ice skate in July at the indoor rink. Fish the Kayderosseras Creek, a Class-A trout stream, or try out Saratoga Lake, often referred to as the Bass Capital of the World. The museums and specialty boutiques are excellent; when you tire of exploring, the springs and spas will revive you. Classical music and dance enthusiasts can enjoy a picnic dinner while great orchestral selections and ballets are performed under the stars. Lovers of Victorian architecture can stroll down a side street or two, where they will spot grand old mansions and exquisite gardens. With all of this, Saratoga Springs also offers the best Thoroughbred horse racing in the world. Each July and August this quiet place pulses with the color, crowds, and excitement of the famed Saratoga Racetrack, where the best jockeys and horses vie for enormous winnings and fame. In addition, there are horse auctions and polo matches, and the public is invited to just about every event. You can spend a month in Saratoga Springs and still not experience all it has to offer. The only thing you must not do is miss it!

GUIDANCE **Saratoga County Chamber of Commerce** (518-584-3255, 800-526-8970), 28 Clinton Street, Saratoga Springs 12866; www.saratoga.org.

Saratoga Springs Urban Cultural Park Visitor Center (518-587-3241), 297 Broadway (Drink Hall), across the street from Congress Park, is open daily in July and August. This well-located information center is a good place for summer visitors to find out what's going on in town upon arrival.

GETTING THERE *By car:* Saratoga Springs (approximately 200 miles from New York City and Boston and 30 miles from Albany) is located north of Albany on I-87 (the Northway), exits 13N through 15.

By air: **Albany International Airport** (518-242-2299) is less than a half-hour drive from Saratoga. **Saratoga County Airport** (518-885-5354), Richmor Aviation, Ballston Spa, has charter service available every day. Call them for detailed information.

By bus: **Adirondack Trailways** (518-583-7490, 800-858-8555), 135 South Broadway, Saratoga Springs, provides service to Albany, Boston, and New York City as well as other destinations.

MEDICAL EMERGENCY Saratoga Hospital (518-587-3222), 211 Church Street, Saratoga Springs.

✳ To See

Children's Museum at Saratoga (518-584-5540), 69 Caroline Street. Open Labor Day through June Tuesday through Saturday 9:30–4:30, Sunday noon–4:30; July through Labor Day also open on Mondays. Admission fee. This unique museum offers children ages one to nine a chance to explore the world, from the local community to the international level. Interactive exhibits allow them to run a general store, make giant bubbles, and "freeze" their shadows. A tree house, fire truck, science section, movie theater, and two toddler areas are also popular with young visitors. Special events have included art workshops and magic shows. The museum is so centrally located that a visit can be combined with shopping or stops at the Canfield Casino Museum and park.

Congress Park (518-584-6920), Broadway and Circular Street. Open daily year-round. Part of the daily life of Saratoga Springs a century ago was "taking the waters," and Congress Park was a popular watering hole. The wealthy who came to Saratoga Springs each summer to escape the plagues and stink of the industrial cities would stay at the area's fine hotels and stroll along the park's pathways to various fountains (see *Springs & Spas*). Today the park has lovely plantings, places to sit and ponder the past, and some interesting decorative offerings. Daniel Chester French's statue *The Spirit of Life* greets visitors near the entrance (he also created the renowned seated president's statue in the Lincoln Memorial), and two huge, lovely urns called "Day" and "Night" bloom with flowers each summer. Tucked in the back of the park is a small reflecting pool with the most popular of the park's denizens: a pair of Triton figurines that shoot out streams of water and are nicknamed Spit and Spat. Enjoy walking among the columns in the Italian Gardens. Also located in the park is **Canfield Casino.** (Open May through October 10–4, closed January. Hours vary widely November through April, so call ahead. Admission fee.) The Canfield Casino was once one of the most famous gambling establishments in the country. Today it is home to a museum and art gallery.

The **Saratoga Historical Society** maintains a lovely series of rooms that offer vignettes of life in Saratoga Springs during the Gilded Age of the late 19th century, when Lillian Russell, Diamond Jim Brady, and a host of others sparkled each night over the gaming tables. Downstairs in the museum's art gallery there are changing exhibits of works by local and regional artists. The museum also hosts crafts shows each summer and fall. (During the racing season, the casino becomes the site of one of the most glamorous society events in the old style:

philanthropist Mary Lou Whitney's "fantasy" parties, where guests may enjoy visiting Oz or watching Cinderella arrive in a real pumpkin coach. Of course, this is not a public event, but if you are in the area, you can watch the Saratoga glitterati arrive. A one-of-a-kind event, really.)

National Bottle Museum (518-885-7589), 76 Milton Avenue (Route 50), Ballston Spa (7 miles south of Saratoga Springs on Route 50). Donations appreciated. Open year-round: June through September, daily 10–4; October through May, Monday through Friday 10–4. This museum focuses on the history of the handmade bottle. Until 1903 bottles were handmade, not manufactured. The permanent collection consists of approximately 2,000 bottles, but there are also changing exhibits that borrow from collections throughout the nation. When I visited, there was an exhibit of blue-decorated stoneware bottles, a bottle-dating exhibit that explained how to recognize various marks made on the glass by hand tools, and a cross-section of a privy dig (many bottles are often found in old privies since during winter they had to be stored in a place where a hole had been dug in the ground).

Make sure to stop at the working glass studio across the street, owned by the museum; classes in glass-blowing and workshops with internationally renowned guest artisans are offered. And every June the museum has a bottle show and sale, featuring antique bottle dealers from throughout the East Coast (see *Special Events*).

National Museum of Dance (518-584-0400), South Broadway. Open May through October Tuesday through Sunday 10–5, November through April

CONGRESS PARK OFFERS GREENERY AND SCULPTURES ALONG WITH ITS WORLD-FAMOUS SPRINGS.

Saratoga County Chamber of Commerce

Saturday and Sunday 10–5. Admission fee. This is the only museum in the country dedicated to preserving the history and art of dance in America, and it does a good job. Changing exhibits feature costumes, artwork, personalities, and choreography of American dance. Videos help place various dances in their historical settings, and it is one of the few places where dance enthusiasts may get up close to the costumes and accessories of their favorite dance "characters." Special events include talks and films; call for a schedule of events.

National Museum of Racing and Hall of Fame (518-584-0400), 191 Union Avenue. Open year-round. Monday through Saturday 10–4:30, Sunday noon–4:30. During racing season, daily 9–5. Closed holidays. Admission fee. This museum is one of the most modern sport exhibits in the world, and it is a must-see for anyone who ever enjoyed the sight of a racehorse blasting out of a starting gate. The film *Race America* is an introduction to the racetrack, and throughout the various galleries video and audio exhibits let visitors experience the sounds and sights of racing. Silks, fine paintings, furniture, and historic items all tell the story of the thoroughbred in America; the museum covers nearly 300 years of history. Special exhibits held in smaller galleries feature art and photography from contemporary artists. Even if you've never placed a bet in your life, the gift shop will immediately turn you into a horse fan.

Harness racing fans will want to visit the **Saratoga Harness Racing Museum and Hall of Fame** (518-587-4210), 352 Jefferson Street, which is located at the Saratoga Harness Raceway and offers memorabilia and artwork depicting the history of harness racing (free).

New York State Military Museum & Veterans Research Center (518-583-0184), 61 Lake Avenue. Open year-round Tuesday through Saturday 10–4. (The research center is closed on Saturday; only the museum is open.) Admission fee. Some 10,000 military artifacts—(weapons, artillery, flags, and more) from New York State's participation in military conflicts, dating from the War of 1812 to Desert Storm—are displayed in this armory built in 1898. (Visitors will see the largest battle flag collection in the world, with over 1,700; most of the flags are from the Civil War, but they range from the War of 1812 to the Gulf War. The Veterans Research Center contains 2,000 volumes and 6,000 photographs (half of the photos are from the Civil War era). This is a great stop for Civil War buffs, particularly those interested in New York State involvement. Note that there are no federal records in the research center, just those from the State of New York.

Saratoga Automobile Museum (518-587-1935), Spa State Park. Open May through Labor Day daily 10–5, October through April Tuesday through Sunday 10–5. This museum is housed in a restored 1930s Saratoga Water Bottling Plant in the park. Dozens of classic cars are on display, including a 1928 sedan once owned by Charles Lindbergh and a 1931 Duesenberg Model J Roadster.

Tang Teaching Museum and Art Gallery (518-580-8080), Skidmore College, 815 North Broadway. Open Tuesday through Sunday 10–5. The two-story building that houses this relatively new museum (it opened in 2000) was designed by Antoine Predock. Paid for by a gift from the Chinese-born American businessman Oscar Tang, whose daughter and wife both graduated from Skidmore, the museum covers postwar art, giving preference to visual work with an aural component. In addition to fine art, the Tang has a few peripheral exhibits (films, performances) in progress and some intriguing auditory treats, including collaborative exhibits with Skidmore's science and history departments.

HISTORIC SITE **Saratoga National Historic Park** (518-664-9821), Routes 4 and 32, Stillwater. Open daily year-round 9–5; closed holidays. Park road for bikers open seasonally. The **Philip Schuyler House** is open daily Memorial Day weekend through Labor Day. Admission fee. The battle of Saratoga turned the tide of the American Revolution, and history buffs will enjoy spending a day here. The British hoped to cut New York into sections with a three-pronged attack and destroy communications among the areas. At Saratoga the supposedly untrained, undisciplined American troops won the field, and history was changed. Your tour should begin at the battlefield visitors center, where dioramas, maps, and explanatory exhibits show how the battle was fought and won. Weapons, uniforms, and other items are on display, and because the battle was such a large one, it is necessary to read the material before you set out on the 10-mile self-guided driving tour. Markers at each stop explain what went on during the battle. At the Schuyler House, memorabilia of General Philip Schuyler and his wife show what life was like for people who lived through the battle and the days after. There is even a monument on the field to a leg: Benedict Arnold was wounded in the leg during the battle and became a hero—until he later turned traitor. Special events, including military encampments, are held at the park throughout the year (call for a schedule).

SPRINGS & SPAS Saratoga is famous for its springs, many of which are still open. A spring-tasting guide is available from the **Urban Cultural Center** opposite Congress Park (see *Guidance*). The center is only open in July and August, but it has small exhibits on the history of Saratoga Springs and its commerce. The springs in Saratoga each have their own chemical makeup and characteristics; there are explanatory signs at each spring and, usually, paper drinking cups. Just remember that too much of the spring water might not sit well with your digestive system; try no more than a sip or two to start. You can also find lots of bottled spring water at shops in Saratoga or at the spas.

High Rock Park (go north on Broadway, make a right onto Lake Avenue, then a left onto High Avenue). You can sample water from Old Red, the Peerless, and the Governor Springs here. These were the original public springs of Saratoga Springs, and each one has its own distinctive taste; Old Red, so called because of its high iron content, was considered good for the complexion.

Congress Park, on Broadway, houses Congress Spring, located underneath an elaborate pavilion. Its waters were some of the first to be bottled and sold commercially in the early 19th century. Also in the park, along the path, are the Columbian Spring, Congress 3, and, in the northeast corner, Freshwater Spring. Across from the park, on Spring Street, the Hathorn No. 1 Spring is a popular stop on a hot summer's day; it has a small seating area and lovely plantings surround it.

Saratoga Spa State Park (from the center of town, take Route 9 south to the Avenue of Pines, on the right, and follow that into the park; the site is well marked. It isn't far from the highway), has springs and bathing facilities (see *Green Space*). Built in the 1930s, the **Lincoln Mineral Baths** (518-583-2880) is open year-round: October through May, Wednesday through Sunday 9–4; June and September, daily except Tuesday 9–4, Friday and Saturday until 5, and Thursday until 7; July and August daily (same schedule as June and September but open Tuesday). You must call for reservations. In operation since 1930, the mineral baths have a rather institutional atmosphere, with individual porcelain tubs separated by simple stalls used as a private dressing area. During the bath you are submerged in a soothing deep tub of naturally carbonated mineral water heated to body temperature. The effervescence creates a feeling of relaxation that continues after the bath when you are then wrapped in warm sheets and left to rest. There are 16 different minerals in the spring feeding the Lincoln Baths, including sodium, potassium, and calcium. They are reputed to help those who suffer from arthritis and muscle pain. After soaking, you may then choose to have a massage, facial, or mud wrap. The experience is wonderful—and very reasonably priced since the baths are state-operated. These aren't luxurious surroundings (the place may be old, but it is well-maintained); however, soaking in their deep tub is something I'd like to do every week instead of annually! Drinking springs throughout the park include Island Spouter (the only spouting geyser east of the Mississippi), Hayes Well (with an inhaling hole), Orenda Spring, Coesa, and Ferndale. A marked walking path leads to many of the springs—a lovely stroll on a summer afternoon. There is no charge for tasting the springs.

The Crystal Spa (518-584-2556), 120 South Broadway (diagonally across from Saratoga Spa State Park), is a relatively new addition to Saratoga's tradition, having been in business for just over 15 years. Built on the same property where you will find the Rosemary Spring, the Crystal Spa has 19 rooms and 35 employees, marble floors, modern amenities, and offers a luxurious pampering experience—quite a different atmosphere from the Lincoln Baths. Here the serenity of the spa (no cell phones allowed) draws over 25,000 people each year for mineral baths, saunas, and massages. There are moderately priced packages, particularly midweek off-season. There is even a moderately-priced 64-unit motel (the Grand Union Motel—see *Lodging*), on the premises. Open year-round, it is advisable to book appointments four to six weeks in advance.

WALKING TOUR A walk through Saratoga Springs gives visitors a chance to see the great variety of architectural styles in vogue during the 19th and early 20th centuries, but it would be impossible to list all the houses that are worth looking at. A self-guided tour is usually available at the information booth near Congress Park or from the Saratoga Chamber of Commerce, 28 Clinton Street. Scores of homes offer a look at Italianate, Gothic Revival, Queen Anne, Romanesque, and other styles popular with the upper-middle class and wealthy residents of the city. The **Batcheller Mansion,** corner of Whitney and West Circular, is a fantasy of French Renaissance and Eastern influence (see *Lodging*); the **Jumel Mansion,** 129 Circular Street, was the summer home of the infamous Madame Jumel, one-

AN EAST-SIDE HOME IN DOWNTOWN SARATOGA SPRINGS

Saratoga County Chamber of Commerce

time wife of Aaron Burr; the **Adelphi Hotel,** on Broadway, recalls the hotels of the past, with tall columns and many arched windows. Several streets and areas you may want to enjoy for their architectural wealth include Broadway, Circular Street, Franklin Square, Clinton Street, Lake Avenue, and Union Avenue. All the homes are private, but their beauty can easily be appreciated from the sidewalk (or the window of a car if you are tired and prefer driving).

Saratoga's main thoroughfare is Broadway, which has won numerous awards for its main-street restoration. There are dozens of shops, galleries, and places of interest to check out—an Irish specialty store, rare-book shops, clothing boutiques— both fashionable and funky, fine glass and porcelain, jewelry, and more. Don't forget to wander the side streets just off Broadway (Phila, Spring, and Caroline), where many other surprises await the intrepid walker. One of my favorite book-stores anywhere is **The Lyrical Ballad** (518-584-8779), 7 Phila Street, just off Broadway, an enormous emporium housed in an old bank. You can wander through room after room (the old vaults and inner recesses of the building), and discover thousands of used and rare books, maps, and literary treasures that will surprise and delight. On a hot summer day, this is the perfect escape from the crowds and the sizzling sidewalks.

For those who want organized orientation, there are guided one-hour walking tours ($2 per person) July through Labor Day, Tuesday through Thursday mornings at 10:30. Just meet at the visitors center, 297 Broadway, and wear comfortable shoes!

✳ To Do

BICYCLING **All Outdoors** (518-587-0455), 35 Van Dam Street, rents mountain-biking equipment.

The Bike Shop (518-587-7857), 35 Maple Avenue, rents both mountain bikes and road bikes. They are open Monday through Friday 10–6, until 5 on Saturday.

BOATING **Fish Creek Marina** (518-587-9788), on Saratoga Lake. From town, take Route 29 east, and make a right on Staffords Bridge Road (about 2 miles out of town). Go another 1.5 miles over the bridge, and you'll see the marina. Open May through September Thursday through Sunday from noon on. Rent canoes, kayaks, rowboats here; there's a Mexican cantina on the premises that serves up burritos, tacos, and cold drinks. Learn how to crew from a certified instructor, but call in advance to arrange lessons. Large pavilion available for barbecues and campfires. The most dramatic sunset can be seen from this spot on the lake—people come from all over Saratoga to see it!

Point Breeze Marina (518-587-3397), on Saratoga Lake. Open daily April through November 9–6. This is a place to rent just about anything you want: canoes, kayaks, rowboats, pontoon boats, speedboats, and fishing boats. They have it all.

Saratoga Boat Works (518-584-BOAT), on Saratoga Lake. Open most of the year, except December, from 7–6. At the north end of the lake, near the bridge, just past the racetrack, this full-service marina is a good place to rent power boats or pontoon boats. If you want to water ski, this is where to rent the necessary equipment, as well.

CANOEING & KAYAKING **Fish Creek Marina** (518-587-9788), on Saratoga Lake. They rent kayaks, canoes, and give lessons and guided tours. Groups welcome. Open in-season.

Saratoga Outfitters (518-584-3932), 268 Broadway. This is the place to go if you want to rent a kayak; they provide instruction and guides, as well. Open year-round.

CROSS-COUNTRY SKIING **Saratoga Spa State Park** (518-584-2535). A network of marvelous groomed trails here should delight cross-country skiers of all abilities.

FARM STANDS AND PICK-YOUR-OWN FARMS Among the many things Saratoga is famous for is melon; more specifically Hand melons, named after the family that first grew them. **The Hand Melon Farm** (518-692-2376) is located 13 miles east of Saratoga Springs on Route 29; the melons are usually ready to go from late July through mid-September. They are sweet and resemble cantaloupes; you will see signs for them at many farm stands. You can also pick your own strawberries in June; raspberries may be picked in September. The farm stand is open May through September.

A great deal of excellent produce is raised on local farms, as well. At **Ariel's Vegetable Farm** (518-584-2189), 194 Northern Pines Road, 5 miles north of Saratoga Springs (open April through September), visitors can pick their own berries, buy fruit and vegetables off the stand, or take a tour of the farm; daily 9–6 in-season.

Bowman Orchards (518-371-7432), Sugar Hill Road, Rexford (open September and October), has pick-your-own apples. **Riverview Orchards** (518-371-2174), Riverview Road, Rexford, has pick-your-own apples (September and October) and farm tours. They are open daily August through December 10–5, Friday through Sunday 10–5 the rest of the year.

The **Saratoga Farmers Market** (518-893-2669), is held at High Rock Park (take Broadway north to Grover Street and watch for signs) May through October, every Wednesday evening 3–6 and Saturday 9–1. You can also sample more of the famous local waters there.

FISHING Head out to **Saratoga Lake** early in the morning, and stop at one of the marinas or bait and tackle shops you will see around the lake for information on the local fishing scene (see—*Boating*).

GOLF **Eagle Crest Golf Club** (518-877-7082), Ballston Lake. Open April through October, 6 AM–8 PM. The 18-hole, par-72 championship course is fairly open—a good bet for novices. Also on the premises: a driving range, par-3 course, miniature golf course, restaurant, and snack bar.

Pioneer Hills Golf Course (518-885-7000), Ballston Spa. Open mid-April through October, weather permitting. This 18-hole, par-70 championship course has a restaurant and bar on the premises. In the summer months, golfers will enjoy the large outdoor patio (canopy covered), a nice place to enjoy refreshments after playing.

Saratoga Lake Golf Club (518-581-6616), 35 Grace Moore Road. Open April through October, 6:30 AM–8:30 PM. This 18-hole, par-72 course was designed in what was once the middle of a forest. Although not a championship course, it is quite challenging. The course has shorter distances for each hole, but there are many elevation changes. Accuracy will help you do well here. They are fairly new to the golf scene in Saratoga, having opened in the autumn of 2000. The snack bar is catered by Panza's Restaurant. (see *Dining Out*).

Saratoga Mini Golf (518-581-2841), 54 Vista Drive, Wilton. Take Northway to exit 15. Make a right off the exit; the course is three lights down on the right side of the road. This is great stop for families traveling with children; it's only a 5- to 10-minute ride from the downtown area. Enjoy after-game treats from the snack bar after your round of miniature golf.

Saratoga National Golf Club (518-583-GOLF), 458 Union Avenue. Next to Longfellow's restaurant. Open late April through mid-November, depending on the weather, 7 AM–sunset. This beautifully maintained 18-hole, par-72 championship golf course has 24 bridges, several wetland areas, and is reminiscent of courses in South Carolina. The club opened in 2001, and *Golf Digest* magazine rated it the fifth best new course in the country. Call to reserve a tee time over the phone with a credit card 30 days in advance during summer months or a week or two in advance at other times of the year.

Saratoga Spa Golf Course (518-584-2006), Saratoga Spa State Park. Open April through October, weekdays 6 AM–dusk, weekends from 5 AM. This beautifully maintained 18-hole, par-72 championship course boasts that no two holes touch each other. The towering pine trees make the surroundings special, and the prices are exceedingly reasonable. There is also a driving range, restaurant, and complete facilities. The Victorian Pool is adjacent to the golf course (see *To Do—Swimming*). They will take reservations one week in advance if you call 518-584-2008 to reserve a tee time. This is the way to go, particularly in the summer months.

HORSE RACING Saratoga Equine Sports Center (518-584-2110), Nelson Avenue. Open year-round, but call for racing dates and post times, which vary seasonally. Admission fee. Formerly a plain harness track, the Sports Center was often overshadowed by its sassier cousin, the Saratoga Race Course. But it has expanded and now offers lots of excitement to anyone who enjoys harness racing, polo, barrel, and rodeo events. Visitors can enjoy watching horses vie for purses on the world's fastest half-mile trotting and pacing track, which, unlike the "flats," is open 140 days a year. (The backstretch area contains the only pool in the state located on the grounds of a racetrack and reserved solely for the use of horses.) There are two polo fields and an outdoor arena with more than 200 acres and 1,100 stalls for the equine patrons. Special events include country-music shows (Countryfest brings platinum headliners to the area), carriage-driving competitions, and craft fairs.

"BREAKFAST AT SARATOGA" IS A POPULAR WAY TO ENJOY THE HORSES AND JOCKEYS UP CLOSE

Saratoga County Chamber of Commerce

Saratoga Race Course (518-584-6200 in-season; 718-641-4700 out of season), Union Avenue. Open for six weeks from late July through Labor Day only; call for specific dates, which change each season. Closed Tuesday. Admission fee. The Saratoga racetrack is a hub of activity for a month and a half, and it is busy from early in the morning until the late afternoon. Rub shoulders with celebrities, rail birds, and just plain people; dress in jeans and T-shirts or elegant suits and hats; the choice is yours, and the ghost of Damon Runyon hovers over all. You can begin with "Breakfast at Saratoga" (7–9:30 AM; get there early; free admission), a popular way for people to enjoy the horses and jockeys close up. An announcer keeps things lively as the horses and their riders breeze by. Handicapping seminars—very useful for novice bettors—are held at the track and are announced at breakfast; the seminar times are also posted throughout the track. Breakfast is also served daily in the clubhouse dining room, in an outdoor tent, and buffet style in the box seats; outside, a continental breakfast is served near the clubhouse. Visitors can enjoy a tour of the backstretch area, as well, where the horses board during the racing season. The tour is escorted, and the area is viewed from an observation "train"; sign up for the tour early during breakfast.

The track opens to the racing crowd at 11 AM weekdays and 10:30 weekends. Although there is lots of parking and seating available, remember one thing: The crowds can be large, and the track is smaller than many modern racetracks. Get there early for good viewing. You can park in an official track lot or at a private lot. The latter cost more, but the former fill up quickly; again, get there early so at least you have a selection. Bring your own chair if possible, and remember that both restaurant food and snacks, though usually good, can be very expensive. You are allowed to bring coolers into the track. Both steeplechases and flat races are held throughout the season; check the daily racing forms to see exactly who is racing in what. Races begin (post time) at 1 PM weekdays, 12:30 weekends, rain or shine.

ICE SKATING **Saratoga Spa State Park** (518-584-2535), South Broadway. There is an outdoor rink here in-season, weather permitting. Call for hours, which change depending on the weather. There is open adult hockey here.

Saratoga Springs Ice Rinks (518-583-3462), Weibel Avenue. There are two rinks here and they accommodate both hockey and figure skating. Open year-round except from mid-April to late June. Call for a schedule, which varies from week to week. Weibel rink is Olympic size, and the Vernon rink is smaller. Both offer family skate sessions, public skates, open adult figure and hockey sessions.

POLO You can't play polo unless you have your own string of ponies, but you can watch in-season at Saratoga. The players come from all over the world and are the best in their sport. Matches are held Tuesday, Friday, and Sunday, June through September, but call for hours and a complete schedule (518-584-8108). The events are held at Lodge Field on Nelson Avenue, or Whitney Field, out Seward Street. To get to the polo grounds at Whitney Field, go north on Broadway, turn left onto Church Street, go about 0.5 mile, and make a right onto Seward Street. Go 1 mile to the railroad overpass, and turn right; the polo field is on the left.

SWIMMING **Brown's Beach** (518-587-8280), on Saratoga Lake, exit 12 off Northway. (Make a right off exit, go 3 miles; you will come to the lake. Make a right, and go 1 more mile north; the beach is on the left side of the road.) Open Memorial Day through Labor Day; weekends only until end of June 10–6, then daily. Admission fee. This 250-long, 25-foot-wide, but only 4-foot deep beach area has a terrific shallow swim area that is great for little children. The adjacent marina offers kayak, canoe, and paddleboat rentals. Snack bar, with burgers, fries, hot dogs, and ice cream on the premises.

Saratoga Spa State Park (518-584-2000), South Broadway. There are two pools in the park, and both are open to the public. The **Victoria Pool** opens Memorial Day weekend and remains open daily until Labor Day, 10–6. Admission fee. There is a smaller pool here for young children in addition to the larger pool. The **Peerless Pool** is open from late June to Labor Day, also daily 10–6. Admission and parking fee. This Olympic-sized pool is a great place to cool off after a day at the races or walking the streets of the city. If you have small children, however, the Victoria Pool is probably a better choice.

YMCA (518-583-9622), 262 Broadway. Indoor pool only. Open year-round; call for information on public swimming sessions, which change daily. There are family swim times, as well. The pool is 25 yards long and 5 lengths wide; temperature is usually around 84 degrees.

✳ Green Space

Bog Meadow Nature Trail (518-587-5554). Open year-round. Free. (From Broadway make a right onto Route 29 east. Go through the traffic light at Weibel Avenue; the trail entrance is about 500 feet farther on the right.) This 2-mile nature trail is ideal for people traveling with children. It's fairly flat and goes through the wetlands just outside town. You can run or walk in the warm-weather months and cross-country ski or snowshoe in the winter. Parking area.

Congress Park (518-587-3550). Open year-round. This is a lovely city park to stroll through, particularly after shopping on Broadway (see *To See—Springs & Spas*).

East Side Recreation Field (518-587-3550), Lake Avenue. (Make a right turn on Lake Avenue, and go about 1.5 miles. The field is on the right side, just after the East Avenue light.) Open year-round. This 20-acre park is free; it has an excellent skateboard park (open daily May through October—a small fee is charged for this activity only). There is also a wading pool for small children as well as tennis courts, playground, basketball courts, and a quarter-mile paved circular track that's great for Rollerblading and running.

Saratoga Spa State Park (518-584-2535), 1 mile south of Saratoga Springs on Route 9. Open year-round. This park is free; there is a small charge for swimming and the bathhouses. This 2,000-acre park is a gem; clean, wide open, full of activities to keep visitors busy—and located only minutes from Saratoga Springs. Listed on the National Register of Historic Places, the park is home to the Saratoga Performing Arts Center, known as SPAC (see *Entertainment*) and the Gideon Putnam Hotel (see *Lodging*) as well as the Lincoln Park Baths (see *Springs & Spas*). Recreation opportunities abound in Spa Park: Three pools, tennis courts, streamside trails for walking, and two golf courses (reservations required) are open during the summer months; in the winter months, cross-country skiing, ice skating, and even a speed-skating oval are available. Special film evenings, nature walks, tours, and other special events are held throughout the year (call for a schedule).

Yaddo (518-584-0746), Union Avenue (Route 9P). Open year-round, but the gardens are at their height from June through August. Free. The rose gardens here are superb, and visitors are welcome to walk among the paths and enjoy the

VISITORS ARE WELCOME TO ENJOY THE SUPERB GARDENS AT YADDO, THE
RENOWNED ARTISTS' RETREAT CLOSE TO DOWNTOWN SARATOGA SPRINGS.

fountains, roses, plantings, and peaceful seating areas. Yaddo, once a private
home, is now an artists' retreat offering residencies to professional creative
artists working in virtually all media and used by both the famous and the
someday-to-be-famous; the site offers a respite from the August frenzy of racing
and the society scene. *Note:* Mid-June through Labor Day Saturday and Sunday
at 11 AM (also Tuesday during racing season) a guided rose-garden tour is given.
A small fee is charged.

✳ Lodging

A note on lodging—and dining—in
Saratoga Springs: The Spa City is a
wonderful place to visit and spend a
day or a week. As in many other
resort areas, prices range from moderate to expensive. But during the
"season"—late July through Labor
Day, when thoroughbred racing is the
main event—prices can go sky high,
and accommodations may be difficult
to obtain (some places are booked
solid as early as April). Restaurants
can be crowded, expensive, and difficult to obtain reservations for—that is,
unless you know someone. I'm not
suggesting that you pass up the excitement that is Saratoga Springs during
the summer—it's still a great time to
visit—but be prepared to pay top
price for lodging and dining out. I
prefer to go in May and October,
when the city is much calmer, and the
weather is still beautiful. If you are
going to visit the area during the summer, you may want to consider staying
in Albany (see "City of Albany"),
which is about a half-hour south.

Note: All listings are in Saratoga Springs 12866 unless otherwise indicated. They are organized by type of accommodation: hotel, motel, or inn/bed & breakfast.

Hotels

Adelphi Hotel (518-587-4688), 365 Broadway. ($$$) This grand Victorian hotel, constructed in 1877 and recently renovated, is located in the heart of Saratoga, and it exudes elegance and charm, transporting visitors back to another era. There are 39 rooms, including 18 suites of varying sizes; two have private balconies. Every room is different, but all are elaborately decorated in the Victorian style, and most have queen-sized beds. A Saratoga tradition is to air oneself on the balcony in the afternoon; if you want to do so, ask for a room facing Broadway, since those are the rooms with balconies. The peaceful courtyard within the hotel looks out on a beautiful old-fashioned swimming pool. The Grand Lobby, with its stenciled walls and ceilings, opens up into the Café Adelphi, a bar-café that is a popular local gathering spot (see *Eating Out*). The café serves desserts and coffee from 5 PM on and is an oasis away from the bustle of Broadway just outside the hotel. A continental breakfast is served to guests (on the piazza, which overlooks Broadway, in the warm-weather months). Children are welcome. Open year-round.

Gideon Putnam Hotel (800-732-1560, 518-584-3000), Saratoga Spa State Park. ($$$) This historic Georgian-style resort hotel is set in the 2,200-acre park, a few minutes' walk from the Saratoga Performing Arts Center (see *Entertainment*) and minutes away from the track and downtown Saratoga Springs. In addition to 102 double rooms, 18 parlor and porch suites are available. The service is quite good, and guests may choose to have meals included in the rate. In fact, several packages are available, so inquire about them, particularly if you will be staying midweek or off-season. Children welcome. Open year-round.

The Inn at Saratoga (800-274-3573, 518-583-1890), 231 Broadway. ($$$) This establishment combines the modern comforts of a hotel and the charming touches of an inn. There are 38 rooms and suites, all decorated in Victorian style. A restaurant downstairs serves dinner daily, and the Sunday brunch features live jazz. Continental breakfast is served. Children welcome. Open year-round.

Saratoga Arms (518-584-1775), 497 Broadway. ($$) This concierge hotel, with 16 rooms, in the middle of the downtown area, is perfect for those who want to be within walking distance of shops, restaurants and cultural activities. It is housed in a brick building that dates back to 1870, and is filled with grand staircases, ornate moldings and ceiling medallions. Every room is beautifully restored and custom decorated with period pieces and antiques; the rooms also have phones, TVs and data ports. Many have working fireplaces. The antique wicker furniture on the wraparound porch overlooking Broadway is a great place to get comfortable and relax after sightseeing or attending the races. A full breakfast is served. (At this writing, a fitness room and small spa are in the works, scheduled to open in 2004.) Children over the age of 12. Open year-round.

Motels

Adirondack Inn (518-584-3810), 230 West Avenue. ($$) Located on

3.5 acres, yet only five blocks from Broadway, this inn offers visitors either a private cottage or a standard motel room. All rooms, however, have cable TV and refrigerators. There is an outdoor pool, barbecue grill, and shuttle-bus service to the race course. A continental breakfast is served, but a four-day minimum stay is required in-season. Children welcome. Open year-round.

Grand Union Motel (518-584-9000), 120 South Broadway. ($) There are 64 clean, quiet, well-maintained rooms at this reasonably priced motel located between the race course and SPAC. There is an outdoor pool for swimming, and guests will enjoy taking the waters at the Rosemary Spring on the property (see *Springs & Spas*). The Crystal Spa on the premises offers a variety of services: from mud and seaweed body wraps to scalp treatments, facials and aromatherapy. Children welcome. Open year-round.

Saratoga Motel (518-584-0920), 440 Church Street. ($) Set on 5 acres, located only a few miles from downtown, this small motel has nine rooms, all with air-conditioning and refrigerators, two with kitchenettes. There is no breakfast served and there is no swimming pool, but the queen-sized beds are comfortable. Good value.

Inns/Bed & Breakfasts

Batcheller Mansion (518-584-7012), 20 Circular Street. ($$$) Built in 1873 by George Sherman Batcheller, an attorney and judge, this magnificent structure is resplendent with beautiful gardens and architectural details that will delight history buffs. In fact, President Ulysses S. Grant slept here shortly after the house was built. They still host guests in the timeless tradition of grace and ease reminiscent of

a century long gone. The nine graciously appointed rooms, four with fireplaces, offer a warm and inviting reprieve from the outside world. This is the perfect spot for a romantic getaway. The luxurious surroundings include a plush sitting room and a library where you can recline on one of the red-velvet sofas. The formal dining room breakfast offers a glorious start to the day, with fresh-squeezed orange juice served in crystal glasses and freshly baked breads and pastries of your choice. No children. Open year-round.

Brunswick B&B (800-585-6751), 143 Union Avenue. ($) This is one of the oldest continuously operating lodging facilities in Saratoga Springs; they have been serving guests since 1886. There are 10 private rooms, 2 of them suites; all are centrally air-conditioned, with a good deal of variety—one room has a gas fireplace; two rooms have Jacuzzis; one suite has a kitchenette. If you are planning to stay for a week during the summer racing season, attractive discount rates are available here, which is unusual. The value for the money is excellent. Children welcome. Open year-round.

Chestnut Tree Inn (888-243-7688, 518-587-8681), 9 Whitney Place. ($$) Named after the last remaining chestnut tree in Saratoga Springs, this inn offers country ambience within walking distance of the racetrack and other points of interest. Continental breakfast is served on the Victorian porch in summer, and the inn is furnished with antiques. Seven rooms, all with private bath. Children welcome. Open May through November.

Circular Manor (518-583-6393), 120 Circular Street. ($$) This 6,000-square-foot Victorian home was built in 1903 by Newton Breeze, a well-known Saratoga architect at the turn of the 20th century. There are five beautifully decorated guest rooms, all with private bath, central air-conditioning, claw-foot tubs, and marble floors. This is a place where you will feel pampered yet comfortable. All the important details have been attended to here: There are beautiful duvets, cotton sheets (300 thread count), and luxurious Egyptian-cotton towels. The full gourmet breakfast (a few choices are available daily) features freshly baked breads, fruit, and wonderful egg creations. Enjoy relaxing on the huge wraparound porch in the heart of Saratoga's historic district, a quiet section of town surrounded by lovely Victorian homes yet only a few blocks away from the shops and restaurants. No children. Open year-round.

The Eddy House (518-587-2340), 4 Nelson Avenue Extension (at Crescent Street). ($$) This B&B, one of the oldest in Saratoga Springs, sits on 1.5 acres of well-tended lawns and gardens, and guests can play badminton or bocce, use the golf net, or just relax. Your hosts will go out of their way to make you feel at home. If you walk or jog in the morning, the location is perfect for a peaceful excursion on foot. In addition to the four private rooms sharing two baths, there are two living rooms, a library, and a screened-in porch for guests' use. A large gourmet breakfast is served daily and may include French toast, eggs, homemade muffins, and other baked goods. No children. Open year-round.

The Fox 'n Hound B&B (866-369-1913), 143 Lake Avenue. ($$) This restored 1904 Colonial-style mansion located in the heart of the city provides a haven of Old-World elegance and European hospitality. There are five guest rooms, all with private bath; two have Jacuzzis, king-sized beds, and private balconies. Guests may sit and relax on the magnificent mahogany wraparound porch or enjoy a swim in the outdoor pool. The owner taught for several years at the Culinary Institute in Hyde Park, and a full gourmet breakfast is cooked to your taste. Children over the age of 14 are welcome. Open year-round.

Geyser Lodge B&B (518-584-0389), 182 Ballston Avenue. ($) For those travelers on a limited budget, this is the place to go in Saratoga. A comfortable Queen Anne–style Victorian dating back to 1896, this spacious, 16-room B&B was once referred to as a "cottage," by the wealthy New York City family who used it as a summer residence. Located near Skidmore College, there are 4 guest rooms; all with private bath and air-conditioning; some have TV and telephone. Full breakfast on weekends; continental during the week. In-ground pool in the backyard. Great value for the money. Children over the age of 12 welcome; but their policy is flexible with younger ones, so be sure to inquire. Open year-round.

Kimberly Inn (518-584-9006), 184 South Broadway. ($) This inn, housed in a structure dating back to the late 1800s, is 0.25 mile from the race course and only 1 mile from SPAC. There are six recently renovated rooms: Five have private bath and kitchenette, one shares a bath with the owner's family, but all have cable TV. There is a beautiful shaded courtyard for relaxing in the warm-weather months. A continental breakfast is served. Children welcome. Open year-round.

The Mansion (888-996-9977, 518-885-1607), 801 Route 29, Rock City Falls, located 7 miles west of town on Route 29. ($$$) This inn was built in 1866 as the summer home of a prominent industrialist, George West, across the street from his Excelsior Mill. (He also invented the folded paper bag and became known as the Paper Bag King!) The inn has had only six owners and is a dream come true for lovers of Victoriana. The mansion has been featured in several publications (in fact, a Chico's catalog was photographed here). Venetian Villa design is the style of the building, which retains its original mirrored fireplaces and elaborate chandeliers. The rooms are comfortably furnished with Victorian antiques, and Mamie Eisenhower's piano is the striking centerpiece of the downstairs library. A full gourmet breakfast is served in the dining room from 7:30 to 9. Guests may use the parlor, the library, walk the grounds, or relax on the porch. This is truly a special spot, and it's worth traveling outside Saratoga Springs to stay here, particularly if you want a respite from the crowds during the summer racing season. The old mill and lovely waterfall across the street from the inn are perfect for taking a short stroll after breakfast. (I enjoyed running on a beautiful road that follows a stream on the grounds of a state fishing preserve, close to the B&B; ask the owners, and they will direct you.) All nine rooms have private bath and individually controlled air-conditioning. Adults only. Open year-round.

181 Phila (518-583-7500), 181 Phila Street. ($$$) The luxurious accommodations at this 19th-century Victorian estate include extraordinary personalized service, an authentic inn in the old style, providing generous hospitality that's not overbearing. There are four suites and a private house, located two blocks from the track and five blocks from the center of downtown. Just some of the features here that reflect host Tara Oliver's attention to detail include velour robes and slippers in your room, a heated in-ground pool, several working fireplaces, a lovely outdoor courtyard with lush plantings, an enormous candlelit hot-tub room with piped-in music of your choice—and private champagne dinners to your order ranging from a lobster barbecue to a full gourmet meal, depending on your desire. Ms. Oliver has been a caterer for several years and served President George W. Bush during his visit to Lake Placid. The atmosphere at 181 Phila enables guests to relax as if they were a guest in a friend's home. Enjoy the pampering of an in-room massage or a family reunion dinner cooked to your specifications.

THE MANSION BED & BREAKFAST

Children over the age of 10 recommended, but they are flexible. Open year-round.

Saratoga Bed & Breakfast (800-584-0920), 434 Church Street. ($) 1.5 miles from Broadway, a five-minute drive to the center of town. This farmhouse B&B dates back to 1860, and the decor is shabby chic: country-style cozy furniture with a variety of antiques throughout. The five rooms all have queen-sized beds, private baths, air-conditioning, and telephones. A full breakfast is served. Children over the age of seven are welcome, but no children are permitted during racing season. Open year-round.

Saratoga Farmstead B&B (518-587-2074), 41 Locust Grove Road. ($$) This bed & breakfast is 2 miles from downtown Saratoga Springs and is located in a restored 18th-century farmhouse. Guests may enjoy six air-conditioned rooms, all with private bath, plus a large gourmet breakfast (many items in-season come from the organic garden on the premises). This is a casual farm setting, a nice change from the rush of downtown in the summer. Bring your binoculars with you; there are a few acres of walking trails filled with wildflowers and birds of all kinds. Children welcome. Open year-round.

Saratoga Sleigh (518-584-4534), 203 Union Avenue. ($$) The location here is attractive to those who want to be near the action: this moderately-priced B&B overlooks the race course. Housed in an historic 1887 Queen Anne Victorian, the four rooms, all with private baths, are filled with antiques. Each room is air-conditioned and has a TV, but there are no telephones. A full breakfast is served.

Children must be over the age of 12. Open year-round.

Six Sisters B&B (518-583-1173), 149 Union Avenue. ($$) This charming establishment, named after the six sisters of one of the owners, is located on the flower-bedecked Union Avenue approach to the racetrack. At Six Sisters guests will enjoy a gourmet breakfast and their choice of four guest rooms or suites, all with private bath and air-conditioning. Only minutes from most of the goings-on in Saratoga Springs, this inn is a lovely place to enjoy a special weekend. Older children welcome. Open year-round.

Union Gables B&B (800-398-1558, 518-584-1558), 55 Union Avenue. ($$) This restored Queen Anne Victorian, circa 1901, is a family-owned and occupied bed & breakfast. Each of the 10 guest rooms is exquisitely decorated to reflect the style of Old Saratoga. Every room has a modern bath, TV, telephone, and a small refrigerator. The establishment is conveniently located near the downtown area and only one block from the thoroughbred racetrack. Children are welcome. Open year-round.

Westchester House B&B (800-581-7613, 518-587-7613), 102 Lincoln Avenue. ($$) Built in high Gothic style—complete with towers, crenellations, and oddments—this charming inn is a fairy tale come true. There are seven rooms, all with private bath, telephones, and data ports. The rooms offer luxury touches like ceiling fans, air-conditioning, and fresh flowers from the surrounding gardens in summer. Downtown Saratoga Springs is a few minutes' walk away, and guests can enjoy sitting on the porch while looking forward to the morning's breakfast of fruit salad, choice of cereal, home-baked goods, and fresh gourmet coffee. Older children only. Open April through November.

✳ Where to Eat

There is a wealth of wonderful restaurants in the Spa City. Some of the establishments listed are popular with both travelers and local residents. I have included my favorite places to eat in Saratoga Springs, whether you are seeking a leisurely gourmet dinner or a quick, informal lunch. All are top-notch. Please note that restaurants are located within the city limits unless otherwise indicated.

Due to the fact that life in Saratoga Springs changes so drastically during the summer racing season, some restaurants may cut back their hours in the winter months. If you are visiting during the months of January through March, especially on a Monday or Tuesday, do call ahead to make sure the restaurant of your choice is open. The days and hours of operation listed here are for *most* months of the year.

DINING OUT **Chez Sophie Bistro** (518-583-3538), 2853 Route 9, Malta Ridge. ($$$) Open Tuesday through Saturday for dinner from 5:30. The French cuisine is first-rate in this elegant spot outside the city. The pâté and escargots are just two of the tempting appetizers, and both the duckling in apricot and green peppercorns and the Black Angus New York strip steak are excellent. Save room for the chocolate mousse. Not recommended for children.

Chianti Il Ristorante (518-580-0025), 208 Broadway. ($$$) Open for dinner daily 5:30–10. Savor new trends in Northern Italian cuisine in this upscale establishment with impeccable service. The chef suggests the capellini with lobster and prawns or

THE SPA CITY OFFERS A WEALTH OF WONDERFUL RESTAURANTS.

Saratoga County Chamber of Commerce

the penne pasta with cannellini beans and sausage. Some of the other entrées include stuffed quail, risotto with porcini and filetto al gorgonzola, and salmon dishes (I sampled one of these, and it was superb). The portions are exceedingly generous, and there are over 300 selections on the wine list. Make sure to leave room for dessert; the tiramisu and chocolate soufflé are excellent. Reservations are not taken here, so it is best to arrive before 6 or after 9 to avoid waiting. Not recommended for young children.

Dine Restaurant (518-587-9463), 26 Henry Street. ($$) Open Tuesday through Saturday for dinner from 5:30; during racing season, every night. International cuisine with an ever-changing menu reflecting what is freshest in-season. The chef combines Asian, French, and Italian cuisine to create exciting, interesting game, beef, seafood, and poultry entrées. The fare here also includes global comfort food, and the meat loaf Wellington is a popular dish. Roasted bison with lobster butter and demi-glace is my favorite. The roasted escolar (a South American tunalike fish) is served with lemon caper beurre blanc. Do save room for one of the mouth-watering, beautifully presented desserts. The owner enjoys the chocolate truffle cake, and Pavlova (meringue with fresh, marinated berries, whipped cream, and house-made ice cream). If you are visiting Saratoga even for a short stay, make sure to dine at Dine at least once. There is a "chef's table" in the kitchen where patrons can taste from 4 to14 courses. Call ahead (reservations are suggested), and try out this dinner with the creator for a unique dining experience!

Eartha's (518-583-0602), 60 Court Street. ($$$) Open daily for dinner 5:30–9:30. A popular spot with diners in the know, this restaurant serves fresh dishes with a Continental flair, including mesquite-grilled seafood, duck, and steaks. There is a small sidewalk patio, and reservations are a must any time. Not recommended for children.

43 Phila Bistro (518-584-2720), 43 Phila Street. ($$) Open daily for dinner from 5. This eclectic New American bistro, its walls decorated with 1940s caricatures of local personalities, features dishes from around the globe. You can sample such tempting entrées as New Zealand lamb, Maryland crabcakes, wild boar, or Jamaican jerk swordfish; there are a number of flavorful vegetarian dishes, as well. All the pasta is homemade, and the pastry chef creates sensational desserts daily. Children welcome.

The Georgian Room at the Gideon Putnam Hotel (518-584-3000), Saratoga Spa State Park. ($$) Open daily for breakfast 7–10:30, until 9:30 on Sunday; lunch 11:30–2; dinner 6–9, until 10 on Friday and Saturday; Sunday brunch 10:30–2. Set in the lovely Spa Park, this hotel restaurant is often packed in the evening before a concert or ballet. The cuisine here combines contemporary American favorites and classic Continental fare. The Sunday brunch is outstanding and well worth the wait (seatings every half hour between 10:30 and 2). Reservations are required for dinner. Children welcome.

Lake Ridge Restaurant (518-899-6000), 35 Burlington Avenue, Round Lake (exit 11 off the Northway). ($$) Open daily except Sunday for lunch

11:30–2:30; dinner 5–9. Chef Scott Ringwood offers fine Continental dining at reasonable prices. The menu includes excellent steaks, seafood, and pasta. The pork rack and breast of duck are imaginatively prepared; they're my favorites. It's worth the drive south of the city. Children welcome.

Little India (518-583-4151), 423 Broadway. Open daily for lunch 11:30–3; dinner 5–10. ($) This tandoori-style restaurant offers a variety of Indian specialties; it's truly a gem and offers some of the best cuisine of its kind you will find anywhere. The mixed grill is the most popular dish and includes chicken, lamb, and beef. Vegetarians will enjoy the pureed spinach casserole with potato and cheese. A number of curry entrées, and different types of Indian breads are available, as well.

The Lodge at Saratoga Raceway (518-584-7988), 1 Nelson Avenue. ($$$) Open daily for dinner 5–10 from mid-July through August only. Continental cuisine with some international touches is served in this elegant yet casual restaurant where the presentation of the fare is first-rate. Try the seared Chilean sea bass with tomatoes, garlic, and olives with arugula salad. The grilled prime New York steak with mashed potatoes, baby vegetables, two homemade steak sauces, and black-pepper butter is wonderful. For dessert, don't pass up the black-satin chocolate cake with brandied cherries and white chocolate ice cream (homemade on the premises). The four-course prix fixe menu ($65 per person) has several choices. Every night diners may enjoy live music from the piano bar. Reservations suggested. Not recommended for children.

Longfellow's Inn & Restaurant (518-587-0108), 500 Union Avenue. ($$$) Open daily for dinner 5–10, Sunday 4–9. Located in an old country estate dating back to the late 1800s, this establishment prides itself on its warm, relaxing ambience. The restaurant is unusual in that it has a waterfall and pond *inside*. The American cuisine here includes several mesquite offerings. In addition to prime rib, rack of lamb, seafood, and pasta entrées, there are some rather imaginative creations. Try the bourbon-glazed salmon or pan-roasted garlic shrimp. There is something on the menu here to please every taste. Children are welcome.

Panza's on the Lake (518-584-6882), 510 Route 9P, Saratoga Lake. ($$) Open Thursday through Sunday for dinner from 5, daily for dinner from 5 during July and August only. Solid Italian American cuisine with a continental flair is what you can enjoy here, along with beautiful views of the lake. There is a full bar with an extensive wine list, and this is a nice place to just enjoy cocktails. Known for his veal dishes, the chef suggests the veal martone (with shrimp, artichoke hearts, and mushrooms). The shrimp sorentino (topped with eggplant, prosciutto, and fresh mozzarella) is another popular entrée. All desserts are homemade on the premises. Children welcome. Reservations suggested.

Sargo's at Saratoga National Golf Club (518-583-4653, ext. 601), 458 Union Avenue (located off exit 14 of I-87; take Route 9P south one mile). Open for lunch Monday through Saturday 11–4; dinner served daily 5–11; Sunday brunch 10–2. Chef Larry Schepici has created a changing menu making use of seasonal ingredients for his regional American cuisine at this fantastic new addition to the Saratoga restaurant scene. House specialties include veal chop Michelangelo, veal lobster Lorenzo, Hudson Valley foie gras, lobster Savanna, and pistachio-encrusted rack of lamb. There is a full-time pastry chef, so save room for the mouthwatering desserts. In the warm-weather months, dine alfresco on the lovely outdoor terrace with its raw bar and sushi station. There is an extensive wine list here. Reservations suggested.

Siro's (518-584-4030), 168 Lincoln Avenue. ($$$) Open daily for dinner in August only. Call for hours, which may vary. This is probably the most popular dinner spot with racegoers. Reservations are required, although the bar area is open and crowded. The food here is Continental, with steak and seafood the specialties. Recommended if you want to continue enjoying the horsey atmosphere—and the crowds—during the evening hours.

Sperry's (518-584-9618), 30 Caroline Street. ($$) Open daily for lunch 11:30–3:30; dinner 5:30–10. This American bistro-style restaurant offers grilled seafood and steak specials, fresh pasta, and sautéed softshell crabs in-season. The homemade pastries and desserts are first-rate: the crème caramel was featured in the *New York Times*. They butcher their own meats here; there is a pastry chef on the premises, and many of the herbs used in the warm-weather months are grown in their own garden. The bar is a favorite of jockeys and trainers. One of Saratoga's most reliable year-round gems. Reservations are recommended.

Springwater Bistro (518-584-6440), 139 Union Avenue. ($$) Open for dinner daily except Tuesday 4–9. Enjoy your meal either in the dining room, with its many window tables, or in the cozy fireplace tapas lounge. In the warm weather, dine alfresco. The excellent American regional cuisine here ranges from veal, shrimp, and lamb shank to salmon, vegetarian, and pasta dishes. Seasonal offerings include wok-charred Hawaiian spear fish and grilled Long Island duckling. There is something for everyone on this varied menu, which highlights traditional favorites imaginatively prepared. Full bar and a particularly nice selection of wines. Children welcome.

Sushi Thai Garden (518-580-0900), 44–46 Phila Street. ($$) Open daily for lunch 11–3; for dinner 5–10. Step off the busy streets of Saratoga Springs into the Far East for a taste of fine, exotic Thai cuisine. They make every dish to order here, with the freshest ingredients. Japanese entrées like chicken teriyaki are offered as well as several vegetarian selections. The sushi bar is excellent. Children welcome.

The Waterfront Restaurant and Marina (518-583-BOAT), 3 miles out of town; take Union Avenue to 626 Crescent Avenue, Saratoga Lake. ($$) Open daily from 11:30 for lunch and dinner. The glass-walled dining room and shoreline deck offer an uninterrupted view of Saratoga Lake and make this casual spot special. Steaks, seafood, pasta, and burgers are served in a relaxing, informal atmosphere. Children welcome.

EATING OUT Adelphi Café (518-587-4688), 365 Broadway. ($$) Dessert and coffee are served after 5 PM year-round, and the pastries are excellent. The Victorian surroundings, which echo the old-time elegance of Saratoga Springs, should not be missed on a walk up Broadway—even if you don't have the time to enjoy a repast in this wonderfully unique café, stop in for a look around.

Beverly's (518-583-2755), 47 Phila Street. ($$) Open daily for breakfast and lunch 8–3. This small café is tucked away on a side street, just off Broadway. The food is fresh and carefully prepared, and the baked goods are excellent. Beverly's is well known for thick slabs of French toast; they will be glad to prepare gourmet take-out lunches for picnics trackside (or anywhere else).

Bruno's (518-583-3333), Union Avenue, opposite Saratoga Racetrack. ($) Open during most months of the year for dinner only 4:30–10. In summer open daily 11:30–11. During racing season, the restaurant opens for breakfast 9–noon, with special egg, bacon, ham, and other creative start-your-day pizzas. Pizza is the specialty here; lovers of that American culinary tradition will not want to pass up Bruno's, where every imaginable type of personal pizza is prepared fresh to your taste in a wood-fired oven. Kids will love it here. The atmosphere is funky 1950s; it's one of my favorite places to eat in town.

Caffè Lena (518-583-0022), 47 Phila Street. ($$) Open Wednesday through Sunday, but hours change depending on the entertainment. Almost all major folk, jazz, and blues artists have appeared at this well-known coffeehouse and nightspot over the years. The food is secondary to the performances, although the coffee, including specialties like iced mocha java, is excellent. Thursday evenings are open-mike nights, and on Sunday

afternoons there are occasionally special programs for children. This is worth a stop, no matter who is on the bill. Not recommended for children in the evening. Call to find out who is featured; a detailed tape recorded message will give you the schedule for an entire week.

Country Corner Café (518-583-7889), 25 Church Street. ($) Open daily 6–2, Sundays 7–2. One of the best breakfasts in town is served until closing time in this cozy café. Try the home-baked breads and muffins with preserves or the fresh fruit pancakes with maple syrup. The hearty soups and sandwiches make this a popular lunch spot with local residents.

Esperanto (518-587-4236), 612 Caroline Street. ($) Open Monday through Saturday, serving lunch and dinner from 11:30 AM–11 PM; Sunday 4–10. Authentic American cuisine, using the freshest ingredients for soups, salads, and healthful sandwiches. There are always a few imaginative daily specials, as well.

Hattie's Chicken Shack (518-584-4790), 45 Phila Street. ($) Open for dinner, Wednesday through Sunday from 5–10. During July and August open for breakfast, lunch, and dinner from 8 AM–10 PM. Since 1938 this is the place Saratogians have been going for Southern-style fried foods: chicken, fish, potatoes and more. There are also hearty pancake breakfasts, and biscuits are served with everything. For lovers of the lost art of the deep fry, this is the place to go. Children are welcome.

Mrs. London's (518-581-1652), 464 Broadway. ($$) Open Sunday, Tuesday through Thursday 7–6, Friday and Saturday until 9. The homemade soups, sandwiches, and wraps are first-rate, and the baked goods are the best in the city. Don't miss this spot for an elegant lunch.

Old Bryan Inn (518-587-2990), 123 Maple Avenue. ($) Open daily at 11 AM for lunch and dinner: there's one menu all day long. This unpretentious country inn is a nice stop for hearty burgers and fries, fresh salads, grilled steaks, and pasta dishes. Try the hot spinach salad or deep-fried cheese sticks with an unusually delicious raspberry sauce. (*Note:* You have to request this latter dish. They no longer put it on the menu, but they still serve it if you ask!) Children welcome.

One Caroline Street Bistro (518-587-2026), 1 Caroline Street. ($$) Open Tuesday through Sunday for dinner 5–10. This family-owned and -operated bistro-style restaurant has live music nightly. The cuisine is an international mix featuring Cajun, Italian, and Asian dishes. The chef tells me that the jambalaya and filet mignon are among the most popular entrées—but adventurous diners won't want to miss the tasty Thai-style bouillabaisse.

The Pink Store (518-584-3840), 119 Clinton Street. ($) Open daily 8–7, Sunday 8–3. This breakfast and lunch eatery has been operated by the same family for over 35 years. The surroundings are casual, and breakfast is served all day. One of the most popular dishes is turkey with mashed potatoes and gravy, a comfort food special that costs just $7. I love their BLT. Children are welcome.

The Parting Glass (518-583-1916), 40 Lake Avenue. ($) Open daily from 11 AM until the early-morning hours. An Irish pub-style restaurant. Try the Guinness-and-black-bean soup served with home-baked bread for a hearty meal. There is entertainment on Friday and Saturday night, and the place is a favorite with the racetrack crowd. Great fun if you enjoy pubs; there's a vast selection of beers and even a serious dart shop. Not recommended for children.

The Putnam Market (518-587-FOOD), 435 Broadway. ($$) Open Monday through Saturday 9–7, Sunday 10–6. Hours are extended during racing season. This gourmet eatery with an open deli and bakery specializes in takeout for picnics if you are heading to SPAC or the track. About a dozen tables are available if you choose to eat at the market, and it's a great place to stop for soup, a sandwich, or a salad while shopping on Broadway. The side dishes, like green beans and hazelnuts topped with a light lemon dressing, are what I enjoy here. I make a meal of a few of these fresh seasonal salad creations—in full view when you enter the store. Sandwiches include items like boneless free-range turkey breast with cheddar cheese and cranberry mayo, and the salmon en croûte is baked to perfection. Menus change seasonally. Save room for the wonderful brownies, cookies, and other dessert treats! Children can't run around here; space is tight.

The Ripe Tomato (518-581-1530), Routes 9 & 9P, Malta. Take Broadway (which becomes Route 9) south out of town for about 5 miles; the restaurant is on the left side of the road, at the junction with 9P. ($$) Open for lunch and dinner Monday through Saturday 11:30–10; Sunday brunch buffet 11–2. This "Italian American Grill" serves affordable meals with exceedingly generous portions. Try the award-winning shrimp and scallop bisque. I enjoy their crab ravioli with pepper-flavored pasta. My friend loves the chicken parmigiana. Every day there are five specials; one of them is a steak entrée, and it's sure to please most meat lovers. Many of the pastas are homemade on the premises. Enjoy standard American favorites here, too, including roast pork and Yankee pot roast. Desserts are sumptuous. Good value for the money. Children welcome.

PJ's Bar-B-Q (518-583-CHIK, 583-RIBS), Route 9 (South Broadway). ($) Open daily at 11:30 AM until closing, serving lunch and dinner. Closed weekdays after Labor Day. You will smell this restaurant before you see it. And the aroma will be irresistible to barbecue aficionados. There are huge barbecue pits behind the place, and they're smoking with racks of chicken, ribs, beef brisket, and pulled pork. Sides include homemade coleslaw, macaroni and potato salads, barbecue beans, and corn on the cob. This is the home of the unique "wick" sandwich and old-fashioned custard ice cream. Also enjoy Sarasodas, PJ's Loganberry fruit beverages, to accompany the thick smoky ribs and chicken. Spicy and satisfying for takeout or eat-in-the-parking-lot. There are hot dogs and burgers for those who don't or won't indulge. Children love the place.

Scallions (518-584-0192), 404 Broadway. ($) Open daily 11–9. A gourmet eatery with a cheerful café atmosphere. Try the unique sandwich combinations, homemade soups, and specialty chicken and pasta dishes. Desserts are first-rate: The carrot cake is the best around. This is a great place to take out a meal for a picnic if you

are heading to the Saratoga Performing Arts Center or the race course.

Shirley's Restaurant (518-584-4532), 74 West Avenue. ($) Open Tuesday through Friday 6 AM–8 PM, Saturday 7 AM–8 PM, Sunday 7–1. This diner has been in the same family now for over 40 years. Lee Bishop, the current owner, explains that Shirley was his mother, hence the name. There are exceedingly reasonable prices here, and the service is efficient and friendly. There are the usual diner standards and daily dinner specials like roast turkey breast and all kinds of overstuffed sandwiches. All pies are homemade on the premises. A great place to go if you are traveling with children.

✳ Entertainment

PERFORMING ARTS Home Made Theater (518-587-4427), at the Spa Little Theater, Saratoga Spa State Park, off Route 9. Open September through April. This theater is open during a calmer time of year in Saratoga Springs. Visitors may enjoy comedy, drama, or children's theater in this venue.

Lake George Opera at Saratoga (518-584-6018), at the Spa Little Theater, Saratoga Spa State Park, off Route 9. Mid-June through mid-July. Two operas are performed in repertory every other night, and some are performed with their own orchestra. The tickets are sold through SPAC, and there are only 500 seats, so it is difficult to get tickets last minute. Opera lovers will enjoy the intimacy of this little theater.

Saratoga Film Forum (518-584-FILM), Saratoga Arts Center Theatre, 320 Broadway. Admission fee. Films are shown on Thursday and

Friday nights and the second Sunday of every month. No reservations are taken; just show up a half-hour before show time.

Saratoga Performing Arts Center (518-587-3330), Saratoga Spa State Park, Route 50, Saratoga Springs. Open from May through early September; schedules, performances, and ticket prices vary. Each summer there are performances here by the New York City Ballet, plus top names in the concert circuit in jazz, rock, and folk visit SPAC, with matinee and evening shows. You can bring a picnic, select items, from the gourmet food carts, or stop at one of the restaurants in town and arrange for an elegant take-along dinner. There is a covered, open-air seating area as well as lawn seats under the stars and plenty of parking. SPAC is but a few minutes' drive from the center of town, but beware: A popular concert can create traffic tie-ups and bottlenecks throughout the area, so plan to get there early. Lawn tickets can be purchased the night of most performances, but it's a good idea to call in advance and inquire about ticket availability.

VENUES PROVIDING MUSIC There are several cafés and restaurants in town that offer wonderful blues, jazz, and dance bands. The schedules (days and hours) vary with the time of the year. If you are visiting and want to hear live music, give the following places a call.

Bailey's Café (518-583-6060), 37 Phila Street; **Caffè Lena** (518-583-0022), 47 Phila Street, **Gaffney's** (518-587-7359), 16 Caroline Street; **High Rock Steak House** (518-583-ROCK), in the Sheraton Hotel at the end of Broadway; **Horseshoe Inn Bar & Grill** (518-587-4909), 1 Gridley Street; **The Inn at Saratoga** (518-583-1890), 231 Broadway, is known for their jazz brunch on Sunday (in-season); **The Newberry Club** (518-581-8329), 388 Broadway, is a dance club; **9 Maple Avenue** (518-583-CLUB), 9 Maple Avenue, offers jazz year-round; **One Caroline Street** (518-587-2026), 1 Caroline Street, has jazz and blues year-round; **The Parting Glass** (518-583-1916), 40 Lake Avenue, is a local haven for Irish music and folk; the **Wishing Well Restaurant** (518-584-7640), Route 9, Wilton, may be out of town a little way, but it offers excellent piano and jazz and features local musicians.

✳ Special Events

The following events are held annually during the month listed. If you know you will be in Saratoga Springs at a particular time, do call to find out the exact dates of these fairs, festivals and events. Attending any of them will enhance your stay in the city.

May: **Encampment at Saratoga National Historical Park** (518-664-9821), Saratoga National Historical Park Battlefield, 648 Route 32, Stillwater. During this weekend, the British encampment at Saratoga is re-enacted. **Saratoga Dressage,** also known as **Saratoga Festival** (518-587-0723), Saratoga Race Course and Equine Center, Union Avenue. Admission fee. The weekend includes precision riding, international exotic all-breed show-horse training, special Olympics riding, carriage, 200 craft exhibitors, dog agility competition, children's activities.

June: **National Bottle Museum Collectors Expo** (518-885-7589),

Saratoga Springs City Center, 522 Broadway. Admission fee. Collectors of bottles from around the country meet here to exhibit and sell their wares. For those who have any interest in old bottles, don't miss this weekend expo! (See *To See.*) **Saratoga Jazz Festival** (518-587-3330), SPAC, Saratoga Spa State Park, Route 50. Admission fee. From noon to midnight, this weekend festival attracts some of the biggest names in jazz from throughout the country. Bring a blanket and picnic; the lawn seats are the best way to experience this.

July: **Hats Off to Saratoga Music Festival** (518-584-3255), various venues in downtown Saratoga Springs. Enjoy an array of music, including jazz, bluegrass, classical, folk, country Latin, Cajun, and Dixieland, during this weekend festival, Friday and Saturday night 7–11. **Heritage Garden Club Flower Show** (518-584-0027), Saratoga Springs City Center, 522 Broadway. Admission fee. This flower show is an annual event sponsored by a local garden club; it's sure to delight gardeners. **Independence Day Celebration** (518-664-9821), Saratoga National Historical Park, 684 Route 32, Stillwater. Hear breaking news of American independence from the town crier. Kids will enjoy this afternoon celebration. At sunset, there are fireworks in Congress Park and the Equine Sports Center. **Saratoga County Fair** (518-885-9701), Saratoga County Fairgrounds, Ballston Spa. Admission fee. From 9 AM to midnight Tuesday through Sunday, enjoy

exhibits, food, rides, shows, animals, and entertainment.

August: **Travers Festival Week** (518-584-3255). This week-long celebration around the race course's midsummer derby, the Travers Stakes—the oldest stakes race. There are numerous events at various locations; so if you're in town, call for information.

September: **Battle of Saratoga Anniversary and Re-enactments** (518-664-9821), Saratoga National Battlefield Park. Admission fee. Enjoy a comedic portrayal of British General Burgoyne. Everyone is in period costumes. There's a festive atmosphere, yet it's also educational. A great place to take the kids. **Saratoga Global Wine and Food Festival** (518-587-3330), SPAC, Route 50. Admission fee. Hundreds of wine merchants and gourmet food purveyors display their tempting wares at this annual event. Anyone interested in food and wine shouldn't miss it.

November: **Victorian Street Walk** (518-587-8635), Broadway and downtown area. Enjoy strolling musicians, street theater, horse-drawn trolley rides, and more. Santa is on hand, and most retail stores in town have an open house with refreshments.

December: **First Night Celebration** (518-584-8262) Broadway and downtown area. The purchase of a button gives you admission to a variety of music and other venues throughout the city, where you'll enjoy Christmas music, jazz, and carols as well as dance and theater performances. The event starts with a 5K race at 5:30 PM and ends at midnight with fireworks.

Columbia County

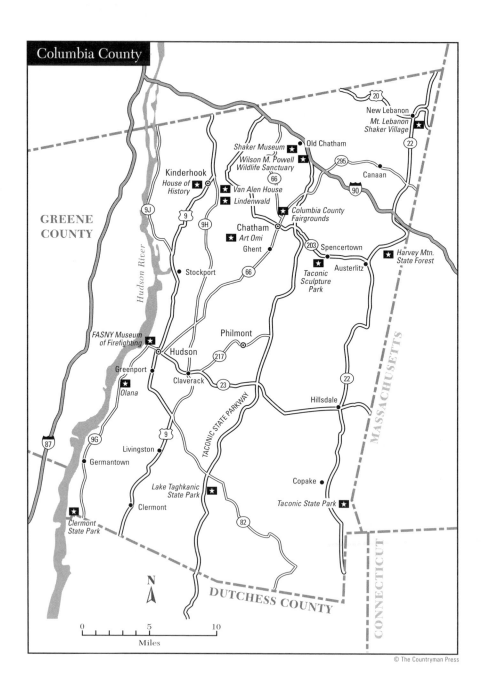

Columbia County

GREENE COUNTY

New Lebanon
Mt. Lebanon Shaker Village

Shaker Museum   Old Chatham
Wilson M. Powell Wildlife Sanctuary
Canaan

Kinderhook
House of History
Van Alen House
Lindenwald
Columbia County Fairgrounds

Chatham
Art Omi
Ghent
Spencertown
Austerlitz
Harvey Mtn. State Forest

Stockport
Taconic Sculpture Park

Hudson River

FASNY Museum of Firefighting
Philmont
Hudson
Greenport
Claverack
Hillsdale

Olana

Livingston
Germantown

Copake
Lake Taghkanic State Park
Taconic State Park
Clermont

Clermont State Park

TACONIC STATE PARKWAY

N

DUTCHESS COUNTY

MASSACHUSETTS

CONNECTICUT

0   5   10
Miles

© The Countryman Press

COLUMBIA COUNTY

F irst the home of the Native Americans who greeted Henry Hudson, Columbia County later attracted Dutch, German, and New England settlers with its river and fertile land. Whaling became a major industry, with the ships moving up the Hudson River and unloading their international cargo at Hudson in the 1830s. The city echoed with the noises of shipping, rope making, trading . . . and prostitution. Fine homes resembling the wood-and-brick extravaganzas of Maine and Massachusetts were built for men and women of substance and sophistication. The unusual is the rule here: a colorful museum filled with firemen's equipment and a library that was once an asylum for the mentally ill. The Shakers built settlements here and led their sober lives, which were also filled with song, dance, and fine craftsmanship. Across the county antiques glow in the windows of well-appointed shops, while the simplicity of Shaker furniture offers its own comment on life. Martin Van Buren lived in Columbia County (in fact, the term *OK* is thought to have originated from Van Buren's nickname, Old Kinderhook). Thoroughbred racehorses are bred, raised, and trained in Columbia County, and every Labor Day weekend the state's oldest county fair brings together folks of all ages in celebration of the harvest's best at the county fairgrounds in Chatham.

GUIDANCE **Columbia County Tourism** (518-828-3375, 800-724-1846), 401 State Street, Hudson 12534; www.columbiacountyny.com.
Columbia County Council on the Arts (518-671-6213), 209 Warren Street, Hudson 12534; www.artscolumbia.org.

GETTING THERE *By car:* Columbia County can be reached from the Taconic State Parkway and by Routes 9, 9H, and 22, all of which run north-south; I-90 (the MassPike in Massachusetts) cuts east-west across the county.
By train: **Amtrak** (800-872-7245) runs regular service between Penn Station in New York City and Hudson (518-828-3379), 69 South Front Street.
By air: **Albany International Airport** (518-242-2200), 737 Albany Shaker Road (exit 4 on the Northway), is less than 30 miles from many parts of

Columbia County. **Columbia County Airport** (518-828-9461), Route 9H, West Ghent.

MEDICAL EMERGENCY Columbia Memorial Hospital (518-828-7601/8500), 71 Prospect Avenue, Hudson.

✳ To See

Columbia County Museum (518-758-9265), 5 Albany Avenue, Kinderhook. This museum, owned by the Columbia County Historical Society, which is also headquartered here, is open May through November Monday through Friday 10–4, Saturday 1–4; December through April open Monday, Wednesday, Friday, and Saturday. The exhibits here include paintings, textiles, and other items that tell the story of Columbia County. The county historical society also administers the **Luykas Van Alen House** and the **James Vanderpoel House** (see *Historic Homes*).

FASNY (Farmers' Association of the State of New York) American Museum of Firefighting (518-822-1875, 877-347-3687), 117 Harry Howard Avenue, Hudson. Open daily year-round 9–4:30 except national holidays. Free. Take a step back in time to the glory days of firefighting at this fascinating museum located next door to the **Firemen's Home.** You will discover the oldest and broadest collection of fire-fighting gear and memorabilia in the United States. Scores of horse-drawn and steam- and gas-powered pieces of equipment are on display, some dating back to the 18th century. Greeting you as you enter the museum is a wooden statue of a volunteer fire chief dressed in patriotic red, white, and blue, complete with stars and golden trumpet. The museum is divided into five halls that house fire-fighting pumps, mobile apparatus, and engines as well as paintings, clothing, banners, photographs, and other memorabilia. A Newsham engine, built in 1725, was used to quench flames in Manhattan houses and saw more than 150 years of use. A delicate silver parade carriage from Kingston, New York, is topped by the figure of a fireman holding a rescued baby. Throughout the museum you will see lots of gleaming brass, bright-red paint, and an oddity or two like ornate firemen's parade trumpets, hand-grenade-style fire extinguishers, and brass fire markers that indicated which fire company had the right to fight a particular fire. There are even modern fire clothes that show the difference in fire-fighting techniques through the years. A September 11th memorial display filled with photographs lists the names of all the firefighters who lost their lives that day. The museum and gift shop consist of 37,000 square feet of memorabilia and exhibits that will be of interest to older children and just about anyone interested in the history of fire-fighting in New York State.

Mount Lebanon Shaker Village (518-794-9500), Route 20, P.O. Box 628, New Lebanon. Open mid-June through October Friday through Sunday 10–5, weekends only after Labor Day. Admission fee. Located on the site of a former Shaker settlement and now part of the Darrow School, the village tour includes an introductory slide show about the Shakers and a walking tour through several buildings, including the stone dairy barn and the meetinghouse.

The Shaker Museum and Library (518-794-9100), 88 Shaker Museum Road,
off County Route 13, Old Chatham. Open daily except Tuesday from May
through October, 10–5; the library is open by appointment at other times.
Admission fee. Although there are several Shaker museums in the country, this
one contains the foremost study collection of Shaker cultural materials, including
journals, letters, and spirit drawings. In the late 18th century a group of English
people immigrated to the colonies with the hope of being allowed to practice
their communal religion. Called Shakers because they danced and moved during
worship services, the group established settlements throughout their new country and became as well known for their fine crafts and innovations as for their
unusual celibate lifestyle. Industry, thrift, and simplicity were their bywords. In
their workshops chairs, seed packets, tin milk pails, and jams were made with
equal skill and care, and today Shaker-made items are still valued for their
beauty and grace. This museum is located in a restored barn and outbuilding;
the collections were gathered by both Shakers and non-Shakers, with the goal of
preserving a culture that is almost gone. All the major Shaker industries are represented at the museum: trip-hammer and washing-machine manufacturing as
well as clothing and broom making. The Shakers are credited with inventing the
circular saw and the revolving bake oven, although they rarely took out a patent,
preferring that the world benefit from their work. The museum also houses a
fine collection of furniture and household items from the various settlements.
Special events are held throughout the season, including crafts workshops, lectures, and concerts.

THE SHAKER MUSEUM AND LIBRARY IN OLD CHATHAM

Courtesy of Columbia County Tourism Department

Taconic Sculpture Park and Gallery (518-392-5757), Stever Hill Road, Spencertown. Open daily 10–5. Free. Roy Kanwit, a working sculptor, has 40 of his works exhibited on his grounds. His home/studio is an enormous stone castle-like structure. Here is a chance to wander through the mind of Gaea and witness the sunset through solar disks. The park attracts a few thousand visitors each year. Older children will love this stop.

HISTORIC HOMES **Clermont State Historic Site** (518-537-4240), located on County Route 6 just off Route 9G in Germantown. Open year-round: April through October, Tuesday through Sunday 11–5; November through March, weekends only 11–4. The grounds are open year-round from 8:30 AM until sunset. Admission fee. Standing on land that was awarded to the Livingston family in 1686, this Georgian mansion remained in the family for nearly three centuries. The family's illustrious history—Judge Robert Livingston wrote the letter of protest to King George just before the Revolutionary War, and Chancellor Robert R. Livingston helped draft the Declaration of Independence—is evident throughout the house. Although Clermont itself was burned by the British during the war, it was later rebuilt around the old walls and foundation. Alterations and additions were made into the late 19th century, so the house today reflects changes wrought by several generations. Clermont's 46 rooms are furnished with family heirlooms and fine examples of period furniture and decorative accessories. A crystal chandelier brought from France in 1802 hangs above the drawing room, where you will also find a French balloon clock made to commemorate the first hydrogen balloon in Paris in 1783. Family portraits decorate the hallways and help visitors sort out the confusing Livingston family tree, and there are exquisite examples of cabinetmaking throughout the mansion.

But as lovely as Clermont is, the setting makes it more so. In fact, the first steamboat, the Clermont, made its way up the Hudson River here in August 1807; that momentous occasion is now commemorated with a celebration every August. The views of the Catskill Mountains across the Hudson River are magnificent; the family purchased as much land as possible to preserve the setting. Tradition holds that the black locust trees flanking the house were planted by many generations of Livingstons. The roses in the Italian walled garden transform the month of June into an enchanting time. Several special events are held at Clermont, including a July Fourth celebration with costumed colonial soldiers, Steamboat Days in August, and a Christmas open house that takes place every weekend in December. There is a small gift shop and visitors center, where you can see a short video that tells the story of the Livingston family. The house tour is not recommended for young children.

Olana (518-828-0135), Route 9G, 1 mile south of the Rip Van Winkle Bridge. Greenport. Open year-round: April through October, Tuesday through Sunday 10–5; November 10–4; December through March, Saturday and Sunday 10–4 or by appointment. The house is viewed by guided tour only, and group size is limited; call to reserve tickets before you go. The grounds can be viewed without a guide at no charge or with a landscape guide for a minimal charge. Admission

Hudson Valley Tourism, Inc.

OLANA, THE PERSIAN-STYLE FANTASY HOME OF HUDSON RIVER SCHOOL
PAINTER FREDERIC CHURCH

fee. Frederic Edwin Church was one of America's foremost artists, a painter who captured the grandeur and mystery of the nation in the 19th century. Church first gained acclaim for his vision of Niagara Falls, a painting that won a medal at the 1867 Paris International Exposition. In 1870 Church and his wife, Isabel, returned from their travels in the Middle East and Europe to their farm in Hudson and began the planning and building of the Persian fantasy that would become known as Olana. Hand-painted tiles on the roof and turrets of the 37-room mansion, situated 460 feet above the river, add touches of pink and green to the sky. Church called his style "personal Persia," and inside you will discover hand-carved, room-sized screens, rich Persian rugs, delicate paintings, decorative pottery and china, and even a pair of gilded crane lamps that look as if they stepped out of an Egyptian wall painting. Olana is also rich in examples of Church's paintings, including *Autumn in North America* and *Sunset in Jamaica*. His studio is still set up as it was in his time. During the holiday season, the house is decorated with elaborate greenery, and Yuletide confections grace the tables. Visitors can hike year-round along the carriage paths and roadways that wind through the property, or take in the Hudson River views; just across the river is Cedar Grove, Thomas Cole's home (see *To See* in "Greene County"), and the place where Church apprenticed as an artist. The 40-minute house tour is not recommended for young children. The visitors center contains an excellent museum shop and offers a short video about Frederic Church and the site. An extensive schedule of weekend art and nature programs feature an array of activities oriented toward families. They are held from Memorial Day weekend through Labor Day weekend on Saturday and Sunday afternoons 1–4; call for a complete listing. There is a marvelous open house in December (see *Special Events*). Olana is one of my favorite places in the Hudson Valley; visit, and you will see why: It is truly a unique treasure.

Luykas Van Alen House (518-758-9265), Route 9H, Kinderhook. After visiting Lindenwald, home of Martin Van Buren, you may want to stop at the Luykas Van Alen House, which is operated by the Columbia County Historical Society. This brick Dutch farmhouse of the early 18th century has been restored to reflect its heritage. The site contains the **Ichabod Crane School House**—a restored one-room schoolhouse open to the public and named after the character in Washington Irving's tale. In fact, Irving based Crane on a local schoolteacher who actually worked in this schoolhouse.

Martin Van Buren National Historic Site (518-758-9689), Route 9H, Kinderhook. Open mid-May through October, Wednesday through Sunday 9–4:30. Admission fee. Known as **Lindenwald,** the house was the home and farm of Martin Van Buren, eighth president of the United States. Built in 1797 and renovated in 1849, the resulting structure is a blend of Federal, Italianate, and Victorian styles. Van Buren was born in Kinderhook (Dutch for "children's corner"), the son of a tavern keeper. He studied law and from Kinderhook embarked on a 30-year political career. At Lindenwald, visitors will see the house Van Buren returned to, to look back on three tumultuous decades of public service. Named after the linden trees on the property, the graceful building—complete with shutters, double chimneys, and arched windows—is today a National Historic Site; it was renovated in recent years to remove or lessen the impact of certain Victorian "improvements." The grounds offer an escape to the peace of rural 19th-century America, but it is inside that the renovations are more evident. A center stairway winds upward through the house, the hundreds of turned spindles so polished that they gleam. The old wallpaper was stripped and replaced with paper appropriate to the era, and furniture and decorative objects finally look as if they belong to the home. The house contains a fine collection of Van Buren memorabilia, and a visit is an excellent way to become acquainted with the president known as the Little Magician because of both his size and his political acumen.

James Vanderpoel House (518-758-9265), Broad Street, Kinderhook. Open Memorial Day weekend through Labor Day, Wednesday through Saturday 10:30–4:30, Sunday 1:30–4:30; call for off-season hours. Admission fee. This site is also called the House of History, and indeed it does present some fine exhibits of life in Columbia County, especially the era when the area was a bustling industrial and whaling center. Built in 1819 for lawyer and politician James Vanderpoel, the Federal house is characterized by delicate ornamentation, including plasterwork ceilings, graceful mantelpieces, and a wide staircase that seems to float to the second floor. The work of several New York cabinetmakers—who created a blend of American pride and European style—is displayed throughout the rooms. A fine selection of paintings, including many by country artists, depicts Columbia County life. The Vanderpoel House holds several special events throughout the year, including a Christmas greens show and a coaching competition.

FOR FAMILIES **Louis Paul Jonas Studios** (518-851-2211), Miller Road, Churchtown. By appointment only. Free. Discover dinosaurs lurking in Churchtown. This renowned workshop produced the dinosaurs that were displayed at the 1963 New York World's Fair (the great reptiles were floated down the Hudson River on a barge for their trip to Queens), and its craftspeople still make full-sized and smaller versions of the reptilian wonders, along with many other finely crafted wildlife sculptures. Jonas was one of the finest animal sculptors in history, with work at the American Museum of Natural History and dozens of other museums and gardens. Today the Jonas gallery resembles the Peaceable Kingdom, with animal models from all eras and environments. Although not open to the general public, group tours are welcome with advance notice. This is one of the least known treasures of the Hudson Valley!

Mud Creek Environmental Learning Center (518-828-4386), Route 66, Ghent. The center, located behind the USDA building, is open year-round 8–4:30, but the nature trail is open all the time to visitors. Free. The nature trail wends its way through wetlands with two loops—one is a mile long, and a shorter loop is about a half-mile long. A number of kiosks along the way provide information about the flora and fauna on the trail. Special programs for groups are available by advance reservation; a full-time educator is on staff to assist visitors from schools and private groups. An interesting stop for families traveling with children between the ages of 3 and 12.

Old Chatham Sheepherding Company (518-794-7733, 888-SHEEP-60), 99 Shaker Museum Road, Old Chatham. Visit this farm, and watch milking the goats and cheese making. They produce several types of sheep's milk cheeses and yogurt and it is the largest sheep dairy farm in the country. The farm began in 1994 with a flock of 150 sheep and there are now more than 1,200 East Friesian crossbred sheep grazing on 600 acres of rolling pastures. They use European methods to create new American original cheeses, which have won awards and been praised in many gourmet food publications. There is a shop on the premises where visitors can purchase the cheeses and yogurt. Farm Day, the last Saturday in April, is when the place is buzzing; it's a great time to visit.

SCENIC DRIVES It is difficult to *avoid* taking a scenic drive in Columbia County—wherever you look, you can see rolling, bright-green meadows, misty ponds, and quiet villages that look the same as they did a century ago. You may find yourself on a bluff overlooking the Hudson River or in a city that recalls the glory of the whaling industry. The roads are well maintained, and you can't get lost for very long.

For a sampling of the county's charms, both Routes 9 and 9H will take you through Hudson, Kinderhook, and Valatie, with plenty of museums, shops, and historic sites to explore. Other routes worth a drive include north-south Route 7 and Route 22, in the eastern part of the county, and Route 82, which runs northwest from the county line at Ancram to near Hudson. Route 11 between Routes 23 and 27, in the town of Taghkanic, has actually received an award for its scenic beauty, having been declared a National Beauty Award Highway (you will see the sign marking this road when you pass by).

One marvelous driving tour through Stuyvesant offers a chance to see many old barns in varied styles, reflecting the agricultural heritage of the town. With over

12,000 acres of tillable land bordering the Hudson River and Kinderhook Creek, the agricultural area of the town of Stuyvesant dates back centuries. You will see "historical roots" barns, with their distinct architectural features; "English roots" barns, which are rectangular in shape; the large square "Dutch roots" barns, with their H shape; and the "German roots" barns, which are rectangular with doors on the long side and rooflines that are higher than the Dutch barns. Begin the tour in the town of Kinderhook south of the Martin Van Buren National Historic Site on Route 9H and bear to the right onto County Route 25. At the intersection of County Routes 25 and 25A, turn left. Proceed for about 2 miles to County Route 46, where you will see three silos across a field on the right. At the T junction with Route 9J, go right for about 0.5 mile to Sharptown Road. Turn right onto Sharptown, where you will see a barn practically in the road; this is a side-hill barn with a lower floor built into the hill, and it is now used as a woodworking shop. Farther along this road you will see the Gleason Farm barns.

WALKING TOUR—HUDSON The city of Hudson, located roughly between Routes 9 and 9G, is rich with the traditions and cultural heritage of its settlers: first the Dutch, then seafarers from Massachusetts and Rhode Island, and later, Quakers and whalers. Carefully designed in the 1780s as a shipping center, with straight streets and "gangway" alleys, ropewalks, wharves, and a warehouse, Hudson was the first city to receive a charter after the Declaration of Independence. Soon whaling and industry took over as the mainstays of the economy, and although Hudson has had its ups and downs since, the city is now in the full flower of a renaissance. On a walking tour of Hudson you will see dozens of architectural styles and hundreds of commercial buildings and homes that have been maintained or restored to their earlier glory. A visitor to the city may want to stop in at the **Columbia County Chamber of Commerce,** 729 Warren Street, and pick up a detailed walking guide. **Columbia County Tourism,** at 401 State Street, can also be a source for the walking guide. But whether or not you follow a specific tour, a walk around several main streets will reveal the architectural heritage of the area. Visitors to Hudson who enjoy antiques will discover some of the best antiques shopping on the East Coast. Many of the shops are located along Warren Street (see *Selective Shopping*) and range in selection from fine European and 18th-century American furniture, glassware, and fine arts to 1950s lamps, textiles, and ephemera.. Many stores are open by chance or appointment, although Thursday through the weekend is a good bet for browsers.

Coming from the south, from Route 9G follow Warren Street west to Front Street (by the river), and park. At Front Street you will see the Parade, an 18th-century park that was kept open for use by the city's inhabitants. From the park, also called Promenade Hill Park, you will have a dazzling view of the Hudson River and the Catskill Mountains, plus the Hudson-Athens Lighthouse built in 1874, used to warn ships off the Hudson Middle Ground Flats. Inside the park you will find a statue of St. Winifred, donated to the city by a man who felt that Hudson needed a patron saint.

The easiest walk in Hudson is up Warren Street, the aforementioned antiques mecca. The architectural styles to be found here include Greek Revival, Federal, Queen Anne, and Victorian. At the **Curtiss House,** 32 Warren Street, look up at the widow's walk, which was built by the house's whaling owner in the 1830s to provide a sweeping view of the river. Some of the houses here sport "eyebrow" windows—narrow windows tucked under the eaves that are often at floor level within the houses. The Adams-style house at 116 Warren Street is considered a rare remnant from the early 19th century and boasts an enclosed private garden.

The 1811 **Robert Jenkins House** (518-828-9764), 113 Warren Street, is open to the public in July and August, Sunday and Monday 1–3 or by appointment. The house serves as the headquarters of the local chapter of the Daughters of the American Revolution and was built by an early mayor of Hudson. The exhibits here offer a look at the city over the past two centuries and contain material on whaling and genealogy, paintings by Hudson River School artists, and other historic items.

At Warren and Fourth Streets is the *Register Star* newspaper building, with its tiny park. Like many other of the buildings here, it has served several purposes: It was a dance hall, an opera house, a county jail, and an assembly hall. Head north on Fourth Street to State Street. The **Hudson Area Library Association,** 400 State Street, is an 1818 stone building guarded by stone lions. The structure has also served as an almshouse, an asylum for the mentally ill, a women's seminary, and a private home. If the building is open, stop in at the second-floor History Room, which has some local memorabilia, prints, and books.

Backtrack to Warren Street, and spend some time looking at the fine 18th- and 19th-century buildings, many of which are undergoing restoration. Other walking areas with interesting architecture include Union Street, East and West Court Streets—appropriately, by the courthouse—and East Allen Street.

✴ To Do

AIRPLANE RIDES **Columbia County Airport** (518-828-9461), Route 9H, Ghent. Richmor Aviation provides scenic flights by special appointment; you can go for a half hour or by the hour.

BICYCLING **Harlem Valley Rail Trail** (518-789-9591). This 12.2-mile paved bicycle/pedestrian path built on the old railroad line that connected New York City, the Harlem Valley, and Chatham, has a few places where it can be accessed. In Ancram, off Route 22, at Undermountain Road; in Copake, take Valley View Road; the Taconic State Park entrance (not to be confused with Lake Taghkanic State Park, below) is near Depot Deli in Copake Falls (see *To Do—Hiking*).

The following parks have excellent paved roadways for bicycling:

Lake Taghkanic State Park (518-851-3631), 1528 Route 82, Taghkanic.

Martin Van Buren Park (518-758-9689), Route 9H (across from the Van Buren home), Kinderhook.

Taconic State Park (518-329-3993), Route 344, off Route 22, Copake Falls.

BOAT CRUISES *The Spirit of the Hudson* (518-822-1014), departs from Waterfront Park in Hudson and offers 1-hour sightseeing cruises on the Hudson River from Memorial Day weekend through October. This company plans to link Hudson, Athens, Catskill, Coxsackie, and Saugerties, but call for a schedule. Brunch and dinner cruises are available as well.

CANOEING AND KAYAKING Columbia County doesn't have an array of outfitters where visitors can rent canoes or kayaks. The state parks are the best places to rent a canoe or rowboat on a lake. However, if you have your own canoe or kayak, the following two spots are wonderful to explore.

Rogers Island (under the Rip Van Winkle Bridge). Row or paddle out to this paradise for bird-watching. There are eagles, waterfowl, and an amazing array of birds that inhabit this intriguing island in the Hudson River between Greene and Columbia Counties.

Stockport Flats, Station Road, Greenport. If you are traveling north on Route 9, look for Station Road, which is on the left, just after you cross the Columbiaville Bridge. This state land offers the perfect place to explore by canoe. There are 250 acres here. I paddled canoe here over 15 years ago and remember the waters of these flats being easy to navigate; a good place for beginners to practice.

FARM STANDS AND PICK-YOUR-OWN FARMS Not only are the lush, rolling farmlands of Columbia County a lovely place to visit, but you will find a remarkably large variety of farm stands and pick-your-own farms here, as well. Along with the traditional apple orchards and berry fields, discover the county's vineyards, melon patches, and cherry orchards, where the selection of the fruit is left up to you. If you go to a pick-your-own-farm, bring along a container, a hat to shade you from the sun, and a long-sleeved shirt to protect you from insect bites, sunburn, and scratches. The delightful thing about the smaller farm stands, which sprout as fast as corn in the summer, is that many of them carry unusual or hard-to-find varieties of corn, apples, and tomatoes.

In Ancram, make sure to stop at **Thompson-Finch Farm** (518-329-7578) on Wiltsie Bridge Road, open daily 9–5, if you love strawberries. Theirs are some of the best you will ever taste—all grown without synthetic fertilizers or pesticides on compost-fed soil.

The **Berry Farm** (518-392-4609), Route 203, Chatham, is a haven for berry lovers, raising everything from gooseberries and currants to boysenberries, strawberries, and even kiwi fruit. Call the farm to find out when the crops are ready to pick.

In Germantown, **Wintje Farms** (518-537-6072), Route 9G, lets you buy or pick apples, cherries, melons, berries, squash, plums, and more.

A truly special farm is found in Ghent on Route 9H, north of Hudson: **Loveapple Farm** (518-828-5048), open July through November, lets you pick your apples, but you can also buy pears, prunes, cherries, and more than a dozen varieties of peaches at the roadside market. The pies and doughnuts are wonderful.

Kinderhook is home to **Samascott Orchard** (518-758-7224), Sunset Avenue (open June through November), which has more than a dozen pick-your-own harvests, including grapes, pears, plums, and strawberries, and just as many varieties of apples.

Near Claverack you will find **Philip Orchards** (518-851-6351), Route 9H, with pick-your-own apples and pears; **Holmquest Farm** (518-851-9629), 516 Spook Rock Road (County Route 29), has fruits and vegetables; and **Bryant Farms** (518-851-9061), Route 9H, is strictly a roadside market but offers a huge selection of fruits, vegetables, and local products. (They also have an indoor flea market year-round on Saturday and Sunday from 9–4.)

The region around the city of Hudson is filled with seasonal farm stands, including **Taconic Orchards** (518-851-7477), Route 82, where you can pick berries and buy everything else imaginable; **Klein's Kill Fruit Farm** (518-828-6082), Route 10, which has sweet, deep-red cherries; and **Don Baker Farm** (518-828-5890), Route 14 (follow signs), with more than seven varieties of apples, both standard and heritage.

If you are north of Hudson, don't miss the **Sunset Meadows Marketplace** (518-851-3000), 3521 Route 9. There is an enormous array of fresh baked goods and local produce as well as a terrific selection of gourmet food products from all over the Hudson Valley. You can also enjoy a cup of gourmet coffee or tea and a pastry in the adjoining café after shopping (see *Eating Out*). The couple who own this establishment moved north from Manhattan and truly enjoy sharing the bounty of the region with visitors.

Valatie is home to **Golden Harvest Farms** (518-758-7683), Route 9, with pick-your-own or already-picked apples and a large roadside stand, and **Yonder Farms** (518-758-7011), Maple Lane, with pick-your-own apples, blueberries, raspberries, and strawberries.

There are three farmers markets in the area. The **Chatham Farmers Market** is held in the parking area of the Kinderhook National Bank, Depot Square, in the village of Chatham on Fridays from 2–6 PM as well as on Mother's Day weekend and Columbus Day weekend. The **Hudson Farmers Market** (518-828-3373), North Sixth Street and Columbia Street, operates June through October, Saturday 9–1. The **Kinderhook Farmers Market** is held in the village square on Route 9 from late spring to mid-October, Saturday, 8–noon.

FISHING The county is filled with deep lakes, clear streams, and stocked ponds and creeks. Keep in mind that a New York State fishing license is required for anyone over the age of 16 partaking of the sport.

The following creeks are stocked by the Department of Environmental Conservation:

Kinderhook Creek. From the county line in New Lebanon at Adams Crossing Road to the county line at Route 20 behind the Lebanon Valley Speedway. Access can be obtained from Route 66 in the town of Chatham at Bachus Road. There is also access to the creek at the bridge in Malden Bridge.

Claverack Creek. At Roxbury Road, off Route 217, a bridge crosses the creek at Hess farm; there is access from the bridge. There is also access on Route 23 at Red Mills, off the south side of the bridge only (not where the falls are); at the bridge on Webb Road (off County Route 29); and on County Route 29 halfway between Webb and Hiscox Roads.

Roeliff Jansen Creek. Access this area from County Route 2 between Elizaville and the Taconic State Parkway; at the junction of County Routes 2 and 19, at Turkey Hill Road; at Buckwheat Road (off Route 9 between County Routes 8 and 6, at the bridge known as Oars Bridge; or about 2 miles south of Hillsdale on Black Grocery Road, which is off Route 22).

There is also fishing at other places in the county, including **Lake Taghkanic State Park,** off Route 82, 3 miles south of the Taconic State Parkway exit. Here you will find year-round fishing with sport fish such as chain pickerel, largemouth, smallmouth, and rock bass, bluegill, pumpkinseed sunfish, yellow perch, brown bullhead, and the occasional cisco in deeper waters. **Taconic State Park,** Route 344 off Route 22, Copake Falls, has **Ore Pond,** where there is stocked trout and other fish native to ponds. **Oakdale Pond,** at Clinton Street and Glenwood Boulevard in Hudson, is stocked annually with trout, and it's a nice family fishing spot. **Queechy Lake,** at the intersection of Route 22 and County Route 30, Canaan, is heavily stocked with trout.

GOLFING **Boston Corners Country Club** (518-329-2800), 390 Undermountain Road, off Route 22, Ancram. Open April through October. Call for hours. This 18-hole, par-71 course offers cart and club rentals. A pro shop is on the premises, and lessons are offered. Snack bar with light fare; cocktails available.

Copake Country Club (518-325-4338), 44 Golf Course Road, off County Route 11, Copake. Open March through November daily 7–7. This 18-hole, par-72 course offers a range of facilities, including riding cart and pull cart rentals, pro shop, lessons, and seasonal memberships. Senior-citizen and group rates offered. There is a fine restaurant on the premises (see *Dining Out*).

Meadowgreens Golf Course (518-828-0663), 1238 Route 9H, Ghent. Open April through October. Call for hours. This nine-hole, par-36 course has both pull cart and riding cart rentals, lessons, and a pro shop. The restaurant/bar on the premises offers outdoor dining in the warm-weather months.

Undermountain Golf Course (518-329-4444), 274 Undermountain Road, off Route 22, Ancram. Open daily April through November 7–7. This 18-hole, par-65 executive course offers club, pull cart, and riding cart rentals, pro shop, lessons, snack bar, practice green. Group rates available.

Winding Brook Country Club (518-758-7054), Route 203, Valatie. Open April through October, Tuesday through Sunday 8–7. This 18-hole, par-70 course is 6,400 yards long. There are lessons, pro shop, pull cart, riding cart, and club rentals as well as group discounts. The restaurant on the premises opens at 11.

The following establishments offer driving ranges, not full golf courses and facilities:

Bryant Farms Driving Range (518-851-9430), Route 9H, Claverack. Open 6:30 AM–7 PM, there are 10 tee boxes with artificial turf, and natural grass for chipping and driving. PGA pro lessons available by appointment.

Campbell's Hillside Driving Range (518-325-4338), 61 Bloody Hill Road, off Route 23, Craryville. Open 7:30 AM–8 PM. Over 300 yards in length; there are grass tees, mats, elevated tees, and lessons available.

Farmer's Range, 2878 Route 203, Valatie. Open daily sunrise to sunset, March through October. This 350-yard range also has a putting green; club rentals available.

Ghent Driving Range (518-672-7996/7922), County Route 9 & Hugo Drive, Ghent. Open Monday through Saturday 8–8, Sunday 11–8. This range is 270 yards; there are 10 tee boxes with separate grass and artificial grass tee area.

HIKING Precautions should be taken when walking through wooded and grassy areas; Lyme disease is transmitted by deer ticks and is *extremely* prevalent in this county. Ticks, which are spread by wildlife, are found in grassy areas as well as in brush, shrubbery, and woodland habitats. Wear appropriate clothing, and be careful if you wander off marked trails for any reason.

Also note that raccoon rabies is present in this part of the state. Don't approach, feed, or touch *any* wild animals you see while walking. If an animal is behaving strangely, report this to a member of the park staff.

In an effort to reduce operating costs, trash receptacles have been removed from many day-use areas. Plastic disposal bags are available for the transport of trash from the park. Dispose of waste responsibly, which will keep user fees low.

Beebe Hill State Forest (518-828-0236), County Route 5, Austerlitz. Open year-round. There is a nice network of trails here, and they're being expanded. Most are of moderate difficulty. In addition to use by hikers and bicyclists, horses, and snowmobiles are permitted on the trails; however, no ATVs are allowed. A 6-mile trail now runs from the top of Beebe Hill to Harvey Mountain, with a lean-to along the way for overnight camping; otherwise, no facilities.

Borden's Pond Preserve, Off Route 203, just outside the village of Chatham. Open year-round, dawn to dusk, this 52-acre preserve provides a nice change of pace after shopping or grabbing a bite to eat in town and is within walking distance of the main village streets. This is a fairly new area, with an old woodland mill pond surrounded by forest land. There is a parking area if you choose to drive.

A PEACEFUL HIKING PATH IN BEEBE HILL STATE FOREST

Dale Evva Gelfand

Drowned Lands Swamp Conservation Area (518-392-5252). 654 County Route 3, Ancram. Open year-round dawn to dusk. This wetland, consisting of 110 acres, is one of the largest in southeastern New York. Home to bog turtles and several species of rare plants, it offers a 0.5-mile steep walk to the summit, Old Croken (an old English word meaning crooked; the path twists and turns). The views of the Taconic Hills and Catskill Mountains from this point, 800 feet above sea level, are wonderful; you can also see the entire drowned lands swamp. There is a lower swamp trail that makes for an easier walk.

Greenport Conservation Area (518-392-5252). Heading south on Route 9 to Greenport, go right onto Joslen Boulevard, across from a condominium complex; then make a right onto Daisy Hill Road. There is a parking area and information kiosk with interpretive brochures detailing the 3.5 miles of trails, which are marked (red, blue, and green). This is a great place for those traveling with children who want to take a short hike; the trails wend their way through meadows, woodlands, and wetlands along the Hudson River. A hand-hewn cedar gazebo overlooking the Hudson is a great spot to rest and enjoy the view.

Harlem Valley Rail Trail (518-789-9591), Undermountain Road, off Route 22, Ancram; Valley View Road, Copake; Taconic State Park entrance near Depot-Deli, Copake Falls. When completed, this paved bicycle/pedestrian path will stretch from Wassaic in Dutchess County to Chatham in Columbia County, and run some 46 miles. It was built on the old railroad bed that connected New York City, the Harlem Valley, and Chatham. Trains stopped running on the Harlem Line north of Dover Plains in 1976. So far the State of New York has purchased 22 miles of land to build this linear park—about half of which lies in southern Columbia County—which is ideal for hiking, bicycling, and cross-country skiing. Those who travel the trail may see many species of birds as well as deer, coyotes, foxes, hawks, turtles, and beavers—or at least their visible dams—to name just some of the wildlife that flourishes here. The trail passes through the hamlets of Amenia and Millerton in Dutchess County to Copake Falls, so hikers can explore these towns along the way.

Harvey Mountain State Forest (518-828-0236), East Hill Road, off Route 22, near I-90 B-3 exit, Austerlitz. Open year-round. Walk either the former logging road or hike through the woods on a marked trail (look for the red blazes) to the top of Harvey Mountain, with a spectacular view (and a picnic table) at the summit. It's about 1.5 miles long and not too difficult. A good choice for those with older children, but keep in mind that there are no facilities here.

Lake Taghkanic State Park (518-851-3631), 1528 Route 82, Taghkanic; direct access off Taconic State Parkway. Open year-round. Admission fee. This 1,569-acre park was donated to the state in 1929 by a descendant of the Livingston family. Find an extended series of hiking and fitness trails here; obtain a map when you enter the park. Overnight camping is available May through October. Facilities include a cabin and cottage area, two bathing beaches, picnic areas, boat rentals, playgrounds, and a ballfield. During the winter visitors can enjoy cross-country skiing, ice fishing, snowmobiling, and ice-skating.

New Forge State Forest (518-828-0236), New Forge Road, off Route 82,

Taghkanic. Open year-round. This state forest consists of 655 acres. A rather easy 2-mile hike on an old logging road goes through the park. Many new trails are in the process of being created.

Pachaquack Preserve (518-758-9806). Elm Street, off Route 203, Valatie. This 43-acre preserve is operated by the town of Valatie, and it's a lovely place for a walk in any season. There are 2 miles of walking trails here, picnic tables, and a gazebo. This is relatively easy walking; the trails follow the Kinderhook Creek, where there is excellent fishing. *Pachaquack* is a Native American word that means "cleared meadow and meeting place."

Taconic State Park (518-329-3993), Route 344, off Route 22, Copake Falls. Open year-round. A 25-mile network of hiking trails here range from very easy to quite difficult in this 5,000-acre park, one of the largest in the Hudson Valley, spanning two counties (Dutchess and Columbia) and bordering Massachusetts and Connecticut. The park runs for 16 miles along the Taconic Ridge, offering spectacular views in many places. This is a good stop for families; there's a small nature center with a few displays, and camping areas are open May through November (however, there is winter camping here: Small cabins may be rented year-round). The historical section of the park includes the Copake Iron Works, which dates back to 1845, when ironmaking was the main industry in town. For over 60 years, iron ore, limestone, and hardwood was taken from local deposits with water power from Bash Bish Creek; 2,500 tons of blast iron, much of which was used for making car wheels, was taken out of the "park." In the 1920s the owner of the foundry sold the site to the state. The cabins that once housed laborers are now rented out as overnight lodging for park visitors.

Wilson M. Powell Wildlife Sanctuary, Hunt Club Road, off County Route 13, Old Chatham. Open year-round, dawn to dusk. This 130-acre sanctuary offers a variety of walks with lovely views of the mountains; some meander around a pond. A marked trail leads you on a 0.5-mile walk to the observation area called Dorson Rock. At the pond, one can observe waterfowl. This is also a good place to go cross-country skiing in the winter.

SWIMMING **Knickerbocker Lake** (518-758-9754), Route 9, just outside the village of Valatie. Open late June to mid-August. This large lake, operated by the town of Kinderhook, has a nice beach, making it a locally popular place to swim, especially for those with young children. It is open to the public; $10 per car.

Lake Taghkanic State Park (518-851-3631), Route 82, Taghkanic. Open Memorial Day weekend through Labor Day. Free. This 156-acre lake has two beaches. The west beach is larger, with boat rentals (rowboats and paddleboats) and volleyball courts; the east beach is good for people traveling with young children. Both beaches have snack-bar concession stands and rest rooms.

Taconic State Park (518-329-3993), Route 344, off Route 22, Copake Falls. Open Memorial Day weekend through Labor Day. Free. This flooded iron ore mine/quarry with a dock allows swimmers to step into 8 feet of water. There is no beach here and it is not recommended for people with small children. There is an adjacent small pond with two feet of water for kids; do come prepared, since there is no snack bar or services, just rest rooms.

✳ Winter Sports

CROSS-COUNTRY SKIING Cross-country skiing in Columbia County is centered in the state parks, where well-marked trails are uncrowded—and free—and natural surroundings are breathtaking. You must bring your own equipment.

Lake Taghkanic State Park (518-851-3631), Route 82 at Taconic Parkway, 11 miles south of Hudson, has skiing and ice-skating.

Clermont State Historic Site (518-537-4240), Route 6 off Route 9G, 10 miles south of the Rip Van Winkle Bridge, offers skiing as does **Taconic State Park** (518-329-3993), east of Route 22 in Copake; **Rudd Pond** (518-789-3059), off Route 22 near Millerton; the **Harlem Valley Rail Trail,** Route 22, off Undermountain Road in Ancram; and **Olana State Historic Site** (518-828-0135), in Hudson.

DOWNHILL SKIING Catamount (518-325-3200), Route 23, Hillsdale, straddles the borders of New York and Massachusetts. It's a popular with skiers of all ages and abilities, beginner to expert. There are 28 slopes and eight lifts as well as a snowboard megaplex, night skiing, lessons, and day care. Catamount offers snowmaking, rentals, and even RV and camping facilities. In summer enjoy grass skiing and mountaincoasters—sort of bobsleds on tracks.

A SNOWBOARDER ENJOYS THE CONDITIONS AT CATAMOUNT IN HILLSDALE.

Courtesy Catamount Ski Area

ICE FISHING Ice fishing is allowed at **Lake Taghkanic State Park** (518-851-3631), Route 82 at Taconic State Parkway, 11 miles south of Hudson, and at **Rudd Pond** (518-789-3059), off Route 22, near Millerton.

✳ Green Space

The Fields Sculpture Park (518-392-7656), Letter S Road, Ghent. From Hudson, take Route 9H north; make a right onto County Route 22, then left onto Letter S Road. Second driveway on the left. Open daily sunrise to sunset. Free. Founded in 1988 as public grounds for viewing contemporary sculpture—as part of the Art

Omi International Arts Center—the park features over 40 sculptures on view now, with works by Liberman, Lipski, Pepper, Highstine, Knowlton, Venet, and others. Each year about 10 new works are added to the park. There are also temporary exhibits at various times of the year, made possible with the assistance of independent curators. This arts center is located on over 150 acres, of which 90 are dedicated to the sculpture park that stretches through rolling fields, wooded knolls, and wetlands. Allow an hour to tour the entire park. Free guided tours are available, with reservation for groups of six or more.

Courtesy Columbia County Tourism Department

THE FIELDS
SCULPTURE PARK STRETCHES THROUGH 90 ACRES OF ROLLING FIELDS, WOODED KNOLLS, AND WETLANDS.

✳ Lodging

The following fine establishments welcome visitors and are my favorite places to stay in Columbia County, but if you need more information about bed & breakfasts, motels, and hotels in the region, contact the **Columbia County Lodging Association** (518-822-8218), P.O. Box 1146, Hudson 12534, www.staycolumbia. com.

Canaan/New Lebanon area
Churchill House Bed & Breakfast (518-766-5852, 800-532-2702), Route 22 and Churchill Road, New Lebanon 12125. ($$) This beautiful 1830 Greek-Revival farmhouse with a wraparound porch is located on 18 acres on the edge of the Berkshires. A lovely stream flows through the property, and guests can enjoy a view of the Taconic Valley and Berkshire Hills. Three rooms and one suite, all with private bath, range in price, so inquire about the variety of accommodations, especially if you are traveling on a budget. Savor the hearty breakfast served in the dining room.

Children over the age of 6 are welcome. Open year-round.

Inn at Silver Maple Farm (518-781-3600), Route 295, Canaan 12029. ($$) This eleven-room inn, including two suites (all with private bath, telephone, and cable TV), is located in a converted barn with wide-board pine floors and exposed beams. Ten acres of woodlands surround the inn, and all rooms have countryside views. The owners live in a house next door. Breakfast includes homemade breads, muffins, fresh fruit, and quiche. Afternoon tea is served at 4. Children welcome. No pets. One room is accessible to the disabled. Open year-round.

Shaker Meadows B&B (518-794-9385), 14209 Route 22, New Lebanon 12125. ($) This 1821 farmhouse located on 50 scenic acres of meadows and hills overlooks a pond. The centrally air-conditioned farmhouse has three large rooms (each with private bath) and three small bedrooms (each with private bath outside the room).

This is an ideal place for a family reunion or large gathering of friends as the farmhouse sleeps 12. A second adjacent building has three guest suites; these rooms have phone, TV, VCR, full kitchen, air-conditioning, living room, and private deck. A dining room, separate from the farmhouse, is where guests are served a hearty full breakfast. During the summer months, make sure to get a pass to the private town beach on Queechy Lake; the innkeepers will provide towels and beach chairs. A minimum stay is never required. Children welcome. Open year-round.

Spencer House B&B (518-794-6500), 466 Route 20, New Lebanon 12125. ($$) Originally the home of Colonel Allen Spencer, who served in the War of 1812, this classic Shaker-style structure is located in a pastoral country setting. You will find plenty of peace and quiet here yet still be conveniently located near a few excellent restaurants. They offer an extended continental breakfast that includes muffins, bagels, fruit, and cereal between 8 and 11 AM. The six rooms (four with private bath and queen-sized beds; two share one bath), are cozy, comfortable, and nicely decorated. Children welcome. Open year-round.

Chatham/Spencertown area
Milk & Honey B&B (518-392-7594), 1214 Route 295, East Chatham 12060. ($) This center hall Colonial home, built in the late 18th century, is located on 8 acres, with wildflower meadows, a fishing pond, and stream. The three rooms, all with private bath (one with a whirlpool and one completely handicapped accessible), are clean and comfortable. A full breakfast is served. Children are welcome. Open year-round.

Spencertown Country House (518-392-5292 or 1-888-727-9980), 1909 County Route 9, Spencertown 12165. ($$) Built in the 19th century, this renovated farmhouse—on 5 landscaped acres next to a dairy farm—is 2 miles from the Taconic Parkway and 3 miles from both Chatham and Spencertown. Nine comfortable guest rooms, all with private bath, phone, TV, and data port, are offered at a range of rates. Those exploring on their own should check out the midweek single-traveler rates, which are excellent value for the money, at half the weekend rates. A full breakfast is served. Children are welcome; however, they must be over the age of 12 to stay in the main house. In a separate carriage house, children of all ages are welcome. Open year-round except the month of January.

Hillsdale area
Aubergine (518-325-3412), Junction Routes 22 and 23, Hillsdale 12529. ($$$) An outstanding example of Dutch-colonial architecture, this inn was built in 1783 by an officer in the Revolutionary War. There are three Palladian windows, a museum-quality corner cupboard, and eight fireplaces with their original mantelpieces. Each of the four guest rooms is decorated differently and simply, and the furniture includes many lovely antiques. Coffee or tea only is served to guests in the morning, though the fine restaurant on the premises serves dinner Wednesday through Sunday (see *Dining Out*). The chef-owner of this establishment views the inn as an extension of his restaurant, a place to retire after a first-rate dinner instead of driving a long distance on dark country roads. Children welcome. Pets by advance reservation only.

Open year-round except the last two weeks of March.

Bell House Bed & Breakfast (518-325-3841), 9315 State Route 22, Hillsdale 12524. ($$) Named for the Bell family, who lived in this house for 140 years until 1970, this elegant 1830 two-story country inn has five rooms, all with private bath; each one is tastefully furnished with early-American antiques. In fact, an antiques shop is on the premises, **Red Fox Antiques** (open Friday through Monday 11–5). A full gourmet breakfast is served outdoors in the summer months, when guests can also enjoy the lovely swimming pool. Children over the age of eight are welcome. Open year-round.

Honored Guest Bed & Breakfast (518-325-9100), 20 Hunt Road, Hillsdale 12529. ($$) Located 2 miles from the Catamount ski area, this 4,000-square-foot house (a Frank Lloyd Wright design built in 1910) is a delightful, comfortable establishment run by an innkeeper who loves her work. Originally the building was a guest house on the 68-acre estate of the architect who built St. Patrick's Cathedral. There are four guest rooms, all with private bath, and they are all on one floor of the three-story structure. A five-course gourmet breakfast is served—complete with home-baked muffins and an exotic fruit course; it includes nothing you would consider making yourself. A favorite offering of mine: the banana-pecan pancakes topped with fresh strawberry sauce. After-noon tea is offered from 4:30–6, with wonderful baked treats; during the winter guests gather around the love-ly fireplace. Expect turndown service at night—complete with romantic

lighting in the room and chocolates on your pillow. Children welcome with advance notice. Open year-round.

Inn at Green River (518-325-7248), 9 Nobletown Road, Hillsdale 12529. ($$) Set on an acre of lawn and gardens above a meadow where Cranse Creek flows into the Green River, this 1830 Federal house is a truly special place for a relaxing weekend. The Green River is a good spot to fish or cool off in the summer months. Tanglewood (in the Berkshires) is just 20 minutes away. A full breakfast is elegantly served in the dining room or on the screened-in porch. The lemon-ricotta pancakes and honey-spice French toast are house specialties. There are seven beautifully decorated rooms, all with private bath; four have gas fireplaces, and two have Jacuzzis. This is a great spot for an anniversary weekend or special occasion. Children over 12 only on weekends; the policy is flexible on weekday nights. Open year-round.

Hudson area
Elizabeth Cottage on Twin Lakes (845-756-3246), 39 North Shore Drive, Elizaville 12523. ($) This charming, one-bedroom cottage, with vaulted ceilings, hand-stenciled wooden floors, wicker furniture, and an antique brass double bed, is located on Twin Lakes, the perfect place for those who enjoy swimming and boating at their doorstep—or a romantic getaway. French doors off the bedroom open up into a lovely flower garden. No breakfast is served to guests, but there is a small kitchen where you can create your own meals and enjoy a relaxing repast outdoors on the tranquil porch. Notice the portrait of Elizabeth, grandmother of the

owner, for whom the cottage is named. Open April through October.

Hudson City Bed & Breakfast (518-822-8044), 326 Allen Street, Hudson 12534. ($$) This wonderful 19th-century Victorian home in the heart of Hudson (on one of the nicest streets in the city) reflects the area's architectural heritage. Ornate ceilings and fireplaces, wainscoting, cornices, and antique lighting are just some of the delightful details you will enjoy in their six air-conditioned guest rooms (all with private bath and king- or queen-sized beds). The innkeeper has over 3,000 videos in his library and since all rooms are equipped with cable TV and VCR, you may enjoy a movie or two . . . or three during your stay. Two of the rooms have claw-foot tubs, so request one of them if you are partial to soaking. A full country breakfast is served. This is the perfect place to stay if you would like to be in town instead of the countryside. The antiques shops and restaurants of Warren Street are only a short walk away. Open year-round.

Inn at Blue Stores (518-537-4277), 2323 Route 9, Hudson 12534. ($$) Built in 1908 and in business for over 15 years, this gracious Arts and Crafts–style inn is one of the nicest in the region, and is located on what was originally a gentleman's farm 10 miles south of the city of Hudson. Guests can enjoy the pool, take a nap on the veranda, or have a cozy chat in front of the fireplace. Decorative accents include stained glass, a clay-tile roof, and black oak woodwork throughout the house. The five rooms (three with private bath; two share a bath) have twin, queen, and king-sized beds, and a full gourmet breakfast is included. No children under 10. Open year-round.

Taghkanic Creek Bed & Breakfast (518-851-6934, 888-876-3084), 624 Old Route 82, Craryville 12521. ($) This bed & breakfast consists of two houses, both Colonial-style structures dating back to the mid-19th century; one was formerly a general store. There are six guest rooms in the houses, all with private bath. Enjoy the in-ground pool on the

THE KINDERHOOK BED & BREAKFAST IN HISTORIC KINDERHOOK

premises a well as an antiques store. A full breakfast is served, and guests can visit nearby Lake Taghkanic State Park for hiking, boating, and swimming. Children are welcome. Open year-round.

Kinderhook/Stuyvesant area
Angel Wing Hollow Bed & Breakfast (518-784-2989), 898 County Route 28, Niverville 12184. ($$) This charming one-bedroom B&B is located in an 1888, fully restored Victorian farmhouse in the hamlet of Niverville (town of Kinderhook). The antiques-furnished room, with private bath, has a claw-foot tub in addition to a stall shower. A full country breakfast is served. Open year-round.

Kinderhook Bed & Breakfast (518-758-1850), 67 Broad Street, Kinderhook 12106. ($$) This majestic center-hall Colonial built in the early 1900s is close to all the historic homes in Kinderhook. If you have never slept in a feather bed, it is one pleasure of country living you should try here—and I'm sure will love as much as I did. All three nicely decorated guest rooms have private bath, air-conditioning, and feather beds. There is a cozy sitting room with a fireplace in the main house where you can socialize with other guests or just relax. During the summer months the grounds are in bloom with beautiful perennial gardens. A continental breakfast is served at 9 in the comfortable country dining room. Midweek and extended-stay discounts are available. There are two dogs in residence, hence the owners regret being unable to accommodate travelers with pets. Children who are well behaved are welcome. Open year-round.

The Van Schaack House (518-758-6118), 20 Broad Street, Kinderhook 12106. ($$$) This Georgian-style historic house was built in 1785 and has had only six owners in 230 years. In 1865 Victorian touches were added, including a slate mansard roof; the porches were built on in the early 20th century. This grand old mansion, decorated with antiques and fine paintings, was once the home of Peter Van Schaack, a prominent 18th-century attorney and close friend of John Jay. His sister married into the Roosevelt family. There are four guest rooms, all with private bath, air-conditioning, TV, VCR, and DVD. You will find a plush bathrobe and bottle of Old Kinderhook water in your room. There is an extensive library for guest use. One of the innkeepers graduated from the Culinary Institute, so the full gourmet breakfast includes freshly squeezed orange juice, terrific breads, and a different egg dish every day. No children. Open year-round, but advance reservations are always required.

✳ Where to Eat

DINING OUT **Aubergine** (518-325-3412), Junction Routes 22 and 23, Hillsdale 12529. ($$$) Open Wednesday through Sunday from 5:30 for dinner only. French-inspired American-country cooking is the style here, in a 1783 brick Dutch Colonial house. The restaurant's warmth and character are the result of meticulous refurbishing. My favorite entrée is the Maine scallop cakes with shiitake mushrooms, scallions, and sprouts, followed by a classic chocolate soufflé for dessert. There are four comfortable rooms here for overnight guests (see *Lodging*).

Backwater Grille (518-781-4933), 42 Queechy Lake Road (County

Route 30), Canaan ($$) Open for dinner Wednesday through Saturday 5–9, Sunday 3–8:30. There is an extensive menu in this lakeside dining spot with lovely views, which was a village grocery 50 years ago. The contemporary Continental cuisine features steaks, seafood, and pasta dishes, along with imaginative daily specials. Children welcome.

Blue Plate (518-392-7711), Central Square, Chatham. ($$) Open Tuesday through Sunday for dinner from 5. This American bistro housed in a Victorian building serves a variety of pastas, steaks, seafood, and salads. Notice the antique copper bar downstairs and wonderful murals. This spot has earned a fine reputation with local residents, weekenders, and travelers.

Charleston (518-828-4990), 517 Warren Street, Hudson. ($$) Open daily Thursday through Monday for lunch 11:30–3:30; dinner 5:30–9:30, until 10 Friday and Saturday. The eclectic international menu emphasizes grilled entrées. The grilled shrimp with spicy Mexican sauce is popular, and the restaurant grows many of its own vegetables and herbs. Selections such as fall-apple chicken as well as many game dishes (including venison and buffalo) are seasonal.

The Greens at Copake Country Club (518-325-0019), 44 Golf Course Road, Copake. ($$) Open daily April through October for lunch 11–3; dinner 5–9. Enjoy American cuisine—steaks, seafood, chicken, and pasta—while looking out over the beautifully manicured golf course. The grilled pork tenderloin, porterhouse steak, and zuppa di pesce are the chef's favorite entrées. There's an informal atmosphere here, and the

children's menu offers a variety of selections. The tavern is separate from the restaurant area, and you can get a meal at the bar any time of day.

Hearthstone (518-325-5600), Route 22, Copake Falls. ($$) Open daily except Wednesday for lunch and dinner 11:30–9; Sunday breakfast is served 8–11:30, dinner 1–9. Located in a country setting surrounded by farmland, the Hearthstone offers three separate dining rooms, all with fireplaces and eclectic decor. The American cuisine features home cooking with baby back barbecue ribs, prime rib, steak, chicken carbonara (chicken served over fettuccine, sautéed in garlic, and topped with a light Alfredo white sauce that has peas, red peppers, bacon, and mushrooms). Desserts are homemade—and both chocolate and coconut cream pies are served. Children's menu available.

Jackson's Old Chatham House (518-794-7373), Village Square, Old Chatham. ($$) Open daily 11:30–10 for lunch and dinner. Enjoy American cuisine in an informal atmosphere at this establishment that has been in business for over 60 years and owned by three generations of the same family. The steaks and prime rib are first-rate; there's also a good selection of seafood and pasta dishes. Children welcome.

Lippera's Restaurant & Bistro (518-392-6600), 29 Hudson Avenue, Chatham. ($$) Open Monday through Thursday 5–9:30, Friday 5–10:30, Saturday 3–10:30, and Sunday 3–9:30. Closed Wednesday October through April. (At this writing, the restaurant is undergoing an expansion; when completed, lunch will also be served.) The international cuisine here includes an array of freshly prepared imaginative entrées featuring steaks, filet mignon, prime rib, seafood, potato-encrusted salmon, fresh trout, linguini with seafood, and several vegetarian dishes. Save room for one of their homemade desserts: key lime pie, chocolate fudge cake, strawberry shortcake, cannoli, flan, peanut-butter mousse, or coconut sorbet. Children welcome.

Mario's (518-794-9495), Routes 20 & 22, New Lebanon. ($$) Open Monday, Wednesday, and Thursday 4–9:30, Friday and Saturday 4–10, Sunday noon–9:30. Closed Tuesday. The Italian American cuisine here is excellent, and the prices are reasonable: There's linguini with white clam sauce, osso bucco Milanese, veal parmigiana, tournedos of beef, and shrimp scampi. Desserts are all made on the premises and include fried ice cream, a variety of homemade gelatos, tiramisu, and chocolate-raspberry mousse cake. Children's portions are offered, and those with young children will feel comfortable here.

Mexican Radio (518-828-7770), 537 Warren Street, Hudson. ($$) In case you are wondering, the song "Mexican Radio" by Wall of Voodoo was released in the early 1980s, and the owners love the song, which is about how rock-and-roll radio got its start when it was banned in the U.S. Hence the name here. . . . Open daily for lunch and dinner 11:30 AM– midnight. This brightly colored, upbeat, candlelit restaurant has a festive atmosphere, with dining rooms on two floors. Everything is made fresh daily, including the salsa. All drinks are made with fresh lime juice, (there are dozens of tequilas for margarita lovers).. Some might call their offerings Mexican comfort food: The burritos, enchiladas, and tacos have imaginative fillings. An array of hot sauces line the tables. There is a large number of vegetarian entrées. Try the Radio roll up—a large deep-fried tortilla filled with vegetables. American touches are integrated into the menu: There are no refried beans or heavy brown sauces here. Their nachos have won awards for the Mexican Radio in New York City. I suggest trying them. The Cajun burrito is a popular entrée—it's filled with shrimp and chorizo sausage. This restaurant, which opened in 2003, is a nice addition to Hudson's restaurant scene. Children welcome.

Paramount Grill (518-828-4548), 225 Warren Street, Hudson. ($$) Open Thursday through Monday 5–9. The international cuisine here features an eclectic mix of dishes, including Cajun shrimp and chicken fajitas. The restaurant is housed in a beautifully restored brick building in downtown Hudson. The ambience is casual yet elegant.

The Pillars (518-794-8007), 860 Route 20, New Lebanon. ($$) Open for dinner Wednesday through Sunday 5–9; Closed for the month of January. The American and Continental cuisine here is reliable and quite decent. The filet of beef Charlemagne—beef tenderloin sautéed with onions and mushrooms topped with Hollandaise sauce—is popular; another favorite is the filet of sole baked with lobster butter and cream. I prefer the grilled sea bass marinated in miso and saki and served with a wasabi soy sauce. Desserts are homemade on the premises; do not pass up the dark chocolate sack filled with chocolate mousse. Children's menu.

Red Dot Bar & Restaurant (518-828-3657), 321 Warren Street, Hudson. ($$) Open Wednesday through Saturday 5–10; Sunday brunch 11–3, dinner 5–9. Eclectic Continental cuisine is served in this bistro: There are burgers, steaks, pasta, duck, and roast chicken. Diners will be delighted to discover the standard favorites done imaginatively and well. A former butcher shop, now completely renovated with a bright red door, the atmosphere is casual and relaxing. The low-key bar is a nice place to enjoy dinner. The French onion soup is excellent; the daily specials are wonderful. Not recommended for children.

Swiss Hütte (518-325-3333), Route 23 Hillsdale. ($$) Open daily for lunch Tuesday through Saturday noon–2, Sunday until 3; dinner Tuesday through Saturday 5:30–9, Sunday 5–9. Hours vary slightly with the season. Overlooking the slopes at the Catamount ski area, the dining rooms here are wood paneled, and the three fireplaces make them warm and cozy. The Swiss chef-owner is both a master chef and a ski racer. The menu features French-Swiss dishes and excellent home-baked pastries.

EATING OUT Brandow's (518-822-8938), 340 Warren Street, Hudson. ($$) Open Tuesday and Wednesday 9–5; Thursday through Saturday until 9. This café/marketplace/bakery offers a taste of SoHo in Hudson, at reasonable prices. The finest, freshest ingredients are used in a menu that changes daily. The pumpkin tortellini, carrot ginger soup, and prosciutto on a bagel with radicchio, balsamic herb mustard, and tomato are just a few of the treats to be sampled here. The buttermilk and sour-cream scones are quite good, and there are fresh juices as well as espresso and cappuccino.

The Cascades (518-822-9146), 407 Warren Street, Hudson ($) Open daily except Sunday 8–4. This café/gourmet deli has just about every type of fresh bagel imaginable. It's a terrific stop for a simple, healthful breakfast or lunch and features homemade soups, salads, and sandwiches. The desserts are sumptuous (try the chocolate silk pie).

Chatham Bakery and Coffee Shoppe (518-392-3411), 1 Church Street, Chatham. ($) Open Monday, Tuesday, Thursday, and Saturday 6–3; Friday 6 AM–8:30 PM; Sunday 6–noon. An institution in Chatham, this family-run restaurant is famous for its baked goods. Other specialties include Wallyburgers, served on homemade bread, and pumpkin doughnuts in the fall. The soups, sandwiches, and coffee are very good. This is a nice stop for breakfast or lunch, and a great place to take the kids.

Claverack Food Mart (518-851-9164) Route 9H, Claverack. ($) Open daily 8–8, Sunday until 2. This is the place to go for enormous sandwiches made with high-quality meats and salads at reasonable prices. A good place to stop if you are planning a picnic and need basic takeout items. Excellent fresh roast beef sandwiches!

The Cottage Restaurant (518-392-4170), Route 295, East Chatham. ($) Open daily except Tuesday 9–9. Enjoy the peaceful country atmosphere and friendly service at this restaurant, where all soups, breads, and desserts are prepared fresh every day. Specials include stir-fried shrimp, Cottage chili, and pastrami surprise (hot pastrami, mushrooms, and cheese on rye). A good place for children.

Earth Foods (518-822-1396), 523 Warren Street, Hudson. ($) Open daily 9–4; Friday through Sunday until 5. The hearty soups (their black bean is excellent), pasta, pizza, wraps, sandwiches and imaginative salads make this a great place to stop for lunch after antiquing in the city. There's a counter, so if you're eating alone, it's a comfortable place to enjoy a meal. Children are welcome.

Fresco's Wood Fired Pizza and Pasta (518-794-9339), Routes 20 & 22, New Lebanon. ($) Open daily 11:30–10. The pizza, pasta, sub sandwiches, and salads are excellent, and the prices are reasonable. Children will particularly enjoy this spot.

Main Street Café (518-758-9000), 3032 Main Street, Valatie. ($) Open Wednesday through Sunday 9 AM–9:30 PM. This is a great place to get a home-cooked turkey sandwich. Or if you prefer wraps, there are several to choose from. Breakfast here includes choices like waffles, pancakes, or homemade muffins baked on the premises. Dinner includes Italian-American favorites like eggplant parmigiana, lasagna, and a variety of pasta dishes. There are also steaks and seafood. Wednesday night is Mexican night. Beer and wine available. Children welcome.

Our Daily Bread (518-392-9852), 54 Main Street, Chatham. ($) Open Wednesday and Thursday 7–4, Friday 7–7, Saturday 8–7, Sunday 8–3. During the summer they are open until 10 PM on Friday and Saturday. Enjoy breakfast, lunch, and dinner (served on weekends only) at this vegetarian restaurant where soups, salads, sandwiches, and quiche are the mainstay.

All breads, cookies, cakes, and pies are baked on the premises. Beer and wine available. Outdoor dining in the summer months. Children welcome.

Random Harvest (518-325-5103), Route 23, Craryville. ($$) Open daily. This charming combination of gourmet shop and country store is an oasis on Route 23. It is filled with fabulous cheeses, salads, breads, and all kinds of tempting baked goods—the perfect stop if you are planning a picnic.

The Red Barn (518-828-5821), Route 9H, West Ghent. ($) Open Thursday through Sunday 11:30–9. Closed November through March. They make their own ice cream and toppings here, which are worth a stop in themselves, but hungry diners will want to try the salads, homemade soups, and hearty sandwiches.

Riverview Café (518-758-8950), 48 Riverview Street, off Route 9J, Stuyvesant. ($$) Open Monday through Thursday 7–3; Friday 7 AM–9 PM; Saturday and Sunday 8–3. This is the only place I know of in Columbia County where you can enjoy a meal by the Hudson River and watch both boats and trains pass by. It is a fairly new addition to the area, having opened in 2002. Breakfast is served all day; I love the blueberry pancakes. For lunch, the various wraps are popular. Friday night dinner includes offerings like red snapper, prime rib, or a vegetarian special. On Fridays they occasionally have Spanish, Italian or Greek night, featuring the cuisine of one nation. Wine and beer are served. Changing exhibits by local artists adorn the walls of the restaurant. Children are welcome.

Sunset Meadows Marketplace (518-581-3000), 3521 Route 9, Hudson. ($) Open daily 9–6; brunch served

Saturdays and Sundays 9–3, featuring soups, quiche, homemade granola, Belgian waffles, omelettes, smoked salmon, breakfast wraps. For lunch try the house salad, Greek Salad, grilled vegetable wrap, or turkey club on whole grain health bread. I love the curried chicken salad.

White Stone Café (518-392-7171), 2337 Route 66, Ghent. ($) Open daily 6 AM–9 PM. The international cuisine here combines American, Greek, Italian, and Mexican specialties. Enjoy pastas, steaks and chops, chicken, sandwiches, omelettes, and hot open-faced sandwiches. The all-you-can-eat buffet option served Friday and Saturday nights and also for Sunday brunch is ridiculously inexpensive. Great for kids.

ENTERTAINMENT Crandell Theater (518-392-3331), Main Street, Chatham. This is one of the few remaining independently owned movie theaters showing first-run films. The single screen, lantern lights, and a balcony with wooden seats make the 1930s theater a landmark. Tickets are a bargain at $3.50—and a box of popcorn will set you back a whole $1.25.

Ghent Playhouse—Columbia Civic Players (518-392-6264), Ghent. The season runs from late September to early June. Offerings range from drama to comedy and musicals. The 2003 productions included *Dracula, Private Lives,* and *H.M.S. Pinafore.*

Hudson Opera House (518-822-1438), 327 Warren St., Hudson. Open year-round, Monday through Saturday noon–5. There is no opera here but rather a cultural center for the city of Hudson, with lectures, performances, readings, and art exhibits. Stop in while you are strolling through Hud-

son and find out what's happening arts-wise.

Mac-Haydn Theatre (518-392-9292), Route 203, Chatham, specializes in summer-stock musical productions. The intimate theater is the perfect venue for all-time favorites like *Oliver!, Oklahoma!, Fiddler on the Roof,* and other performances that will appeal to the entire family.

Tannery Pond Concerts (888-820-1696), off Route 20, New Lebanon. From May through October, weekends at 8 PM, these chamber-music concerts are held in an original Shaker tannery that seats 300. The campus of the Darrow School and Mt. Lebanon Shaker Village is where the tannery is located. This is an unusual and interesting venue, and featured performers have included the Tokyo String Quartet, Susan Graham, Earl Wild, and the Emerson String Quartet.

Pleshakov Music Center (518-671-7171), 544 Warren Street, Hudson, is housed in a beautiful brick and marble-columned building (formerly a bank) that is over a century old. The center features an annual Hudson Valley composer series, regular Sunday-afternoon chamber music, and a Wednesday-evening piano concert series. If you love classical music, make sure to see a performance here.

Spencertown Academy (518-392-3693), Route 203, Spencertown. Built in 1847 as a private school, it is now a cultural arts center where visitors will enjoy films, dance, theater, poetry, lectures, concerts, and a variety of other cultural events. The Academy has a reputation as a leading area venue for great folk music and jazz. Groups of local, regional, and national renown entertain in an intimate setting year-round. There are also workshops, performances, and classes especially for children. The two galleries on the premises feature changing art and crafts exhibits. Do call for a schedule if you will be in the area.

Time & Space Limited, TSL Warehouse (518-822-8448), 434 Columbia Street, Hudson. Open year-round, check performance times; gallery hours are Monday through Saturday 11–3 and by appointment. This is one of the most interesting venues to emerge anywhere in the Hudson Valley in recent years. Housed in a converted bakery, with 8,800 square feet, it is now a performance space offering independent films with talks by filmmakers, art exhibits, and theatrical and musical productions as well as readings and open forums dealing with community issues. This interdisciplinary arts organization, run by two transplanted New Yorkers, was described in the *New York Times* as "making unusual statements in the area ever since they packed up their Manhattan theater company (in 1991) and handed back a $10,000 check to the politically charged National Endowment for the Arts." Make sure to get on the mailing list, and check out the event-filled calendar if you are going to be in Hudson. This is exactly the kind of independent, dynamic programming that is needed everywhere in America today.

✳ Selective Shopping

ANTIQUES When searching for antiques in Columbia County, expect to discover rare and lovely items at shops that are often as well-stocked as many museums. You will see everything from unembellished Shaker rockers to ornate English sideboards,

from fine examples of American folk art to the just plain odd. Quality antiques and shops are located throughout the county, but you may have to look around for bargains; many of the dealers here carry only the best, with prices to match. This is not to say that an English hunt table isn't worth several thousand dollars; just don't expect to find a Shaker table at a yard-sale price since many sellers have relocated from New York City and are savvy about their goods. Shop hours vary widely and by season, so call before you go. Most shops are closed on Wednesday, some on Tuesday.

In the city of Hudson, an antiques hub, Warren Street is a popular haunt, with dozens of shops located in a five-block area. Some have regular hours; others are open by appointment. The best way to enjoy Hudson antiquing is to spend a day wandering the streets and looking around. **Alain Pioton/The Hudson Antiques Center** (518-828-9920), 536 Warren Street, carries fine furniture and decorative objects from the 18th to 20th centuries. **Botanicus Antiques** (518-828-0520), 446 Warren Street, features rare 18th- and 19th-century pieces for the garden. **The Flying Dutchman** (518-822-0664), 510 Warren Street, offers fine linens. Also stop at **Arenskjold Antiques Art** (518-828-2800), 537 Warren Street, which has a nice blend of fine 18th- and 19th-century European antiques, paintings, and Danish Modern furniture. **Hudson House Antiques,** 738 Warren Street, **Doyle Antiques** (518-828-3929), 711 Warren Street, and **Kendon Antiques** (518-822-8627), 508 Warren Street, will all be of interest to antiques buffs.

ART GALLERIES & GIFT SHOPS It is impossible to list every gallery and interesting new shop that opens in the county, especially in Hudson, with its ever-changing, dynamic scene. These are some of my favorite places in the city—and county—at this writing, so do explore and discover much more on your own.

Carrie Haddad Gallery (518-828-1915), 622 Warren Street, Hudson, features prominent local artists in a bright, well-lit open space; exhibits change monthly.

The Fields Sculpture Park (518-392-7656), Letter S Road, Ghent. (See *Green Space*.)

Gallery 512 (518-828-2019), 512 Warren Street, Hudson, has changing exhibits of drawings, painting, sculpture, and photography.

Sarah Y. Rentschler Gallery (518-828-8432), 116 Warren Street, has paintings, sculpture, works on paper, and photography and is worth a stop while walking through the city.

Taconic Sculpture Park and Gallery (518-392-5757), Stever Hill Road, Spencertown. (See *To See*.)

Make sure to stop at the **Hudson Valley Art Center** (518-828-2661), 337 Warren Street, which features a nice selection of handcrafted items, including pottery, jewelry, and metalwork as well as paintings, from local artists. A couple of my favorite gift shops, if you like unusual things: **Shop Naked** (518-671-6336), Warren Street, is a pop-culture lover's heaven. The owner designs terrific T-shirts, and the novelty items, books, and cards are truly special. There is a lovely café in the back of the shop, where you can get coffee, cold drinks, and wonderful desserts. **The Velvet Egg** (518-822-9556), 528 Warren Street, is a beautiful store and carries a fine selection of unique gift items, including a varied offering of regional and fun books.

✳ Special Events

May: **Annual Columbia Land Conservancy Shad Bake and Country Barbecue** (518-392-5252), Clum and Patchen Farm, Livingston, 4:30–8. This benefit festival is held rain or shine on Memorial Day. Activities include a silent auction, music, and an environmental education program in honor of this river fish so important to the area's early economy and diet. There is a shad to enjoy, of course, and chicken and ribs for turf lovers! **Columbia Heritage Tour** (518-537-TOUR). Explore 300 years of architectural treasures during this tour of several homes depicting the unique aspects of Georgian, Federal, Classical Revival, Arts and Crafts, and contemporary styles. Tour 12 private as well as 4 public homes. This is a benefit for the Columbia County Historical Society, Clermont, and the Hudson Opera House.

June: **Antiques Festival at the Luykas Van Alen House** (518-758-9265), Route 9H, Kinderhook. This festival attracts vendors from all over the Hudson Valley, and it's usually held on Father's Day. **Olana Summer Family Fun Weekends** (518-828-0135), Route 9G, Hudson. From early June through August, Saturdays and Sundays 1–4, family-centered activities, including crafts, nature programs, games, and art projects inspired by the Church family's favorite summer pastimes, may be enjoyed at this beautiful state historic site.

July: **4th of July Family Festival at Columbia County Fairgrounds** (518-392-2121), Routes 66 and 203, Chatham. There are vendors, crafts, food, and fireworks; fun for the entire family. A tradition in the county. **Old Fashioned Family 4th of July** (518-537-4240), Clermont State Historic Site, off Route 9G, Clermont. This is a celebration complete with fireworks, all kinds of drinks, food, and activities for the kids. Bring a picnic and enjoy the action by the Hudson, at one of the most beautiful spots along the river. **Falcon Ridge Folk Festival** (860-364-0366, 866-325-2744), Long Hill Farm, Route 23, Hillsdale. This four-day festival of folk music and dance with over 40 acts on four stages includes mainstage concerts, dancing, song swaps, crafts, workshops, ethnic food, activities for the kids. Come for a day, or camp all weekend. Some of the people who have appeared include Arlo Guthrie, Holly Near, Tom Paxton, and Lucy Kaplansky. **Grey Fox Bluegrass Festival** (888-946-8495 for ticket and performance information), Rothvoss Farm, Route 22, off County Route 3, Ancramdale. Considered the best gathering of bluegrass musicians in the East, Grey Fox is a must-stop for anyone who loves banjo, fiddle, singing, or clogging tunes. Held in mid-July, the festival is packed with sets, workshops, pick-up sessions, children's classes, and more. There's camping on-site and lots of family and group activities, including movies, magic shows, and, of course, music. Bluegrass learning sessions take place for all ages and skill levels, and you can enjoy traditional, contemporary, and progressive bands. If you plan to camp, do book a reservation a month or two in advance. **Strawberry**

Shortcake Festival (518-794-9100), Shaker Museum and Library, 88 Shaker Museum Road, Old Chatham. If you love strawberry shortcake, partake of this summer tradition. Children will especially like this event!

August: **Heritage Blues Fest** (518-537-4240), Clermont State Historic Site, off Route 9G, Clermont. Enjoy hearing jazz and blues on the beautifully landscaped grounds of this state historic site along the Hudson River. **Steamboat Days** (518-537-4240), Clermont State Historic Site, off Route 9G, Clermont. In August 1807 the first steam-powered boat made its way up the Hudson from Clermont and this festival with music and fine fare commemorates the event.

September: **Columbia County Fair** (518-392-4121, 758-1811), County Fairgrounds, Routes 66 and 203, Chatham. Held Labor Day weekend. Admission fee. The oldest continuously held fair in the country, this one is still as lively as ever. A five-day celebration, it's less raucous and somewhat smaller than many other county fairs but just as much fun. Horses, sheep, cows, and other livestock are all displayed proudly by 4-H members, while prizewinning vegetables and fruits are shown off in the Grange buildings. Handmade quilts and needlecrafts make a colorful display. Sheep-to-shawl demonstrations and antique gas engines enliven the fairgrounds throughout the week; modern farm machinery has its place here also. But the fair is more than just exhibits—it's also entertainment in the best country tradition. Bluegrass bands, folksingers, and country and western stars entertain the crowds in the evening—and what would a county fair be without the midway games and fair food. Children will love this fair with all the usual fun rides. **Fall Apple Harvest Festival** (518-794-9100), Shaker Museum and Library 88 Shaker Museum Road, Old Chatham. Enjoy apple cider and homemade doughnuts as well as other autumn treats at this celebration on the grounds of the Shaker Museum.

October: **Film Columbia** (518-766-5892), Crandell Theatre, Main Street, Chatham. This film festival is small but will interest film buffs. The Crandell Theatre is a landmark in the town and the county (see *Entertainment*). **Hudson Arts Walk** (518-671-6213), Warren Street, Hudson. All the galleries and the antiques shops are bustling with activity; held Columbus Day weekend. Just walk up and down Warren Street and enjoy.

December: **Olana Open House** (518-828-0135), Route 9G, just south of Hudson. The home of Frederic Church is decorated beautifully for the holiday season, and light refreshments are served. This is a beautiful time to visit Olana and see what it must have been like when the Church family celebrated their traditional Christmas. **Winter Walk on Warren Street** (518-822-1438), Warren Street, Hudson. This lovely tradition is held on the first Saturday in December and begins the holiday shopping season. All the shops are decorated beautifully for the holidays, and most serve refreshments.

Dutchess County 10

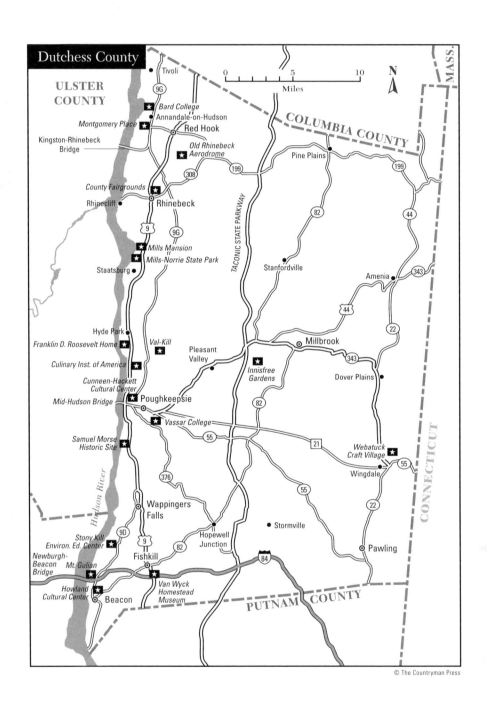

Dutchess County

ULSTER COUNTY

MASS.

Tivoli

0   5   10
Miles

N

9G

Bard College
Annandale-on-Hudson

Montgomery Place

Red Hook

COLUMBIA COUNTY

Kingston-Rhinebeck Bridge

Old Rhinebeck Aerodrome

Pine Plains

199

199

308

199

County Fairgrounds

Rhinecliff

Rhinebeck

82

44

9

9G

Mills Mansion

Mills-Norrie State Park

Staatsburg

Stanfordville

Amenia

343

TACONIC STATE PARKWAY

44

Hyde Park

Franklin D. Roosevelt Home

Val-Kill

22

Pleasant Valley

Millbrook

Culinary Inst. of America

Innisfree Gardens

343

Dover Plains

Cunneen-Hackett Cultural Center

Mid-Hudson Bridge

Poughkeepsie

82

Vassar College

55

21

Samuel Morse Historic Site

Webatuck Craft Village

55

Wingdale

376

55

22

Hudson River

CONNECTICUT

Wappingers Falls

Stormville

Stony Kill Environ. Ed. Center

9D

Hopewell Junction

Pawling

Newburgh-Beacon Bridge

9

82

Mt. Gulian

Fishkill

84

Howland Cultural Center

Beacon

Van Wyck Homestead Museum

PUTNAM COUNTY

© The Countryman Press

DUTCHESS COUNTY

When Henry Hudson sailed up the river that bears his name, one of his crew described the region known today as Dutchess County as "as pleasant a land as one can tread upon." With an area of 800 square miles, Dutchess boasts more than 30 miles of Hudson River shoreline and thousands of acres of farms and fields. The generous forests, impressive mountains, and abundance of wildlife attracted the Dutch first, but the county was named for the Duchess of York and, later, Queen Mary of England. Powerful families controlled local industries like farming, lumbering, and mining and built elegant stone and wood manors overlooking the river and mountains. Today much of the county's past is still visible in the grand homes perched over the Hudson, the gracious villages, and the historic restorations that dot the region. Recent major cultural additions to the landscape, in 2003, include the Fisher Center for the Performing Arts at Bard College and Dia:Beacon arts museum, which draw thousands of visitors to Dutchess County. The near future looks bright for the county, with the Hudson River Institute planned to open in Beacon toward the end of the decade.

GUIDANCE **Dutchess County Tourism Promotion Agency** (845-463-4000, 800-445-3131), 3 Neptune Road, Poughkeepsie 12601; www.dutchess tourism.com.

Rhinebeck Chamber of Commerce (845-876-4778), Route 9, P.O. Box 42, Rhinebeck 12572; www.rhinebeckchamber.com.

Greater Southern Dutchess Chamber of Commerce (845-897-2067), 2482 South Avenue, Wappingers Falls 12590; www.gsdcc.org.

GETTING THERE *By car:* Dutchess County can be reach via I-84, the Taconic State Parkway, or Route 9.

By bus: **Shortline/Coach USA** (201-529-3666, 800-631-8405) 4 Leisure Lane, Mahway, NJ, has daily service to and from New York City, Long Island, and New Jersey to Dutchess County.

By train: **Amtrak** (800-872-7245) has daily service to both Poughkeepsie and Rhinecliff from Penn Station in New York City. **Metro North** (212-532-4900,

800-METRO-INFO) offers daily service to Poughkeepsie and Beacon as well as several other smaller towns in the county.

By air: **Stewart International Airport** (845-564-7200), at the junction of Interstates 87 and 84, New Windsor. There is connecting service to and from the Hudson Valley throughout the country. **Dutchess County Airport** (845-463-6000), 263 New Hackensack Road, Wappingers Falls. **Sky Acres Airport** (845-677-5010), 30 Airway Drive, LaGrangeville.

MEDICAL EMERGENCY **Northern Dutchess Hospital** (845-876-3001, 877-729-2444), 6511 Springbrook Avenue, Rhinebeck.

St. Francis Hospital (845-483-5000), 241 North Road, Poughkeepsie.

Vassar Hospital (845-454-8500), 45 Reade Place, Poughkeepsie.

✳ To See

Culinary Institute of America (845-452-9600), Route 9, Hyde Park. Open year-round, except for vacation periods the last two weeks in July and December. Free. Founded in 1946 as a place where returning veterans could learn useful culinary job skills, the school is today regarded as a premier training institute for those in the food-service and hospitality industries. The grounds of the institute—housed in a former Jesuit seminary—provide visitors with a sweeping view of the Hudson River. Tours can be arranged only for prospective students and groups (12 or more people) with reservations at one of the restaurants (see *Dining Out*). Still, the courtyard has a fine display of carved pumpkins for Halloween and ice sculptures in winter, and autumn usually offers a chocolate festival that is lots of fun, as visitors can sample the wares and watch confectionary experts at work. After breakfast or lunch, take the time to walk around the campus, which overlooks the river.

The Richard B. Fisher Center for the Performing Arts at Bard College (845-758-7900), Annandale-on-Hudson. (Cross the Kingston-Rhinecliff Bridge, and at the first traffic light make a left onto County Route 103. Drive north for 3.5 miles.) Open year-round; call for schedule of events. Experience music and dance performances in the East Coast's only Frank Gehry–designed performing-arts center, which opened in 2003. This unique and controversial venue, an architectural wonder, is worth a visit for all travelers to Dutchess County, even just to see the exterior. There are two theaters: One has 900 seats (the Sosnoff Theater) and is primarily for professional performances, the other has 200 seats (Theater Two) and is used by students in Bard's dance and theater programs. (See *Theater—Dance.*) This performance facility celebrates Bard College's advocacy of the arts. With this remarkable space (the acoustics are phenomenal), Bard will be better equipped to fulfill its commitment to making the arts central to education. Despite the fact that art outside the commercial realm has suffered increasingly in recent years, the aesthetic sphere is vital to freedom and individuality. This building, as a performance space and a work of art in itself, is a statement of the college's mission that the arts are essential to humanity and will endure despite difficult times.

Hyde Park Railroad Station (845-229-2338), 34 River Road, Hyde Park. (Located at the foot of the hill that is formed by West Market Street and River Road, off Route 9.) Open year-round Monday, 7–9 PM; mid-June through mid-September, Saturday and Sunday 11–5; or by appointment. Free. This railroad station was built in 1914, based on a design shown at the Pan American World Exposition of 1898, although trains passed through the region during the 19th century. The building was nearly demolished in 1975, when the Hudson Valley Railroad Society acquired the station and set about restoring it. Almost 30 years later, the station is on the National Register of Historic Places and houses exhibits that tell the story of the area's railroads and history. Model trains run throughout the building, and there are always ferro fans on board to answer your questions. A nice stop along historic Route 9.

Old Rhinebeck Aerodrome (845-752-3200), Stone Church Road, off Route 9, Rhinebeck (watch for signs). Open daily mid-May through October 10–5; weekend air shows mid-June through mid-October at 2 PM. Admission. Viewing stands for the air show are outside, so dress appropriately. One of the most unusual history museums around, the aerodrome is the site for air shows, displays, and demonstrations of aeronautic history. But the finely restored airplanes (or copies with original engines) are not earthbound—they are frequently taken for a spin over the Hudson Valley or used in a make-believe dogfight. Fokkers, Sopwiths, and Curtiss airplanes are found in the museum, which offers guided tours. On Saturday daring men and women reenact flights from the pioneer and Lindbergh eras; World War I battles are saved for Sunday, complete with nefarious villains, beautiful damsels, and brave fighter pilots. Picnic tables and snack bar.

RICHARD B. FISHER CENTER FOR THE PERFORMING ARTS, BARD COLLEGE

Peter Aaron/Esto

Hudson Valley Tourism, Inc.

THE OLD RHINEBECK
AERODROME IS THE SITE
FOR AIR SHOWS, DISPLAYS, AND DEMONSTRA-
TIONS OF AERONAUTIC HISTORY.

Wing's Castle (845-677-9085), Bangall Road, off County Route 57, Millbrook (call for detailed directions). Open May through October, Wednesday through Sunday noon–5. Admission fee. An intriguing site, the "castle" has been under construction for more than 30 years, and work is still in progress. Salvaged materials have gone into the towers, crenellations, cupolas, and arches—don't be surprised if a Victorian birdbath turns up as a sink or a cauldron as a bathtub. A couple of performance events are held here during the summer, and children especially will enjoy a castle tour and meeting interesting owners Peter Wing and his wife, Toni. This is a must-see for travelers interested in architecture and anomalies!

FOR THOSE TRAVELING WITH CHILDREN **Fun Central** (845-297-1010), Route 9, Wappingers Falls. Open late June through Labor Day, Sunday through Thursday 10 AM–midnight; Friday and Saturday until 1 AM; the rest of the year noon–10, Friday and Saturday until midnight. This multiactivity indoor and outdoor recreational facility with miniature golf, bumper boats, an arcade, virtual-reality roller coaster, and laser tag is a great place to stop if you are traveling with children. At night, teenagers hang out here in large numbers; it's best to go earlier in the day with younger children.

Hudson Valley Raptor Center (845-758-6957), 148 South Road, Stanfordville. Open May through October, weekends 1–4; July and August, Friday 1–4; rest of the year, weekdays by appointment only. This educational center offers visitors a chance to discover the beauty and strength of eagles, hawks, and other raptors up close. There are flying demonstrations by the birds, some of which were wounded in the wild, as well as natural history programs. Everyone in the family will learn something here.

Listening Rock Farm (845-877-6335), 78 Sinpatch Road, Wassaic. Open June through October, Saturday and Sunday 7:30–4. For those who want to learn how cheese is made as well as see farm life up close. There is a simple farm kitchen breakfast, and lunch is offered as well as environmental and ecological programs.

Mid-Hudson Children's Museum (845-471-0589), 75 North Water Street (at the waterfront, close to the train station), Poughkeepsie. Open Tuesday through Sunday 11–5; special summer hours in July and August include Monday 11–2. This hands-on museum features permanent and changing exhibits that focus on the sciences and the arts. Children ages 2–12 will enjoy these educational displays, some of which include a horizontal rock climbing wall, a huge play structure of the heart and lungs, and science on wheels that includes a bicycle gyroscope and giant bubble machine.

Splash Down Park and Adventure Island Family Fun Center (845-896-6606), 2200 Route 9, Fishkill. Open daily May through September: Splash Down, 10–7; Adventure Island, Wednesday through Friday 3–9, Saturday 10–9, Sunday 11–9. The multi-activity water park includes waterslides, shipwreck island, a 700-foot river, a pollywog pond for the youngest visitors, miniature golf, water wars, and hoops. Adventure Island has indoor and outdoor amusements, including an arcade, bumper cars and boats, and miniature golf. A good place to go on a sweltering day.

Stony Kill Environmental Education Center (845-831-8780), Route 9D, Wappingers Falls. Open daily year-round; grounds from sunrise–sunset; visitors center Monday through Friday 8:30–4:30, Saturday 9:30–12:30, Sunday 1–4. Part of a 17th-century estate owned by Gulian Verplanck, this nature center was later used as a farm. Today Stony Kill is fulfilling its mission to provide agricultural and natural history programs to the public. The trails are relatively short (the longest is 2 miles), and there are places to study pond life, deciduous forests, swamps, and fields. The bird observation area is a great place to view migrating and native birds, and special events and family-oriented workshops are held throughout the year. The trails and grounds and open sunrise to sunset for hiking, fishing, birding, and snowshoeing.

Trevor Zoo (845-677-3704), The Millbrook School, off Route 44, Millbrook. Open daily 8–5. Free. Started as a teaching zoo in 1936 with the hope that children would better appreciate wildlife if they were familiar with it, the zoo is now a 4-acre site accredited by the American Zoological Association, offering close-up views of more than 150 types of animals, both exotic and indigenous. Red-

WING'S CASTLE, MILLBROOK HAS BEEN A WORK IN PROGRESS FOR OVER 30 YEARS

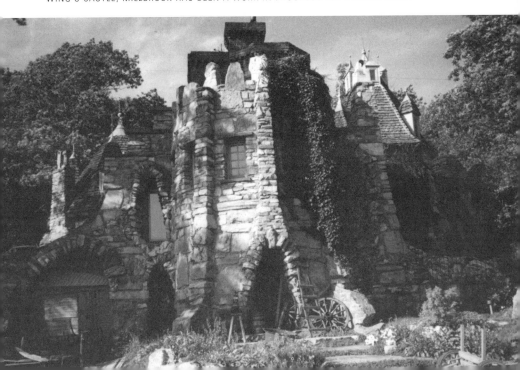

tailed hawks, coatis, otters, swans, and badgers are only some of the zoo's guests. There is a self-guided nature walk and a boardwalk that overlooks a lively marsh.

HISTORIC HOMES Locust Grove, the Samuel Morse Historic Site (845-454-4500), 2683 South Road (Route 9) Poughkeepsie. Open May through Thanksgiving 10–3. Grounds are open 8 AM until dusk, weather permitting. Situated along an old stagecoach route, this 150-acre site known as Locust Grove was the summer home of Samuel Morse. An artist and scientist who changed the way the world communicates (he invented the telegraph and Morse code), he purchased the country residence in 1847 and under the tutelage of architect Alexander Jackson Davis began to transform the house into an Italianate villa with extensive gardens. The house boasts a four-story tower, a skylighted billiard room, and a false stone exterior. Throughout the house decorative items (including china and a then-elegant and new fabric known as denim), furniture, art, and paintings by John James Audubon can be enjoyed. The formal gardens, walking trails, and wildlife sanctuary offer a lovely setting in which to spend an afternoon. There are 145 acres at this site with a network of trails that cover 3 miles through a diverse habitat teeming with wildlife as well as a variety of trees (and wildflowers in season). If you have the time, take a walk on one of the many trails formerly used by wagons and horse-drawn carriages that have been restored. The visitors center, where tours begin with a 10-minute orientation film, distributes a map/trail guide, and the paths are marked with arrowed plaques corresponding to the brochure descriptions. Most are an easy walk. The visitors center also contains the Morse Gallery, with paintings and sculptures by Samuel Morse, as well as his patent model for the telegraph and a display on telegraphic communication.

Madam Brett Homestead (845-831-6533), 50 Van Nydeck Avenue, Beacon. Open April through October, Wednesday through Monday 10–5; weekends in November 10–4:30; first two weekends in December noon–5. Admission fee. When Catheryna and Roger Brett moved to the area now known as Beacon in 1708, they built a homestead of native stone, graced with scalloped cedar shingles and sloping dormers. The house is one of the oldest in Dutchess County and was the center of a 28,000-acre estate. During the Revolutionary War, the homestead was believed to have been a storage place for military supplies as well as a stopping point for such luminaries as Washington, Lafayette, and the Baron von Steuben. The house remained in the family until 1954, when it was purchased by the Daughters of the American Revolution. Today there are 17 rooms of furnishings, porcelain, paintings, books, and tools. The house offers visitors a look back to the time when there were lodgings for slaves, and what is now the front door was the rear: As the town grew around the house, the main street formed at the back of the building, so the doors were switched for the convenience of callers. There was even a well accessible from inside the house—a major convenience in the 18th century. During the summer months stroll through the herb and formal gardens, which are quite beautiful.

Mills Mansion, Staatsburgh State Historic Site (845-889-8851), Old Post Road (off Route 9), Staatsburg. Open April through October, Tuesday through

Saturday 10–5, Sunday 11–5. Closed November. Open December for holiday tours, but hours vary; call ahead. January through March Sunday 11–5. Open year-round by appointment. Admission fee. One of the grand old Hudson River estates, the Mills Mansion has its origins in the 18th century, when Morgan and Gertrude Lewis built a home on the site. The house was destroyed by fire in 1832 and was rebuilt by Ruth Livingston Mills in 1896. Rooms were gilded and plastered, with ornamental balustrades, ceilings, and pilasters. The size of the rooms is still overwhelming, as are the furnishings: dining tables that take 20 leaves; carved, gilded, and floral furniture in the style of Louis XIV, XV, and XVI; and many fine paintings and elaborate tapestries. Incredibly, the house was used primarily as an autumn retreat and then infrequently the remainder of the year. There is a wonderful museum store on-site, and popular annual events include free outdoor summer concerts, an herb festival, a Celtic festival, an antique car show, and a Gilded Age Christmas. This is one historic site where access to the Hudson River is only a short walk away. After the house tour, it's an easy stroll; so if the weather is good, make sure to follow the path down to the water. There are several miles of walking trails on the land surrounding this site (see *To Do—Hiking*).

Montgomery Place (845-758-5461), County Route 103 (River Road, off Route 199), Red Hook. Open April through October, Wednesday through Monday 10–5; weekends in November 10–4:30; first two weekends in December noon–5. Admission fee. A magnificent, Classical Revival–style mansion, Montgomery Place was once the home of Janet Livingston Montgomery, wife of the Revolutionary War general Richard Montgomery. Begun in 1802 and completed three years later, the mansion is the centerpiece of an estate that includes waterfalls (don't miss the stream tumbling down to the Hudson River), footbridges, gardens, and Catskill Mountains views. The building was remodeled in the 1840s and 1860s by the great architect Alexander Jackson Davis and was home to the Livingston family until 1985. Purchased and restored by Historic Hudson Valley, the mansion reflects the family's history rather than one specific era. Gilbert Stuart portraits, Persian tile chairs, Czechoslovakian chandeliers, family china, and rare books are only some of the treasures to be seen on a house tour. Walking the grounds (all 434 acres), visitors can enjoy watching ships on the Hudson and seeing the variety of trees on the property. The over 200-year-old arboretum has some wonderful specimen trees. Special events throughout the year include holiday tours, garden festivals, and a spring wine and food festival (see *Special Events*). Visitors should not pass by the selections at the Montgomery Place farm stand (on Route 9G, just south of the mansion), where heritage tomatoes, homemade jams and apples, grapes, and peaches are sold in glorious ripe color.

Mount Gulian Historic Site (845-831-1872), 145 Sterling Street, Beacon. (Take Route 9D north of I-84 for 0.3 mile, turn left into the Hudson View Park apartments, and then make a left onto Lamplight Street, which becomes Sterling Street, and go to the end of the road.) Open April through October Wednesday through Sunday 1–5; November and December Wednesday and Sunday 1–5 and by appointment. Admission fee. This 44-acre Dutch homestead was the family seat of the Verplancks, prominent Hudson Valley farmers, and offers a place to learn about domestic and agricultural life in the 18th and 19th centuries as it unfolded along the river. Visitors will see a unique Dutch barn that dates back to the 1740s. Mount Gulian was constructed between 1730 and 1740; during the American Revolution it was the headquarters of General von Steuben, who is credited with molding the colonial troops into a fighting force. The house was also where the Society of the Cincinnati was formed in 1783, a fraternal organization for officers that is still in existence. A visit to Mount Gulian includes a tour of the house and the English formal gardens, which have been restored to their former glory; the gardens' history was recorded by James Brown, an escaped slave who worked in them from 1829 to 1868. Special events are held throughout the season: call for a schedule.

Franklin Delano Roosevelt Home (845-229-9115, 800-FDR-VISIT), 4097 Albany Post Road (Route 9), Hyde Park. Open year-round 9–5. Admission fee. Your first stop, the new visitors center, offers an orientation film and a wonderful gift shop as well as a café with refreshments of all kinds. Here you can purchase tickets for the four sites on the property or however many you choose to tour.

The Victorian house, embellished with Georgian touches, was the boyhood home of Franklin Delano Roosevelt. Here Eleanor and Franklin raised their family, entertained heads of state, and shaped world history. The site includes the house, the first presidential library, rose garden, and the site of the Roosevelts' graves. In the house itself, once jokingly called the Summer White House by Roosevelt, family memorabilia, including photos, antiques, and the possessions of Franklin's iron-willed mother, Sara, are displayed. Don't forget to stop at the gravesite and rose garden (exquisite in June). A visit to the FDR Home is a must for any visitor to Dutchess County.

A VISIT TO THE FDR HOME IN HYDE PARK IS A MUST FOR ANY VISITOR TO DUTCHESS COUNTY.
Hudson Valley Tourism, Inc.

Top Cottage (845-229-9115), 7097 Albany Post Road (Route 9), Hyde Park. Open May through October, Thursday through Monday 10–5. Admission fee. (Note that shuttle bus tours leave from the visitors center at the FDR Home and Library, where tickets must be purchased to go to this site.) This hilltop retreat that FDR designed for himself provided a tranquil place for him to get away after he left office. During his third and fourth terms, the cottage was used as a private meeting house for political purposes: forging essential relationships with Winston Churchill and King George VI of Great Britain, among others. It is interesting to see how the cottage was designed to accommodate a wheelchair and meet Roosevelt's physical needs. First opened to the public in 2001, the cottage has been restored to its original appearance during Roosevelt's time. There are displays of memorabilia and photographs throughout the site. Plans are in the works to reopen a pedestrian trail between Val-Kill and Top Cottage in the near future.

Val-Kill, Eleanor Roosevelt National Historic Site (845-229-9115), Route 9G, Hyde Park. Open daily, May through October 9–5; November through April, Thursday through Monday only 9–5. Admission fee. This is the only National Historic Site dedicated to the memory of a first lady. Val-Kill was a favorite spot for Roosevelt family picnics; in 1924 FDR deeded the land to Eleanor for a personal retreat. A Dutch-style stone cottage was built (it is now a conference center), and an existing building was converted into a factory, in keeping with Eleanor's efforts to encourage rural economic development. The factory was later remodeled into a house, which now holds the museum. The small furniture factory was adjacent to the cottage shared with Eleanor Roosevelt's friends, Nancy Cook and Marion Dickerman. The three women met in the early 1920s working for the League of Women Voters. They shared a dedication to politics, education, and progressive reform that motivated their interest in creating Val-Kill Industries, a social experiment that embraced the revival of handicraft traditions to supplement income in an agricultural economy. In this way, young people might choose to remain in the area instead of seeking work in the cities. The economic strains of the Depression put an end to the business in 1937. Visitors can learn more about this experiment, tour the cottage, and enjoy a film biography about Eleanor Roosevelt, *First Lady of the World,* as well as walk the trails on the 180-acre site. Ongoing lectures, seminars, and community programs center around Eleanor Roosevelt's concerns, including solutions to pressing social problems, and an exploration of contemporary values. Call for a schedule of events and changing exhibits.

Vanderbilt Mansion National Historic Site (845-229-9115), Route 9, Hyde Park. Open year-round daily 9–5. Admission fee. This imposing Beaux Arts mansion was used by Frederick Vanderbilt and family as a spring and fall residence. A fine example of Gilded Age living in the 19th century, the mansion was the focus of a large Hudson River estate and was built at a cost of $600,000—a fortune at that time. Lavish furnishings, fine art, and decorative items from around the world are on view throughout the spacious rooms (the living room is 30 feet by 50 feet); visitors can also stroll pathways and take in the breathtaking river panorama. The restored formal Italian gardens feature a reflecting pool, terraces, and a pergola and loggia with three levels of annuals, perennials, and roses; they should not be missed on a visit to the mansion. The wonderful gift shop on the premises is filled with a terrific selection of books and souvenirs. The **Music in the Parks** program (see *Special Events*) is held on the mansion grounds Wednesday nights at 6:30 during July and August. The concerts are free and open to the public. In the event of rain, the concerts are held at Haviland Middle School Auditorium, Route 9G, in Hyde Park.

Wilderstein (845-876-4818), 330 Morton Road, Rhinebeck. Open May through October, Thursday through Sunday noon–4; Thanksgiving through December, weekends only 1–4. Admission fee. The history of this country seat begins in

1852, when Thomas Suckley purchased this riverfront site and commissioned an architect to build an Italianate villa. He named the property "Wilderstein" (wild man's stone) in reference to a Native American petroglyph by a cove on the property. For over 150 years and three generations, Wilderstein was owned by the Suckley family. It is filled with their furniture, paintings, antiques, and other effects, which attest to the lively social history of the estate and the family's relationship to the Hudson Valley. The main-floor rooms were designed by J. B. Tiffany, and Calvert Vaux was responsible for the landscape design. An intricate network of drives, walks, and trails wind throughout the property, so make sure to explore a few of them when you visit. This site is listed on the National Register of Historic Places; it's a gem, and will intrigue both scholars and those interested in life in the region during the 19th century.

MUSEUMS The Center for Curatorial Studies and Art in Contemporary Culture at Bard College (845-758-7598), Route 9G, north of Rhinebeck, Annandale-on-Hudson. Open year-round Wednesday through Sunday 1–5. Free. Founded in 1860 as a men's school, today Bard College is a coeducational institution known for its emphasis on the creative arts. In 1992 this 9,500-square-foot exhibition space opened at Bard to house the college's permanent collection, the core of which is the Marieluise Hessel Collection of 1,000 works of painting, sculpture, photography, and video from the 1960s to the present. Hessel founded the center with a generous gift to the college, and the building contains a museum and research library as well as the college's master's program in curatorial studies. Hessel's goal, to support the creation of a place for study of late 20th-century arts, was realized, and the museum's changing exhibits encourage experimental approaches to the contemporary visual arts. Student shows are presented in the winter and spring; museum shows take place in the summer and fall. After visiting the museum, take a stroll to two lovely centerpieces of the campus: the Hudson River estate houses Blithewood and Ward Manor. There are gardens and a Victorian gatehouse nearby as well as the Fisher Center for the Arts (see *To See*), which make the Bard College a nice stop any time of year.

Dia:Beacon (845-440-0100), 3 Beekman Street, Beacon. Open year-round; mid-May through Columbus Day, Thursday through Monday 11–6; the rest of the year Friday through Monday 11–4. The museum is located off Interstate 84 and Route 9D. Follow signs to the railroad station. Admission fee (members and children under 12 free). In 2003 this 240,000-square-foot museum, on a 31-acre site along the banks of the Hudson River (adjacent to 90 acres of riverfront parkland and the Beacon railroad station), opened its doors to the public. Housed in a restored printing facility built in 1929 by Nabisco, the expansive light-filled galleries are illuminated almost entirely by natural light, displaying the large-scale works in Dia's renowned collection of American art of the 1960s and 1970s. Since 1974 Dia Art Foundation has become internationally recognized as one of the world's most influential contemporary art institutions. The name "Dia," taken from the Greek word meaning "through," was chosen to suggest the foundation's role in enabling extraordinary artistic projects that might not be realized without financial assistance. Dia's permanent works include art by Joseph Beuys, Dan

Flavin, Donald Judd, Agnes Martin, Richard Serra, and Andy Warhol. The art of this period often represented a radical departure in practice from conventional work, and much of it was large-scale. In addition to holding one of the world's foremost collections of work by artists who came of age in the 1960s and 1970s, Dia maintains long-term site-specific projects in the American West, Manhattan, and elsewhere. Modern-art aficionados will particularly enjoy this museum; most people will enjoy the structure itself, which is as interesting as the art within its walls.

Franklin D. Roosevelt Presidential Library & Museum (800-FDR-VISIT), 4079 Albany Post Road (Route 9), Hyde Park. Open April through October 9–6; November through March 9–5; Research library year-round Monday through Friday 9–5. Admission fee. The museum has both permanent and changing exhibits that reflect the impact both Eleanor and Franklin Roosevelt had on their times and world events during the first half of the 20th century. Visitors will enjoy detailed displays on the lives and careers of the Roosevelts as well as an array of interactive exhibits. Walking through this museum is like taking a historic tour the first 50 years of the 20th century; the site is a must-visit for World War II buffs (see *Historic Homes—FDR Home*). Also on the site are FDR's boyhood home and the gravesites of both Eleanor and Franklin. The museum shop at the Henry A. Wallace Visitors Center (named for FDR's first vice-president) should be your first and last stop.

Van Wyck Homestead Museum (845-896-9560), Routes 9 and I-84, 1 mile south of Fishkill. Open Memorial Day weekend through October, Saturday and Sunday 1–4, and by appointment. Local history library Tuesday 7–9 PM and Saturday 10–noon. Admission fee. Guides in period costume escort visitors through the Dutch Colonial house, built in 1732 by Cornelius Van Wyck and untouched by any changes after a 1757 addition. During the Revolution, the house served as a depot and courtroom, and it is also believed to have been the inspiration for the setting of James Fenimore Cooper's *The Spy*. The homestead is furnished with 18th-century pieces, and visitors can examine artifacts recovered from surrounding archaeological sites, see several Hudson Valley portraits, and enjoy changing exhibits and events.

Vassar College Francis Lehman Loeb Art Center (845-437-5632/7745), 124 Raymond Avenue off Route 44/55, Poughkeepsie. Open Tuesday through Saturday 10–5, Sunday 1–5. Free. When Matthew Vassar founded the college in 1861, he not only broke new ground by making it a women's college, but he also made it the first college to have an art gallery and museum. The gallery's permanent collection consists of more than 16,500 pieces, including Hudson River School landscapes, Whistler prints, a large photography collection, European coins, armor, and sculpture; it spans the history of art from ancient Egypt to contemporary America. Shows and exhibits change on a regular basis, and after enjoying the art, visitors can walk around the campus, with its lakes, gardens, amphitheater, and rare trees. Docent-led tours by appointment only—call 845-437-7745. Stop in at the chapel to see the Tiffany windows. Also on the campus is the **Warthin Geological Museum** (Ely Hall, open year-round; summer hours by appointment), which houses a large collection of mineral, gem, and fossil exhibits.

After visiting Vassar, a drive through the city of **Poughkeepsie**, with its several historic districts, is worthwhile. **Clinton House** (845-454-0605), on the corner of Main and North White Streets, is the headquarters of the Dutchess County Historical Society, where visitors can see exhibits of local history (open by appointment only); they also maintain the **Glebe House** (845-454-0605), 635 Main Street, which dates back to 1767 and has been restored to represent a typical home of the late-18th and early-19th centuries (open Tuesday–Friday 10–3 or by appointment). At 185 Academy Street you will discover **Springside National Historic Site** (845-471-0183), which offers tours by appointment only. Even if you don't take the tour, however, walk the 20 acres of carriage roads on this site, the work of America's first native-born landscape architect, Andrew Jackson Downing, and the last surviving example of his work. Go south off Montgomery Street to reach Garfield Place, one of the most beautiful streets in the city. A residential area in the 1850s, the huge homes have been kept up ever since. The houses, which span several periods, boast turrets, towers, cupolas, and Hudson River bracketing. Academy Street from Montgomery to Holmes Street is still a gracious residential area with ornate Victorian houses, as is the Union Street Historic District (cross Market Street and continue down Union to Grand Street). In the 1760s Union was a path to the river, and later it was the German-Irish area of town. Notice the cast-iron details on the brick-and-clapboard buildings. This area is now the Little Italy of Poughkeepsie. Lower Mansion Avenue, off North Bridge Street, has fine examples of 19th-century architecture, although there are many modern buildings, as well.

SCENIC DRIVES In Dutchess County almost any drive is a scenic one. Even the Taconic Parkway, which is now over 50 years old, offers more of a country drive than a trip on a major highway, and there are commanding views of distant mountains and lovely vistas along its length. The roads of this region are well marked, both with direction and historic-site signs, and the county publishes a series of detailed, self-guided driving tours that are keyed to roadside markers (Call Dutchess County Tourism to request the brochure: 845-463-4000, 800-445-3131).

Don't be afraid to follow the back roads of the county on your own with the assistance of a good map. The following are just a few suggestions of roads that will take you through farmland and villages and along the river. Route 9 is the old stagecoach road that once was the main route to Manhattan; there are many restorations and historic sites along this road, but these days it can be clogged with traffic, particularly during rush hour and on Saturdays. Route 9G takes you past old homes and gracious stone walls. Route 44/55 catches up with the Taconic, which is, despite being a parkway, a lovely road to travel. Route 199 runs from east to west toward Connecticut, and the views are more like New England than New York.

WALKING TOURS **Beacon.** Nestled between the majestic Hudson Highlands and the Hudson River, the city of Beacon is being reborn. Beacon is in the midst of a Renaissance, which includes the opening of Dia:Beacon museum, the renovation of the Riverfront Park and Beacon Landing, and an explosion of shops, galleries, and restaurants springing up on Main Street. At one time the city was accessible by rail, steamboat, ferry, and trolley, and Beacon became a hot spot for people from the city looking for a change of scenery. In 1900 a group of local businesspeople formed the Incline Railway Association to erect a cable railway to the top of Mount Beacon. The railway—a monument to the ingenuity of the engineers of the day—was built on a steep grade of 65 percent and transported passengers to the summit at 1,150 feet. Opened in 1902, the railway carried 60,000 passengers during its first season. At the top was the Beacon Crest Hotel and a casino that offered breathtaking views; both were destroyed by fire in 1932 and were never rebuilt. Mount Beacon was the most popular day-trip destination in the Hudson Valley at the turn of the 20th century, and over 3 million people rode the rail in its 75 years of operation. Today, Mount Beacon park is again welcoming visitors. During the post–World War II years, the economy of the city went into decline, but in the early 1990s restoration efforts began. Over the past 10 to 15 years, artists have settled in the city, and with the arrival of Dia:Beacon, the community has new energy and life as a creative center.

Walk up and down Main Street, anchored by historic districts featuring numerous architectural treasures that are home to antiques shops, boutiques, and tony eateries. Try to visit on a **Second Saturday** of the month, when there are art openings, readings, and musical performances throughout the city. **Collaborative Concepts** (845-838-1516), 348 Main Street, open Wednesday through Sunday noon–5, is a nonprofit organization dedicated to presenting contemporary art. A 6,500-square-foot gallery and sculpture garden with a schedule of changing exhibits, this venue has become a place to feature the area's growing community of professional artists. **Beacon Project Space** (845-831-1277), 240 Main Street, open Wednesday through Saturday noon–5, is an intimate gallery that presents programs on contemporary art and culture. **Van Brunt Gallery** (845-838-2995), 460 Main Street, features changing exhibits with the emphasis on abstract art with high energy that is "edgy or provocative," according to the owner. **Riverfront Park** offers picnic areas and fishing access; the **Beacon Landing** is the 23-acre waterfront property managed by Scenic Hudson that is being revitalized. Plans include a trail that will pass by **Dia:Beacon** (see *To See—Museums*) and connect city residents with the river. A former city library, designed by Richard Morris Hunt, the **Howland Cultural Center** (845-838-4988) features decorative exterior, brickwork, and a grand interior crowned by ornate wood vaulting; it is open Thursday through Sunday 1–5 or by appointment. A wonderful new bookstore, **World's End** (845-831-1760), 532 Main Street, has a great selection of used books as well as regional titles. **Hudson Beach Glass** (845-724-5088), 162 Main Street, is a three-story firehouse that has been converted into a gallery complete with its own glassblowing studio. **Minetta Brook** (845-831-4129), 4–6 South Chestnut Street, is a public art organization that commissions artists to create work related to sites in the region. The work is shown in many of Beacon's galleries. The initial financing for this organization came from Lee Balter, chairman of the Tallix art foundry, a longtime area resident and founding patron of Watershed, a preservation organization. A stop here will give you background on the exciting changes in the city of Beacon.

Millerton. An idyllic Victorian village with sophisticated shops in a beautiful rural setting, this hamlet is best explored on foot. **Oblong Books,** an oasis in the heart of town since 1975 and renowned for its eclectic selection of books and music, is a great place to start your walking tour. There are several antiques shops, a glassworks, and an array of interesting places to explore.

Red Hook. The town was possibly named when Hendrik Hudson anchored off its shore in October 1609, and the crew noted the brilliant red sumac and Virginia creeper that covered the hook-like peninsula of Cruger's Island. Another theory is that the name became attached to the town from the red-painted barns at Tivoli, then called Hoffmans' Mills, once part of Rhinebeck. The early population of the area was concentrated in Red Hook, once known as Hardscrabble, and Tivoli. The location contributed to the growth of water-powered mills, wool processing factories, fishing, and river transport in the 18th century. The 19th century was when dairy and fruit farms sprang up, tool and tin making burgeoned, and tobacco processing thrived. The railroad was built in the 1850s, and freight (and tourists) traveled largely by train until the early 20th century. The population has more than doubled from 4,500 in 1955 to about 10,000 at the start of the 21st century, when an influx of people was drawn by the technology and electronics industries. Make sure to visit **Mansion Row,** the old Fraleigh Store (now the **Lyceum Theater**) built in 1875, and the **Tobacco Factory** at the corner of Tobacco Lane and Broadway (the main street). At the intersection of Cherry Street and North Broadway is the **Elmendorph Inn** (circa 1760), a Federal-style structure with a Dutch gambrel roof listed on the National Historic Register. One of the two earliest buildings in the village, it was a former stagecoach stop and tavern as well as the site of the town's first kindergarten. Saved from the wrecking ball through a community effort, the inn has a working kitchen fireplace and a reconstructed beehive oven. (Open most Tuesdays or by appointment; it is the headquarters for the Egbert Benson Historical Society.) For detailed information on several of the town's buildings, request the walking tour map of the village from **Dutchess County Tourism Promotion** (845-463-4000, 800-445-3131).

Rhinebeck. This village is rich in architectural delights, and a walk through town can make the history of families like the Roosevelts, Livingstons, and Beekmans come alive. The Beekman Arms, in the center of town, is one of the oldest inns in the United States (see *Lodging*); across the street, the corner department store is housed in a Civil War-era building. The post office was reconstructed in 1938 under the direction of Franklin Delano Roosevelt; it is a replica of a 1700 Dutch house and contains murals by local artists. If you amble down Route 9 and along the side streets, you will discover Gothic Revival homes, Georgian-style churches, and houses with mansard roofs, arched windows, and Second Empire touches.

Tivoli. This lovely, tranquil town is filled with historic buildings. The Watts De Peyster Hall (fireman's hall) in the center of town was built in 1898 and given to the village by a local landowner, John de Peyster, who was a fireman in New York City while he attended Columbia College in the 1840s. At one time the hall contained a courtroom and community meeting rooms; today it houses the Tivoli Free

Library and provides administrative offices for the village government. De Peyster's house, the original carriage house and entrance to the Rose Hill estate built in 1860, named for the family's ancestral home in Scotland, is now a private residence and may be seen from Woods Road. The town got its name from a Frenchman, Peter de Labigarre, who bought land on the waterfront in the 1790s. He wanted to design the town with a central square in the European style, but the project went bankrupt, and he had to abandon the plan. A plaque on the brick wall at the end of Friendship Street marks the location of his home, named Le Chateau de Tivoli; he had envisioned an ideal community named after the Tivoli in Italy.

WINERIES **Alison Wines & Vineyards** (845-758-6335), Pitcher Lane (off Route 9, 3 miles north of the village of Red Hook, on the Greig Farm). Open daily May through October 11–6; November and December, weekends only 11–5. This is the county's newest winery, and their pinot noir is dry and delicious. They also offer two styles of chardonnay, and all wine making and barrel aging is done on the premises, in a converted dairy barn that dates back to the 19th century. Tours and tastings are offered to visitors. This is a beautiful spot where you can enjoy panoramic views of the Catskill Mountains and shop in the adjacent Greig Farm Market (or pick your own produce on the farm in-season).

Cascade Mountain Winery & Restaurant (845-373-9021), 835 Cascade Mountain Road (off Route 82A—watch for signs), Amenia. Open Thursday through Monday 11–5. This respected winery, which offers tours and tastings, has won accolades from both oenophiles and connoisseurs of fine food. There is a wonderful restaurant on the premises (See *Where to Eat—Eating Out*).

Clinton Vineyards & Winery (845-266-5372), 212 Schultzville Road, Clinton Corners. Open year-round for tours and tastings Friday through Sunday 11–5:30 or by appointment. This small, picturesque, family-run winery specializes in seyval blanc, champagne, and dessert wines.

Millbrook Vineyards & Winery (800-662-WINE), 26 Wing Road, Millbrook. Open for tours and tastings daily September through May noon–5, June through August 11–6. They have the largest 100 percent vinifera vineyard in the Hudson Valley region. Production follows French techniques. They offer chardonnay, pinot noir, and cabernet wines. There are summer concerts and art exhibits, so call ahead to see what's happening if you are planning to visit the winery during July or August.

✳ To Do

AIRPLANE RIDES & BALLOONING **New England Helicopter, Inc.** (845-496-7928, 800-836-3541), Dutchess County Airport, New Hackensack Road, Wappingers Falls, arranges customized scenic tours of the Hudson Valley by air. Call ahead to schedule a trip.

The primary season for a hot-air balloon trip is April through October, but flights are available year-round, weather conditions permitting. **Blue Sky Balloons** (888-999-2461), 99 Teller Avenue, Beacon, organizes balloon festivals as well as flights and lessons. Flights are always within two hours after sunrise or two hours before sunset. This company uses only FAA-certified pilots and balloons and has over 30 years of experience.

BICYCLING **The Harlem Valley Rail Trail** (845-297-1224, 518-789-9591). Two paved sections of this 20-mile rail trail are open, and the Dutchess County section, about 8 miles, runs from Amenia to Millerton. There is access to the bike trail in both towns: in Millerton, Railroad Plaza, across from the gazebo; in Amenia, at the Mechanic Street parking lot.

Mid-Dutchess Trailway (845-486-2925). This 12-mile bike path runs from Hopewell Junction north to the city of Poughkeepsie.

Mills-Norrie State Park (845-889-4646), off Route 9, Staatsburg. Open dawn to dusk. This 1,000-acre state park offers several bicycle paths, which are easily accessed from the entrance to the park off Route 9.

Wilbur Boulevard Trailway (845-451-4100), Poughkeepsie. This trailway runs along Wilbur Boulevard in the city and town of Poughkeepsie. The paved length is 1.2 miles.

The following state highway corridors in Dutchess County have been designated as part of a regional system of state bike routes: **Route 9D, Route 52, Route 82, Route 199,** and **Route 308.** While this system of state bike routes is intended to provide safe bicycling facilities, it is imperative to be extra cautious when bicycling on these roads. For further information on the best bicycling in the county, contact the **Mid-Hudson Bicycle Club** (845-635-1184) in Poughkeepsie. They have a wealth of information about both road and mountain biking; they also sponsor social events and an annual group ride (see *Special Events*).

BOAT CRUISES If you want to spend an afternoon on the Hudson River relaxing on a tour boat, passing elegant old estates, being dazzled by autumn's painted trees, your best bet is to head across the river to Newburgh or Kingston (see *Boat Cruises* in "Orange County" and "Ulster County"). However, there are a few options to explore in Dutchess County.

Hudson Maritime Services (845-265-7621), Beacon Municipal Dock, Beacon. Open Monday through Friday 4–9 PM, Saturday, Sunday, and holidays 8 AM–9 PM. Private sightseeing trips are available on the *Manitou*, a 25-foot sloop; an 18-foot powerboat can also be chartered.

Hudson River Sloop *Clearwater* (845-454-7673), 112 Little Market Street, Poughkeepsie. Call Monday through Friday 9–5 to find out dates, times, and locations of the sloop as well as public sail schedule.

***River Rose* Tours and Cruises** (845-565-4210), Poughkeepsie and Newburgh docks. The *River Rose* is a Mississippi-style paddle wheeler, offering sightseeing cruises and charters. There's an open upper deck and a fully enclosed, climate-controlled main deck. Call for a schedule. Departures are from Newburgh, across the Hudson River from Beacon.

Sloop *Woodie Guthrie* (845-297-7697), Beacon Railroad Plaza, Beacon. Open July through October, Monday through Friday 6:30 PM. Free. This wooden sailboat is a replica of a Hudson River ferry sloop; it goes out on the Hudson River weekday evenings only during the summer and fall season.

CROSS-COUNTRY SKIING Dutchess County was made for cross-country skiing, with low hills that slope down toward the river, open meadows turned liquid silver by moonlight, and secret paths that cross streams and disappear into the pines. Many of the area's trails are maintained by towns and villages, and most are quiet. The following state and county parks offer cross-country skiing during the winter months. Since the weather is often exceedingly changeable, do call ahead to check conditions.

James Baird State Park (845-452-1489), 1 mile north of Route 55 on the Taconic Parkway, LaGrange. Open dawn to dusk. Free. Some 600 acres, including several miles of scenic wooded trails. A full-service restaurant overlooking the golf course is open to the general public and golfers alike.

Bowdoin Park (845-298-4600), 85 Sheafe Road, Wappingers Falls. Open 9–5. Free. There are 300 acres to explore for skiing and sledding.

Ferncliff Forest (845-876-3196), Mt. Rutsen Road, Rhinebeck. Open dawn to dusk. Free. This 200-acre park is a gem and less crowded than some of the other parks in the county.

Mills-Norrie State Park (845-889-4646), off Route 9, Staatsburg. Open dawn to dusk. This 1,000-acre state park offers several wooded trails for skiing, some of which have Hudson River views. The park also has picnic and sledding areas.

Edward R. Murrow Park (845-855-1131), Lakeside Drive & Old Route 55, Pawling. Open 10–7 May through August. Nature trails for hiking, children's play area, lake beach, and picnic area, and tennis courts; 86 acres. Admission fee.

Taconic State Park, Rudd Pond Area (518-789-3059), County Route 62, Millerton. Open 8 AM–dusk. Free but parking fee. There are 225 acres here with several trails.

Wilcox Park (845-758-6100), Route 199, Stanfordville. Free. There are 615 acres here with some lovely trails that go around the lake; they are not marked, however.

FARMERS MARKETS, FARM STANDS, AND PICK-YOUR-OWN FARMS June's ripe strawberries, summer blueberries, and jewel-like raspberries are three of the most popular crops in Dutchess County. But the harvest doesn't end with the berries: there are asparagus, apples, and big-bellied pumpkins for picking later in the season. Farm stands sprout like corn along the back roads: many are small, homey places where fresh cider and doughnuts lure you inside. Pick-your-own farms often have roadside signs indicating which crop is ready for harvest. For your own comfort, bring along a hat, sunscreen, and a container for the pickings, although you can buy a bucket or boxes at the farms. Harvest times vary with the weather and the temperature, so call before you go. Farmers markets are usually held on weekends; call the county Cooperative Extension Service, Monday through Friday 8:30–4:30, for information (845-677-8223), 2715 Route 44, Farm & Home Center, Millbrook.

Public Farmers Markets

Arlington (845-876-7756), Vassar College Campus, Raymond and Collegeview Avenues, Poughkeepsie. Open June through October, Thursday 3–7.

Beacon, Veterans Place and Main Street, next to the post office. Open June through October, Friday 3–8.

Millbrook (845-677-5300), Front Street, Millbrook. Open May through October, Saturday 9–1.

Pleasant Valley (845-677-5300), Maggiacomo Lane, Key Food Market Place, June through October, Friday 3–7.

Poughkeepsie (845-471-9478), 372 Main Street at Hudson Valley Foodworks, Poughkeepsie. Open late May through October, Friday 10–3.

Rhinebeck (845-876-4778), Village Parking Lot, East Market Street, Rhinebeck. Open Memorial Day weekend through October, Sunday 10–2.

Organic Produce

Community Supported Agriculture (CSA) projects bring fresh—and often organic—produce directly to consumers. Shareholders pay in advance for a portion of the farm's seasonal production to cover the farmer's costs. In return they get a weekly portion of the farm's produce. The following are a few such farms: **Poughkeepsie Farm Project** (845-485-8984), **Sisters Hill Farm** (845-868-7048) in Stanfordville, and **Still Point Community Farm** (845-373-8010) in Amenia.

A couple of places where travelers can pick up organic produce are **McEnroe Organic Farm Market** (518-789-4191), Routes 22/44 in Millerton, which is open daily year-round, and **Green Horizons Organic Farm** (845-855-5555), South Dingle Road in Pawling, which is open April through September for pick-your-own vegetables and pumpkins in season.

In Clinton Corners don't miss **La Terre Garlic Farm** (845-266-4320, 800-909-2272), 105 Field Road, off County Route 19. They are open mid-June and July and September through January. Closed August and February to mid-June. Farm shop is open Saturday and Sunday 11–3. The organically grown garlic here is first-rate. There are seven varieties of hard-neck garlic and elephant garlic from September 1 through the end of the year and garlic scapes in mid-June.

Pick Your Own & Farm Stores

Greig Farm (845-758-1234), Pitcher Lane, Red Hook (off Route 9G, 3 miles north of town; follow signs), has acres of fields that are available for self-harvesting, as well as a wonderful farm market. Berries, beans, apples, pumpkins, and peaches are only some of the seasonal treats; you will also find a winery, greenhouse, and extensive herb and cut-your-own flower gardens on the site. This is one of the largest and most popular stops for pick-your-own in the county and visiting all the farm has to offer could take a couple of hours if you spend time in the fields, as well.

Also in Red Hook is **Montgomery Place Farm Market** (845-758-6338), at the junction of Routes 9G and 199, open June through October, where there is a good selection of fruits and vegetables in-season. A conveniently located roadside stand by the Kingston-Rhinecliff Bridge, open May through December, is

Migliorelli Farm Market (845-757-3276), at the corner of River Road and Route 199, Rhinebeck. They offer homemade products in addition to apples, berries, pumpkins, squash, and other vegetables, depending on the time of year you stop by. Also in nearby Rhinebeck, make a stop at **Wonderland Farm** (845-876-6760), 191 White Schoolhouse Road, which carries coveted springtime asparagus for picking in addition to pumpkins and Christmas trees later in the year. They also have hayrides for the kids in autumn.

In the southern part of the county, be sure to stop at **Keepsake Farm Market** (845-897-2266), East Hook Cross Road, Hopewell Junction, where you can pick cherries, blueberries, raspberries, strawberries, and peaches during spring and summer and apples and pumpkins in the fall. The market offers homemade baked goods plus freshly pressed cider and doughnuts in-season. There's live entertainment and children's activities on weekends in autumn as well as hayrides, a petting zoo, and hay bales for the kids to play on. This is a terrific stop, particularly for those traveling with children. Also in Hopewell Junction is **Kohlmaier Farm Market & Greenhouses** (845-226-5028), 689 Route 376, open April through December, where you will find apples, berries, pumpkins, vegetables, and all kinds of plants. They do not, however, have pick-your-own—it's strictly a market/greenhouse. There are special activities, including hayrides, so call ahead. In nearby Wappingers Falls is **Secor Farms** (845-452-6883), 63 Robinson Lane, open June through August and the month of October, for pick-your-own strawberries, which they are known for, as well as apples, berries, and pumpkins in autumn. The kids will enjoy going on a hayride here, as well.

In Poughkeepsie, there are a few places worth visiting. **Adams Fairacre Farm** (845-454-4330), 765 Dutchess Turnpike, is a fantastic farm market/supermarket with a lovely gift shop and garden center. Just behind Adam's, in the same parking lot, is **The Pastry Garden** (845-473-5220), 749 Dutchess Turnpike, which has some of the best eclairs and baked goods—don't miss this spot, especially if you have a sweet tooth! Not far from there is **Lewis Country Farm,** Overlook & DeGarmo Roads, which offers fresh produce, homemade baked goods, and a lovely, large gift shop. **Piggots Farm Market** (845-297-3992), 46 Spring Road, Poughkeepsie, stocks fruit and vegetables along with local maple syrup, eggs, and honey. There are hayrides in the autumn, and tours of the farm can be arranged by calling ahead. **Red Oaks Mill Farm** (845-463-0032), 12 Red Oaks Mill Road, LaGrange (take Route 55 east from Poughkeepsie), is open May through November for pick-your-own apples, berries, pumpkins, and more, depending on the time of year. They have a gift shop on the premises and hayrides during the autumn. In Pleasant Valley, visit **Wigsten's Farm Market** (845-635-1570), Wigsten Road, which is open June through October for picking your own fruits or vegetables, depending on the season. They have an array of home-baked goods and local gourmet products, as well.

Farther east in Dutchess County is **Blueberry Park** (845-724-5776), 2747 County Route 21, Wingdale, which lives up to its name: stocking only pick-your-own blueberries in July and August (that is the only time of year they are open). Farm tours are offered here, as well, with advance notice. **Barton Orchards** (845-227-2306), County Route 7 (the Beekman Poughquag Road), in

Beekman, is open May through December for pick-your-own crops, including berries of all kinds, apples, pumpkins, Christmas trees, and vegetables. This is a wonderful place to visit, especially with children; autumn hayrides and special events throughout the season.

GOLF Several courses are open to the public in Dutchess County. Hours change with the season, and courses may be more or less crowded, depending on the time of year and time of day. Most are open from April through mid-November. There is sometimes a waiting list during the summer months. Do call ahead to reserve a tee time, particularly on weekends. Just about all the courses open at 6 AM on weekends and 7 AM weekdays.

James Baird State Park Golf Course (845-452-6959), 1 mile north of Route 55 off Taconic Parkway, LaGrange. This 18-hole championship course designed by Robert Trent Jones Sr. has a clubhouse, driving range, putting green, pro shop, lessons, restaurant—and reasonable prices.

Beekman Country Club (845-226-7700), 11 Country Club Road, Hopewell Junction. This 27-hole championship course has first-rate facilities that include a clubhouse, driving range, putting green, pro shop, cart rental, and restaurant. There are special rates for junior golfers. Do call a week in advance for a tee time.

Branton Woods Golf Club (845-223-1600), 178 Stormville Road, Hopewell Junction. This new (opened in 2003) 18-hole course is open year-round, weather permitting. There is a pro shop, driving range, putting green, lessons, clubhouse, excellent restaurant, and snack bar.

Thomas Carvel Country Club (518-398-7101), Ferris Road, Pine Plains. This 18-hole championship course offers a driving range, clubhouse, putting green, club rentals, lessons, and restaurant on the premises.

Casperkill Country Club (845-433-2222), 2330 South Road, Route 9, Poughkeepsie. This 18-hole championship golf course was designed by Robert Trent Jones Sr. There is a clubhouse here as well as a driving range, putting greens, pro shop, lessons, cart and club rental, and snack bar.

College Hill Golf Course (845-486-9112), 145 North Clinton Street, Poughkeepsie. This nine-hole course is inexpensive and has junior rates; good for novice golfers.

Dinsmore Golf Course (845-889-4071), Mills-Norrie State Park, Route 9, Staatsburg. This 18-hole course is the second oldest golf course in the country. There is a clubhouse, pro shop, putting green, and restaurant. The views of the Hudson River and Catskill Mountains are wonderful here, especially when the leaves are off the trees!

Dutcher Golf Course (845-855-9845), 135 East Main Street, Pawling. This nine-hole course is the oldest public course in America. There is a pro shop, putting green, and snack bar; cart and club rentals.

Fishkill Golf Course (845-896-5220), junction of Route 9 and I-84, Fishkill. There is a nine-hole course, driving range, and miniature golf course here as well as a pro shop, practice greens, club rental, and restaurant.

Harlem Valley Golf Club (845-832-9957), Wheeler Road, Wingdale. This nine-hole course is a good place for novice golfers.

The Links at Union Vale (223-1000), 153 Parliman Road, Union Vale. This 18-hole links-style course is quite challenging. There is a clubhouse, driving range, putting green, pro shop, and restaurant on the premises. Lessons and cart rental available.

McCann Memorial Golf Course (845-454-1968), 155 Wilbur Boulevard, Poughkeepsie. This 18-hole championship course also has a driving range, putting greens, pro shop, snack bar, and fine restaurant on the premises. Lessons and cart rentals available.

Red Hook Golf Club (845-758-8652), 650 Route 199, Red Hook. This 18-hole championship course with clubhouse, putting and chipping green, driving range, pro shop, and restaurant on the premises also offers lessons, cart and club rentals. Soft spikes required.

Silo Ridge Country Club (845-373-9200), Route 22, Amenia. This 18-hole championship course has a clubhouse, driving range, pro shop, club rentals, outdoor pavilion, and restaurant. Junior and senior rates.

Vassar Golf Course (845-473-1550), Vassar College Campus, Raymond Avenue, Poughkeepsie. This nine-hole course is inexpensive and great for beginners. There are junior and senior rates; club and cart rentals available.

HIKING **Appalachian Trail** (845-454-4936). Thirty miles of the AT pass through southeastern Dutchess County. Within the county there are 4,000 acres of protected parkland with hiking, backpacking, snowshoeing, and cross-country skiing and five overnight use areas. Look for trailheads—marked by AT trail crossing signs—at the following locations: Route 52, 4 miles east of the Taconic Parkway, with parking on the north side of the road; Route 55, west of Pawling, near the Route 292 intersection, with parking just west of the trail crossing; Route 22, north of Pawling, between Route 68 and the DOT parking area, north of Route 68 and Hurds Corners Road. Free. Open year-round.

Harlem Valley Rail Trail (518-789-9591). There are 20 miles of scenic paved trail, linking villages and parks on the rail bed from Amenia and Millerton to Copake Falls in Columbia County. There is access to the trail at Railroad Plaza in Millerton and in Amenia on Mechanic Street. Free. Open year-round.

Hyde Park Trail (845-229-9115). There are 8.5 miles of hiking trails connecting several parks and historic sites. Bikes are not permitted, and access is behind the FDR Presidential Library. Free. Open year-round.

Mills-Norrie State Park (845-889-4646), off Route 9, Staatsburg has 1,000 acres of woodlands with hiking trails, marina, boat launch, picnic areas, and a golf course; it's also near Mills Mansion (see *To See—Historic Homes*). Free. Open year-round.

Edward R. Murrow Park (845-855-1131), Lakeside Drive and Old Route 55, Pawling. Open May through August 10–7. Admission fee. There are several hiking trails on this 86-acre site, which also has a lake with small beach for swimming, restaurant, and picnic pavilions.

Pawling Nature Reserve (914-244-3271), Quaker Lake Road, Pawling. This 1,000-acre reserve has miles of hiking trails amid mountains, fields, woods, and ponds. Free. Open year-round.

Stissing Mountain Fire Tower (518-398-5069), off Lake Road 1.2 miles from Route 199, Pine Plains, has an elevation of 1,492 feet. The 90-foot lookout tower is reached by following a hiking trail from the base of the mountain, the 2nd oldest mountain in the Western Hemisphere. Incredible views of three states, along with an interesting piece of local history: the fire tower, a structure that has nearly disappeared from the face of the Hudson Valley. Enjoy watching eagles, hawks, and vultures in flight. Open year-round; free.

Thompson Pond Preserve (914-244-3271), Lake Road, 1.2 miles from Route 199, Pine Plains. Open year-round; free. After climbing Stissing Mountain, check out this multi-acre reserve with its fields, woods, and pond areas.

Wilcox Park (845-758-6100), Route 199, Stanfordville. Open year-round, this 615-acre site has the amenities of a larger park, along with hiking trails suitable for a family outing. Free park entry.

HORSEBACK RIDING Calypso Farm (845-266-4664), 25 Seelbach Lane, Staatsburg. This equestrian center offers lessons, training, and a children's summer-riding program. They are open year-round by appointment only.

Cedar Crest Farm (518-398-1034), 2054 Route 83, Pine Plains. Open year-round Tuesday through Sunday 8:30–5. This equestrian center offers lessons in show-jumping, cross-country, and dressage to riders of all abilities.

The Southlands Foundation (845-876-4862), 5771 Route 9, Rhinebeck. Open year-round Wednesday through Monday. Call to schedule time. This equestrian farm is located on 200 acres overlooking the Hudson River. They offer lessons, pony rides, and a weekend riding package, which includes overnight accommodations.

Western Riding Stables (518-789-4848), 228 Sawchuck Road, Millerton. This unique western riding experience takes visitors on trail rides, horseback camping pack trips, and daily and overnight excursions. Lessons, hayrides, sleigh rides, and pony rides available. Groups welcome. Hours change seasonally, so call and check before you go.

Willowbrook Farm (845-266-4522), Willow Lane, Clinton Corners. Open by appointment only. A professional staff offers training, lessons, and boarding.

SWIMMING Edward R. Murrow Park (845-855-1131), Lakeside Drive & Old Route 55, Pawling. Open daily May through August 10–7. Admission. This 86-acre park has a wonderful lake with a small beach; perfect for young children.

Sylvan Lake Beach Park (845-221-9889), 18 McDonnells Lane off County Route 9, Beekman. Open Memorial Day weekend through Labor Day 8–8. Free except for parking fee.

Taconic State Park, Rudd Pond Area (518-789-3059), County Route 62,
Millerton. Open Memorial Day weekend through Labor Day daily 11–7. Admission fee per vehicle. There is a small beach area; a good place for young children. The pond is 8 feet deep in the swimming area. There is fishing, row boat rentals, picnic area, bicycling.

Wilcox Park (845-758-6100), Route 199, Stanfordville. Open weekends Memorial Day weekend through Labor Day 10–7. Admission fee per vehicle for non-Dutchess County residents. This manmade lake (6–7 feet deep) is lovely and offers a good-sized beach where you can relax with lots of shade nearby. Hiking trails surrounding the lake provide an easy walk after your swim. This park is nice for bicycling, as well.

✳ Green Space

Fishkill Ridge Conservation Area (845-473-4440), Fishkill. (Take 52 west, off Route 9, through town and make a left on Maple Avenue; at the end turn right and cross the bridge. Make a left onto Old Town Road, then a right on Sunnyside Road, and follow to the end. Bear left, then right, and continue up the hill to the parking area.) This 1,900-acre area of the ridge, the northern gateway to the Hudson Highlands, is filled with wildlife and offers stunning views of the Hudson River and surrounding Catskills. There are excellent trails as well which connect to the Hudson Highlands State Park (see *Hiking* in "Putnam County") and Mount Beacon.

Hudson River Research Preserve (845-758-7010/7012), Tivoli Bay, Annandale-on-Hudson. Located on the Bard College campus (and the Tivoli Bays Wildlife Management Area), this preserve has 1,700 acres that can be hiked (there are six trails) or enjoyed as part of the various public programs that are offered throughout the year. Call for information on guided canoe trips, organized walks, and other events, or stop in at the new visitors center adjacent to the Tivoli Free Library on Broadway (the main street) in Tivoli between 10 and 2 on Saturday (hours vary during the week, so call before you go). Be aware that hunting, fishing, and trapping are permitted in-season in this wildlife management area.

Hyde Park Trail (845-473-4440), Hyde Park. Trailheads are at both the FDR home and Vanderbilt Mansion at intersection of East Market Road and Route 9. This 8.5-mile trail system runs along the Hudson River and links three National Historic Sites—the Vanderbilt Mansion, the FDR Home, and the Eleanor Roosevelt National Historic Site (Val-Kill)—with Hyde Park's Riverfront Park. There are five trail sections, and bicycling is permitted only on the 1.5 mile unpaved Val-Kill loop.

Innisfree Gardens (845-677-8000), Tyrrel Road (1.75 miles from the Taconic Parkway overpass on Route 44; make a right onto Tyrrel Road), Millbrook. Open May through October, Wednesday through Friday 10–4; Saturday, Sunday and holidays 11–5. Admission fee. Inspired by the Eastern cup garden, these individual "garden pictures" draw the attention to a particular object, setting it apart by establishing an enclosure around it. Following the tradition of Asian artists, garden founder Walter Beck used natural formations as well as terraces, walls, and paths to keep specific areas in "tension," believing that moving rocks or plants only an inch or so would destroy the effect. Visitors can stroll these public gardens and enjoy this visual laboratory and garden notebook. There is a picnic area for use by visitors; no pets are permitted, and there is very limited handicapped access.

Institute of Ecosystem Studies (845-677-5359), Route 44A, Millbrook. Open April through September, Monday through Saturday 9–6, Sunday 1–6; October through March same days and hours, but they close at 4. Free, but stop at the Gifford House Visitor and Education Center for an access permit. There are more than 1,900 acres of nature trails and plant collections at this educational and research facility. Public ecology programs, perennial gardens, and a tropical greenhouse (where you will find pineapples and banana trees) highlight a stop at these lovely grounds. A great stop if you are traveling with older children.

Poet's Walk Romantic Landscape Park (845-473-4440), County Route 103, Red Hook. (Cross the Kingston-Rhinecliff Bridge heading east; turn left at the first traffic light—River Road. The entrance to the park is 0.6 mile farther on the left.) This 120-acre park offers magnificent views of the Hudson River, Kingston-Rhinecliff Bridge, and Catskill Mountains. There are 2 miles of trails, along with rustic cedar pavilions—and benches—when you want to rest and take in the scenery. This is a wonderful place to stop and take a walk while touring Dutchess County by car.

Wethersfield Estate and Gardens (845-373-8037), 214 Pugsley Hill Road off County Route 86, Amenia. Formal gardens open June through September Wednesday, Friday, and Saturday noon–5; house by appointment only. This 10-acre formal garden created by Chauncey D. Stillman (1907–1989) is arranged in the classical style, like the Italian villas of the 17th century. It is a garden of scenic views and statues, bursting with colorful flowers. There is an east garden, cupid fountain, arbor vitae arch, and allee as well as cutting, water, and inner gardens, a knot garden south terrace, pine terrace, peacock walk, belvedere, and rune stone (designed from a 9th century Swedish original). Stillman's house is a Georgian-style Colonial, with the highest point on the property offering panoramic views of the Catskills to the west and the Berkshires to the north. It is filled with his collection of antiques, paintings, sculptures, and fine furniture. Stillman, an early conservationist, ran one of the first estates in Dutchess County to use soil-and-water-conservation farming techniques. He constructed 12 ponds for irrigation and prevention of soil erosion, rotated crops on contour strips, reforested, and employed organic farming methods. Today both field crops and livestock are raised, and the farm carries on the tradition of conservation. Stillman's interests went beyond agriculture and horticulture and extended to horses. He had a good-sized stable on the property and acquired 22 carriages, which he had restored; most date from 1850 to 1910 and can be seen by appointment, along with the interior of the house. Although these gardens are only open limited days and hours, they are worth seeing if you enjoy horticulture.

❄ Lodging

Northwestern Dutchess County (Red Hook, Rhinebeck, Rhinecliff, Staatsburg, Hyde Park)

Beckrick House on Chumley's Pond (845-876-6416), 27 Beckrick Drive, Rhinebeck. ($) Located on 3 acres in a parklike setting, just over the Kingston-Rhinecliff Bridge, this country ranch-style house has four rooms, three with private bath and one with bath outside the room. There are paddleboats for use by guests in the summer months. Full gourmet breakfast. Midweek and off-season rates available. Children over the age of 12 welcome. Open year-round.

Beekman Arms (845-876-7077), 6387 Mill Street (Route 9), Rhinebeck. ($$) The oldest inn in America, the Arms is steeped in history and antiques. Located on the main road in town, shops and restaurants are just outside the door. There are 19 rooms, all with private bath. If you want a quieter place—a restaurant and tavern *are* downstairs (see *Dining Out*)—ask about the Delamater House, a gingerbread fantasy that dates back to 1844 and is operated by the Beekman Arms. Children welcome. Open year-round.

The Belvedere (845-889-8000), 10 Old Route 9, Staatsburg 12580. ($$$) *Belvedere* means beautiful view, and there is a wonderful one from this restored Greek-Revival mansion overlooking the Hudson River with the Catskill Mountains as a backdrop. In addition to the lavish accommodations in the main house, there are accommodations within a separate carriage house facing the mansion. All have individual entrances and private bath. Each room has a unique character and is decorated with antiques and American folk art. During the winter months a hearty country breakfast is served fireside in the main dining room. In warmer weather breakfast is served alfesco in a pavilion gazebo overlooking the fountain and pond. There is also an in-ground pool. Open year-round.

The Bitter Sweet Bed & Breakfast (845-876-7777), 470 Wurtemburg Road, Rhinebeck. ($$) This 1770 Dutch Colonial situated on 150 acres has seven rooms, all with private bath and air-conditioning and filled with antiques. A full breakfast is served. Children over the age of five. Open April through December.

Bryndelbrook (845-876-6618), 167 River Road, Rhinebeck. ($$$) The two-bedroom barn apartment on this historic estate dates back to the early 19th century and is located on one of the most beautiful roads in the Hudson Valley. Set on 50 acres with meadows, gardens, ponds, and in-ground pool, the main house and barns were formerly the property of Vincent Astor. In fact, the railroad bed he built for his private railroad now serves as a scenic walking trail through the back 42 acres of woodlands here. This home away from home offers the warmth and coziness of a rustic, antiques-filled country barn with all the modern amenities: handmade quilts and designer towels and linens as well as air-conditioning, satellite TV, VCR, washer and dryer. On arrival, the refrigerator will be stocked with whatever you desire for a gourmet breakfast of your choice (although you will have to prepare it yourself!). Children welcome (the barn sleeps five people). Open year-round.

CD Diplomat B&B (845-757-4305), 82 Walker Hill, Red Hook. ($$$) There are three rooms with private bath, central air-conditioning, TV. An English Tudor house built in 1990, completely renovated, this house is located on 4 wooded acres with a view of the Hudson River and Catskill Mountains. Full gourmet breakfast cooked to your order. Less expensive mid-week prices available Monday through Thursday nights. Well-behaved children only. Open year-round.

Delamater House (845-876-7080), 6433 Montgomery Street (Route 9), Rhinebeck 12572. ($$) This romantic country inn is located in the heart of town. There are seven separate buildings, and four are historic structures. Walk to the restaurants and shops when staying in any of the 44 rooms, all with private bath, air-conditioning, phone, refrigerator, TV, and fireplace. There are five suites and five rooms with kitchenettes. Continental breakfast is served. Children are welcome. Open year-round.

The Gables at Rhinebeck B&B (845-876-7577), 6358 Mill Street (Route 9), Rhinebeck. ($$) An 1860s cottage carpenter Victorian home with 17 gables has three rooms, all with private bath, air-conditioning, TV, and queen-sized beds; large claw-foot tubs in some bathrooms. Full gourmet, candlelit breakfast; afternoon refreshments served daily. Mid-week and seasonal discounts available. Children welcome over the age of 10. Open year-round.

The Grand Dutchess (845-758-5818), 7571 Old Post Road (North Broadway), Red Hook 12571. ($$) This Victorian Italianate mansion built in 1874 is located on 1 acre and is within walking distance of the shops and restaurants in town. There are six rooms; four have private bath, and two share a bath. A full breakfast is served, and children over the age of six are welcome. Open year-round.

Hideaway Suites (845-266-5673), 439 Lake Drive, Rhinebeck 12572. ($$) Enjoy secluded elegance in the middle of a forest. The three suites and three guest rooms all have private bath, king-sized beds, air-conditioning, TV, and phone. Most have a fireplace, Jacuzzi, wet bar, and private deck. Located 1 mile from the Omega Institute. Open year-round.

Journey Inn Bed & Breakfast (845-229-8972), One Sherwood Place, Hyde Park 12538. ($$) Situated directly across from the entrance to the Vanderbilt Mansion and grounds (where guests can easily take a morning walk or run), this comfortable, cozy B&B is chock-full of fascinating memorabilia from the travels of the owners. There are two master suites, one with a king-sized bed, and four bedrooms, all with private bath. Children welcome over the age of nine. Open year-round.

The Merrill House (845-758-9162), 710 Salisbury Turnpike, Rhinebeck. ($$$) There are three rooms on 25 acres in this majestic, 40-year-old Colonial-style house, formerly a residence of ad agency Ogilvy & Mather's owner. The three guest rooms have private bath, 400-count cotton sheets, planked wood floors, and air-conditioning (no TV, VCR, or phone—they are available only in the living room); outdoors there is a beautiful heated swimming pool with a deck surrounded by gorgeous gardens. The English Room, with cathedral ceiling and king-sized bed, is filled with English antiques and has its own spa, complete with grotto shower, and private sauna room. The French Room, with a king-sized bed and French antiques, is smaller but also regal. The Italian Room has a 16th-century queen-sized bed, with antiques from Italy. The owner, who studied at the Culinary Institute, serves a full gourmet breakfast on Wedgewood china with Waterford crystal and sterling silver. While expensive on weekends, those who stay for an extended period—or during the week—will receive substantial savings with discounted rates. No young children. Open year-round.

Olde Rhinebeck Inn (845-871-1745), 340 Wurtemburg Road, Rhinebeck. ($$$) Listed on the National Register of Historic Places, this early-American farmhouse, built before the Revolutionary War by Dutch Palatine settlers, retains many of its original architectural details including hand-hewn chestnut beams and wide-plank floors. The three rooms, each with their own charm, combine authentic touches with the modern amenities. One room offers a Jacuzzi and private balcony overlooking the spring-fed pond. The large suite has a queen-sized canopied bed with adjoining sitting room. All rooms have private bath, satellite TV, air-conditioning, refrigerator, plush terry-cloth robes, and fresh-cut flowers. Full gourmet breakfast. A two-night minimum stay required on weekends May through November. Children not permitted. Open year-round.

Red Hook Inn (845-758-8445), 31 South Broadway, Red Hook 12571. ($$) There are six rooms with private bath in this 156-year-old Federal-style house, converted to a charming inn

with a restaurant and tavern downstairs (see *Dining Out*). A Continental breakfast is served to guests. Children are welcome. Open year-round.

Rhinecliff Bed and Breakfast (845-876-3710), corner of William and Grinnell Streets, Rhinecliff. ($) This 1860 Victorian home on the banks of the Hudson River offers views of a different sunset every night! Located by the train station and only 2 miles from the town of Rhinebeck, this cozy home has three rooms (they share two baths), all with air-conditioning and cable TV. The front porch has a view of the river, and there is an in-ground swimming pool on the premises. The rates are among the least expensive in Dutchess County; the B&B has been operating since 1980. Children are welcome (the owner is a retired schoolteacher). Open year-round.

Veranda House (845-876-4133), 6487 Montgomery Street (Route 9), Rhinebeck 12572. ($$) This charming Federal house built in 1845 was once a farmhouse, and for almost a century served as a church parsonage. Located in the Rhinebeck Village Historic District, three blocks from the center of town, it features five cozy rooms, all with private bath. The Rose Room, with its queen-sized four-poster bed and lacy canopy, is my favorite. Guests are invited to enjoy the library, TV, VCR, and living room with fireplace. The terrace overlooks the garden and is a nice place to relax in the warm-weather months. Children over 12 are welcome. Open year-round.

Whistlewood Farm (845-876-6838), 52 Pells Road, Rhinebeck ($$) This distinctive B&B is also a working horse farm located on 40 acres with miles of walking trails through beautiful woodlands. Animals abound here.

DUTCHESS COUNTY

The living room has a stone fireplace and a view of the paddock area, and there are antiques, including a player piano, throughout the house. A hearty farm breakfast with home-baked muffins, breads, and jams is served daily. The four bedrooms have private bath with Jacuzzi and private patio; two cottages have fireplaces, one has a hot tub. Guests may use the entire house. Note that the owner offers deeply discounted rates during the week (Monday through Thursday nights) to single travelers. Children and pets are welcome. Open year-round.

Southwestern Dutchess County (Beacon, Fishkill, Hopewell Junction, Poughkeepsie)

Bykenhulle House Bed & Breakfast (845-221-4182), 21 Bykenhulle Road, Hopewell Junction 12533. ($$) A Georgian Colonial set on 6 acres, this house has five large bedrooms featuring four-poster beds and antiques, all with private bath. There are six fireplaces, a sun room, flower gardens, and swimming pool. Two of the rooms have Jacuzzis, and two have fireplaces. A full gourmet country breakfast is served on fine china in the formal dining room. No children. Open year-round.

Hilton Garden Inn (845-896-7100), 21 Westage Drive, Fishkill. ($$) There are 111 rooms in this new hotel at the junction of Route 9 and I-84. All have high-speed Internet access, refrigerator, microwave, and coffeemaker in addition to the usual hotel amenities. There is an indoor pool, fitness center, 24-hour business center (with fax, computer, and photocopy machine). Children welcome. Open year-round.

THE INN AT ROSE HILL FARM

Richard Segalman

The Inn at the Falls (845-462-5770), 50 Red Oaks Mill Road, Poughkeepsie 12603. ($$$) This inn blends the luxury of a plush resort and the atmosphere of a country estate. Nestled next to a waterfall, the inn has rooms decorated in English, Oriental, and American-country styles. A continental breakfast is delivered to your room. Twenty-four rooms and 12 suites have private bath, Jacuzzi, phone, TV, VCR. Children welcome. Open year-round.

The Inn at Rose Hill Farm (845-677-5611), 86 Barmore Road, LaGrangeville. ($$$) This establishment provides the independent traveler with a B&B experience that is quite different from the standard one. There are five guest rooms in this French Provincial house built in the 1930s: all have featherbeds with fine linens, private bath, central air-conditioning, stereo, flat-screen TV, and data ports. Reminiscent of a miniature resort in style, the inn is located on 100 acres, with an outdoor heated pool and Jacuzzi, tennis court, mountain bikes for guest use, and a licensed massage therapist available on request. There's a 12-seat barrel-shaped projection room on the premises, a wonderful small theater, complete with surround sound, and guests may choose from over 300 movies in the owner's extensive film collection. So in the event of inclement weather, one need not head to the mall! There are miles of hiking trails on the property, and a full gourmet breakfast is served. Children are not permitted. Open year-round except the month of January.

The Residence Inn (845-896-5210), Route 9, Fishkill 12524. ($$$) Part of the Marriott hotel chain, there are 139 suites here, each with the usual modern amenities as well as fireplace and kitchen. A continental breakfast is served. An outdoor pool, whirlpool, and exercise room are on the premises (passes to nearby All Sport Fitness Center are given to all guests). Children welcome. Open year-round.

Central Dutchess County (Bangall, Clinton Corners, Millbrook, Stanfordville)

A Cat in Your Lap Bed & Breakfast (845-677-3051), 62 Old Route 82 and The Monument, Millbrook 12545. ($) There are two barn studios here with private bath, king-sized bed, and fireplace. The garden studio is a little smaller, but also charming. The village of Millbrook is within walking distance. A hearty breakfast is served, and these elegant accommodations come at rock-bottom prices. Open year-round.

Bullis Hall (845-868-1665), 88 Hunns Lake Road, Bangall ($$$) Some of the luxurious suites in this beautifully decorated, completely renovated historic inn have fireplaces, and others have Jacuzzis, but all overlook the beautiful gardens. Staying here is like going away to a well-staffed elegant home. One guest told me there is nothing quite like this north of 93rd Street. After spending a night at Bullis Hall, I tend to agree. The room price includes breakfast and an open bar as well as dinner in the antiques-filled dining room with its 18th-century atmosphere. The fare is first-rate, prepared by a Culinary Institute–trained chef, and the service is excellent all-around. Relais & Château has given this establishment their hard-won stamp of approval. Your host, Addison Berkey, is a former New York publisher; he and his

his wife, Lauren, will make you feel welcome . . . and regal. A wonderful place to celebrate a special occasion. An unusual feature here: Guests may use the shooting clubs nearby. Children at the discretion of the owner. Open year-round.

Calico Quail (845-677-6016), Route 44, Mabbettsville (near Millbrook) 12545. ($) This classic 1830s farmhouse is set on a parklike property that has a Chinese bridge and pond, complete with boat. Service is the watchword here, and guests enjoy fresh flowers, antiques, homemade pastries, and breakfast in the Tavern Room. There are three rooms—two share a bath, and one has a private bath. No children. Closed in February and March; otherwise, open year-round.

Millbrook Country House (845-677-9570), 506 Sharon Turnpike, Millbrook. ($$) The four guest rooms in this delightful 1808 center-hall Colonial, all with private bath and central air-conditioning, are decorated with many 18th-century Italian antiques and paintings. Imported linens are featured on all the beds, which adds a nice touch, and guests can spend time around any of the several fireplaces. The wonderful gardens (both flower and herb) are filled with modern sculptures, a nice counterpoint to the antiques. Guests will enjoy a full gourmet breakfast with homemade jams and syrups; the omelettes use herbs from the garden during the summer months. Breakfast is served any time at your convenience between 7 and 10. Afternoon tea is available between 4 and 5. Those interested in art and antiques will particularly appreciate a stay here. Reduced midweek rates avail-

BULLIS HALL, BANGALL

O/O Communications

able. Children welcome over the age of 10. Open year-round.

The Porter House Bed & Breakfast (845-677-3057), 17 Washington Avenue, Millbrook. ($$) There are five rooms in this renovated stone building dating back to 1912. Each room has a private bath, air-conditioning; one has a fireplace. A continental breakfast is served. Within walking distance to all the attractions in the village; a good bet for those who want to stay in Millbrook rather than out in the countryside. Children over the age of 12 welcome. Open year-round.

Eastern Dutchess County (Amenia, Dover Plains, Millerton)
Alpen Haus Bed & Breakfast (845-373-9568), 49 Powder House Road, Amenia. ($$) This new Victorian-Colonial-style house up high overlooking the town of Amenia has two rooms, both with private bath, central air-conditioning, and TV as well as a large deck for use in summer months. A full breakfast with freshly baked breads, fresh fruit, and cereal is served. Children over the age of eight. Open year-round except the month of January.

Old Drovers Inn (845-832-9311), 196 East Duncan Hill Road (off Route 22), Dover Plains. ($$$) This historic inn is coupled with a fine restaurant downstairs (see *Dining Out*). There are antiques in the four guest rooms (all have private bath); three rooms have fireplace. Breakfast is served in the Federal Room. Children over the age of 12 and small dogs are welcome. Open year-round Thursday through Tuesday; closed the first two weeks of January.

Simmons Way Village Inn (845-789-6235), 53 Main Street (Route 44),

Millerton. ($$$) Built originally as a modest merchant's home in 1854, the Village Inn was remodeled in 1892 into an elegant Victorian by the new bank-president owner and now boasts nine rooms with private bath, filled with down pillows, fine linens, antiques, and canopied beds. Enjoy a continental breakfast in your suite, in the dining room, or on the front porch. There is a restaurant on the premises, as well. Children are welcome. Open year-round.

Troutbeck Inn & Conference Center (845-373-9681), Leedsville Road, Amenia 12501. ($$$) This English country estate on 600 acres is an executive retreat during the week, but on weekends it's a relaxed getaway. Fronted by sycamores and a brook, the slate-roofed estate has leaded-glass windows, walled gardens, antiques, and an outdoor pool and tennis courts. The 42 rooms and 6 suites, all with private bath and 9 with fireplace, are beautifully decorated. Not recommended for children. Open year-round.

✳ Where to Eat
DINING OUT

Northwestern Dutchess County (Tivoli, Red Hook, Rhinebeck, Staatsburg, Hyde Park)
Agra Tandoor (845-876-7510), 5856 Route 9 South,Rhinebeck. ($) Open for lunch noon–2:30; dinner 4:30–10; Sunday brunch noon–3. Enjoy the finest South and North Indian food in the area's finest Indian restaurant. They offer vegetarian and meat dishes as well as enticing weekly specials. Try the buffet dinner on Wednesdays from 5–9:30 for excellent value. Children welcome.

China Rose (845-876-7442), 100 Shatzell Avenue, Rhinecliff. ($$) Open every day except Tuesday 5–10, until 11 on weekends. Enjoy patio dining with a view of the Hudson River during the warm-weather months in this Chinese bistro. The cuisine is exceptional, with selections like the house special noodle soup, shrimp with basil, scallops with black beans, beef with double mushrooms, or pork with eggplant (my favorite). There is a choice of pork fried, steamed white, or brown rice to accompany your meal. The ice cream offered includes flavors like almond cookie, which comes from Manhattan's Chinatown; the tangerine sherbet is also delicious. More expensive than most Chinese restaurants but worth it. Children welcome. No reservations taken.

Cripple Creek (845-876-4355), 18 Garden Street, Rhinebeck. ($$$) Open daily except Tuesday for dinner

THE CULINARY INSTITUTE'S NEWEST RESTAURANT VENUE, THE COLAVITA CENTER.

Courtesy CIA

from 5. The eclectic American cuisine in this fine establishment includes mouth-watering entrées like marinated grilled lamb on risotto with roasted garlic rosemary sauce or seared sea scallops on spinach and truffle-crushed potatoes with red wine sauce. Make sure to save room for the signature dessert: warm chocolate mousse cake. It is one of the best desserts I've ever experienced. Zagat named Cripple Creek one of the top restaurants in the region; *Wine Spectator* commended their wine list. There are wonderful touches that enhance the dining experience here—rose petals on the fine cloth napkins (which are black to ensure a lintless lap if you are wearing black!), complimentary reading glasses, even Gameboys and other electronic games for the children in your party to occupy them while waiting for their meal. Live piano music nightly. Open year-round.

Culinary Institute of America (845-471-6608), Route 9, Hyde Park. ($$) Hours vary. There are five restaurants at this world-famous culinary institution, where the food is prepared and served by the students under the guidance of world-class chefs. Except for weekdays at St. Andrew's Café and the Apple Pie Bakery Café (see *Eating Out*), reservations are essential, and should be made several weeks in advance; the wait is usually well worth it. **American Bounty Restaurant** offers the best in the way of American regional cuisine: Try smoked turkey with black-pepper pasta and cream, then a Mississippi riverboat for dessert. Visitors are served in a comfortable dining room. **Caterina d'Medici Restaurant** is now located in the newest venue, **Colavita Center for**

Italian Food and Wine, which specializes in Northern Italian food like tricolor pasta diamonds with prosciutto. The menu features the culinary traditions of various regions of Italy, and the decor is reminiscent of the architecture and landscape of Tuscany. There are six dining areas, including a formal dining room with Venetian chandeliers and the Al Forno room, with a casual antipasto bar, open kitchen, and wood-fired ovens. The **Escoffier Room** has classical haute cuisine, such as pheasant with morels and fillet of sole with lobster mousse. **St. Andrew's Café** is less formal and offers healthful dishes that are delicious, as well, like grilled salmon fillet with tomato-horseradish sauce and chocolate-bread-pudding soufflé for dessert. They also provide diners with a computer printout of the food's nutritional analysis. **Apple Pie Bakery Café** (845-905-4500), open Monday through Friday 8–6:30, is a great place to stop for lunch or a midday snack. The salads, sandwiches, cakes, pies, and breads are first-rate.

Gigi (845-876-1007), 6422 Montgomery Street (Route 9), Rhinebeck. ($$) Open Tuesday through Sunday for lunch noon–2:45; dinner Tuesday through Thursday and Sunday 5–9, Fridays and Saturdays 4:30–10, Sunday 4:30–9. Late-night menu Tuesday through Saturday for one hour after the kitchen closes. A casual restaurant, relatively new to town (since 2002), featuring Hudson Valley Mediterranean cuisine, with an emphasis on local ingredients in-season. Skizza bianca (white pizza with mozzarella and goat cheese, figs, pears, sweet red onion, and fresh arugala, topped with white truffle oil) is a unique creation, so do try it. Other popular choices are the pastas made on the premises, and the 28-ounce rib-eye steak served with Tuscan fries. For dessert there is excellent cheesecake with caramel sauce or lemon brûlée with cranberries. Menus change seasonally, and regional Italian specials are offered daily with a prix fixe four-course tasting menu nightly ($28.95 weekdays, $34.95 weekends).

Julia & Isabella (845-758-4545), Route 9, Upper Red Hook, 2 miles north of the intersection of Route 199. ($$) Open for dinner Wednesday–Saturday 5–10, Sunday 5–9. Enjoy international cuisine, seasonal outdoor dining, and live music at this wonderful restaurant offering imaginative dishes in an informal atmosphere. The hormone-free New Zealand rib-eye steaks and grilled calamari with garlic sauce are popular entrées. Atkins and vegetarian friendly.

Le Petit Bistro (845-876-7400), 8 East Market Street, Rhinebeck. ($$$) Open for dinner Thursday through Monday 5–10. This charming, intimate French bistro is a great place to stop for dinner on a special occasion; the food and service are consistently excellent, and everything is prepared to order. All entrées are served with a fresh mixed salad. Excellent wine list. Not recommended for children.

Max's Memphis Barbecue (845-758-6297), Route 9, Red Hook. ($$) Open Tuesday through Sunday 5–10. Max's southern regional cooking is based on family recipes and includes traditional barbecue dishes like Memphis John's barbecue pulled pork plate and Big Mike's famous slow-smoked pork ribs. There are crabcakes, smoked brook trout, barbecued chicken, and a veggie sampler from a menu sure to appeal to just about everyone at this lively restaurant. Children welcome.

Mina (845-758-5992), 29 West Market Street, Red Hook. ($$) Open Friday through Sunday for dinner from 5:30; reservations are necessary. This intimate, multiethnic restaurant borrows from French, Italian, and American cuisines, combining both New- and old-world styles of cooking, to create exciting, eclectic fare that has been recognized nationally. The owner was trained at the Culinary Institute; her grandmother was named Wilhelmina, which is where the name is derived. The place is cozy with a relaxed ambience, like dining in your own home. The menu changes weekly, making use of the freshest local ingredients, many organically grown. (The chicken is free-range from a nearby Hudson Valley farm.)

P. J. McGlynn's (845-758-3102), Route 9, Rhinebeck. ($$) Open daily 11:30–10, Friday and Saturday until 11. The complete Sunday brunch with a cocktail costs $7.95 (without a drink it's $5.95); it's one of the best culinary bargains in the county, served from 11:30–2. Closed Thanksgiving and Christmas Day only. The specialty at this American steakhouse is farm-raised lamb (and it's the only restaurant in the state where the owner raises and serves his own lamb), although the pork dishes are also popular. The roasted-garlic mashed potatoes and 16-ounce prime rib with horseradish cream sauce are excellent. There are seafood entrées and seared fillet of yellow-fin tuna for surf lovers. There is lots of Irish decor, with wooden booths and tables giving the place a rustic ambience. Children welcome.

Osaka (845-876-7338), 18 Garden Street, Rhinebeck; and 74 Broadway, Tivoli (845-757-5055). ($$) Open for lunch Monday through Friday 11:30–2:30; dinner served daily at 5. Eat in or take out from this first-rate, informal Japanese restaurant at two locations in Dutchess County. The sushi is some of the best to be had in the Hudson Valley. The grilled fish daily special and chicken teriyaki are excellent. They are accompanied by soup or salad. There is also a chef's special lunch box of the day for those considering picnic fare. A seat at the bar offers a great view of the sushi chefs at work. Children welcome.

Portofino (845-889-4711), 57 Old Post Road, Staatsburg. ($$) Dinner is served daily except Monday from 4 in this moderately priced Northern Italian restaurant that also features Continental specialties. The town of Staatsburg, 5 miles south of Rhinebeck, is a quiet hamlet tucked away from the bustle of Route 9, and this restaurant is worth a stop when passing through the area. A popular place with local residents. Reservations are not taken.

Quail Hollow Restaurant (845-266-8822), 360 Hibernia Road, Salt Point. ($$) Open for dinner Wednesday through Sunday from 5–9, until 10 Friday and Saturday. Enjoy comfortable country dining in a barn-red building dating back to 1908. The lovely downstairs dining room has exposed wood beams and an inviting stone fireplace, with a 20-foot pine bar upstairs. The fare is American with Mediterranean and French influences, but the chef incorporates cuisines from around the world. Enjoy shredded duck salad to start, and entrées including herb-crusted prime rib of beef, New Zealand rack of lamb, salmon tapenade (grilled salmon with a kalamata olive and caper purée served with wild rice and summer vegetables). There is always a chef's special vegetarian dish and a pasta selection (made daily on the premises). On Wednesday and Thursday try the chef's special four-course dinner. Reservations are recommended on weekends. Children welcome.

Red Hook Inn (845-758-8445), 31 South Broadway, Red Hook. ($$) Open Wednesday through Sunday for dinner 5–10. Enjoy American and Continental favorites in this Federal-style, over-160-year-old building that houses the restaurant as well as an inn (see *Lodging*). Pan-fried trout with pecans and lemon and grilled pork chop with garlic mashed potatoes and greens are only a couple of the tasty entrées available. For dessert, try the chocolate soufflé cake or espresso crème caramel. Espresso and cappuccino are served, along with a selection of fine teas. Children welcome.

Santa Fe (845-757-4100), 52 Broadway, Tivoli. ($$) Dinner daily except Monday 5–10. Enjoy traditional Mexican favorites like tacos and enchiladas in a festive atmosphere. The goat cheese in the enchiladas is locally made. Children welcome. Great margaritas with a number of tequilas from which to choose.

Terrapin (845-876-3330), Route 9, Rhinebeck. ($$) Bistro open daily for lunch and dinner 11 AM–midnight, until 2 AM weekends. Dinner is served daily in the dining room 5:30–10. There are actually two restaurants (together they seat 150) housed in one building here—a large, informal bar/bistro and a more formal restaurant with a spacious dining room. A

former Baptist church that dates back to the 18th century, the cathedral-ceilinged structure has been completely renovated. The New American cuisine featured in the dining room fuses Asian, southwestern, and Italian flavors. For those who prefer lighter fare, try the innovative bistro menu with organic beefburgers, free-range chicken wings, fresh salads, and a create-your-own sandwich option. Children welcome.

Traphagen Restaurant at the Beekman Arms (845-876-7077), 4 Mill Street, Rhinebeck. ($$) Open daily for lunch and dinner; Sunday brunch 10–3. This Hudson Valley institution is housed in the oldest inn in America (see *Lodging*) and dates back to 1766. Hearty breakfast and weekend brunch are particularly good. If you decide to dine here, try the Dutch-style turkey pot pie (made with free-range turkey) and roasted root vegetables. Children welcome.

Southwestern Dutchess County (Poughkeepsie, Wappingers, Hopewell Junction, Fishkill, Beacon)
Angelo's (845-831-2292), 47 East Main Street, Beacon. ($$) Open for lunch and dinner Tuesday through Saturday 11:30–10, Sunday 3–10; jazz on Sundays 4–7 and on Thursday 7–10. The Italian-American fare at this family restaurant is decent and the portions good-sized. A good place to go with children.

Aroma Osteria (845-298-6790), 114 Old Post Road, off Route 9, Wappingers Falls. ($$) Open daily for dinner from 5. Lunch served Tuesday through Saturday 11:30–2:30. The rustic Italian cuisine is served in a lovely country setting. There is an extensive wine list and many wines by the glass. The meal begins with rustic bread and olive oil. The antipasti of bruschetta al pomodoro and steaming Prince Edward Island mussels in a broth of extra-virgin olive oil, garlic, and fresh herbs are fine appetizers. Everything is prepared to order. Children welcome.

Il Barilotto (845-897-4300), 1113 Main Street, Fishkill. ($$) Open Monday through Saturday for lunch and dinner. Enjoy Italian cuisine with a contemporary flair in this trattoria and wine bar housed in an historic 1870 brick building with a romantic ambience and old-world charm.

Beech Tree Restaurant (845-471-7279), 1 Collegeview Avenue, Poughkeepsie. ($$) Open daily for lunch and dinner Monday through Saturday 11:30–11:30; Sunday brunch served 11:30–3; dinner 5–11. This is a popular place with both local residents and the Vassar College community. Entrees like grilled shrimp over asparagus risotto with roasted red peppers, or house smoked spare ribs with sweet lime barbecue sauce and new potato salad, are served with a small salad. Brunch selections are imaginative and include crème Anglaise French toast with raspberry-maple syrup; eggs may be accompanied by Jugtown Mountain no-nitrate bacon or rabbit ginger sausage. The bar is a busy place on Friday nights.

The Blue Fountain (845-226-3570), 940 Route 376, Hopewell Junction. ($$) Open for lunch Tuesday through Friday 11–3; dinner served daily 4–10. The Italian-American cuisine here includes the standard steaks, seafood, chicken, and veal dishes. My favorites are the zuppa di pesce—an enormous platter of shrimp, mussels, clams, scallops, sole, and calamari over linguine—and the steak *au poivre*. Fresh bread is always accompanied by a serving of roasted red peppers in herbed olive oil. The dining room tables all have a view of a huge fountain. The Marinaro brothers, who operate this establishment, owned a restaurant in the Bronx for many years. There is a good-sized children's menu, and families are welcome. Excellent value.

The Brass Anchor (845-452-3232), 31 River Point Road, Poughkeepsie. ($$) Open for lunch and dinner daily from 11:30. Seafood is the specialty here. In the warm-weather months enjoy dining outdoors overlooking a marina and the Hudson River.

Brothers Trattoria (845-838-3300), 465 Main Street, Beacon. ($–$$) Open daily 11–10. A tradition in Beacon for the past 7 years, this is a good place to go for pizza and pasta as well as standard Italian favorites, particularly if you are traveling with children. The newly renovated dining room is lovely, with an informal yet elegant atmosphere and classy decor. Dinner entrées range from $10.95 to $22.95. Children's menu available.

The Haymaker (845-486-9454), 718 Dutchess Turnpike, Poughkeepsie. ($$) Open for lunch Monday through Saturday 11–2:30; dinner daily 5–9, until 10 on Friday and Saturday, Sunday 5–9. The American regional cuisine here is prepared with the freshest local ingredients. The service is first-rate, and the portions are generous. I can't recommend this restaurant highly enough for both lunch and dinner. A little bit of SoHo in Poughkeepsie.

The Inn at Osborne Hill (845-897-3055), 150 Osborne Hill Road, Fishkill. ($$) Open for lunch Monday through Friday 11:30–2:30; for dinner Monday through Saturday at 5. The creative husband-and-wife team who run this restaurant both graduated from the Culinary Institute. The American regional cuisine is particularly imaginative and includes such selections as breast of pheasant with cranberries and green peppercorns as well as linguine with rock shrimp, scallions, mushrooms, and tomatoes in lobster cream sauce. The wine cellar is extensive, with many difficult-to-find selections.

Inn at Stone Creek (845-227-6631), 31 Route 376, Hopewell Junction. ($$) Open for dinner Tuesday through Sunday 5–10. Regional American cuisine is featured here; the chef is Culinary Institute trained. Pistachio-crusted rack of lamb and the petit rack of veal are specialties of the house. Located in a restored manor house that dates back to 1741, this is a lovely place to enjoy a relaxing meal while listening to live jazz (Friday evenings) or piano music (Saturday nights). Children's menu available.

Isabella (845-485-9999), 309 Titusville Road, Poughkeepsie. ($$) Open for lunch Tuesday through Friday noon–3; dinner Monday through Saturday 5–10, Sunday 4–9. Reservations suggested. This restaurant offers a wonderful selection of Mediterranean and eclectic European cuisine. Enjoy a variety of dishes, including a wonderful seasonal menu, in an intimate setting. Both the Sicilian pizza with mushrooms, spinach, or artichokes and the 10-ounce filet mignon covered in gorgonzola cheese are tempting dinner options. There are also grilled fish entrées. The flatbed wraps of chicken parmigiana,

Genoa salami, and prosciutto or lobster ravioli are some of the lunch offerings. The white-bean and truffle soup is excellent. If you have room for dessert, the tiramisu is a good choice.

Le Pavillon (845-473-2525), 230 Salt Point Turnpike (Route 115), Poughkeepsie. ($$) Open for dinner Monday through Saturday 5:30–10; reservations required. This over-200-year-old brick farmhouse provides an elegant dining setting. Serving French country cuisine, the specialties are game, fish, and seasonal dishes. Not recommended for children.

Mojo Grill (845-226-1111), 942 Route 376, Wappingers Falls. ($$) Open daily for lunch and dinner noon–9:30, Sunday 1–9:30. The work of local artists decorates the walls in this lively, colorful restaurant featuring eclectic American cuisine with Latin and Asian touches. Local organic produce is used in-season. Choose from entrées like jumbo gulf shrimp, mussels with jalapeños and tomatillos, or filet mignon. Weekday nights there are sandwiches on the menu, including pulled pork, grilled steak with sautéed onions and Monterey jack cheese, and oyster po'boy accompanied by sweet-potato fries. Live music Wednesday through Saturday nights. Children welcome.

Oasis (845-463-0100), 1820 Route 376 (New Hackensack Plaza), Wappingers Falls. ($$) Open for dinner Wednesday through Saturday 5–10, Sunday 3–8. The two owners hail from Oaxaca, Mexico, and Ecuador and have created a Latin-American menu featuring New Spanish cuisine and the foods of Puerto Rico, Cuba, and Mexico. Start off with the guacamole, prepared fresh at your table. I enjoyed the excellent seafood paella.

Equadoran seviche, shrimp with salsa Oasis, and salmon Caribe are some of the other seafood specialties. The meat entrées range from a 14-ounce grilled rib-eye steak to Puerto Rican roasted pork (heavily seasoned with garlic) and Cuban-style pot roast (stuffed with ham and Spanish sausage). All include soup or salad. For dessert, the flan is first-rate, but the fire ball—a huge ball of ice cream doused in rum and flamed tableside—provides a dramatic finale to any meal. Children welcome.

O'Sho (845-297-0540), 763 South Road, Poughkeepsie. ($$) Open for lunch Monday through Friday 11:30–2:30; dinner served daily from 5. Hibachi-style chicken and steak are the specialty, but the sushi is also very good. Dine in an elegant Japanese-style steakhouse. Delightful atmosphere. Children welcome.

Piggy Bank (845-838-0028), 448 Main Street, Beacon. ($$) Open Tuesday through Thursday 11–9:30, Friday and Saturday noon–10:30 Sunday noon–9. Located in a converted turn-of-the-20th-century bank building with a unique interior (the original vault is the wine cellar and centerpiece of the bar), the authentic Southern barbeque is at its best here: slow cooked, moist, and tender. Try the ribs, chicken, pulled pork, wings, chili—even the vegetarian dishes. All desserts are baked fresh daily on the premises. On Rack Attack Tuesdays enjoy all-you-can-eat ribs. Live music every Friday night. Outdoor dining in the warm-weather months. Children's menu.

Pippy's (845-483-7239), 2 Delafield Street, Mount Carmel Square, Poughkeepsie. Open daily except Monday for dinner 4–10. Pippy was the nick-name of the owner's father, who was born and brought up in Mount Carmel, the Little Italy of Poughkeepsie. The Southern Italian specialties here are first rate—try the zuppa di pesce, fried calamari, and a delicious appetizer: prosciutto wrapped shrimp with gorgonzola cheese served with a white Tuscan bean salad. Desserts are excellent as well—there is tiramisu, triple chocolate cake, and, of course, cannoli. They opened in 2000 and have become a popular neighborhood restaurant with a relaxed yet elegant ambience. Children's menu.

Spanky's (845-485-2294), 85 Main Street, Poughkeepsie. ($$) Open for lunch Monday through Friday 11:30–3; early-bird dinner specials 4–6; dinner served daily from 5 on Saturday, Sunday 4–9. The tasty Cajun cuisine here is a refreshing change from the usual fare (which is also available on the extensive menu). There is jambalaya, gumbo, crawfish, ribs, all the traditional Southern favorites, in addition to burgers, sandwiches, and salads. A casual yet warm atmosphere compliments the spicy menu selections and makes this spot one of the most appealing places to dine in downtown Poughkeepsie. Children are welcome.

Union House (845-896-6129), 1108 Main Street, Fishkill. ($$) Open daily for dinner 5–10. Steak lovers take note: This is a place where you can get prime dry-aged Western steaks, ranging from filet mignon to New York strip. There is T-bone and the house specialty: porterhouse for two ($59). There is also a nice selection of seafood entrées (Chilean sea bass, twin lobster tails, or herb-crusted Atlantic salmon) as well as other tempting dishes like New Zealand rack of lamb and lemon-pepper roasted chicken. The restaurant is named Union House since it was formerly the Union Hotel 150 years ago. Children's welcome; children's menu.

Northeastern Dutchess County (Millerton, Pine Plains, Millbrook, Amenia, Dover Plains)

Allyn's Restaurant & Café (845-677-5888), Route 44, Millbrook. ($$) Open daily except Tuesday for lunch 11:30–4; dinner from 5:30; Sunday brunch 11:30–4. Housed in a 200-year-old converted church, first opened by chef Allan and host Denise Katz in 1986. Meals begin with a variety of breads and a white-bean spread. Regional specialties and Continental favorites are served in two dining rooms—one is elegant, the other more informal. I have often dined at the intimate, cozy bar. The fare and service here is absolutely first-rate—consistently. I love the Maryland lump crabcakes with Dijon béarnaise and black-bean salsa as an appetizer, and the double-cut New Zealand lamb chops are my favorite entrée. The emphasis is on fresh, local items as well as game in-season. The restaurant tends to get crowded on weekends, so be sure to make a reservation.

Les Baux (845-677-8166), 152 Church Street, Millbrook. ($$) Named after Les Baux, a picturesque, medieval village in France, with narrow streets filled with ruins and stone houses, this cozy bistro is run by a Frenchman who worked at a fine restaurant in Les Baux. For lunch or a light dinner, there is a variety of wonderful salads; the onion soup and steamed mussels are superb. For dinner, the French comfort food offered includes grilled sirloin steak, rack of lamb, salmon filet with mustard sauce, filet of sole, and pork tenderloin. The restaurant opened in 2003 and quickly became popular with Millbrook residents.

Old Drovers Inn (845-832-9311), Route 22, Dover Plains. ($$$) Open daily for dinner 5–10. Lunch is served Friday through Sunday noon–3. Long ago this former tavern catered to the drovers who transported cattle to New York City for sale. Today the more than 250-year-old building (it has had only three deed transfers in its history!) is home to an appealing restaurant that serves dishes such as cheddar-cheese soup, breast of pheasant in champagne sauce, and chocolate truffle cake. I love their wonderful key lime pie. Children welcome.

Stissing House Restaurant & Tavern (518-398-8800), Corner of Route 82 & Route 199, Pine Plains. ($$) Open for dinner Friday and Saturday 5–10, Sunday through Thursday 5–9; Saturday lunch and Sunday brunch 11:30–3. Housed in an historic structure that has been a tavern for over 100 years, this establishment offers American regional cuisine in an informal, relaxed atmosphere. There is live music Friday night at 8. Children welcome.

The Links at Union Vale Restaurant (Player's Pub) (845-223-1002), 153 North Parliman Road, Union Vale. ($$) Open daily for breakfast, lunch, and dinner during golf season; the rest of the year open for dinner only, but call ahead for hours. There are two menus here—one features pub fare (hearty burgers, wraps, salads, and sandwiches), and diners sit at tables or the bar overlooking the golf course; in the back room (open after golf season ends) diners will enjoy an elegant, candlelit ambience with Continental cuisine on weekends (Friday, Saturday, and Sunday and brunch) that includes steaks, seafood, and nightly specials. For breakfast here, I love the piping-hot Irish oatmeal served with steamed milk and dried fruit—it's some of the best I've had anywhere. My lunch favorite is the hand-carved roasted turkey on whole-wheat bread with a savory pesto mayonnaise. Children welcome in both venues.

Southeastern Dutchess County (Pawling, Stormville, Wingdale)

Guidetti's (845-832-6721), Pleasant Ridge Road, Wingdale. ($$) Open Thursday through Saturday for dinner 5–10, Sunday 4–8:30. This restaurant serves fine Northern Italian cuisine. If you find yourself in eastern Dutchess County, dinner here is consistently good. Children welcome.

Harrald's (845-878-6595), Route 52, Stormville. ($$$) Open Thursday through Saturday for dinner from 6. Enjoy old-fashioned elegance in a 200-year-old Tudor-style house with candlelight atmosphere and specials like Maryland jumbo lump crabmeat cakes and trout meunière. The six-course dinner is prix fixe for $67.50. Not recommended for children.

McKinney and Doyle Fine Foods Café (845-855-3875), 10 Charles Colman Boulevard, Pawling. ($$) Open for lunch Wednesday through Friday 11:30–3; dinner Wednesday through Saturday 6–9:30, Sunday 5–9; Saturday and Sunday brunch 9–3. This old-fashioned, high-ceilinged storefront café has exposed brick walls, a mix of booths and tables, and lots of local

memorabilia in the decor. The eclectic cuisine includes such unusual treats as grilled shrimp with Thai peanut sauce over angel-hair pasta and breast of duck with peppercorns and applejack-soaked figs. An excellent bakery operates out of the café, so don't skip dessert. Sour cream apple pie and raspberry linzertorte are just a couple of the tempting creations.

EATING OUT

Northwestern Dutchess County

Bread Alone Bakery & Café (845-876-3108), 45 East Market Street, Rhinebeck. ($) Open daily 7–7. The homemade soups, hearty sandwiches, and terrific breads offered here make this informal eatery a renowned stop among locals for breakfast, lunch, or takeout. Children welcome.

Calico Restaurant & Patisserie (845-876-2749), 9 Mill Street, Rhinebeck. ($$) Open for lunch Wednesday through Saturday and Sunday for brunch 11:30–2:30. Dinner served Wednesday through Saturday 6–9. This cozy spot is great for an elegant lunch. I recommend the smoked salmon with capers and the chicken-salad sandwich. The pastries are excellent. Children welcome.

Hyde Park Brewery (845-229-8277), 514 Albany Post Road, Hyde Park. ($) Open daily for lunch Monday through Saturday 11–5, Sunday noon–4; dinner daily 5–10, Sunday from 4. They brew their own beer here (approximately 1,000 barrels per year) and there are six different kinds to choose from, both light and dark varieties. (Notice the huge bags of malt barley stacked by the rest rooms.) The fare includes creative international specials at reasonable prices. Thursday at dinner is Tex-Mex night, and the chef's specials include fajitas, enchiladas, burritos, and quesadillas, with some rather unique touches. My favorite menu item is the portobello club sandwich, which is grilled portobello mushrooms layered with mozzarella, roasted red peppers, spinach, and pesto mayo. A great stop for lunch, conveniently located across the road from the home of FDR. Children welcome.

Luna 61 (845-758-0061), 61 East Market Street, Red Hook. ($) Open Wednesday through Sunday 5–9; until 10 weekends. The organic vegetarian cuisine here includes an eclectic mix of flavors using the freshest ingredients. The salads, chili, and veggie burgers are wonderful. Sandwiches are offered on the dinner menu (a couple of choices are falafel or PLT, a vegetarian rendition of BLT substituting portobello mushrooms for bacon and dressed with wasabi mayonnaise). There is a cafe atmosphere here that makes this a wonderful stop for those seeking healthful, tasty cuisine. Children welcome.

Milagros (845-757-5300), 73 Broadway, Tivoli. ($) Open Monday through Saturday 7 AM–5 PM, Sunday 8:30 AM–4 PM. This eatery, located in a renovated historic landmark church, serves an eclectic mix of healthy, tasty international favorites made from fresh Hudson Valley ingredients. Enjoy tapas, overstuffed sandwiches, and salad plates as well as Indian-, Middle Eastern–, and Asian-inspired dishes. A full deli offers an array of eat-in or takeout items.

Mill House Panda Restaurant (845-876-2399), 21 West Market Street, Rhinebeck. ($$) Open Tuesday through Friday for lunch 11:30–3:30; dinner 3:30–9:30, Saturday 4–10, Sunday 1–9. This Cantonese Chinese restaurant elegantly prepares every dish to order. The Peking duck and walnut shrimp are excellent. I thought the tofu vegetable soup was among the best I've had anywhere. Children welcome.

Pandemain (845-876-2454), 18 Garden Street, Rhinbeck. ($) Open daily 6:30–6:30. *Pandemain* is a medieval term that means "the bread of royalty" or "the best bread," often used for the sacrament in church in the Old World. And the baked goods here, made from scratch on the premises every day, are first-rate. Enjoy both sweets (cookies, brownies, pastries) and savories (breads, scones, focacce), while relaxing at one of the few attractively decorated tables. Soups and sandwiches are also offered using the freshest local ingredients. Opened in 2001, this establishment has a loyal, local following: It's off the main drag and provides a quiet oasis in the village. Full tea service is available any time of day, featuring Northern Port Tea, a single estate, unblended imported tea headquartered in Rhinebeck. Try the Assam—or one of the other excellent choices—which can be purchased by the bag. Children welcome.

Samuel's (845-876-5312), 42 East Market Street, Rhinebeck. ($) Open daily 8–6. This small confectionary and coffee shop is the perfect place to enjoy a cup of high-quality coffee, tea, or hot chocolate after browsing the stores in town. The cookies and biscotti are delicious. Children will be delighted by the attractively displayed penny candy and gourmet jelly beans. There is also a variety of truffles, hand-dipped chocolates, and sugar-free sweets.

Schemmy's Ltd. (845-876-6215), 19 East Market Street, Rhinebeck. ($) Monday and Thursday 9–9, Friday 9 AM–10 PM, Saturday 8 AM–10 PM, Sunday 8–7. Closed Tuesday and Wednesday except during the summer months, when they are open every day. Serving breakfast, lunch, and light dinner, this old-fashioned ice cream parlor with a counter and booths throughout features homemade soups, sandwiches, and salads. There is outdoor dining on the patio in the rear of the restaurant during the warm-weather months. Children welcome.

The White Rabbit Coffee House & Café (845-758-6500), 40 Market Street, Red Hook. ($) Open Monday through Friday 7–7, Saturday and Sunday 7:30–7. The fare here includes sandwiches, soups, wraps, veggie burgers, and lots of vegan options. The Hudson Valley coffee company coffee is served here, and there is a list of over 50 different caffeinated and decaf teas. The baked goods (muffins, scones, and vegan desserts) are baked on the premises, and some of the other pastries are obtained locally. A gathering place for Bard students, with an atmosphere reminiscent of a 1960s coffeehouse. Children welcome.

Southwestern Dutchess County
Amore Pizzeria & Café (845-635-5555), 18 West Road, Pleasant Valley; located in the Saw Mill Plaza. ($) Open daily 11:30 AM–9:30 PM. This is a great choice for all the Italian favorites in addition to pizza. A particularly good stop if you are traveling with children.

Apple Pie Bakery Café at the Culinary Institute (845-905-4501), Culinary Institute, Route 9, Hyde Park. Open Monday through Friday 8–6:30. Enjoy fine, fresh soups, salads, sandwiches, and pizzas at exceedingly reasonable prices in this eatery where students in baking and pastry arts programs run the show. It's a wonderful stop for breakfast, lunch, or a light dinner as well as takeout. Children welcome.

Busy Bee (845-452-6800), 138 South Avenue, Poughkeepsie. ($$) Open for lunch Monday through Friday 11–3; dinner served Wednesday through Saturday 5:30–9. This small gourmet eatery offers elegance in an informal café atmosphere. The first time I had lunch here, I enjoyed sesame-crusted Asian grilled tuna salad with cellophane noodles and wasabi cream. My companion loved the grilled hamburger with portobello mushroom steak fries and garlic aioli. The eclectic menu offers a similar range of imaginative dinner choices. Make sure you experience dessert; the warm chocolate timbale with fresh strawberries and whipped cream and New York cheesecake with passion fruit sauce were wonderful.

Café Maya and the Beacon Tavern (845-838-9000), Main Street, Beacon. Open daily except Tuesday for dinner from 5. This lovely restaurant once located only in Cold Spring (see *Eating Out* in "Putnam"), has another location in Dutchess County as of 2003. Their nachos Maya—tortilla chips topped with refried beans, melted cheese, jalapenos, guacamole, and sour cream—and black-bean soup topped with red onion and shredded cheese are both hearty and quite good. I enjoyed the fajita Maya, which arrives at the table on a sizzling skillet and combines sliced chicken, steak, and shrimp with onions and peppers in a tasty marinade with all the fixings. The Beacon Tavern, adjacent to the café, with old-world ambience, has been operating for over a century, and it's housed in a building that dates back to 1871. Children welcome.

Caffè Aurora (845-454-1900), 145 Mill Street, Poughkeepsie. ($) Open daily 10–9; closed at 5 on Monday. This café offers the ambience of Little Italy—located in the quaint, quiet Mount Carmel area of downtown Poughkeepsie. Enjoy cannoli, eclairs, butter cookies, and probably the best cappuccino and espresso in the county. In the warm weather, have dessert at the outdoor tables, and listen to the regulars speaking animatedly in Italian. Live music on weekends. This neighborhood café is one of the best things about Poughkeepsie! Children welcome.

Chthonic (pronounced "Thonic") Clash Coffeehouse (845-831-0359), 418 Main Street, Beacon. ($) Open daily 8 AM–midnight. Enjoy coffee, tea, baked goods, live music, games, and art at this eclectic gathering place in the heart of Beacon, run by an art dealer from Manhattan. The name means "of the earth," and in addition to changing art exhibits, there are poetry readings, live music, and chess tournaments in this cozy living room–like space. This is a place where local creative people can get together to exchange ideas—and visitors will feel at home. Children welcome.

Cup and Saucer Tea Room (845-831-6288), 165 Main Streeet, Beacon. ($) Open Tuesday through Sunday for breakfast, lunch, and brunch during the summer months (July and August) only. Call for hours. Do make a reservation for High Tea, which is served

on two Sundays each month. This Victorian tearoom, decorated with tea-time accessories throughout, serves up hot grilled sandwiches, veggie and grilled chicken salads, quiche, soups, and desserts. Specialties of the house include the portobello club and tuna nicoise.

DD's Pizza (845-452-1754), 300 Hooker Avenue, Poughkeepsie. ($) Open daily 11–10. For some of the freshest pizza you can find in the county, head to Dominick's place. He and his brothers are always behind the counter in the open kitchen, preparing your pizza before your eyes—and their mother is always in the back, helping out. I enjoy the salads here (always made to your order, never in advance). It's truly a family business, and the decor hasn't changed since they opened 30 years ago. Children welcome.

Demitasse Cafe (845-485-8707), 202 Main Street, Poughkeepsie. ($) Open Monday through Friday 6 AM–11 PM; Saturday 7 AM–11 PM; Sunday 7 AM –8 PM. This Italian-style coffee shop is ideal for art and history fanatics. Visitors can take in the landscapes painted on the walls while savoring paninis, crepes, and pastries—among other delicacies. The sweet and savory dishes are complemented by an immense menu of tea and coffee concoctions such as Snickers mocha espresso and chocolate peanut butter crunch coffee. Take your time trying everything in the plush café surroundings, as the owner says, it is the type of place to get away from life's problems; they aren't about to rush anyone out.

Gino's Restaurant (845-297-8061), Route 9, Wappingers Falls; in Lafayette Plaza, 1.6 miles south of the Galleria. ($) Open daily noon–10.

Enjoy Italian-style home cooking in this family-owned and operated casual dining spot. They offer a range of pizzas, pasta dishes, heros, and sandwiches in addition to Italian favorites like lasagna, veal parmigiana, calamari, and many more. Children welcome.

Julie's Restaurant (845-452-6078), 49 Raymond Avenue, Poughkeepsie. ($) Open Monday through Thursday 7 AM–8 PM; Friday and Saturday until 3; Sunday 8–2. Julie and her husband serve up wonderful breakfast wraps (try the Vassar or Greek wraps, my favorites) along with pancakes, omelettes, and great oatmeal. Lunches include burgers, salads, sandwiches, and soups accompanied by homemade macaroni salad or coleslaw. This is a popular local spot with a loyal following. Children welcome.

LuLu's Café (845-486-9851), 380A Main Street, Poughkeepsie. ($) Open for breakfast, lunch and dinner daily 7 AM–9 PM, Sunday they close at 6. In this dinerlike setting enjoy tasty, inexpensive Mexican specialties prepared by a chef who ran restaurants in Mexico before emigrating to Dutchess County in 1991. Try the mole poblano or steak tacos, which are served in soft, flat shells topped with lots of tender strips of grilled steak. There are also burgers, salads, and sandwiches here. Cash only. Children welcome.

Longobardi's Restaurant & Pizzeria (845-297-1498), Route 9, Wappingers Falls; in Imperial Plaza. ($) Open daily 11:30–9:30. This informal eatery is a perfect stop for lunch or dinner when shopping on Route 9. One of my favorite dishes here is the grilled chicken salad; I also like their

pasta e fagiole soup. They offer the full range of Italian favorites, including pizza, pasta, and calzone as well as seafood, veal, and eggplant dishes. Everything is prepared to order. Children's menu.

96 Main (845-454-5200), 96 Main Street, Poughkeepsie. ($$) Open Monday through Thursday 11 AM–2 AM, Friday and Saturday until 4 AM, Sunday 5–11 PM. Formerly a college hangout known as The Derby, this restaurant has been transformed into an upscale eatery and tavern by two Culinary Institute graduates. The lovely brick-walled dining room with mahogany bar is elegant yet casual, and the black-and-white photos of Poughkeepsie dating back to the 19th century add a nice touch to the decor. The Mediterranean cuisine with an Italian accent includes steaks, chicken, seafood, wood-fired oven pizzas, and veal, with side dishes like wild mushroom risotto and vermicelli noodles. There are at least a half-dozen beers on tap and several more by the bottle. There is live music on Friday and Saturday night and a late-night bar menu.

Palace Diner (845-473-1576), 294 Washington Street, Poughkeepsie. ($) This well-established gathering place near Marist College, just off Route 9, has been a mainstay of the community. It's popular for lunch among local attorneys and politicians. In addition to the usual diner fare, there are Greek and international dishes as well as an array of daily specials. The portions are generous and the desserts are quite good. Children welcome.

Saigon Café (845-473-1392), 6A LaGrange Avenue, off Raymond Avenue near Vassar College, Poughkeepsie. ($) Open Monday through Saturday lunch 11:30–3; dinner 5–9:30, Sunday 5–9. This is a casual dining spot that has Vietnamese cuisine, and it's quite good. Try the imperial rolls with shrimp, fresh mint, and cilantro. There is an excellent selection of chicken, beef, seafood, and vegetarian dishes. For those who have never dined on Vietnamese cuisine, this is a good place to try it.

Tiramisu (845-227-8707 or 4877), 810 Route 82, Hopewell Junction. ($) Open daily 8 AM–10 PM; dinner begins at 4. This family-oriented eatery features brick oven–baked pizzas of all kinds, terrific pasta dishes, and the excellent chicken Tiramisu ($12.95), which includes chicken breast, roasted red peppers, onions, artichokes accompanied by pasta in a light marinara sauce. Relaxed, informal atmosphere. Children are welcome and the reasonable prices are hard to beat.

Vassarview Café (845-473-6000), 5 Collegeview Avenue, Poughkeepsie. ($) Open Monday through Saturday 11–4. This sunny, pleasant café offers excellent fare at reasonable prices. Soups are prepared fresh daily. The turkey club sandwich (they roast their own turkey here) is enormous and one of the best I've had anywhere; the chicken salad is excellent, as well, and is served in a sandwich or on top of the garden salad. There are wraps, burgers, hot sandwiches, and Greek specialties like spinach pie, souvlaki, pastitio, and moussaka. The chef-owner, Spyros, is always on the premises making sure patrons are satisfied. Children welcome.

Northeastern Dutchess County
Cascade Mountain Winery Restaurant (845-373-9021), Flint Road, Amenia. ($$) Open April

through mid-November, Thursday through Monday for lunch 11:30–3:30; Saturday dinner 5:30–9. It's a beautiful drive to this winery in the countryside, and those who have lunch here will enjoy the first-rate regional bistro cuisine using the freshest local fruits, vegetables, cheeses, and products like heirloom duck, chicken, and quail. Everything is complimented, of course, by the winery's various offerings. Try the smoked-pheasant sausage wrap or fresh mozzarella with heirloom tomato and fresh basil sandwich for lunch. There is patio dining in nice weather.

Crumpets (518-398-1600), Route 199, Pine Plains. ($) Open daily except Tuesday 7–3. Breakfast is served all day here. There are homemade soups, hearty sandwiches, and pies baked on the premises. Enjoy patio dining in the warm weather. Children welcome.

Desserticus Café (845-858-1400), 5979 Route 82, Stanfordville. ($) Open Monday through Friday 8–3:30, Saturday 8 AM–9:30 PM; Sunday 8–6:30. Although you might imagine only desserts being served at this eatery, they have terrific lunches, as well. The owner was trained at the Culinary Institute. Offerings include mouthwatering brownies, pastries, pies, and cookies. Chocoholics will be delighted with the range of choices. Children will love it.

Happy Days Café (845-677-6244), Washington Hollow Plaza at the junction of Routes 82 and 44, Millbrook. ($) Open daily for breakfast, lunch, and dinner. This is a fun place to take the kids. The decor is vintage 1950s, and the food is American favorites: burgers, wraps, steak, and seafood.

Jeanie Bean & Company (845-266-3800), 2411 Salt Point Turnpike (take Salt Point exit off Taconic Parkway, and travel 0.5 mile east), Clinton Corners. ($) Saturday and Sunday 10–4. Where would the British Empire be without fish-and-chips? The codfish is dipped in batter, deep fried until golden brown, and served with chips as well as Jean's coleslaw. The best way to enjoy it is with a sprinkle of Sarson's vinegar over this English soul food. This is just one example of Jean Bean's British-style lunch offerings (there is also shepherds pie, bangers and mash, ploughman's lunch, and Scottish belted Galloway cheeseburger in a pita pocket with HP sauce, tomato, and Spanish onion). Having lunch here in Clinton Corners brings back memories of the British countryside. For dessert there are scones, English trifle, London Fog, and coconut bread pudding, accompanied by Jeanie's Best breakfast tea served piping hot in a Brown Betty teapot (they don't serve coffee!).

Lia's Mountain View (518-398-7311), Route 82, Pine Plains. ($) Open daily except Monday for lunch and dinner 11:30–10, Sunday 4–9. Italian home cooking combined with a lovely view of the mountains. Try spiedini, white pizza, calzone, and the excellent desserts. Tuesday is prime rib night (starting at $11.95), Wednesday is pasta night, and Thursday there are complete dinner specials for $11.95. Children welcome.

Mabbettsville Market (845-677-5284), 3809 Route 44, Millbrook. ($$) Open Tuesday through Saturday 7–6, Sunday 8–4. This gourmet market with a small outdoor patio and dining area is filled with tempting dishes that include fresh soups, quiches, and salads (dilled tuna, sesame noodle, and lemon-basil chicken are just a few). The sandwich choices include smoked turkey and cucumber with herbed mayo, grilled vegetables, goat cheese and olivada, and rare roast beef with horseradish sauce. From the wood-burning grill, there are free-range rotisserie chickens, pork or chicken satay, and shrimp and scallop kebobs. The phenomenal baked goods include fallen-chocolate soufflé, fresh-fruit tarts, and assorted cheesecakes, all baked on the premises. The place is somewhat pricey but well worth it. The weekend residents of Millbrook love it—and there is a growing local following.

Spumoni Gardens (845-398-1961), Church Street (Route 199), Pine Plains. ($) Open April through October, Monday through Saturday noon–11, Sunday 2–22. The owner says visitors to his establishment will enjoy a touch of Europe in Pine Plains. He offers pleasant outdoor dining in an interestingly designed *biergarten* during the warm-weather months. There is also live entertainment; call in advance for a schedule. The international fare includes pizza, pasta, bratwurst, salads, and burgers.

The Tin Horn Tavern (845-677-5600), Franklin Avenue, Millbrook. ($$) Open Thursday, Friday, and Monday for lunch noon–4:30, Saturday and Sunday 11–4:30; dinner served 5–10. The American cuisine here features local produce in season with an emphasis on organic items. There is always a soup and fish of the day. Menu choices include free-range chicken, fresh fish, and 21-day aged Black Angus rib-eye steak, which is wonderful. All the mouth-watering desserts are made on the premises.

Outdoor dining and bar from Memorial Day weekend through October. Monthly wine dinners showcase different nations of the world. Children welcome.

Southeastern Dutchess County

Beekman Square Restaurant (845-223-3401), 2515 Route 55, Poughquag 12570. ($) Open daily for breakfast, lunch, and dinner 6 AM– 10 PM and 11 on Friday and Saturday nights. International cuisine. Early in the day enjoy three-egg omelettes, chocolate-chip or banana-walnut pancakes, cinnamon-raisin French toast, or Belgian waffles at this neighborhood restaurant. Their French onion soup, grilled chicken Caesar salad, terrific quesadillas, focacce sandwiches (they make their own breads here), or Beekman Square burger (with bacon, onions, mushrooms, and cheese), are my favorites for lunch. Bourbon Street ribs marinated in homemade light barbecue sauce as well as steaks, broiled fish, and pasta are all reasonably priced. Children welcome; there is a children's menu.

✳ Entertainment

Dutchess County offers an enormous amount of theater, dance, and stand-up comedy, and the choices keep growing. So after you have enjoyed an excellent repast at one of the region's fine restaurants, enjoy some first-rate entertainment.

THEATER & DANCE Bardavon 1869 Opera House (845-473-2072), 35 Market Street. Poughkeepsie. Open year-round. First named the Collingwood Opera House, this elegant concert hall was constructed in 1869 and is the oldest continually

operating theater in New York state. The dramatic dome ceiling has sheltered everything from movies and rock concerts to ballet and dramatic theater. Mark Twain, Frank Sinatra, Sarah Bernhardt, John Phillip Sousa, and Al Pacino are among the entertainers to have performed on the 816-square-foot stage. After being added to the National Register of Historic Places in 1978, the Bardavon has undergone over $3 million worth of renovations. It is the perfect place to enjoy a symphony, drama, musical, old-time movie, contemporary musician, or comedian. When you are visiting Dutchess County, it's worth calling to see what's being showcased.

Center for Performing Arts at Rhinebeck (845-876-3080) Route 308, Rhinebeck. Open year-round. Call for a performance schedule. This multipurpose cultural and education center features dramatic plays, musicals, dance, concerts, lectures, staged readings, and workshops. There are children's shows, as well.

County Players Falls Theatre (845-298-1491), 2681 West Main Street, Wappingers Falls. Four or five productions are offered annually by this community-theater group. The work usually consists of traditional Broadway fare. The theater is large, the seats are comfortable, and the production I attended was light entertainment well done.

Fisher Center for Performing Arts at Bard College (845-758-7900), County Route 103, Annandale-on-Hudson. Internationally distinguished performing arts center, designed by renowned architect Frank Gehry, has two theaters offering music, opera, drama, and dance performances (see *To See*).

Kaatsban International Dance Center (845-757-5106), 120 Broadway, Tivoli. Open year-round. This performance center for all types of dance as well as a working retreat center is dedicated to the growth, advancement, and preservation of professional dance. Located in a renovated space on a spectacularly scenic 153-acre setting (a former horse farm) overlooking the Hudson River and Catskill Mountains, Kaatsban — Dutch for "playing field"—presents an array of multiethnic dance companies. The former Callendar House farm, developed by the Livingston family in the 18th century and turned into a horse farm by the Osborne family, is now home to three dance studios, one of which serves as a 160-seat public theater. The historic barns and cottage were designed at the turn of the 20th century in the shingled Arts and Crafts style. There are open rehearsals here in addition to workshops, world premieres, and performances. Call for a schedule.

Powerhouse Theater (845-437-7235), Summer Theater at Vassar College, 124 Raymond Avenue, Poughkeepsie. June, July and August only, Tuesday through Saturday 8 PM, Saturday and Sunday 2 and 8. Admission fee. For the past 20 summers, New York Stage and Film, in conjunction with Vassar, presents new plays premiered in a professional-theater venue. The name is derived from the actual powerhouse on the Vassar campus, built in 1912 to accommodate the college's changeover from gas to electric power. In 1973 the original structure was reinvented as a black-box theater and renamed the Hallie Flanagan Davis Powerhouse Theater, in memory of the legendary dramatist who created the Experimental Theater at

POWERHOUSE THEATER, VASSAR COLLEGE

Dixie Sheridan

Vassar College. Past productions have been of excellent quality and have featured the likes of Juliana Margulies, Kyra Sedgwick, David Strathairn, Jill Clayburgh, and John Heard, to name just some of the actors who have been a part of this dynamic venue. The Powerhouse Theater also offers free outdoor Shakespeare. Don't miss seeing a production here if you are in the Dutchess County area during the summer months. Call for a schedule.

MISCELLANEOUS VENUES **Bananas Comedy Club** (845-462-3333), Best Western Inn, 2170 Route 9, Pough-keepsie. Shows are Friday 9:30 PM, Saturday 8 and 10:30 PM. See live stand-up comedy with performers from television, films, Las Vegas, and Atlantic City in this hotel nightclub that draws a good-sized local following.

The Chance (845-471-1966), 6 Cran-nell Street, Poughkeepsie. This down-town nightclub showcases national musical acts including rock and roll, country, R&B, and blues. There is usually entertainment on weekend evenings, but call in advance for the schedule. Show times vary.

Rhinebeck Chamber Music Soci-ety (845-876-2870), 6436 Mont-gomery Street, Rhinebeck. Concerts are held at the Church of the Messiah in town every month from September through April. Call for dates and times. String quartets and chamber ensembles are featured.

Towne Crier Café (845-855-1300), 130 Route 22, Pawling. Open Wednes-day through Sunday evenings, this club presents live folk, jazz, blues, and zydeco artists with an array of per-formers, theater, vaudeville and chil-dren's concerts. Call for a schedule.

Upstate Films (845-876-2515, 866-FILM-NUT), 6415 Montgomery Street (Route 9), Rhinebeck. Open year-round. There are two to three films daily in the two theaters here (matinees on holidays, weekends, and some Fridays), and you won't find the usual mall offerings. Provocative international cinema is featured, including foreign, independent, documentary, and animated films. Guest speakers appear regularly—filmmakers, scholars, and critics—often to discuss their work after it is screened. This is a local treasure, especially in these days of mostly meaningless commercial movies. Upstate has a large local following, so get there early since the theaters are rather small. Go to www.upstate-films.org for schedules.

✳ Selective Shopping

ART & CRAFT CENTERS/GALLERIES
Barrett Art Center (845-471-2550), 55 Noxon Street, Poughkeepsie, exhibits distinguished Hudson River School and other American artists.

Collaborative Concepts Gallery (845-838-1516), 348 Main Street, Beacon, focuses on contemporary art and exhibitions, including works by nationally known artists. They have two arts in residence studios here as well as a slide-file registry.

Cunneen Hackett Cultural Center (845-471-1221), 12 Vassar Street, Poughkeepsie, has theater, dance, and art shows on its annual schedule. The center is housed in two restored Vic-torian buildings, and regional art and artists are usually featured.

Gilmor Glassworks (518-789-6700), 2 Main Street, Millerton, is open daily 10–5. Their hand-blown glass has been made at this working studio since 1977. Enjoy watching the bowls, ornaments, vases, and special pieces being created before your eyes. Call ahead for the glass-blowing schedule.

Howland Cultural Center (845-831-4988), 477 Main Street, Beacon, sponsors exhibits, concerts, and workshops year-round in a 130-year-old building designed by famed architect Richard Morris Hunt. Call for a schedule.

Hudson Beach Glass (845-831-3116), 162 Main Street, Beacon. Open Tuesday through Sunday 10–5. There are four artists whose hand-cast glass, using an ancient process, is exhibited here. Both sculptural and functional objects are on display and for sale.

Arnold Larson, Inc. (845-724-5502), 2575 Route 55, Poughquag, is open Monday through Friday 9–5, Saturday 10–4. Glass blowing is done on the premises by masters of this craft. The glass factory and gift shop sell a variety of items.

Mill Street Loft (845-471-7477), 455 Maple Street, Poughkeepsie, is a multicultural arts-educational center that sponsors shows, workshops, and a unique art camp for kids.

Phoenix Pottery (845-855-5658), 34 Coulter Avenue, Pawling, is open by appointment only. Wheel-thrown stoneware for the kitchen and a choice of everything from lamps to mugs in an array of glazes. Classes offered for both adults and children.

Albert Shahinian Fine Art (845-454-0522), 198 Main Street, Poughkeepsie. Open Thursday through Saturday 1–6, Sunday 1–5, or by appointment. Contemporary regional, West Coast, and Hudson River art, with exhibits changing monthly.

Webatuck Craft Village (845-832-6522), Route 55 and Dogtail Corner Road, Wingdale. Open year-round, but hours vary with the season, so call ahead. Many crafters closed on Monday and Tuesday. Free, although admission is charged for special festivals. Webatuck was once a village of artists' studios and workshops along the Ten Mile River. Today visitors can stop in at a variety of shops that sell glass, pottery, furniture, and more. Special events include a river festival in May and a harvest festival in October, offering color and action on the site itself.

AUCTIONS AND ANTIQUES Lovers of antiques and collectibles will have a field day in Dutchess County, where it seems that every village and hamlet boasts a selection of fine antiques shops. Clocks, vintage clothing, fine china, Hudson River School paintings, and rare jewels are all waiting for a home, and it's easy to spend an afternoon looking for that one-of-a kind treasure. The search is made even easier at antiques centers that offer a cluster of dealers under one roof and regular hours year-round.

The **Annex Antiques and Accessories** (845-758-2843), 23 East Market Street, Red Hook, is filled with Victorian and country furniture, jewelry, collectibles, and Americana. Call **George Cole Auctions, Inc.** (845-758-9114), 7578 North Broadway, also in Red Hook, for a schedule of auctions.

Beekman Arms Antique Market & Gallery (845-876-3477), Route 9, is located behind the Beekman Arms Hotel (see *Lodging*); open daily 11–5. **Hammertown Barn** (845-876-1450), Route 9, Rhinebeck and 3201 Route

199, Pine Plains (518-398-7075) has country wares, folk art, and primitives. Farther south at the **Hyde Park Antiques Center** (845-229-8200), 4192 Route 9, Hyde Park, there are more than 50 dealers and a large range of specialty collectibles and antiques. They are open daily 10–5. The **Village Antique Center at Hyde Park** (845-229-6600), 4321 Albany Post Road (Route 9), features about 20 dealers, and they stock lots of pine and oak furniture, silver, glassware, books, and more.

Going east in the county, the **Ole Carousel Antique Center** (845-868-1586), 6208 Route 82, Stanfordville, offers a large collection of books, records, and miniatures. In Millbrook there are three centers: the **Millbrook Antiques Mall** (845-677-9311) at 8801 Franklin Avenue, has many dealers of 18th-century furniture; the **Village Antiques Center** (845-677-5160), 3278 Franklin Avenue, has dozens of quality dealers with merchandise in categories as diverse as decorative items and sporting collectibles; the **Millbrook Antiques Center** (845-677-3921), 3283 Franklin Avenue, has nearly 50 different "mini shops." These shops are all open Monday through Saturday 11–5, noon–5 on Sunday.

✳ Special Events

Last Sunday in April, Memorial Day weekend, July 4th weekend, first weekend in August, Labor Day weekend, Columbus Day weekend, and first Sunday in November: **Stormville Airport Antique Show & Flea Market** (845-221-6561), Route 216, Stormville, features more than 600 vendors with antiques, collectibles, arts and crafts, and apparel—new merchandise as well as old treasures to be found here. Free. This event is held rain or shine from dawn to dusk.

May: **Revolutionary War Living History Weekend** (845-831-8172), Mount Gulian Historic Site, off Route 9D just north of I-84, Beacon. Admission fee. Open 10–5. See the 10th British and Continental Armies' encampment. There is a battle re-enactment at 2 PM both Saturday and Sunday, with cannons, crafts, music, military drills and food. **Antique Car Show and Swap Meet** (845-876-3554), Dutchess County Fairgrounds, Route 9, Rhinebeck. Admission fee. This is one of the largest weekend car shows in the Northeast, including hot rods and custom vehicles on Saturday and pre-1977 unmodified antique/classic cars on Sunday. There is a car corral and swap meet, handcrafts building, and food court. The **Hudson River Striped Bass Derby** (845-297-9308) takes place on the river between the George Washington Bridge and the Troy Dam and is open to anyone over the age of 12. You may fish from shore or from a boat. Begins at midnight on Friday and Saturday. There is a weigh-in on Saturday from 10–7 and Sunday 10–5 at several stations. Admission fee to compete. Prizes are given. **Springtime Cajun Zydeco Dance Festival** (845-724-5270), Clinton Corners Recreation Park, Clinton Hollow Road (County Route 18), Clinton Corners. Admission fee. This celebration of Cajun-Creole culture includes dancing, fine fare, music workshops, Louisiana cooking demos, children's games, and an array of vendors. An unusual festival in the region! **Rhinebeck Antiques Show** (845-876-4001), Dutchess County Fairgrounds, Route

9, Rhinebeck. Admission. Saturday 10–5, Sunday 11–4. There are nearly 200 exhibitors, with an emphasis on furniture, folk art, decorative accessories, vintage jewelry, clothing, and clocks. Wide range of prices. **Mid-Hudson Balloon Festival** (845-454-1700), Waryas Park and other sites, Main Street, Poughkeepsie. Free, but there is a fee for rides. Hot-air balloon flights are given morning (6 AM) and evening (6 PM), weather permitting. This is nice family entertainment, with rides for the kids and a variety of vendors. **Spanky's Crawfish Festival** (845-485-2294), Spanky's Restaurant, 85 Main Street, Poughkeepsie. Live crawfish are flown in from New Orleans for crawfish boils and other dishes. There's live music and a festive atmosphere at both lunch and dinner. **Music in the Parks** (845-229-8086), at both Vanderbilt National Historic Site in Hyde Park and Staatsburgh State Historic Site in Staatsburg. From Memorial Day weekend through August, there is a series of free outdoor concerts. This is the time to get the blankets and lawn chairs, pack a picnic, and enjoy the evening overlooking the Hudson River with the sounds of the area's fine bands. Call for a schedule.

June: **St. Anthony Street Festival** (845-454-0340), 11 Mount Carmel Place, Poughkeepsie. Our Lady of Mount Carmel parish kicks off the summer season with this festival of plentiful Italian food, live music, children's activities, and games of chance. Free. Thursday through Sunday evenings 5–8. **Hudson Valley Wine and Food Festival** (845-758-5461), Montgomery Place, River Road, Annandale-on-Hudson. Admission. Saturday and Sunday 11–6. There is

lots of fine food and wine tastings, gourmet delicacies, farmers market, cooking demos, and workshops, along with live music at this annual celebration of the bounty of the region. **Father's Day Ice Cream Social** (845-229-6432), Italian Gardens at Vanderbilt Mansion, Hyde Park. Free. 1–4. Enjoy ice cream with an array of toppings and refreshments. Dads get a free scoop of ice cream. Children's activities and games. **Scarborough Faire Herb & Garden Festival** (845-889-8851), Staatsburgh State Historic Site (Mills Mansion), Old Post Road off Route 9, Staatsburg. Admission fee. Children under 12 are admitted free with a paying adult. Open 11–5. There are herb and garden lectures, entertainment, children's activities, and culinary demonstrations as well as gourmet food items. **Locust Grove Lawn Concert Series** (845-454-4500), Samuel Morse Historic Site, 2683 Route 9, Poughkeepsie. Free. Begins at 2 PM, rain or shine. These concerts on Sunday afternoons from late June through late July feature wonderful local groups. Do call for a schedule.

July: **Bard Summerscape** (845-758-7900), Bard College, Annandale-on-Hudson. This performing-arts festival includes music, dance, opera, and film. It runs from late July through mid-August, so call for a schedule of events.

Latin American Festival (845-463-0409), Riverfront Park, Beacon. Free. Open noon–8:30. There is entertainment, food, arts and crafts, and children's activities. Parking at the Metro North train station.

August: **Vintage Motorcycle & Tractor Day** (845-752-3200), Old

Rhinebeck Aerodrome Museum, 44 Stone Church Road, Rhinebeck. Admission. Open 10–5. Visiting vintage motorcycles and tractors are in the courtyard, in addition to regular air shows at 2 PM. **Hudson Valley Antique Bottle Show** (845-677-3638), Millbrook Firehouse, Millbrook. Admission. Open 9–3. Bottle dealers from throughout the Northeast display and sell a wide variety of antique, collectible, rare, and unusual bottles and Depression glass. **Dutchess County Fair** (845-876-4001), County Fairgrounds, Route 9, Rhinebeck. Held Tuesday through Sunday, toward the end of the month, open daily from 10–midnight. Admission fee. For the biggest—and some say the best—county fair in the Hudson Valley, a stop at this event is in order. The fairgrounds include large display buildings, show arenas, a racetrack, food stands, and more. Plenty of livestock is displayed, and name entertainment is offered. The colorful, noisy midway attracts all ages, and the rides will please the adventurous and the not-so-adventurous alike.

September: **Hudson River Valley Ramble** (800-453-6665). Over 100 guided walking, hiking, kayaking, biking and equestrian events are held in 10 counties during the 3rd weekend in September. There are 20 sites in Dutchess County, with planned activities including Stony Kill, Harlem Valley Rail Trail, the Poets' Walk, Tivoli Bays, Pawling Trail, Appalachian Trail, and Stissing Mountain. Call for a schedule of events and locations. **Celtic Day at Mills Mansion** (845-889-8851), Old Post Road, off Route 9, Staatsburg. Admission. Open 11–5. This Celtic celebration on the Hudson includes pipe bands, Celtic music,

dance workshops, sheepdog herding, clan tent displays, and food.

October: **Crafts at Rhinebeck** (845-876-4001), Dutchess County Fairgrounds, Route 9, Rhinebeck. Admission fee. Open Saturday 10–6, Sunday 10–5. This juried crafts show has more than 350 artists who work in glass, wood, leather, ceramics, metal sculpture, and jewelry. There is a specialty food section, wine tasting, music, hayrides, and children's activities. **Harvest Festival at Webatuck Craft Village** (845-832-6522), Route 55, Wingdale. Free. Open 10–5. Enjoy crafts and food, entertainment, harvest produce, games, and music along the Ten Mile River. **Harvest Fair** (845-758-5461), Montgomery Place, River Road, Annandale-on-Hudson. Admission fee. Open Saturday and Sunday 10–5. Seasonal entertainment, crafts, farm market, hay rides, cider pressing, and games. **Rhinebeck Antiques Fair** (845-876-4001), Dutchess County Fairgrounds, Route 9, Rhinebeck. Admission fee. Open Saturday 10–5, Sunday 11–4. See nearly 200 exhibitors of furniture (both formal and country), folk art, jewelry, and quilts at this annual gathering. **Dutchess County Country Tour** (845-677-3002), at various sites throughout the county. Admission fee. Open 9:30–4. Celebrate rural tradition with this annual day of farm-and hunt-country tours. It is best to purchase tickets to this event in advance, so call early for information. Sites change each year. **Fall Foliage Bike Ride** (845-897-5199), Freedom Park, Skidmore Road, LaGrange. Entry fee. 8 AM–1 PM. There are both 10- and 30-mile courses through winding countryside. This is a benefit to raise money for children with cancer. **NYS**

Sheep & Wool Festival (845-876-4001), Dutchess County Fairgrounds, Route 9, Rhinebeck. Admission fee. Open Saturday 10–5, Sunday until 4. See 175 vendors, including wool artists, culinary displays, spinning and weaving demonstrations, sheep and alpaca sales. **Gem & Mineral Show** (845-471-1224), Mid-Hudson Civic Center, 14 Civic Center Plaza, Poughkeepsie. Admission. Open Saturday and Sunday 11–5. There are usually around 30 dealers at this annual show, which features gemstones, minerals, fossils, fluorescent minerals, and jewelry. There are museum-quality specimens from New York State Academy of Mineralogy. **Gathering of Old Cars** (845-889-8851), Staatsburgh State Historic Site, Old Post Road off Route 9, Staatsburg. Admission. Open 11–4. This get-together for antique autos at Mills Mansion, sponsored by the Red Hook Car Club, is a wonderful way to visit this site and enjoy its marvelous location on the Hudson River. **Beacon Sloop Club's Pumpkin Festival** (845-831-6962), Metro North train station, Beacon. Free. Open noon–6. Enjoy music, environmental displays, food, and pumpkins at this riverfront festival.

November: **Taste of the Hudson Valley** (845-431-8707), Culinary Institute of America, Route 9, Hyde Park. Free. Open 1–4. There are cooking demonstrations, seminars, wine and food tastings, book signings, and auctions. **Railroad Exposition** (845-297-0901), Mid-Hudson Civic Center, 14 Civic Center Plaza, Poughkeepsie. Admission fee. Open 10–3. This annual event, held the second Sunday in November, offers operating railroad layouts, dealer tables, modeling demonstrations, and exhibits.

December: **Historic Hyde Park Christmas Celebration** (845-229-9115), Vanderbilt Mansion, FDR Home, Val-kill. Free. Friday and Saturday of the first weekend in December 6–9 PM. There are an array of activities, music, refreshments, and beautiful holiday decorations to delight visitors at the open-house festivities that continue throughout the month. Call for a schedule. Also, a number of tree lightings, parades, and open houses take place at the historic sites and great estates throughout the county during the month of December. Call Dutchess County Tourism Promotion for a list of these events if you are visiting at the holiday season.

Putnam County

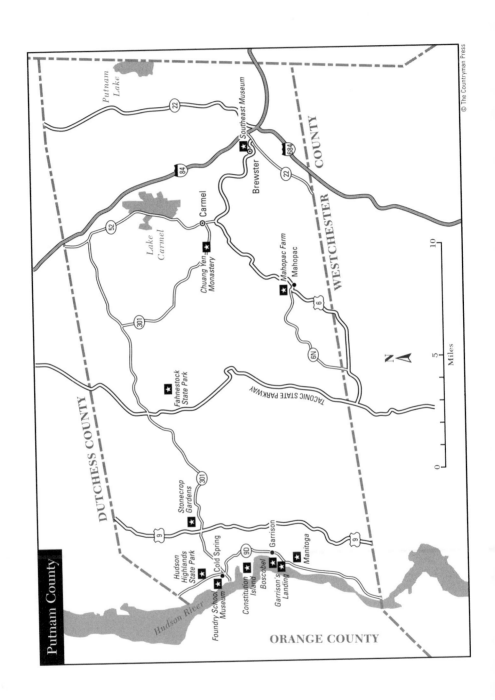

Putnam County

DUTCHESS COUNTY

WESTCHESTER COUNTY

ORANGE COUNTY

Hudson River

Putnam Lake

Lake Carmel

Carmel

Brewster

Southeast Museum

Chuang Yen Monastery

Mahopac Farm

Mahopac

Fahnestock State Park

Stonecrop Gardens

Hudson Highlands State Park

Cold Spring

Foundry School Museum

Constitution Island

Boscobel

Garrison's Landing

Garrison

Manitoga

TACONIC STATE PARKWAY

N

Miles

0   5   10

© The Countryman Press

PUTNAM COUNTY

One of the gateways to the Hudson Highlands, Putnam County offers splendid river views, lots of outdoor entertainment, and a chance to see small-town America before it disappears. In Cold Spring the tiny shops and riverside gazebo are charming reminders of a more leisurely past. Up north, the Federal mansion called Boscobel (which came within hours of being demolished) has been restored to its former elegance. A spring walk through the gardens there offers thousands of flowers in full color, blooming with scent. There are also acres of wetlands, lakes, forests, and meadows in Putnam, beckoning the hiker, walker, and nature lover. A very different outdoor environment was created at Manitoga, where industrial designer Russel Wright constructed Dragon House, a unique home built into the wall of a quarry. In Putnam you can drive along rustic roads, smell apple blossoms, see houses that date back to before the Revolution, stop at an art gallery, or just laze away an afternoon watching the Hudson. Route 9D from the Bear Mountain Bridge goes past many historic areas. Route 9 is the old Albany Post Road and has been in constant use for more than two centuries. Just an hour from Manhattan, Putnam County can seem a century away, with a pace and a grace all of its own.

GUIDANCE **Putnam County Visitors Bureau** (845-225-0381, 800-470-4854), 110 Old Route 6, Building 3, Carmel 10512; www.visitputnam.org.

GETTING THERE *By train:* The **Metro North** (Harlem and Hudson Lines) stop in Brewster, Garrison, and Cold Spring.

By car: Interstate 84, Route 684, the Taconic State Parkway, and Routes 9 and 9D all go through the county.

MEDICAL EMERGENCY **Putnam Hospital Center** (845-279-5711), Stoneleigh Avenue, Carmel.

✳ Villages

Cold Spring. This lovely river town was founded in the 18th century and, according to local folklore, got its name from George Washington's comment on the water found at a local spring. Cold Spring received an economic boost in the 19th century when it became the site of one of the largest iron foundries in the United States. The town's West Point Foundry produced everything from weapons to some rather unusual furniture, some of which can be seen at the Tarrytown home of Washington Irving in Westchester County.

On Main Street you can visit "antiques row," where many dealers own or share shops that specialize in everything from rare books and vintage clothing to knick-knacks and brass beds. If you continue down Main Street to the railroad tracks, you will find a plaque commemorating Washington's visit. The bandstand here was constructed for riverside concerts—now it provides a wonderful place to look across the river to Storm King Mountain, which, true to its name, is the center of many storms. At the corner of Main and West Streets, follow West Street south to Market to see the Chapel of Our Lady (845-265-2781). This one-room Greek Revival chapel was built in 1834 for workers at the foundry; it is the oldest Roman Catholic church in the region and was one of the most popular subjects for painters and artists of the Hudson River School. The chapel looks across the river, but you may have to wait to get in on weekends because it's popular for weddings.

Garrison. The Landing, which overlooks the Hudson River at the railroad station, is the town's hub. Walk down to the riverside gazebo, which was used as the set for the filming of *Hello, Dolly!* The Landing is also home to the Garrison Art Center (845-424-3960), which holds exhibits, auctions, workshops, and special events, including an art fair, throughout the year.

STORM KING MOUNTAIN AS SEEN FROM THE VILLAGE OF COLD SPRING

Putnam Visitors Bureau

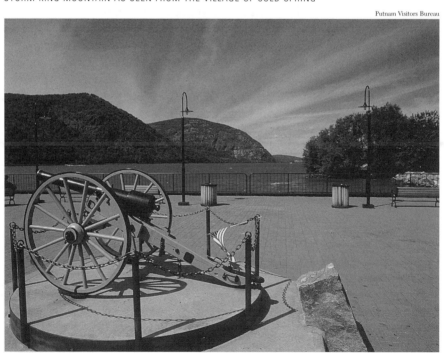

Chuang Yen Monastery (845-228-4287), 2020 Route 301, Carmel 10512. Open year-round 9:30–dusk. The monastery houses the largest Buddhist statue in the Western Hemisphere as well as many other unique shrines, statues, and pieces of art. The library has over 70,000 books, the majority of them Buddhist texts. A morning meditation session and seminar is held every Sunday, followed by a vegetarian lunch. Visitors are welcome to participate.

Foundry School Museum of the Putnam Historical Society (845-265-4010), 63 Chestnut Street, Cold Spring. Open March through December, Tuesday through Thursday 10–4, Saturday and Sunday 2–5. Free. The original Foundry School served the children of Irish immigrants and apprentices who were employed at the West Point Foundry; today the 1820 building is a small museum. The exhibits offer a look at local history, including the Civil War artillery weapons (the Parrott gun was developed by a West Point officer) that were constructed here, and there are also small collections of paintings and furniture. There is even a horse-drawn cutter, once owned by Julia Butterfield, who is said to have received the sleigh from the tsarina of Russia. The **West Point Foundry Preserve** is past the museum, at the south end of Chestnut Street and Route 9D (at bridge). This 87-acre landscape is listed on the National Register of Historic Places. The restored wetlands here may be viewed from a short loop trail that follows Foundry Brook.

Mahopac Farm (845-628-9298), Route 6, Baldwin Place, Mahopac. Open daily April through October 10–5. Small admission fee per family. This is a fun stop if you are traveling with children. There is a petting zoo, pony rides, and hayrides (in the Halloween season).

Putnam Art Council Art Center (845-628-3664), 255 Kennicut Hill Road, Mahopac. Open year-round Tuesday through Friday 9–3, Sunday 1–4. Fee charged for workshops. This cultural organization has a gallery with annual and changing exhibits, as well as workshops in visual and performing arts for children and adults. There are concerts, lectures, and special events offered throughout the season.

Southeast Museum (845-279-7500), 67 Main Street, Brewster. Open April through December, Tuesday, Wednesday, Friday, and Saturday 10–4. Suggested donation. This Victorian-style building houses a small museum with an eclectic local collection. There are permanent exhibits on the Borden Dairy Condensory (condensed milk was developed by a Putnam County resident), the construction of the Croton Water System (a project remarkable for engineering innovations), the American circus, Harlem Line Railroad, and a large collection of minerals from local mines. Local history is also a focus of this museum.

HISTORIC HOME **Boscobel Restoration** (845-265-3638), Route 9D, Garrison-on-Hudson. Open April through October, Wednesday through Monday 9:30–4:30; March, November, and December until 3:30. Admission fee. Standing on a bluff overlooking the Hudson River, the country mansion known as Boscobel looks as if it had spent all of its nearly 200 years in peace and prosperity. But appearances can be deceiving. Statesman Morris Dyckman, a Loyalist of Dutch ancestry, began building the mansion in 1805 for himself and his wife, Elizabeth Corne Dyckman, and their family. But he died before it was completed. Designed in the Federal style, Boscobel was furnished with elegant carpets, fine porcelain, and furniture from the best workshops in New York. The house remained in the family until 1888; from then on it had various owners, including the federal government. In 1955 the government decided it no longer needed Boscobel, and the house was sold for $35 to a contractor, who stripped it of many of its architectural details and sold them off. Local people were so incensed that they tracked down the sections that had been sold; they salvaged and restored the other parts of the house, and, finally, purchased land on which to re-erect the building. Today visitors to Boscobel will see the house as it was, complete with elegant staircase, fine decorative objects, and period furniture made by New York craftspeople. (It is requested that visitors wear broad-heeled walking shoes to tour the home, which helps to preserve the floors and rugs.)

Boscobel's grounds are enchanting, as well. At the Gate House you can see the home of a middle-class family of the era and explore the Orangerie, a 19th-century greenhouse. In spring and summer the gardens at Boscobel blaze with thousands of flowers, including tulips, daffodils, roses, pansies, and wildflowers. Special events are held all season, such as a rose festival, concerts, candlelight holiday tours, and workshops in horticultural and American crafts. From mid-June to August, there is the annual Hudson Valley Shakespeare Festival, with several different plays performed on the grounds in a tent (call 845-265-9575 for schedule).

HISTORIC SITES Old Southeast Church (845-279-7429), Route 22 (Old Croton Turnpike), Brewster. Open June to Labor Day, Sunday 2–5. Free. Founded

ONE OF THE GARDENS AT BOSCOBEL RESTORATION

Charles Lyle

in 1735 by Elisha Kent, this is the church that most of the tenant farmers of the area attended in the 18th century; the present building was built in 1794. Guides in period dress take visitors through the structure.

Town of Carmel Historical Society (845-628-5300), 40 McAlpine Street. Open May through November, Sunday 2–4 and by appointment. Free. An interesting stop for history buffs, the center was donated by a general of the Civil War. Displays include a general store, an exhibit on local history, and decorative accessories of the period.

✳ To Do

FARM STANDS AND PICK-YOUR-OWN FARMS **Green Chimneys Farm Stand** (845-279-2995), Putnam Lake Road, Brewster, is open June through September, Wednesday through Saturday 3–6, and offers organically grown vegetables raised by the students of the Green Chimneys School.

Maple Lawn Farm Market (845-424-4093), Route 9, Garrison, is open daily March through December and stocks seasonal produce, baked goods, cider, and Christmas trees.

Philipstown Farm Market (845-265-2151), Route 9, Cold Spring, offers fruit, vegetables, flowers, imported foods, and Christmas trees in-season; open daily March through December, 8–7.

Ryder Farm (845-279-3984), Starr Ridge Road, Brewster, has 125 acres of organically grown raspberries on its pick-your-own family farm, in operation for over 200 years. Open August and September (call for hours since the season is weather dependent).

Salinger's Orchards (845-279-3521), Guinea Road, Brewster, has a wide selection of local fruit and vegetables; a cider mill and bakery offer tempting treats to visitors. Open daily June to August, 9–6.

GOLF The lush greens of Putnam County golf courses lure golfers of all abilities. You may want to call before you go since some of the courses are semiprivate and might have special events scheduled. All charge fees for use and cart rentals.

Centennial Golf Club (845-225-5700), Simpson Road, Carmel. Open daily April through November. Enjoy a 27-hole, Larry Nelson–designed course, practice facilities, and world-class services.

Garrison Golf Club (845-424-3604), Route 9, Garrison, is open daily 7–7 April through November.

Highlands Country Club (845-424-3727), Route 9D Garrison, is open daily 7–6 April through December,.

Putnam Country Club at Lake MacGregor (845-628-3451), Hill Street, Mahopac, has 18 holes and is 6,750 yards in length; open daily 7–6 April through November.

Vails Grove Golf Course (845-669-5721), Route 121, Brewster, has nine holes. The course is open to the public April through November, weekdays 7:30–6, weekends after 12:30.

HIKING & OUTDOOR ACTIVITIES **Clarence Fahnestock Memorial State Park** (845-225-7207), Route 301, east of the Taconic Parkway, Carmel. Open year-round. Free. This 12,000-acre park consists of swamp, lake, forest and meadow and was assembled through donations of land from private and state organizations. Several hiking trails, including part of the Appalachian Trail, wend in an out of the park; there are also fishing ponds, Canopus Beach, boat rentals, ice-skating areas, and cross-country ski trails. Fees are charged for boats and for swimming, and you must bring your own equipment for winter sports and fishing. The park also sponsors performing-arts programs and has provisions for camping, although you must call ahead to make reservations. The park's marked 1.5-mile Pelton Pond Nature Trail follows the perimeter of a pond formed when an old mine shaft was dammed. You can picnic in this area or watch the woods from a small pavilion. Hikers will want to look for the 8-mile stretch of Appalachian Trail that crosses the park, the Three Lakes Trail—with its varied wildflowers and views—and Catfish Loop Trail, which cuts through the abandoned settlement once known as Dennytown. Since many of these trails cross one another, you should look for signs and trail blazes along the main park roads, which include Route 301, Dennytown Road, and Sunk Mine Road. If you plan to go fishing in the park, you will need a state license. When you visit, be sure to stop at the park headquarters first, where you can pick up a list of special events (some nice programs for children are offered in summer) and free trail maps and fishing guides. Some facilities are accessible to the disabled.

Hudson Highlands State Park (845-225-7207), Route 9D, Cold Spring. There are approximately 4,200 acres in this enormous park. However, there are a few particularly scenic hiking trails that meander through the eastern portion of the Highlands, in Putnam. The Breakneck Ridge Trail begins just north of the tunnel on Route 9D, 2 miles north of the village of Cold Spring. Look for the white blazes. The Washburn Trail begins on Route 9D 1 mile north of Cold Spring, passes an abandoned quarry, then rises steeply before reaching the summit. This trail ends at the beginning of the Notch Trail (blue blazes). The White Rock/Canada Hill Trail begins where the white-blazed part of the Appalachian Trail crosses Route 9 (at the junction of Route 403). Where the AT turns left to ascend the ridge, follow the yellow blazes, which end at the Osborn Loop (blue blazes). Continue to the junction with the Sugarloaf South Trail (red blazes). A side trip to the top of Sugarloaf South offers great views up the river to West Point. The Osborn Loop turns south along the western flank of the mountain, then turns uphill to reach its southern terminus at the Appalachian Trail. Follow north along the ridge, and descend to the junction with the Carriage Connector. This loop is about 6.5 miles long; if you include the side trip up Sugarloaf South, add another mile.

Manitoga/Russel Wright Historic Site & Nature Sanctuary (845-424-3812), Old Manitou Road and 9D, Garrison. Open year-round, but hours vary, so call ahead to check. Admission fee. Daily tours. The name of this center is taken from the Algonquian word for "place of the spirit," and the philosophy of Manitoga lives up to its name. Here people and nature are meant to interact, and visitors are encouraged to experience the harmony of their environment. The center was designed by Russel Wright, who created a 5-mile system of trails that focus on specific aspects of nature. The Morning Trail is especially beautiful early in the day, the Spring Trail introduces the hiker to wildflowers, and the Blue Trail wanders over a brook and through a dramatic evergreen forest (the trail system hooks up with the Appalachian Trail). You will find a full-sized reproduction of a Native American wigwam, which was constructed with traditional methods and tools. The site is used as an environmental learning center, and many special programs are offered here. There are workshops in art, poetry, photography, and botany, along with guided nature walks and concerts. You can visit Dragon Rock, the grass-walled cliff house built by Wright. Manitoga is a place where human design and the natural world reflect and inspire each other.

Manitou Point Preserve (845-473-4440), Mystery Point Road, Garrison. (Take Route 9D north for 2 miles from Bear Mountain Bridge. Make a left on Mystery Point Road. Entrance is at the dead end.) This 136-acre retreat once belonged to the Livingston family. Enjoy 4 miles of lush trails that wind through Manitou Marsh, past woods and the Cooper Mine Brook ravine, along the banks of the Hudson. You will pass the restored Livingston mansion, which is now the national headquarters for Outward Bound and not open to the public.

Taconic Outdoor Education Center (845-265-3773), Clarence Fahnestock Memorial State Park, 775 Mountain Laurel Road, Cold Spring. Free. This state-run center is situated on 500 acres and holds classes and workshops year-round. Boat, swim, fish, or just stay overnight in one of the park's cabins and enjoy the experience at **Highland Lodge** (reservations for camping required).

Other parks include **Pudding Street Multiple Use Area** (845-256-3000), Pudding Street, Putnam Valley; **California Hill Multiple Use Area** (845-256-3000), Gordon Road, Kent; **White Pond Multiple Use Area** (845-256-3000), White Pond Road, Kent; **Big Buck Mountain Multiple Use Area** (845-256-3000), Farmers Mills and Ressique Road, Kent; **Ninham Mountain Multiple Use Area** (845-256-3000), Gypsy Trail and Mount Ninham Road, Kent; and **Cranberry Mountain Wildlife Management Area** (845-256-3000), Stagecoach Road, Patterson.

✳ Green Space

Thousands of acres of Putnam County are dedicated to public use and outdoor education. Most parks are free, but some charge use fees for special events, camping, and swimming; activities include nature studies, birding, hiking, walking, ski touring, and boating.

Constitution Marsh Wildlife Preserve (845-265-2601), access off Route 9D, 0.25 mile south of Boscobel in Garrison. Open May through November, Tuesday through Sunday 9–5. Trails are open, but visitors must make reservations if they would like a tour. A National Audubon Society haven for nature lovers who enjoy birding along the river and spotting rare wildflowers in spring. There is a board-walk to make viewing easier and a self-guided nature tour.

Graymoor (845-424-3671), Route 9, near Route 403, Garrison. Open daily year-round 10–5. Free. Founded by the Episcopal Church in 1898, this historic site is home of the Franciscan Friars of the Atonement. Today the site is an ecumenical retreat center, with nature trails and access to the Appalachian Trail.

Stonecrop Gardens (845-265-2000), Stonecrop Lane, off Route 301 (2.5 miles east of Route 9), Cold Spring. Admission fee. Open by appointment only on Tuesdays, Wednesdays, Fridays, and the first and third Saturday of each month, April through October, 10–4. This 63-acre tranquil refuge set above the village of Cold Spring and surrounded by the Hudson Highlands is the former home of Anne and Frank Cabot. There are 12 acres of magnificent gardens, including woodland, water, rock, and grass gardens. According to the British-born director, several student interns live and work at Stonecrop each year to learn gardening techniques. Summer is the time to see the ferns as well as the wisteria pavilion, which overlooks the pond garden, and the enclosed flower garden is bursting with color during the warm-weather months. There are also bamboo groves and foliage throughout the fall. Don't miss the horticultural rarities on display here, like *Gunnera manicata*, the largest herbaceous plant in the world, native to Brazil. Stonecrop boasts two of these. Every season has something beautiful to offer, so remember to call in advance if you are a garden aficionado.

✳ Lodging

Some of the following inns offer special packages for extended stays or midweek visits. Call for reservations and rate information.

The Bird and the Bottle Inn (845-424-3000), Route 9, Garrison 10524. ($$$) For history buffs, this is a great place. Constructed in 1761, the building has had a romantic and colorful past. Each room has a fireplace and period furnishings that include a canopied or four-poster bed. A full breakfast is served to guests in the restaurant dining room downstairs (see *Dining Out*). Two double rooms have private bath; there is also one suite and one cottage. Children under the age of 12 are not permitted. Open year-round except part of January.

The Country House Inn (845-228-5838), 1457 Peekskill Hollow Road, Kent 10512; 5 miles west of Carmel. ($$) Here you will find four charming, antiques-filled suites, each with a private bath, in a beautiful setting. Open year-round.

Heidi's Inn (845-279-8011), Route 22, Brewster 10509. ($) This quiet, simple, comfortable inn has 38 rooms, all with private bath. A continental breakfast is included with the reasonable room rates. They are open year-round.

Hudson House Inn (945-265-9355), 2 Main Street, Cold Spring 10516. ($$$) The second oldest continuously operating inn in New York State, Hudson House is completely restored and filled with antiques. In addition to quaint bedrooms, there is a cozy lounge, river views, and an exquisite garden. Twelve rooms with private bath; one suite. A full breakfast is served. Children welcome. Open year-round.

Mallard Manor (845-628-3595), 345 Lakeview Drive, Mahopac 10541. ($) Open year-round. Two bedrooms share a bath in this 25-year-old Colonial with old-world charm. The history of Mahopac is depicted in paintings in the stairwell and foyer. Guests can enjoy a hearty breakfast with views of the flowering gardens in-season.

Pig Hill Inn (845-265-9247), 73 Main Street, Cold Spring 10516. ($$$) This Georgian brick town house is a most unusual place to stay. Each guest room is furnished in a different style, and all have a fireplace—and if you fall in love with the rocking chair or anything else in your room, you can buy it. All breads and cakes are home-made. Breakfast in bed is offered, as is a morning meal in the dining room. Five rooms with private bath (one is a Jacuzzi); four others share two baths. Open year-round.

Plumbush Inn (845-265-3904), Route 9D, Cold Spring 10516. ($$$) Now you can stay at this famous restaurant on an 1867 estate. Period furnishings fill the rooms, and, of course, the food is superb (see *Dining Out*). Three rooms with private bath. Open year-round Wednesday through Sunday. Older children only.

✳ Where to Eat

DINING OUT The Arch (845-279-5011), Route 22, Brewster. ($$$) Open for lunch Wednesday through Friday noon–2:30; dinner Wednesday through Sunday 6–10; Sunday brunch and lunch served noon–2:30. An ele-gant, intimate spot filled with antiques and separated into three small dining rooms with fireplaces and lots of airy windows. The chef specializes in Continental cuisine with a French touch. The menu changes seasonally; game is the specialty in fall. Reservations and jackets for men are required.

The Bird and Bottle Inn (845-424-3000), Route 9, Garrison. ($$) Open Wednesday through Sunday for din-ner 6–9; Sunday brunch noon–2. Established in 1761 and originally known as Warren's Tavern, this restaurant was a major stagecoach stop between New York and Albany. The inn still retains a colonial ambi-ence, with wood-burning fireplaces,

beamed ceilings, wide-plank floors, and authentic antiques. Dinner is prix fixe; the specialties include salmon, grilled swordfish, Black Angus steak, and for dessert, crème brûlée. Reser-vations suggested; jackets required for men. Not recommended for young children.

Capriccio (845-279-2873), Route 22, Brewster. ($$$) Open daily for lunch noon–2:30; dinner 5:30–9:30. Enjoy a lake and countryside view from this fine restaurant, which is housed in a large white-clapboard house. North-ern Italian specialties include pasta, shrimp, and lamb. Reservations are required on weekends; jackets are rec-ommended for men. Not for children.

Cathryn's Tuscan Grill (845-265-5582), 91 Main Street, Cold Spring. ($$) Open for lunch and dinner noon–10:30; Sunday brunch noon–3. The Northern Italian cuisine here is first-rate, and so is the wine list. Dine al fresco, in a gardenlike setting. Fan-tastic homemade pastas, fine grilled fish, and hearty beef selections.

HUDSON HOUSE: THE SECOND OLDEST CONTINUOUSLY OPERATING INN IN NEW YORK STATE.
Putnam Visitors Bureau

Downey's Mahopac Beach Restaurant (845-628-8436), 825 South Lake Boulevard (Route 6N) Mahopac. ($$) Open daily noon–9, weekends until 10. This is a wonderful place to have drinks and appetizers lakeside in the warm-weather months. The indoor dining room has a view of the lake that is just as good as outdoors. There isn't gourmet food here but rather an eclectic mix of bar food and fresh fish. The spinach-and-artichoke dip with Tuscan bread is tasty; try that and pass on the calamari and meat entrées. Stick with the seared tuna, poached salmon, and tilapia. Limited wine list; many beers and frozen drinks are offered, however.

Hudson House Restaurant (845-265-9355), 2 Main Street, Cold Spring. ($$) Open for lunch Thursday through Monday 11:30–3:30; dinner Wednesday through Saturday 5–9:30; Sunday brunch 11–3, dinner 4:30–9. Country touches fill this charming 1832 landmark building, and the dining rooms have Hudson River views. Specialties include lobster tortellini and New Zealand rack of lamb. Desserts are superb. Children's menu.

Le Bouchon (845-265-7676), 76 Main Street, Cold Spring. ($$) Open daily except Tuesday noon–9:30.This brasserie/café is owned by a native of France's Alsace region. A couple of the tempting offerings include prosciutto-wrapped trout with Basque vegetables and sea scallops with morel and pencil asparagus. Diners may enjoy a variety of imaginative dishes from salmon strudel and escargot to three types of mussels and salad niçoise.

Northgate at Dockside Harbor (845-265-5555), 1 North Street, Cold Spring. ($$) Open Wednesday through Sunday for lunch 11:30–3;

dinner 5–10. The emphasis here is on basic American regional cuisine, with steaks, seafood, and pasta dishes as mainstays. A great stop during the summer; most tables have a magnificent view of the Hudson River. Enjoy outdoor dining, weather permitting.

Plumbush Inn (845-265-3904), Route 9D, Cold Spring. ($$) Open for dinner Wednesday through Sunday 5:30–10. A restored Victorian home, complete with antiques and cozy paneled rooms. Both dining rooms have fireplaces and candlelight. During the summer, dine on the spacious porch overlooking the grounds. There is a live-trout tank and lots of attention to service. Not recommended for children.

Riverview Restaurant (845-265-4778), 45 Fair Street, Cold Spring ($$) Open Tuesday through Sunday for lunch noon–3; for dinner 5:30–10; Sunday brunch from noon. The Italian cuisine here is hearty, and the place is popular with locals. The wood-fired brick-oven pizza is the specialty. Enjoy the river view while dining on the terrace, weather permitting.

EATING OUT Café Maya Mexican Kitchen (845-265-4636), 3182 Route 9, Cold Spring. ($) Open for lunch and dinner daily except Tuesday 11:30–9. Authentic Mayan cuisine in a cozy atmosphere with an open kitchen. Serving specialties from the Yucatan peninsula like cochnita pibil: boneless tender pork marinated in sour cebille orange juice with achiote (Mayan spices). A terrific variation on the standard Mexican fare. Try it.

Cold Spring Depot Restaurant (845-265-2305), 1 Railroad Avenue Cold Spring. ($) Open daily for lunch 11–4:30; dinner 4:30–10. A casual restaurant housed in a restored train station where, to the delight of rail fans, trains still pass by several times a day. Burgers and fries are hearty, and there are wraps, ribs, and steaks. Children welcome.

East Side Kitchen (845-265-7223), 124 Main Street, Cold Spring. ($) Open Tuesday through Sunday for lunch and dinner 11:30–9:30. This casual, family-oriented restaurant has the feel of a 1940s diner. They serve traditional American favorites as well as some wonderful variations on standard fare, such as fettuccine with wild mushroom and black olive ragout served with chicken or shrimp. Egg creams, milkshakes, and soda floats are available at "the milk bar." Limited beer and wine list.

Foundry Café (845-265-4504), 55 Main Street, Cold Spring. ($) Open Monday through Friday 6–5, Saturday and Sunday 8–5. Naturally healthy foods (low fat, whole grain, and tasty) are the specialty here, prepared in the spirit of regional America. Home-baked goods and hearty soups are prepared fresh daily.

Papa John's Pizzeria & Restaurant (845-265-3344), Route 9, Garrison. ($) Open daily 11–10. This family restaurant, featuring pizza, pasta, sandwiches, and fantastic calzone, is patronized by local residents who enjoy simple, decent Italian food at reasonable prices.

Red Rooster Drive-In (845-279-8046), 1566 Route 22, Brewster. ($) Open Monday through Wednesday 10 AM–11:30 PM, Thursdays and Sundays until midnight, Friday and Saturday, until 1 AM. This old-fashioned, immaculate drive-in with wonderful outdoor eating area (there's even lots of shade) is housed in an A-frame decorated with red-and-white stripes topped with a huge ice cream cone. The kids will love the burgers, hot dogs, fish-and-chips, and fries. For the more health conscious, there is a charbroiled chicken breast sandwich on the menu. The milkshakes are one of the best items here, making this a great snack stop. The miniature golf course on the premises is owned and operated by the restaurant. Fast food with cache!

Texas Taco (845-878-9665), Route 22, Patterson. ($) Open daily 11:30–9:30. In business for more than 30 years, this unique Tex-Mex restaurant has a talking parrot and a monkey that lives out back. Owner Rosemary Jamison is from Texas and started out with a pushcart in front of New York's Plaza Hotel. The chili dogs, franks and chips, and burritos are delicious. This one is worth going out of the way for!

✴ Special Events

February: **Winterfest** (845-265-3773), Outdoor Education Center, 75 Mountain Laurel Lane, Cold Spring; 9–4. Free. Enjoy a pancake breakfast, nature walks, crafts, and winter sports at this annual festival, which is wonderful for young children.

March: **Sap to Syrup** (845-265-3773), Outdoor Education Center, 75 Mountain Laurel Lane, Cold Spring; 9–3. Free. Watch demonstrations of tapping trees, boiling and producing syrup. There is also a pancake breakfast.

May: **The Riverkeepers Annual Shad Picnic** (845-446-8676, 845-265-4010), Boscobel Restoration, 1601 Route 9D, Garrison; 12–5. Contact the Riverkeepers' office for more information and tickets. **City Dweller's Weekend** (212-532-4900, 800-METRO-INFO), Boscobel Restoration, 1601 Route 9D, Garrison.

In cooperation with Metro North. Take the train to Cold Spring Station and the shuttle bus to Boscobel to enjoy shopping in Cold Spring Village. Reservations required. Call for ticket information and reservations. Weekends also in June, September, and October. **Boscobel in Bloom Weekend** (845-265-3638), Boscobel Restoration, 1601 Route 9D, Garrison. See the beautiful landscape and gardens at their peak. Garden tours and woodland trails available.

June: **Cold Spring Antiques Show** (845-265-4414), Mayor's Park, Fair Street, Cold Spring; 9–5. Admission $5. There are 60 dealers selling antiques on the bank of the Hudson River. **Hudson Valley Shakespeare Festival** (845-265-9575), Boscobel Restoration, 1601 Route 9D, Garrison. Reservations required. Call for specific productions and prices. **Circle of 1,000 Drums** (845-225-0381, 800-470-4854), Veterans Memorial Park, Gipsy Trail Road, Carmel; 12–5. Admission and parking free. This is a multicultural event good for children and includes drum making, games, music, food, and entertainment.

July: **Summer Music Sundays in Cold Spring** at the bandstand on Main Street, Cold Spring. Admission free. Enjoy jazz, folk, rock, etc. **Annual Putnam 4-H Fair** (845-278-6738), Veterans Memorial Park, Gipsy Trail Road, Carmel. Admission and parking free. This is a true country fair, featuring animals, exhibits, entertainment, and food.

August: **Garrison Art Center Annual Fine Arts and Crafts Fair** (845-424-3960), Garrison's Landing Riverfront Park, 23 Garrison's Landing, Garrison; 10–5. Suggested donation of $5 for adults. Shop at 70 vendors on the Hudson River. **Daniel Nimham Intertribal Pow Wow** (845-225-0381, 800-470-4584), Veterans Memorial Park, Gipsy Trail Road, Carmel; 10–5. Admission and parking free. Enjoy Native American singers, dancers, crafters, foods.

September: **Big Band Evening and Sunset Picnic** (845-265-3638), Boscobel Restoration, 1601 Route 9D, Garrison; 6–8. Admission $12. Bring a picnic supper, and enjoy the views of the Hudson River; then dance to the music of a 20-piece jazz orchestra, recreating the swinging sound of the big-band era. Reservations required. **Woodland Ramble** (845-265-3638, ext. 115), Boscobel Restoration, 1601 Route 9D, Garrison; 10:30–12. Admission $7. Go on a walking tour of the Woodland Trail in conjunction with the Hudson River Valley National Heritage Area Ramble Weekend. **Annual Brewster Founder's Day Street Fair** (845-279-2477), Main Street, Brewster; 10–4. Free. Enjoy rides, family entertainment, vendors, food.

October: **Annual Putnam Storytelling Festival** (845-628-5585), Taconic Outdoor Education Center, 12 Dennytown Road, Cold Spring; 12–5. Free. **Fall Cold Spring Antiques Show** (845-265-4414), Mayor's Park, Fair Street, Cold Spring; 9–5. Admission $5. Browse 60 antiques dealers selling outdoors on the bank of the Hudson River.

December: **Traditional Candlelight Tours** (845-265-3638, ext. 115), Boscobel Restoration, 1601 Route 9D, Garrison; 5–8. Admission fee. Go on a candlelight tour of Boscobel, decorated for the holidays. Reservations required.

Westchester County

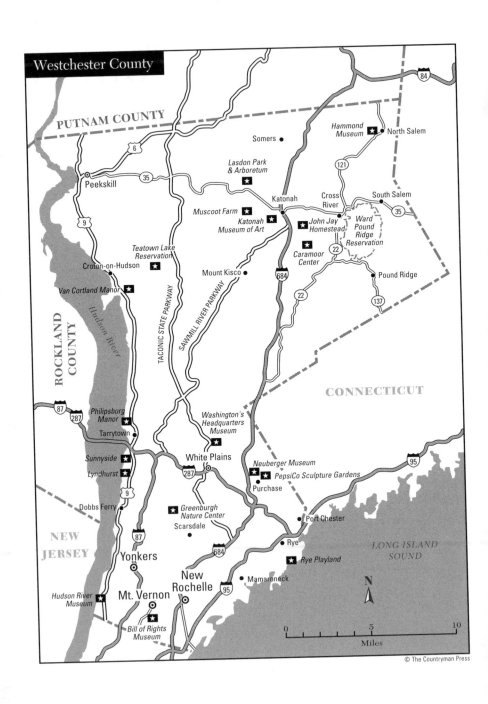

Westchester County

PUTNAM COUNTY

84

Hammond
Museum ★ North Salem

Somers ●

6

121

Lasdon Park
& Arboretum
★

35

Peekskill

Katonah

Cross
River

South Salem

35

9

Muscoot Farm ★

Katonah
Museum of Art ★

John Jay ★
Homestead

Ward
Pound
Ridge
Reservation

Teatown Lake
Reservation ★

Croton-on-Hudson ●

Mount Kisco ●

684

Caramoor ★
Center

22

Van Cortland Manor ★

Pound Ridge ●

22

137

ROCKLAND
COUNTY

Hudson River

TACONIC STATE PARKWAY

SAWMILL RIVER PARKWAY

CONNECTICUT

87

Philipsburg
Manor ★

287

Tarrytown ●

Washington's
Headquarters
Museum ★

95

Sunnyside ★

White Plains

287

Lyndhurst ★

Neuberger Museum
★ ★ PepsiCo Sculpture Gardens

9

Purchase

Dobbs Ferry ●

★ Greenburgh
Nature Center

87

Scarsdale ●

Port Chester ●

NEW

684

● Rye

LONG ISLAND
SOUND

JERSEY

Yonkers

★ Rye Playland

New
Rochelle

● Mamaroneck

N

Hudson River ★
Museum

Mt. Vernon

95

★
Bill of Rights
Museum

0   5   10

Miles

© The Countryman Press

WESTCHESTER COUNTY

Home of the unexpected. Westchester—which calls itself the Golden Apple—can be a nature preserve, a riverfront mansion, a 17th-century Dutch house tucked just off the old Post Road, or a bustling shopping district. The county has made extraordinary attempts to preserve both its history and its natural environment. Although Westchester borders New York City, it is an area replete with parks and nature preserves that offer an enormous selection of children's activities and special events for visitors. Washington Irving described the enchantment of Westchester in his short stories, immortalizing Tarrytown and the Headless Horseman. On historic Route 9 visitors will be awed by the Gothic castle called Lyndhurst and the working Dutch mill at Philipsburg Manor. From the Pinkster Festival in spring to December's candlelight tours of historic sites, Westchester is fun to visit year-round.

GUIDANCE Westchester County Office of Tourism (914-995-8500, 800-833-WCVB), 222 Mamaroneck Avenue, Suite 100, White Plains 10605; www.westchesterny.com.

GETTING THERE *By car:* Westchester is accessible from I-87, I-95, Route 684, and Route 9.

By train: **Amtrak** (800-872-7245), provides service from New Rochelle to stations on the Boston-Washington Northeast corridor. There is service from Croton-Harmon and Yonkers to upstate New York, Montreal, Chicago, and points west. **Metro North** (800-METRO-INFO) operates commuter trains with 43 station stops in Westchester on 3 lines. There is daily service to Grand Central Station in Manhattan as well as to points north.

By bus: **Adirondack Trailways** (800-858-8555) offers service to various towns in Westchester from the Port Authority in Manhattan. The **Bee-line System** (914-813-7777) offers countywide bus service with over 55 routes and express service to Manhattan.

By air: **Westchester County Airport** (914-995-4860), offers scheduled airline and charter services and corporate flights.

MEDICAL EMERGENCY **White Plains Hospital Medical Center** (914-681-0600), Davis Avenue at East Post Road, White Plains.

Northern Westchester Hospital Center (914-666-1254), 400 East Main Street, Mount Kisco.

Phelps Memorial Hospital Center (914-366-3590), 701 North Broadway, Sleepy Hollow.

Hudson Valley Hospital Center (914-737-9000), 1980 Crompond Road, Peekskill.

✳ To See

GARDENS **Hammond Museum and Japanese Stroll Garden** (914-669-5033), 28 Deveau Road, off Old Route 124, North Salem. Open May through October, Wednesday through Sunday noon–4. Admission fee. This small Asian arts museum with a 4-acre Japanese-inspired garden offers a chance to stop back into the Edo period of Japanese history. Created by Natalie Hays Hammond in memory of her parents, these gardens are actually are 13 small landscapes, including a Zen garden, as well as many species of trees and flowers (cherry, katsura, quince, azalea, peony, and iris, among others). Each section is beautifully appointed and has a symbolic meaning: In the reflecting pool, for example, five water lilies represent humanity, justice, courtesy, wisdom, and fidelity. The museum displays a mix of art, antiques, and collectibles, but it is the gardens that must not be missed. The **Terrace Café** on the grounds serves refreshments and lunch.

The Lady Bird Johnson Demonstration Garden at the Native Plant Center (914-785-7870), 75 Grasslands Road, Valhalla. Open year-round daily 7 AM–11 PM. This center informs visitors about the importance of low-maintenance native plants, which support birds, bees, and butterflies. The 2-acre demonstration garden consists solely of plants and wildflowers indigenous to the northeastern United States. Designed for summer and fall color, no pesticides or fertilizers are used in the garden.

Donald M. Kendall Sculpture Gardens at PepsiCo Headquarters (914-253-2001), Anderson Hill Road, Purchase. Open daily year-round dawn to dusk. Free. Here, on 168 acres, visitors will see 45 large sculptures by Rodin, Giacometti, Nevelson, Moore, and Noguchi. Carefully landscaped with paths, reflecting pools, and fountains, the gardens (filled with trees, shrubs, and herbaceous plants), bloom from early spring until fall. Picnicking is permitted.

Lasdon Park and Arboretum (914-864-7260), Route 35, Somers. Open year-round daily 8–4; until 6 Memorial Day weekend through Labor Day. This lush 243-acre park has a 30-acre arboretum with a formal azalea garden, a magnolia and lilac collection, a rare native American-chestnut grove, and a dwarf conifer collection of pines, spruces, firs, and cypress. Another feature is the Chinese garden with plant species native to China, including cherry trees and butterfly bushes. There is a plant shop on the premises.

Pruyn Sanctuary Butterfly and Hummingbird Garden (914-666-6503), 275 Millwood Road (Route 133), Chappaqua. Open year-round daily from dawn to dusk. Guided group tours are available by appointment. A 92-acre parcel of protected open space, this garden features over 125 types of annual and perennial flowering plants selected to be food or nectar plants for butterflies and hummingbirds, including asters, irises, lavender, lilies, and snapdragons. A drip pool attracts birds. Over 25 species of butterflies and moths and two dozen species of birds are drawn to the garden. Plants have identification labels.

Stone Barns Center for Food and Agriculture (914-366-6200), 630 Bedford Road, Pocantico Hills 10591. ($$) This newly opened educational center—which is under the direction of David Rockefeller and is located on the 4,000-acre Rockefeller estate—thrives on its natural production of locally grown food. Prior to dining, visitors have an opportunity to tour the grounds that produce what they are eating. Visitors may then indulge in delicacies devoid of fertilizers, pesticides, and herbicides in the center's renovated cow barn, which hosts the **Blue Hill Restaurant,** open Wednesday through Sunday for dinner. Here visitors may relax and dine on American cuisine featuring local, seasonal ingredients, including fresh fish, organic chicken and beef, and a wide variety of Hudson Valley products. Those in a hurry can experience homegrown goodness in the ambience of the **Blue Hill Café,** located in the public courtyard, a perfect stop for a light lunch or refreshments. The Stone Barns Center is a unique learning experience for Hudson Valley travelers yet also offers a culinary experience that reconnects consumers to the natural world. (*Note:* Since this establishment was not yet open at press time in early 2004, do visit their web site for the most current information: www.stonebarnscenter.org.)

Untermyer Park and Gardens (914-377-6429), 945 North Broadway (Route 9), Yonkers. Open year-round daily dawn to dusk. This historic Grand Beaux Arts garden was created in the early 20th century by attorney Samuel Untermyer. The extensive grounds offer breathtaking Hudson River views. Renovated architectural elements such as a Greek-style amphitheater, fountains and canals characterize the grounds. The gardens feature annuals, perennials, and a large collection of indigenous trees and shrubs.

HISTORIC HOMES **Caramoor Center for Music and the Arts** (914-232-5035), Girdle Ridge Road, off Route 22, Katonah. Open year-round, but hours vary with the season; call for a schedule. Admission fee. Built in the 1930s by lawyer and banker Walter Tower Rosen, this 117-acre estate was meant to be the setting for Rosen's magnificent collection of fine art from Europe and the Orient. The house itself was created by combining entire rooms (55 in all) from European villas with an American "shell." The result is a unique, magical building that provides an architectural tour of the world in a few hours. Rosen's bedroom, for example, was taken from an Alpine cottage; in his wife's room is a headboard made for Pope Urban VIII; the music room is from a 16th-century Italian villa; portions of the outdoor theater are from the south of France. Throughout the house are thousands of breathtaking pieces of priceless needlework, tapestries, porcelain, furniture, and art, some of which date from the Middle Ages and China's golden age. Tours are offered, and lectures are given by art historians who illustrate their talks with pieces from the collections. Don't miss the exquisite gardens at Caramoor, where fine statuary is set among evergreens and flowers. Caramoor is also the site of a world-renowned music festival, which is presented each summer (see *Special Events*). The Venetian Theater is a showcase in itself and was built around 15th-century Venetian columns; operas and concerts take center stage on warm evenings, while chamber concerts are offered in the Spanish Courtyard. Concertgoers are allowed to picnic on the grounds before shows. Special events are also held throughout the year, including Renaissance Day, crafts and antiques shows, and holiday tours.

Jasper F. Cropsey Home and Studio (914-478-1372), 49 Washington Avenue, Hastings-on-Hudson. Open weekdays by appointment only. Free. Although you have to call in advance to view this site, it is well worth the extra effort. Cropsey was a member of the Hudson River School of painters as well as an architect (he designed part of the New York City railroad system), and his Gothic home has about 100 of his works, including paintings, sketches, and studies. The furniture spans those styles that appealed to the Victorian taste, and the artist's studio is part of the tour. Maintained by a private foundation, the site also offers visitors a short video about Cropsey's life and times.

Horace Greeley House and New Castle Historical Society (914-238-4666),100 King Street, Chappaqua. Open year-round, Tuesday through Thursday 1–4, Saturday noon–4. Free. A crusading editor of the *New York Tribune*, 1872, presidential candidate, foe of slavery, and a women's rights advocate, Greeley lived here during the summer months from 1864 through 1872. There is a guided tour of the furnished house, which has been restored in keeping with the era and is listed on the National Register of Historic Places. Exhibits focus on the history of New Castle and this famous native son, with a collection of

HORACE GREELEY HOUSE, CHAPPAQUA

Greeley family furniture, memorabilia, papers, and books. The period perennial and herb gardens include unusual species indigenous to the area and plants once used for medicinal purposes. Museum gift shop on the premises. The Chappaqua Antiques Show has been held here every October since 1976 (see *Special Events*).

John Jay Homestead (914-232-5651), 400 Route 22, Katonah. Open April through November, Wednesday through Saturday 10–4, Sunday noon–4. Admission fee. This 18th-century farmhouse was home to five generations of Jays. As president of the Continental Congress, first chief justice of the Supreme Court, minister to Spain, and Foreign Affairs Secretary, John Jay—the most famous member of the family—held some of the most influential appointments in the new country's government. He retired to this homestead in 1801, and the house reflects the changes wrought by his descendants. Family portraits grace the walls, and the kitchen has an impressive beehive oven along with the hearth. Various styles of furniture and decorative items can be viewed, and the tour adds an interesting dimension to America's early years. The homestead also hosts special events, including candlelight tours during the winter holidays.

Hudson Valley Tourism, Inc.

KYKUIT, THE GRAND ROCKEFELLER ESTATE IN TARRYTOWN.

Kykuit (914-631-9491), Route 9, Tarrytown. Tours begin from Philipsburg Manor. Open mid-April through October, daily except Tuesday. Admission fee. Tours are two hours in length and are not recommended for children under the age of 12. John D. Rockefeller, the founder of Standard Oil, delegated the task of building Kykuit, his home, to his son, John D. Rockefeller Jr. The neo-Classical country house and its gardens were completed in 1913, and Kykuit remains one of the finest and best-preserved Beaux Arts homes in America. Governor Nelson Rockefeller lived here from 1960 to 1979. The gardens contain masterpieces by Henry Moore, Alexander Calder, and Louise Nevelson, and there are special tours that focus on the landscapes around the estate. The house is furnished with antiques, fine ceramics, and paintings; a coach barn contains vintage automobiles and carriages.

Lyndhurst (914-631-4481), 635 South Broadway (Route 9), Tarrytown. Open mid-April through October, Tuesday through Sunday 10–5; November through mid-April, weekends 10–3:30. Admission fee. The term Gothic Revival may bring to mind castles, turrets, and crenellations, but it won't prepare a visitor for the wealth and magnificence of Lyndhurst. Built in 1838 for William Paulding, a former New York City mayor, the house and grounds were enlarged by the Merritt family. Lyndhust was later owned by the notoriously wealthy Jay Gould. Much of the furniture, paintings, and decorative accessories are original to the mansion, which was owned by the Goulds until 1961, when it was given to the National Trust. The rooms are sumptuous, and many are decorated in "faux" material—a substance made to resemble something else. Ironically, in the case of marble, imitating it with wood and paint often cost more than real marble would have (some of the mineral "marble" was actually limestone quarried at Sing Sing prison). Each room is filled with rare furniture, artwork, and decorative pieces: Tiffany glass and windows are outstanding highlights. Outside in the gardens are magnificent roses, a children's playhouse, a conservatory with brick paths, and nature paths among the dozens of different trees, ferns, and plantings.

Washington Irving's Sunnyside (914-591-8763), West Sunnyside Lane (off Route 9). Tarrytown. Open April through December, daily except Tuesday 10–5 (closing time is 4 in November and December); during March, Saturday and Sunday 10–4. Closed January and February. Admission fee. Washington Irving once referred to his home as being "as full of angles and corners as an old cocked hat," and indeed the charming, wisteria-draped home of the author of *The Legend of Sleepy Hollow* and *Rip Van Winkle* is an original. Irving purchased the small estate in 1835 and soon began to remodel it, adding weathervanes, gables, and even an Oriental-style tower. There is much locally made furniture, and some furnishings from Irving's time, including his desk and many of his books, remain. The kitchen was considered a modern wonder; a large hotwater heater was fed from the nearby pond by a gravity-run system. Every year Sunnyside is lovingly decorated for the holiday season, and candlelight tours are held (see *Special Events*) that recall Irving's pleasure at seeing his home bustling with relatives and guests. The grounds are carefully attended and overlook the Hudson River and the railroad tracks; Irving made a deal with the railroad, allowing it to pass through his land if trains would stop to pick him up for the trip to New York. You can stroll along the paths, picnic near the Little Mediterranean (a pond), watch the swans, see the icehouse root cellar, and visit the "necessary." (Note that boat trips leave from New Jersey and Manhattan during the spring, summer, and fall to visit Sunnyside and Philipsburg Manor. Call 800-53-FERRY for a schedule.)

Van Cortlandt Manor (914-271-8981), South Riverside Avenue, Croton-on-Hudson. Open April through October, daily except Tuesday 10–5; November and December, weekends only 10–4. Closed January through March. Admission fee. This manor originally consisted of 86,000 acres of land. The main floors of the present manor house were built in 1748; the house remained in the Van Cortlandt family until the middle of the 20th century. As supporters of the American Revolution, the Van Cortlandts were hosts to such luminaries as Washington, Franklin, and Lafayette. Inside the house there is a blend of styles and periods, reflecting the history of the family. One of the most impressive items is the fowling gun, a huge firearm that was fired into a flock of birds and reduced hunting time considerably! Outside, the gardens beckon flower lovers, and the Long Walk—a brick path that leads to the **Ferry House**, a nearby inn and tavern—wanders by well-maintained flower beds and herb gardens. Special events are held throughout the year, with Autumn Market Days, candlelight tours, and colonial-crafts workshops among the most popular. The Ferry House

has been restored and furnished with Hudson Valley pieces and offers a rare
look into the social life of the colonial period. Notice the familiar white-clay
pipes—they were for rent, with the ends broken off for each new smoker. The
Ferry House is open for tours, as well.

HISTORIC SITES **Old Dutch Church and Burying Grounds** (914-631-1123),
42 North Broadway (Route 9), Tarrytown. There are cemetery tours every Sunday at 2, Memorial Day weekend through October. At other times of the year, by
appointment only. Free. One of the oldest churches in New York State, this stout
stone building was erected in 1685 and is still used, albeit infrequently, for services. Surrounding the church is the fascinating Sleepy Hollow Cemetery, where
visitors can read old Dutch and English tombstones. Washington Irving is buried
here (his grave site is a National Historic Landmark), and the cemetery was
reputed to be the spot where a headless Hessian ghost resided, giving rise to *The
Legend of Sleepy Hollow.*

The Marble School (914-793-1900), 388 California Road, Eastchester. Open
by appointment. Admission fee. Although you have to make arrangements with
the Eastchester Historical Society to visit this site, if you are interested in seeing
a school of the past, by all means go. Built of locally quarried "marble" (actually
limestone), the school is furnished in the style of the 19th century, with many
antique toys and games still available for playtime. A good collection of children's
books from the past is also contained in the society's archives.

Philipsburg Manor (914-631-3992), Route 9, North Tarrytown. Open April
through December, daily except Tuesday 10–5 (closing time is 4 in November
and December); March, Saturday and Sunday 10–4. Closed January and February. Admission fee. Once the center of a 17th-century estate of more than 50,000
acres, Philipsburg Manor was founded by Frederick Philipse, an immigrant
Dutch carpenter. The manor was in the middle of a bustling commercial empire,
which included milling and trading concerns. For almost a century the Philipses
were respected colonists; then the family fled to England as Loyalists during the
Revolution, and their landholdings were broken up, which is why they are not as
well-known as other prominent colonial families.

Tours of the manor begin in the basement, where the dairy and slave cooking
quarters are, rather than through the front door. Some of the rooms feature
reproductions of period pieces that can be touched. The front hall contains documents like the 1750 house inventory—and advertisements for runaway slaves.
At the two-story stone house and office building, the rooms have been restored
to their earlier simplicity. The house was not the main residence of the family, so
it was not furnished lavishly, but there are several bedrooms, a kitchen, and the
counting office to explore. The mill, still run by waterpower, continues to grind
meal for the kitchen (you can purchase the flour in the gift shop), and turns out
500–1,000 pounds of flour annually. The resident miller explains the intricacies
of a millwright's job, how waterpower turns corn into flour, and so on, all the
while working the dusty, noisy machinery.

Outside by the barn and the outbuildings, where costumed guides go about the
business of working a small farm, vignettes depicting life at the time are acted

out. They show that the North, too, depended on slavery for economic survival. In *Trying Times*, a pair of interpreters play Albert the overseer, at his desk in the main house, and Susan, the enslaved woman, who supervised the dairy operations. Their dramatic conversation, where Susan seeks permission to visit a family member who had been sold, expresses some of the complexities of their relationship and reveal negotiations that might very well have gone on at the time. This site has not shied away from the ugly, yet realistic, aspects of early-American culture; children will understand more about slavery from such dramatic enactments. A clear sense of how America came together on the backs of different cultures is communicated at this site—which is rare anywhere. I commend Philipsburg Manor for their progressive approach to colonial history and hope other sites follow their lead. Special events are held throughout the year, including sheep shearing and spinning demonstrations, so call for a schedule (see *Special Events*).

MUSEUMS St. Paul's Church National Historic Site (914-667-4116), 897 South Columbus Avenue. Mount Vernon. Open year-round, Monday through Friday 9–5; special weekend programs. Free. Few people realize that the 18th-century libel trial of John Peter Zenger led directly to the establishment of the Bill or Rights in 1791; fewer still know that this all took place in Mount Vernon, and that an unusual site preserves the story. Begin your visit with a tour of St. Paul's Church, which was founded in 1665 (the present building dates from 1763). The church has a highly carved bishop's chair from 1639 as well as one of the oldest working church organs in the country. You will also see the Freedom Bell, sister of Philadelphia's Liberty Bell and cast at the same time in the same London foundry. At one time the church was used as a courthouse during the week, and lawyers, including Aaron Burr, presented their cases here. The museum is located in the former carriage house and has exhibits that recall America's drive to guarantee essential freedoms. Displays include historic dioramas and panels, a working printing press, and papers and prints that describe America's historic dedication to individual rights. There are self-guided sections of the museum; guided tours are available, as well.

Hudson River Museum (914-963-4550), 511 Warburton Avenue, Yonkers. Open year-round, Wednesday through Sunday noon–5; Friday noon–9 May through September. Admission fee. When financier John Bond Trevor built a 19th-century mansion called Glenview on a rise overlooking the Hudson River, he probably never envisioned it becoming a museum, but when the house was purchased by the city of Yonkers, that is what happened. And a lucky thing too. Period artwork, clothing, furniture, and decorative accessories are displayed throughout the mansion; the museum is located in a separate wing and contains science and art exhibit areas. The Red Grooms bookstore is a favorite stop with visitors, and the Andrus Space Planetarium (the only public planetarium in the area and one of the few in the Northeast) can take you on a journey through the universe with its Zeiss star machine. There are special events at this site all year, so it is best to call ahead for a schedule. You can even plan a birthday party for youngsters in the planetarium; call for reservations.

Katonah Museum of Art (914-232-9555), Route 22 at Jay Street, Katonah. Open Tuesday through Saturday 10–5, Wednesday until 8 (free after 5), Sunday noon–5. Admission fee. This lively teaching museum was founded in 1953 to display the best art of the past and present and foster arts education. There are exhibits by museum members, an annual local studio tour, and changing displays, which may range from a look at the creations of fashion designers to Navajo rugs or modern art. Special events and shows are held year-round, and the museum is well worth a stop. There is also an outdoor sculpture garden.

Neuberger Museum of Art (914-251-6100), Purchase College Campus, 735 Anderson Hill Road, Purchase. Open Tuesday through Friday 10–4, Saturday and Sunday 11–5 except national holidays. Masterpieces of modern art by Avery, Hopper, O'Keeffe, Pollack, and others are displayed in several galleries at this extraordinary teaching museum. There is also an important collection of African art, and selections from Nelson Rockefeller's collection of ancient art are exhibited. An outdoor sculpture area with works by Henry Moore, Andy Goldsworthy, and Alexander Liberman should not be overlooked. This is one of Westchester County's finest cultural resources, with 16 changing exhibitions annually. The museum offers lectures, workshops, tours, performances, and concerts throughout the year. There is a gift shop and café on the premises.

Peekskill Museum (914-736-0473), 124 Union Avenue, Peekskill. Open June through December, Saturday 1–3. Free. This local history museum is housed in the Herrick House, one of Peekskill's most famous Victorian houses. The museum features three permanent exhibits that reveal how well-to-do New Yorkers lived in "the country": the Ladies Victorian Bedroom, the Mario Boyle Children's Room, and the Peekskill Stove Collection, plus other artifacts relating to the city's history, including some Revolutionary War cannons. After visiting the museum, visit the **Peekskill Artists District Open Studios** (914-734-1894) and see how painters, sculptors, and photographers have moved to the downtown area, encouraging a renaissance in the city (see *Special Events*).

Reader's Digest **Tour** (914-241-5125), Route 117, Pleasantville. Tours are offered Monday through Friday; reservations are required. Not many

THE HUDSON RIVER MUSEUM IN YONKERS IS A GREAT PLACE FOR FAMILIES.

Hudson Valley Tourism, Inc.

people know that the headquarters of *Readers's Digest* also houses an outstanding collection of impressionist and postimpressionist artworks. Paintings by Monet, Renoir, Chagall, and others and sculpture by masters like Modigliani and Brancusi are on view throughout the building. This is a special stop for an art lover but not recommended for children.

Somers Historical Society and Museum of the Early American Circus (914-277-4977), Routes 100 and 202, Somers. Open year-round, Thursday 2–4 and the second and fourth Sunday of every month 1–4. This unusual museum is located in the historic Elephant Hotel, probably the only hotel in the world built in memory of an elephant. Recalling the birth of the American circus in the 18th century, the hotel was erected by showman Hachaliah Bailey (a distant relation of the Bailey of Barnum & Bailey), who imported the first elephant to America in 1796. Called Old Bet, the elephant journeyed with Bailey up and down the eastern seaboard as part of a traveling menagerie until it was shot by a suspicious farmer in Maine. Today the former hotel houses a museum full of circus memorabilia, posters, photographs, a miniature big top, and exhibits of local history.

Square House Museum (914-967-7588), 1 Purchase Street, Rye. Open year-round, Tuesday through Friday 1–3:30. Admission fee. This 1760 Federal farmhouse and tavern once hosted George Washington, and today the five restored rooms offer a fascinating look at 18th-century life. In the tavern room, visitors learn that the term "bar and grill" derives from barkeepers having secured a wooden covering over the bar at night to avoid having the liquor stolen. In the kitchen a beehive oven (the interior was shaped like an old-fashioned bee skep) and open hearth are still used by museum staff. There was also an early medical office in the building, and you'll discover that the barber, who was also the surgeon, would wrap bloody cloths around a stick to indicate that he was open for business; the origin of the striped pole still used by barbers today.

Washington's Headquarters Museum (914-949-1236), 140 Virginia Road, North White Plains. Built in 1738 by the Miller family, the house served as Washington's headquarters before the fighting on Miller Hill, which concluded the Battle of White Plains on November 1, 1776. The museum contains Colonial artifacts and Washington's table and chairs. Miller Hill, Westchester's only preserved battlefield, can be visited after touring the house. Open by appointment only.

Yorktown Museum (914-962-2970), 1974 Commerce Road, Yorktown Heights. Open year-round, Sunday 1–4 or by appointment. Free, but donations are accepted. A unique collection of dollhouses and miniature landscapes depicting Victorian homes, street scenes, and stores is on display, as are exhibits of Mohegan Indian life and furnished period rooms circa 1750–1850, railroad memorabilia, and local history.

WINERIES **North Salem Vineyard** (914-669-5518), Hardscrabble Road, North Salem (watch for signs). Open year-round, Saturday and Sunday 1–5. Free. This small, privately owned vineyard produces several wines and welcomes guests to sample its products. There is a short tour. Wine and snack shop on the premises. A picnic area is also available to visitors.

Prospero Winery (914-769-6870), 134 Marble Avenue, Pleasantville. (Located off exit 27 of the Saw Mill River Parkway.) Open Tuesday through Sunday. Free. You can taste quite a variety of wines in their tasting room: cabernet sauvignon, chardonnay, merlot, Zinfandel, and more. This is a relatively new addition to the winery scene in the Hudson Valley.

✳ To Do

BICYCLING If bicycling is your passion, plan to take part in **Bicycle Sundays** (May through September, except holiday weekends, 10–2), when the Bronx River Parkway is closed to vehicular traffic. Call 914-185-PARK, and request trail maps for the Bronx River Pathway, North County Trailway, South County Trailway, Briarcliff-Peekskill Trailway, and Old Croton Aqueduct State Historic Park, which have free bike paths that are open year-round. In-line skating is also welcome in most of these areas.

Briarcliff-Peekskill Trail (914-864-PARK). This county-owned linear park runs 12 miles from the town of Ossining to the Blue Mountain Reservation in Peekskill.

Bronx River Pathway (914-864-PARK). This 807-acre park extends 13.2 miles in three distinct segments. It is excellent for road biking, hiking, and walking.

Old Croton Aqueduct State Historic Park (914-693-5259). This level, 26-mile trail from Croton Dam south to Van Cortlandt Park in the Bronx passes through 11 towns and offers striking panoramas of the Hudson River at several points. The trail follows the route of the aqueduct, which carried water to New York City from 1842 to 1955. Most of this structure lies beneath the trail and has been designated a National Historic Landmark.

North County Trailway (914-864-PARK). There are 22 miles of county-owned trail, running from Mount Pleasant north to the Putnam County Line in Yorktown.

South County Trailway (914-864-PARK). This 5.2-mile county-owned trail runs from Hastings to Elmsford.

BOAT CRUISES **Hudson Highlands Cruises** (845-534-7245). On the last Saturday of the month from May through October, the excursion boat *Commander* offers a three-hour narrated cruise to the Hudson Highlands, leaving Peekskill at 12:30 PM from Riverfront Park, passing West Point, Fort Montgomery, Garrison, Constitution Island, and the Bear Mountain Bridge. Advance reservations required.

Hudson Valley Riverboat Tours (914-788-4000). Open May through October for Saturday afternoon (2–5) and Sunday evening (5–8) cruises plus Wednesdays in July and August. This historic refurbished paddle wheeler, *The River Queen,* sails on the Hudson from the Sixth Street dock in Verplanck. Northbound cruises pass Bear Mountain and West Point, while southbound cruises pass Croton Point Park. Advance reservations required.

New York Waterway (800-53-FERRY). Enjoy specially themed sightseeing cruises up the Hudson River from New York City to Sleepy Hollow to visit

Lyndhurst, Kykuit, Sunnyside, and Philipsburg Manor. A two-hour northbound Hudson River tour departs from and returns to Tarrytown on weekends and holidays, mid-May through October. Weekend getaway cruises leaving Saturday and returning Sunday are also available. Call for schedule and reservations.

New York Sailing School (914-235-6052). Open April through November for sunset sails, Tuesday through Sunday nights, departing from New Rochelle at 6:30. Do bring a picnic dinner and drinks. Overnight cruises are available with sleeping accommodations on the vessel. Call for information and reservations.

CROSS-COUNTRY SKIING Westchester County offers a large number of places to cross-country ski when the weather cooperates. For information on ski conditions, clinics, and workshops, call 914-864-PARK before you go. The following places offer marked trails:

Blue Mountain Reservation, Welcher Avenue, Peekskill; **Cranberry Lake Preserve,** Old Orchard Street, North White Plains; **Lenoir Preserve,** Dudley Street, Yonkers; **Marshlands Conservancy,** Route 1, Rye; **Mountain Lakes Park,** Hawley Road, North Salem; **Rockefeller State Park Preserve,** Route 117, Pocantico Hills; **Saxon Woods Park,** Mamaroneck Road, White Plains; **Ward Pound Ridge Reservation,** Routes 35 and 121, Cross River.

FARM STANDS AND PICK-YOUR-OWN FARMS Even though Westchester is more built up than many other Hudson River counties, farm stands provide fresh local produce during the summer and fall harvest seasons. Farmers markets are held in many towns, and they are a great way to sample the bounty of the county!

Outhouse Orchards (914-277-3188), Hardscrabble Road, Croton Falls, offers tours; you can pick apples in the fall, or shop at the stand year-round, where you will find fresh vegetables, jams, and other treats.

Stuart's Fruit Farm (914-245-2784), 62 Granite Springs Road, Granite Springs, is open daily April through October 9–6; November and December 9–5; Closed January through March. They sell a large selection of fruits and vegetables in-season.

Westchester Greenhouses (914-693-2935), 450 Secor Road, Hartsdale, is open year-round, Saturday and Sunday 9–6. They offer plants, fresh produce, cider, jams, and honey.

Wilkens Fruit and Fir Farm (914-245-5111), 1335 White Hill Road, Yorktown. Open daily 11–5. Pick your own apples and peaches in-season Saturday and Sunday 10–4:30. Choose and cut Christmas trees after Thanksgiving through mid-December, 10–4.

The following **farmers markets** are popular with local residents and visitors to the county. Try to visit at least one on your travels through Westchester.

Bronxville Farmers Market (914-923-4837), Pondfield Road. Late June through October, Saturday 9–1:30. Excellent seasonal fruits and vegetables.

Hartsdale Farmers Market (914-993-1507), Train Station Plaza. Late June through October, Saturday 9–2. Visit here for seasonal produce and flowers, home-baked breads and pastries.

Hastings-on-Hudson Farmers Market (914-923-4837), Maple Avenue (next to the library). Mid-June through mid-November, Saturday 8:30–2. They sell wine, organic produce, breads, pastries, cut flowers, potted plants, and poultry.

Mount Vernon Farmers Market (914-699-7200), 107 West Fourth Street. From mid-July through October, Wednesday 8:30–2:30, you will find fresh produce at the Neighborhood Health Center.

New Rochelle "Green Seasons" (914-654-2186), Main Street, in front of city hall. Every Friday from the end of June to late November, 8–3, you will find all kinds of fruits and vegetables in-season as well as home-baked breads, pies, jams, and doughnuts.

Ossining Farmers Market (914-923-4837), Main and Spring Streets. Mid-June through mid-December, Saturday 8:30–2. Enjoy organic produce, cheeses, meats, produce, wines, breads, pastries, cut flowers, honey, and jams.

Peekskill Farmers Market (914-737-2780), Bank Street. Mid-June through October, Saturday 8–2. There is produce, dairy items, poultry, baked goods, plants, herbs, soaps, and bath products, in addition to live entertainment.

Pleasantville Farmers Market (914-769-0273), Manville Road, across from Wheeler Avenue. Late June through October, Saturday 8:30–1, they offer organic produce, wine, breads, cider, eggs, pastries, and cut flowers.

Tarrytown Farmers Market (914-631-1885), Patriot Park, 125 North Broadway (Route 9). Mid-June through October, there is organic produce, honey, eggs, wine, flowers, potted plants, and musical entertainment to enjoy as you stroll around.

White Plains Farmers Market (914-422-1336), Main and Court Streets. Mid-June through mid-November, Wednesday 8–4, you will find organic produce, baked goods, plants, and more.

Yonkers Farmers Market (914-963-3033), St. John's Courtyard, 1 Hudson Street. Early July through October, Thursday 9–4. The offerings here include fresh produce, bakery items, homemade jams, and a flea market.

FOR FAMILIES **Playland** (914-925-2701), Playland Parkway, off I-95, Rye. Different sections of the park are open year-round, although hours vary widely during the season, so call ahead. Open mid-May through Labor Day and weekends only in the month of September. A true old-fashioned amusement park and National Historic Site, Rye's Playland is an architectural gem. Built in 1928, this was the first amusement park constructed according to a complete plan where recreational family fun was the focus. Fortunately, the park's family atmosphere and art deco style are still here to be enjoyed. Set on the beaches of Long Island Sound, Playland offers a famous 1,200-foot boardwalk, a swimming pool, gardens, a saltwater boating pond (paddleboats can be rented), a beach, and, of course, there are 50 rides and an amusement area. Seven original rides are still in use: Among them are the carousel (with a rare carousel organ and painted horses), the Dragon Coaster (a rare wooden roller coaster), and the Derby Racer (horses zip around a track). Fireworks and special entertainment, including free musical revues, go on all summer; in winter the three ice-skating rinks at Playland are open to the public.

Muscoot Farm (914-864-7282), Route 100, Somers. Open daily May through October, 10–4; until 6 Memorial Day weekend through Labor Day. Free, but there are workshops on the premises that charge a fee. A showplace for the farming techniques of the 19th-century, this 777-acre interpretive farm offers a look at life in a bygone era. Built in 1885 by a pharmacist (*muscoot* means "something swampy," in a local Native American language), visitors today can view a variety of farm animals and displays of vintage farm equipment, tour historic farm buildings and enjoy hayrides. Muscoot also has a series of trails that wind through ferns and wildflowers, along which animals and an amazing number of birds make their homes; there are ponds, wetlands, and meadows to explore, as well.

GOLF Westchester is famous for some prestigious professional golf tournaments hosted in the county; five county-owned courses are open to the public:

Dunwoodie (914-231-3490), Wasylenko Lane, Yonkers, is an 18-hole, par-70 course with pro shop, driving range, snack bar, and restaurant. **Maple Moor** (914-995-9200), North Street, White Plains is an 18-hole, par-71 course with pro shop, snack bar, and restaurant. **Mohansic** (914-862-5283), Baldwin Road, Yorktown Heights, is an 18-hole course, par 70, with pro shop, driving range, snack

PLAYLAND IN RYE IS A TRUE OLD-FASHIONED AMUSEMENT PARK AND A NATIONAL HISTORIC SITE.

Hudson Valley Tourism, Inc.

bar, and restaurant. **Saxon Woods** (914-231-3461), Mamaroneck Road, Scarsdale, is an 18-hole, par-71 course with pro shop, restaurant, and locker rooms. **Sprain Lake Golf Course** (914-231-3481), Grassy Sprain Road, Yonkers, is an 18-hole course, par 70, with pro shop, snack bar, and restaurant.

Semiprivate golf courses include: **Doral Golf Club** (914-939-5500), Anderson Hill Road, Rye Brook, 9 holes, par 35; **Lake Isle Park** (914-961-3453, ext. 206), White Plains Road, Eastchester, 18 holes, par 70; **Loch Ledge Golf Course** (914-962-8050), Route 188, Yorktown Heights, 18 holes, par 71; and **Pound Ridge Country Club** (914-764-5771), High Ridge Road, Pound Ridge, has an 18-hole course and restaurant on the premises.

HIKING There are over 40 county-owned parks in Westchester, and the **Department of Parks, Recreation and Conservation** (914-864-PARK) can provide an extensive list of places to hike. These are my favorite spots, but do refer to the Green Space section in this chapter for additional areas that should not be overlooked.

Franklin D. Roosevelt State Park (914-245-4434), 2957 Crompond Road, off the Taconic Parkway, Yorktown Heights, is open year-round 8 AM–dusk and has hiking and cross-country ski trails, a huge outdoor pool that is accessible to the disabled, and boating on Mohansic Lake and Crom Pond.

Indian Brook Assemblage (914-244-3271), Mount Holly Road, Lewisboro, is really a collection of smaller parks and preserves maintained by the Nature Conservancy. Lakes, waterfalls, ponds, and trails form a perfect getaway for the outdoors lover, and the hiking ranges from a leisurely walk to a challenging climb.

Marshlands Conservancy (914-835-4466), Route 1, Rye. Marked trails take the hiker through fields and woods and along the seashore. This is a great spot for birders, and a small nature center offers exhibits on the natural history of Long Island Sound.

More hiking is found at the **Mianus River Gorge** (914-244-3271), Mianus River Road, Bedford, and along the **Old Croton Aqueduct** (914-693-5259), Route 129, to the Croton Dam Plaza. The latter hike is a total of 30 miles, but both hikers and cyclists can follow as much or as little of the trail as they want. Stop at the plaza spillway, which was considered an engineering marvel in its day.

HORSEBACK RIDING **River Ride Equestrian Center** (914-633-0303), 960A California Road, Eastchester, is open Wednesday through Sunday for both English and Western riding lessons. There is a petting zoo on the premises.

ICE SKATING Since schedules vary from month to month, do call the ice rinks for hours. Make sure to specify if you are interested in figure skating, ice hockey, public sessions or freestyle time. There are three indoor rinks at Playland (see *For Families*), and at the following locations:

Ebersole Ice Rink (914-422-1348), Lake Street, White Plains. There are public skating sessions every day here for both ice hockey players and figure skaters.

Edward J. Murray Memorial Skating Center (914-377-6469), 348 Tuckahoe Road, Yonkers, is open Wednesday through Sunday for figure skating, speed-skating, and ice hockey.

Hommocks Ice Rink (914-834-1069), Boston Post Road and Weaver Street, Larchmont, is open daily. Call for hours.

New Roc City (914-637-7575), Le Count Place, New Rochelle, features two world-class ice rinks with figure skating, ice hockey, and clinics. Daily public skating sessions.

Westchester Skating Academy (914-347-8232), 91 Fairview Park Drive, Elmsford, has 2 NHL-size ice rinks with classes and rentals. Open year-round; call for hours.

SWIMMING Those who want to go to the beach can enjoy the one at **Playland Park** in Rye (914-813-7000, see *For Families*). There are some other nice beaches, as well:

Blue Mountain Reservation Beach (914-862-5275), Welcher Avenue, Peekskill, has beaches, a pool, and extensive recreation areas.

Croton Point Park and Beach (914-862-5290), Croton-on-Hudson, overlooks the Hudson River, and has special events during the summer months. There is also a swimming pool, recreation hall, and playing fields.

Osceola Beach and Picnic Grounds (914-245-3246), Jefferson Valley, is a good place to go with small children. Snack bar, picnic tables, family atmosphere.

Spruce Lake at Mountain Lake Park (914-669-5793), Hawley Road, North Salem. This lake is open Saturday, Sunday, and holidays only from Memorial Day weekend through Labor Day. Rowboats and canoes are available for rental by advance reservation.

✳ Green Space

Westchester County may be a bustling area for big business and corporate headquarters, but you will also find dozens of lovely public parks and outdoor facilities throughout the region.

Blue Mountain Reservation (914-862-5275), Welcher Avenue, Peekskill. Open year-round. Situated in the northwestern part of the county, this recreation area has a large lake for swimming in the summer and ice skating during the winter. There are facilities for hiking, fishing, and picnicking. Camping is available in the Trail Lodge, which has a dining hall and large fireplace.

Cranberry Lake Preserve (914-428-1005), Old Orchard Street off Route 22, North White Plains. Open year-round. This lovely preserve consists of 135 acres of unspoiled wetlands and hardwood forests. The park has a 10-acre pond with trails and boardwalks, so visitors can observe life in an aquatic habitat. You will also find fishing, cross-country ski trails, and hiking. A small lodge offers interpretive programs and seasonal exhibits.

Croton Point Park (914-271-3293), Croton Avenue (off Route 9), Croton-on-

Hudson. Open year-round. This park is located along the banks of the Hudson
River and features a pool, canoe-launching area, recreation hall, and ball fields.
The location is ideal for fishing, hiking, and picnicking. Cabins, lean-tos, and
facilities for tents and trailers are also available.

Greenburgh Nature Center (914-723-3470), 99 Dromore Road, off Central
Avenue, Scarsdale. Open daily year-round. Situated on 32 acres, this innovative
nature center offers visitors a chance to explore several environments, including
woodlands, a vineyard, orchards, and cultivated gardens. More than 30 different
species of trees can be found in the preserve, along with wildflowers, ferns, and
a host of songbirds. At the center's museum, see a Nunatak, an Inuit word meaning "hill of stone," animal exhibits, descriptive displays that explain some of the
area's natural history, and a glass beehive. You can also pick up maps here to use
on the self-guided nature walks. Many special events are held at the nature center, from concerts on the lawn to art exhibits.

Marshlands Conservancy (914-835-4466), Route 1, Rye. Open year-round.
There is an environmental education center with changing exhibitions and four
saltwater aquaria at this 137-acre wildlife sanctuary. The unique character of the
conservancy lies in the diversity of habitats preserved within its boundaries,
including woods, fields, freshwater ponds, a salt marsh, and shore. Paths
throughout the conservancy lead to these points of interest.

Rockefeller State Park Preserve (914-631-1470), Route 117, Pocantico Hills.
Open year-round from 8 AM to sunset. Find a variety of habitats here, including
wetlands, woodlands, meadows, fields, and a lake. Miles of hiking trails, which
during the winter become cross-country ski trails, will delight outdoors lovers,
and for horseback riders, there are beautiful bridle paths. The visitors center
hosts exhibits of local and historical interest. This preserve is truly a county
treasure, private land opened to the public through the generosity of the Rockefeller family.

Rye Nature Center (914-967-5150), 873 Boston Post Road, Rye. Open daily
9–5 year-round. A small nature center (under 50 acres), this is a nice stop if you
are traveling with children. The museum has exhibits of local plants and animals,
and there are some mini exhibits about nature. Take the 2.5 mile walk, described
in a guide you can pick up at the museum. Picnic area available to visitors.

Scenic Hudson Park at Irvington (845-473-4440). From I-287, exit 9, take
Route 9 south for 1.6 miles. At the light turn right onto Main Street and continue to the end. Make a right on North Astor Street, a left on Bridge Street, cross
the railroad tracks, and continue bearing to the left. The park is on the right,
past Bridge Street Properties. This 12-acre site, with views of the Manhattan
skyline, the Palisades, and Tappan Zee Bridge, is continually being transformed
into parkland. Scenic Hudson Land Trust saved the area from development.
There is a promenade, small boat launch, and ball fields.

Teatown Lake Reservation (914-762-2912), Spring Valley Road, Ossining.
Take exit 134 off the Taconic, and then follow Grant's Lane to Spring Valley
Road. Open daily year-round; museum open Tuesday through Saturday 9–5.
Free. This 400-acre reservation has marked nature walks and hiking trails, a

museum, and outdoor exhibits. Wildflowers are abundant here in the spring, and there is an unusual selection of fences. Visitors can enjoy viewing waterfowl and other animals at a large lake; inside the museum are live exhibits of local animals and plants.

Ward Pound Ridge Reservation (914-864-7317), Routes 35 and 121, Cross River. Open year-round. Free. Ward Pound Ridge is the largest park in Westchester, covering more than 4,700 acres. There are miles of trails for cross-country skiing, sledding, snowmobiling, hiking, and horseback riding. There are also several places to go fishing and to picnic. You can easily spend a day here. On weekends there are often nature programs for children and families.

Westmoreland Sanctuary (914-666-8448), Chestnut Ridge Road, Mount Kisco. Open year-round, Monday through Saturday 9–5, Sunday 10:30–5. Free, but fees are charged for some workshops and special events. The sanctuary is an active site, with more than 15 miles of walking and hiking trails, wildlife displays, and exhibits of local natural history. There are workshops, lectures, and events all year, including "Building Bat Houses," seasonal hikes, birdsong identification walks, Earth Day celebrations, even a search for the first ferns of spring! An excellent site for a family visit.

Also see *To See—Gardens.*

✳ Lodging

Westchester County is home to many conference centers and fine hotels, which offer visitors everything from saunas and spas to fine dining. Visitors who prefer B&B establishments will have difficulty finding one. Due to the restrictive zoning regulations in most Westchester communities, such businesses are rare. After extensive research, I discovered only two places in the county that fit into this category—one in Mount Kisco and the other in Croton-on-Hudson.

Alexander Hamilton House (914-271-6737), 49 Van Wyck Street, Croton-on-Hudson 10520. ($$) This Victorian house dates back to 1889 and has eight luxurious rooms; two have Jacuzzis and five have fireplaces. The bridal chamber is on the third floor and has a king-sized bed, skylights, and pink-marble fireplace. All rooms have private bath, TV, telephone, and high-speed Internet access.

Crabtree's Kittle House (914-666-8044), 11 Kittle Road, Chappaqua. ($$) This over-200-year-old building has been an inn since the 1930s, when it attracted film stars like Henry Fonda and Tallulah Bankhead. One of the only inns in Westchester, the Kittle House is moderately priced for the area. Continental breakfast is served, and children are welcome. There are 12 rooms with private bath, telephone, cable TV, and high-speed Internet access. Guests can enjoy the fine restaurant on the premises, as well (see *Dining Out*).

HOTELS AND CONFERENCE CENTERS
The following full-service hotels and conference centers welcome individual guests as well as groups.

The Castle at Tarrytown (914-524-6366), 400 Benedict Avenue, Tarrytown 10591. ($$$) Open year-round. Only 25 miles north of Manhattan, perched in splendor on 10 hilltop acres overlooking the majestic Hudson River, is this establishment—an authentic castle and one of the oldest and grandest historic landmarks in the region. The main tower rises 75 feet, the highest point in Westchester County. Built between 1897 and 1910 by the son of a Civil War general, the Castle has changed little in the last 100 years. Much of the hewn-oak girders, beams, woodwork, and some of the furniture were brought over from Europe. The innkeepers are European, and the service is excellent. Today a luxury inn, gourmet restaurant (the Equus; see *Dining Out*), and special-events facility, this is one of the most magical, romantic spots anywhere. The accommodations include five enormous suites that range from 750 to 900 square feet. For a special occasion, ask for the tower suite—it is magnificent and has fantastic views of the river and mountains; I will always remember my stay there. Spacious living rooms, working fireplaces, and luxurious bathrooms are standard. Each suite includes color cable TV, in-room fax, and mini bar, and most have a fireplace. All guest rooms are nonsmoking.

Courtyard by Marriott (914-631-1122, 800-589-8720), 475 White Plains Road, Tarrytown 10591. ($$) This relatively small (139 rooms), moderately priced hotel, where guests can enjoy relaxing in the Jacuzzi and pool or simply sit in the scenic courtyard, offers special weekend rates in the winter months. The Courtyard Café serves breakfast daily.

Crowne Plaza (914-682-0050, 800-PLAINS-2), 66 Hale Avenue, White Plains 10601. ($$) This hotel, with 400 guest rooms and an indoor pool, whirlpool, sauna, and exercise room,

also has a restaurant on the premises where guests can get breakfast, lunch, and dinner daily.

Dolce Tarrytown House (914-591-8200, 800-553-8118), East Sun Lane, exit 9 off I-287, Tarrytown 10591. ($$) There are 212 rooms here in this beautiful, completely renovated castlelike structure. Guests can enjoy indoor and outdoor pools, a fitness center, racquetball, sauna, Jacuzzi, and tennis courts. There is also a full-service restaurant on the premises.

Doral Arrowwood (914-939-5500, 866-241-8752), Anderson Hill Road, exit 8E off I-287, Rye Brook 10573. ($$$) This full-facility resort of 374 rooms is located on 114 wooded acres. You will find a nine-hole golf course, indoor-outdoor pools, tennis and squash courts, along with a sauna and Universal gym. The atrium dining room is a multilevel restaurant that overlooks the grounds and gardens and serves excellent food. Weekend packages are available during the spring and summer. Children are welcome.

Hampton Inn (914-592-5680, 800-HAMPTON), 200 Tarrytown Road, Elmsford 10523. ($$) There are 156 rooms in this moderately priced hotel. A fitness room and outdoor pool are available to guests, and a deluxe continental breakfast is served from 6–10. Open year-round.

Hilton Rye Town (914-939-6300 or 800-HILTONS), 699 Westchester Avenue, Rye Brook 10573. ($$) This hotel has 436 guest rooms, indoor and outdoor pools, saunas, whirlpool, tennis courts, and an exercise room. There are two restaurants: **Tulip Tree** serves casual, inexpensive fare; **Penfield's** serve gourmet American cuisine (see *Dining Out*).

Ramada Inn (914-273-9090, 800-2-RAMADA), 94 Business Park Drive, exit 3 off I-684, Armonk 10504. ($$) This 140-room, newly renovated hotel has an exercise room and outdoor pool as well as complimentary shuttle service to and from Westchester County Airport. A restaurant is on the premises.

Renaissance Westchester Hotel (914-694-5400), 80 West Red Oak Lane, White Plains 10604. ($$$) This 364-room full-service hotel has an indoor pool, sun deck, whirlpool, sauna, exercise room, and tennis and volleyball courts. Located on 30 wooded acres, there are nice dining facilities in **The Woodlands Restaurant** overlooking the grounds. Special weekend rates.

Westchester Marriott (914-631-2200, 800-228-9290), 670 White Plains Road, exit 1 off I-287 or exit 9 off I-87, Tarrytown 10591. ($$$) The hotel has 444 guest rooms, an indoor pool, sauna, whirlpool, and fitness center. **Allie's Restaurant** serves Continental cuisine; **Ruth's Chris Steakhouse** serves excellent porterhouse steaks in an elegant atmosphere every evening from 5. There is also a nightclub, **Gambits,** and a sports bar, **The Pub,** on the premises. The location is excellent, close to many of the historic attractions in Tarrytown.

✳ Where to Eat

Westchester is fortunate to have hundreds of eateries, in all price ranges and to please all tastes. I only wish I had the time and money to sample all of them—a daunting task. The following were selected from my personal experience traveling throughout the county; they are only some of the fine choices available. Since the county is large, restaurants are grouped by geographic area (northeast, northwest, southwest, southeast, and central). Don't be afraid to try the broad spectrum of places—ranging from Indian and Thai to Italian and Continental—that can be found in this restaurant-intensive region of the Hudson Valley!

Northwestern Westchester (Including Peekskill, Croton, Ossining)

Cactus Jack (914-526-2222), 3258 East Main Street, Mohegan Lake; 210 Saw Mill River Road, Elmsford (914-345-3334). Open daily 11:30–10. Southwestern cuisine is served with a Mexican touch. Sample the fajitas, which are excellent, whether you order the steak, shrimp, or chicken. Children welcome.

Churrasqueira Ribatejo (914-941-5928), 39 Spring Street, Ossining. ($) Open every day 11–10 for lunch and dinner. This family-run Portuguese diner, an informal eatery where you can watch your food being prepared on an open grill, is a real find. The barbecued chicken (or meat) and spicy shrimp with rice and fresh vegetables are piled high on the plate, and the prices here are difficult to beat. The fresh fish (red snapper) and steaming clams in garlic broth are my favorite dishes. For a quick takeout choice (and there's a lot to choose from), go with the homemade cod cakes. Children welcome.

Dudley's (914-941-8674), 6 Rockledge Avenue, Ossining. ($$) Open for lunch Monday through Friday noon–2:30; dinner served daily 6–9:30, Sunday 5:30–8:30. The American cuisine here includes breast of duck, sea scallops, swordfish, and grilled baby pheasant. The sirloin steak is also a popular entrée. A terrific, moderately priced neighborhood restaurant.

India House (914-736-0005), 199 Albany Post Road, Montrose. ($$) Open daily for lunch 11:30–2; dinner 5–10. Lots of greenery surrounds this attractive restaurant. The dining rooms are decorated to resemble a colorful, handmade tent, with walls hung with antique tapestries. Tandoori lamb, chicken, and shrimp dishes are the specialty. The vegetarian entrées are excellent, and everything can be prepared from mild to very hot and spicy—just let the server know your preference. Children welcome.

Iron Horse Grill (914-741-0717) 20 Wheeler Avenue, Pleasantville. ($$$) Open for dinner Tuesday through Saturday from 5. Located around the corner from the Jacob Burns Film Center (see *Entertainment*) in the renovated waiting room of the Pleasantville train station, this establishment specializes in contemporary American cuisine in elegant surroundings. A favorite appetizer of mine is the tuna sashimi with seaweed. Entrées include breast of duck with rhubarb chutney, rack of lamb with polenta, and fillet of yellowtail sole, all creatively presented. Outdoor dining on the patio in the warm-weather months. The prix fixe menu offers excellent value. Good wine list with moderately priced selections.

Monteverde (914-739-5000), Bear Mountain Bridge Road, Peekskill. ($$) Open Monday, Wednesday, Thursday, and Friday for lunch noon–2:30; dinner 5:30–9:30, Saturday 5:30–9:30, Sunday noon–8:30. This 18th-century stone mansion was built by the Van Cortlandt family and is now an outstanding restaurant. Great views of the river and a rural setting make this stop a treat in summer for fine Continental cuisine.

Papillon (914-941-9771), 21 Campwoods Road (off route 133), Ossining. ($) Open Tuesday through Saturday for breakfast 9–11:30 and lunch 11:30–3, Sunday 10:30–2. Dinner served Thursday through Saturday 6–9:30. Formerly an old-fashioned soda fountain and coffee shop, this funky, charming neighborhood restaurant is run by a husband (chef) and wife (baker) who offer hearty food at reasonable prices. Breakfast includes homemade chocolate-chip scones, pancakes, and maple-walnut French toast; there are imaginative wraps, fresh creative salad choices, or overstuffed sandwiches for lunch. The eclectic cuisine combines French, Asian, and contemporary American elements. Try the artichoke reggiano appetizer with minced artichoke hearts, roasted red peppers, garlic and parmigiana cheese served over warm home-baked bread; for an entrée the coq au vin is a good choice. Wine and beer are served. Children welcome. Call in advance to make reservations for the Epicurean dinners, held twice each month; they're a bargain, and you can go alone: seating is at long communal tables.

Susan's (914-737-6624), 12 North Division Street, Peekskill. ($$) Open Tuesday through Saturday for lunch 11:30–3; dinner 5–10. Eclectic international cuisine is served in this informal country bistro. The grilled breast of duck with garlic mashed potatoes, Turkish baked-stuffed eggplant, and salmon strudel with spinach and wild rice are just a few of the excellent dinner entrées. All breads and desserts are made fresh daily on the premises. Children welcome.

Umami (914-271-5555), 325 South Riverside Avenue, Croton-on-Hudson. ($) Open for dinner Sunday through Thursday 5:30–10, Friday and Saturday until 11. Pronounced *oo-MAH-mee*, the word refers to an amino acid present in various acidic foods that gives them a more complex taste. Diners in this intimate, simply furnished eatery will enjoy citrus flavors and interesting food combinations. The imaginatively prepared international cooking features specialties like coconut lime soup with chicken, shrimp, or vegetables; mini tacos with seared tuna guacamole and wasabi-laced sour cream; Peking duck quesadilla; or Thai-style curry. Try the Blue Pig ice cream for dessert. This restaurant opened in 2002 and has a dedicated local following. Reasonable prices for healthful delicious creations.

Zephs' (914-736-2159), 638 Central Avenue, Peekskill. ($$$) Open Wednesday through Sunday at 5:30 for dinner. Set in a reclaimed factory building, Zephs' serves American cuisine with a fresh twist. Choices may include Moroccan lamb, potato-crusted salmon, tomato tart, salt and pepper squid, fresh fruit cobblers, mud cake, and rich custards. Many of the herbs are grown by the owners, and summer diners can enjoy the outdoor patio area. Reservations are necessary.

Northeastern Westchester (Including North and South Salem, Katonah, Mt. Kisco, Pound Ridge, Chappaqua)

Auberge Maxime (914-669-5450), Route 116, North Salem. ($$$) Open Thursday through Monday for lunch at noon and dinner at 6. Enjoy classical French cuisine with a nouvelle touch in this lovely country inn. Comfortable chairs and beautifully appointed tables grace the dining room, and the six-course prix fixe dinner includes such treats as duck with pear and fresh ginger sauce and hot and cold soufflés.

Bacio Trattoria (914-763-2233), Corner of Routes 35 and 121, Cross River. ($$) Open for lunch Tuesday through Saturday 11–3, Sunday 12:30–3; dinner Tuesday through Thursday 5–9:30, Friday and Saturday until 10, Sunday 3–9. This intimate restaurant has a large outdoor patio for al fresco dining in the summer months; there is a relaxed leisurely pace about the service. The grilled calamari is excellent, and so is the white-bean soup and roasted-vegetable ravioli with walnut sauce. Lemon risotto with grilled scallops and monkfish fillet in cherry tomato and garlic sauce are also popular here. For dessert try the apple pie à la mode. Moderately priced wine list. Children's menu.

The Blue Dolphin Ristorante (914-232-4791), 175 Katonah Avenue, Katonah. ($) Open daily except Sunday for lunch 11–3; dinner 5–10. This family-owned and -operated Italian restaurant housed in a diner-like building, is a mainstay in town. Don't miss the ziti blue dolphin, fried calamari, and excellent soups. The prices are exceedingly reasonable and the service is friendly. A wonderful choice for those traveling with children.

Café Antico (914-242-7490), 251 Lexington Avenue. Mount Kisco. ($$) Open for lunch Monday through Saturday 11:30–3:30; dinner Sunday through Wednesday 3:30–11, Thursday through Saturday until midnight; Sunday brunch 11:30–3. A dark, romantic, candlelit atmosphere prevails in this late-night spot where dinner is served until midnight on weekends. A great place to enjoy drinks, antipasto, terrific salads, or one of the excellent pasta dishes. Live music (usually jazz) on Fridays from 9:30 on.

Crabtree's Kittle House (914-666-8044), Route 117, Mount Kisco. ($$$) Open for lunch Monday through Friday noon–2:30; dinner served daily 5:30–10; Sunday brunch noon–2:30. The American cuisine here has Italian, French, and Asian influences. The menu changes daily, but the excellent roasted free-range Hudson Valley chicken with black truffles is a specialty of the house. There is an award-winning wine cellar here. The pastry chef suggests the Alsatian cheesecake with huckleberry sauce—one of his favorites. Live jazz on Friday and Saturday night.

Finch Tavern (914-277-4580), 592 Route 22, Croton Falls. ($$$) Open for lunch Tuesday through Friday 11:30–2:30; dinner Tuesday through Thursday 5:30–10, Friday and Saturday until 11, Sunday 5–9. The creative American regional cuisine begins with excellent bread and high quality olive oil in this Victorian-style structure where an enormous mural of horses covers one of the walls. The appetizers are served in generous portions, and one could certainly make a meal from two of them. The Maryland crabcake with rémoulade sauce is excellent, as is the Asian marinated tuna tartare with avocado puree and cucumber mango salad. The lamb shank and Atlantic salmon are favorite entrées of mine. Decadent desserts include three different tropical sorbets and apple walnut tart with cinnamon caramel sauce and vanilla ice cream.

The Fish Cellar (914-666-4448), 213 Main Street, Mount Kisco. ($$) Open for dinner Tuesday through Saturday 5–10. If you have a craving for oysters or clams from a huge raw bar or desire a steamed (or grilled) lobster, head to this delightful restaurant. A blackboard by the bar lists the latest selections from cold-water fishing areas, guiding diners to order the freshest fare available. The Copper River wild salmon is phenomenal, but the season is a short one—just two weeks in June. A side salad is actually included with dinner entrées, a rarity these days. For those who enjoy exceedingly fresh seafood, a stop here is a must.

The Flying Pig (914-666-7445), 1 Kirby Plaza, Mount Kisco. ($$) Open for lunch Monday through Saturday 11:30–3; dinner Wednesday through Sunday 6–9:30; Sunday brunch 10–3. Located in the Mount Kisco train station, this café-market serves and sells Hudson Valley organic farm fare; the menu changes seasonally, and offerings depend on what is available locally. The rack of lamb is excellent; the pork is meaty and tender (the animals are grass-fed, which makes an enormous difference in the taste). Spinach in phyllo pastry is another of my favorite items on the menu at this eatery with healthful food and reasonable prices. After 3 PM Tuesday through Friday, coffee, hot chocolate, and cider are free. Children are welcome.

Inn at Pound Ridge (914-764-5779), 258 Westchester Avenue, Pound Ridge. ($$$) Open Tuesday through Friday for lunch noon–2:30; dinner 6–9; Sunday brunch noon–2. The American cuisine here includes rack of lamb, roasted duck, sautéed pork chops, and grilled swordfish, served in a New England–style country inn with rustic elegance. The menu is contemporary, yet familiar, and all breads and desserts are made fresh daily on the premises. The proprietor enjoys the mudslide pie with Kahlúa and Bailey's Irish Cream or coconut flan with roasted pineapple to top off the meal. Jackets preferred for men at dinner. Reservations suggested.

La Camelia (914-666-2466), 234 North Bedford Road, Mount Kisco. ($$) Open daily except Monday for lunch noon–3; dinner from 6; Sunday brunch noon–3:30, with classical guitarist on occasion. One of the best Spanish restaurants you will find anywhere in the county, La Camelia is located in a landmark, nearly 150-year-old building. Northern Spanish cuisine is the specialty and includes gazpacho, shrimp Catalan, squid with angel hair pasta, and homemade desserts. Children welcome.

La Tulipe Desserts (914-242-4555), 455 Lexington Avenue, Mount Kisco. ($) Open Thursday through Saturday 7:30–6:30; Sunday 8–2. Closed Monday and for two weeks in January and August. You will feel transported to a European patisserie when you see the phenomenal marzipan fruits, handmade truffles, lemon tartlets with meringue cones, and other tempting treats displayed here. The young owner hails from Holland, where he studied baking; he also went to school in Paris to learn his craft. The finest ingredients are used in all the creations in this unassuming oasis of desserts. A rare find, and definitely worth a stop if you are in the area.

Le Chateau (914-533-6631), Route 35, South Salem. ($$$) Open daily except Monday for dinner at 6. This French restaurant with old-world charm is situated on 32 wooded acres and offers magnificent sunset views and lavishly decorated dining rooms. House specialties include wild mushroom soup, salmon in parchment, and quail in raspberry sauce. An assortment of mousses set in crème anglaise are served for dessert. This is a perfect choice for a special occasion; Le Chateau is elegant, and the cuisine and service are first-rate.

L'Europe (914-533-2570), Route 123, South Salem. ($$$) Open for lunch Wednesday through Saturday noon–2:30; dinner 6–9:30; Sunday brunch noon–2:30, dinner 3–8. This traditional French dining establishment, reminiscent of an English club, serves outstanding cuisine. Specialties include grilled salmon, duck with five different sauces, and rack of lamb. The tempting desserts include chocolate or raspberry soufflé with Grand Marnier. Business casual attire; jackets preferred at dinner for men. You might not think it, but children are warmly welcomed here. Reservations suggested.

Nino's (914-533-2671), 355 Route 123 South Salem. ($$) Open daily for lunch 12–3; dinner from 5–10. This simple restaurant serving Northern Italian cuisine is run by five brothers. Try the fried calamari and grilled veal chops. The Dover sole with lemon, white wine, and garlic is another of my favorites from the extensive menu. And save room for one of the treats from the multitiered dessert cart. Not recommended for children.

Purdy's Homestead (914-277-2301), 100 Titicus Road, North Salem. ($$) This renovated 18th-century farmhouse surrounded by an intricate wrought-iron fence was constructed by the Purdy family in 1775. There are fireplaces, beautiful wide-plank wood floors, tables with lots of room between them, and a porch for outdoor dining in the summer months. Warm, delicious cheddar biscuits begin the meal; however, breads and entrées change seasonally. The salsify and oyster soup is excellent. For an entrée, there is baked brook trout, sea scallops, or rack of lamb, all served with fresh vegetables. Sweet potato pie accompanies the lamb in wine sauce with fresh mint. Portions are generous, and that includes desserts. Try the pumpkin cheesecake topped with poached cranberries or apple tart with pecan ice cream.

Central Westchester (Including White Plains, Larchmont, Scarsdale, Hartsdale Area)

Auberge Argenteuil (914-948-0597), 42 Healy Avenue, Hartsdale. ($$$) Open daily except Monday for lunch 11:30–2:30 and dinner 5:30–9:30; Sunday noon–7. In June, July, and August no lunch served. Set in a building that was a speakeasy in the 1920s, this restaurant is hidden high up in a wooded area above Central Avenue. Specialties include lobster bisque, veal with wild mushrooms, and a superb ice cream bombe. Not recommended for children.

Harry's of Hartsdale (914-472-8777), 230 East Hartsdale Avenue, Hartsdale. Open daily for lunch 11:30–3; dinner 3–10:30. This steakhouse is also known for its raw bar, which offers shrimp, lobster, crabmeat, and clams. I could dine at least twice a week at the oyster bar that serves at least six types of oysters (which vary seasonally). They sell over

3,000 oysters a week. In addition to steaks, chicken, pasta, and fish entrées are served. Family atmosphere—children are welcome.

Lusardi's (914-834-5555), 1885 Palmer Avenue, Larchmont. ($$) Open daily for lunch and dinner noon–10:30. The Northern Italian cuisine here has a Mediterranean accent; it's served in an informal atmosphere. Enjoy veal Martini, homemade pasta stuffed with spinach and porcini mushrooms, or artichoke salad with arugula, Parmesan cheese, and diced cherry tomatoes. Children welcome.

Mulino's (914-761-1818), 99 Court Street, White Plains. ($$) Open for lunch Monday through Friday 11:30–4; dinner 4–11:30; Saturday dinner only 5-midnight. The Northern Italian cuisine here is quite good, and the tables look out on a courtyard garden with waterfalls. This is the gathering place of several politicians in Westchester County, White Plains being the county seat, and the location of the restaurant is in the downtown area. Enjoy rack of lamb, veal chop, fresh fish, including Dover sole, and save room for the tempting desserts. Children are welcome.

Olde Stone Mill (914-771-7661), 2 Scarsdale Road, Tuckahoe. ($$). Open for lunch Monday through Saturday 11:30–3; dinner 5–10, Sunday 3–9. Housed in a renovated century-old mill on the banks of the Bronx River, this restaurant has spacious, bright dining rooms and beautiful views, along with wonderful reasonably priced food. The imaginative American cuisine includes lobster seviche or beet and goat cheese salad for appetizers; both are first-rate. The rack of lamb coated with herbed and buttered bread crumbs, served with roasted potatoes and fresh-cooked spinach was excellent. The pumpkin cheesecake and carrot cake are among the mouthwatering desserts.

Pete's Saloon (914-592-9849), 8 West Main Street, Elmsford. ($$) Open daily 11:30–midnight. This informal eatery with a busy bar serves classic American favorites, including a variety of burgers, steaks, sandwiches, and salads. The stuffed pork chops and lemon chicken are two popular entrées. There are over 40 bottled beers available as well as 9 beers on tap; and there are 30 different single-malt scotches to choose from. Entertainment five nights a week starting at around 10 PM.

Ray's Café (914-833-2551), 1995 Palmer Avenue, Larchmont. ($$) Open for lunch Monday through Friday noon–3; dinner 3–10, Saturday 3–10:30, Sunday 3–9:30. This Chinese restaurant serves Shanghai-style cuisine. The crispy shrimp with honey walnuts is excellent, as is the sesame chicken. You can also order crispy or steamed whole fish, prepared to order the way you like it. Children welcome.

Rustico (914-472-4005), 753 Central Park Avenue, Scarsdale. ($$) Open Monday through Saturday 11:30–10, Sunday 4–10. Northern Italian cuisine with a French influence is the style of cooking here. There are standard favorites like veal scaloppini as well as an array of pasta dishes (all pasta is homemade on the premises). The gnocchi and fettuccine are excellent.

Watercolor Café (914-834-2213), 2094 Boston Post Road, Larchmont. ($$) Open for lunch Monday through Saturday 11:30–3:30; dinner daily 4–9:30; Sunday brunch noon–3. This restaurant derives its name from the decor: watercolor paintings by local artists. The contemporary American cuisine includes such intriguing dishes as hoisin-barbecued chicken, grilled shrimp over angel hair pasta served with basil cream sauce, and pecan-crusted salmon. Live music on Wednesday through Saturday nights; call to check the schedule.

Southwestern Westchester (River Towns: Tarrytown, Irvington, Hastings, Dobbs Ferry)

Blu (914-478-4481), 100 River Street, Hastings-on-Hudson. ($$) Open for lunch Monday through Friday 11:30–2:30; dinner Monday through Saturday 5–10, Sunday 4–8; Sunday brunch 11:30–2:30. There are great views of the Hudson River from the dining room and deck here, the perfect place to enjoy clams and oysters in-season. The Blu Cobb salad, grilled lamb chops, grilled red snapper, and sesame salmon are just some of the offerings to be found at this delightful bistro. Their chocolate malteds are made the old-fashioned way, so if you're an aficionado, this is where to order one. Children welcome.

Buffet de la Gare (914-478-1671), 155 Southside Avenue, Hastings-on-Hudson. ($$$) Open for lunch Thursday and Friday noon–2; dinner Tuesday through Saturday from 6. Enjoy classical French cuisine in a relaxing ambience. Everything here is prepared to order, and the desserts should not be passed up. The fine reputation of this establishment, long a favorite with local residents, has spread throughout the county.

Chart House (914-693-4130), High Street, Dobbs Ferry. ($$) Open for dinner Monday through Saturday at 5, Sunday noon–9. This contemporary restaurant has a magnificent view of the Palisades, the Tappan Zee Bridge, and the New York City skyline. If you want to dine and look out at the Hudson River, this is a good place to go. Specialties include prime rib, thick steaks, and an enormous selection of seafood and fish entrées. Their mud pie is famous throughout the area. Children are welcome.

Equus Restaurant at the Castle at Tarrytown (914-631-3646), 400 Benedict Avenue, Tarrytown. ($$$) Open daily for lunch and dinner and Sunday brunch. This is one of the most romantic spots in the region, located in a castle constructed almost 100 years ago. The restaurant has several elegantly appointed rooms as well as an enclosed veranda with magnificent views of the Hudson River. The Oak Room is constructed of wood brought from Germany. The smoked fillet of Black Angus beef with sweet potato tamale, corn truffles, and chipotle bordelaise is wonderful. You might also try medallions of venison in-season with warm mango and green peppercorn sauce or a root vegetable stew *en papillote*. Save room for the beautifully presented and mouthwatering desserts.

Harvest on Hudson (914-478-2800), 1 River Street, Hastings-on-Hudson. ($$$) Open for lunch Monday through Friday noon–2:30; dinner Monday through Thursday 5–10, Friday and Saturday until 11, Sunday 5–9. This huge mission-style building at the edge of the Hudson offers wonderful views of the river as well as their own herb and vegetable gardens. The eclectic contemporary American cuisine includes ahi tuna seared and served with rice, wasabi vinaigrette, and seaweed salad as well as an array

of pastas, quail, sea scallops, and steak entrées. There are covered and open patio areas for al fresco dining in the warm-weather months. Live entertainment on Friday nights 9–1. The sorbets and chocolate mousse are highly recommended. The drinks here are expensive, however.

Horsefeathers (914-631-6606), 94 North Broadway, Tarrytown. ($$) Open daily at 11:30 for lunch and dinner. Saturday and Sunday brunch served 11:30–4. One of the first "grazing" restaurants in the county, Horsefeathers continues to offer great cafe food like burgers, steaks, and overstuffed sandwiches and wraps. The atmosphere is casual and comfortable, and children are welcome.

Main Street Café (914-524-9770), 24 Main Street, Tarrytown. ($$) Open for lunch Tuesday through Saturday noon–3; dinner 5–10; Sunday brunch noon–3 and dinner 3–9. A casual stop for bistro food and jazz entertainment, this restaurant features contemporary American cuisine including a wide variety of pasta entrées, steaks, fresh seafood, and an extensive wine list.

Santa Fe (914-332-4452), 5 Main Street, Tarrytown. ($$) Open daily for lunch and dinner 11:30–10. You can get steak, chicken, shrimp, and even shark fajitas at this colorful Mexican dining spot. For taco lovers there is a make-your-own taco basket, and diners are served chicken or beef, beans, rice and peppers, and other fixings from which they can create their own meal. One of the most unusual and delicious dishes is the shrimp and crab enchiladas with blue corn tortillas. Children are welcome.

Sunset Cove (914-366-7889), 238 Green Street (the Washington

Irving Boat Club), Tarrytown. ($$) Open for lunch Monday through Saturday 11:30–3; dinner daily 5–11, Sunday brunch 11:30–3.The views of the Hudson are wonderful, especially if you dine outdoors on the large sweeping patio at the river's edge at sunset. The sun goes down behind the Palisades in full view of the Tappan Zee Bridge, while boats pass by. If you opt to drink and have a light meal, try the calamari or clams on the half shell. Entrées that are quite good are the Moroccan chicken with polenta, rack of lamb with Gorgonzola, and grilled salmon. For dessert, the pear tart or Sunset sundae are good bets. Children welcome.

Sushi Mike's (914-591-0054), 146 Main Street, Dobbs Ferry. ($$) Open for lunch weekdays except Tuesday 11:30–3; dinner daily except Tuesday 4:30–10, Sunday 3–10. In addition to the expected sushi, sashimi, and teriyaki dishes of Japanese restaurants, there are several unusual offerings here. Try the grilled yellowtail cheek (*hamachi kama*), *negitoro* (finely chopped yellowtail and mild Japanese leek), or Sushi Mike's roll. The Fantastic Roll is huge, wrapped in white seaweed, and filled with salmon, tuna, yellowtail, flying fish roe, avocado, and vegetables. For dessert there is mochi, a sweet rice paste that has ice cream in the center. Children welcome.

Thai Garden (914-524-5003), 128 Cortlandt Street, Sleepy Hollow. ($) Open for dinner Tuesday through Sunday 5–10. The festive decor here includes masks of Buddha and prints depicting life in the Thailand of a bygone era. The chef is a master of vegetable and fruit carving, so get ready for an exciting presentation that complements the first-rate Thai cuisine. For first-timers, try the Thai Garden sampler appetizer. The grilled chicken satay or skewered jumbo shrimp (on bamboo skewers) are quite good, and for the more adventurous there are Thai dumplings, whole red snapper, and boneless roasted duck in red curry with coconut milk and basil. The server will inquire at the beginning of the meal just how spicy you like your meal. Try Thai iced tea or Singha, the Thai beer, both a good accompaniment to the array of exotic flavors.

Zuppa (914-376-6500), 59 Main Street, Yonkers. ($$) Open for lunch Monday through Friday 11:30–2:30, Sunday 11:30–3; dinner Monday through Thursday 5–10, Friday and Saturday 5–11, Sunday 5–9. Live music on Wednesday, Friday, and Saturday evenings. Enjoy relaxed dining at this spacious, comfortable restaurant and bar, located by the waterfront area of Yonkers. The renovated *Gazette Press* factory building provides a wonderful ambience for this elegant new (2003) establishment, which boasts a plethora of imaginative Italian dishes, including perciatelli pasta with lobster and roasted garlic or porterhouse steak with oyster mushrooms. Diners may choose from a wide variety of international wines as well as an outstanding selection of desserts, including a heavenly slice of warm chocolate cake topped with caramel ice cream.

Southeastern Westchester (Including Rye, Rye Brook, Mamaroneck, Eastchester, and New Rochelle)

Aberdeen (914-835-0880), 278 Halstead Avenue, Harrison. ($$) Open for lunch and dinner Monday through

Friday 11:30–10, Saturday and Sunday 11–10. Enjoy the fresh ingredients of over 125 entrées at this authentic Cantonese restaurant. Dishes are light and savory, with strategically mingled flavors, and if you order fish, you will have an opportunity to inspect it before preparation. Indulge in chicken, duck, pork, or beef dishes—and even frogs legs—or such entrées as scallop and bean curd with black-bean sauce and beef with snow peas and oyster sauce. The huge fish tank will delight the kids!

Abis (914-698-8777), 406 Mamaroneck Avenue, Mamaroneck. ($$) Open for lunch Monday through Saturday 11:30–2:30; dinner served daily 5:30–10. This lovely Japanese restaurant serves teriyaki dishes as well as sushi and sashimi.

Bayou (914-668-2634), 580 Gramatan Avenue, Mount Vernon. ($$) Open daily for lunch and dinner 11:30–11. The Cajun Creole cuisine includes stuffed pork chops, jambalaya, gumbo, and mudbugs (boiled crawfish). For those who prefer less adventurous fare, steak, sandwiches, and burgers are offered, as well.

Coromanbel Cuisine of India (914-235-8390), 30 Division Street, New Rochelle. ($$) Open daily for lunch noon–2:30; dinner 5–10. Authentic Indian cuisine is served in an atmosphere of Indian decor and music. The menu features tandoori specialties as well as classical Indian curries and vegetable fritters. There is an exotic dessert consisting of frozen milk with cashews, raisins, and saffron, which should be tried if you have never sampled it.

Eastchester Fish Gourmet (914-725-3450), 837 White Plains Road, Scarsdale. ($$$) Open for lunch Thursday and Friday 11:30–2:30; Dinner Sunday through Thursday 5–9:30, Friday and Saturday until 11. Nautical decor adorns this classic fish and seafood restaurant a few doors away from the Eastchester Fish Market. An array of consistently first-rate dishes are imaginatively prepared with interesting fruit, vegetable, and herb reductions that complement the fish. To start, try jumbo crabcake with pickled sweet red pepper or tuna and salmon carpaccio with pear, ginger, and lime. Enjoy swordfish with black olive butter as an entrée, or Dover sole with sweet anise. Piano music on weekends. Children welcome.

Emilio (914-835-3100), 1 Colonial Place, Harrison. ($$$) Open for lunch Tuesday through Friday noon–2:30; dinner Tuesday through Saturday 5:30–10:30, Sunday 5–9. This regional Italian restaurant is housed in a Colonial-style house; as one enters the large main dining room, you can't help but notice the huge antipasto table. Fresh pasta, made on the premises daily, is excellent. The spinach lasagna and wild-mushroom ravioli are my favorites. The menu changes seasonally, and in the winter months there are interesting game dishes from which to choose. Children welcome.

F.I.S.H. (914-939-4227), 102 Fox Island Road, Port Chester. ($$) Open for lunch Wednesday through Sunday 11:30–3; dinner served daily 5:30–10; until 11 Thursday through Saturday. Late night bar menu on weekends. This lively, waterfront restaurant (Fox Island Seafood House) uses local organic produce, and their fried calamari, Caesar salad, crabcakes, and fish specials are first-rate. Landlubbers should note that there are meat dishes offered, and they serve up decent steaks.

Koo (914-921-9888), 17 Purdy Avenue, Rye. ($$) Open for lunch every day except Sunday 11:45 AM –3 PM; dinner served daily 5–10 and until 11 weekend nights. This unassuming Japanese dining spot features excellent sushi, sashimi, and tempura dishes, along with fusion creations that are particularly flavorful and worth trying. Don't miss the green apple sorbet for dessert. Children welcome.

Le Provencal Bistro (914-777-2324), 436 Mamaroneck Avenue, Mamaroneck. ($$) Open daily for lunch and weekend brunch noon–3; dinner 6–10. Enjoy home-style cooking found in French bistros. On Mondays, all-you-can-eat mussels cost only $17.50. There is excellent foie gras, along with comfort foods like lamb sirloin and chicken with lentils and carrots. For dessert, enjoy chocolate-mousse cake or biscotti. Children welcome.

La Panetiere (914-967-8140), 530 Milton Road, Rye. ($$$) Open for lunch Monday through Friday noon–2:30; dinner Monday through Saturday 6–9:30. Sunday 1–8:30; dinner served all day long. Housed in a building that dates back to the 1800s, with a Provencal interior featuring exposed beams, stucco walls, and a huge grandfather clock, this is one of the finest restaurants in the county. Appetizer specials include warm oysters with leeks, duck terrine with truffles and pistachios, and fresh foie gras; entrées include squab, venison, and Dover sole filled with puree of artichokes. A six-course prix-fixe menu is available and is a good value. This is a place to go to celebrate a special occasion.

Penfield's (914-939-6300), 699 Westchester Avenue, Rye Brook. ($$$) Open for dinner Monday–

Saturday 6–10. This restaurant, located in the Rye Town Hilton, features upscale American cuisine. Try the rack of lamb or fresh fillet of Dover sole. Save room for one of the marvelous desserts.

Satsumaya (914-381-0200) 576 Mamaroneck Avenue, Mamaroneck. ($$) Open for dinner Tuesday–Sunday 5–10. There is a sushi bar at this Japanese restaurant, which serves a variety of tempura and teriyaki selections. The noodle dishes are a specialty of the house.

Seaside Johnnie's (914-921-6104), 94 Dearborn Avenue, Oakland Beach, Rye. ($$) Open for lunch Monday through Saturday 11–4, Sunday until 3; dinner menu available all day until 11 every night; Friday and Saturday until midnight. Enjoy magnificent views of Long Island Sound from the dining room, and in the warm weather, dine on the large open terrace, where you can watch the sea gulls and take in the fresh salty air. There are cherry-stone clams, steamers, fried calamari, barbecued ribs, and grilled swordfish, which are all prepared decently. Stick with ice cream for dessert. Children welcome.

Underhill's Crossing (914-337-1200), 74½ Pondfield Road, Bronxville. ($$) Open daily 11:30–10. The eclectic Asian-fusion cuisine ranges from pizza, sandwiches and burgers, to veal, lamb and salmon entrées. Every dish is prepared to order. This eight-year-old restaurant is popular with local residents.

✳ Entertainment

Bendheim Performing Arts Center (914-472-3300, ext. 403), 999 Wilmot Road, Scarsdale. This theater, with over 200 seats, offers a distinctive entertainment experience—musical and theatrical performances, comedy acts, lively lectures with leading intellectuals, and a wide variety of children's programs.

Jacob Burns Film Center (914-747-5555), 364 Manville Road, Pleasantville. If you will be in the area, check out this three-screen theater that features foreign, independent, documentary, and classic films. There are retrospectives, film festivals, and special series offerings year-round. The historic theater, which dates back to 1925, closed its doors in 1987. But thanks to Friends of the Rome Theater, it reopened in 2001. Close to 3,000 memberships were sold within the first two months, and the cinema has become a cultural phenomenon, drawing moviegoers from all over the county. Two of the three theaters collaborate with the Film Soceity of Lincoln Center, and the advisory committee includes Martin Scorcese, Christopher Reeve, Glenn Close, Susan Sarandon, and Richard Gere. You do not have to be a member to attend a movie; call for a schedule.

Caramoor Center for Music and the Arts (914-232-5035), 149 Girdle Ridge Road, Katonah. This Katonah Landmark (see *Historic Homes*) is home to the annual Caramoor International Music Festival, one of the top five outdoor festivals in the country (see *Special Events*). For eight weeks every summer the two outdoor theaters here are filled with music created by the world's best classical, operatic and jazz artists. There are other performances in the warm-weather months; call for a schedule.

Emelin Theatre (914-698-0098), 153 Library Lane, Mamaroneck. This theater has been in operation for over 30 years, and offers exceptional entertainment in 11 different series including theater, family programs, classical music, folk, jazz, holiday performances, klezmer, bluegrass, children's offerings, film, and lectures. Call for a schedule.

Fleetwood Stage (914-654-8949), 44 Wildcliff Drive, New Rochelle. This professional Equity theater offers a wide range of programming, including new plays and Shakespeare, during 35 weeks of the year. There are also workshops in playwriting.

Northern Westchester Center for the Arts (914-241-6922), 272 North Bedford Road, Mount Kisco. Open Monday through Friday 9–9; Saturday and Sunday hours vary, so call ahead. There are changing art exhibits, concerts, recitals, and a poetry series. Art, dance, music, theater, and creative writing classes are offered year-round.

Paramount Center for the Arts (914-739-2333), 1008 Brown Street, Peekskill. This restored 1,000-seat movie palace of the 1930s offers quality arts and entertainment, ranging from classical to pop, comedy to drama, art exhibits, independent films, and children's programs. The theater's facade contains its original 2,000-bulb marquee with running chase lights.

Performing Arts Center (914-251-6200), SUNY Purchase, Anderson Hill Road, Purchase. There are five theaters here that offer more than 70 events annually in dance, classical music, jazz, and more. Call for a schedule.

Philipsburgh Performing Arts Center (914-964-8977), 2–8 Hudson Street at Getty Square, Yonkers.

From its opening 98 years ago, the ballroom was a legendary performance and party hall. Now renovated and in use for the first time in over 30 years, this center offers a program of performances, exhibits, and arts education workshops for children and adults. There is chamber music, jazz, dance, and choral and orchestral performances, as well as film and lectures. Call for a schedule.

Tarrytown Music Hall (914-631-3390), 13 Main Street, Tarrytown. This national landmark dates back to 1885. The 840-seat theater has Queen Anne, Victorian, and art deco elements, and is home to the Jazz Forum Arts Series, folk blues, children's performances, classical music, and musical theater. Call for a schedule of events.

Westchester Broadway Theatre (914-592-2222), One Broadway Plaza, Elmsford. Enjoy popular musical revivals in this intimate dinner theater where all 450 seats have a great view of the 30-by-35-foot stage. Before the show, enjoy a three-course meal served at your table. This is the longest-running year-round Equity theater in the state of New York.

Westchester Community College (914-785-6567), 75 Grasslands Road, Valhalla. A mixture of musical, dance, and theatrical performances are offered here as well as a Friday evening film series. Call for a schedule.

Westchester County Center (914-995-1050), 198 Central Avenue, White Plains. There is a 100-seat Little Theatre in this multipurpose facility as well as a 12,800-foot exhibit hall with changing shows throughout the year. Call for a schedule of events.

Yorktown Stage (914-962-0606), 1974 Commerce Street, Yorktown Heights. This 600-seat regional theater offers professional musical productions and plays. There are children's events, classical music, and dance. Call for a schedule.

✳ Selective Shopping

Westchester County is often synonymous with shopping. The county has many charming downtown shopping districts in villages like Briarcliff Manor, Pleasantville, Chappaqua, Mount Kisco, Bedford, and Katonah. The best way to see the interesting small boutiques, bookstores, and specialty shops is to wander through these towns at a leisurely pace. The following selection of antiques stores, auctions, and shopping centers is by no means comprehensive but rather is intended as a guide to discovering the shopper's paradise that exists in the county.

Antiques and Auctions

In Bedford Hills, visit the **Antiques Marketplace** (914-242-9846), 297 Bedford Road, which carries thousands of pieces dating back to 1850, including furniture, jewelry, paintings, lamps, and decorative accessories for gifts or home. They are open Tuesday through Saturday 11–5. Also in town is **Archi-Treasures** (914-666-4242), at 215 Railroad Avenue, which specializes in antiques, architectural salvage, and vintage items. They are open Monday through Saturday 10–5. **Bedford Salvage Company** (914-666-4595), 2 Depot Plaza, has fine architectural salvage and European and American country antiques. Open Tuesday through Friday 11–4, Saturday 11–5, or by appointment.

In Cross River, don't miss **The Yellow Monkey Antiques** (914-763-

5848), 792 Route 35, with 8,000 square feet of elegant European country furniture and accessories like glassware, china, and linens plus custom design services. They are open Tuesday through Sunday 1–5:30.

In Hastings-on-Hudson, there is **Riverrun Rare Book Room** (914-478-1339), 12 Washington Avenue, open daily 11–5, with over 200,000 books in categories ranging from Shakespeare and James Joyce to history, travel, art, and poetry. There are 10,000 American fiction titles alone. Used and rare-book aficionados won't want to miss this wonderful store.

In Larchmont, **Designer's Corner** (914-834-9170), 2082 Boston Post Road, specializes in fully restored vintage and antique chandeliers, sconces, and lamps as well as antique furniture and accessories. **Dualities Antiques and Art, Inc.** (914-834-2773), 2056 Boston Post Road, has paintings, sculpture, fine porcelain ceramics, glass, silver, and decorative objects. They have been in business for almost 30 years and are open Monday through Saturday 10–5. **Milestones Antiques & Collectibles, Inc.** (914-833-3133), 2134 Larchmont Avenue, with turn of the century antiques (1890–1920) and collectibles of all types including vintage or postwar classic items, lamps, tables, and prints. Open Tuesday through Sunday 1–6.

In Tarrytown, there are several antiques shops along Main Street. **The Arcadia Shoppe** (914-631-7884), 23 Main Street, offers antiques, fine art, jewelry, furniture, and accessories; open Wednesday through Sunday, noon–5. **Belkind Bigi Antiques Ltd.** (914-524-9626), 19 Main Street, has both antiques and contemporary furniture and gifts. They are also open Wednesday through Sunday, noon–5. **Bittersweet Antique Center** (914-366-6292), has an array of things including books, jewelry, porcelain, quilts, and country items. Open Wednesday through Sunday noon–5:30. Also on Main Street is **Michael Christopher Antiques** (914-366-4665), 23 Main Street; **Remember Me Antiques** (914-631-4080), 9 Main Street; **Tarrytown Antiques Center** (914-366-4613), 25 Main Street; and **Tarrytown Art & Antiques Company** (914-524-9626), 19 Main Street. All are open Wednesday through Sunday, noon–5.

There are two major auction services in the county: **Campbell's** (914-734-7414), 1000 North Division Street, Peekskill, which holds auctions every other week, usually on Wednesday evenings from 6–9. Preview of items begins at noon on the day of the auction. **Corcoran & Clarke, Inc.** (914-833-8336), 20 North Avenue, Larchmont, holds auctions every four weeks on Monday evenings, beginning at 6. Preview of items is held the weekend before the auction, Saturday and Sunday 10–6.

Shopping Centers

Cross County Shopping Center (914-968-9570), Yonkers. Open daily 10–9. This is the county's largest mall, with over a million square feet of space across several buildings joined by a promenade. There are over 100 stores here.

Empire State Jewelry Exchange & Flea Market (914-939-1800), Port Chester. Open Friday through Sunday; call for hours, which vary with the season. This exchange/flea market has over 100 vendors with new merchandise.

Manufacturers Outlet Center
(914-241-8503), Mount Kisco. There
are over 30 stores with name-brand
items sold at discounted prices.

Vernon Hills Shopping Center
(914-472-2000), Eastchester. Several
upscale stores; hours vary with the
establishment. This is not an enclosed
mall but an outdoor shopping center.

The Westchester (914-683-8600),
White Plains. There are over 150 fine
stores in this 830,000-square-foot mall
featuring upscale amenities like valet
parking, bronze sculptures, and marble and carpeted floors.

✳ Special Events

April: **Washington Irving's Birthday Celebration** (914-631-8200),
Sunnyside, Route 9, Tarrytown.
Admission fee. There are shadow
puppet performances, storytellers,
crafts, games, and food at this annual
event, which is especially fun for children. **Sheep to Shawl** (914-631-
8200), Philipsburg Manor, Route 9,
Sleepy Hollow. Admission fee. Scot-
tish border collies exhibit their sheepherding skill, plus enjoy shearing,
wool dyeing, and cloth-weaving
demonstrations at this annual spring
event.

May: **Annual Flower Festival** (914-
965-4027), Philipse Manor Hall State
Historic Site, Yonkers. Free. There
are plant and flower sales, arts and
crafts, and music at this festival welcoming the spring season. **White
Plains Cherry Blossom Festival**
(914-422-1336), Tibbets Park, White
Plains. Free. Asian-influenced activities and entertainment amid the flowering cherry blossom trees: origami
workshops, Taiko drummers, tea ceremonies, and karate exhibitions.
Spring Fest (914-864-7282), Mus-

coot Farm Somers. Admission fee.
This family event includes music,
sheep shearing, pony rides, and children's activities. **Pinkster** (914-631-
8200), Philipsburg Manor, Sleepy
Hollow. Admission fee. A multicultural
festival recreating an African American
celebration of spring in colonial times
with music, dance, food, and revelry.
Shadfest (914-864-PARK), Croton
Point Park, Croton-on-Hudson.
Admission fee. This annual celebration
of the arrival of shad season includes
shad and other seafood tastings, musical entertainment, and boat races.

Late May–early June: **Westchester
County Fair** (914-968-4200), Yonkers
Raceway, Yonkers. Admission fee. For
over 20 years this county fair has featured rides, shows, games, food, and
performances of all kinds. Usually it is
held for two weeks—the last week in
May and the first week in June.

May and September: **Crafts at Lyndhurst** (914-631-4481), Lyndhurst Historic Site, Route 9, Tarrytown. The
craft shows are usually held the third
weekend of May and the third weekend of September, Friday and Sunday
10–5, Saturday 10–6. Admission fee.
This spectacular crafts fair has
become a Westchester tradition for
more than a 15 years. Craftspeople
from across the country participate—
potters, jewelers, fiber artists, and
glassmakers. There is a children's tent
with activities, so parents can shop in
the huge tents unimpeded. A tour of
the Lyndhurst mansion is available at
a discount to those who attend the
show. Food vendors offer an array of
delicious treats. Be sure to get there
early and beat the crowds.

June: **Great Hudson River Revival**
(800-67-SLOOP), Croton Point Park,
Croton-on-Hudson. Free. This

weekend-long riverside festival of music, art, and environmental activism is held to support the work of the historic sloop *Clearwater.* Enjoy performances by well-known musicians in addition to founder and folk legend Pete Seeger. **White Plains Outdoor Arts Festival** (914-422-1336), Tibbets Park, White Plains. Free. An outdoor showcase of the work of fine artists, craftspeople, jewelers, and sculptors from the region. Performances, demonstrations, and a variety of fare. **Tarrytown Street Fair** (914-631-1705), Main Street, Tarrytown. Free. Outdoor festival with live music, food, crafts, and an array of vendors. **Peekskill Artist District Open Studio** (914-737-6039), downtown Peekskill. Free. Visitors can meet over 35 artists in their studios and see an array of their work.

Mid-June through mid-August: **Caramoor International Music Festival** (914-232-1252), Caramoor Center for Music and the Arts, Katonah. Admission fee. This internationally renowned outdoor music festival features symphonic and chamber music, opera, jazz, and pops. Picnicking is allowed on the magnificent grounds.

July: **Fourth of July Fireworks: Mamaroneck** (914-777-7784), Mamaroneck Harbor; **New Rochelle** (914-654-2086), Hudson Park and Five Island Park; **Peekskill** (914-737-2780), Riverfront Green; **Playland** (914-813-7000), Rye; **Yonkers** (914-377-6450), City Recreation Pier. **Independence Day Festivities** (914-591-8763), Sunnyside, Tarrytown. Admission fee. Celebrate July 4th in 19th-century style, with a pie-judging contest, town ball game, slack-rope walkers, and juggling. Pic-

nicking on the grounds is permitted. **Asian Arts Festival** (914-669-5033), Hammond Museum and Japanese Stroll Garden, North Salem. Admission fee. This annual family festival includes Chinese lion dancers, Tibetan dance and music, Japanese folk dancing, martial arts, children's crafts, and Asian food.

August: **Peekskill Celebration & Victorian Ice Cream Social** (914-736-2000), Peekskill Riverfront Green and downtown. Free. This city-wide event includes tall ships, fireworks over the Hudson River, kayak trips, arts and crafts, carnival rides, a car show, and more. The ice-cream social downtown features horse-and-buggy rides, High Tea, Victorian homes tours, an ice cream–eating contest, croquet, and storytelling. **18th Century Dinners** (914-631-8200, ext. 618), Van Cortlandt Manor, Croton-on-Hudson. Admission fee. Four Saturday nights in August. Enjoy dining in an historic setting on cuisine from recipes dating back to the 18th century, served by wait staff attired in period costume. Harpsichord music sets the mood for the festivities of an era long gone.

September: **Church Tower Walk** (914-667-4116), St. Paul's Church National Historic Site, Mount Vernon. Free. Visitors may enjoy a guided tour up the wooden staircase in the 225-year-old church tower, which leads to the historic 1758 Freedom Bell, cast in London at the same foundry that produced the Liberty Bell of Philadelphia. Annual **Hudson River Valley Ramble** (800-453-6665). Some events free, some admission fee. Weekend-long region-wide festival—held the third weekend of September—of nature walks, guided hikes, biking, and kayaking. Call for schedule of activities and locations. **Armonk Outdoor Art Show** (914-273-9706), North Castle Community Park, Armonk. Admission fee. This juried art show and sale of fine art includes works in oil, acrylic, and watercolor as well as photography, sculpture, and mixed media.

Labor Day through Halloween: **Hudson Heritage Festival** (1-800-833-WCVB). Held throughout Westchester County, this festival celebrates the river and historic heritage of the region. Each river town struts its stuff, with fairs, cruises, and other special events. It's a great way to enjoy autumn in the county.

October: **Chappaqua Antiques Show** (914-238-4666), Horace Greeley House, 100 King Street, Chappaqua. This show has become an October tradition in Chappaqua with many vendors from around the northeast; it also offers an opportunity to tour a historic home. **Tarrytown Halloween Parade** (914-631-8389), Broadway to Patriot's Park. Free. People of all ages parade down Broadway in costume, and the array of floats will delight just about anyone. **Teatown Fall Festival** (914-762-2912, ext. 10), Teatown Lake Reservation, Ossining. This family festival includes fun, food, music, hayrides, storytelling, pumpkin carving, and birds of prey demonstrations.

November: **Pound Ridge Historical Society Antiques Show** (914-698-3442), Fox Lane High School, Bedford. Admission fee. Nearly 50 international dealers of antique furniture, jewelry, artwork, rare books, porcelain clocks, and other decorative accessories exhibit their wares annually

at this show. **Turkey Scavenger Hunt** (914-723-3470), Greenburgh Nature Center, Scarsdale. Admission fee. Turkey token hunt along the nature trails, followed by refreshments; a perfect outing for those with young children. **Thanksgiving Day Parade** (914-632-5700), North Avenue to Main Street, New Rochelle. Free. This is the county's largest parade, with 18 marching bands, 15 floats, and over 1,000 marchers. **Thanksgiving Weekend in Sleepy Hollow Country** (914-631-8200), Sunnyside, Philipsburg Manor, Van Cortlandt Manor. Admission fee. Visit these historic sites decked out in festive decor, and discover the holiday traditions of the 18th and 19th centuries on special tours led by costumed guides.

December: **Classic Toy Trains Display** (914-737-2780), downtown Peekskill. Free. This mesmerizing collection of original Lionel trains from the 1940s and 1950s is displayed annually during the month of December. Train buffs and children will be delighted. **Holiday Candlelight Evenings** (914-631-8200, ext. 628/618), Sunnyside, Van Cortlandt Manor. Admission fee. Enjoy special holiday tours of these candlelit historic sites on weekend evenings in December, with caroling and hot cider around the bonfire. Call for exact times. **Holiday Candlelight Evenings at Lyndhurst** (914-631-4481), Route 9, Tarrytown. The elaborately decorated mansion is bathed in candlelight during weekend evenings in December; enjoy live music, hot cider, and dessert treats in a festive atmosphere. Call for exact times.

INDEX

B

Bacio Trattoria, 386
Backstage Studio Productions, 145
Backwater Grille, 283–84
Bailey's Café, 258
Bailiwick Ranch/Catskill Equestrian Center, 192
Bakery, The (New Paltz), 142
bald eagles, 39, 69, 73, 272, 298, 316; Eagle Institute, 71
Baldwin Vineyards, 47, 105
Ballard Honey, 164
ballooning: Dutchess County, 309–10, 346; Greene County, 207; Orange County, 48
Ballston Lake, 241
Ballston Spa, 259; sights/activities, 235, 241
Balsam Shade Resort, 207
Bananas Comedy Club, 343
Bangall: lodging, 323–25
Bannerman's Castle, 49, 53
Bard College, 304; performing arts, 296, 341; sights/activities, 304, 317; special events, 346
Bard Summerscape, 346
Bardavon 1869 Opera House, 341
Barking Dog Antiques, 147
Barnsider, The, 224
Barnsider Tavern, 62
Barrett Art Center, 343
Barryville: eating, 85–86; lodging, 80; shopping, 89; sights/activities, 71, 74–75
Barthels Farm Market, 109
Barton Orchards, 313–14
Basement Bistro, The, 199–200
Bash Bish Creek, 277
Batcheller Mansion, 238, 247
Bayou, 393
beaches. See swimming
Beacon, 306–7; eating, 329–33, 336–37, 337; lodging, 322–23; shopping, 343, 344; sights/activities, 300, 301–2, 304–12; special events, 345, 346, 348; trav-

eling to, 37, 295–96
Beacon Dia Center, 304–5, 307
Beacon Landing, 307
Beacon Project Space, 307
Beacon Tavern, 336–37
Bear Café, 130–31
Bear Creek Café, 202
Bear Creek Landing Family Sport Complex, 184
Bear Mountain Bridge, 46, 351
Bear Mountain Inn, 28
Bear Mountain State Park, 26–27; beaches, 53; bicycling, 24; eating, 31; hiking, 25; ice skating, 52; lodging, 28
Bear Mountain Zoo, 26, 44
Bear Spring Mountain State Park, 164, 166
Bearsville: eating, 130–31, 133
Beaverkill Angler, 77
Beaverkill Creek, 76–77, 165
Beaverkill Trout Hatchery, 77
Beaverkill Valley Inn, 128–29
Beck, Walter, 317–18
Beckrick House on Chumley's Pond, 319
Bed by the Stream, 121
Bedford Hills: shopping, 396
Bedford Salvage Company, 396
Beebe Hill State Forest, 275
Beeb's, 57
Beech Tree Restaurant, 330
Beekman Arms, 308, 319, 329, 344
Beekman Country Club, 314
Beekman Square Restaurant, 341
Bee-line System, 365
Belkind Bigi Antiques Ltd., 397
Bell House Bed & Breakfast, 281
Belleayre Mountain, 114, 117, 118; special events, 151, 152–53
Belleayre Mountain Fall Festival and Concerts, 152–53

Belleayre Music Festival, 151
Bell's Coffee Shop, 202
Bellvale Farms, 62–63
Belvedere, The, 319
Belvedere Country Inn, 173
Bendheim Performing Arts Center, 394–95
Benedictine Hospital, 94
Benmarl Winery, 105–6
Bennett's Berry Patch, 188
Benson's, 135
Berman, Bob, 96
Bernie's Holiday Restaurant, 84
Berry Farm, 272
Best Western Nyack on Hudson, 28
Bethel: sights/activities, 70, 78, 80
Bethel Woods Center for the Arts, 70
Bethel Woodstock Museum, 70
Betsy Ross Park, 26
Beverly's, 255
Bevier House, 97
Bicentennial Trails, 25
Bicycle Depot (New Paltz), 108
bicycling: Albany, 218–19, 229; Columbia County, 271; Delaware County, 162–63; Dutchess County, 310, 347; Greene County, 187; Rockland County, 24; Saratoga Springs, 239–40; Ulster County, 107–8; Westchester County, 375
Big Band Evening and Sunset Picnic, 362
Big Buck Mountain Multiple Use Area, 357
Big House Brewing Company, 227
Big Indian: eating, 138, 144–45; lodging, 128–30
Big Pond (Andes), 163
Bike Shop (Saratoga), 240
Birchcreek Inn, 129
Bird and the Bottle Inn, 358, 359
Bird-On-A-Cliff Theatre Company, 146